The FRANCHISE
REDBOOK

Easy-to-Use Facts and Figures

ROGER C. RULE

OASIS
PRESS

The Oasis Press®/ PSI Research
Central Point, Oregon

Published by The Oasis Press®/PSI Research
© 1999 by ████████████

This publication is designed to provide accurate and authoritative information in regard to the subject matter covered. It is sold with the understanding that the publisher is not engaged in rendering legal, accounting, or other professional service. If legal advice or other expert assistance is required, the services of a competent professional person should be sought.

> — *from a declaration of principles jointly adopted by a committee of the American Bar Association and a committee of publishers.*

Editor: Constance C. Dickinson

Book Designer: Constance C. Dickinson

Compositor: Jan Olsson

Franchise Information Designer: Eric Saltzen, Elsware Ltd.

Cover Designer: Steven Burns

Please direct any comments, questions, or suggestions regarding this book to The Oasis Press®/PSI Research:

Editorial Department
P.O. Box 3727
Central Point, OR 97502
(541) 479-9464
info@psi-research.com *e-mail*

The Oasis Press® is a Registered Trademark of Publishing Services, Inc., an Oregon corporation doing business as PSI Research.

The ten positive developments for franchising is reprinted, with permission of the publisher, from *Franchising and Licensing: Two Ways to Build Your Business* © 1991 Andrew J. Sherman. Published by AMACON, a division of the American Management Association. All rights reserved.

Rule, Roger C.
    The franchise redbook: easy-to-use facts and figures / Roger C. Rule
    p. cm. — (PSI successful business library)
    Includes index.
    ISBN 1-55571-484-6
    1. Franchises (Retail trade)—United States Directories.
    2. Franchises (Retail trade)—Canada Directories. I. Title
    II. Series.
    HF5429.235.U5R847   1999
    658.8'708—dc21   99-37189

Printed in the United States of America
First edition 10 9 8 7 6 5 4 3 2 1

 Printed on recycled paper when available.

*This book is dedicated with love and admiration
to my oldest son, Robin Sean Rule,
who, concurrently with the first printing of this book,
attained his Master of Business Administration*

Table of Contents

Part II: Franchise Industries Facts and Figures

Part III: Alphabetical Tables Listing Franchises by Category

Part IV: Appendices

Preface

In the field of observation, chance only favors minds which are prepared.
— Louis Pasteur

The Franchise Redbook is to be an easy-to-use reference of companies offering franchises, in the United States and Canada, that have continuing plans for expansion. As a source book, the material is presented in a unique style and is as complete and current as possible. It is a collection of data valuable to all who are involved in the world of franchising.

- Marketing and sales department directors and executives of corporate franchisor companies,
- Managers and office personnel of existing franchisees,
- Prospective franchisors and franchisees, and
- Franchise suppliers, consultants, attorneys, advertisers, statisticians, and others who provide support services.

While there are several other reference books available, *The Franchise Redbook* is comprehensive, up-to-date, and by far the most user-friendly for comparative analyses.

There are 1,214 of the most prolific and profitable franchise corporations in the United States and Canada represented within this volume. Some 1,780 different, customized questionnaires were computer generated with each franchisor's information on its own tailored form. They were then distributed for return via a self-addressed envelope or by facsimile. Appendix C is a sample of the questionnaire. The overall response was overwhelming, resulting in the very latest information straight from the franchisors.

Since franchisors have provided all of the material for Part II, Franchise Industry Facts and Figures, the publisher cannot claim responsibility for the accuracy of the information. However, the franchisor's data should be accurate and truthful, because it could jeopardize their creditability and possible future relationships with prospective franchisees, investors, and suppliers if the information were misleading.

If you request a franchisor's information packet and disclosure document and discover that the information differs from the data published here, give precedence to the information in the franchisor's documents. The disclosure document, in particular, is regulated for accuracy under threat of prosecution, possibly resulting in fines or imprisonment, or both, and should be the most reliable source of information.

It is our goal to provide the most timely and accurate compendium possible, so if you find any contradictions or errors in the *Redbook*, please use the form provided after the index to report the discrepancies for correction in the next edition. Your comments and suggestions as to how to enhance the usefulness of the *Redbook* are also welcome.

New franchisors who want to be included in the next edition can fill out and send in the Redbook Questionnaire in the back of this book or on one retrieved from the website:

www.elsware.com/redbook/

Questionnaires received up to six months prior to publication of the next edition will be processed for inclusion in the next edition.

Despite the fact each franchisor's questionnaire was customized, a process was designed to make updating as simple as possible. At the completion of the data collection for this first edition, the task of preparing for subsequent editions was begun with the goal of continually increasing the number of fields and the usefulness of the information to be included.

Part I

Basics of Franchising

Chapter 1

About Franchising

I do not believe you can do today's job with yesterday's methods and be in business tomorrow.
— NELSON JACKSON

This compendium of facts about North American franchises provides details and statistics unavailable anywhere else in a single source. The scope and accessibility of the information makes this an ideal source for anyone wanting to contact or to locate facts about existing franchises.

- Potential franchisees,
- Existing franchisees and franchisee managers,
- Franchise affiliates and support-businesses,
- Franchises, franchise corporate planners, and subfranchisors,
- Franchise consultants, attorneys, and accountants,
- Franchise trade association and trade publication staff members, and
- Statisticians.

For those looking into the possibilities of franchising, Part I, chapters 1 and 2, provides basic information on franchising and how to maximize your chances for success when choosing to become a franchisee. Chapter 3 explains how you can get the most out of and best use the thousands of facts about the franchises contained in Part II.

Part II, Franchise Industries Facts and Figures, begins with a summary of key averages for the 142 business specialties selected. It is followed by the comparative guide to financial and other fundamental information from more than 1,200 franchises — contact information is included. You will find the information particularly useful when selecting a franchise, doing market and competitive analyses, preparing a marketing plan, completing a business plan, preparing contact lists, or doing other research on franchises in the United States and Canada.

Franchising's Growing Success

The U.S. Census Bureau conducts an economic census every five years — in years ending with 2 and 7 — but they do not publish the results until two years later. While this bureau has formerly tracked some franchised sales versus nonfranchised sales, they have since discontinued this practice, last using this method of recordkeeping in the 1987 Economic Census. At that time, projections showed that sales through franchised outlets accounted for one-third of all retail sales of products and services in the United States. The results of the next, 1992, census showed retail sales of products and services totalled $3.5 trillion.

Franchising's major trade organization, the International Franchise Association (IFA), reveals that studies conducted on one hundred different industry specialties in well over 650,000 locations in this country by independent consulting agencies and the University of Kentucky, Louisville, indicate that franchise sales will account for nearly one-half of all sales around the turn of the millennium. In the results of one of the independent studies, John Naisbitt — the Naisbitt Group, *The Future of Franchising* — wrote over ten years ago that franchise sales would increase to one-half of all retail sales by the year 2010. His projection appears to have been conservative. Adding to this are the several new markets opening in countries around the world which has created a surge of international franchising.

Opportunities abound for the proliferation of franchises, which translates into the possibility for more people to get into lower risk businesses and to realize their dreams. As more people looking to go into business for themselves become aware of the franchise advantage, there will be more potential franchisees searching for the right franchise with which to associate. Companies and entrepreneurs that develop and franchise a unique and efficient business format can benefit from this potential force of prospective franchisees by entering into mutually beneficial alliances with them, thus strengthening their own companies.

Definitions

In general, franchising is a method of sales expansion by a successful company wanting to distribute its product, service, or method of business through retail outlets owned independently by others. The successful company allows these independently-owned retail outlets to use its trade name, trademarks, or marketing techniques with defined controls, for payment of fees.

The International Franchise Association, defines a franchising system as:

"a continuing relationship in which the franchisor provides a licensed privilege to do business, plus assistance in organizing, training, merchandising, and management in return for a consideration from the franchisee."

There are three commonly understood types of franchising: product franchising, licensing franchising, and business-format franchising. The first two have existed the longest. In product franchising, occasionally called distributor franchising, a parent company simply grants other companies the right to sell its product, or products. Examples of this are Singer sewing machines, as distributed in the 19th Century, and 20th Century automobile dealerships and gasoline service stations.

License franchising, which deals with trademark or trade name licensing, has also existed since the19th Century. In this system, the parent company gives licensees the right to use the parent company's trademark or trade name in the operation of their business. Examples are soft drink bottling companies.

The third and newest type, business-format franchising, is the focus of this text. The older two types of franchising are on a fast decline, while business-format franchising — where a franchise duplicates it's business format — is flourishing. In order to distribute products or services to the consumer through a method of business operation, business-format franchising involves two separate business entities:

- The company, or franchisor, that developed the system and lends the use of its name or trademark; and

- An independently owned outlet, or franchisee, that buys the right to operate a business under the franchisor's name or trademark.

A business-format-franchising program has three major components:

- An identity. A trade name often identified by a symbol protected by registration such as a trademark or service mark for the exclusive use of the franchising system.

- A business format. A system of operating a daily business that a franchisor can transfer to individual franchisees.

- A continuous financial arrangement. An initial fee paid up front by the franchisee for establishing the franchise and for start-up costs. In addition, ongoing royalties paid by the franchisee, usually based on a percentage of sales revenues, are paid to the franchisor in exchange for its ongoing support activities on behalf of the franchisee.

The Federal Trade Commission (FTC) recognizes business format franchising under the terminology of package franchising. While the FTC has its definition for franchise as do each of the fifteen states that require franchise registration, these all seem to differ slightly. Though California was the first state to pass a franchising law, its definition is complete and representative. The California Business and Professions Code, Section 2001, defines franchise as:

Franchise means a contract or agreement, express or implied, whether oral or written, between two or more persons by which:

- A franchisee is granted the right to engage in the business of offering, selling, or distributing goods or services under a marketing plan or system prescribed in substantial part by a franchisor;
- The operation of the franchisee's business pursuant to that plan or system as substantially associated with the franchisor's trademark, service mark, trade name, logo type, advertising, or other commercial symbol designating the franchisor or its affiliates; and
- The franchisee is required to pay, directly or indirectly, a franchise fee.

A contract, called the franchise agreement, legally controls the bond between the franchisor and the franchisee.

The franchisee is an independent owner of his or her business who supplies nearly all the capital to set up the outlet and contracts with the franchisor to obtain the right to use the components of the system under a financial arrangement. The franchisor provides its idea, its identity, its perfected business format, agreed upon ongoing support, and in some cases, a product.

Multilevel Franchising

When a franchisor wants to capitalize on rapid growth, to dominate or infiltrate a new geographic area, with lower costs than it normally takes through the usual methods of franchisee development, the franchisor can implement multilevel franchising. There are three accepted types: regional franchising, area development franchising, and subfranchising.

In regional franchising, sometimes referred to as master franchising, the franchisor designates one of the existing franchisees a regional (or master) franchisee. The franchisor then delegates the regional franchisee the responsibilities of enlisting other franchisees and providing them with the initial training and support typically provided by the franchisor. After opening, the franchisor then assumes the normal ongoing support for all the franchisees.

The agreement between the franchisor and the regional franchisee spells out the obligations and duties of both parties and usually sets a period for the regional franchisee to perform the objective. The regional franchisee shares in future royalty fees paid to the franchisor by the franchisees that the regional franchisee enlists; this sometimes includes a percentage of the advertising royalties as well.

While the franchisor pays the regional franchisee according to their agreement, the fees and ongoing support between the franchisor and the franchisees go unchanged from the franchisee's perspective. In this arrangement, since the regional franchisee's future payments are a function of the gross sales of the franchisees that it selects and trains, it behooves the regional franchisee to screen the prospective franchisees as diligently as the franchisor would.

In area development franchising, an outside investor or syndicate of investors is granted exclusive rights by the franchisor to develop a specific, even broad, territory. The investors then develop the franchise units within their area, either owning them directly or retaining shares or percentages of ownership in the businesses of franchisee units. In this system, the area developer pays the franchisor an initial franchise fee, just as a franchisee would, and the area developer has a specified period to develop a certain number of outlets. The franchisees that the area developer establishes pay their franchise fees and ongoing royalties to the franchisor. However, the area developer, because of its retained ownership percentage, shares in the net profit of the franchisees it has established and of the outlets that the area developer may own directly.

Subfranchising is probably the simplest of the three multilevel processes. Similar to regional franchising and area developer franchising, there is a middle entity. In this case, it is a subfranchisor that has a specific area to develop. To accomplish this, the subfranchisor selects other franchisees, again similar to regional franchising and to some facets of area development franchising, except there is no retained ownership. The franchisor may or may not require the subfranchisor to own and operate an outlet in its territory.

Different from both of the other systems, the franchisor has very little to do with the franchisees of the subfranchisor. The franchisees deal directly with the subfranchisor who provides initial training, site selection, lease negotiation, and other support services that are commonly the franchisor's responsibilities. The franchisees pay their initial franchise fees and royalties to the subfranchisor, who pays a portion to the franchisor. In this scenario, the subfranchisor becomes the franchisor of the specified territory. The weakness in this system is that the subfranchisor may not have the longevity, the business acumen, the financial backing, or the ongoing support equal to that provided by the franchisor. If a prospective franchisee is considering buying into this type of arrangement, it is necessary to check out the credentials and background of the subfranchisor.

Also, it is important for franchisees to know the terms and conditions of the agreement between the subfranchisor and the franchisor. Any agreement made between the franchisee and the subfranchisor should be congruent with the agreement between the subfranchisor and the franchisor.

The Franchise Advantage

According to the U.S. Department of Commerce, 80 percent of all nonfranchised small businesses fail — many within their first year of business. In contrast, less than 3 percent of all new franchises fail in their first year of business, and approximately 90 percent are still operating after ten years. Erwin J. Keup, author of the *Franchise Bible*, states that the statistics are even better, with less than 2 percent of new franchises discontinued over the first three-year period. In the world of franchising, this comparison of business success to failure between franchised businesses and nonfranchised businesses is called "the franchise advantage."

Stated in relevant terms, a small business that is not in a franchise system is four and half times less likely to succeed than one that is. In addition, the few small businesses that are not franchised but do succeed earn only 80 percent as much as their franchised counterparts. With these statistics, if you are thinking of going into business for yourself and you want to optimize your chances for success, you can hardly ignore the overwhelming advantages the franchise system offers.

Describing the franchise advantage in his book, *Franchising for Free*, Dennis L. Foster states that "... nine out of ten franchise businesses succeed for at least five years, whereas eight out of ten nonfranchise startups never make it past the first year."

In his book on setting up a franchise system, *Franchising and Licensing: Two Ways to Build Your Business*, published by AMACON (American Management Association), Andrew J. Sherman lists ten reasons (or "positive developments") for this trend in franchising. They are reprinted here with permission:

- A growing interest from the commercial banking and venture capital industries in franchising, which should lead to more loans and investments being made in franchises and franchisees

- Franchises joining forces, sometimes through master franchises or joint ventures and sometimes through domestic and international mergers and acquisitions, in order to offer combination franchises (for example, pizza and ice cream or mufflers and transmissions), operational and administrative efficiencies, and franchised mini-malls

- An increasing commitment from our nation's schools and universities to recognize franchising as a separate educational discipline

- An increased number of U.S.-based franchises entering into international markets, which positively contributes to our trade deficit and the spirit of American innovation

- A deliberate effort by franchises, subfranchisors, and state and local governments to expand the role of women and minority groups in franchising

- A growing commitment among existing franchises to set up franchisee advisory councils, awards programs, regional and national meetings and seminars, and other programs to ensure that franchisees receive the support and recognition that they deserve

- The downsizing of corporate America coupled with a troubled economy is causing the layoffs of many well-trained executives who are candidates for franchises, leading to an even higher level of sophistication and financial strength of our nation's franchisees

- An increasing number of Fortune 500 companies [are] entering the franchising area (such as Prudential Insurance Company, Merrill Lynch, Ashland Oil, S. C. Johnson, Union Carbide, First Interstate Bancorp), which in turn has resulted in new-unit and conversion franchising within new and often previously fragmented industries such as banking, real estate, insurance, and financial services

- Further growth predicted by the International Franchise Association within some of the franchising industries that have traditionally been the strongest, such as home improvement, cleaning services, businesses aids and services, fast food, automotive repair, lodging and leisure, equipment rental, convenience stores and educational services and unprecedented growth is expected in the franchising of health care services, child care services and food delivery services

- The maturation and growth of many of our nation's franchises, forcing the entrepreneurial and free-wheeling management styles of the company's founders to the wayside, to be replaced by more seasoned corporate executives and management systems†

Advantages of Joining a Franchise

In the United States franchising has become the most efficient operational method for guaranteeing the success of a small business. The major advantage of joining a franchise is the higher chance of success as indicated by the statistics of the franchise advantage. Specifically, the reasons for this are:

- Established name recognition. Consumers are usually familiar with the franchise name or its trade or service marks.

- Co-op marketing. The franchisor and its franchisees pool their resources in developing advertising and promotional programs at low cost. This allows a franchise system to project a strong image of a large independent company for each of the franchisees.

- Bulk purchasing power. Collectively, franchise outlets have a stronger purchasing power than small independent businesses. This gives them an economy of scale that translates into lower cost of goods and services.

- Training and training time. The franchisor trains franchisees to operate an efficient business format that has taken years and substantial dollars to develop and replicate. The training period to teach this proven method of operation is a relative short time, usually measured in weeks.

- Management experience. The franchisor provides its wealth of management expertise and assistance to its franchisees because the franchisor has a vested interest with its success directly linked to its franchisees.

---

† Reprinted, with permission of the publisher, from *Franchising and Licensing: Two Ways to Build Your Business*© 1991 Andrew J. Sherman, Published by AMACON, a division of the American Management Association, All rights reserved.

• Other support assistance. Besides training and management, the franchisor routinely offers other support services included in the ongoing royalties, or at very low cost.

If you have picked up this book because you are interested in becoming a franchisee, and the advantages of joining a franchise have bolstered your intent, Chapter 2 can be especially helpful with your search and selection.

Becoming a Franchisee

We do not meet with success except by reiterated efforts.
— Françoise de Maintenon

Franchising has become the most efficient operational method for guaranteeing the success of a small business. One of the key factors in this success is careful selection by both franchisor and franchisee.

Care in selection is paramount, for both franchisor and franchisee, for this kind of mutual relationship to have long term success. Therefore, if you are a prospective franchisee wanting to buy a franchise, be prepared for a lengthy qualifying process, on your part and on theirs. Once it is complete, you will sign an agreement and your business relationship will begin.

The franchisor provides a new franchisee with a business strategy and a standard operations manual. The franchisor's initial involvement is to assist the franchisee in getting the new outlet started. Specifically, the responsibilities of this initial assistance are to: select a site, often negotiate a lease, train the franchisee, assist in hiring, train franchisee staff, equip the facility, establish supply lines, and assist in a Grand Opening and the first or more weeks of operation. In effect, this amounts to setting the franchisee up in business. After this initial assistance, the franchisor continues to provide ongoing support to maintain consistency and quality control. For all of this, you will pay an initial franchise fee, and perhaps other charges, and an ongoing royalty based on a percentage of gross sales. You will continue to pay these royalties, usually monthly, throughout the period of the franchise agreement. Generally, you will pay an advertising royalty, also, for your franchisor's assistance with nationwide or regional advertising.

Evaluating Yourself as a Prospective Franchisee

Before buying a franchise, or any business, be ready to examine yourself. The most common objectives of prospective franchisees are: the desire to be ones own boss, to make ones own decisions, or to live where one wants to while producing a livelihood. You must have a strong inner motivating force. Naturally, you will be attracted to the potential profits, but those who prosper share certain traits: they are positive, enthusiastic, ambitious, energetic, and have clear and realistic financial goals, in addition to the other traits already mentioned. Above all, the most potentially helpful quality is simply to enjoy your business. If you can gain both personal and professional satisfaction from the business and have fun running it, you are ahead in the game.

Ask yourself if you are willing and capable of making the sacrifices necessary to succeed. Many emotional and mental qualities come into play. At least initially, are you ready and willing to sacrifice family time, recreation, and other pleasures for long hours of hard work? Do you have the initiative to be self-driven? Are you capable of mentally and emotionally dealing with financial uncertainty? If you have a family, are they supportive and able to deal with the uncertainties? Are you and they prepared to sacrifice the family time initially required to get the business running smoothly? Do you understand what self-employment is really about?

Most franchises require that you enjoy working with other people. Can you manage people? How organized are you? Potential franchisors will help you answer these questions about yourself. Some will even insist that you complete a self-survey of these basic and other specific qualities. However, most franchisors find themselves hard pressed to turn you down if you qualify financially, and if they believe that you are qualified to operate your own business.

When an established franchise invests in you, your success adds to its success. Conversely, your failure would add to its record of unsuccessful operations, something most reputable franchisors want to safeguard against. They do not want to have to explain unsuccessful franchisees.

If a franchisor only checks to see that you have the needed capital and credit for the investment, you will have to take an objective look in the mirror and ask these questions of yourself. Moreover, while family and friends can make a significant impact on your decisions, they may not be very objective at the outset when it comes to answering important self-evaluating questions.

In the process of selecting your franchisor, you will have to evaluate whether you and your franchisor are a good match for each other. When a franchisor's business philosophy and methods are compatible with yours, the relationship can be ideal — ultimately one of mutual respect.

When you operate a franchise, you give up a measure of independence in return for the franchisor's success formula. In addition, you will regularly pay royalties for your franchisor's on-going support. These exchanges of benefits are what increase the potential for the success for both you and your franchisor. Care in selection, for both franchisor and franchisee, is paramount for this kind of mutual relationship to have long term success.

Choosing the Right Franchise

Before selecting a franchise, there are two basic decisions you must make. First, you must choose the product or service you want to manage and market for the long haul. Then you must choose the geographic area where you can successfully market and sell the product or service. Even if you have already made your decisions regarding these two elements, you might want to reexamine them in light of their important considerations.

Before selecting a product or service, check out those that interest you with companies in the same type of business, with their customers and competitors, and with other consumers. It is important to get reliable opinions as to the product's or service's appeal — its marketability. In your survey, you will want to find answers to the following questions:

- Can you "get behind" the product or service. Can you endorse it, stand by it and feel comfortable promoting it with enthusiasm?
- Does the product or service have quality? Is it something that is reputable?
- Does it have a competitive edge?
- Is it already market proven? If not, is there evidence the market exists?
- Is the product or service competitively priced?
- Is the product or service nationally known?
- Are there trademarks or patents involved?
- Does the franchisor furnish guarantees or warranties?
- Is the target market for the product or service a specialty market? For instance, is it seasonal or for teenagers or for a specific economic class?
- Can the product or service become obsolete? Particularly, is the product or service so new that it may only be a trend or a fad, doing well now but for how long?
- Does the industry for this product or service have room to develop new products or services in the future?

After you are convinced that you know which product or service you want to franchise, turn your focus to the second element, the location. Since your livelihood will depend on your ability to sell your product or service in the area you choose, evaluate the sales potential and the market need in your area. If there is not enough market for your product or service, no matter how hard you work or how great your product or service is, you will not be successful until there is.

If you can check sales data of similar or related businesses in your region to get an idea of how a franchise might do, by all means do so. The local Chamber of Commerce and planning department, trade associations, and people in the market area may all be helpful. Here are some questions to answer in choosing the right market area:

- Is there already a competitive product or service in your area? Does it do well?
- Is the potential product or service that you are planning to sell better than others already on the market?
- Is the product or service competitively priced? Would it offer something new or different to the area?
- How does the franchised product or service compare with those existing in your local market, especially as to price and quality?
- Was there ever a franchise of your product or service in the area?
- Are there already too many companies competing for the same business in your area?
- Are there any ideal locations available in your area for your product or service?
- Is the purchase or lease price of the prospective facility affordable?
- Are there any restrictions imposed on the products or services or the location by local, state, or federal governments?
- Is the population in your area changing; is it expanding or declining or changing in composition?
- Are there any competitive franchises already looking into this area?
- Are they already in the planning stage?

Evaluating a Franchise

In doing your due diligence, here are some basic guidelines to use in assessing a franchise and its appropriateness for your business goals.

- Determine the reputation and reliability of the franchisor. Resources are other franchisees, trade and consumer protection organizations, and credit agencies or investor service organizations.
- Assess the adequacy of the support assistance for your needs.
- Evaluate the area's demand for the franchise products or services for each location you are considering.
- Establish what all the start-up costs are, including your working capital requirement.
- Develop financial pro formas using the franchisor's numbers to forecast your profitability.
- Evaluate the terms in the franchise agreement by thoroughly going through it with an attorney familiar with franchising.
- Determine if your choice of franchisor and product or service are best suited for the targeted location.

There are several publications you will find helpful for accomplishing these tasks, see Other Resources for Franchisees at the end of this chapter.

Questions to Ask Other Franchisees

Other franchisees in the system can enlighten you about their initial opening costs, whether or not these were higher than the franchisor originally estimated and whether profit forecasts were, and are, realistic. They can also tell you about their own experiences of the ongoing support assistance. In general, they can inform you of any complaint they might have about the franchisor. At a minimum you will want to ask:

- How long have you owned your franchise?
- Is your franchise profitable?
- In which month did you reach your break-even point in the first year?
- Have you made approximately the same profit that was forecast in the disclosure document?
- Were your opening costs consistent with the original projections in the disclosure document?
- Are you satisfied with the franchisor?
- Are you satisfied with the product or service?
- Is the operations manual clear, up-to-date, and adequate?
- Are you satisfied with the marketing and promotional assistance provided by the franchisor?
- Was the initial training sufficient for you to operate your business?
- What business training did you have in addition to your franchise training?
- Are deliveries of goods provided by the franchisor timely?
- Is the franchisor fair and amicable to work with?
- Does the franchisor listen to your concerns?
- Have you or other franchisees you've heard of had any disputes with the franchisor? What was their nature? Were they resolved fairly?
- Do you know of any disputes between the franchisor and the government? Do you know of any disputes with competitors?

When contacting existing franchisees, have your list of questions prepared. You may want to use the Franchise Questionnaire and Evaluation at the end of this chapter which includes the questions above.

Information from Public and Private Organizations

Besides analyzing the disclosure document and interviewing other franchisees, part of your research on the franchisor should include inquiries to the Federal Trade Commission, trade organizations, consumer protection organizations, and credit agencies or investor service organizations. If complaints to the FTC exist, they are on file with the sources' names and telephone numbers.

Federal Trade Commission
Franchise Rule Coordinator
Bureau of Consumer Protection

Pennsylvania Avenue at 6th Street, NW

Washington, D.C. 20580

(202) 326-3135

Internet: http://www.ftc.gov/bcp/franchise/franrulmkg.htm

e-mail: FRANPR@ftc.gov

Trade Organizations

The International Franchise Association (IFA), formed in 1960, serves the interests of companies involved in franchising. The IFA encourages high standards and diligently screens potential members. The association's executive committee approves members who must observe a comprehensive code of business ethics.

To become a full member, a company must:

- Have been in business for at least two years,
- Have satisfactory references,
- Have a $ 100,000 net worth and a satisfactory financial condition,
- Have at least ten franchise units with one having been in business for at least two years, and
- Have met state and federal disclosure requirements.

There is a provision for associate members that are either new to franchising or do not otherwise meet all of the requirements of full membership. If you are interested in a franchisor that is not a member of the IFA, you should find out the reason.

In addition to the IFA, there are two other major American franchise associations listed below. A list of the international franchise associations are located in Appendix B.

International Franchise Association

1350 New York Avenue, NW, Suite 900

Washington, DC 20005

(202) 628-8000

FAX: (202) 628-0812

Internet: http://www.franchise.org

e-mail: ifa@franchise.org

American Association of Franchisees and Dealers

P.O. Box 81887

San Diego, California 92138-1887

(800) 733-9858

FAX: (619) 209-3777

Internet: http://www.aafd.org/

e-mail: Benefits@AAFD.org

American Franchisee Association

53 West Jackson Boulevard, Suite 205

Chicago, Illinois 60604

(312) 431-0545

FAX: (312) 431-1469

Internet: http://infonews.com/franchise/afa

e-mail: afa@infonews.com

The IFA's counterpart in Canada is the Canadian Franchise Association (CFA), founded in 1967. Besides regular and associate memberships, similar to the IFA, the CFA also offers affiliate memberships to companies that provide products or services to franchisors.

Canadian Franchise Association

5045 Orbitor Drive, Building 12, Unit 201

Mississauga, Ontario

Canada L4W 4Y4

(905) 625-2896

FAX: (905) 625-9076

Another organization is Women in Franchising (WIF). Its objective is to form a national network for women involved in franchising, from the executive level of franchisors to franchisees and potential franchisees. The WIF regularly receives inquiries from women who would like to become business owners. They send these to all franchisor members as leads. The WIF guarantees 1,200 leads per year, which provides their members with a valuable service in attracting prospective franchisees.

Women in Franchising

53 West Jackson Boulevard, Suite 205

Chicago, IL 60604

(312) 431-1467

FAX: (312) 431-1469

Internet: http://infonews.com/franchise/wif

e-mail: wif@infonews.com

Consumer Protection Organizations

When companies have complaints against franchises, they often file these with their local Better Business Bureau (BBB). Filed complaints are normally on record with the BBB in the same city as the franchisor's headquarters. If you cannot easily locate the local BBB, send a self-addressed, stamped envelope with your inquiry on the franchise system you are investigating to the national BBB:

Council of Better Business Bureaus, Inc.

4200 Wilson Boulevard, Suite 800

Arlington, Virginia 22203-1838

(703) 276-0100

Internet: http://www.bbb.org/about/aboutcouncil.html

e-mail: ehasychak@cbbb.bbb.org

You can also check on franchisors at consumer protection and securities divisions in many states. These are offices of consumer affairs in the states' departments of commerce.

Investor Service Organizations

For more detailed financial information on a particular franchisor, you can go to credit agencies or investor service organizations such as Dun & Bradstreet, Moody's, and Standard & Poor's. These will let you know if the franchisor pays its creditors in a timely manner, or if its operation is highly leveraged from debt financing.

Dun & Bradstreet

One Diamond Hill Road
Murray Hill, NJ 07974-1218
(908) 665-5000
(800) 234-3867
FAX: (908) 665-5803
Internet: http://www.dbisna.com/customer/menu.htm
e-mail: feedback on web site

Moody's Investor Service

99 Church Street
New York, NY 10007
(212) 553-1658
Internet: http://www.moodys.com/directry/dirindex/html
e-mail: feedback on web site

Standard & Poors Research Reports

c/o Government Information Services
12350 Imperial Highway
Norwalk, CA 90650
(800) 582-1093
FAX: (562) 868-4065
Internet: http://www.colapublib.org/fyi/
e-mail: coffman@cerfnet.net

Established Franchisor versus New Franchisor

Another consideration in your discovery of a franchise system is to determine the age and size of a company and whether these factors should have any bearing on your decision. While there is nothing wrong with buying into a new company — less than two years old — usually it is less risky to go with an older, established business. There are at least ten advantages of contracting with an established franchisor

- Established name recognition.
- Much more regional or national advertising.
- Much less chance of franchisor financial failure.
- Experienced management. The organization has moved beyond the entrepreneurial stage of being run by a founder to the more sophisticated stage of being run by a management organization and having a network of field representatives.

- Less chance of being overtaken by strong competitors in a price or advertising war.
- More refined training and support services.
- Better purchasing power with established price discounts.
- More likely to have franchise financing available.
- More established and efficient working prototype or company-owned stores.
- Improved assistance from existing qualified franchise owners through advisory councils.

However, there are several disadvantages to choosing an established franchisor, as well.

- Less desirable choices of location for new franchisees. The best choices are frequently reserved for veteran owners.
- Less locations to choose for all franchisees.
- Less opportunity of multi-unit ownership.
- Higher franchise fees and royalties.
- Higher original investment required.
- Lack of personal attention from key personnel of the franchise corporation.
- Less opportunity for growth and profit potential — profit being more stable and controlled.
- Higher chances that there is a larger markup on franchisor furnished items — leases, fixtures, inventory, supplies, products, or services.
- Less enthusiasm by the consumer for products or services that may be "old hat."
- Tougher requirements for applicants.

Review these advantages and disadvantages as they pertain to your goals and to your potential franchisor.

Site Selection

In the world of real estate, the three priorities most often noted for buying the best real estate are: location, location, and location. This does not end in the world of real estate. It is equally true for the site selection of any small business, because it is key to the success of a small business. It is also true that even an average-run business can be successful if it has a customer base who frequent it due to the convenience of its location. For a new business in an excellent location, the success can be awesome. The franchisee of such a business is out front in the race for profits and with a properly run business, it will stay that way.

While every business can have a best location, there are some franchises where location does not play such a vital role. If the location matters for your business, then it is important to put this in its proper perspective. In this case, place as much importance on the site selection process as you do for your choice of franchises. Some important aspects to consider are:

- Suitability,
- Market proximity,
- Traffic volume from counts (which side of the street and what times of the day for both vehicular and foot traffic),
- Visibility,
- Accessibility,
- Cost effectiveness,
- Interior space requirements,
- Exterior site requirements, and
- The terms of the purchase or lease.

You can find in-depth information on site selection in the book *Location, Location, Location* by Luigi Salvaneschi, published by The Oasis Press.

Meeting Your Prospective Franchisor

After your initial inquiry to the franchisor by telephone, letter, or form response to an advertisement, the franchisor usually follows up with a reply or information packet. The information packet may include detailed financial and legal information, but generally, the franchisor will not send these until you have been accepted as a qualified franchisee candidate. Usually, the first correspondence includes an application for you to fill out, so the franchisor can proceed to evaluate you, to find out your level of interest, and to verify if you qualify as a viable franchisee candidate. These can be very rigorous. When they are, it simply means that the company is making a strong attempt to establish sound relationships with its franchisees.

Then within seven to ten days, a representative will call you to see if you have received the information and to schedule a personal appointment. Your first meeting will be with a franchisor representative. That person may be:

- A field sales representative employed by the company,
- A field sales representative commissioned to handle your area exclusively,
- A sales representative working for an independent brokerage that has several franchisor accounts, or possibly
- A subfranchisor or area developer with a license agreement for your area.

The first meeting is usually informal. The purpose of this meeting will be to establish your acquaintance, so it is a good idea to have your spouse present. In compliance with state and federal law, the representative will give you the disclosure document if you have not already received it. It includes important background, financial, and legal information about the franchisor and a list of operating franchisees that you can interview during your intense investigation.

In addition, you will probably receive the capital and cash requirements, so you can decide whether you are financially qualified. Typically at this point, you will also receive a copy of the franchise agreement to take with you for review. Reputable franchisors will not expect you to sign it until after the qualification process, your attorney review, negotiation, and of course, a final agreement is reached. By law, you have a minimum of ten days after receiving the disclosure document before the franchisor can accept your signature or your deposit. It is during this period, often up to thirty days, you will perform your due diligence.

Early in the meeting, attempt to discover the extent of authority that the sales person has as a representative of the franchisor. If he or she makes any promises or forecasts that are not clear in the disclosure document or the franchise agreement, put these in writing and submit them to the franchisor for clarification.

If there are several principals involved in the ownership of the franchisor, attempt to find out their financial involvement to make a judgment as to how strong their commitment is to the future of the business. Also, in addition to the company's financial statements, ask to see the profit and loss statements of the prototype unit or any other company-owned units. If the franchisor is reluctant to give you these financial statements, request that a copy of the statements be sent to your attorney for review.

Often, but not always, you will attend several meetings with corporate management personnel, so they can interview and evaluate you. But you will have at least one more meeting after the franchisor has determined you are qualified, and you have completed your due diligence and are ready to commit to becoming one of their franchisees. You will meet with other management personnel at a regional or headquarters office for signing the franchise agreement. It is customary, again at this meeting, to have your spouse accompany you.

If you check out several franchisors, you will find that their procedures and policies differ. These steps describe a minimum response to potential franchisee inquiries.

Legal Obligations and Documents

There are several documents you will need to read and understand. The two primary ones are the disclosure document, usually called the Uniform Franchise Offering Circular, and the franchise agreement. In addition, you may have to sign a lease for your location. You will want to go over all of these documents with your attorney before committing to anything. The laws established are for your protection, but without your due diligence and the counsel of a franchise attorney, you could face some unexpected surprises.

Due Diligence

In the world of business and real estate purchases, the concept of *due diligence* is synonymous with *discovery*. As a buyer, you will have a specified period, often referred to as a feasibility period, to determine for your own satisfaction whether the business or property being purchased will serve the purpose for which it is intended. While it is the duty of the seller to disclose all facts "as known," it is still your responsibility to discover those not known. If it turns out there are problems, it is better to learn of these before the transaction closes. This is true for making any investment and especially for buying a franchise. The research to discover potential problems requires doing your homework, often called doing your due diligence.

Uniform Franchise Offering Circular

The International Franchise Association was instrumental in getting the Franchise Disclosure Act passed. On October 21, 1979, the Federal Trade Commission issued a trade regulation Rule 436, called the FTC Franchise Rule. It requires that all franchisors provide to each would-be buyer, a disclosure document. This can either be in the format of the Franchise Rule offering circular provided by the FTC or in the format of the Uniform Franchise Offering Circular (UFOC) prescribed by the North American Securities Administrators' Association (NASAA). A franchisor must give the disclosure document to a potential franchisee on or before the first personal appointment and at least ten business days before the signing of a franchise agreement and payment of fees.

Fifteen states followed the FTC's lead and have passed registration acts requiring disclosure documents. These are: California, Hawaii, Illinois, Indiana, Maryland, Michigan, Minnesota, New York, North Dakota, Oregon, Rhode Island, South Dakota, Virginia, Washington and Wisconsin. All other states follow the FTC Rule as their regulatory guideline. See Appendix A for state contact information. The front page of the disclosure document will identify whether or not the document is published according to federal or state law, or both.

The disclosure document is required to include information replete with truth and disclosure of all facts relating to 23 subjects which are usually in the order of the UFOC format.

1. **The Franchisor, Affiliates, and Background** identifies the franchisor its affiliates, and predecessors and describes their business experience.

2. **Experience of Franchisor Officers, Directors, and Management Personnel** covers the business experience of persons affiliated with the franchisor: officers, directors, and management personnel responsible for franchise services, training, and other facets of the franchise program.

3. **Franchisor Litigation** is a history of the franchisor's and any of the above personnel's involvement in lawsuits.

4. **Franchisor Bankruptcy** is a history of the franchisor's and any of the above personnel's involvement in any bankruptcies.

5. **Initial Franchise Fees and Payment** covers the financial requirements to obtain the franchise. This is an up-front fee that you make to the franchisor to use its business format and trade or service marks or trade names for a specified period. In addition, this fee usually

includes services like opening assistance and, for conversions, design and layout of premises.

6. **Royalties and Other Fees** is a disclosure of recurring or fixed fees or payments required after the franchise opens. This is commonly an ongoing monthly payment, based on a specified percentage of the gross monthly sales. Sometimes, however, it can be a fixed fee or a variation of one or both. For these fees, the franchisor regularly provides you support services, management, joint marketing, updating of the business format, and new product development.

7. **Original Investment** is an estimated cost (by way of a low-high range) of your initial investment, including all expenses required for setting you up in business.

8. **Required Goods and Services from the Franchisor** includes any requirements for the purchase or lease of goods and services used in the franchise from the franchisor, the franchisor's affiliates, or other designated sources. This normally spells out a percentage of goods and services required to be purchased by you from the franchisor. To ensure the quality of the goods and services, it is common for franchisors to insist that this be 100 percent.

   This section also specifies the period in which you are required to pay for these goods and services. Usually, franchisors provide you the same credit terms as do others in the trade, like 30 or 60 days credit.

9. **Controlled and Specified Goods and Services** (from approved suppliers) includes any restrictions on the quality of goods and services used in the franchise. This includes any requirement that you purchase such goods and services in accordance with specifications provided by the franchisor, affiliates of the franchisor, or other designated sources.

10. **Financing Assistance** is a disclosure of any assistance available from the franchisor or its affiliates in financing the purchase of the franchise.

11. **Franchisor Obligations** is a description of supervision, assistance, or other ongoing services including training and other things, such as site assistance provided by the franchisor.

12. **Exclusive Territory** is a disclosure of any territorial protection granted to you. The size of the territory can vary depending on the nature of business and the franchise agreement; however, the franchisor will not set up other franchisees within this territory.

13. **Trademarks, Service Marks, Trade Names, Logo Types, and Other Commercial Symbols** includes all of those licensed to you for your use.

14. **Patents and Copyrights** is a description of the patents and copyrights owned by the franchisor and the terms and conditions under which you may use them.

15. **Personal Participation Requirement** states the extent to which you personally participate in the operation of the business or is a requirement that you must operate the franchise business.

16. **Marketing Restrictions** includes what you may or may not sell as to goods and services offered by the franchisor or by others.

17. **Provisional Changes to the Franchise Agreement** includes transfer of ownership and the terms in which either you or the franchisor can modify the agreement. Terms and other relevant information covered are renewal, termination, repurchase, modification, and assignment.

18. **Arrangements with Public Figures** is a disclosure of your responsibility to include the involvement of any celebrities or public figures in the franchise.

19. **Franchise Sales, Profits, or Earnings** includes projected and other figures that might be actual, average, or forecast numbers. This full disclosure shows the basis for any earnings claims that the franchisor makes to you. It also discloses percentages of actual results achieved by existing franchises.

20. **Past, Current, and Future Franchisees** gives the numbers of franchises that are existing, projected, terminated, turned down for renewal, and repurchased. This section includes a list of the names and addresses of other franchisees, but it does not need to include all of them.

21. **Financial Statements** shows the franchisor's financial status.

22. **Contracts** discloses a copy of the franchise agreement and any other contracts that you will execute, such as license agreements, guarantees, lease assignments.

23. **Acknowledgment of Receipt** is a statement that you sign to establish proof that you have received the offering circular.

While federal statutes require the above, they do not provide for a means of determining whether or not the information submitted by the franchisor is truthful or accurate. It would be illegal for the franchisor to be other than truthful, but it still behooves you, as a prospective buyer of a franchise, to use due diligence and investigate the accuracy and legitimacy of the disclosure document. If it is fraudulent, inaccurate, or incomplete, this could be a violation of federal or state law and should be reported to the FTC. If the disclosure document provided to you does not include all of the information discussed here, obtain the missing details from the franchisor.

While it is important to research and verify the information in the UFOC, you will probably not find any misrepresentations as they would expose the franchisor to legal remedy. However, what you do need to do is spot check the document. Once you are comfortable that it is current and accurate, you can use it to locate other franchisees, prepare your financials, and make your projections.

Your Franchise Agreement

As an element of your franchise selection process, the franchise agreement is something else for you to review thoroughly. This is a legal contract, between you and the franchisor, spelling out the terms and conditions and the rights and obligations of both parties. The franchisor provides the basic agreement, written by its attorney(s). This agreement is the mortar that holds everything together between you and your franchisor.

Prospective franchisees often do not try to understand the franchise agreement — one of the Ten Common Mistakes of Prospective Franchisees (see below). It is imperative that you have an attorney that knows franchising review the franchise agreement. If you do not know of one, refer to the Yellow Pages of any major city, or look up attorney members in the International Franchise Association and the American Association of Franchisees and Dealers. Both of these associations and the On-line Directory have long lists of specialized franchise attorneys and contact information on the Internet.

International Franchise Association

Internet: http://www.franchise.org [go to: Search Guide, Suppliers & Consultants, Attorney]

American Association of Franchisees and Dealers

Internet: http://www.aafd.org//LegaLine.htm

On-Line Directory of Franchise Attorneys

Internet: http://www.franchise-update.com/law/attorney.html

Since your franchisor's typical agreement is standardized, there is very little that is subject to change. However, you can negotiate minor changes in the main document and major revisions with exhibits, addenda, and amendments prepared by your attorney, or even by way of separate or supplemental agreements. Just make sure you get everything in writing and leave nothing open to verbal promises or projections.

While there are as many franchise agreements as franchisors, there are several common elements fundamental to most agreements. The few that vary from franchisor to franchisor are identified with asterisks and descriptions of the differences follow.

1. Grant of franchise
2. Term of franchise*
3. Name of franchise
4. Location of franchise
5. Obligations of franchisee
6. Initial franchise fee
7. Franchise service fees; reporting and audits
8. Advertising fund
9. Training assistance
10. Operation of the business format
11. Representations by franchisor
12. Representations by franchisee
13. Relationships of the parties
14. Renewal and renewal fee*
15. Assignment

16. Termination*
17. Procedures after termination
18. Remedies for breach, and methods of enforcement, of the agreement*
19. Attorney fees
20. Amendment
21. Waiver
22. Approvals
23. Construction and venue
24. Severability
25. Binding of successors
26. Exclusive property

You may require legal interpretation of some of the provisions and clauses. Specifically, seek professional advice to understand these items and key legal clauses within the provisions of your contract.

- Term of franchise — ranges from three to fifteen years or more, but ten is the most common.
- Renewal and renewal fees — most have standard renewal policies, some allow a renewal for the same period at no additional cost, others ask an additional fee to renew the contract.
- Termination — there are three ways: 1) the time period expires, 2) you opt to withdraw from the franchise early, or 3) your agreement is cancelled under breach of contract.
- Remedies for breach and methods of enforcement of the agreement — if, after being warned, you continue to conduct your business in a manner that is adverse to the franchise image and business, the franchisor can terminate the franchise agreement. Likewise, you can seek legal recourse if the franchisor does not adhere to the terms and conditions of the agreement.
- Your rights, including exclusivity of territory.
- The obligations of the franchisor.
- Restrictions placed on you to enter into business after termination.
- Restrictions placed on you to reassign the franchise.
- The method by which conflicts are resolved.

Your Lease

Because lease negotiation assistance is often included as support assistance by franchisors, and because this may be one of the first services you need, whether or not your potential franchisor provides this service should be resolved early as a matter of due diligence. If so, find out to what extent. At one end of the scale, many franchisors offer to be the lessors for their franchisees. At the other end, if your franchisor service is weak or nonexistent in this department, you may want a different franchisor, or you will find it necessary to handle your own lease negotiation. If you have a proposed lease agreement, show this to your franchisor. If you are starting from scratch, go through a reputable Realtor. When it is time to negotiate the lease, have an attorney assist in reviewing the agreement, especially if leases are new to you. Some essential elements of lease negotiation are:

- Check to see if the lease conforms to the cost guidelines suggested by your franchisor.
- Coordinate the period of the lease with the period of your franchise agreement.
- Avoid a percentage lease in favor of a fixed rental agreement. In a percentage lease, you pay a percentage of your gross sales to the lessor.
- Look for hidden costs. If the monthly payments are triple net, you will be responsible to pay the agreed rent plus all costs of maintenance and repair as well as property taxes and insurance.
- Attempt to get several months free rent, especially during the downtime before business opening.
- Have your attorney draw up or add an addendum to the lease for an equipment waiver to be signed by the lessor. This will provide protection of your interest in the equipment in case of default of the lease.
- Reserve the right to sublet or assign the lease in the event you sell your franchise.
- Make sure the parking is adequate. Get a specific number of spaces written into the lease.
- Do not sign a lease on an "as is" basis. You will not have any recourse upon the discovery of problems.
- Make sure the lease commission is the responsibility of the lessor, if a Realtor is involved.

Ten Common Mistakes of Prospective Franchisees

To insure your success, you will want to avoid as many mistakes as possible. Here are the ten most common mistakes made by prospective franchisees in their pursuit of buying a franchise.

1. Not reading, understanding, or asking questions about the disclosure document. These documents are typically long, sometimes eighty pages, but it is very important that you read and understand each item, 1–23 of the UFOC. As you read the document, keep notes on those areas that are confusing and unclear. While you may want your attorney's opinion, give the franchisor the benefit of the doubt and first ask its representatives to explain their understanding. Then check the remainder of your concerns with your attorney. Check the document's date. If it is current, you may want to request a previous document for comparison.

   One of the most common problems between new franchisees and the franchisor is a misunderstanding as to responsibilities. Among other things, this can cause problems in meeting the schedule for Grand

Opening dates. Read the disclosure document and the franchise agreement carefully as to your responsibilities. Also pay attention to the stated obligations of the franchisor, especially item eleven of the UFOC. Do not assume the franchisor is responsible for details of a particular support service. If it is not spelled out, get it in writing. List all of your concerns, and clarify which duties, obligations, and responsibilities belong to whom.

2. Not understanding or having an inaccurate or incomplete interpretation of the franchise agreement and other legal documents to be signed. You and your attorney should carefully review the franchise agreement, lease or real estate agreements, and any other contracts. First, make a list of questions to go over with your attorney, then present your concerns to the franchisor. Get the franchisor's clarifications in writing. There may be very little that you can change in these standardized agreements, but things can be added. There is no reason the franchisor cannot give you additional documentation to clarify something in the agreement that is confusing to you or your attorney.

3. Not seeking sound legal advice. Locate and retain an attorney, preferably one experienced in franchising. For some suggested sources, see Your Franchise Agreement in this chapter.

4. Not verifying oral representations of the franchisor. You can avoid this mistake if you take the proper precautions. You may want to tape record all your meetings with the franchisor. If you ask permission to do so, it is generally admissible in court if the need arises later. It also lets the company representatives know that you are tracking their words. You can do this politely, but if you prefer, take compendious notes of all your meetings. Later, review and summarize the details of your discussion, noting any items requiring clarification. Send a registered letter to the franchisor and a copy to the representatives memorializing your notes with a request for their response to any items you want clarified. Do not leave anything unresolved.

   Due diligence also includes verification. If there have been any oral representations, of which you are uncertain, try to verify these with previous and current franchisees as well as through additional meetings with the franchisor. As stated in item 2 above, get anything orally promised in writing if it differs from other literature and the disclosure document.

5. Not contacting enough current franchisees. The section of the disclosure information on "Past, Current and Future Franchisees" is a valuable starting point for locating franchisees. It is imperative to discuss any concerns you may have with existing franchisees. If the franchisor gives you a tour, which includes two or three franchisees, get back to them later and ask any questions that could have been confrontational or embarrassing if asked in front of the franchisor. Another important factor here is to find out whether the franchisor

has introduced you to specific franchisees compensated for their help to solicit new franchisees. Ask them directly, then follow up with letter stating their answers to your questions. It is surprising how an inaccurate response might change once it is in writing.

Other than the franchisees introduced to you by the franchisor, to get a true picture, you can survey others listed in the disclosure document not versed in soliciting prospective franchisees. Find out from them if the franchisor has a reputation for honesty and fair dealing. It is of paramount importance to contact existing franchisees of the franchisor to verify their experience of the accuracy of previous disclosure documents. Also, ask their opinions of the accuracy and completeness of the current one. Further, you can solicit their help in verifying any other information not provided in the disclosure document.

When interviewing other franchisees, try to cover a large cross section of franchisees. Seek answers from those that:

• Are in different locations,
• Have one franchise,
• Have multiple franchises,
• Have been in business a long time,
• Are still new,
• Are successful, and
• Are not doing so well.

For the latter, try to determine the reasons. Specifically, ask the franchisees if they feel that the franchisor exercises too much control, or not enough. Is the franchisor always willing to help? Has the franchisor held up its end of the obligations regarding ongoing support assistance and training? There is a Franchisee Questionnaire and Evaluation you can use located at the end of this chapter.

Information from franchisees about their first year in business and their experience with the franchisor can be extremely enlightening. Under the FTC requirement, while the offering circular must disclose a list of existing franchisees, this record does not have to be complete. If you find the list provided to you is incomplete, ask the franchisor for a complete registry.

6. Not confirming the reasons for failed franchises. Locate some franchise outlets that are closed, sold, or have changed ownership to company-owned, and find out the reasons for their change of status. Contact the original owners and get their stories. If no two are alike, you may want to pay them less heed. If, on the other hand, there is a common story, the underlying problem may be something you want to avoid. Nevertheless, for fairness, get the franchisor's version.

7. Not having enough working capital. Make sure you have enough capital to cover every cost associated with the business including all pre-opening costs, enough set aside for your family budget, and enough operating cash for the business to make it through the break-even point.

8. Not recognizing the need for financing, not knowing how to make a proper loan request, and not developing a true and accurate financial statement. If business accounting is not your forte, solicit the help of a good accountant.

9. Not meeting the franchisor's key management personnel at their headquarters and the field representative assigned to your territory. Quite often, the sales representative will do such a good job in building your confidence that you may not bother with trying to meet the other important personnel or traveling to the headquarters before signing the franchise agreement. Do not make this mistake. Meet the other franchisor personnel and verify the information provided by the sales representative.

   After the franchisor defines your territory, also meet the field representative or district supervisor that will be working with you. It is important that your personalities are sufficiently harmonious to be able to work effectively together. Although you may not be able to determine this at first, you can find out the field representative's length of time on the job, training, and other experience levels. If you foresee problems, it is better to address them and try to work them out before you sign the agreement.

10. Not analyzing your market in advance. While the franchisor may help with site selection, it is still your responsibility to decide for yourself whether a particular location is desirable and promising. It is important to confirm the market for your product or service in this area.

    If competition exists, there are several things to consider. Do the competitors have any weaknesses that you will be able to avoid in your business to capture more market? Are the competitors so strong that their market saturation may be hard for you to penetrate? If a local competitor dominates the market, entering it may turn into a competitive struggle that will increase your working capital requirement.

    Also, evaluate your franchisor's marketing strategy; find out the amount of advertising and promotional dollars intended to help. Although helpful, it is not a good idea to rely totally on your franchisor for your market research. It is to your advantage to do your own market analysis and to develop your own marketing plan.

    If your findings support a strong market for a "virgin" area, you may want your agreement to include a right of first refusal to buy additional franchised outlets in the subject territory before the franchisor considers other prospective franchisees. If you consider this, you will be under a timetable to expand according to the franchisor's goal. If you can not meet the stated expansion goal, you will forfeit the area.

    If you are looking into a franchised area controlled by a subfranchisor, research the subfranchisor with the same determination and persistence you used evaluating the franchisor — maybe even more.

While these ten mistakes are the most common, there are others. By knowing these and second-guessing the rest, you can adequately prepare yourself to execute your due diligence prior to buying a franchise. Several of these topics, in particular marketing, financing, and business plan issues, are covered in *No Money Down Financing for Franchising*, which is described below along with other valuable resources.

Even after you have decided to focus on a specific franchise, do not forget to check out your franchisor's competitors and some of their franchisees. Although you should consider the source, franchisors competing with the one you are evaluating will gladly give you stories about your prospective franchisor. Of course if you find them, this is usually true of your franchisor's unhappy franchisees as well. The Franchisee Questionnaire and Evaluation located at the end of this chapter can be helpful in making this comparison.

Other Resources for Franchisees

There are several books available from The Oasis Press and other publishers that you can use to assist you in your search for the American dream of owning your own business and to improve your chances of success with your new franchise business. You may want to become acquainted with some of these resources before contacting franchisors, reading the franchisor's materials, and starting your due diligence.

The Complete Franchise Book by Dennis L. Foster, published by Prima Publishing and Communications, provides advice and guidance by one of America's foremost franchise consultants from answering a newspaper ad and choosing the right company to negotiating a fair contract and opening your doors.

Franchise Bible: How to Buy a Franchise or Franchise Your Own Business by Edwin J. Keup, published by The Oasis Press, is a virtual one-stop resource for what you'll need to know to buy that franchise you've been dreaming of. This book, written by an attorney and franchising specialist, will save you time and dollars. It provides you with sample legal documents, several evaluation forms and checklists, and the Uniform Franchise Offering Circular Guidelines.

Franchise Selection: Separating Fact from Fiction by Raymond J. Munna, Attorney, published by A. H. Granite Publishers, is an in-depth approach to evaluating franchise options, how to locate hot opportunities, how to avoid pitfalls, and what to look for in franchise agreements.

Know Your Market by David B. Frigstad, published by The Oasis Press, contains successful competitor research techniques that can facilitate your franchise selection

Location Location Location by Luigi Salvaneschi is published by The Oasis Press. As the title implies, location is the most important ingredient for success for any business that depends on customers finding it. This covers all the criteria and is written by a master in the industry — he has been the

Vice President in charge of real estate for McDonald's, Senior Vice President responsible for new markets and locations for Kentucky Fried Chicken, and President of Blockbuster Entertainment Corp.

No Money Down Financing for Franchising by Roger C. Rule, published by The Oasis Press, is an essential source book on financing methods and resources for franchisees. In addition, it guides you through each step of creating a business plan — including determining your working capital requirements and other financial needs, doing a market analysis, and developing a marketing plan. It is illuminated by a complete, sample business plan and several graphs for highlighting probability ratios.

Owning Your Own Franchise by Herbert Rust, published by Prentice Hall, is an insider's guide to success that describes how to take the risk out of selecting, buying, and operating a franchise.

Start Your Business: A Beginner's Guide, 3rd Edition, published by The Oasis Press, is "One of the 40 top small business books," according to *Inc.* magazine. It discusses both franchise and nonfranchise issues and the resources you will require to get your business up and running.

Franchising is a wonderful way of doing business with the least amount of risk and, consequently, the best chance of success. The world of franchising welcomes you to add to that success.

Franchisee Questionnaire and Evaluation

Questions Responses:	Franchisee 1	Franchisee 2	Franchisee 3	Franchisee 4
☐ How long have you owned your franchise?				
☐ Is your franchise profitable?				
☐ Where was the break-even point in the first year?				
☐ Have you made the profit forecast in the disclosure document?				
☐ Were your opening costs consistent with the original projections in the disclosure document?				
☐ Are you satisfied with the franchisor?				
☐ Are you satisfied with the product or service?				
☐ Is the operations manual adequate?				
Is it too controlling?				
Is it clear and easy to follow?				
Is it updated regularly?				
☐ Are you satisfied with the marketing and promotional assistance provided by the franchisor?				
☐ What business training did you have in addition to your franchise training?				
☐ Was the initial training period long enough or too long? Was it sufficient for you to run the operation?				
☐ Do you feel that the additional training, if any, was necessary for the successful operation of your franchise?				
☐ Are deliveries of goods provided by the franchisor timely?				
☐ Is the franchisor fair and amicable to work with?				
☐ Does the franchisor listen to your concerns?				
☐ Have you or other franchisees that you have heard of had any disputes with the franchisor?				
What was the nature of each of them?				
Were they resolved fairly?				
☐ Do you know of any disputes between the franchisor and the government?				
☐ Do you know of any disputes with competitors?				
☐ _____				
☐ _____				
☐ _____				
☐ _____				

Respondent Information

1. Date: _____

   Franchisee Name: _____

   Location: _____

   _____

   Phone: _____

   E-mail: _____

2. Date: _____

   Franchisee Name: _____

   Location: _____

   _____

   Phone: _____

   E-mail: _____

3. Date: _____

   Franchisee Name: _____

   Location: _____

   _____

   Phone: _____

   E-mail: _____

4. Date: _____

   Franchisee Name: _____

   Location: _____

   _____

   Phone: _____

   E-mail: _____

Evaluation of Most Important Questions

Item: _____

_____

_____

_____

Item: _____

_____

_____

_____

Item: _____

_____

_____

_____

Conclusions

_____

_____

_____

_____

_____

Chapter 3

How to Use Part II

What is the virtue and service of a book? Only to help me live less gingerly and shabbily.
— CHRISTOPHER MORELEY

Part II, Franchise Industries Facts and Figures, is an easy-to-use reference of most of the companies offering franchises in the United States and Canada. The format is designed for your easy viewing and quick comparative analyses. The three-tiered alphabetical outline locates franchise information, first by industry, next by business specialty, and then by franchise. If you do not find the business specialty you are looking for, you will probably find it in the other category located last in the specialty list.

All of the franchise information is laid out on facing pages, or spreads. Left facing pages are in table format for easy comparison of the 33 fields of information on up to eight competing franchises. Right facing pages present 18 fields of more descriptive information on the same companies, such as contact information, products or services description, and field support and training provided. This two-page spread format enables you to make the fastest comparative review of a specific franchise with its competitors and to access its contact information.

The quickest way to locate a specific franchise is by using the Index. To find the several franchises within a business specialty, such as Hamburgers or Automobile Rentals, use the Table of Contents. In addition to these aids, there are seven tables in Part III that allow you to find franchises by categories such as start-up costs, average franchise fee, geographic area, products and services, and royalty percentages.

Descriptions and Explanations for Information Spreads

The title lines at the top of each page of the two-page spread include: 1) the industry classification, 2) the business specialty subclassification, and, in cases where the number of franchises in a business specialty category has several consecutive pages, 3) the spread number and number of spreads for that specialty within parentheses.

There are twenty-eight different industries, based on the IFA industry classifications, that appear alphabetically. In addition, there are 142 business specialty subclassifications including "other" (listed last) alphabetically listed within their respective industries. See the Table of Contents for the complete list.

Content Summary of Left-facing Pages

Column Headings	One to eight franchise names. This may be either the franchise's marketing or corporate legal name.	
Data Description	**Sample Responses and Explanations**	**Abbreviations**
Start-up Cost	Example: $10,000 or $10,000–40,000	$10K or $10–40K

This is an estimate of the required start-up cost, according to the franchisor. An entry of $10K means that $10,000 is needed to open the franchise. A low to high range, such as $10–40K, indicates there are variances due to geographic location, type and method of acquiring site locations, financing, and working capital needed. If the number or range appears low, a prospective franchisee should request a copy of the UFOC from the franchisor and further clarification. In addition to the obvious costs, such as rent deposits, opening inventory and salaries, it is up to the franchisee to find out the built-in assumptions:

• The amount of working capital included,

• The assumed break-even point, and

• The amount of draw included for the franchisee's family to live on.

Consultants, and most franchisors, caution franchisees not to make risky consessions to meet the working capital model. There is an extensive discussion about estimating the working capital requirement in *No Money Down Financing for Franchising*, published by The Oasis Press.

Franchise Fee	Example: $15,000	$15K

This is the up-front fee a franchisee pays to the franchisor for opening an outlet — occasionally there is a range, from low to high. The franchise fee, is a one-time assessment (nonrecurring). Franchisors generally consider this amount to be a reimbursement of costs incurred to start a franchisee in business: advertising (amortized over all new franchisees), qualifying, assisting in site selection and lease negotiation, training, grand opening, and other initial support. Some franchisors will help finance the fee. A prospective franchisee with a particular field of interest should look at all the franchisors in the selected business specialty to find the average of this fee, then compare it to specific franchisor numbers. Characteristically the more renowned a franchisor is, the higher their fee — justified due to the greater advantages to the franchisee.

Data Description	Sample Responses and Explanations	Abbreviations
Royalty	Example: Four percent of gross sales	4%

Typically, this is a percentage of gross sales a franchisee pays directly to the franchisor on a periodic basis, usually monthly, but sometimes weekly, bimonthly, or quarterly. Sometimes this is a fixed periodic fee or a combination of a fixed fee plus a percentage. Refer to the franchisor's disclosure document and franchise agreement for specific language.

The royalty is the franchisee's cost of doing business under the franchisor's license and provides for benefits such as national or regional advertising, a highly visible and recognizable name, strong buying power (which reduces costs), and other support services. Royalties pay for the extensive overhead costs of providing support service, administration, and research and development, as well as the profit of the franchisor.

Advertising Fee   Example: Two percent of gross sales   2%

This is a percentage of the franchisee's gross sales, usually about 2 percent. Occasionally, instead of basing it on sales, franchisors assess a flat fee. The amount spent for collective advertising for a franchise system is one of the best buys in franchising. If franchisees were to spend their own funds to obtain the same benefits from advertising that the coop advertising pool provides, the cost to each franchisee is estimated at two to three times the amount. Again, because of cost differences, sometimes this is a low to high range. It is more expensive to set up a new franchisee in a new area than it is to set up a new franchisee in an established area; however, only a few franchisors list a low to high range.

Financing Provided   Yes or No   Y/N

This entry, which will be expanded in future editions, refers to whether the franchisor provides financial assistance, either directly or indirectly, to franchisees in helping them get started in business. As to types of financing assistance, this may include direct assistance, such as leases or loans by the franchisors, or indirect assistance. Indirectly, franchisors may introduce a franchisee to special lenders that are involved with the franchisor for this purpose. In some cases, the franchisor will become a co-signer for a promising prospective franchisee.

Experience Required   Yes or No   Y/N

Some franchisors require franchisees to have a background in business or experience in their particular field — a muffler franchisor may only want franchisees with automotive experience or a restaurant franchisor may want a franchisee with experience in restaurants. Most franchisors have no experience requirement and, instead, provide the necessary training to their prospective franchisees for running their outlets.

Passive Ownership   Allowed, discouraged, or not allowed   A/D/N

This indicates whether the franchisor will allow, will not allow, or discourages a franchisee from buying, as an investor, then hiring an on-site manager to operate the business. Most franchisors want the franchisee to be the manager and operator of the business. Some franchisors allow passive ownership providing that specific guidelines are met, or after the franchisee's operation meets certain success requirements. A franchisor is most likely to accept passive ownership after the franchisee displays a certain level of success, then wishes to become a multiple franchise owner.

Data Description	Sample Responses and Explanations	Abbreviations
In Business Since	Example: 1952, a specified year	1952
	This represents the year the company first started, the founding year of the business, not the founding year of the franchise (see next).	
Franchised Since	Example: 1955, a specified year	1955
	This is the year that the company first became a franchisor. Many times, there is a big difference between this year and the first year of the business. To the prospective franchisee, it may be important that the franchisor has some time under its belt in franchising. For most prospective franchisees, it is better to see fewer years as an independent outlet or chain and more years as a franchisor.	

Franchised Units (last 3 years)

	1996	Example: 700 franchised outlets for 1996	700
	1997	Example: 750 franchised outlets for 1997	750
	1998	Example: 810 franchised outlets for 1998	810

These entries indicate the number of franchised outlets owned and operated by franchisees, as opposed to company-owned outlets within the system. Compare these three numbers with those for Company Owned and Number of Units (below). Are the trends for all three the same? Are the franchised units increasing or decreasing?

If franchised units are increasing rapidly, does the franchisor have adequate financing and support staff to handle the increase? If the numbers are sporadic, is this in line with economic trends or is there some other reason? If decreasing, refer to the next discussion under Company Owned.

Company Owned (last 3 years)

	1996	Example: 56 franchisor-owned outlets, 1996	56
	1997	Example: 49 franchisor-owned outlets, 1997	49
	1998	Example: 52 franchisor-owned outlets, 1998	52

These entries show the numbers of outlets that the company has owned, or owns, during the recent three-year period. Again, compare these numbers with the franchised units and the total units. Are the numbers of company-owned units increasing or decreasing? With three years of this information, you can see a trend. Typically, increasing would be positive, showing that the franchisor is investing in its own system, convinced of its long-term profitability. However, exercise caution when company-owned units are increasing in the system. Are the outlets the company is adding new start-up businesses or are they mostly takeover franchisee units?

If the company-owned units are buyouts of existing franchisees, a prospective franchisee, in his or her due diligence, should contact the buyout franchisees and determine the reasons behind the sales. In some instances, franchisors have bought out an existing unit to satisfy and stop litigation from an unhappy franchisee. Sometimes the company will take over an existing franchisee to keep the franchisee from being a blemish to the franchise record of success, a statistic reported in the Uniform Franchise Offering Circular.

Data Description		Sample Responses and Explanations	Abbreviations
Company Owned (continued)		If, however, the company-owned outlets are mostly increasing due to start-up businesses, the company must be very comfortable with its ability to create successful outlets. Also, more company-owned units can indicate how committed the franchisor is to the success of the operation.	
		Finally, if these numbers are decreasing, compare with the trends of the franchised units and of the total units to see how this plays into the overall growth of the system.	
Number of Units	U.S.	Example: 56 franchise units in the United States	56
	Canada	Example: 79 franchise units located throughout Canada	79
	Foreign	Example: 2 franchise units in other countries	2
		The numbers represent the total number of outlets that the franchisor currently has in each of three markets: the United States, Canada and all other countries. Those franchisors that have wide geographic influence and have been able to sustain it for several years are typically mature franchisors, with extensive name recognition.	
Projected New Units	U.S.	Example: 26 franchise units are projected for the United States	26
	Canada	Example: 9 new franchise units are projected for Canada	9
	Foreign	Example: 2 more franchise units are projected for other countries	2

This is a number of outlets projected for development in the year succeeding the three-year history listed above.

The franchise advantages are well understood for joining a healthy franchise system that is growing — better purchasing power, a larger coop advertising pool, and stronger name recognition — however, the disadvantages of rampant growth may mean that the franchisor is near overload. It may not be able to afford, in terms of both money and effective human resources, to continue adequate ongoing support, research and development, and quality control. The system can lose consistency, which devalues image. For these reasons, it is important to evaluate Projected New Units with the history of the franchise.

First look at the year in the entry, Franchised Since. Then compare that and the three-year trend with the overall history. You can make a mathematical projection from this data. When you compare your finding with the forecast given by the franchisor, it may seem realistic or exaggerated. If the franchisor's forecast doesn't seem logical, you are encouraged to find out why, especially if you have interest in this franchisor.

As an example, suppose ABC Hamburgers started franchising in 1953. During these 45 years, it has developed 400 outlets. Given that the first few years are normally susceptible to slow growth and recessions and attrition have taken their tolls, their overall history shows a growth rate of approximately ten a year. Now they project for 1999 that they will have 70 new units and 470 total outlets. While the increases in the last three years show 12 and 18 (from 360 in 1996, to 372 in 1997, and 400 in 1998), a projection of probably 24 to 30 would be more realistic as an optimistic forecast unless new financing or other influences are factors. (In future years, you can look back at previous editions of *The Franchise Redbook* to weigh the accuracy of these franchisor forecasts.)

Data Description	Sample Responses and Explanations	Abbreviations
Corporate Employees	Example: forty employees	40

This is a number entry that shows the number of full-time staff employed by the franchisor. Compare this number to the number of outlets; usually, the franchisor with the highest ratio of employees to outlets offers more and has a better capability to provide ongoing support assistance.

| Contract Length | Example: ten years for initial agreement and five years for first renewal | 10/5 |

The first entry is the number of years the initial franchise agreement remains in effect. The second number indicates the length of time, in years, of the first renewal period. A third number, when given, is the length of the second renewal period.

While most franchisors have a consistent and fixed period for the contractual term of their franchise agreement, some offer different term lengths to franchisees within their own system. This may have to do with varying lengths of time for pre-existing regional franchise agreements and area development or subfranchise agreements with third parties of multilevel agreements. It could also involve geographic factors.

Generally, the longer the period, the better for the franchisee. You do not want to invest the time and capital into building up your business, only to lose it because the franchise agreement expires. At a minimum, you should coordinate the period of the franchise agreement with the period of your lease for the facility.

| Expand in Territory | Yes or No | Y/N |

This entry refers to the right of a franchisee to set up other units within an exclusive territory. Usually there are quota requirements, but if you are successful and there is a demonstrated need for additional units within your territory, the franchisor will grant the right to expand. If the franchisor allows this important right, the entry is Yes.

| Full-time Employees | Example: Four full-time franchisee employees are recommended | 4 |

Many franchisors indicate an exact number of employees needed for the average outlet, while some indicate a minimum and a maximum depending on the amount of business anticipated. It usually includes the franchisee's services.

| Part-time Employees | Example: Twenty-one part-time franchisee employees are recommended | 21 |

Typically, this is an average number that is required throughout the system. Part-time employees can keep your overhead expenses down, because part-time employees will often work for lower wages. Full-time status is usually the basis for additional employee benefits.

| Conversions | Yes or No | Y/N |

This answers the question of whether the franchisor allows an existing independently-owned and nonfranchised business in the same industry to convert to a franchised outlet. Kentucky Fried Chicken is famous for using this procedure in their early days of it's expansion activity, but conversions are not always popular. They can mean a major overhaul of the facility to conform to specifications and, although training is a requirement, existing business owners often have difficulty conforming to the business format administered and controlled by the franchisor.

Data Description	Sample Responses and Explanations	Abbreviations
Site Selection Assistance	Yes or No	Y/N

This entry indicates whether the franchisor does or does not provide some form of site selection assistance. While location is important for all businesses, it is critical for some and can mean the difference in success or failure regardless of how much the money, advertising, or hard work is put into the business. For these site-sensitive businesses, responsible franchisors should have specific guidelines and a Location Data Report with enough information to support a specific site selection.

If the entry is No, franchisees are on their own regarding this important decision and should become familiar with all the information they can find on the principles of site selection. For more information, see Selecting Your Site in Chapter 2.

Data Description	Sample Responses and Explanations	Abbreviations
Lease Negotiation Assistance	Yes or No	Y/N

If lease negotiation assistance is provided as a support assistance by the franchisor, it will assist a franchisee in negotiating the initial lease for the actual site location. For most franchisees, this service is an important advantage, since few have the experience that the franchisor does in real estate leasing. If it is not provided, the entry is No, so franchisees must handle this responsibility on their own. For more details, see Your Lease, in Chapter 2.

Data Description	Sample Responses and Explanations	Abbreviations
Site Space Required	Example: 1,800 square feet are required for the facility	1800

This number represents the average number of square feet required or a suggested range from low to high of interior space square-footage.

Data Description	Sample Responses and Explanations	Abbreviations
Development Agreement	Yes or No	Y/N

A Yes or No indicates whether the franchisor allows this type of multi-level structure. These agreements with the franchisor give an investor the exclusive right to develop a specific, often broad, territory.

Usually, the area developer pays a large up-front fee for the right to develop its territory and must meet a specified schedule for developing a specific number of outlets. To a new franchisee, this can be attractive because, oftentimes, the area developer provides more financial assistance than is otherwise provided by the franchisor. For more information, see Multilevel Franchising in Chapter 1.

Data Description	Sample Responses and Explanations	Abbreviations
Development Agreement Term	Example: The initial contract period is five years	5

When allowed, this is the contract period in the initial agreement for area development.

Data Description	Sample Responses and Explanations	Abbreviations
Sub-franchising	Yes or No	Y/N

A Yes means that the franchise system allows subfranchising. For those that do, franchisees should establish exactly with whom they are dealing, the franchisor or one of its subfranchisors.

Subfranchising differs from the area development arrangement in that the subfranchisor's position is like that of a franchisor to its franchisees. It is important for franchisees to know the terms and conditions of the agreement between the subfranchisor and the franchisor. See the discussion on subfranchising under Multilevel Franchising in Chapter 1.

Content Summary of Right-facing Pages

Data Description	Data Entry Samples and Explanations	Abbreviated Responses
Franchise Company Name	MegaBucks International This is sometimes stated as the marketing name of the franchise, rather than its legal name.	franchisor's
Address	1234 Walnut Street	standard
City	Kansas City	standard
State or Province	MO This is the franchisor's U.S. state or Canadian province.	standard postal
Postal Code	64110-2356	standard postal
Country	USA This is the franchisor's country — U.S.A. or Canada.	standard
Product or Service Byline	Commercial Real Estate This byline provided by the franchisors briefly describes their products or services, usually in abbreviated text.	franchisor's
Phone	(816) 622-3400 This is the franchisor's contact telephone number.	standard
Accepts Collect Calls?	Yes If collect calls are permitted, the entry will be Yes. It will be No, if they are not.	Yes or No
Toll Free	(800) MEGABUCK This is the corporate or franchisor's toll-free telephone number; sometimes with a prefix of 888.	800 or 888 number
FAX	(816) 622-3401 This is the corporate or franchisor's facsimile number.	facsimile number
Internet	www.MEGABUCK.com This is the corporate or franchisor's Internet web page address.	no abbreviations
Suitable Sites	FB, SF, SC. OC, RM These are the types of spaces or sites permitted for franchise outlets. There are twenty different abbreviations used for the type of space that a franchisor allows:	*Redbook* abbreviations

Type of site	Abbreviation	Type of site	Abbreviation
Anchored Center	AC	Mall	M
Auto Mall	AM	Office Complex	OC
Executive Suite	ES	Office and Storage	OS
Depends on Area	DA	Power Center	PC
Free-standing Building	FB	Regional Mall	RM

Data Description	Data Entry Samples and Explanations					Abbreviated Responses
Suitable Sites (continued)	Food Court	FC		Strip Center	SC	FC, HO, IP, K, LI, SC, SF, WF, WR, O
	Home Office	HO		Storefront	SF	
	Industrial Park	IP		Waterfront Area	WF	
	Kiosk	K		Warehouse	WR	
	Light Industrial	LI		Other	O	

Concentration

200 in PA, 82 in CA, 74 in MA

standard

These are the three states and/or provinces with the highest volume of outlets with the state or province abbreviation for this entry together with a corresponding number representing the number of outlets for that state or province. These entries show the franchisor's highest areas of concentration of franchised outlets. Concentration is an indicator of the quality of support assistance and coop advertising in a region. If a prospective franchisee is considering opening an outlet in a new state or a totally new area, the franchisor may not be in a position to give equal support or services to this franchisee. In such cases, the franchisee should ascertain the interest and commitment level of the franchisor toward this pioneering effort before making a final commitment.

Expansion

NW, W

standard region

This entry indicates where this specific franchise plans to expand within the United States or outside of the country. Some franchisors respond "All", meaning anywhere and everywhere in the United States. Others list a standard state or regional abbreviation, or combination thereof.

Registered

ALL, CA

standard

Currently, fifteen states (CA, HI, IL, IN, MD, MI, MN, ND, NY, OR, RI, SD, VA, WA, and WI) and the District of Columbia require registration through their own regulatory agencies. All other states allow the franchisor to follow the Federal Trade Commission (FTC) Rule 436. The FTC requires submission of specific information to be disclosed by franchisors to prospective franchisees under Rule 436. For more information on registration and the UFOC, see Uniform Franchise Offering Circular in Chapter 2.

An entry here may list any combination of the abbreviations for the fifteen registration states, or "All" indicating it is registered in all U.S. registration states.

Field Support

DP, CP, EO, ST, O, FC, H

Redbook abbreviations

This field indicates what ongoing support assistance is provided by the franchisor and paid for by the franchisee through recurrent royalty payments. Some franchisors provide more services than others. Entries with dollar symbols ($) indicate that the support service is available, but at extra cost to the franchisee.

Data Description	Data Entry Samples and Explanations			Abbreviated Responses

Field Support (continued)

Field Support Service	If included	If at extra cost
Central Data Processing	DP	$DP
Central Purchasing	CP	$CP
Evaluation of Operations	EO	$EO
Field Training	ST	$ST
Store or Grand Opening	SO	$SO
Inventory Control	IC	$IC
Franchisor Conferences	FC	$FC
Telephone Hotline	H	$H
Newletter	N	$N

Training Provided

1 week at corporate HQ
3–4 days on-site
Ongoing as needed

standard

These entries show months, weeks or days, and the location. Franchisors could use up to three lines of text to describe the training they provide new franchisees. The example, a typical entry, indicates the franchisor provides one week of training at its corporate headquarters, three to four days in the field at the franchisee's site, and ongoing training and/or support as required by the franchisee.

Typically, the first stage of the training process is at franchisor headquarters, so a new franchisee can learn the business format and the methods of operation developed by the franchisor. Some franchisors arrange to have the first-stage training at a prototype outlet or at one of their regional locations. Topics frequently cover the basics of running a small business, as well as the proprietary systems, formulae and shortcut methods developed exclusively by the franchisor for its organization. The length of time of this training varies.

Field training usually includes on-the-job training, dry runs, and store opening preparation. Evaluation and final testing generally follow.

These descriptions provide more detailed information for an entry of "ST" under the Field Support data.

Part II
Franchise Industries Facts and Figures

Summary of Franchise Industry Statistics

Statistical figures referring to economic events are historical data. They tell us what happened in a nonrepeatable historical case.

— LUDWIG EDLER VON MISES

This summary provides some key averages for each business specialty. The dollar amounts are shown in thousands of dollars.

Industry	Specialty	Start-up Cost	Franchise Fee	Royalty	Advertizing Fee
Apparel Industry	Clothing	$134.2	$18.5	4.8%	0.7%
	Formal Wear	$120.6	$13.8	6.9%	1.0%
	Jewelry	$159.7	$29.2	3.3%	0.8%
Automotive Industry	Auto Accessories	$128.7	$21.3	3.3%	1.7%
	Oil Change, Lube	$293.1	$21.2	5.1%	3.6%
	Parts, Tools	$178.8	$ 9.8	1.7%	0.3%
	Rentals	$209.1	$24.1	3.6%	1.1%
	Repair: Body	$130.4	$19.2	5.2%	1.2%
	Repair: Brakes	$ 99.6	$19.1	5.0%	2.5%
	Repair: Exhaust, Brakes, Suspension	$157.8	$22.3	4.2%	3.0%
	Repair: General	$132.8	$21.7	3.7%	3.7%
	Repair: Transmission	$105.9	$23.4	6.9%	1.9%
	Repair: Tune-ups	$103.5	$16.4	5.2%	2.2%
	Repair: Windshield, Glass	$ 33.7	$11.4	4.8%	1.9%
	Repair: Other	$ 90.3	$19.8	4.4%	1.3%
	Sales, Brokerage	$460.7	$26.3	4.5%	0.7%

Industry	Specialty	Start-up Cost	Franchise Fee	Royalty	Advertizing Fee
Automotive Industry	Tires	$234.5	$17.2	3.8%	1.5%
	Wash, Detail, Protect	$141.2	$23.8	5.3%	2.2%
	Other Automotive	$1,162.6	$14.1	1.8%	1.1%
Beauty Industry	Cosmetics	$ 86.2	$12.6	2.5%	1.2%
	Hair Care	$100.8	$26.0	5.7%	2.1%
Business Service Industry	Accounting, Collections	$ 28.8	$18.1	5.1%	1.5%
	Advertising, Promotion	$ 27.1	$17.8	2.7%	0.3%
	Brokerage, Sales	$ 25.2	$12.2	3.0%	0.3%
	Finance	$ 56.5	$24.9	2.0%	1.5%
	Job Training	$ 92.1	$22.9	8.4%	0.8%
	Signs	$ 95.5	$25.5	5.5%	0.2%
	Telecom, Internet	$ 66.9	$31.1	1.5%	0.0%
	Other Business Service	$127.6	$24.2	4.4%	1.0%
Child Development Industry	Child Care	$ 77.3	$20.8	6.7%	2.0%
	Child Education	$345.3	$33.4	4.4%	0.5%
	Child Fitness	$ 38.8	$16.3	6.6%	1.0%
	Other Child Development	$ 93.5	$17.2	4.2%	0.6%
Cleaning and Repair Industry	Carpet, Upholstery, Drapery	$ 31.9	$13.5	3.0%	0.3%
	Commercial Cleaning	$ 59.2	$21.1	6.5%	0.7%
	Lawn Care, Landscaping	$142.9	$17.4	5.1%	1.6%
	Residential Cleaning	$ 35.1	$15.6	5.5%	1.2%
	Surface Restoration	$ 42.8	$14.9	2.8%	0.5%
	Vinyl Repair	$ 34.5	$23.5	5.8%	0.5%
	Other Cleaning and Repair	$ 66.6	$14.6	5.6%	0.7%
Construction Industry	Closet Systems	$158.8	$29.4	5.4%	2.0%
	Kitchens, Baths, Cabinets	$ 50.0	$11.9	3.9%	1.1%
	Repair, Reconstruction	$ 36.6	$18.8	4.0%	0.3%
	Windows, Doors, Siding	$ 88.6	$11.8	2.8%	0.1%
	Other Construction	$101.4	$26.7	3.2%	0.3%
Consumer Service Industry	Consumer Finance	$ 78.5	$16.2	3.0%	0.8%
	Dating Services	$ 22.6	$12.3	3.0%	0.0%
	Dry Cleaning, Laundry	$157.0	$18.6	4.1%	1.0%
	Income Tax	$ 26.1	$ 7.6	6.5%	2.3%
	Packaging, Mailing, Shipping	$ 86.4	$29.8	5.0%	1.5%
	Personal Services	$ 90.4	$19.5	5.1%	1.4%
	Special Event Services	$ 36.9	$13.0	4.0%	1.0%
	Other Consumer Service	$113.0	$26.9	11.0%	0.6%
Education Industry	Computer Training	$217.4	$35.8	7.3%	0.7%
	Other Education	$ 89.6	$24.2	5.3%	1.4%
Food Industry	Candy	$117.6	$20.8	4.3%	0.3%
	Coffees, Teas	$198.3	$24.8	5.4%	1.4%
	Convenience Stores	$304.1	$13.1	2.9%	0.6%
	Health Food, Vitamins	$126.5	$24.9	5.2%	1.4%

Industry	Specialty	Start-up Cost	Franchise Fee	Royalty	Advertizing Fee
Food Industry	Snack Foods	$175.6	$12.9	3.6%	0.3%
	Other Food	$264.7	$22.5	7.9%	1.0%
Health Industry	Adult Fitness	$366.3	$10.5	5.0%	0.0%
	Medical Supplies	$111.5	$23.3	3.4%	0.5%
	Optical Supplies	$530.8	$20.0	7.7%	6.7%
	Weight Loss and Control	$ 74.6	$14.0	3.0%	0.9%
Human Resources Industry	Executive-search Personnel	$ 70.7	$48.3	6.3%	0.2%
	General Personnel	$105.5	$14.1	5.9%	0.5%
	Medical Personnel	$139.4	$22.3	4.1%	0.3%
	Temporary Personnel	$ 87.7	$16.8	10.7%	0.0%
	Other Human Resources	$135.3	$12.5	1.3%	0.8%
Interior Design Industry	Carpet	$ 91.0	$17.2	4.0%	0.3%
	Furnishings	$163.4	$22.8	3.4%	0.8%
	Window Coverings	$ 61.6	$16.7	6.0%	0.8%
	Other Interior Design	$123.2	$24.2	4.0%	2.0%
Lodging Industry	Campgrounds	$139.0	$24.0	7.0%	1.5%
	Hotels, Motels	$5,540.0	$23.0	4.4%	1.3%
Pets Industry	Pet Care	$ 46.0	$13.3	4.5%	1.3%
	Pet Supplies	$149.9	$19.2	3.7%	0.4%
Photography Industry	Photography	$ 63.0	$23.9	4.2%	0.8%
Printing and Copying Industry	Printing and Copying	$217.5	$23.3	5.1%	0.9%
Publishing Industry	Publishing	$ 48.9	$16.8	3.8%	0.0%
Quick-service Industry	Bakery: Bagels	$245.6	$24.3	4.4%	1.5%
	Bakery: Cinnamon Rolls	$122.5	$25.0	5.5%	1.5%
	Bakery: Cookies	$157.8	$23.1	5.6%	1.9%
	Bakery: Doughnuts	$471.1	$15.2	4.4%	2.2%
	Bakery: Muffins	$249.1	$25.0	6.0%	1.6%
	Bakery: Pretzels	$127.3	$18.9	5.7%	0.5%
	Bakery: Other	$277.6	$27.6	5.4%	1.3%
	Frozen: Ice Cream	$228.2	$18.4	3.4%	1.8%
	Frozen: Soft-serve	$290.6	$26.9	4.5%	4.1%
	Frozen: Yogurt	$152.9	$19.2	4.3%	1.9%
	Frozen: Other	$263.6	$20.2	4.1%	1.7%
	Juices & Smoothies	$122.6	$19.1	5.0%	0.5%
	Meals: Cheese-steak	$169.8	$20.0	5.0%	2.5%
	Meals: Chicken, Turkey	$384.7	$18.2	4.8%	2.7%
	Meals: Hamburgers	$499.1	$30.4	5.6%	2.6%
	Meals: Hot Dogs	$208.1	$17.0	4.0%	1.4%
	Meals: Italian	$140.0	$26.7	5.3%	0.7%
	Meals: Mexican	$253.8	$21.9	5.0%	1.9%
	Meals: Oriental	$211.9	$14.4	6.0%	2.3%
	Meals: Sandwiches, Soups, Salad	$216.0	$19.8	5.7%	1.4%
	Meals: Seafood	$443.9	$17.8	4.8%	3.8%

Industry	Specialty	Start-up Cost	Franchise Fee	Royalty	Advertizing Fee
Quick-service Industry (continued)	Meals: Steak, BBQ	$823.5	$27.4	4.2%	1.3%
	Meals: Submarine Sandwiches	$147.8	$14.6	5.3%	2.3%
	Pizza: Dine-in or Delivery	$257.2	$18.1	4.2%	1.8%
	Pizza: Take and Bake	$ 95.0	$20.0	2.5%	0.5%
	Other Quick-service	$253.9	$22.2	4.6%	1.3%
Real Estate Industry	Property Inspection	$ 39.7	$18.7	4.9%	1.3%
	Other Real Estate	$ 36.3	$13.7	5.1%	1.3%
Restaurant Industry	Barbecue	$799.8	$40.0	3.9%	2.6%
	Burgers	$999.2	$36.7	4.0%	0.8%
	Diner Style	$226.3	$15.0	4.5%	0.3%
	Family Style	$839.7	$53.2	4.3%	2.2%
	Italian	$519.2	$33.3	4.7%	2.0%
	Mexican	$168.0	$18.3	3.8%	2.3%
	Oriental	$ 99.6	$35.0	6.0%	0.3%
	Specialty Style	$1,201.5	$70.8	4.5%	1.3%
	Steak Houses	$1,190.1	$30.4	3.6%	1.1%
	Other Restaurant	$758.0	$33.0	4.2%	0.9%
Retail Industry	Art, Prints, Framing	$119.1	$24.2	5.2%	1.6%
	Books, Audiobooks	$398.9	$29.3	3.0%	0.9%
	Computer Sales and Service	$103.5	$15.7	2.9%	0.8%
	Discount Stores	$184.6	$30.1	4.8%	2.0%
	Electronics	$159.9	$21.1	2.6%	0.6%
	Flowers	$ 43.3	$38.3	4.0%	1.0%
	Games, Hobby	$154.2	$20.9	3.4%	0.6%
	Gifts	$154.9	$24.6	4.9%	0.9%
	Hardware	$130.3	$26.5	3.0%	1.8%
	Music, Video	$178.0	$20.5	4.6%	1.3%
	Nature, Ecology	$269.9	$26.1	3.8%	0.6%
	Party Supplies	$270.2	$30.7	4.3%	0.0%
	Water	$ 78.8	$ 8.2	2.6%	0.0%
	Other Retail	$146.0	$20.0	4.5%	0.9%
Security Systems Industry	Security Systems	$111.8	$22.0	4.0%	1.0%
Sports and Recreation Industry	Apparel, Equipment	$181.8	$24.1	4.0%	1.9%
	Golf Specialty	$289.5	$30.5	2.9%	0.9%
	Memorabilia, Collectibles	$135.8	$21.4	4.6%	1.0%
	Tanning	$100.0	$12.4	3.9%	2.3%
	Other Sports and Recreation	$329.3	$13.2	7.3%	0.3%
Travel Industry	Travel	$ 71.2	$16.3	2.0%	0.7%

Franchise Industries Information Spreads

Every man, as long as he does not violate the laws of justice, is left perfectly free to pursue his own interest his own way, and to bring both his industry and capital into competition with those of any other man ....

— ADAM SMITH

For easiest comparison, the information — provided by U.S. and Canadian franchise corporations responding to the *Redbook* questionnaire — is presented on two-page spreads. The industries, and the specialties within them, are shown at the top of each page. When a specialty requires multiple spreads, it is noted within parentheses. Other hints for quickly locating precisely what you are searching for are at the beginning of Chapter 3.

Also in Chapter 3, you will find explanations of the terms and abbreviations used: on pages 36–42 (for left-facing pages) and on pages 42–45 (for right-facing pages). In addition, there are valuable tips on how you can transform the numbers into useful information.

The franchises that participated were sortable into these 28 IFA industry classifications.

Apparel	Health	Quick-service: Juices, Smoothies
Automotive	Human Resources	Quick-service: Meals
Beauty	Interior Design	Real Estate
Business Service	Lodging	Restaurants
Child Development	Pets	Retail
Cleaning and Repair	Photography	Security Systems
Construction	Printing and Copying	Sports and Recreation
Consumer Service	Publishing	Travel
Education	Quick-service: Bakery	
Food	Quick-service: Frozen	

Apparel Industry   Clothing

	Around Your Neck	Heel Quik	Jacadi	Just Legs	Panda Shoes	Shoe Stop	Sox Appeal	Totally Kool
Startup Cost	41.9K-70.7K	6K-138.5K	183K-313K	95K-110K	80K-125K	25K-130K	98K-210K	260.2K
Franchise Fee	12.5K-25K	2.5K-17.5K	20K	15K	25K	15K	20K	24.5K
Royalty	7%	4%	4%	5.5-3.5%	4%	5%	5%	5%
Advertising Fee		2%	1%	0%	.5%		1%	1%
Financing Provided	N	Y	N	Y	N	N	N	Y
Experience Required		N	N				N	N
Passive Ownership		A	N	D	D	N	D	D
In Business Since	1991	1984	1988	1992	1972	1984	1986	1993
Franchised Since	1997	1985	1992	1995	1974	1985	1986	1996
Franchised Units 1996							8	0
1997	1	675	15	8	58	12	8	0
1998			16				6	1
Company Owned 1996	1						0	1
1997	1	2	2	2	4	9	0	1
1998			3				0	1
Number of Units U.S.		181	17	0	0	21	6	
Canada		0	2	10	62	0	0	
Foreign		496	385	0	0	0	0	
Projected New U.S.			8				4	
Canada			0					
Foreign			20					
Corporate Employees		10	4	3	8	5	3	
Contract Length		20/10/10	7/7	10/10	5/lease	10/10	10/10	10/10/10
Expand in Territory		Y	Y	Y	Y	Y	Y	
Full-Time Employees		1-4	2-3	2	3	2	2	
Part-Time Employees			2-3	2	2	1	3	
Conversions		Y	N	Y	Y		N	Y
Site Selection Assist.		Y	Y	Y	Y	Y	Y	
Lease Negotiation Assist.		Y	N	Y	Y	Y	Y	
Site Space Required		100-600	1000	500-700	800	300-600	500-700	2800-4200
Development Agreement		Y	Y	Y	N	N	N	N
Develop. Agree. Term			7	5				
Sub-franchising		N	N	Y	N	Y	N	

Apparel Industry   Clothing

Around Your Neck
16415 Addison Rd #135
Dallas, TX 75248
Direct sales of mens clothing/image consulting
Phone: 972-713-9797   Accepts collect calls?
Toll Free: FAX:
Internet:
Suitable Sites:
Concentration:
Expansion:
Registered:
Field Support:
Training:

Heel Quik
1730 Cumberland Point Dr #5
Marietta, GA 30067
Shoe repair, specialty leather refinishing, hand-made shoes/boot
Phone: 770-951-9440   Accepts collect calls? N
Toll Free: 800-255-8145   FAX: 770-933-8268
Internet: hqcorp@bellsouth.net
Suitable Sites: AC, K, M, PC, RM, SC, SF
Concentration: 18 in GA, 13 in FL, 5 in CA
Expansion: All United States, Canada, Foreign
Registered: CA,FL,IL,IN,MD,MI,MN,NY,SD,VA,WA,WI
Field Support: EO, ST, SO, FC, H, N
Training: 2 weeks training cntr Atlanta, GA
store opening support

Jacadi
72 Parkway E
Mount Vernon, NY 10552
Upscale apparel, shoes, furniture, cosmetics for newborn-size 12
Phone: 914-667-2183   Accepts collect calls? N
Toll Free: FAX: 914-665-0416
Internet: jacadi@juno.com
Suitable Sites: FB, M, RM, SF
Concentration: 6 in CA, 3 in NY, 2 in TX
Expansion: All United States, Canada, Foreign
Registered: CA,FL,IL,NY
Field Support: CP, EO, $ST, SO, $FC, H, N
Training: 3-5 days minimum in New York
3 days on-site

Just Legs
935 Richmond Ave
Victoria, BC V8S-3Z4   CANADA

Phone: 250-595-8934   Accepts collect calls?
Toll Free: FAX: 250-595-8935
Internet:
Suitable Sites: RM
Concentration: 10 in BC
Expansion: All United States, Canada, Foreign
Registered:
Field Support: DP, EO, ST, SO, IC, FC
Training: 20 days Vancouver, BC

Panda Shoes
305 Marc Aurele Fortin Blvd
Laval, PQ H7L-2A3   CANADA

Phone: 514-622-4833   Accepts collect calls?
Toll Free: FAX: 514-622-2939
Internet:
Suitable Sites: RM
Concentration: 38 in PQ, 12 in ON, 9 in BC
Expansion: N, Canada
Registered:
Field Support: CP, EO, ST, SO, IC, FC, N
Training: 2 weeks Toronto, ON
2 weeks on-site

Shoe Stop
611 Market St #1 & 3
Kirkland, WA 98033

Phone: 425-889-1446   Accepts collect calls?
Toll Free: 800-275-3503   FAX: 425-889-4560
Internet:
Suitable Sites: RM, SC, SF
Concentration: 13 in WA, 11 in CA, 3 in OR
Expansion: NW and SE
Registered: CA,OR,WA
Field Support: EO, ST, SO, IC, $FC, H, N
Training: 4-6 weeks in-store

Sox Appeal
6321 Bury Dr Ste 2
Eden Prairie, MN 55346
Socks & hosiery fashion & basic items for men, women, children
Phone: 612-937-6162   Accepts collect calls? N
Toll Free: 800-899-8478   FAX: 612-934-5665
Internet:
Suitable Sites: OTHER
Concentration: 3 in MN, 3 in PA
Expansion: All United States
Registered: MN
Field Support: EO, ST, SO, IC, FC, H, N
Training: 4-5 days corporate office
1 week on-site

Totally Kool
1599 Fence Row Dr
Fairfield, CT 06430
Children's/mom's retail clothing
Phone: 203-256-9944   Accepts collect calls? N
Toll Free: FAX:
Internet:
Suitable Sites: DA, FB, M, PC, RM, SC, SF
Concentration: 2 in CT
Expansion: New England + Mid Atlantic
Registered:
Field Support:
Training:

Apparel Industry

Formal Wear

	Gent's Formal Wear	Gingiss Formalwear						
Startup Cost	45K-75K	119.7K-242.7K						
Franchise Fee	10K-15K	15K						
Royalty	8%	4.5-7%						
Advertising Fee		2%						
Financing Provided	N	N						
Experience Required		N						
Passive Ownership	D	D						
In Business Since	1981	1936						
Franchised Since	1991	1968						
Franchised Units 1996								
1997	2	207						
1998		195						
Company Owned 1996								
1997	1	32						
1998		38						
Number of Units U.S.	3	238						
Canada	0	0						
Foreign	0	0						
Projected New U.S.		15						
Canada								
Foreign								
Corporate Employees	2	49						
Contract Length	5/5	10/10						
Expand in Territory	Y	Y						
Full-Time Employees	2	2						
Part-Time Employees	1	4						
Conversions	Y	Y						
Site Selection Assist.	Y	Y						
Lease Negotiation Assist.	Y	Y						
Site Space Required	1000	1100-1200						
Development Agreement	N	Y						
Develop. Agree. Term		5						
Sub-franchising	Y	N						

Apparel Industry

Formal Wear

Gent's Formal Wear
404 E Wright St
Pensacola, FL 32501

Phone: 904-434-3272   Accepts collect calls?
Toll Free: FAX:
Internet:
Suitable Sites: FB, SC
Concentration: 2 in FL, 1 in MS
Expansion: SE
Registered: FL
Field Support: DP, CP, EO, $ST, SO, IC, $FC
Training: 2 weeks home office
1 week on-site

Gingiss Formalwear
2101 Executive Dr
Addison, IL 60101-1482
Formalwear specialist, rental & sales of men's & boys formalwear
Phone: 630-620-9050   Accepts collect calls? N
Toll Free: 800-621-7125   FAX: 630-620-8840
Internet: www.gingiss.com
Suitable Sites: FB, M, PC, RM, SC, SF
Concentration: 32 in CA, 37 in IL, 35 in TX
Expansion: All United States, Canada
Registered: CA,FL,IL,IN,MD,MI,MN,NY,OR,RI,VA,WA,WI
Field Support: CP, EO, ST, SO, IC, FC, N
Training: 2 weeks corporate HQ
on location, regional advisors
confidential operations manual

Apparel Industry   Jewelry

	Elegance Jewelry	Fast-Fix Jewelry Repairs	Rodan Jewellers/ Simply Charming				
Startup Cost	99/KIT	30K	200K-500K				
Franchise Fee	0	25K	50K-75K				
Royalty	0%	5%	5%				
Advertising Fee	0%	0	2-2.5%				
Financing Provided	N	Y	Y				
Experience Required		N					
Passive Ownership	A	D	N				
In Business Since	1990	1984	1976				
Franchised Since	1995	1987	1982				
Franchised Units 1996		70					
1997	1	72	12				
1998		88					
Company Owned 1996		0					
1997	265	2	0				
1998		0					
Number of Units U.S.	1	84	0				
Canada	265		12				
Foreign	0	4	0				
Projected New U.S.		24					
Canada							
Foreign		1					
Corporate Employees	1	8	5				
Contract Length	5/5	10	5-7/3-5				
Expand in Territory	Y	Y	N				
Full-Time Employees	1	2	2-3				
Part-Time Employees		1	3-4				
Conversions		Y	N				
Site Selection Assist.	N	Y	Y				
Lease Negotiation Assist.		Y	Y				
Site Space Required		150-750	400-1000				
Development Agreement	N	Y	N				
Develop. Agree. Term		VAR.					
Sub-franchising	N		N				

Apparel Industry   Jewelry

Elegance Jewelry
25 Kenmount Rd #202
St John's, NF A1B-1W1 CANADA

Phone: 709-726-1515   Accepts collect calls?
Toll Free: FAX:
Internet:
Suitable Sites: HO
Concentration: 1 in NF
Expansion: All United States, Canada
Registered:
Field Support:
Training: by mail

Fast-Fix Jewelry Repairs
1750 N Florida Mango Rd #103
West Palm Beach, FL 33409
Jewelry & watch repair while you wait
Phone: 561-478-5292   Accepts collect calls? N
Toll Free: 800-359-0407   FAX: 561-478-5291
Internet: fastfix@bellsouth.net
Suitable Sites: AC, K, RM
Concentration: 18 in FL, 14 in TX, 9 in CA
Expansion: All United States, Canada, Foreign
Registered: CA,FL,HI,IL,IN,MD,MI,MN,ND,NY,OR,RI,SD,VA,WA,WI,DC
Field Support: DP, CP, EO, ST, SO, FC, H, N
Training: complete on-site training
continuing support & services
national & regional conferences

Rodan Jewellers/ Simply Charming
4259 Canada Way #246
Burnaby, BC V5G-1H1 CANADA

Phone: 604-438-1625   Accepts collect calls?
Toll Free: FAX: 604-438-1635
Internet: www.rodan.com
Suitable Sites: RM
Concentration: 12 in BC
Expansion: N, Canada
Registered:
Field Support: CP, EO, ST, SO, FC, N
Training: 2 weeks HQ
4-6 months HQ and on-site

Automotive Industry   Auto Accessories

	Auto Accent Centers	Auto One Glass & Accessories	Truck Options					
Startup Cost	70K-120K	52K-70K	160K-300K					
Franchise Fee	14.9K	24K	25K					
Royalty	5%	5%	4%/$1333/MO					
Advertising Fee	1%		4%					
Financing Provided	Y	N	Y					
Experience Required								
Passive Ownership	D		A					
In Business Since	1985	1984	1987					
Franchised Since	1992	1984	1996					
Franchised Units 1996		28						
1997	5	29	3					
1998								
Company Owned 1996		1						
1997	7	1	2					
1998								
Number of Units U.S.	12		5					
Canada	0		0					
Foreign	0		0					
Projected New U.S.								
Canada								
Foreign								
Corporate Employees	25		5					
Contract Length	10/10		10/10					
Expand in Territory	N		Y					
Full-Time Employees	3		3					
Part-Time Employees	1		1					
Conversions	Y		Y					
Site Selection Assist.	Y		Y					
Lease Negotiation Assist.	Y		Y					
Site Space Required	2000-2500		4000-7000					
Development Agreement	Y		Y					
Develop. Agree. Term	NEG.		10					
Sub-franchising	N		N					

Automotive Industry

Auto Accessories

Auto Accent Centers

6550 Pearl Rd
Parma Heights, OH 44130

Phone: 216-888-8886   Accepts collect calls?
Toll Free: 800-567-3120   FAX: 216-888-4333
Internet:
Suitable Sites: FB, SC
Concentration: 10 in OH
    Expansion: OH and Bordering
    Registered:
Field Support: DP, CP, EO, ST, SO, IC, FC, H, N
    Training: 2 weeks corporate HQ
           1 week on-site

Auto One Glass & Accessories

2301 E Michigan Ave
Jackson, MI 49202
Auto/truck accessories,security,auto glass,detailing
    Phone: Accepts collect calls?
Toll Free: 800-922-8861   FAX:
Internet:
Suitable Sites:
Concentration:
    Expansion: NE,S,SE,MW
    Registered:
Field Support:
    Training:

Truck Options

5865 University Blvd W
Jacksonville, FL 32216

Phone: 904-731-7548   Accepts collect calls?
Toll Free: 800-463-7978   FAX: 904-731-3558
Internet:
Suitable Sites: FB, SF
Concentration: 3 in FL, 1 in FA, 1 in MD
    Expansion: All United States
    Registered: FL,MD,VA
Field Support: $DP, $CP, EO, ST, SO, IC, $FC, H, N
    Training: 4 weeks Jacksonville, FL

Automotive Industry   Oil Change, Lube (Spread 1 of 2)

	Express Oil Change	Grease Monkey International	Indy Lube	Jiffy Lube International Inc	Lube Depot	LubePros International, Inc.	Mister Mobile On-Site Oil Changes	Oil Butler International
Startup Cost	550K-800K	500K-750K	250K-450K	139K-159K	118.7K-157.4K	170K-200K	15.25K-67.6K	9K-18K
Franchise Fee	17.5K	28K	7.5K	35K	12.5K	25K	19.5K	3K-7K
Royalty	3-5%	5%	5%	TO 5%	5%	5%	4%	7%
Advertising Fee	3-5%	1%	5%			5%		2%
Financing Provided	Y	Y	Y	Y	Y	N	Y	Y
Experience Required						N		
Passive Ownership	D	D	D			A		D
In Business Since	1979	1978	1986	1979	1995	1978	1990	1987
Franchised Since	1983	1979	1989	1979	1995	1985	1996	1991
Franchised Units 1996				787	20		0	
1997	30	188	8	908	26	24	0	104
1998						24		
Company Owned 1996				506	1		1	
1997	28	30	20	551	1	12	1	1
1998						12		
Number of Units U.S.	58	198	28			36		89
Canada	0	0	0			0		4
Foreign	0	20	0			0		12
Projected New U.S.								
Canada								
Foreign								
Corporate Employees	25	55	10			7		9
Contract Length	10/10	15/15	20/5-10			20/10/10		10/5
Expand in Territory	N	Y	Y			Y		Y
Full-Time Employees	10	4	4			6		1-2
Part-Time Employees		2	2					1
Conversions	Y	Y	N					
Site Selection Assist.	Y	Y	Y			Y		Y
Lease Negotiation Assist.	Y	Y	Y			N		
Site Space Required	3500	15000	2100			1800		
Development Agreement	Y	Y	Y			N		Y
Develop. Agree. Term			20					
Sub-franchising	N	N	N			N		N

Automotive Industry

Express Oil Change
190 W Valley Ave
Birmingham, AL 35209

Phone: 205-945-1771   Accepts collect calls?
Toll Free: 800-945-1771   FAX: 205-940-6026
Internet:
Suitable Sites: FB
Concentration: 54 in AL, 2 in FL, 2 in MS
Expansion: SE
Registered: FL
Field Support: CP, EO, ST, SO, IC, FC, H, N
Training: 6-8 weeks w/ managers at Alabama
1-2 weeks w/crews in Alabama

Grease Monkey International
216 16th St Ste 1100
Denver, CO 80202-5125

Phone: 303-534-1660   Accepts collect calls?
Toll Free: 800-364-0352   FAX: 303-534-2906
Internet:
Suitable Sites: FB
Concentration: 52 in CO, 15 in CA, 12 in NJ
Expansion: All United States, Canada, Foreign
Registered: CA,FL,HI,IL,IN,MD,MI,MN,ND,NY,OR,RI,SD,VA,WA,WI,DC
Field Support: CP, EO, ST, SO, IC, FC, H, N
Training: 1 week Denver, CO

Indy Lube
6515 East 82nd St #209
Indianapolis, IN 46220
Quick lube services
Phone: 317-845-9444   Accepts collect calls?
Toll Free: 800-326-5823   FAX: 317-577-3169
Internet: www.indylube.com
Suitable Sites: FB
Concentration: 22 in IN, 6 in MN
Expansion: Midwest
Registered: IN
Field Support: $DP, $CP, EO, ST, SO, IC, FC, H, N
Training: 2-3 weeks HQ

Jiffy Lube International Inc
PO Box 2967
Houston, TX 77252-2967
Fast oil change
Phone: 713-546-6272   Accepts collect calls?
Toll Free: FAX:
Internet:
Suitable Sites:
Concentration:
Expansion: All United States
Registered:
Field Support:
Training:

Lube Depot
1237 W Fourth St
Mansfield, OH 44906
Oil change & lubrication services
Phone: 419-529-5669   Accepts collect calls?
Toll Free: FAX:
Internet:
Suitable Sites:
Concentration:
Expansion: All United States, Canada, Foreign
Registered:
Field Support:
Training:

LubePros International, Inc.
1630 Colonial Pkwy
Inverness, IL 60067

Phone: 847-776-2500   Accepts collect calls? N
Toll Free: 800-654-5823   FAX: 847-776-2542
Internet:
Suitable Sites: FB
Concentration: 27 in IL, 7 in WI
Expansion: Central, North Central
Registered: IL,IN,MN,WI
Field Support: EO, ST, SO, FC, H, N
Training: 10 days Rockford, IL

Mister Mobile On-Site Oil Changes
5592 61st N
Saint Petersburg, FL 33709
Motor vehicle lubrication services
Phone: 813-545-5823   Accepts collect calls?
Toll Free: FAX:
Internet:
Suitable Sites:
Concentration:
Expansion: SE
Registered:
Field Support:
Training:

Oil Butler International
1599 Route 22 W
Union, NJ 07083

Phone: 908-687-3283   Accepts collect calls?
Toll Free: FAX: 908-687-7617
Internet:
Suitable Sites: OC
Concentration: 21 in TX, 13 in CA, 8 in CO
Expansion: All United States, Canada, Foreign
Registered: CA,FL,IL,MD,MI,NY,VA,WA
Field Support: CP, EO, ST, IC, FC, N
Training: 4 days 2 weeks union, NJ

Automotive Industry

Oil Change, Lube (Spread 2 of 2)

	Oil Can Henry's International	Q Lube	Speedee Oil Change & Tune-Up	Valvoline Instant Oil Change	Victory Lane Quick Oil Change			
Startup Cost	130K-650K	350K-750K	186K-765.5K	81K-193K	80K			
Franchise Fee	25K	25K	30K	25K	20K			
Royalty	5.50%	2.5-4.5%	6%	4-6%	6%			
Advertising Fee	8%	6%	8%	6-8%	1%			
Financing Provided	Y	Y	N	Y	Y			
Experience Required								
Passive Ownership	N	D	D	A	D			
In Business Since	1978	1977	1980	1988	1980			
Franchised Since	1987	1977	1982	1988	1986			
Franchised Units 1996								
1997	34	126	128	133	13			
1998								
Company Owned 1996								
1997	1	450	6	381	10			
1998								
Number of Units U.S.	35	548	121	514	23			
Canada	0	28	0	0	0			
Foreign	0	0	13	0	0			
Projected New U.S.								
Canada								
Foreign								
Corporate Employees	9	120	16	84	11			
Contract Length	10/10	15/15	15/5/5	15/5/5	10/10			
Expand in Territory	Y	Y	Y	Y	Y			
Full-Time Employees	4-6	4-5	6	4	5			
Part-Time Employees	5-9	1-2	2	2				
Conversions	Y	Y	Y	Y	Y			
Site Selection Assist.	Y	Y	Y	Y	Y			
Lease Negotiation Assist.	N	Y	Y	Y	Y			
Site Space Required	15000	12000-15000	2700	15000	1500			
Development Agreement	Y	Y	Y	Y	Y			
Develop. Agree. Term	NEG.	3-5	15		5			
Sub-franchising	N	N	N	N	Y			

Automotive Industry

Oil Can Henry's International
1200 NW Front Ave #690
Portland, OR 97209
Automotive lubrication & filter maint.

Phone: 503-243-6311	Accepts collect calls?
Toll Free: 800-765-6244	FAX: 503-228-5227

Internet:
Suitable Sites: FB
Concentration: 15 in OR, 6 in CA, 5 in FL
  Expansion: NW, SE, FL
  Registered: CA,FL,MD,OR,VA,WA
Field Support: EO, $ST, SO, $FC, H, N
  Training: 5 weeks Portland, OR

Speedee Oil Change & Tune-Up
159 Hwy 22 E PO Box 1350
Madisonville, LA 70447

Phone: 504-845-1919	Accepts collect calls?
Toll Free: 800-451-7461	FAX: 504-845-1936

Internet:
Suitable Sites: FB
Concentration: 50 in CA, 22 in LA, 10 in MA
  Expansion: All United States, Canada, Foreign
  Registered: CA,VA,FL,HI
Field Support: EO, ST, SO, FC, N
  Training: 3 days HQ
        2-4 weeks local office
        1-2 weeks shop

Victory Lane Quick Oil Change
405 Little Lake Dr
Ann Arbor, MI 48103

Phone: 734-996-1196	Accepts collect calls?
Toll Free:	FAX: 734-996-4912

Internet:
Suitable Sites: FB, SC
Concentration: 21 in MI, OH, IN
  Expansion: Midwest
  Registered: MI
Field Support: CP, EO, ST, SO, IC, FC, N
  Training: 1 week corporate office

Q Lube
1385 W 2200 South
Salt Lake City, UT 84119

Phone: 801-975-4731	Accepts collect calls?
Toll Free: 800-526-4648	FAX: 801-975-4627

Internet: www.qlube.com
Suitable Sites: FB
Concentration: 57 in TX, 53 in IN, 49 in WA
  Expansion: All United States, Canada
  Registered: CA,FL,HI,IL,IN,MD,MI,MN,ND,NY,OR,RI,SD,VA,WA,WI,DC
Field Support: $DP, CP, EO, ST, SO, IC, $FC, H, N
  Training: 10 days salt Lake City, UT
        5-7 days pre-opening franch loca
        1 week after opening

Valvoline Instant Oil Change
3499 Blazer Pkwy
Lexington, KY 40509

Phone: 606-357-7070	Accepts collect calls?
Toll Free: 800-622-6846	FAX: 606-357-7049

Internet: www.valvoline.com
Suitable Sites: FB
Concentration: 74 in OH, 61 in MI, 51 in MN
  Expansion: SE,NW,SE,NE, Canada, Foreign
  Registered: CA,FL,HI,IL,IN,MD,MI,MN,ND,NY,OR,RI,SD,VA,WA,WI,DC
Field Support: DP, CP, EO, ST, SO, IC, $FC, H, N
  Training: 2 days Lexington, KY
        3 weeks opt. train

Automotive Industry

Parts, Tools

	Batteries Plus	Champion Auto Stores	FCI Franchising Inc	Matco Tools	Mighty Distribution System of America Inc			
Startup Cost	185K-225K	225K-450K	150K+	50K-127K	72K-154.4K			
Franchise Fee	25K	0	0	0	12.9K-34.8K			
Royalty	3-4%	0%	0	0%	5%			
Advertising Fee	1%	0%		0%	.5%			
Financing Provided	Y	Y	Y	Y	Y			
Experience Required	N			N	N			
Passive Ownership	N	D		A	A			
In Business Since	1988	1956	1989	1979	1963			
Franchised Since	1992	1961	1995	1993	1970			
Franchised Units 1996			0		144			
1997	74	130	0	1225	144			
1998	175				145			
Company Owned 1996			0		4			
1997	19	48	0	22	4			
1998	19				4			
Number of Units U.S.	93	178		1200				
Canada	0	0		0				
Foreign	0	0		0				
Projected New U.S.	40				6			
Canada	0				1			
Foreign	0							
Corporate Employees	39	150		180	45			
Contract Length	15	ANNUAL		10/10	10			
Expand in Territory	N	Y		Y	Y			
Full-Time Employees	3-4	3		1	3			
Part-Time Employees		4-6			1			
Conversions	N	Y		Y	Y			
Site Selection Assist.	Y	Y		N	Y			
Lease Negotiation Assist.	Y	Y			N			
Site Space Required	1800-2000	4000-8000			3500			
Development Agreement	N	N		Y	N			
Develop. Agree. Term				3				
Sub-franchising	N	N		N	N			

Automotive Industry
Parts, Tools

Batteries Plus
625 Walnut Ridge Dr #106
Hartland, WI 53029
Batteries for all types of uses, retail & commercial
Phone: 414-369-0690   Accepts collect calls? N
Toll Free: 800-274-9155   FAX: 414-369-0680
Internet: www.batteriesplus.com
Suitable Sites: FB, SC
Concentration: 15 in WI, 12 in MN, 17 in FL
Expansion: All United States
Registered: CA,FL,HI,IL,IN,MD,MI,MN,ND,NY,OR,SD,VA,WA,WI,RI
Field Support: DP, EO, ST, SO, IC, FC, H, N
Training: 4 weeks corporate HQ
10 days on-site

Champion Auto Stores
9353 Jefferson Hwy
Maple Grove, MN 55369

Phone: 612-391-6655   Accepts collect calls?
Toll Free: 800-621-4227   FAX: 612-391-7540
Internet: www.championauto.com
Suitable Sites: FB, SC, SF
Concentration: 83 in MN, 19 in WI, 16 in NE
Expansion: Midwest, North Rocky MT.
Registered:
Field Support: DP, CP, EO, ST, $SO, $IC, FC, H, N
Training: 3-4 weeks Minneapolis, MN

FCI Franchising Inc
18872 Hwy 169 N
Saint Joseph, MO 64505
Auto parts
Phone: Accepts collect calls?
Toll Free: 800-451-6742   FAX:
Internet:
Suitable Sites:
Concentration:
Expansion:
Registered:
Field Support:
Training:

Matco Tools
4403 Allen Rd
Stow, OH 44224-1096
Precision mechanics hand tools, service equip & diagnostic comp.
Phone: 330-929-4949   Accepts collect calls? N
Toll Free: 800-368-6651   FAX: 330-929-1526
Internet: www.matcotools.com
Suitable Sites:
Concentration:
Expansion: All United States, Canada
Registered: CA,FL,HI,IL,IN,MD,MI,MN,ND,NY,OR,RI,SD,VA,WA,WI,DC
Field Support: DP, CP, EO, ST, SO, IC, FC, H, N
Training: 6 days classroom stow, OH
3 weeks on-site

Mighty Distribution System of America Inc
50 Technology Pk
Norcross, GA 30092
Wholesale distribution of original equipment quality auto parts
Phone: 770-448-3900   Accepts collect calls? N
Toll Free: 800-829-3900   FAX: 770-446-8627
Internet: www.mightyap.com
Suitable Sites: FB, OS, WR
Concentration:
Expansion: All United States, Canada, Foreign
Registered: CA,FL,HI,IL,IN,MD,MI,MN,ND,NY,OR,RI,SD,VA,WA,WI,DC
Field Support: DP, CP, EO, ST, SO, IC, FC, H, N
Training: extensive initial & ongoing training
support to owners & sales people

Automotive Industry

Rentals (Spread 1 of 2)

	Affordable Car Rental	Budget Car & Truck Rental	Discount Car & Truck Rentals	Dollar Rent A Car	Dollar Rent A Car (Canada)	Joe Loue Tout Rent All	Payless Car Rental System	Practical Rent A Car
Startup Cost	$VAR.	VAR.	150K-250K	100K-2M	150K-300K	50K-1M	VAR.	25K-100K
Franchise Fee	3.5K+	20K	VAR.	12.5K+	10K-50K	20K	6K-250K	2.5K-100K
Royalty	0	5%	6-8%	7%	7%	4%	3-5%	FLAT/CAR
Advertising Fee	0	2.5%	0%	INCLUDED	2%	3%	1-3%	0%
Financing Provided	N	Y	Y	Y	Y	Y	Y	Y
Experience Required								
Passive Ownership	N	D	N	N	D	D	D	D
In Business Since	1981	1958	1980	1965	1966	1979	1971	1989
Franchised Since	1981	1960	1984	1966	1990	1982	1971	1989
Franchised Units 1996								
1997	95	2482	180	827	39	85	67	134
1998								
Company Owned 1996								
1997	0	544	23	69	3	0	0	0
1998								
Number of Units U.S.	95	960	23	266	0	0	41	134
Canada	0	375	170	76	42	85	0	0
Foreign	0	1458	10	554	0	0	26	0
Projected New U.S.								
Canada						10		
Foreign								
Corporate Employees	9	300	40	400	10	5	46	8
Contract Length	PERPETUAL	5/5	10/5/5	10/10	5/5	5/5	5/5	10/10
Expand in Territory	Y	Y	Y	Y	Y	Y	Y	Y
Full-Time Employees	1	VAR	3	VAR	3	2	4	2
Part-Time Employees	2		1		1	1-4	2	1
Conversions		Y	Y	Y	Y	Y	Y	Y
Site Selection Assist.	N	Y	Y	N	Y	Y	Y	Y
Lease Negotiation Assist.		Y	Y	N	Y		Y	Y
Site Space Required		15000	1500	2000	1200	2000		1000
Development Agreement	N	N	Y	Y	Y	N	Y	N
Develop. Agree. Term			10	VAR.	3		5	
Sub-franchising	N	Y	Y	N	Y	N	Y	N

Automotive Industry   Rentals (Spread 1 of 2)

Affordable Car Rental
96 Freneau Ave #2
Matawan, NJ 07747

Phone: 732-290-8300   Accepts collect calls?
Toll Free: 800-631-2290   FAX:
Internet:
Suitable Sites: FB
Concentration:
Expansion: All United States
Registered: FL,IL,IN,MD,MI,NY,RI,VA
Field Support: EO, ST, IC, FC, H, N
Training: 2 days corporate in New Jersey

Budget Car & Truck Rental
4225 Naperville Rd
Lisle, IL 60532

Phone: 630-955-7360   Accepts collect calls?
Toll Free: FAX: 630-955-7811
Internet:
Suitable Sites: FB
Concentration: 108 in CA, 107 in FL, 57 in AZ
Expansion: All United States, Canada, Foreign
Registered: CA,FL,HI,IL,IN,MD,MI,MN,ND,NY,OR,RI,SD,VA,WA,WI,DC
Field Support: $CP, EO, ST, SO, FC, H, N
Training: 1 week corp office, ON-site

Discount Car & Truck Rentals
720 Arrow Rd
North York, ON M9M-2M1 CANADA

Phone: 416-744-0123   Accepts collect calls?
Toll Free: 800-263-2355   FAX: 416-744-0624
Internet: www.discountcar.com
Suitable Sites: FB, SC, SF
Concentration: 86 in ON, 36 in PQ, 12 in AZ
Expansion: All United States, Canada, Foreign
Registered: CA,FL,HI,IL,IN,MD,MI,MN,ND,NY,OR,RI,SD,VA,WA,WI,DC
Field Support: DP, CP, EO, ST, SO, $IC, $FC, $H, N
Training: 2-4 weeks North York, ON

Dollar Rent A Car
5330 E 31st St
Tulsa, OK 74153

Phone: 918-669-3103   Accepts collect calls?
Toll Free: 800-555-9893   FAX: 918-669-3006
Internet: www.dollarcar.com
Suitable Sites: AM, FB, SC, SF
Concentration: CA, TX, ON
Expansion: Not FL,MA,VT,NH,NV,AR,UT,MT, Canada, Foreign
Registered: CA,FL,HI,IL,IN,MD,MI,MN,ND,NY,OR,RI,SD,VA,WA,WI,DC
Field Support: $DP, CP, EO, ST, SO, FC, H, N
Training: 3 days HQ orientation
2 weeks on-site field training
1 week autoMAtion

Dollar Rent A Car (Canada)
1027 Yonge St, 3rd Fl
Toronto, ON M4W-2K9 CANADA

Phone: 416-969-1190   Accepts collect calls?
Toll Free: 800-254-7561   FAX: 416-969-9582
Internet:
Suitable Sites: FB
Concentration: ON, BC, PQ
Expansion: N, Canada
Registered: AB
Field Support: CP, EO, ST, SO, IC, FC, H
Training: 5 days Toronto, ON

Joe Loue Tout Rent All
28 Rue Vanier
Chateauguay, QC J6J-3W8 CANADA

Phone: 514-692-6268   Accepts collect calls? N
Toll Free: 800-361-2020   FAX: 514-692-2848
Internet: www.joelouetout.ca
Suitable Sites: FB, HO, SC, SF
Concentration: 11 in ON, 1 in MB, 1 in SK
Expansion: Canada
Registered:
Field Support: CP, EO, ST, SO, FC, H, N
Training: 1 week office
1 week at store

Payless Car Rental System
2350 N 34th St N
Saint Petersburg, FL 33713
Auto rentals/auto sales
Phone: 813-321-6352   Accepts collect calls?
Toll Free: 800-729-5255   FAX: 813-323-3529
Internet:
Suitable Sites: FB, SC, SF
Concentration: 7 in AK, 5 in FL
Expansion: All United States, Canada, Foreign
Registered: CA,FL,HI,IL,IN,MD,MI,MN,NY,ND,OR,RI,VA,WA,WI,DC
Field Support: CP, EO, ST, SO, FC, H, N
Training: 3 days corporate office
4 days on-site

Practical Rent A Car
1500 E Tropicana Ave #123
Las Vegas, NV 89119

Phone: 702-798-0025   Accepts collect calls?
Toll Free: 800-424-7722   FAX: 702-798-4739
Internet:
Suitable Sites: FB, SC, SF
Concentration: 20 in WA, 14 in PA, 10 in OK
Expansion: All United States, Foreign
Registered: CA,FL,HI,IL,IN,MD,MI,MN,ND,NY,OR,RI,SD,VA,WA,WI,DC
Field Support: $DP, CP, EO, $ST, SO, FC, H, N
Training: 4.5 days HQ

Automotive Industry

Rentals (Spread 2 of 2)

	Rent 'N Drive	Rent-A-Wreck of America	Thrifty Car Rental (Canada)	Thrifty Rent-A-Car	Rental of America Inc	U-Save Auto	Wheelchair Getaways		
Startup Cost	28K-46K	32.8K-209K	200K-500K	150K+	72.5K-203.5K	38K-100K		
Franchise Fee	20K	5K+	15K+	VAR.	15K	17.5K		
Royalty	6%	6%/$30/CAR	5%	5%	VAR.	$550/VAN/YR		
Advertising Fee	1%	2%/$7/CAR	3%	2.5%		$550/VAN/YR		
Financing Provided	Y	Y	Y	Y	Y	Y		
Experience Required	N				N	N		
Passive Ownership	D	D	N	N		D		
In Business Since	1990	1973	1965	1950	1979	1988		
Franchised Since	1996	1978	1965	1952	1979	1989		
Franchised Units 1996	0				411			
1997	1	417	150	1122	439	32		
1998	1	450			450			
Company Owned 1996	1				1			
1997	1	0	10	8	1	0		
1998	1	0						
Number of Units U.S.	2	415	480	515		32		
Canada		0	159	132	9	0		
Foreign		2	467	475	2	0		
Projected New U.S.	6							
Canada								
Foreign								
Corporate Employees	6	26	465	539	25	2		
Contract Length	10/5/5	10/5	10/5	10/5	3	10/10		
Expand in Territory	Y	Y	Y	Y	Y	Y		
Full-Time Employees	1	1	3			2		
Part-Time Employees	2		2					
Conversions	Y	N	N	Y		N		
Site Selection Assist.	Y	Y	Y	Y	Y	Y		
Lease Negotiation Assist.	Y	N	N	N	N	N		
Site Space Required	650	1500				500		
Development Agreement	N	N	N	N	Y	N		
Develop. Agree. Term								
Sub-franchising	N	N	N	Y	N	N		

Automotive Industry

Rent 'N Drive
1919 South 40th St Ste 202
Lincoln, NE 68506
Used car, truck and van rentals
Phone: 402-434-5620   Accepts collect calls? N
Toll Free: 800-865-2378   FAX: 402-434-5624
Internet: www.franchisedevelopers.com
Suitable Sites: FB, SF
Concentration: 2 in NE
Expansion: All United States
Registered:
Field Support: $CP, EO, ST, SO, H, N
Training: 1 week NE
1 week on-site

Rent-A-Wreck of America
11460 Cronridge Dr #120
Owings Mills, MD 21117
Car rental franchises
Phone: 410-581-5755   Accepts collect calls? N
Toll Free: 800-421-7253   FAX: 410-581-1566
Internet: www.rent-a-wreck.com
Suitable Sites: AM, FB, OS, SC, SF
Concentration: 53 in CA, 33 in NY, 24 in NJ
Expansion: All United States, Foreign
Registered: CA,FL,HI,IL,IN,MD,MI,MN,ND,NY,OR,RI,SD,VA,WA,WI,DC
Field Support: EO, ST, $SO, $FC, $H, N
Training: 1 week in Baltimore, MD

Thrifty Car Rental (Canada)
6050 Indian Line
Mississauga, ON L3P-1K2 CANADA

Phone: 905-612-1881   Accepts collect calls?
Toll Free: 800-612-1893   FAX: 905-612-1893
Internet: www.thrifty.com
Suitable Sites: AM, ES, DA, FB, RM, SC, SF
Concentration:
Expansion: All United States, Canada, Foreign
Registered: CA,FL,HI,IL,IN,MD,MI,MN,ND,NY,OR,RI,SD,VA,WA,WI,DC
Field Support: CP, EO, ST, $SO, IC, $FC, $H, N
Training: 1 week on-site
1 week HQ

Thrifty Rent-A-Car
5310 E 31st St
Tulsa, OK 74135
Vehicle rentals, leasing & parking
Phone: 918-669-2853   Accepts collect calls?
Toll Free: 800-532-3401   FAX: 918-669-2061
Internet: www.thrifty.com
Suitable Sites: ES, DA, FB, RM, SC, SF
Concentration:
Expansion: All United States, Canada, Foreign
Registered: CA,FL,HI,IL,IN,MD,MI,MN,ND,NY,OR,RI,SD,VA,WA,WI,DC
Field Support: CP, EO, ST, SO, IC, $FC, $H, N
Training: 5 days HQ in Tulsa, OK

U-Save Auto Rental of America Inc
4780 I-55 N, Ste 300
Jackson, MS 39211
New & used auto rentals
Phone: 601-713-4333   Accepts collect calls? N
Toll Free: 800-438-2300   FAX: 601-713-4330
Internet: jackie.mclaughlin@usave.net
Suitable Sites:
Concentration: NC, MA, OH
Expansion: All United States, Canada, Foreign
Registered:
Field Support:
Training:

Wheelchair Getaways
PO Box 605
Versailles, KY 40383-0605
Rental or long-term leasing of wheelchair accessible vans
Phone: 606-873-4973   Accepts collect calls?
Toll Free: 800-536-5518   FAX: 606-873-8039
Internet: wheelchair-getaways.com
Suitable Sites: FB, HO, RM, SF
Concentration: 4 in FL, 3 in CA, 2 in NY
Expansion: All United States, Canada, Foreign
Registered: CA,FL,IL,IN,MD,MI,NY,VA,DC,MN
Field Support: SO, $FC, H, N
Training: 1 day corporate HQ, frn site

Automotive Industry   Repair: Body (Spread 1 of 2)

	Abra Auto Body & Glass	Custom Auto Restoration Systems	Dent Doctor	Dent Zone	DentPro	Auto Appearance Centers EndRust	Painting & Bodyworks Maaco Auto	Painting & Bodyworks (Canada) Maaco Auto
Startup Cost	229.6K-422.6K	1K-10K	40K-49K	15K-24K	51K-65K	90K	189.9K	195K
Franchise Fee	22.5K	N/A	7.8K-22.8K	20K	25K+	VAR.	30K	25K
Royalty	5%	0%	6%	8%	7%	0%	8%	8%
Advertising Fee	3%	0%	0%	1%	2% OPT	0%	$750/WK.	$500/WK
Financing Provided	N	N	Y	Y	Y	Y	Y	N
Experience Required	Y		N	N	N			N
Passive Ownership	A		A	D	D	A	N	N
In Business Since	1984	1984	1986	1993	1991	1969	1972	1972
Franchised Since	1987	1986	1990	1997	1993	1970	1972	1972
Franchised Units 1996				0	36			
1997	36	841	27	1	42	55	505	505
1998	28		30	1	48			
Company Owned 1996				1	3			
1997	18	257	3	1	4	0	0	0
1998	35		3	1	3			
Number of Units U.S.	63	584	28	2	46	55	458	459
Canada	0	131	2		0	0	40	41
Foreign	0	126	0		2	0	7	6
Projected New U.S.	30		10	10	3			
Canada	0				0			5
Foreign	0		2		0			
Corporate Employees	600+	6	5	6	6	6	125	11
Contract Length	10/10	N/A	10/10/10	10/5/5	10/5/5	INDEFIN.	15/5	15/5
Expand in Territory	Y	Y	Y	Y	Y	Y	Y	Y
Full-Time Employees		1	2	1	1	2	11	8
Part-Time Employees				1	1	1		
Conversions	Y		Y	Y	Y		N	Y
Site Selection Assist.	Y	N	Y	Y	N	Y	Y	Y
Lease Negotiation Assist.	Y	N	Y	Y	N	Y	Y	Y
Site Space Required	8000-15000		2000	750		2000	7500-10000	8000
Development Agreement	Y	N	Y	N	N	Y	N	N
Develop. Agree. Term	5					5		
Sub-franchising	N	N	N	N	N	Y	N	Y

Automotive Industry

Abra Auto Body & Glass
6601 Shingle Creek Pkwy #200
Brooklyn Center, MN 55430

Phone: 612-561-7220   Accepts collect calls?
Toll Free: 800-536-2334   FAX: 612-561-7433
Internet:
Suitable Sites: AM, FB
Concentration: 28 in MN, 7 in TN, 6 in WI
Expansion: Central, South, SE
Registered: IL,IN,MI,MN,ND,SD,WI
Field Support: $DP, CP, EO, ST, SO, IC, $FC, H, N
Training: 2-4 weeks training ctr Minneapolis
       6 weeks on-site

Custom Auto Restoration Systems
479 Interstate Ct
Sarasota, FL 34240

Phone: 941-378-1193   Accepts collect calls?
Toll Free: 800-736-1307   FAX: 941-378-3472
Internet: www.autorestoration.com/cars/
Suitable Sites:
Concentration: PA, AL, TX
Expansion: All United States, Canada, Foreign
Registered: FL
Field Support: H, N
Training: 1-2 weeks Sarasota, FL

Dent Doctor
11301 W Markham
Little Rock, AR 72211
Paint free dent repair of minor dents, door dings & hail damage
Phone: 501-224-0500   Accepts collect calls? Y
Toll Free: 800-946-3368   FAX: 501-224-0507
Internet: www.dentdoctor.usa.com
Suitable Sites: AM, FB, SF
Concentration: 5 in TX, 4 in CO, 4 in TN
Expansion: All United States, Canada, Foreign
Registered: MI,CA,IN,IL,NY,WA
Field Support: CP, EO, ST, SO, FC, H, N
Training: 5 weeks little rock, AR
       1 week franchisee's home area

Dent Zone
1919 South 40th St Ste 202
Lincoln, NE 68506
Paintless dent repair service
Phone: 402-434-5620   Accepts collect calls? N
Toll Free: 800-865-2378   FAX: 402-434-5624
Internet: www.franchisedevelopers.com
Suitable Sites: FB, SF
Concentration: 1 in TX, 1 in NE
Expansion: All United States
Registered:
Field Support: $CP, EO, ST, SO, H, N
Training: 3-4 weeks Dallas, TX

DentPro
2801 Whipple Rd
Union City, CA 94587
Paintless dent repair system of auto body repair
Phone: 510-429-5100   Accepts collect calls?
Toll Free: 800-868-3368   FAX: 510-429-5099
Internet: www.dentpro.com
Suitable Sites: HO
Concentration: 21 in CA, 5 in ID, 2 in NV
Expansion: All United States, Canada
Registered: CA
Field Support: CP, EO, ST, SO, FC, H, N
Training: 6 weeks Union City, CA

EndRust Auto Appearance Centers
1155 Greenbriar Dr
Bethel Park, PA 15102

Phone: 412-831-1255   Accepts collect calls?
Toll Free: FAX: 412-833-3409
Internet:
Suitable Sites: FB, HO, RM, SC, SF
Concentration: 20 in PA, 12 in OH, 8 in WV
Expansion: All United States
Registered: CA,FL,HI,IL,IN,MD,MI,MN,ND,NY,OR,RI,SD,VA,WA,WI,DC
Field Support: EO, ST, SO, IC, FC, N
Training: 1 week on-site
       continual follow-up

Maaco Auto Painting & Bodyworks
381 Brooks Rd
King Of Prussia, PA 19406

Phone: 610-265-6606   Accepts collect calls?
Toll Free: 800-296-2226   FAX: 610-337-6176
Internet: www.maaco.com
Suitable Sites: FB
Concentration: 36 in CA, 21 in PA, 24 in NJ
Expansion: All United States, Canada
Registered: CA,FL,HI,IL,IN,MD,MI,MN,ND,NY,OR,RI,SD,VA,WA,WI,DC
Field Support: DP, CP, EO, ST, SO, IC, FC, H, N
Training: 4 weeks King of Prussia, PA
       3 weeks on-site

Maaco Auto Painting & Bodyworks (Canada)
10 Kingsbridge Garden Cir #501
Mississauga, ON L5K-3K6 CANADA
Auto painting & body work
Phone: 905-501-1212   Accepts collect calls? Y
Toll Free: 800-387-6780   FAX: 905-501-1218
Internet:
Suitable Sites: AM, FB, IP, LI, SC, SF, OTHER
Concentration: 18 in ON, 7 in AB, 6 in BC
Expansion: N, Canada
Registered: AB
Field Support: DP, CP, EO, ST, SO, IC, FC, H, N
Training: 4 weeks school
       7 weeks on-site

Automotive Industry

	Miracle Auto Painting & Body Repair						
Startup Cost	215K-275K						
Franchise Fee	35K						
Royalty	5%						
Advertising Fee	5%						
Financing Provided	Y						
Experience Required	N						
Passive Ownership	D						
In Business Since	1953						
Franchised Since	1964						
Franchised Units 1996							
1997	33						
1998							
Company Owned 1996							
1997	5						
1998							
Number of Units U.S.	38						
Canada	0						
Foreign	0						
Projected New U.S.	2						
Canada							
Foreign							
Corporate Employees	20						
Contract Length	10/10						
Expand in Territory	Y						
Full-Time Employees	10						
Part-Time Employees	2						
Conversions	Y						
Site Selection Assist.	Y						
Lease Negotiation Assist.	Y						
Site Space Required	7500-10000						
Development Agreement	Y						
Develop. Agree. Term	5						
Sub-franchising	Y						

Automotive Industry   **Repair: Body (Spread 2 of 2)**

Miracle Auto Painting & Body Repair
3157 Corporate Pl
Hayward, CA 94545
Body & collision repairs, auto refinishing
    Phone: 510-887-2211   Accepts collect calls? N
    Toll Free: 877-MIR-ACLE   FAX: 510-887-3092
    Internet: www.miracleautopainting.com
Suitable Sites: AM, DA, FB, IP, LI, SC
Concentration: 28 in CA, 7 in TX, 1 in AZ
    Expansion: Western
    Registered: CA,OR,WA
Field Support: $DP, $CP, EO, ST, SO, $IC, FC, N
    Training: 10 days HQ
              10 days on-site

Automotive Industry

Repair: Brakes

	American Brake Service	Brake Centers of America	The Brake Shop	Tilden for Brakes Car Care Centers			
Startup Cost	110K-119K	50K-90K	39K-86K	131K-171.5K			
Franchise Fee	19.5K	12K	20K	25K			
Royalty	6%	6%	8%	6%/$350/WK			
Advertising Fee	6%	4%		3%/$175/WK			
Financing Provided	Y	Y	Y	Y			
Experience Required		N					
Passive Ownership	D	N	D	D			
In Business Since	1991	1989	1987	1923			
Franchised Since	1991	1996	1989	1996			
Franchised Units 1996							
1997	17	0	82	9			
1998		0					
Company Owned 1996							
1997	0	6	16	0			
1998		8					
Number of Units U.S.	17	8	98	9			
Canada	0	0	0	0			
Foreign	0	0	0	0			
Projected New U.S.		2					
Canada							
Foreign							
Corporate Employees	4	4	15	4			
Contract Length	10/10	17/10	20/10	10/5/5			
Expand in Territory	Y	Y	Y	Y			
Full-Time Employees	3	3	3	4			
Part-Time Employees	2	1		2			
Conversions	Y	Y	Y	Y			
Site Selection Assist.	Y	Y	Y	Y			
Lease Negotiation Assist.	Y	Y	Y	Y			
Site Space Required	3000	2500	1500-4000	5000			
Development Agreement	Y	Y	Y	Y			
Develop. Agree. Term		OPEN	20	10			
Sub-franchising	Y	Y	N	N			

Automotive Industry

American Brake Service

3715 Northside Pkwy NW Bldg 300 #195
Atlanta, GA 30327

    Phone: 404-262-7005   Accepts collect calls?
    Toll Free: 800-362-7005   FAX: 404-262-0810
    Internet: www.americanbrakeservice.com
Suitable Sites: FB, SC
Concentration: 6 in MA, 6 in GA, 2 in MN
    Expansion: All United States
    Registered: IN
Field Support: EO, $ST, SO, IC, FC, H, N
    Training: 2 weeks Atlanta, GA

Brake Centers of America

35 Old Battery Rd
Bridgeport, CT 06605
True brake specialty shop
    Phone: 203-336-1995   Accepts collect calls? N
    Toll Free: FAX: 203-336-1995
    Internet: brakesusa@aol.com
Suitable Sites: AC, AM, FB, SC
Concentration: 8 in CT
    Expansion: NE
    Registered: NY
Field Support: CP, EO, $ST, $SO, IC, H, N
    Training: 80 hours Norwalk, CT

The Brake Shop

31900 Utica Rd Ste 202
Fraser, MI 48302

    Phone: 810-415-2800   Accepts collect calls?
    Toll Free: 800-747-2113   FAX: 810-415-2812
    Internet:
Suitable Sites: AM, FB, M, SC
Concentration: 36 in MI, 8 in OH, 7 in NY
    Expansion: All United States
    Registered: MI
Field Support: EO, ST, SO, FC, H, N
    Training: 1 week training center
            1 week on-site

Tilden for Brakes Car Care Centers

1325 Franklin Ave #165
Garden City, NY 11530

    Phone: 516-746-7911   Accepts collect calls?
    Toll Free: 800-845-3367   FAX: 516-742-4499
    Internet:
Suitable Sites: FB
Concentration: 8 in NY, 1 in FL
    Expansion: All United States, Canada
    Registered: CA,FL,MD,NY,VA
Field Support: DP, CP, EO, ST, SO, IC, FC, H
    Training: 2 weeks home office
            1 week franchisee's store

Automotive Industry   Repair: Exhaust, Brakes, Suspension (Spread 1 of 2)

	Car-X Muffler & Brake	Lentz USA Service Centers	Meineke Discount Mufflers	Merlin's Muffler & Brake	Midas (Canada)	Minute Muffler And Brake	Monsieur Muffler	Mr. Front-End
Startup Cost	204K-263K	75K-95K		138K-164K	250K	150K-250K		150K
Franchise Fee	20K	20K	25K	26K-30K	25K	0-25K	10K	10K
Royalty	5%	0-7%	5-7%	4.9%	5%	0%	5%	4%
Advertising Fee	5-7%	0	10%		5%	0%	2%	1%
Financing Provided	N	Y	Y	Y	N	N	N	Y
Experience Required	N	N	N		N	N	N	
Passive Ownership	D	D	D		N	D	D	D
In Business Since	1971	1983	1972	1975	1955	1969	1956	1973
Franchised Since	1973	1989	1972	1975	1961	1977	1976	1993
Franchised Units 1996	119			47			65	
1997	124	25		53	215	120	73	1
1998	129	28	889		237		83	
Company Owned 1996	53	11		8			15	
1997	53	11		3	32	1	10	1
1998	53	11	4		10		0	
Number of Units U.S.	182	39			0	0	0	0
Canada		0			247	119	83	2
Foreign		0			0	2	0	0
Projected New U.S.	10	7					0	
Canada							4	
Foreign							0	
Corporate Employees		10	100+		330	13	0	5
Contract Length	15/5	10/10	15		20/20	ON-GOING	5	UNLIM./20
Expand in Territory	Y	Y	Y		Y	Y	Y	N
Full-Time Employees	4	3			4-5	3-5	3	4
Part-Time Employees		2			4-5	1	2	
Conversions	Y	Y	Y		Y	Y		Y
Site Selection Assist.	Y	Y	Y		Y	Y	Y	Y
Lease Negotiation Assist.	Y	Y	Y		Y	Y	N	Y
Site Space Required	5000	3600	3000		5000	3200-3500		4000
Development Agreement	Y	Y	N		N	N	N	N
Develop. Agree. Term	VAR.	10						
Sub-franchising	N	N	N		N	Y	N	N

Automotive Industry

Repair: Exhaust, Brakes, Suspension (Spread 1 of 2)

Car-X Muffler & Brake
8430 W Bryn Mawr #400
Chicago, IL 60631
Brakes, exhaust, ride control, steering systems, a/c, tires, oil
Phone: 773-693-1000   Accepts collect calls?
Toll Free: 800-359-2359   FAX: 773-693-0309
Internet: dmaltzma@carx.com
Suitable Sites: FB
Concentration: 59 in IL, 25 in MN, 21 in MO
Expansion: MW,S,SE,SE
Registered: FL,IL,IN,MD,MI,MN,NY,RI,VA,WI,DC
Field Support: EO, ST, SO, $FC, H, N
Training: 5 weeks HQ
2 weeks franchisee's shop

Lentz USA Service Centers
1001 Riverview Dr
Kalamazoo, MI 49001
Repair of brake, steering & exhaust systems, oil changes & a/c
Phone: 616-342-2200   Accepts collect calls? N
Toll Free: 800-354-2131   FAX: 616-342-9461
Internet: www.lentzusa.com
Suitable Sites: FB, SC
Concentration: 23 in MI, 10 in IN, 6 in IL
Expansion: All United States, Canada, Foreign
Registered: FL,IL,IN,MD,MI
Field Support: CP, EO, ST, SO, IC, FC, H, N
Training: 2 weeks Kalamazoo, MI
1 week on-site

Meineke Discount Mufflers
128 S Tryon St #900
Charlotte, NC 28202
Automotive service - under car specialists
Phone: 704-377-8855   Accepts collect calls?
Toll Free: 800-634-6353   FAX: 704-358-4706
Internet: www.meineke.com
Suitable Sites: FB
Concentration:
Expansion: All United States, Canada
Registered:
Field Support: DP, EO, ST, SO, FC, H, N
Training:

Merlin's Muffler & Brake
1 N River Ln #206
Geneva, IL 60134
Brakes/exhaust/suspension/oil & lube
Phone: 630-208-9900   Accepts collect calls?
Toll Free: 800-652-9900   FAX:
Internet:
Suitable Sites:
Concentration:
Expansion: S,SE,MW
Registered:
Field Support:
Training:

Midas (Canada)
105 Commander Blvd
Agincourt, ON M1S-3X8 CANADA

Phone: 416-291-4261   Accepts collect calls?
Toll Free: FAX: 416-291-0635
Internet: midas.canada@sympatico.ca
Suitable Sites: AC, ES, FB, IP, OTHER
Concentration: 126 in ON, 33 in PQ, 33 in BC
Expansion: N, Canada
Registered: AB
Field Support: DP, CP, EO, ST, $FC, H, N
Training: 2 days head office
in-store as needed

Minute Muffler And Brake
1600 - 3rd Ave S
Lethbridge, AB T1J-0L2 CANADA

Phone: 403-329-1020   Accepts collect calls?
Toll Free: 888-646-6833   FAX: 403-328-9030
Internet: www.minutemuffler.com
Suitable Sites: FB
Concentration: 25 in BC, 24 in AB, 18 in ON
Expansion: N, Canada, Foreign
Registered: AB
Field Support: CP, EO, ST, $SO, IC, $FC, H, N
Training: 1-10 weeks head office
1-2 weeks on-site

Monsieur Muffler
9061 Boul Pie Ix
Montreal, PQ H1Z-3V6 CANADA

Phone: 514-593-3752   Accepts collect calls? Y
Toll Free: 800-363-7131   FAX: 514-326-9634
Internet: yjutras@belroncanada.com
Suitable Sites: DA, FB
Concentration: 76 in QUE, 7 in ONT
Expansion: Canada
Registered:
Field Support: DP, CP, EO, ST, SO, IC, FC, N
Training:

Mr. Front-End
192 Northqueen St
Etobicoke, ON M9C-1A8 CANADA

Phone: 416-622-9998   Accepts collect calls?
Toll Free: FAX: 416-622-9999
Internet:
Suitable Sites: FB
Concentration: 2 in ON
Expansion: N, Canada
Registered:
Field Support: DP, CP, EO, ST, SO, FC
Training: Ontario

Automotive Industry   **Repair: Exhaust, Brakes, Suspension (Spread 2 of 2)**

	One Stop Undercar	Muffler & Brake Shops / Top Value					
Startup Cost	292K-460K	105K-160K					
Franchise Fee	40K-80K	10K-15K					
Royalty	5%	2-5%					
Advertising Fee	3%	3%					
Financing Provided	N	Y					
Experience Required		N					
Passive Ownership	D	D					
In Business Since	1993	1977					
Franchised Since	1993	1980					
Franchised Units 1996		38					
1997	10	38					
1998		35					
Company Owned 1996		12					
1997	4	9					
1998		6					
Number of Units U.S.	14	41					
Canada	0	0					
Foreign	0	0					
Projected New U.S.		5					
Canada		2					
Foreign		0					
Corporate Employees	7	33					
Contract Length	20/20	10/5/5					
Expand in Territory	Y	Y					
Full-Time Employees	8	2-3					
Part-Time Employees		VAR.					
Conversions		Y					
Site Selection Assist.	N	Y					
Lease Negotiation Assist.	N	Y					
Site Space Required	3500	2500-3600					
Development Agreement	Y	Y					
Develop. Agree. Term	5	VAR.					
Sub-franchising	N	N					

Automotive Industry   **Repair: Exhaust, Brakes, Suspension (Spread 2 of 2)**

One Stop Undercar
14831 Myford Rd #A
Tustin, CA 92780

Phone: 714-505-2600   Accepts collect calls?
Toll Free: FAX: 714-505-1817
Internet:
Suitable Sites: WR
Concentration: 13 in CA
Expansion: SE
Registered: CA
Field Support: ST, SO, IC, $FC, $N
Training: 4 weeks orange county, PA

Top Value Muffler & Brake Shops
36887 Schoolcraft
Livonia, MI 48150
Service for brakes, mufflers, shocks, suspension, front-end, a/c
Phone: 734-462-3633x207   Accepts collect calls? Y
Toll Free: 800-860-8258x207   FAX: 734-462-1088
Internet: www.top-value.com
Suitable Sites: AM, FB
Concentration: 34 in MI, 6 in OH, 1 in IN
Expansion: MI,OH,IN,N.KY, Canada
Registered: IN,MI
Field Support: CP, EO, ST, SO, IC, FC, H, N
Training: 3 weeks operations, marketing, etc. at HQ
1 week on-site
grand opening

Automotive Industry   **Repair: General**

	King Bear Auto Service Centers	The Master Mechanic	Saf-T Auto Centers						
Startup Cost	150K-250K	125K-175K	32K-65K						
Franchise Fee	25K	25K	15K						
Royalty	5%	6%	$500/MO						
Advertising Fee	7%	3%	1%						
Financing Provided	Y	Y	Y						
Experience Required	N	Y							
Passive Ownership	D	D	D						
In Business Since	1973	1979	1978						
Franchised Since	1974	1983	1985						
Franchised Units 1996									
1997	29	25	7						
1998		29	9						
Company Owned 1996									
1997	1	1	2						
1998		0	1						
Number of Units U.S.	30	0	10						
Canada	0	29	0						
Foreign	0	0	0						
Projected New U.S.									
Canada		4							
Foreign									
Corporate Employees	6	5	3						
Contract Length	25	20/OPEN	10/10						
Expand in Territory	N	Y	Y						
Full-Time Employees	2	3-4	2						
Part-Time Employees	1	1-2							
Conversions	Y	Y	N						
Site Selection Assist.	Y	Y	Y						
Lease Negotiation Assist.	Y	Y	Y						
Site Space Required	3500	4000	2000						
Development Agreement	N	Y	Y						
Develop. Agree. Term		10							
Sub-franchising	N	Y	N						

Automotive Industry   Repair: General

King Bear Auto Service Centers
130 - 29 Merrick Blvd
Springfield Gardens, NY 11434
Full service auto repair & used car facility
    Phone: 718-527-1252   Accepts collect calls? N
    Toll Free: 800-311-5464   FAX: 718-527-4985
    Internet: www.kingbearautofranchise.com
Suitable Sites: AC, AM, DA, FB, LI, SC
Concentration: 30 in NY
    Expansion: NE, Canada, Foreign
    Registered: NY
Field Support: CP, EO, ST, SO, IC, FC, H, N
    Training: 2 weeks corporate center
            on-site as needed
            assist in hiring, etc.

The Master Mechanic
1989 Dundas St E
Mississauga, ON L4X-1M1 CANADA
General automotive repair
    Phone: 905-629-3773   Accepts collect calls?
    Toll Free: FAX: 905-629-3864
    Internet:
Suitable Sites: FB, M, RM, SC, SF
Concentration: 29 in ON
    Expansion: N, Canada
    Registered:
Field Support: DP, CP, EO, ST, SO, FC, H, N
    Training: 1 week classroom
            4 weeks training shop
            2 weeks on-going on-site

Saf-T Auto Centers
121 N Plains Industrial Rd Unit H
Wallingford, CT 06492
Owner operated repair shop
    Phone: 203-294-1094   Accepts collect calls? Y
    Toll Free: 800-382-7238   FAX: 203-269-2532
    Internet: www.saftauto.com
Suitable Sites: FB, SC
Concentration: 10 in CT
    Expansion: Connecticut
    Registered: FL
Field Support: DP, CP, EO, ST, SO, IC, FC, H, N
    Training: 1 month on-site

Automotive Industry   Repair: Transmission

	AAMCO Transmissions	American Transmissions	Cottman Transmission	Kennedy Transmission	Lee Myles Transmissions	Mister Transmission	Speedy Transmission Centers	Transmission USA
Startup Cost	150K-175K	80K-120K	95K-115K	95K	98K-127K	75K-90K	50K-80K	125K
Franchise Fee	30K	25K	25K	17.5K	25K	25K	14.5K	25K
Royalty	7%	7%	7.50%	6%	7%	7%	7%	7%
Advertising Fee		3%/$400/WK.	$550/WK	2-6%	4.5%	7%	$100/MO	$100/MO
Financing Provided	N	Y	Y	N	Y	N	Y	Y
Experience Required	N			N	N	N	N	
Passive Ownership	N	N	N	N	N	D	D	N
In Business Since	1963	1981	1962	1962	1947	1963	1983	1990
Franchised Since	1963	1985	1964	1971	1964	1969	1983	1990
Franchised Units 1996				16				
1997	716	11	202	17	73	89	28	149
1998				19	86	87		
Company Owned 1996				3				
1997	2	0	5	2	0	0	0	4
1998				1	0			
Number of Units U.S.	695	11	206	20	86	0	28	153
Canada	23	0	1		0	87	0	0
Foreign	0	0	0		0	0	0	0
Projected New U.S.	30			2			10	
Canada	8					3		
Foreign								
Corporate Employees	200	5	45	4	15	12	5	
Contract Length	15/15	15/15	15/15	15/15	25/15/5/5	10/10	20/10	20/20
Expand in Territory	Y	Y	Y	N	Y	Y	Y	Y
Full-Time Employees	5	5	3-4	4-5	4	4-5	4	3-5
Part-Time Employees		1	1	0			1	
Conversions	Y	Y	Y	Y	Y	Y	Y	Y
Site Selection Assist.	Y	Y	Y	Y	Y	Y	Y	Y
Lease Negotiation Assist.	Y	Y	Y	Y	Y	Y	Y	Y
Site Space Required	4000	3200	3000-4000	3400	3000	2600	2400	4000
Development Agreement	N	N	Y	N	Y	N	Y	Y
Develop. Agree. Term			6		15		10	
Sub-franchising	N	N	N	N	N	N	Y	N

Automotive Industry   Repair: Transmission

AAMCO Transmissions
One Presidential Blvd
Bala Cynwyd, PA 19004

Phone: 610-668-2900   Accepts collect calls? N
Toll Free: 800-223-8887   FAX: 610-617-9532
Internet: www.aamco.com
Suitable Sites: AM, FB, M, SF
Concentration: 109 in CA, 62 in FL, 45 in NY
Expansion: All United States, Canada
Registered: CA,FL,HI,IL,IN,MD,MI,MN,ND,NY,OR,RI,SD,VA,WA,WI,DC
Field Support: EO, ST, SO, IC, FC, H, N
Training: 4 weeks home office Philadelphia
1 week center location

American Transmissions
38701 Seven Mile Dr #105
Livonia, MI 48152-1058

Phone: 734-591-9411   Accepts collect calls?
Toll Free: 800-380-4609   FAX: 734-591-2482
Internet:
Suitable Sites: FB
Concentration: 9 in MI, 2 in FL
Expansion: MI, FL
Registered: FL,MI
Field Support: DP, EO, ST, SO, IC, FC, H, N
Training: 14 days home office, Livonia, MI

Cottman Transmission
240 New York Dr
Fort Washington, PA 19034

Phone: 215-643-5885   Accepts collect calls?
Toll Free: 800-394-6116   FAX: 215-643-2519
Internet: www.cottman.com
Suitable Sites: AM, FB, M, SC
Concentration: 38 in PA, 18 in NJ, 16 in MI
Expansion: All United States, Canada, Foreign
Registered: CA,FL,IL,IN,MD,MI,MN,NY,RI,VA,WA
Field Support: EO, ST, SO, IC, FC, H, N
Training: 3 weeks ft. Washington, PA
1 week on-site

Kennedy Transmission
410 Gateway Blvd
Burnsville, MN 55337
Service & repair of auto & manual transmission domestic & import
Phone: 612-894-7020   Accepts collect calls? Y
Toll Free: 800-968-7388   FAX: 612-894-1849
Internet: www.kennedytrans.com
Suitable Sites: AM, FB
Concentration: 18 in MN, 1 in SD, 1 in ND
Expansion:
Registered: MN,ND,SD,WI
Field Support: EO, ST, SO, H, N
Training: 2 weeks classroom
1 week in operating store
ongoing on-site

Lee Myles Transmissions
140 Route 17 N
Paramus, NJ 07652
Repair, replace & service auto/manual transmissions & related
Phone: 201-262-0555   Accepts collect calls?
Toll Free: 800-533-6953   FAX: 201-262-5177
Internet: www.leemyles.com
Suitable Sites: AM, FB, M, SC
Concentration: 30 in NY, 15 in NJ, 14 in AZ
Expansion: All United States, Canada
Registered: CA,FL,MD,NY,OR,RI,VA,WA,DC IL WI
Field Support: DP, EO, ST, SO, IC, H, N
Training: 1-2 weeks corporate office
ongoing on-site operational assistance

Mister Transmission
30 Wertheim Ct #5
Richmond Hill, ON L4B-1B9 CANADA
Transmission repair service
Phone: 905-886-1511   Accepts collect calls?
Toll Free: 800-373-8432   FAX: 905-886-1545
Internet: mrt@idirect.com
Suitable Sites: AM, FB, SC, SF
Concentration: 63 in ON, 13 in BC, 3 in MB
Expansion: N, Canada
Registered:
Field Support: EO, ST, SO, FC, H, N
Training: 1 week head office
1 week on-site

Speedy Transmission Centers
902 Clint Moore Rd #216
Boca Raton, FL 33487
Centers repair, rebuild & recondition auto & std transmissions
Phone: 561-995-8282   Accepts collect calls? N
Toll Free: 800-336-0310   FAX: 561-995-8005
Internet: www.speedytransmission.com
Suitable Sites: AM, FB, IP, LI, SC
Concentration: 18 in FL, 4 in GA, 2 in CA
Expansion: SE and NE, Foreign
Registered: FL
Field Support: EO, ST, SO, IC, FC, H, N
Training: 2 weeks home office
1 week on-site

Transmission USA
4444 W 147th St
Oak Forest, IL 60452

Phone: 708-389-5922   Accepts collect calls?
Toll Free: 800-377-9247   FAX: 708-389-9882
Internet:
Suitable Sites: AM, FB, SC
Concentration: 27 in TX, 22 in GA, 19 in IL
Expansion: All United States, Foreign
Registered: CA,FL,IL,IN,MI,NY,VA
Field Support: $DP, EO, ST, SO, IC, FC, H, N
Training:

Automotive Industry

Repair: Tune-ups

	Diagnostic & Tune-Up Centers	Auto-Lab	Certicare	Econo Lube N' Tune	Milex Tune-Ups And Brakes	Precision Tune Auto Care	Tunex International, Inc.		
Startup Cost	70K-90K	VAR.		61K-135.86K	125K	142K-203K	126.5K-163.1K		
Franchise Fee	20K	VAR.		9.5K	25K	25K	19K		
Royalty	5% W/CAP	VAR.		6.5%	7%	7.50%	5%		
Advertising Fee	4% W/CAP				DEPENDS	9.0%	$600/MO		
Financing Provided	N	N		Y	Y	Y	N		
Experience Required							N		
Passive Ownership	D				N	D	D		
In Business Since	1984	1990		1973		1975	1974		
Franchised Since	1984	1988		1978	1996	1978	1975		
Franchised Units 1996		243		185			15		
1997	40	156		214	12	569	20		
1998							23		
Company Owned 1996		0		36			5		
1997	0	0		28	0	0	3		
1998							2		
Number of Units U.S.	44				12	478	24		
Canada	0				0	1	0		
Foreign	0				0	90	1		
Projected New U.S.									
Canada									
Foreign									
Corporate Employees	8					52	6		
Contract Length	10/10				20/20	10/5	10/10		
Expand in Territory	Y				Y	Y	N		
Full-Time Employees	4				3-5	6	4		
Part-Time Employees	2					1-2			
Conversions	Y				Y	Y			
Site Selection Assist.	Y				Y	Y	Y		
Lease Negotiation Assist.	Y				Y	Y	Y		
Site Space Required	2500					3000	2750		
Development Agreement	N				Y	Y	Y		
Develop. Agree. Term						5	10		
Sub-franchising	N				N	Y	Y		

Automotive Industry   **Repair: Tune-ups**

Auto-Lab Diagnostic & Tune-Up Centers
15965 Jeanette St
Southfield, MI 48075

Phone: 248-559-2784   Accepts collect calls?
Toll Free: FAX: 248-557-7931
Internet: www.wfcnet.com
Suitable Sites: FB, SC
Concentration: 35 in MI, 5 in IN
Expansion: Midwest - MI, IN and OH, Canada, Foreign
Registered: IN,MI
Field Support: EO, ST, SO, FC, H, N
Training: 2 weeks HQ
1 week on-site

Certicare
200 E Randolph St
Chicago, IL 60601
Auto services center
Phone: 312-856-7872   Accepts collect calls?
Toll Free: FAX:
Internet:
Suitable Sites:
Concentration:
Expansion: All United States
Registered:
Field Support:
Training:

Econo Lube N' Tune
4911 Birch
Newport Beach, CA 92660
Auto lube & tune/brakes/other services
Phone: Accepts collect calls?
Toll Free: 800-628-0253   FAX:
Internet:
Suitable Sites:
Concentration:
Expansion: NE,S,SE,SE,W,NW
Registered:
Field Support:
Training:

Milex Tune-Ups And Brakes
4444 W 147th St
Midlothian, IL 60452

Phone: 708-389-5922   Accepts collect calls?
Toll Free: 800-377-9247   FAX: 708-389-9882
Internet: www.moranindustries.com
Suitable Sites: AM, FB, SC
Concentration: 12 in IL
Expansion: All United States, Foreign
Registered: IL
Field Support:
Training: 3 weeks in-center training
1 week training facility

Precision Tune Auto Care
PO Box 5000 748 Miller Dr SE
Leesburg, VA 20177

Phone: 703-777-9095   Accepts collect calls?
Toll Free: 800-231-0588   FAX: 703-777-9190
Internet: www.precision-tune.com
Suitable Sites: FB, SC, SF
Concentration: 40 in MI, 38 in FL, 32 in GA
Expansion: All United States, Canada, Foreign
Registered: CA,HI,IL,IN,MD,MN,NY,ND,RI,SD,VA,WA,WI
Field Support: CP, EO, ST, SO, IC, FC, H, N
Training: 2 weeks Leesburg, VA

Tunex International, Inc.
556 East 2100 S
Salt Lake City, UT 84106
Diagnostic service & repair of ignition/fuel system, ac, exhaust
Phone: 801-486-8133   Accepts collect calls?
Toll Free: 800-448-8639   FAX: 801-484-4740
Internet: www.tunex.com
Suitable Sites: AM, FB, SC, SF
Concentration: 14 in UT, 4 in CO, 1 in AZ
Expansion: Inter-Mountain, SE, Foreign
Registered:
Field Support: EO, ST, SO, IC, H, N
Training: 1 week corporate HQ
1 week on-site

Automotive Industry   Repair: Windshield, Glass

	Apple Auto Glass	Chip King	Novus Windshield Repair	Superglass Windshield Repair				
Startup Cost	65K-95K	30.5K	5.3K	9.5K-28.5K				
Franchise Fee	5K	20K	15K	5.4K				
Royalty	5%	5%	6%	3%				
Advertising Fee	2.5%	2%	2%	1%				
Financing Provided	Y	Y	Y	Y				
Experience Required			N					
Passive Ownership	D	A	D	D				
In Business Since	1983	1993	1972	1992				
Franchised Since	1983	1995	1986	1993				
Franchised Units 1996			454					
1997	126	38	462	156				
1998			473					
Company Owned 1996			13					
1997	2	6	13	0				
1998			13					
Number of Units U.S.	0	0	486	143				
Canada	128	44	71	1				
Foreign	0	0		12				
Projected New U.S.			30					
Canada		6	3					
Foreign								
Corporate Employees	23	10	40	6				
Contract Length	10/10	5/15	10	10/10				
Expand in Territory	Y	Y		Y				
Full-Time Employees	3	1		2				
Part-Time Employees		1						
Conversions	Y	Y	N	Y				
Site Selection Assist.	Y	Y	N	N				
Lease Negotiation Assist.	Y	Y	N	Y				
Site Space Required	2500	120						
Development Agreement	N	N	Y	Y				
Develop. Agree. Term				10/10				
Sub-franchising	N	N	Y	N				

Automotive Industry   Repair: Windshield, Glass

Apple Auto Glass
360 Applewood Cres
Concord, ON L4K-4V2 CANADA

Phone: 905-669-7800   Accepts collect calls?
Toll Free: FAX: 905-669-7821
Internet:
Suitable Sites: SC
Concentration: 86 in ON, 12 in NS, 11 in NB
Expansion: N, Canada
Registered: AB
Field Support: $DP, CP, $ST, $SO, $FC, H, N
Training: var. head office

Chip King
1200 S Service Rd W #2
Oakville, ON L6L-5T7 CANADA
Stone chip repairs, windshield replace, insurance inspections
Phone: 905-825-9567   Accepts collect calls?
Toll Free: 800-603-4465   FAX: 905-825-9627
Internet:
Suitable Sites: FB, RM
Concentration: 27 in ON, 6 in NS, 4 in NB
Expansion: All United States, Canada
Registered:
Field Support: $DP, CP, EO, ST, SO, IC, FC, N
Training: 1-1.5 weeks home office, Oakville, ON
1.5 weeks on-site

Novus Windshield Repair
10425 Hampshire Ave S
Minneapolis, MN 55438
Mobile windshield repair & replacement
Phone: 612-944-8000   Accepts collect calls? N
Toll Free: 800-328-1117   FAX: 612-944-2542
Internet: www.novuswsr.com
Suitable Sites:
Concentration:
Expansion: All United States, Canada, Foreign
Registered: CA,FL,HI,IL,IN,MD,MI,MN,ND,NY,OR,RI,SD,VA,WA,WI,DC,AB
Field Support: CP, EO, ST, $FC, H, N
Training: 8.5 days factory training
1 week in the field
annual workshops, internet exchange

Superglass Windshield Repair
6101 Chancellor Dr #200
Orlando, FL 32809

Phone: 407-240-1920   Accepts collect calls?
Toll Free: 888-771-2700   FAX: 407-240-3266
Internet:
Suitable Sites:
Concentration: 10 in NJ, 8 in FL, 8 in GA
Expansion: All United States, Canada, Foreign
Registered: CA,FL,IL,MI,OR,SD,VA
Field Support: $DP, CP, EO, ST, SO, IC, FC, H, N
Training: 5 days Orlando, FL
5 days exclusive franchisee terr

Automotive Industry

Repair: Other

	Aero-Colours	Airbag Options	Airbag Service	Altracolor Systems	Cartex Limited	Certigard/Petro-Canada	Tuffy Auto Service Centers	
Startup Cost	55K	4K	75K-100K	15.2K-34.9K	23.5K	250K	161K-213K	
Franchise Fee	25K	10K	25K-35K	9.9K	23.5K	20K	20K	
Royalty	4-7%	7%	8.5%	$95/WK	$300	5%	5%	
Advertising Fee	0		2%	0%	0%	2%	5%	
Financing Provided	Y	Y	N	Y	Y	N	Y	
Experience Required	N		N	N	N			
Passive Ownership	A		A	N	D	N	D	
In Business Since	1985	1996	1992	1988	1987	1973	1970	
Franchised Since	1993	1997	1995	1991	1988	1987	1971	
Franchised Units 1996	49		12					
1997	53	0	18	185	85	142	188	
1998	56		30		8			
Company Owned 1996	4	0	1					
1997	4	1	1	0	1	4	16	
1998	4		1		1			
Number of Units U.S.	54		29	185	86	0	204	
Canada			1	0	0	146	0	
Foreign	2			0	0	0	0	
Projected New U.S.	20		10	30				
Canada			6		0			
Foreign	2				0			
Corporate Employees	14		11	5	6	20	44	
Contract Length	10		15/5	15/5	5/5	5/5	15/10	
Expand in Territory	Y		Y	Y	Y	Y	Y	
Full-Time Employees	2-5		1	1	6	6	4-6	
Part-Time Employees					1	1		
Conversions			Y	N	Y	Y	Y	
Site Selection Assist.	Y		N	Y	N	Y	Y	
Lease Negotiation Assist.	Y		N	N		Y	Y	
Site Space Required	2000					500-750	3700	
Development Agreement	N		N	Y	N	N	Y	
Develop. Agree. Term				15				
Sub-franchising	Y		N	Y	N	N	Y	

Automotive Industry

Repair: Other

Aero-Colours
6971 Washington Ave S #102
Minneapolis, MN 55439-1508
Mobile auto paint repair process serve dealership, fleet, indiv.
 Phone: 612-942-0490   Accepts collect calls?
 Toll Free: 800-696-2376   FAX: 612-942-0628
 Internet:
Suitable Sites: IP, WR
Concentration: 19 in CA, 7 in AL, 6 in TX
 Expansion: All United States, Foreign
 Registered: CA,FL,IN,MD,MI,NY,VA,WI
Field Support: DP, CP, EO, ST, SO, FC, H, N
 Training: 2 weeks HQ
  2 weeks on-site in territory

Airbag Options
1414 W Randol Mill Rd #200
Arlington, TX 76012
Airbag deactivation services
 Phone: 817-461-6000   Accepts collect calls?
 Toll Free: FAX:
 Internet:
Suitable Sites:
Concentration:
 Expansion: All United States, Canada, Foreign
 Registered:
Field Support:
 Training:

Airbag Service
1045 12 Ave NW Ste F2
Issaquah, WA 98027
Mobile airbag system repair for the collision industry
 Phone: 425-391-9664   Accepts collect calls? N
 Toll Free: 800-224-7224   FAX: 425-391-6721
 Internet: www.airbagservice.com
Suitable Sites: AM, DA, FB, HO, IP, OC
Concentration: 7 in TX, 4 in CA, 3 in WA
 Expansion: All United States, Canada, Foreign
 Registered:
Field Support: ST
 Training: technical, administration

Altracolor Systems
111 Phlox Ave
Metairie, LA 70001
Mobile auto paint restoration system
 Phone: 504-454-7233   Accepts collect calls? N
 Toll Free: 800-678-5220   FAX: 504-454-7233
 Internet: www.concentric.net/altra
Suitable Sites: HO, OTHER
Concentration: 22 in NC, 18 in VA, 12 in SC
 Expansion: All United States, Canada, Foreign
 Registered: CA,FL,IN,MI,MN,OR,RI,WA,WI
Field Support: EO, ST, SO, IC, FC, H, N
 Training: 4 days New Orleans, LA
  1 week home territory
  +3 days 90 days after startup

Cartex Limited
42816 Mound Rd
Sterling Heights, MI 48314
Mobile service business specialize in interior repair
 Phone: 810-739-4330   Accepts collect calls?
 Toll Free: 800-421-7328   FAX: 810-739-4331
 Internet:
Suitable Sites: AM, FB, HO, IP, LI, OC, SF
Concentration: 16 in CA, 11 in FL, 7 in TX
 Expansion: All United States, Canada, Foreign
 Registered: CA,FL,HI,IL,IN,MD,MI,MN,NY,VA,WA,DC,AB,OR
Field Support: CP, EO, ST, FC, H, N
 Training: initial training on location in field
  on-going thru corp office

Certigard/Petro-Canada
150 - 6th Ave S W
Calgary, AB T2P-3E3 CANADA

 Phone: 403-296-8000   Accepts collect calls?
 Toll Free: FAX: 403-296-3030
 Internet:
Suitable Sites: OTHER
Concentration: 53 in ON, 24 in BC, 23 in AB
 Expansion: N, Canada
 Registered: AB
Field Support: EO, ST, SO, IC, FC, N
 Training: 5-10 days HQ
  on-going Toronto/Montreal

Tuffy Auto Service Centers
1414 Baronial Plaza Dr
Toledo, OH 43615

 Phone: 419-865-6900   Accepts collect calls?
 Toll Free: 800-228-8339   FAX: 419-865-7343
 Internet: www.tuffy.com
Suitable Sites: FB
Concentration: 67 in OH, 65 in MI, 16 in IL
 Expansion: Reg. States, OH,IA,PA,NJ,KY
 Registered: FL,IL,IN,MD,MI,MN,NY,VA,WI
Field Support: EO, ST, SO, IC, FC, H, N
 Training: 4 weeks Toledo, OH

Automotive Industry   Sales, Brokerage

	Auto Purchase Consulting	Easyriders	J. D. Byrider Systems					
Startup Cost	57K	350K-500K	300K-1.5M					
Franchise Fee	15K	25K	39K					
Royalty	8%	3%	2.5%/.5%					
Advertising Fee	0%	2%	1750/MO					
Financing Provided	N	N	Y					
Experience Required	N	Y	N					
Passive Ownership	N	N	A					
In Business Since	1984	1993	1989					
Franchised Since	1997	1994	1989					
Franchised Units 1996								
1997	2	28	85					
1998		30						
Company Owned 1996								
1997	1	4	9					
1998		2						
Number of Units U.S.	0	31	90					
Canada	0	1	4					
Foreign	0	0	0					
Projected New U.S.	6	10	15					
Canada	0		1					
Foreign	0		0					
Corporate Employees		12	67					
Contract Length	7/7	5/5	10/10					
Expand in Territory	Y	Y	Y					
Full-Time Employees	1-2	4-6	10					
Part-Time Employees		2-3	0					
Conversions	Y	Y	Y					
Site Selection Assist.	Y	Y	Y					
Lease Negotiation Assist.	Y	Y	Y					
Site Space Required	200-400	8000	5000					
Development Agreement	N	N	Y					
Develop. Agree. Term			5					
Sub-franchising	N	N	N					

Automotive Industry   Sales, Brokerage

Auto Purchase Consulting
9841 Airport Blvd #1517
Los Angeles, CA 90045
Professional new car & truck buying, financing, leasing
Phone: 310-670-2886   Accepts collect calls? N
Toll Free: 800-756-4227   FAX: 310-670-5603
Internet: www.autopurchaseconsulting.com
Suitable Sites: AC, ES, OC
Concentration: 3 in CA
Expansion: All United States
Registered: CA
Field Support: DP, CP, EO, ST, SO, FC, H
Training: 10 days comprehensive at HQ
2 days on-site initial
ongoing

J. D. Byrider Systems
5780 W 71st St
Indianapolis, IN 46278
5-10 yr. old used car, sub-prime financing
Phone: 317-387-2345   Accepts collect calls? N
Toll Free: 800-947-4532   FAX: 317-387-2373
Internet: www.jdbyrider.com
Suitable Sites: AM, FB
Concentration: 22 in IN, 13 in OH, 7 in CO
Expansion: All United States, Canada
Registered: CA,FL,IL,IN,MI,MN,ND,NY,RI,SD,VA,WA,WI,AB
Field Support: DP, CP, EO, ST, SO, IC, $FC, H, N
Training: 16 days JDB corporate office
varied on-site

Easyriders
28210 Dorothy Dr
Agoura Hills, CA 91301
Full service aftermarket motorcycle shop
Phone: 818-879-6114   Accepts collect calls?
Toll Free: FAX: 818-889-5214
Internet: www.easyriders.com
Suitable Sites: FB, SC
Concentration: 3 in OH, 2 in GA, 2 in NC
Expansion: All United States, Canada, Foreign
Registered: CA,FL,IL,IN,MD,MI,MN,ND,NY,OR,RI,VA,WA,WI,DC,SD
Field Support: DP, CP, EO, ST, SO, IC, FC, H, N
Training: 5 days Columbus, OH
in-store/set-up as needed

Automotive Industry   **Tires**

	Active Green + Ross Tire & Automotive Centre	Big O Tires	Team Tires Plus Ltd	Tire Time Rentals	Tire Warehouse Central			
Startup Cost	115K-200K	180K-270K	273K-467K	96.5K-393.5K	100K-250K			
Franchise Fee	25K	21K	10K-30K	20K	0			
Royalty	5%	2%	3%	6%	3%			
Advertising Fee	2.5%	2-4%			2%			
Financing Provided	Y	Y	N	Y	N			
Experience Required					N			
Passive Ownership	N	D			D			
In Business Since	1982	1962	1976	1994	1971			
Franchised Since	1983	1967	1981	1995	1989			
Franchised Units 1996			25	19	20			
1997	25	433	34	21	20			
1998					20			
Company Owned 1996			47	1	27			
1997	4	7	52	1	27			
1998					27			
Number of Units U.S.	0	403			47			
Canada	29	37			0			
Foreign	0	0			0			
Projected New U.S.					10			
Canada					0			
Foreign					0			
Corporate Employees	9	50			43			
Contract Length	5/5	10			7			
Expand in Territory	Y	Y			Y			
Full-Time Employees	4+				5			
Part-Time Employees					3			
Conversions	Y	Y			Y			
Site Selection Assist.	Y	Y			Y			
Lease Negotiation Assist.		Y			Y			
Site Space Required	3000-5000				5000			
Development Agreement	N	Y			N			
Develop. Agree. Term								
Sub-franchising	Y	Y			N			

Automotive Industry   Tires

Active Green + Ross Tire & Automotive Centre
580 Evans Ave
Toronto, ON M8W-2W1 CANADA

Phone: 416-255-5581	Accepts collect calls?
Toll Free:	FAX: 416-255-4793

Internet:
Suitable Sites:
Concentration: 29 in ON
    Expansion: N/A, Canada
    Registered: N
Field Support:
    Training: head office & on-site

Big O Tires
11755 E Peakview Ave PO Box 3206
Englewood, CO 80111

Phone: 303-790-2800	Accepts collect calls?
Toll Free: 800-622-2446	FAX: 303-790-0225

Internet:
Suitable Sites: FB
Concentration: 146 in CA, 46 in AZ, 36 in CO
    Expansion: All United States, Canada, Foreign
    Registered:
Field Support: DP, CP, EO, $ST, SO, IC, $FC, H, N
    Training: 5 weeks Denver, CO

Team Tires Plus Ltd
600 W Travelers Tr
Burnsville, MN 55337
Tires & automotive services

Phone:	Accepts collect calls?
Toll Free: 800-754-6519	FAX:

Internet:
Suitable Sites:
Concentration:
    Expansion: MW
    Registered:
Field Support:
    Training:

Tire Time Rentals
305 Brown St
Big Spring, TX 79720
Rent-to-own tires & custom wheels

Phone: 915-263-6832	Accepts collect calls?
Toll Free:	FAX:

Internet:
Suitable Sites:
Concentration:
    Expansion: CA
    Registered:
Field Support:
    Training:

Tire Warehouse Central
492 Main St PO Box 486
Keene, NH 03431-0486
Retail sales & service of tires, wheels, auto parts, accessories

Phone: 603-352-4478	Accepts collect calls? N
Toll Free: 800-756-9876	FAX: 603-352-2398

Internet:
Suitable Sites: FB
Concentration: 19 in NH, 11 in ME, 10 in MA
    Expansion: New England, New York
    Registered: NY,RI
Field Support: DP, CP, EO, ST, SO, IC, FC, H, N
    Training: 2-4 weeks Keene, NH
               2-4 weeks on-site

Automotive Industry

Wash, Detail, Protect

	The Car Wash Guys/Gals	Colors On Parade	Shine Factory	Spot-Not Car Washes	Ziebart Tidycar			
Startup Cost	62.4K-75K	40K-100K	125K	622K-1.1K	100K-161K			
Franchise Fee	20K	5K-35K	10K-50K	25K	24K			
Royalty	$700/MO	7%+23%	8%	5%	5-8%			
Advertising Fee	0%	N/A	5%	1%	5%			
Financing Provided	Y	N	N	Y	Y			
Experience Required	N	N						
Passive Ownership	A	D	D	D	D			
In Business Since	1979	1989	1979	1968	1954			
Franchised Since	1997	1991	1979	1985	1962			
Franchised Units 1996								
1997	8	245	31	36	469			
1998		280						
Company Owned 1996								
1997	53	0	0	0	18			
1998		2						
Number of Units U.S.	61	280	0	36	265			
Canada	0	0	31	0	50			
Foreign	0	0	0	0	253			
Projected New U.S.		50						
Canada								
Foreign								
Corporate Employees		23	4	18	100			
Contract Length	5/20	15/15	5/5	10/5/5	10/10			
Expand in Territory	Y	Y	Y	Y	Y			
Full-Time Employees	1	1	3	2	2			
Part-Time Employees	3		2	3	3			
Conversions	Y		Y	Y	Y			
Site Selection Assist.	N	Y	Y	Y	Y			
Lease Negotiation Assist.	Y	Y	Y	Y	Y			
Site Space Required			4000	40000	500			
Development Agreement	Y	Y	Y	Y	Y			
Develop. Agree. Term		15	5					
Sub-franchising	N	N	Y	N	N			

Automotive Industry

Wash, Detail, Protect

The Car Wash Guys/Gals
5699 Kanan Rd #130
Agoura Hills, CA 91301
Mobile car wash turnkey franchise
      Phone: 888-927-4489   Accepts collect calls? Y
      Toll Free: 888-879-8783   FAX: 888-927-4425
      Internet: www.carwashguys.com
Suitable Sites:
Concentration: 58 in CA, 2 in AZ, 1 in NV
      Expansion: FL,TX,ID,OR,HI,WA, Foreign
      Registered: CA,FL,HI,WA
Field Support: DP, CP, EO, ST, SO, IC, FC, H, N
      Training: 40 hours Agoura hills, CA
               40 hours franchisee territory

Colors On Parade
5201 Brookhollow Pkwy #A
Norcross, GA 30071
Mobile on-site auto reconditioning svcs, paint/dent/interior rep
      Phone: 770-368-4112   Accepts collect calls?
      Toll Free: 800-726-5677   FAX: 770-368-4116
      Internet: www.colors.net
Suitable Sites: HO
Concentration: 32 in FL, 29 in FA, 31 in CA
      Expansion: All United States, Foreign
      Registered: CA,FL,HI,IL,IN,MD,MI,MN,NY,VA,WA,WI
Field Support: CP, EO, ST, FC, H, N
      Training: 3 weeks Myrtle Beach, SC

Shine Factory
3519 - 14th St SW 2nd Fl
Calgary, AB T2T-3W2   CANADA

      Phone: 403-243-3030   Accepts collect calls?
      Toll Free: FAX: 403-243-3031
      Internet:
Suitable Sites: FB, SC
Concentration: 12 in NS, 12 in AB, 4 in BC
      Expansion: N, Canada
      Registered: AB
Field Support: EO, ST, SO, IC, FC, H
      Training: 2 weeks training center
               2 weeks on-site

Spot-Not Car Washes
2011 W 4th St
Joplin, MO 64801-3297

      Phone: 417-781-2140   Accepts collect calls?
      Toll Free: 800-682-7629   FAX: 417-781-3906
      Internet:
Suitable Sites: FB
Concentration: 10 in AR, 10 in IL, 8 in IN
      Expansion: Midwest, South and SE
      Registered: IL,IN,MI,WI
Field Support: CP, EO, ST, SO, IC, FC, H, N
      Training: 17 days Joplin, MO & OJT site

Ziebart Tidycar
1290 E Maple Rd, PO Box 1290
Troy, MI 48007-1290

      Phone: 248-588-4100   Accepts collect calls?
      Toll Free: 800-877-1312   FAX: 248-588-0718
      Internet:
Suitable Sites: FB
Concentration:
      Expansion: All United States, Canada, Foreign
      Registered: CA,FL,HI,IL,IN,MD,MI,MN,ND,NY,OR,RI,SD,VA,WA,WI,DC
Field Support: $DP, CP, EO, ST, SO, IC, $FC, H, N
      Training: 3-6 weeks mngmnt & tech home office

Automotive Industry   Other Automotive (Spread 1 of 2)

	21st Century Auto Alliance	ATL International	Dealer Specialties Int'l Inc	Marine Services, Inc. Naut-A-Care	Petro Stopping Centers	Planet Earth Recycling	Rennsport	Travelcenters of America, Inc.
Startup Cost	~8K	120K-130K	7.7K-31.9K	47.8K-120.8K	10M	60K-85K	47K-146K	
Franchise Fee	4.5K	25K	2.5K	25K-30K		10K	25K	
Royalty		7%	$.6/UNIT	$500/MO		3%	6%	
Advertising Fee		8%		$125/MO		1%	1%	
Financing Provided	Y	Y	Y	Y	N	Y	Y	N
Experience Required	N			Y	Y			Y
Passive Ownership	D	N		A	D	D	N	N
In Business Since	1986	1985	1989	1991	1974	1990	1985	
Franchised Since	1995	1985	1996	1995		1995	1996	
Franchised Units 1996	14		68	0				
1997	14	450	137	1		3	0	
1998	15			2				40
Company Owned 1996	1		0	1				
1997	2	0	0	1		1	1	
1998	2			2				106
Number of Units U.S.	15	450		4	50	4	1	
Canada	0	0		0	0	0	0	
Foreign	0	0		0	0	0	0	
Projected New U.S.	10			6	7			
Canada	2			0	0			
Foreign	1			2	0			
Corporate Employees	3	75		4		5	3	
Contract Length	10	15/5X3		10/10/10	20	10/15	10/10	5/3/3
Expand in Territory	Y	Y		Y	Y	Y	N	Y
Full-Time Employees		5		2	175	1-3	5	
Part-Time Employees					25			
Conversions		Y		Y	N		N	
Site Selection Assist.	N	Y		N	Y	N	Y	Y
Lease Negotiation Assist.	Y	Y		N	N		Y	N
Site Space Required		3000					3000	20000
Development Agreement	N	N		N	Y	N	N	N
Develop. Agree. Term								
Sub-franchising	N	N		N	N	Y	N	N

Automotive Industry

Other Automotive (Spread 1 of 2)

21st Century Auto Alliance
1117 Woodbury #C
Independence, MO 64050-4725
Data collection & window sticker service to auto dealers
     Phone: 861-252-1322   Accepts collect calls?
    Toll Free: 800-580-8696   FAX: 861-254-9727
    Internet: www.21aa.com
Suitable Sites: HO, OS, SC, WR, OTHER
Concentration: 3 in SC, 2 in MO
    Expansion: Most, Canada, Foreign
    Registered:
Field Support: $EO, $ST, H, N
    Training: 2 days computer skills & marketing at HQ

ATL International
8334 Veterans Hwy
Millersville, MD 21108

     Phone: 410-987-1011   Accepts collect calls?
    Toll Free: 800-935-8863   FAX: 410-987-3060
    Internet: www.usa.nia.com/atl
Suitable Sites: AM, FB, M, SC
Concentration: 50 in CA, 35 in TX, 30 in MD
    Expansion: All United States, Canada, Foreign
    Registered: CA,FL,IL,IN,MD,MI,MN,NY,OR,RI,VA,WA,WI,DC
Field Support: CP, EO, ST, SO, IC, FC, H, N
    Training: 2 weeks corporate office
          1 week center

Dealer Specialties Int'l Inc
60-A S American Wy
Monroe, OH 45050
Used-car window stickers
     Phone: Accepts collect calls?
    Toll Free: 800-647-8425   FAX:
    Internet:
Suitable Sites:
Concentration:
    Expansion: All United States
    Registered:
Field Support:
    Training:

Naut-A-Care Marine Services, Inc.
610 Newport Center Dr #700
Newport Beach, CA 92660-6442
Boat to boat oil changing, bilge steam cleaning & carpet clean
     Phone: 714-760-9699   Accepts collect calls?
    Toll Free: FAX:
    Internet:
Suitable Sites: WF
Concentration: 2 in CA
    Expansion: S,SE,W,NW, Foreign
    Registered: CA,FL
Field Support:
    Training: 1 week Newport Beach Harbor
          1 week franchisee harbor

Petro Stopping Centers
6080 Surety Dr
El Paso, TX 79905
Full facility interstate travel plazas
     Phone: 915-779-4711   Accepts collect calls? N
    Toll Free: 800-331-8809x7300   FAX: 915-774-7391
    Internet: lglines@petrotruckstops.com
Suitable Sites:
Concentration: PA, VA, IN
    Expansion: Limited
    Registered: FL,IL,IN,MD,MI,MN,ND,NY,OR,RI,SD,VA,WA,WI
Field Support: DP, CP, EO, ST, SO, FC, H, N
    Training:

Planet Earth Recycling
7928 State Rd PO Box 65311
Philadelphia, PA 19155-5311

     Phone: 609-768-0310   Accepts collect calls?
    Toll Free: 800-471-4684   FAX: 215-333-6830
    Internet:
Suitable Sites:
Concentration: 1 in FL, 1 in WI, 1 in IL
    Expansion: All United States
    Registered: IL,WI
Field Support: CP, EO, ST, IC, FC, H, N
    Training: 5 days corporate office, PA
          1-2 days franchisee's area

Rennsport
10390 Alpharetta St #620
Roswell, GA 30075

     Phone: 770-992-9442   Accepts collect calls?
    Toll Free: FAX: 770-643-4806
    Internet: www.rennsport.com
Suitable Sites: FB
Concentration:
    Expansion: All United States
    Registered:
Field Support: EO, $ST, $FC
    Training: 30-65 days Atlanta, GA

Travelcenters of America, Inc.
24601 Center Ridge Rd #300
Westlake, OH 44145-5634
Travelcenters on major hwys serving pro truck driver & motorist
     Phone: 216-808-3012   Accepts collect calls?
    Toll Free: 800-872-7496   FAX: 216-808-3307
    Internet:
Suitable Sites:
Concentration:
    Expansion: All United States
    Registered:
Field Support:
    Training:

Automotive Industry

Other Automotive (Spread 2 of 2)

	Yipes Stripes						
Startup Cost	40K-75K						
Franchise Fee	32K						
Royalty	5%/$500						
Advertising Fee	0%						
Financing Provided	Y						
Experience Required							
Passive Ownership	D						
In Business Since	1972						
Franchised Since	1988						
Franchised Units 1996							
1997	25						
1998							
Company Owned 1996							
1997	1						
1998							
Number of Units U.S.	26						
Canada	0						
Foreign	0						
Projected New U.S.							
Canada							
Foreign							
Corporate Employees	2						
Contract Length	5/5						
Expand in Territory	Y						
Full-Time Employees	1						
Part-Time Employees							
Conversions							
Site Selection Assist.	Y						
Lease Negotiation Assist.							
Site Space Required							
Development Agreement	Y						
Develop. Agree. Term	10						
Sub-franchising	N						

Automotive Industry

Other Automotive (Spread 2 of 2)

Yipes Stripes
PO Box 775, 520 Court St
Dover, DE 19903-0775

Phone: 302-736-1735
Accepts collect calls?
Toll Free: 800-947-3755
FAX: 302-736-2693
Internet:
Suitable Sites: HO
Concentration: 7 in OH, 3 in MO, 3 in PA
Expansion: All United States
Registered:
Field Support: CP, $EO, $ST, $SO, FC, H, N
Training: 2 weeks Dover, de

Beauty Industry   Cosmetics

	Aloette Cosmetics	Beneficial Health & Beauty	Biozhem Skin Care Centers	Merle Norman Cosmetics	Perfumes Etc.	The T O L Franchise Group		
Startup Cost	55K-86.3K	100K	75K-125K	35K-170K	10K-50K	96K-132K		
Franchise Fee	20K	15K	15K	0	1K-10K	20K		
Royalty	5%	3%	0%	0%	2%	5%		
Advertising Fee	N/A	4%	0%	0%	3%	0		
Financing Provided	Y	Y	N	Y	N	N		
Experience Required				N	N	N		
Passive Ownership	D	D	D	A	A	D		
In Business Since	1978	1981	1992	1931	1992	1983		
Franchised Since	1978	1990	1992	1989	1996	1987		
Franchised Units 1996					1	6		
1997	79	26	2	2042	2	5		
1998					3	5		
Company Owned 1996					3	1		
1997	3	2	8	5	3	0		
1998				6	4	0		
Number of Units U.S.	50	10	10	1940	0			
Canada	32	0	0	97	7			
Foreign	0	18	0	9	0			
Projected New U.S.				60	4	2		
Canada				10	10	0		
Foreign					3	0		
Corporate Employees	25	7	4	640	25			
Contract Length	5/10	10/5	10/5	UNLIMITED	5	10		
Expand in Territory	Y	Y	N	Y	Y			
Full-Time Employees	3	2	2	2	1			
Part-Time Employees		2	1	2-5	2			
Conversions		Y	N	Y	Y	Y		
Site Selection Assist.	N	Y	Y	Y	Y			
Lease Negotiation Assist.	N	Y	Y	Y	Y			
Site Space Required	1000	1200-2500	600-1800	450-800	500-2000	700-1200		
Development Agreement	N	Y	N	N	Y	Y		
Develop. Agree. Term		10			5			
Sub-franchising	N	N	N	N	Y	Y		

Beauty Industry   ## Cosmetics

Aloette Cosmetics
1301 Wright's Ln E
West Chester, PA 19380

Phone: 610-692-0600   Accepts collect calls?
Toll Free: 800-256-3883   FAX: 610-692-2390
Internet:
Suitable Sites: HO, LI
Concentration: 18 in ON, 4 in BC, 3 in PQ
   Expansion: All United States, Canada
   Registered:
Field Support: EO, ST, SO, $FC
   Training: 2 days ops training at franchise
      2 days sales training @franchise

Beneficial Health & Beauty
1780 West 500 South
Salt Lake City, UT 84104

Phone: 801-973-7778   Accepts collect calls?
Toll Free: 800-367-0990   FAX: 801-973-8836
Internet:
Suitable Sites: FB, HO, SC, SF
Concentration: 6 in CA, 2 in HI, 2 in WI
   Expansion: All United States, Canada, Foreign
   Registered: CA,HI,IL,MI,MN,NY,ND,OR,WA,WI
Field Support: CP, EO, ST, SO, $IC, FC, H, N
   Training: 2 days local area
      4 days practical Salt Lake City UT
      weekly on-site

Biozhem Skin Care Centers
32240 Paseo Adelanto #A
San Juan Capistrano, CA 92675

Phone: 714-488-2184   Accepts collect calls?
Toll Free: 800-270-8237   FAX: 714-488-2191
Internet:
Suitable Sites: RM
Concentration: 3 in CA, 2 in OK
   Expansion: All United States, Canada, Foreign
   Registered:
Field Support: CP, EO, ST, SO, IC, FC, H, N
   Training: 1 week San Juan Capistrano CA

Merle Norman Cosmetics
9130 Bellanca Ave
Los Angeles, CA 90045

Phone: 310-641-3000   Accepts collect calls?
Toll Free: 800-421-6648   FAX: 310-337-2370
Internet: www.merlenorman.com
Suitable Sites: AC, DA, M, PC, RM, SC
Concentration: 291 in TX, 99 in GA, 103 in AL
   Expansion: All United States, Canada
   Registered: CA,FL,HI,IL,IN,MD,MI,MN,ND,NY,OR,RI,SD,VA,WA,WI,DC,AB
Field Support: $DP, CP, EO, ST, SO, IC, FC, H, N
   Training: 2 weeks Los Angeles CA

Perfumes Etc.
871 Islington Ave Unit 2
Toronto, ONT M8Z-4N9 CANADA
Market brand name fragrances & cosmetics
Phone: 416-253-3717   Accepts collect calls? Y
Toll Free: 888-737-3678   FAX: 416-253-7757
Internet: perfumes@pathcom.com
Suitable Sites: K, M, PC, SF, WR
Concentration: 3 in ONT
   Expansion: All United States, Canada, Foreign
   Registered:
Field Support: CP, EO, ST, SO, IC, FC, H, N
   Training: in-house via company store

The T O L Franchise Group
515 Bath Ave
Long Branch, NJ 07740
Retail discount cosmetics & fragrances
Phone: 732-229-7278   Accepts collect calls? N
Toll Free: 800-929-3083   FAX: 732-222-1762
Internet:
Suitable Sites: AC, M, PC, RM, SC, SF, WF
Concentration:
   Expansion: Canada, Foreign
   Registered:
Field Support: EO, SO, IC, H, N
   Training: extensive on-site training

Beauty Industry   **Hair Care (Spread 1 of 2)**

	City Looks Salons Int'l	Cost Cutters Family Hair Care	Custom Cuts	Fantastic Sams	First Choice Haircutters (U.S.) Inc.	Great Clips	H R C Int'l Inc	Hairlines
Startup Cost	75.5K-152.5K	42.5K-112.5K	100K-125K	60K-125K	70K-80K	86.6K-127.6K	53K-118K	100K-150K
Franchise Fee	12.5K-19.5K	12.5K-19.5K	25K	20K-30K	25K	17.5K	10K-25K	35K
Royalty	4%	6%	10%	$191/WK	7%	6%	6%	8%
Advertising Fee	4%	4%	4%	$100/WK	3%	5%		3%
Financing Provided	Y	Y	N	Y	Y	N	N	N
Experience Required	Y	N		N				
Passive Ownership	N	A	A	D	N	D		A
In Business Since	1963	1982	1985	1974	1980	1982	1971	1963
Franchised Since	1970	1982	1986	1976	1982	1983	1994	1994
Franchised Units 1996	52						6	
1997	63	739	6	1295	155	927	7	1
1998	38	810		1301				
Company Owned 1996	1						6	
1997	1	22	26	5	105	11	0	4
1998	1	81		5				
Number of Units U.S.		841	32	1174	48	912		5
Canada		0	0	15	212	26		0
Foreign	28	0	0	88	0	0		0
Projected New U.S.	10	100		120				
Canada				6				
Foreign	10			0				
Corporate Employees	70	80	15	14	850	130		60
Contract Length	15	15/15	10/10	10/10	10/5	10/5/5		10/10
Expand in Territory	Y	Y	Y	Y	Y	Y		N
Full-Time Employees	7	6	12	8-12	5-7	3		1
Part-Time Employees	3	3	2	2-6	2-4	5		2-3
Conversions		Y		Y	Y	N		
Site Selection Assist.	Y	Y	Y	Y	Y	Y		Y
Lease Negotiation Assist.	Y	Y	Y	Y	Y	Y		Y
Site Space Required	1500	900-1200	1000-1400	1000-1600	800-1000	1000-1200		1000
Development Agreement	Y	Y	Y	Y	Y	N		N
Develop. Agree. Term	VAR.	VAR.	5	10	15			
Sub-franchising	N	N	N	Y	N	Y		N

Beauty Industry   Hair Care (Spread 1 of 2)

City Looks Salons Int'l
300 Industrial Blvd N E
Minneapolis, MN 55413
Full-service, upscale hair care salon products & services
   Phone: 612-331-8500 Accepts collect calls? N
   Toll Free: FAX: 612-331-2821
   Internet:
Suitable Sites: M, PC, RM
Concentration: 21 in MN, 7 in IA, 2 in PA
  Expansion: IL,IN,MI,MN,ND,WI, Foreign
  Registered: IL,IN,MI,MN,ND
Field Support:
   Training: 1 week home office
       1 week on-site
       on-going available

Cost Cutters Family Hair Care
300 Industrial Blvd NE
Minneapolis, MN 55413
Value priced, family hair care salon products & services
   Phone: 612-331-8500 Accepts collect calls? N
   Toll Free: 800-858-2266 FAX: 612-331-2821
   Internet:
Suitable Sites: AC, M, PC, RM, SC
Concentration: 105 in WI, 83 in MN, 60 in CO
  Expansion: All United States, Canada, Foreign
  Registered: CA,FL,HI,IL,IN,MD,MI,MN,ND,NY,OR,RI,SD,VA,WA,WI,DC
Field Support: EO, ST, SO, $FC, H, N
   Training: 1 week national HQ
       1 week on-site
       ongoing available

Custom Cuts
13846 Manchester Rd
St Louis, MO 63011

   Phone: 314-391-1717 Accepts collect calls?
   Toll Free: FAX: 314-227-3351
   Internet:
Suitable Sites: SC
Concentration: 19 in MO, 7 in IL, 6 in KS
  Expansion: All United States
  Registered: IL
Field Support: $DP, $EO, ST, SO, $FC
   Training: 4 weeks St Louis MO

Fantastic Sams
1400 N Kellogg #E
Anaheim, CA 92807

   Phone: 714-701-3471 Accepts collect calls? N
   Toll Free: 800-441-6588 FAX: 714-779-3422
   Internet: www.fantasticsams.com
Suitable Sites: AC, FB, SC
Concentration: 185 in CA, 139 in FL, 99 in TX
  Expansion: All United States, Canada, Foreign
  Registered: CA,FL,HI,IL,IN,MD,MI,MN,ND,NY,OR,RI,SD,VA,WA,WI,DC
Field Support: $CP, EO, ST, SO, FC, N
   Training: 1 week Anaheim
       ongoing within region

First Choice Haircutters (U.S.) Inc.
10014 North Dale Mabry
Tampa, FL 33618

   Phone: 813-964-9779 Accepts collect calls? Y
   Toll Free: 877-964-2111 FAX: 813-961-2395
   Internet:
Suitable Sites: SC
Concentration: 151 in ON, 32 in FL, 22 in AB
  Expansion: NE, SE, Midwest, Canada
  Registered: FL,IL
Field Support: CP, EO, ST, SO, FC, H, N
   Training: 1 week home office classroom
       15 days on-site

Great Clips
3800 W 80th St #400
Minneapolis, MN 55431-4419

   Phone: 612-893-9088 Accepts collect calls?
   Toll Free: 800-999-5959 FAX: 612-844-3443
   Internet:
Suitable Sites: SC
Concentration: 102 in MN, 93 in CO, 72 in MO
  Expansion: All United States, Canada
  Registered: CA,FL,IL,IN,MD,MI,MN,ND,NY,OR,SD,VA,WA,WI,DC,AB
Field Support: DP, CP, EO, ST, SO, $IC, FC, H, N
   Training: 3 days Minneapolis MN
       2.5 weeks local mkt

H R C Int'l Inc
1971 W 190th St
Torrance, CA 90504
Hair replacements
   Phone: 310-516-6614 Accepts collect calls?
   Toll Free: FAX:
   Internet:
Suitable Sites:
Concentration:
  Expansion: CA, Foreign
  Registered:
Field Support:
   Training:

Hairlines
656 E Golf Rd
Arlington Heights, IL 60005-4061

   Phone: 847-593-7900 Accepts collect calls?
   Toll Free: 800-424-7911 FAX: 847-593-7955
   Internet:
Suitable Sites: OC
Concentration: 5 in IL
  Expansion: Midwest
  Registered: IL
Field Support: CP, EO, ST, SO, IC, H
   Training: 4 weeks Chicago IL

Beauty Industry   Hair Care (Spread 2 of 2)

	Lemon Tree - A Unisex Haircutting Est.	Lord's & Lady's Hair Salons	Men's Hair Now	Pro-Cuts	Snip N' Clip Haircut Shops	Sport Clips	We Care Hair
Startup Cost	37.5K-70.6K	50K-175K	125K-225K	100K-130K	60K-80K	75K-125K	60.7K-132.3K
Franchise Fee	10K	25K	25K-200K	25K	10K	15K	12.5K-19.5K
Royalty	6%	6%	6%	0-6%	5%	6%	6%
Advertising Fee	$400/MO	0%	3%	5%	1%	$250/WK	
Financing Provided	Y	Y	N	Y	Y	Y	Y
Experience Required	N			N	N	N	
Passive Ownership	D	D	N	D	A	A	
In Business Since	1974	1975	1972	1982	1976	1995	1985
Franchised Since	1974	1980	1994	1983	1986	1995	1986
Franchised Units 1996	73						140
1997	75	22	0	176	42	11	122
1998	69				44	17	
Company Owned 1996	0					3	11
1997	0	0	3	24	51	4	0
1998	0				53	4	
Number of Units U.S.	69	22	3	200	93	21	
Canada	0	0	0	0	0	0	
Foreign	0	0	0	0	0	0	
Projected New U.S.	8			20		30	
Canada				0			
Foreign				0			
Corporate Employees	5	6	3	29	10	12	
Contract Length	15/15	10/10	10/10	10/10	5/5	5/5	
Expand in Territory	Y	Y	N	Y	Y	Y	
Full-Time Employees	4-6	6	8-10	6	4	8	
Part-Time Employees	3	8		2	2	4	
Conversions	Y	Y	N	N		N	
Site Selection Assist.	Y	Y	Y	Y	Y	Y	
Lease Negotiation Assist.	Y	Y	Y	Y	Y	Y	
Site Space Required	800-1200	1500	2200	1200	1000	1200	
Development Agreement	Y	N	Y	Y	Y	Y	
Develop. Agree. Term	NEG.		10				
Sub-franchising	N	N	Y	N	N	N	

Beauty Industry

Lemon Tree - A Unisex Haircutting Est.
3301 Hempstead Trnpk
Levittown, NY 11756
Affordable prices and quality service for the whole family
Phone: 516-735-2828   Accepts collect calls?
Toll Free: 800-345-9156   FAX: 516-735-1851
Internet: www.lemontree.com
Suitable Sites: FB, SC, SF
Concentration: 65 in NY, 1 in CN, 2 in PA
Expansion: NJ,CT,PA,MD,NY
Registered: FL,MD,NY
Field Support: EO, ST, SO, IC, FC, H
Training: 1 week franchise HQ
1 week in-shop upon opening

Lord's & Lady's Hair Salons
450 Belgrade Ave
Boston, MA 02162

Phone: 617-323-4714   Accepts collect calls?
Toll Free: FAX: 617-323-4059
Internet:
Suitable Sites: RM
Concentration: 18 in MA, 3 in NH, 1 in CT
Expansion: NE
Registered:
Field Support: DP, CP, EO, ST, SO, IC, FC, H
Training: 5 days Boston MA

Men's Hair Now
515 Madison Ave #300
New York, NY 10022

Phone: 212-832-0707   Accepts collect calls?
Toll Free: 800-835-4247   FAX: 212-832-0942
Internet: www.menshair.com
Suitable Sites: OC
Concentration: 2 in NY, 1 in NJ
Expansion: NE
Registered: NY
Field Support: EO, $ST, SO, $IC, $FC, H
Training: 2 weeks NY

Pro-Cuts
500 Grapevine Hwy #400
Hurst, TX 76054-2708
Family haircare centers providing quality haircuts, affordable $
Phone: 817-788-8000   Accepts collect calls? N
Toll Free: 888-PRO-CUTS   FAX: 817-788-0000
Internet: www.procuts.com
Suitable Sites: AC, FB, SC
Concentration: 149 in TX, 18 in OK, 9 in OH
Expansion: SE, Midwest
Registered: IN
Field Support: $CP, EO, ST, SO, $FC, H, N
Training: 3 days franchise support office
on-going support

Snip N' Clip Haircut Shops
7910 Quivira Rd
Lenexa, KS 66215
Budget price family haircut shops, open 7 days & nights, n appt
Phone: 913-438-1200   Accepts collect calls? N
Toll Free: 800-622-6804   FAX: 913-438-3456
Internet:
Suitable Sites: SC, SF
Concentration: 39 in KS, 30 in MO, 12 in AR
Expansion: Midwest, West, SE
Registered: CA,FL,IL,IN,MI,MN
Field Support: EO, ST, SO, FC, H, N
Training: 5 days on-site

Sport Clips
PO Box 3000-266
Georgetown, TX 78627
Sports-themed haircutters for men & boys
Phone: 512-869-1201   Accepts collect calls? N
Toll Free: 800-872-4247   FAX: 512-869-0366
Internet: sportclips.com
Suitable Sites: AC, PC, RM, SC
Concentration: 16 in TX, 5 in NY
Expansion: TX,UT
Registered: CA,NY
Field Support: CP, EO, ST, SO, IC, FC, H, N
Training: 10 days franchisee, 3 days TX
10 days manager in Austin, TX
3 days locally for stylists

We Care Hair
300 Industrial Blvd
Minneapolis, MN 55413
Hair care, beauty supplies & tanning
Phone: Accepts collect calls?
Toll Free: 800-345-7811   FAX:
Internet:
Suitable Sites:
Concentration:
Expansion: All United States
Registered:
Field Support:
Training:

Business Service Industry

Accounting, Collections

	AccounTax Services	Accounting Business Systems	Acctcorp	E.K. Williams & Co.	LedgerPlus	Padgett Business Services		
Startup Cost	10K	11.5K-15K	15K-60K	41K-45K	12.4K-25.4K	40K-60K		
Franchise Fee	2.5K	9.5K	10K-20K	35K	12K	34.5K		
Royalty	5%	$150/MO.	8%	8-2%	6%	9-4.5%		
Advertising Fee	2%	0%	3%	2%	2%	0%		
Financing Provided	Y	Y	Y	Y	Y	Y		
Experience Required	Y		N			Y		
Passive Ownership	D	N	D	D	A	D		
In Business Since	1979	1989	1955	1935	1989	1966		
Franchised Since	1981	1991	1994	1947	1990	1975		
Franchised Units 1996			9					
1997	3	36	16	156	205	450		
1998			19					
Company Owned 1996			3					
1997	1	2	3	0	2	0		
1998			4					
Number of Units U.S.	1	38	19	155	206	283		
Canada	3	0	0	1	0	120		
Foreign	0	0	0	0	1	0		
Projected New U.S.						320		
Canada						130		
Foreign								
Corporate Employees	8	4	20	18	7	20		
Contract Length	5/5	10/10	5	10/10	10/10	20/20		
Expand in Territory	Y	Y	Y	N	Y	Y		
Full-Time Employees	1	1	1		1	1		
Part-Time Employees	1	1	2	1		2		
Conversions	Y		Y	Y	Y	Y		
Site Selection Assist.	Y	N	Y	N	N	N		
Lease Negotiation Assist.	Y		Y		N			
Site Space Required	600		300		400	300-600		
Development Agreement	N	N	N	N	Y	N		
Develop. Agree. Term					10			
Sub-franchising	N	N	N	N	Y	N		

Business Service Industry   **Accounting, Collections**

AccounTax Services
499 Ray Lawson Blvd #32
Brampton, ON L6Y-4E6 CANADA
Accounting, bookkeeping, taxation & financial planning
    Phone: 905-453-3220   Accepts collect calls? N
Toll Free: FAX: 905-453-9562
Internet:
Suitable Sites: ES, HO, M, OC, RM, SC, SF
Concentration: 2 in ON, 1 in BC
    Expansion: All United States, Canada, Foreign
    Registered: CA,FL,HI,IL,IN,MD,MI,MN,ND,NY,OR,RI,SD,VA,WA,WI,DC
Field Support: $DP, $CP, $EO, $ST, SO, IC, $FC, $H, N
    Training: 2 weeks Toronto, ON
        1 week on-site

Accounting Business Systems
1260 Palmetto Ave #C
Winter Park, FL 32789

    Phone: 407-644-5400   Accepts collect calls?
Toll Free: 800-227-7504   FAX: 407-869-0077
Internet:
Suitable Sites:
Concentration: 8 in FL, 3 in GA, 3 in TX
    Expansion: All United States
    Registered: FL,OR,WA
Field Support: $FC, N
    Training: 5 days winter park, FL

Acctcorp
7414 NE Hazel Dell Ave #209
Vancouver, WA 98665
Collection of past due accounts
    Phone: Accepts collect calls? N
Toll Free: 800-844-4024   FAX: 360-694-5924
Internet: franchiseeacctcorp.com
Suitable Sites: HO, OC, OTHER
Concentration: 6 in WA, 3 in CA, 3 in ID
    Expansion: All United States, Foreign
    Registered: CA,FL,HI,OR,WA,IN,MD
Field Support: $CP, EO, ST, SO, $FC, H, N
    Training: 3 weeks Vancouver, WA

E.K. Williams & Co.
1020 N University Parks Dr PO Box 3146
Waco, TX 76707

    Phone: 254-745-2424   Accepts collect calls?
Toll Free: 800-992-0706   FAX: 254-745-2566
Internet: www.ekwilliams.com
Suitable Sites:
Concentration: 29 in CA, 13 in FL, 10 in TX
    Expansion: All United States, Canada
    Registered: CA,FL,HI,IL,IN,MD,MI,MN,ND,NY,OR,RI,SD,VA,WA,WI,DC
Field Support: DP, CP, EO, ST, FC, H, N
    Training: 2 weeks Waco, TX
        1 week 1 of 3 regional offices

LedgerPlus
401 St Francis St
Tallahassee, FL 32301

    Phone: 850-681-1941   Accepts collect calls?
Toll Free: 888-643-1348   FAX: 850-561-1374
Internet: www.ledgerplus.com
Suitable Sites:
Concentration: FL, NC, CA
    Expansion: All United States, Canada
    Registered: CA,FL,HI,IL,IN,MD,MI,MN,NY,OR,RI,VA,WA,WI
Field Support: $CP, EO, ST, FC, N
    Training: 5 days Tallahassee, FL

Padgett Business Services
160 Hawthorne Park
Athens, GA 30606
Monthly accounting & tax for small business
    Phone: 706-548-1040   Accepts collect calls? Y
Toll Free: 800-323-7292   FAX: 706-543-8537
Internet: smallbizpros.com
Suitable Sites: ES, HO, OC
Concentration: 67 in ON, 38 in QC, 26 in GA
    Expansion: All United States, Canada
    Registered: CA,FL,HI,IL,IN,MD,MI,MN,ND,NY,OR,RI,SD,VA,WA,WI,DC
Field Support: EO, ST, SO, FC, H, N
    Training: 2.5 weeks Athens, GA

Business Service Industry   Advertising, Promotion (Spread 1 of 2)

	Adventures In Advertising	Bright Beginnings	Business Information Int'l Inc	Connect.Ad	Greetings	Impressions On Hold International	Merchant Advertising Systems	Mobil Ambition USA LC
Startup Cost	35K-45K	5K	19.5K-116.5K	25K-30K	15K-30K	40K	17K-29K	65K-100K
Franchise Fee	27.5K	50K	12.5K+	9.5K	15K	37K	13.5K-25.5K	10K-15K
Royalty	4%	2-5%	0	3%	5%	4%	0%	600-1K
Advertising Fee	1%	0		3%	0%	1%	0%	
Financing Provided	Y	Y	Y	Y	N	Y	N	N
Experience Required		N						
Passive Ownership	D	D		D	D	D	D	
In Business Since	1979	1986	1994	1995	1984	1991	1985	1995
Franchised Since	1994	1986	1995	1996	1990	1994	1987	1995
Franchised Units 1996		3	22					12
1997	80	5	15	10	5	70	2	39
1998		7						
Company Owned 1996		20	0					2
1997	0	22	0	1	3	5	9	1
1998		22						
Number of Units U.S.	76			10	8	75	11	
Canada	4	0		0	0	0	0	
Foreign	0	0		1	0	0	0	
Projected New U.S.		8-10				10		
Canada		0				0		
Foreign		0				0		
Corporate Employees	19	5			2	50	4	
Contract Length	10/10	5/5/5		10/10	10/5	10/10	10/10	
Expand in Territory	Y	Y		Y	Y	Y	Y	
Full-Time Employees	1	2			1		3	
Part-Time Employees	0	2-6			1		1	
Conversions	Y	Y						
Site Selection Assist.	N	Y		N	Y	N	Y	
Lease Negotiation Assist.		N					Y	
Site Space Required					250		5	
Development Agreement	Y	N		N	N	N	Y	
Develop. Agree. Term							10	
Sub-franchising	N	N		N	N	N	Y	

Business Service Industry   Advertising, Promotion (Spread 1 of 2)

Adventures In Advertising
400 Crown Colony Dr
Quincy, MA 02169

Phone: 617-472-9901   Accepts collect calls?
Toll Free: 800-432-6332   FAX: 617-472-9976
Internet: www.advinadv.com
Suitable Sites: HO
Concentration: 12 in WA, 9 in MA, 9 in CA
    Expansion: All United States, Canada
    Registered: CA,FL,HI,IL,IN,MD,MI,MN,ND,NY,OR,RI,SD,VA,WA,WI,DC
Field Support: $DP, EO, ST, $FC, H, N
    Training: 2 weeks HQ Quincy, MA

Bright Beginnings
1150 Main St #D
Irvine, CA 92614
Upscale community advertising/neighbor welcoming service
    Phone: 714-752-2772   Accepts collect calls? N
    Toll Free: FAX: 714-833-3773
    Internet: brightbeginnings.net
Suitable Sites: HO, OS
Concentration: 26 in CA
    Expansion: All United States
    Registered:
Field Support: $EO, ST, SO
    Training: sales, computer, art & design
                management

Business Information Int'l Inc
22 N Front #620
Memphis, TN 38103
Direct marketing information
    Phone: 901-578-3282   Accepts collect calls?
    Toll Free: FAX:
    Internet:
Suitable Sites:
Concentration:
    Expansion: Canada
    Registered:
Field Support:
    Training:

Connect.Ad
1000 W Mc Nab Rd #236
Pompano, FL 33069

Phone: 954-942-5070   Accepts collect calls?
    Toll Free: FAX: 954-942-0701
    Internet: www.connectad.com
Suitable Sites: HO
Concentration:
    Expansion: All United States, Canada, Foreign
    Registered: CA,FL,HI,IL,IN,MD,MI,MN,ND,NY,OR,RI,SD,VA,WA,WI,DC
Field Support: FC, N
    Training: 1 week Ft. Lauderdale, FL

Greetings
PO Box 25623
Lexington, KY 40524

Phone: 606-272-5624   Accepts collect calls?
    Toll Free: FAX:
    Internet:
Suitable Sites: HO
Concentration: 5 in KY, 2 in TN, 1 in IL
    Expansion: SE, NE, MW
    Registered: N
Field Support: $CP, EO, ST, FC, N
    Training: 5 days Lexington, KY
                5 days franchisee location

Impressions On Hold International
6218 S Lewis #116
Tulsa, OK 74136
"On hold" advertising service (on hold telephone messages)
    Phone: 918-744-0988   Accepts collect calls?
    Toll Free: 800-580-4653   FAX: 918-744-0989
    Internet:
Suitable Sites: HO
Concentration:
    Expansion: All United States, Canada
    Registered: CA,FL,HI,MD,MI,NY,VA,WA
Field Support: DP, CP, EO, ST, $FC, $H, N
    Training: 5 days corporate office
                2 days on-site

Merchant Advertising Systems
4115 Tiverton Rd
Randallstown, MD 21133-2019

Phone: 410-655-3201   Accepts collect calls?
    Toll Free: FAX: 410-655-0262
    Internet:
Suitable Sites: RM
Concentration: 5 in MD, 3 in PA, 2 in VA
    Expansion: All United States, Canada
    Registered: FL,MI,OR,VA,DC
Field Support: CP, EO, ST, SO, IC, FC, H, N
    Training: 1 week HQ
                1 week franchisee's territory

Mobil Ambition USA LC
5353 N Federal Hwy #304
Fort Lauderdale, FL 33308
Advertising system
    Phone: 954-493-8440   Accepts collect calls?
    Toll Free: FAX:
    Internet:
Suitable Sites:
Concentration:
    Expansion: Canada, Foreign
    Registered:
Field Support:
    Training:

Business Service Industry   Advertising, Promotion (Spread 2 of 2)

	Marketing Concepts Inc	Performance Points for Profits	Profit-On-Hold	Resort Maps Franchise Inc	Tee Signs Plus	Trimark	Val-Pak Direct Marketing	Direct Mail Advertising Yellow Jacket
Startup Cost	25K	5K	5K	3.6K-8.7K	15.95K-23.95K	27.5K-47K	VAR.	27K
Franchise Fee	25K	6K	5K	8.5K	11.9K	19.5K	1K	25K
Royalty	10%	0	3%	10%	40/SIGN/YR	$0.50/AD	0%	$15/COUPON
Advertising Fee			0	0		N/A	0%	$3/COUPON
Financing Provided	N	N	N	N	N	N	Y	N
Experience Required				N		Y		
Passive Ownership			A			N	D	D
In Business Since	1992	1970	1991	1988	1992	1969	1968	1991
Franchised Since	1995	1975	1992	1993	1996	1978	1989	1991
Franchised Units 1996	2	16		14	0			
1997	2	16	1	26	2	31	244	13
1998				35				
Company Owned 1996	1	2		21	0			
1997	1	2	4	14	0	0	9	0
1998				12				
Number of Units U.S.			5	9		34	211	13
Canada			0			0	42	0
Foreign			0			0	0	
Projected New U.S.				9		6		
Canada				1		1		
Foreign						0		
Corporate Employees			4	4		30	1100	10
Contract Length			5/5	10/10		10/10	10/5	15/15
Expand in Territory			Y	Y		Y	Y	Y
Full-Time Employees			1	1		1	VAR	1
Part-Time Employees			1	0		1		
Conversions			Y	N		Y	Y	Y
Site Selection Assist.			N	Y		N	N	N
Lease Negotiation Assist.				N		N		
Site Space Required			500					
Development Agreement			N	N		Y	N	Y
Develop. Agree. Term						2		15
Sub-franchising			N	Y		Y	N	N

Business Service Industry   Advertising, Promotion (Spread 2 of 2)

Performance Marketing Concepts Inc
4155 E Jewell Ave #1000
Denver, CO 80222
Marketing seminars/products/consulting
    Phone: 303-584-0146   Accepts collect calls?
    Toll Free: FAX:
    Internet:
Suitable Sites:
Concentration:
    Expansion: Canada, Foreign
    Registered:
Field Support:
    Training:

Points for Profits
PO Box 2424
La Mesa, CA 91943
Proof-of-purchase ad plan for broadcast stations
    Phone: 619-588-0664   Accepts collect calls?
    Toll Free: FAX:
    Internet:
Suitable Sites:
Concentration:
    Expansion: CA
    Registered:
Field Support:
    Training:

Profit-On-Hold
3401 Ridgelake Dr #108
Metairie, LA 70002

    Phone: 504-832-8000   Accepts collect calls?
    Toll Free: 800-569-4653   FAX: 504-828-2141
    Internet:
Suitable Sites: HO
Concentration: 5 in LA
    Expansion: TX
    Registered:
Field Support: $DP, CP, EO, ST, $SO, IC, $FC, H, N
    Training: 2 weeks home office

Resort Maps Franchise Inc
Old High School / Rte 100 Box 726
Waitsfield, VT 05673
Business & tourist information maps
    Phone: 802-496-6277   Accepts collect calls? N
    Toll Free: 800-788-5247   FAX: 802-496-6278
    Internet: resortmaps@mudriver.com
Suitable Sites: HO
Concentration: 8 in NJ, 3 in CT, 2 in VT
    Expansion: CA,HI,MD,NY,RI,VA, Canada, Foreign
    Registered: CA FL HI MD NY RI VA
Field Support: ST, H
    Training: 3 days HQ
              7 days on site

Tee Signs Plus
PO Box 878
Pleasant Grove, UT 84062
Golf course tee signs/bench advertising
    Phone: 801-785-5832   Accepts collect calls?
    Toll Free: FAX:
    Internet:
Suitable Sites:
Concentration:
    Expansion: All United States
    Registered:
Field Support:
    Training:

Trimark
184 Quigley Blvd
New Castle, DE 19720
Direct-mail advertising in print on behalf of local business
    Phone: 302-322-2143   Accepts collect calls? N
    Toll Free: 888-321-6275   FAX: 302-322-9910
    Internet: trimark@universal.dca.net
Suitable Sites: HO
Concentration: 4 in PA, 3 in NY, 1 in FL
    Expansion: All United States, Canada, Foreign
    Registered: FL,HI
Field Support: $CP, $EO, ST, $FC, $H, N
    Training: 40 hours corporate HQ
              40 hours on-site

Val-Pak Direct Marketing
8605 Largo Lakes Dr
Largo, FL 33773

    Phone: 813-393-1270   Accepts collect calls?
    Toll Free: 800-237-6266   FAX: 813-392-0049
    Internet: www.valpak.com
Suitable Sites:
Concentration:
    Expansion: All United States, Canada
    Registered: CA,FL,HI,IL,IN,MD,MI,MN,ND,NY,OR,RI,SD,VA,WA,WI,DC
Field Support: $DP, EO, ST, $FC, H, N
    Training: 5 days home study
              5 days HQ
              var. on-site

Yellow Jacket Direct Mail Advertising
23101 Moulton Pkwy #110
Laguna Hills, CA 92653

    Phone: 714-951-9500   Accepts collect calls?
    Toll Free: 800-893-5569   FAX: 714-859-0899
    Internet:
Suitable Sites: HO
Concentration: 10 in CA, 3 in AZ
    Expansion: SE
    Registered: CA,HI
Field Support: CP, EO, ST, FC, H, N
    Training: 1-2 weeks corporate office

Business Service Industry

Brokerage, Sales

	Confidential Business Connection	Empire Business Brokers	Mergers & Acquisitions International	Business Group, Inc. Proventure	Sunbelt Business Brokers	VR Business Brokers		
Startup Cost	52K-100K	5K	VAR.	35K-50K	5K-50K			
Franchise Fee	15.5K-31K	8.9K	10K	10K	5K-10K	7K-19.8K		
Royalty	6%	$150/MO	$375/QTR	6%	3-6K/YR	4.5-7.5%		
Advertising Fee	2%	0%	N/A	0%	0	$100/MO		
Financing Provided	N	Y	N	Y	Y	N		
Experience Required	N	N						
Passive Ownership	D	A	N	D	N	N		
In Business Since	1997	1981	1969	1979	1978	1979		
Franchised Since	1998	1989	1979	1981	1993	1979		
Franchised Units 1996	1							
1997	2	49	60	5	130	63		
1998	1	53						
Company Owned 1996	0	2						
1997	0	2	0	4	1	0		
1998	0	2						
Number of Units U.S.	1	49	52	9	130	63		
Canada	0	2	0	0	0	0		
Foreign	0	0	8	0	1	0		
Projected New U.S.	6	24						
Canada	1	2		1				
Foreign	0	2		3				
Corporate Employees	2	5	3	2	7	10		
Contract Length	10/10	20/10	10/10	10/10	ON-GOING	7/5/5/5		
Expand in Territory	Y	Y	N	Y	Y	Y		
Full-Time Employees	3	1		2	INDEP	2-3		
Part-Time Employees	1	0	1	2				
Conversions	N	Y		Y	Y	Y		
Site Selection Assist.	Y	Y	N	Y	N	Y		
Lease Negotiation Assist.	Y	Y		Y		N		
Site Space Required	750	500		500	1000	300		
Development Agreement	N	Y	Y	N	N	Y		
Develop. Agree. Term		5	25					
Sub-franchising	N	Y	Y	N	N	Y		

Business Service Industry

Confidential Business Connection
4155 E Jewell Ave #1010
Denver, CO 80222
Franchise seller/buyer matching, business brokerage, consulting
Phone: 303-759-2334   Accepts collect calls? N
Toll Free: 888-446-1414   FAX: 303-584-0793
Internet:
Suitable Sites: ES, FB, OC, PC, SC
Concentration: 1 in CO
    Expansion: All United States, Canada
    Registered:
Field Support: $EO, $ST, SO, N
    Training: 4 days HQ
           3 days on-site
           ongoing fee basis

Empire Business Brokers
336 Harris Hill Rd
Buffalo, NY 14221
Existing business & franchise sales, financial brokering
Phone: 716-677-5229   Accepts collect calls? N
Toll Free: FAX: 716-677-0955
Internet: www.empirebusinessbrokers.com
Suitable Sites: HO, OC, SF
Concentration: 6 in GA, 4 in OH, 3 in NY
    Expansion: All United States, Canada, Foreign
    Registered: CA,FL,HI,IL,IN,MD,MI,MN,ND,NY,OR,RI,SD,VA,WA,WI,DC
Field Support: $DP, $CP, EO, ST, SO, FC, H, N
    Training: 1 week at home office
           incl classroom, video &
           audio tapes, manuals

International Mergers & Acquisitions
4300 N Miller Rd #230
Scottsdale, AZ 85251

Phone: 602-990-3899   Accepts collect calls?
Toll Free: FAX: 602-990-7480
Internet:
Suitable Sites:
Concentration: 7 in AZ, 4 in CA, 3 in NY
    Expansion: All United States, Canada, Foreign
    Registered: CA,FL,HI,IL,IN,MD,MI,MN,ND,NY,OR,RI,SD,VA,WA,WI,DC
Field Support: DP, FC, N
    Training: 3 days world HQ
           2 days creative work sessions

Proventure Business Group, Inc.
PO Box 338
Needham Heights, MA 02494
Business brokers, intermediary, M & A for private companies
Phone: 781-444-8278   Accepts collect calls? N
Toll Free: FAX: 781-444-0565
Internet: proventure@aol.com
Suitable Sites: ES, FB, HO, OC
Concentration: 8 in MA, 1 in NH
    Expansion: New England, Canada, Foreign
    Registered:
Field Support: EO, ST, SO, $FC, N
    Training: 1 week HQ

Sunbelt Business Brokers
2 Amherst St
Charleston, SC 29403
Business brokerage
Phone: 803-853-4781   Accepts collect calls?
Toll Free: 800-771-7866   FAX: 803-853-4135
Internet: www.sunbeltnetwork.com
Suitable Sites: FB
Concentration: 14 in FL, 10 in NC, 9 in GA
    Expansion: All United States, Canada, Foreign
    Registered: CA,FL,IL,MD,MI,NY,VA,HI
Field Support: EO, ST, FC, H, N
    Training: 2 days various regional centers

VR Business Brokers
1151 Dove St #100
Newport Beach, CA 92660

Phone: 714-975-1100   Accepts collect calls?
Toll Free: 800-377-8722   FAX: 714-975-1940
Internet:
Suitable Sites: ES
Concentration: 10 in CA, 9 in FL, 4 in NC
    Expansion: All United States, Canada, Foreign
    Registered: CA,FL,IL,MD,MI,OR,WA
Field Support: $EO, $ST, $FC, N
    Training: 2 weeks classes Newport Beach, CA

Business Service Industry   Finance

	American Lenders Service Co.	Interface Financial Group	Money Concepts (Canada)	Paceco Financial Services				
Startup Cost		50K-100K	80K	22K-120K				
Franchise Fee		25K	49.5K	25K				
Royalty		8%	VAR.	7%/$150/WK				
Advertising Fee		1%	2%/5K MAX	3%				
Financing Provided	Y	N	N	Y				
Experience Required	N							
Passive Ownership		D	D	A				
In Business Since	1978	1971	1984	1952				
Franchised Since	1978	1991	1985	1995				
Franchised Units 1996	92							
1997	93	41	94	1				
1998	94							
Company Owned 1996	3							
1997	8	0	0	10				
1998	16							
Number of Units U.S.	110	17	0	11				
Canada		24	94	0				
Foreign		0	0	0				
Projected New U.S.	12							
Canada								
Foreign								
Corporate Employees	103		25	30				
Contract Length		10/10	5/1	5/5/5/5				
Expand in Territory	N	Y	Y	N				
Full-Time Employees			4	2				
Part-Time Employees		1						
Conversions	Y			Y				
Site Selection Assist.	Y	N	Y	Y				
Lease Negotiation Assist.	Y	N	Y					
Site Space Required			750-1000	1000				
Development Agreement	N	Y	Y	Y				
Develop. Agree. Term			5	5				
Sub-franchising	N		N	N				

Business Service Industry   Finance

American Lenders Service Co.
PO Box 7238
Odessa, TX 79760
Collateral recovery (repossession service) for commercial lender
- Phone: 915-332-0361   Accepts collect calls? N
- Toll Free: FAX: 915-332-1065
- Internet: www.americanlenderssrv.com
Suitable Sites:
Concentration: 16 in TX, 8 in NC, 6 in CA
- Expansion: All United States
- Registered: CA,FL,HI,IL,IN,MD,MI,MN,ND,NY,OR,RI,SD,VA,WA,WI,DC
Field Support: CP, EO, SO, FC, N
- Training: administrative
marketing assistance

Interface Financial Group
4521 Pga Blvd #211
Palm Beach Gardens, FL 33416

- Phone: 905-475-5701   Accepts collect calls?
- Toll Free: 800-387-0860   FAX: 905-475-8688
- Internet: www.interface financial.com
Suitable Sites: HO
Concentration: 7 in ON
- Expansion: All United States, Canada, Foreign
- Registered: CA,FL,IL,MI,MN,NY,VA,WA & FTC DISCLOSURE STATES
Field Support: ST, SO, H
- Training: 3 days + on-site

Money Concepts (Canada)
180 Attwell Dr #501
Etobicoke, ON M9W-6A9 CANADA

- Phone: 416-674-0450   Accepts collect calls?
- Toll Free: 800-661-7296   FAX: 416-674-4785
- Internet:
Suitable Sites:
Concentration: 53 in ON, 21 in BC, 5 in NB
- Expansion: N, Canada
- Registered: AB
Field Support: DP, $CP, EO, ST, FC, H, N
- Training: 2 weeks head office

Paceco Financial Services
1301 W Main
Duncan, OK 73533

- Phone: 405-256-3140   Accepts collect calls?
- Toll Free: 800-811-7223   FAX: 405-252-5222
- Internet:
Suitable Sites: SC
Concentration: 11 in OK
- Expansion: Central and NW
- Registered:
Field Support: DP, $CP, EO, ST, SO, $FC, H, N
- Training: 3 weeks Duncan, OK & on-site

Business Service Industry   Job Training (Spread 1 of 2)

	Barbizon Schools of Modeling	Boston Bartenders School Associates	ExecuTrain	John Casablancas Modeling/Career Center	Leadership Management, Inc.	Institute of Health Careers	Metropolitan Model Managers Int'l	Professional Dynametric Programs/PDP
Startup Cost	47K-67.5K	30K	200K-250K	100K-200K	N/A	6.7K-29.9K	5KCDN-10K CDN	31.5K-49.5K
Franchise Fee	19.5K-35K	6.9K	30K	15K-35K		9.9K	15K+CDN	29.5K
Royalty	7.50%	10%	6-9%	7%	0%	5%	10%	0-30%
Advertising Fee	2.5%		1.5%	3%	0%			0%
Financing Provided	Y	N	Y	N	Y	N	N	Y
Experience Required								N
Passive Ownership	D	D	D	N	D			D
In Business Since	1939	1968	1984	1979	1965	1993	1996	1978
Franchised Since	1968	1995	1986	1979	1965	1996	1996	1980
Franchised Units 1996						0	1	
1997	63	3	183	48	365	0	1	27
1998								21
Company Owned 1996						1	1	0
1997	0	6	35	0	0	1	1	0
1998								0
Number of Units U.S.	90	9	173	40	365			20
Canada	2	0	4	1	0			4
Foreign	4	0	41	7	0			3
Projected New U.S.								2
Canada								1
Foreign								2
Corporate Employees		2	110	6	25			6
Contract Length	10/10	10/10	7/7	10/5/5	1			7/3
Expand in Territory	Y	Y	Y	Y	N			Y
Full-Time Employees		2	15-20	4	VAR			1-2
Part-Time Employees		1		6-8				
Conversions	Y		N	Y				
Site Selection Assist.	Y	Y	Y	Y	N			N
Lease Negotiation Assist.	Y	Y	Y					
Site Space Required		1000	3500	1800-2500				
Development Agreement	N	N	N	N	N			N
Develop. Agree. Term								
Sub-franchising	N	N	N	N	N			N

Business Service Industry

Barbizon Schools of Modeling
2240 Woolbright Rd #300
Boynton Beach, FL 33426

Phone: 561-369-8600   Accepts collect calls?
Toll Free: FAX: 561-369-1299
Internet:
Suitable Sites:
Concentration: 11 in CA, 7 in NY, 6 in FL
Expansion: All United States, Canada, Foreign
Registered: CA,HI,IL,MD,MN,NY,VA,WA
Field Support: EO, ST, SO, FC, N
Training: var. home office
     var. on-site

Boston Bartenders School Associates
PO Box 176
Wilbraham, MA 01095

Phone: 413-596-4600   Accepts collect calls?
Toll Free: 800-357-3210   FAX: 413-596-4630
Internet:
Suitable Sites:
Concentration: 4 in MA, 2 in CT, 2 in RI
Expansion: All United States, Canada
Registered: RI
Field Support: DP, SO, IC, FC, H
Training: 2 weeks Springfield, MA

ExecuTrain
4800 Northpoint Pkwy
Alpharetta, GA 30202

Phone: 770-521-6271   Accepts collect calls?
Toll Free: 800-437-2034   FAX: 770-521-6283
Internet: www.exec>train.com
Suitable Sites: FB
Concentration:
Expansion: N, Canada, Foreign
Registered: CA,FL,HI,IL,IN,MD,MI,MN,ND,NY,OR,RI,SD,VA,WA,WI,DC
Field Support:
Training: 5 days gm training
     5 days instructor training
     5 days sale training

John Casablancas Modeling/Career Center
111 E 22nd St 4th Flr
New York, NY 10010

Phone: 212-420-0655   Accepts collect calls?
Toll Free: FAX: 212-473-2725
Internet:
Suitable Sites: RM, SC
Concentration: 5 in FL, 2 in OH, 2 in PA
Expansion: NW, SE, Foreign
Registered: CA,IL,MI,NY,VA,WI
Field Support: $CP, EO, ST, SO, $FC, $N
Training: 2-3 days New York

Leadership Management, Inc.
4567 Lake Shore Dr
Waco, TX 76710

Phone: 254-776-2060   Accepts collect calls?
Toll Free: 800-365-7437   FAX: 254-757-4600
Internet:
Suitable Sites:
Concentration:
Expansion: All United States, Canada
Registered: CA,FL,HI,IL,IN,MD,MI,MN,ND,NY,OR,RI,SD,VA,WA,WI,DC
Field Support: EO, ST, FC, H
Training: 1-3 weeks

Metropolitan Institute of Health Careers
5201 Westbank Expwy, #315
Marrero, LA 70072
Continuing education/seminars
Phone: 504-347-8704   Accepts collect calls?
Toll Free: 888-289-6442   FAX:
Internet:
Suitable Sites:
Concentration:
Expansion: IL
Registered:
Field Support:
Training:

Model Managers Int'l
696 Dufferin St
Toronto, ON M6K-2B5 CANADA
Modeling courses & related services
Phone: 416-588-8806   Accepts collect calls?
Toll Free: FAX:
Internet:
Suitable Sites:
Concentration:
Expansion: N, Canada
Registered:
Field Support:
Training:

Professional Dynametric Programs/PDP
750 E Hwy 24 Bldg I
Woodland Park, CO 80866
Integrated management systems for development of human capital
Phone: 719-687-6074   Accepts collect calls?
Toll Free: 800-632-1127   FAX: 719-687-8587
Internet: www.pdpnet.com
Suitable Sites: ES, HO, OC
Concentration: 2 in CA, 2 in CO, 2 in TX
Expansion: All United States, Canada, Foreign
Registered: CA,FL,HI,WA
Field Support: DP, CP, EO, $ST, IC, $FC, N
Training: 2 weeks corporate HQ
     3 days client location

Business Service Industry   Job Training (Spread 2 of 2)

	Renaissance Executive Forums	Sandler Sales Institute	Turbo Management Systems Ltd.					
Startup Cost	50K-100K	41.5K-758.3K	10K					
Franchise Fee	49.5K	35K	24K					
Royalty	20%	$908	10%					
Advertising Fee	0%	N/A	2%					
Financing Provided	N	Y	N					
Experience Required			N					
Passive Ownership	N	D	N					
In Business Since	1994	1983	1985					
Franchised Since	1994	1983	1995					
Franchised Units 1996			0					
1997	42	182	1					
1998			2					
Company Owned 1996			1					
1997	1	0	1					
1998			1					
Number of Units U.S.	43	171	3					
Canada	0	11	0					
Foreign	0	0	0					
Projected New U.S.			10					
Canada			2					
Foreign			2					
Corporate Employees	13	26	6					
Contract Length	10/10	5/5/5/5	10					
Expand in Territory	Y	Y	Y					
Full-Time Employees	1	1						
Part-Time Employees		1						
Conversions			Y					
Site Selection Assist.	N	N	Y					
Lease Negotiation Assist.	N		Y					
Site Space Required								
Development Agreement	Y	N	N					
Develop. Agree. Term	5							
Sub-franchising	N	N	Y					

Business Service Industry

Job Training (Spread 2 of 2)

Renaissance Executive Forums
875 Prospect St #302
La Jolla, CA 92037

Phone: 619-551-6600   Accepts collect calls?
Toll Free: FAX: 619-551-8777
Internet:
Suitable Sites: ES
Concentration: 17 in CA, 5 in IL, 3 in MI
    Expansion: All United States, Canada, Foreign
    Registered: CA,FL,HI,IL,IN,MD,MI,MN,ND,NY,OR,RI,SD,VA,WA,WI,DC
Field Support: DP, $CP, $EO, $ST, $H, N
    Training: 12.5 days La Jolla, CA

Sandler Sales Institute
10411 Stevenson Rd
Stevenson, MD 21153

Phone: 410-653-1993   Accepts collect calls?
Toll Free: 800-669-3537   FAX: 410-358-7858
Internet: www.sandler.com
Suitable Sites:
Concentration: 15 in PA, 14 in OH, 12 in TX
    Expansion: All United States, Canada
    Registered: CA,FL,IL,IN,MD,MI,MN,ND,NY,OR,RI,SD,VA,WA,WI
Field Support: FC, H, $N
    Training: 4 days home office
           1 day home office

Turbo Management Systems Ltd.
36280 NE Wilsonville Rd
Newberg, OR 97132
Management/customer service/leadership/sales training
Phone: 503-625-1867   Accepts collect calls?
Toll Free: 800-574-4373   FAX:
Internet:
Suitable Sites: HO
Concentration: 1 in OR, 1 in MO, 1 in PA
    Expansion: Canada, Foreign
    Registered:
Field Support: CP, ST, FC, H, N
    Training: 30 days home office

Business Service Industry

	American Sign Shops	ASI Sign Systems Inc	FastSigns	Sign-A-Rama	Signs By Tomorrow	Signs First	Signs & More In 24	Signs Now
Startup Cost	55K-75K	147K-207K	125K	80K-90K	83K-151K	20K-65K	45K-99K	56.2K-115.1K
Franchise Fee	15K	35K-100K	20K	37.5K	19.5K	10K-15K	13K	19.8K
Royalty	6%	5%	6%	6%	2.5-5%	6%	3-4%	5%
Advertising Fee	0%		2%	0%	0%	0%	0%	0%
Financing Provided	Y	Y	Y	Y	Y	Y	Y	Y
Experience Required			N	N	N			
Passive Ownership	D		N	D	N	D	A	D
In Business Since	1985	1977	1985	1986	1986	1966	1991	1983
Franchised Since	1987	1978	1986	1987	1987	1989	1992	1986
Franchised Units 1996		34						
1997	43	34	394	350	68	41	5	284
1998			424	425	79	40		
Company Owned 1996		0						
1997	0	0	0	0	1	1	2	0
1998			0	0	1	2		
Number of Units U.S.	43		353	324	79	42	7	218
Canada	0		9	6	0	0	0	26
Foreign	0		59	20	0	0	0	40
Projected New U.S.			21	95	18	5		
Canada			3	15				
Foreign			12	55				
Corporate Employees	6		74	37	15	5	4	11
Contract Length	20/20		20/10	35	20/20	10/10	10/10	20/20
Expand in Territory	N		Y	Y	Y	Y	Y	Y
Full-Time Employees	3		3	1-5	3	1	3	2
Part-Time Employees	1				1		1	1
Conversions	N		Y	Y	Y			Y
Site Selection Assist.	Y		Y	Y	Y	Y	Y	Y
Lease Negotiation Assist.	Y		Y	Y	Y	Y	Y	N
Site Space Required	1200-1400		1200-1600	1200	1600	1500	1500	1200
Development Agreement	N		Y	Y	Y	Y	N	N
Develop. Agree. Term			VAR.	VAR.	10	10		
Sub-franchising	N		Y	N	N	N	N	N

Business Service Industry

American Sign Shops

3803-B Computer Dr #200
Raleigh, NC 27609

Phone: 919-787-1557   Accepts collect calls?
Toll Free: 800-966-2700   FAX: 919-787-3830
Internet: www.amerisign.com
Suitable Sites: SC
Concentration: 15 in NC, 9 in MI, 4 in OH
Expansion: East Of Rocky Mountains
Registered: FL,IL,MI,VA
Field Support: EO, $ST, SO, FC, H, N
Training: 8 hours home study
2 weeks home office
1 week franchisee location

ASI Sign Systems Inc

3890 W NW Hwy #102
Dallas, TX 75220
Finished architectural signs/planning svcs.
Phone: 214-352-9140   Accepts collect calls?
Toll Free: FAX:
Internet:
Suitable Sites:
Concentration:
Expansion: HI,MD,NY,VA, Canada, Foreign
Registered:
Field Support:
Training:

FastSigns

2550 Midway Rd #150
Carrollton, TX 75006
Computer generated signs & graphics produced in one day
Phone: 972-447-0777   Accepts collect calls? N
Toll Free: 800-827-7446   FAX: 972-248-8201
Internet: www.fastsigns.com
Suitable Sites: AC, SC
Concentration: 47 in TX, 34 in CA, 24 in FL
Expansion: All United States, Canada, Foreign
Registered: CA,FL,HI,IL,IN,MD,MI,MN,ND,NY,OR,RI,SD,VA,WA,WI,DC,AB
Field Support: EO, ST, SO, FC, H, N
Training: 3 weeks new owner in Dallas, TX
field & regional training

Sign-A-Rama

1601 Belvedere Rd
West Palm Beach, FL 33406

Phone: 561-640-5570   Accepts collect calls? Y
Toll Free: 800-776-8105   FAX: 561-640-5580
Internet: www.sign-a-rama.com
Suitable Sites: SC, SF
Concentration:
Expansion: All United States, Canada, Foreign
Registered: CA,FL,IL,IN,MD,MI,MN,ND,NY,OR,RI,SD,VA,WA,WI
Field Support: EO, ST, SO, IC, FC, H, N
Training: 2 weeks west palm beach FL
80 hours minimum on-site

Signs By Tomorrow

6460 Dobbin Rd
Columbia, MD 21045
All types of computer generated signs, graphics & lettering
Phone: 410-992-7192   Accepts collect calls? Y
Toll Free: 800-765-7446   FAX: 410-992-7675
Internet: www.signsbytomorrowusa.com
Suitable Sites: AC, FB, SC, SF
Concentration: 15 in PA, 11 in MD, 8 in NJ
Expansion: All United States, Canada
Registered: CA,FL,HI,IL,IN,MD,MI,MN,ND,NY,OR,RI,SD,VA,WA,WI,DC
Field Support: CP, EO, ST, SO, IC, FC, H, N
Training: 2 weeks HQ
2 weeks on-site
various advanced classes as appropriate

Signs First

813 Ridge Lake Blvd #390
Memphis, TN 38120
Retail, computerized sign store w/ strong showroom design & svc
Phone: 901-682-2264   Accepts collect calls?
Toll Free: 800-852-2163   FAX: 901-682-2475
Internet:
Suitable Sites: SC
Concentration: 13 in MS, 11 in TN, 3 in CO
Expansion: All United States
Registered: FL
Field Support: DP, CP, EO, ST, SO, IC, FC, H, N
Training: 3 weeks Memphis TN
1 week location of store

Signs & More In 24

1739 St Mary's Ave
Parkersburg, WV 26101

Phone: 800-424-7446   Accepts collect calls?
Toll Free: 800-358-2358   FAX: 304-422-7449
Internet: www.signs-and-more.com
Suitable Sites: FB
Concentration: 4 in PA, 2 in WV, 1 in OH
Expansion: Midwest, South Atlantic
Registered:
Field Support: CP, EO, ST, SO, IC, FC, H, N
Training: 2 weeks Parkersburg WV
1 week on-site

Signs Now

4900 Manatee Ave W #201
Bradenton, FL 34209

Phone: 941-747-7747   Accepts collect calls?
Toll Free: 800-356-3373   FAX: 941-747-5074
Internet: www.signsnow.com
Suitable Sites: SC
Concentration: 20 in FL, 21 in BC, 8 in OR
Expansion: All United States, Canada, Foreign
Registered: CA,FL,HI,IL,IN,MD,MI,MN,ND,NY,OR,RI,SD,VA,WA,WI,DC
Field Support: EO, ST, SO, FC, H, N
Training: 3-4 weeks regional mgr store
1-2 weeks own store

Business Service Industry

	Custom Sign Centres / Vinylgraphics							
Startup Cost	90K							
Franchise Fee	25K							
Royalty	8%							
Advertising Fee	0%							
Financing Provided	Y							
Experience Required								
Passive Ownership	N							
In Business Since	1983							
Franchised Since	1990							
Franchised Units 1996								
1997	14							
1998								
Company Owned 1996								
1997	0							
1998								
Number of Units U.S.	0							
Canada	14							
Foreign	0							
Projected New U.S.								
Canada								
Foreign								
Corporate Employees	8							
Contract Length	10/5							
Expand in Territory	Y							
Full-Time Employees	3							
Part-Time Employees								
Conversions	Y							
Site Selection Assist.	Y							
Lease Negotiation Assist.	Y							
Site Space Required	1500							
Development Agreement	Y							
Develop. Agree. Term	15							
Sub-franchising	Y							

Business Service Industry

Vinylgraphics Custom Sign Centres
36 Apple Creek Blvd
Markham, ON L3R-4Y4   CANADA

Phone: 905-415-9809   Accepts collect calls?
Toll Free: 800-265-7446   FAX: 905-415-9424
Internet:
Suitable Sites: SC
Concentration: 14 in ON
Expansion: All United States, Canada, Foreign
Registered:
Field Support: CP, EO, ST, $SO, FC, H, N
Training: 5 weeks Toronto on

Business Service Industry

Telecom., Internet

	IC Solutions Inc	IMBC	Quik Internet	Z Land, Inc.				
Startup Cost	20K+	100K	35K	95K-130K				
Franchise Fee	7.5K	62K	25K	30K				
Royalty	6%	$5K/MO	10	0				
Advertising Fee			3					
Financing Provided	N	Y	N	Y				
Experience Required			N	N				
Passive Ownership			N	D				
In Business Since	1997	1996	1996	1995				
Franchised Since	1997	1997	1996	1996				
Franchised Units 1996			12	0				
1997	8	2	30	1				
1998			100	10				
Company Owned 1996		0	0	0				
1997	1	1	0	1				
1998			0	3				
Number of Units U.S.			100	12				
Canada			5					
Foreign			8	1				
Projected New U.S.			100	400				
Canada			30					
Foreign			150	5				
Corporate Employees			16	50				
Contract Length			10	7				
Expand in Territory			Y	Y				
Full-Time Employees			1	6-7				
Part-Time Employees			1	0				
Conversions			N	Y				
Site Selection Assist.			Y	N				
Lease Negotiation Assist.			N	N				
Site Space Required			200					
Development Agreement			Y	N				
Develop. Agree. Term			15					
Sub-franchising			N	N				

Business Service Industry   Telecom., Internet

IC Solutions Inc
    9800 Centre Pkwy #550
    Houston, TX 77036
Internet & telecommunications services
        Phone: 713-773-1200   Accepts collect calls?
        Toll Free: FAX:
        Internet:
    Suitable Sites:
    Concentration:
        Expansion: All United States, Canada, Foreign
        Registered:
    Field Support:
        Training:

IMBC
    1000 John #208
    Troy, MI 48083
Interactive internet broadcasting
        Phone: 248-599-1415   Accepts collect calls?
        Toll Free: FAX:
        Internet:
    Suitable Sites:
    Concentration:
        Expansion: CA,MI,NY,ND,SD,WI
        Registered:
    Field Support:
        Training:

Quik Internet
    2533 N Carson St Ste 3743
    Carson City, NV 89706
Full service Internet access
        Phone: 949-054-8217   Accepts collect calls? N
        Toll Free: 888-784-5266   FAX: 949-548-0569
        Internet: www.quik.com
    Suitable Sites: ES, OC
    Concentration:
        Expansion: All United States, Canada, Foreign
        Registered: CA,FL,HI,IL,IN,MD,MI,MN,ND,NY,OR,RI,SD,VA,WA,WI,DC,AB
    Field Support: DP, CP, EO, ST, SO, IC, FC, H, N
        Training:

Z Land, Inc.
    1221 E Dyer Rd #290
    Santa Ana, CA 92705-5635
Internet-based business solutions
        Phone: 714-708-8580   Accepts collect calls? N
        Toll Free: FAX:
        Internet: www.zland.com
    Suitable Sites: ES, IP, OC
    Concentration: 2 in CA, 2 in NJ
        Expansion: All United States, Canada, Foreign
        Registered: CA,IL.MD,MI,WI
    Field Support: ST
        Training: initial and ongoing

Business Service Industry

Other Business Service (Spread 1 of 3)

	Bevinco	Commission Express	Comprehensive Business Services	Estrella Insurance	Fortune Practice Management	Franklin Traffic Service	General Business Services	Hq Business Centers
Startup Cost	25K-35K	48.3K-148.5K	35.9K-57.4K	99.5K-125K	20K-50K	25K	41K-45K	500K-2M
Franchise Fee	22.5K	10K-20K	12.5K	39.5K	42K	25K	35K	30K-100K
Royalty	$12/AUDIT	VAR.	4%/$15/WK.	3-4%	10%	VARIABLE	2-8%	2-2.4%
Advertising Fee	$2/AUDIT		1%/$15/WK.	1%	5%	N/A	2%	0%
Financing Provided	Y	N	Y	N	N	Y	Y	N
Experience Required	N				N			
Passive Ownership	N		N	D	D	A	D	N
In Business Since	1987	1991	1949	1980	1990	1969	1962	1972
Franchised Since	1990	1996	1965	1997	1991	1985	1962	1977
Franchised Units 1996		1						
1997	135	3	287	3		1	347	178
1998					31			
Company Owned 1996		0			2			
1997	1	1	6	35	2	2	0	0
1998					2			
Number of Units U.S.	80		241	38	31	3	343	132
Canada	36		42	0		0	1	4
Foreign	20		4	0		0	3	42
Projected New U.S.					5			
Canada								
Foreign								
Corporate Employees	4		25	30	4	70	18	30
Contract Length	5/5		10/5	7/7	5	5/5	10/10	PERPETUAL
Expand in Territory			Y	N		Y	N	Y
Full-Time Employees	1-3		4	3		1		8
Part-Time Employees	1-3		1	1			1	
Conversions			Y	Y			Y	Y
Site Selection Assist.	N		N	Y		N	N	N
Lease Negotiation Assist.			N	Y				N
Site Space Required			500-1500	800				15000
Development Agreement	Y			Y		N	N	Y
Develop. Agree. Term	5			10				
Sub-franchising	N		N	N	N	N	N	Y

Business Service Industry

Other Business Service (Spread 1 of 3)

Bevinco
250 Consumers Rd Ste 1103
Toronto, ON M2J-4V6 CANADA
Liquor inventory auditing service for bars & restaurants
Phone: 416-490-6266   Accepts collect calls?
Toll Free: 888-238-4626   FAX: 416-490-6899
Internet: www.bevinco.com
Suitable Sites:
Concentration: 6 in OH, 7 in MI, 6 in NJ
    Expansion: All United States, Canada, Foreign
    Registered: CA,FL,HI,IL,IN,MD,MI,MN,ND,NY,OR,RI,SD,VA,WA,WI,DC
Field Support: DP, $CP, ST, FC, H, N
    Training: 5 days corp classroom Toronto
           3-5 days in-field

Commission Express
8408 Arlington Blvd #103
Fairfax, VA 22031
Real estate commission factoring
Phone: 703-560-5500   Accepts collect calls?
Toll Free: FAX:
Internet:
Suitable Sites:
Concentration:
    Expansion: All United States, Canada, Foreign
    Registered:
Field Support:
    Training:

Comprehensive Business Services
26722 Plaza Dr
Mission Viejo, CA 92691

Phone: 714-348-5100   Accepts collect calls?
Toll Free: 800-323-9000   FAX: 714-348-5126
Internet: www.comprehensive.org
Suitable Sites: FB, SC, SF
Concentration: 39 in ON, 33 in CA, 23 in IL
    Expansion: All United States, Canada, Foreign
    Registered: CA,FL,HI,IL,IN,MD,MI,MN,ND,NY,OR,RI,SD,VA,WA,WI,DC
Field Support: EO, ST, $FC, H, N
    Training: 3 weeks corporate HQ
           3 weeks & 3 days in-field

Estrella Insurance
3750 W Flagler St
Miami, FL 33134

Phone: 305-443-2829   Accepts collect calls?
Toll Free: FAX: 305-448-1816
Internet: www.estrella-ins.com
Suitable Sites: FB, RM, SC, SF
Concentration: 38 in FL
    Expansion: Florida
    Registered: FL
Field Support: DP, CP, EO, ST, SO, FC
    Training: 8 weeks Miami, FL

Fortune Practice Management
9191 Towne Centre Dr #500
San Diego, CA 92122
Dental/health care consulting co, affiliated w/ Anthony Robbins
Phone: 619-535-1784   Accepts collect calls? N
Toll Free: 800-628-1052   FAX: 619-535-6387
Internet:
Suitable Sites: HO
Concentration: 6 in CA, 3 in WA, 3 in AZ
    Expansion: All United States, Canada, Foreign
    Registered: CA,FL,IL,IN,MI,NY,OR,WA
Field Support:
    Training:

Franklin Traffic Service
PO Box 100
Ransomville, NY 14131

Phone: 716-731-3131   Accepts collect calls?
Toll Free: FAX: 716-731-2705
Internet:
Suitable Sites:
Concentration: 2 in NY, 1 in MN
    Expansion: SE, Midwest
    Registered: NY
Field Support: DP, CP, EO, $ST, N
    Training: 3 weeks Ransomville, NY

General Business Services
1020 N University Parks Dr PO Box 3146
Waco, TX 76707

Phone: 254-745-2525   Accepts collect calls?
Toll Free: 800-583-6181   FAX: 254-745-2566
Internet: www.genbusiness.com
Suitable Sites:
Concentration: 29 in TX, 25 in CA, 23 in FL
    Expansion: All United States, Canada, Foreign
    Registered: CA,FL,HI,IL,IN,MD,MI,MN,ND,NY,OR,RI,SD,VA,WA,WI,DC
Field Support: DP, CP, EO, ST, FC, H, N
    Training: 2 weeks Waco, TX

Hq Business Centers
120 Montgomery St #2350
San Francisco, CA 94104

Phone: 415-781-7811   Accepts collect calls?
Toll Free: 800-480-2020   FAX: 415-781-8034
Internet: www.hqnet.com
Suitable Sites: OC
Concentration:
    Expansion: All United States, Canada, Foreign
    Registered: CA,FL,MI,MN,NY,RI,VA
Field Support: CP, ST, $FC, $H, N
    Training: 2 weeks various locations

Business Service Industry

Other Business Service (Spread 2 of 3)

	Jay Roberts & Associates	Knowledge Development Centers Inc	Auto Insurance Agencies / Look No-Fault	Magis Fund Raising Specialists	Management Associates / Manufacturing	Mister Money - USA	The Office Alternative	Rynker Ribbon Xchange Inc.
Startup Cost	VAR.	208.77K	5K-50K	28.5K	15K-25K	64K-200K	47K	55K
Franchise Fee	2K	35K	2K	7.5K	6K-8K	21.5K-24.5K	22.75K	25K
Royalty	VAR.	5%	15%	8%	5%	3-5%	6%	$600/MO
Advertising Fee	NA		2%	2%	1%/$500	1%		2%
Financing Provided	Y	Y	Y	Y	N	Y	N	Y
Experience Required								N
Passive Ownership	N		D	N	N	A		A
In Business Since	1965	1993	1988	1991	1982	1977	1983	1989
Franchised Since	1981	1994	1993	1991	1992	1995	1986	1994
Franchised Units 1996		3					10	
1997	30	10	29	6	6	13	10	29
1998								
Company Owned 1996		2					2	
1997	2	0	3	3	1	12	2	3
1998								
Number of Units U.S.	32		32	6	7	26		0
Canada	0		0	3	0	0		30
Foreign	0		0	0	0	0		0
Projected New U.S.								6
Canada								12
Foreign								
Corporate Employees	5		3	2	20	8		14
Contract Length	OPEN/OPEN		10/5/5	5/5	10/10	5/5		5/5
Expand in Territory	Y		Y	Y	Y	Y		Y
Full-Time Employees	2		1	2	1	3		2
Part-Time Employees			1	4		1		
Conversions			N	Y	Y	Y		
Site Selection Assist.	N		Y	N	Y	Y		Y
Lease Negotiation Assist.	N		Y		Y	Y		N
Site Space Required			500	500		2000-6000		350
Development Agreement	Y		Y	Y	N	N		Y
Develop. Agree. Term								
Sub-franchising	N		N	Y	N	N		N

Business Service Industry

Other Business Service (Spread 2 of 3)

Jay Roberts & Associates
81 N Chicago St #200
Joliet, IL 60432-1362

Phone: 815-722-0683   Accepts collect calls?
Toll Free: FAX: 815-722-4750
Internet:
Suitable Sites: ES, DA, HO
Concentration: 2 in IL, 2 in NY, 2 in CA
Expansion: All United States
Registered:
Field Support: DP, EO, ST, $FC, N
Training: 1 week Joliet, IL

Knowledge Development Centers Inc
445 Hutchinson Ave #120
Columbus, OH 43235
Training facility rentals
Phone: 614-888-2444   Accepts collect calls?
Toll Free: FAX:
Internet:
Suitable Sites:
Concentration:
Expansion: CA,IN,MD,MI,MN,NY
Registered:
Field Support:
Training:

Look No-Fault Auto Insurance Agencies
32620 Cherryhill Rd
Garden City, MI 48135

Phone: 248-552-1127   Accepts collect calls?
Toll Free: FAX: 248-552-4030
Internet:
Suitable Sites: FB, SF
Concentration: 32 in MI
Expansion: Michigan
Registered: MI
Field Support: EO, ST, SO, FC, H
Training: 30 days canton, MI

Magis Fund Raising Specialists
845 Heathermoor Ln #202
Perrysburg, OH 43551
Assist and act as counsel to non-profit organizations campaigns
Phone: 419-244-6711   Accepts collect calls? N
Toll Free: FAX: 419-244-4791
Internet:
Suitable Sites: HO
Concentration: 3 in MI, 3 in OH, 3 in ON
Expansion: All United States, Canada
Registered: CA,FL,HI,IL,IN,MD,MI,MN,ND,NY,OR,RI,SD,VA,WA,WI,DC
Field Support: $DP, CP, $EO, $ST, SO, $FC, N
Training: 1 week home study
1 week support service center
1 week on-site

Manufacturing Management Associates
1301 W 22nd St #500
Oak Brook, IL 60523

Phone: 630-575-8700   Accepts collect calls?
Toll Free: 800-574-0308   FAX: 630-574-0309
Internet: www.consult-mma.com
Suitable Sites:
Concentration: 3 in IN, 2 in IL
Expansion: All United States, Canada
Registered: IL,IN,MI,WA
Field Support: $DP, SO, FC, H, N
Training: 8-10 days Chicago, IL

Mister Money - USA
238 Walnut St
Fort Collins, CO 80524

Phone: 970-221-4391   Accepts collect calls?
Toll Free: 800-827-7296   FAX: 970-490-2099
Internet: www.mistermoney.com
Suitable Sites: FB, SF
Concentration: 7 in CO, 5 in IA, 2 in WY
Expansion: West, Midwest, South, Foreign
Registered: FL,IL,MN,WI
Field Support: DP, CP, EO, ST, SO, IC, H
Training:

The Office Alternative
5151 Monroe St #200
Toledo, OH 43623
Office space & support services
Phone: 419-841-4700   Accepts collect calls?
Toll Free: 800-843-1040   FAX:
Internet:
Suitable Sites:
Concentration:
Expansion:
Registered:
Field Support:
Training:

Rynker Ribbon Xchange Inc.
8566 Fraser St #200
Vancouver, BC V5X-3Y3 CANADA
Recycling print media cartridges: ribbons, inkjets, lasers
Phone: 604-322-9421   Accepts collect calls? N
Toll Free: FAX: 604-322-1658
Internet: rynker@dowco.com
Suitable Sites: HO
Concentration: 17 in BC, 4 in AB, 7 in ON
Expansion: All United States, Canada
Registered: AB
Field Support: CP, ST, FC, H, N
Training: 8 days head office
3 days franchisee territory

Business Service Industry

Other Business Service (Spread 3 of 3)

	Service Center	Tradebank International	Universal Business Consultants	World Trade Network	Your Office USA			
Startup Cost	1K-50K	50K	10K	135K	250K-350K			
Franchise Fee	1K-35K	30K	30K+	12K	38K			
Royalty	5.30%	N/A	10%	7%	6% MINIMUM			
Advertising Fee	0%	N/A		3%	2%			
Financing Provided	Y	Y	N	Y	Y			
Experience Required								
Passive Ownership	A	D		D	A			
In Business Since	1991	1987	1989	1993	1989			
Franchised Since	1992	1995	1995	1993	1989			
Franchised Units 1996			5					
1997	8	18	6	40	99			
1998								
Company Owned 1996			1					
1997	1	8	1	1	1			
1998								
Number of Units U.S.	9	20		5	1			
Canada	0	6		1	6			
Foreign	0	0		35	93			
Projected New U.S.								
Canada								
Foreign								
Corporate Employees	2	15		3	10			
Contract Length	10/10	5/2-5		10/15	10/10			
Expand in Territory	Y	Y		N	N			
Full-Time Employees	1	1		1	2			
Part-Time Employees				1				
Conversions		N		Y	Y			
Site Selection Assist.	Y	Y		N	Y			
Lease Negotiation Assist.		Y		N	Y			
Site Space Required	300	600-1000		400	5000			
Development Agreement	N	N		N	Y			
Develop. Agree. Term					10			
Sub-franchising	N	N		N	N			

Business Service Industry

Other Business Service (Spread 3 of 3)

Service Center
5202 E Mt View Rd
Scottsdale, AZ 85253

Phone: 602-998-1616 — Accepts collect calls?
Toll Free: 800-729-7424 — FAX: 602-998-4091
Internet:
Suitable Sites: SC
Concentration: 2 in TX, 2 in AZ, 2 in CA
Expansion: All United States
Registered: CA,FL,HI,IL,IN,MD,MI,MN,ND,NY,OR,RI,SD,VA,WA,WI,DC
Field Support: SO, H
Training: 1 week Las Vegas, NV

Tradebank International
4220 Pleasantdale Rd
Atlanta, GA 30340-3523

Phone: 770-239-3177 — Accepts collect calls?
Toll Free: 800-899-1111 — FAX: 770-239-3113
Internet: www.tradebankonline.com
Suitable Sites: FB, OC, SC, SF
Concentration: 7 in GA, 4 in AL, 3 in TN
Expansion: All United States, Canada, Foreign
Registered: FL,MI,OR
Field Support: DP, EO, ST, SO, $FC, H
Training: 1 week Atlanta, GA
1 week franchised territory

Universal Business Consultants
7624 Tanglecrest Dr
Dallas, TX 75240
Business referral network
Phone: 972-702-0345 — Accepts collect calls?
Toll Free: 800-460-9000 — FAX:
Internet:
Suitable Sites:
Concentration:
Expansion: All United States, Canada
Registered:
Field Support:
Training:

World Trade Network
580 Lincoln Park Blvd #255
Dayton, OH 45429

Phone: 937-298-3383 — Accepts collect calls?
Toll Free: 800-227-3772 — FAX: 937-298-2550
Internet: www.wnetwork.com
Suitable Sites: OS
Concentration: 2 in CA, 1 in WI, 1 in OH
Expansion: All United States, Canada, Foreign
Registered: FL
Field Support: $ST, $FC, N
Training: 5 days Dayton, OH

Your Office USA
1455 Frazee Rd #100
San Diego, CA 92108

Phone: 619-297-4100 — Accepts collect calls?
Toll Free: 888-950-1700 — FAX: 619-297-4199
Internet: www.yourofficeusa.com
Suitable Sites: FB, OC
Concentration: 2 in ON, 1 in CO
Expansion: All United States, Canada, Foreign
Registered: CA,FL,HI,IL,IN,MD,MI,MN,ND,NY,OR,RI,SD,VA,WA,WI,DC
Field Support: DP, CP, EO, ST, SO, $FC, H, N
Training: 1 week San Diego, CA

Child Development Industry

Child Care

	Baby's Away	Child Care Learning Center	Tutor Time Private Home Day Care	Wee Watch				
Startup Cost	16K-25K	175K-200K	24K					
Franchise Fee	8K	42K	12.5K					
Royalty	7%	6%	6-8%					
Advertising Fee	3%	1% NATIONAL	2%					
Financing Provided	Y	Y	N					
Experience Required	N							
Passive Ownership	A	D	N					
In Business Since	1990	1980	1984					
Franchised Since	1994	1990	1987					
Franchised Units 1996								
1997	19	260	50					
1998	20							
Company Owned 1996								
1997	7	11	0					
1998	6							
Number of Units U.S.	21	270	0					
Canada	7	0	50					
Foreign	0	1	0					
Projected New U.S.	3							
Canada								
Foreign								
Corporate Employees	1	83	9					
Contract Length	10/5/5	10/10	5/20					
Expand in Territory	Y	Y	N					
Full-Time Employees	1	20	2					
Part-Time Employees		15	1					
Conversions	Y		Y					
Site Selection Assist.	Y	Y	N					
Lease Negotiation Assist.	N	Y						
Site Space Required		10						
Development Agreement	Y	Y	N					
Develop. Agree. Term		10						
Sub-franchising	N	Y	N					

Child Development Industry

Child Care

Baby's Away
3131 S. Vaughn Way Ste 523
Aurora, CO 80014
Baby equipment & supplies rental for traveling/visiting parents
    Phone: 303-596-8864   Accepts collect calls?
    Toll Free: 800-571-0077   FAX: 303-750-6664
    Internet: www.csd.net/~babyaway
Suitable Sites: HO
Concentration: 4 in CO, 3 in CA, 3 in SC
    Expansion: All United States
    Registered: CA,FL,IL
Field Support: $CP, EO, ST, IC, H, N
    Training: 2 days corporate HQ CO
          2 days franchisee's residence

Tutor Time Child Care Learning Center
621 N W 53rd St #450
Boca Raton, FL 33487

    Phone: 561-994-6226   Accepts collect calls?
    Toll Free: 800-275-1235   FAX: 561-994-2778
    Internet:
Suitable Sites: FB
Concentration: 33 in FL, 30 in NY, 18 in TX
    Expansion: 28 States, Canada, Foreign
    Registered: (PENDING),CA,FL,MD,MN,NY,VA,WA(PENDING)
Field Support: $DP, $CP, EO, ST, SO, IC, H, N
    Training: 2 weeks corporate HQ
          on-site various locations
          their location

Wee Watch Private Home Day Care
105 Main St
Unionville, ON L3R-2G1   CANADA

    Phone: 905-479-4274   Accepts collect calls?
    Toll Free: FAX: 905-479-9047
    Internet:
Suitable Sites:
Concentration: 38 in ON, 12 in BC
    Expansion: All United States, Canada
    Registered:
Field Support: CP, EO, ST, FC, H, N
    Training: 4 days home office
          3 days on-site

Child Development Industry

Child Education (Spread 1 of 2)

	Academy of Learning	ComputerTots / Computer Explorers	FutureKids (Canada)	FutureKids Inc	Genius Kid Academy	The Goddard Schools	Imagine That Discovery Museums	Kiddie Academy International
Startup Cost	200K-300K	22.7K-42.1K	100K-142.9K	35K-65K	50K-70K	160K	425K-525K	180K-260K
Franchise Fee	30K	15K-29.9K	50K	35K	50K	30K	25K	40K
Royalty	0%	6%/$250 MIN	10% + $360	VAR.	12%	7%	6%	7%
Advertising Fee	$400/MO.	1%	2%/$250		0%		0%	0%
Financing Provided	N	Y	N	N	Y	Y	N	Y
Experience Required		N						N
Passive Ownership	N	N	D		D		D	A
In Business Since	1987	1983	1983	1983	1992	1986	1992	1981
Franchised Since	1987	1988	1989	1989	1993	1988	1994	1992
Franchised Units 1996				656		21		
1997	154	224	596	889	3	26	3	40
1998								
Company Owned 1996				0		10		
1997	3	2	0	0	1	10	0	11
1998								
Number of Units U.S.	7	128	243		0		3	51
Canada	140	0	31		2		0	0
Foreign	10	92	322		1		0	0
Projected New U.S.		138						18
Canada		0						
Foreign		130						
Corporate Employees	30	18	1		1		3	30
Contract Length	10/10	10/10	10/10		5/5		10/10	10/5/5
Expand in Territory	Y	Y	Y		Y			Y
Full-Time Employees	5	1	VAR		1		3	10-20
Part-Time Employees	2	5			2		15	2
Conversions	Y		N					Y
Site Selection Assist.	Y	Y	Y		Y		Y	Y
Lease Negotiation Assist.	Y	N	Y		Y		Y	Y
Site Space Required	3000		1000		800-1000		15000	7500-13000
Development Agreement	Y	N	Y		N		N	N
Develop. Agree. Term			1.5					
Sub-franchising	N	Y	Y		N		N	N

Child Development Industry

Child Education (Spread 1 of 2)

Academy of Learning
5 Bank St #202
Attleboro, MA 02703

Phone: 508-222-0000   Accepts collect calls?
Toll Free: 800-750-8973   FAX: 508-222-8007
Internet: www.academyol.com
Suitable Sites: OTHER
Concentration: 50 in ON, 16 in BC, 9 in AB
Expansion: NE, Canada, Foreign
Registered: NY,RI,AB
Field Support: EO, ST, SO, $FC, H, N
Training: 2 weeks training center
2 days head office
1 week on-site

ComputerTots / Computer Explorers
10132 Colvin Run Rd
Great Falls, VA 22066
International computer enrichment program for children 3-12
Phone: 703-759-2556   Accepts collect calls? N
Toll Free: 800-531-5053   FAX: 703-759-7411
Internet: www.computertots.com
Suitable Sites: HO, OC
Concentration: 15 in CA, 8 in TX, 8 in FL
Expansion: All United States, Canada, Foreign
Registered: CA,FL,HI,IL,IN,MD,MI,MN,NY,ND,OR,RI,VA,WA,WI,DC
Field Support: $CP, $EO, $ST, $FC, H, N
Training: 7 days great falls, VA

FutureKids (Canada)
18 Crimson Millway
Willowdale, ON M2L-1T6 CANADA

Phone: 416-445-6488   Accepts collect calls?
Toll Free: 800-205-5437   FAX: 416-445-5750
Internet:
Suitable Sites: SC, SF
Concentration: 58 in CA, 26 in NY, 14 in ON
Expansion: N, Canada, Foreign
Registered: AB
Field Support: CP, EO, ST, $SO, FC, H, N
Training: 2 weeks Los Angeles, CA

FutureKids Inc
5777 W Century Blvd #1555
Los Angeles, CA 90045-5678
Computer literacy education
Phone: 310-337-7006   Accepts collect calls?
Toll Free: FAX:
Internet:
Suitable Sites:
Concentration:
Expansion: All United States, Foreign
Registered:
Field Support:
Training:

Genius Kid Academy
398 Steeles Ave W #214
Thornhill, ON L4J-6X3 CANADA

Phone: 905-886-1920   Accepts collect calls?
Toll Free: FAX: 905-886-4919
Internet:
Suitable Sites: FB, RM
Concentration: 2 in ON
Expansion: All United States, Canada, Foreign
Registered:
Field Support: $CP, $ST, SO, FC, N
Training: 4 weeks Toronto, ON
4 weeks London, ON

The Goddard Schools
381 Brooks Rd
King Of Prussia, PA 19406
Preschool learning center
Phone: Accepts collect calls?
Toll Free: 800-272-4901   FAX:
Internet:
Suitable Sites:
Concentration:
Expansion: All United States
Registered:
Field Support:
Training:

Imagine That Discovery Museums
PO Box 493
New Vernon, NJ 07976

Phone: 973-267-2907   Accepts collect calls?
Toll Free: 800-820-1145   FAX: 973-445-1917
Internet:
Suitable Sites: FB, SC
Concentration: 2 in NJ, 1 in MD
Expansion: All United States
Registered: FL,MD
Field Support: DP, CP, EO, ST, SO, IC, H
Training: 2 weeks e Hanover, NJ

Kiddie Academy International
108 Wheel Rd
Bel Air, MD 21015
Early child care learning centers w/ age appropriate curriculum
Phone: 410-515-0788   Accepts collect calls? N
Toll Free: 800-554-3343   FAX: 410-569-2729
Internet: www.kiddieacademy.com
Suitable Sites: FB, LI, M, OC, PC, SC, SF
Concentration: 19 in MD, 12 in NJ, 9 in NY
Expansion: East Of Mississippi
Registered: CA,FL,IL,IN,MD,MI,MN,NY,OR,RI
Field Support: $DP, CP, EO, ST, SO, H, N
Training: 2 weeks owner train., corp. HQ
1 week dir. train., corp. HQ
3-5 days staff training

Child Development Industry   Child Education (Spread 2 of 2)

	Quality Learning Centers	Kids R Kids	Learning Express	Little Scientists	Odyssey Art Centers	Primrose Schools	TechnoKids		
Startup Cost	1.3M-1.7M	203K-354K	25K-50K	1K-39K	1.3M-1.8M	75K-85K		
Franchise Fee	37.5K	30K	25K	24K	48.5K	20K		
Royalty	5%	5%	7%/$350	6%	7%	6%		
Advertising Fee		2%	1%	2%	1%	0%		
Financing Provided	Y	Y	Y	N	Y	N		
Experience Required			N	N	N			
Passive Ownership		D	D	D	N	N		
In Business Since	1985	1987	1995	1974	1982	1993		
Franchised Since	1988	1990	1996	1995	1989	1993		
Franchised Units 1996	50			2				
1997	54	63	6	3	67	12		
1998				2	93	17		
Company Owned 1996	0			1				
1997	0	0	2	1	1	1		
1998				1	1			
Number of Units U.S.		63	8	3	93	0		
Canada		0	0		0	2		
Foreign		0	0		0	14		
Projected New U.S.				5	25			
Canada					0	3		
Foreign					0	28		
Corporate Employees		12	15	2	22	6		
Contract Length		10/5	10/10	10	11/10/10	10/10		
Expand in Territory			Y	Y	N	Y		
Full-Time Employees		2	2		16	2		
Part-Time Employees		8-10	6		10	1		
Conversions			N	Y		Y		
Site Selection Assist.		Y	N	Y	Y	N		
Lease Negotiation Assist.		Y		Y	Y	N		
Site Space Required		3000	250-500	250	6500-8500	800		
Development Agreement		Y	Y	N	N	Y		
Develop. Agree. Term		10	TBA			10		
Sub-franchising		N	Y	N	N	Y		

Child Development Industry

Child Education (Spread 2 of 2)

Kids R Kids Quality Learning Centers
5300 Oak Brook Pkwy #135
Norcross, GA 30093
Child care centers
    Phone: 770-279-7777   Accepts collect calls?
    Toll Free: FAX:
    Internet:
Suitable Sites:
Concentration:
    Expansion: SE,S,MW,SE,W,NW
    Registered:
Field Support:
    Training:

Learning Express
76 Farmers Row
Groton, MA 01450

    Phone: 978-448-2333   Accepts collect calls?
    Toll Free: 800-924-2296   FAX: 978-448-2333
    Internet: www.learningexpress.com
Suitable Sites: FB, RM, SC, SF
Concentration: 14 in MA, 6 in TX, 6 in NJ
    Expansion: All United States
    Registered: CA,FL,IL,IN,MD,MI,MN,ND,NY,OR,RI,SD,VA,WA,WI,DC,AB
Field Support: EO, ST, SO, IC, FC, H, N
    Training: 1 week Brookline, MA
              1 week Sunnyvale, CA
              1 week Dallas, TX

Little Scientists
200 Main Street
Ansonia, CT 06401
Hands-on after-school science learning ages 3-10
    Phone: 203-732-3522   Accepts collect calls?
    Toll Free: 800-322-8386   FAX: 203-736-2165
    Internet: www.little-scientists.com
Suitable Sites: HO, OS
Concentration: 5 in CT, 2 in NJ, 2 in MA
    Expansion: All United States, Canada, Foreign
    Registered: CA,FL,IL,NY,VA,WA,DC
Field Support: $CP, $EO, ST, $IC, FC, H, N
    Training: 5 days Ansonia, CT

Odyssey Art Centers
Box 512
Tarrytown, NY 10591
Art classes / fine art based upon art history
    Phone: 914-631-7148   Accepts collect calls? N
    Toll Free: FAX: 914-631-7148
    Internet: www.odysseyart.com
Suitable Sites: ES, FB, HO, OC, SF, WR
Concentration: 3 in NY
    Expansion: NE, Canada, Foreign
    Registered: NY
Field Support: DP, CP, EO, ST, SO, IC, FC, H, N
    Training: 2 weeks intensive training in
              the unique method of
              creative art based on history

Primrose Schools
199 S Erwin St
Cartersville, GA 30120
Quality educational child-care w/ emphasis on devel. Whole child
    Phone: 770-606-9600   Accepts collect calls? N
    Toll Free: 800-745-0677   FAX: 770-606-0020
    Internet:
Suitable Sites: FB
Concentration: 33 in GA, 39 in TX, 9 in NC
    Expansion: Midwest, SE, SE, CO
    Registered: FL,MI
Field Support: EO, ST, SO, FC, H, N
    Training: 1 week corporate office
              1 week on-site (school)
              1 week in-school mentor program

TechnoKids
145 Peyside Dr
Oakville, ON L6L-5Y1   CANADA

    Phone: 905-829-4171   Accepts collect calls? N
    Toll Free: 800-221-7921   FAX: 905-829-4172
    Internet: technokids.com
Suitable Sites: SC
Concentration: 2 in ON, 1 in AB
    Expansion: All United States, Canada, Foreign
    Registered:
Field Support: $EO, $ST, SO, $FC, H, N
    Training: 2 weeks head office

Child Development Industry

	Gymboree	Gymn' Around Kids	Gymsters, Inc.	Head Over Heels	J.W. Tumbles, A Children's Gym	Kinderdance International	The Little Gym International, Inc.	Pee Wee Workout
Startup Cost	80K-150K	5K-9.5K	7.8K-12.5K	20K-30K	85K-110K	6K-20.6K	110K-150K	2K-2.3K
Franchise Fee	35K	8.5K	12K	12.5K	25K	6.5K-15K	37.5K	1.5K
Royalty	6%	8%	7%	8%	$2400/YR.	6-15%	8%	10%
Advertising Fee	1.75K	0%	3%	0%	0%	3%	1%	0%
Financing Provided	N	N	N	Y	N	Y	Y	N
Experience Required			Y		Y	N		
Passive Ownership	N	N	D	A	D	D	D	D
In Business Since	1976	1987	1980	1990	1985	1979	1992	1986
Franchised Since	1978	1994	1988	1993	1993	1985	1992	1987
Franchised Units 1996	365							
1997	384	2	9	8	3	50	90	38
1998	391		7				110	
Company Owned 1996	13							
1997	12	2	1	2	2	1	3	1
1998	15						5	
Number of Units U.S.	286	4	8	9	3	50	87	37
Canada	22	0	0	1	0	1	0	1
Foreign	83	0		0	1	0	12	1
Projected New U.S.	15		4		2		24	
Canada	5							
Foreign	10						2	
Corporate Employees	16	1	4	5	8	5	18	
Contract Length	10/10	3/1	5/5	20/10	5/5	10/10	10/10	5/5
Expand in Territory	Y	Y	Y	Y	Y	Y	Y	Y
Full-Time Employees	1	1	1	2	1	1+	2	
Part-Time Employees	3	1-2		5	2	1	2-3	1
Conversions	N			N	N		Y	
Site Selection Assist.	N	Y	Y	N	Y	N	Y	N
Lease Negotiation Assist.	N	N	N		Y	N	Y	
Site Space Required	1800				2000		3500	
Development Agreement	N		N	Y	Y	N	N	N
Develop. Agree. Term								
Sub-franchising	N	N	N	Y	N	N	N	Y

Child Development Industry

Child Fitness (Spread 1 of 2)

Gymboree
700 Airport Blvd #200
Burlingame, CA 94010
Parent-child participation play program
Phone: 650-579-0600   Accepts collect calls? N
Toll Free: FAX: 650-696-7452
Internet: www.gymboree.com
Suitable Sites: AC, M, RM, SC, SF
Concentration: 49 in CA, 32 in NY, 31 in NJ
   Expansion: All United States, Canada, Foreign
   Registered: CA,FL,HI,IL,IN,MD,MI,MN,NY,OR,RI,SD,VA,WA,DC,AB,WI
Field Support: CP, ST, $FC, H, N
   Training: 6 days HQ
             twice yearly regional
             3 days annual meeting

Gymn' Around Kids
705-A Seminole Dr
West Columbia, SC 29169

   Phone: 803-794-1471   Accepts collect calls?
   Toll Free: 800-543-6167   FAX: 803-892-5631
   Internet:
Suitable Sites: OC
Concentration: 3 in SC, 1 in NC
   Expansion: All United States
   Registered:
Field Support: $CP, $ST, $IC, $FC, H, N
   Training: 3-5 days South Carolina

Gymsters, Inc.
6111 Paseo Pueblo Dr
San Jose, CA 95120-2741
Mobile fitness program for children ages 2-12
   Phone: 408-997-6997   Accepts collect calls? N
   Toll Free: FAX: 408-997-6997
   Internet:
Suitable Sites: HO
Concentration: 6 in CA, 1 in OH
   Expansion: All United States, Canada, Foreign
   Registered: CA,FL,HI,IL,IN,MD,MI,MN,ND,NY,OR,RI,SD,VA,WA,WI,DC
Field Support: $CP, $EO, ST, $IC, $FC, H, N
   Training: 6 days San Jose, CA

Head Over Heels
2106 Cahaba Rd
Birmingham, AL 35223

   Phone: 205-879-6305   Accepts collect calls?
   Toll Free: 800-850-3547   FAX: 205-877-8377
   Internet:
Suitable Sites: HO
Concentration: 2 in AL, 2 in TN
   Expansion: All United States, Canada, Foreign
   Registered:
Field Support: $DP, CP, EO, ST, SO, $IC, $FC, H, N
   Training: 1 week Birmingham, AL
             1 week on-site

J.W. Tumbles, A Children's Gym
12750 Carmel Country Rd #102
San Diego, CA 92130
Instruction in basic gymnastics & tumbling, 4 mo thru 9 yr olds
   Phone: Accepts collect calls? N
   Toll Free: 800-886-2532   FAX: 619-756-7719
   Internet: www.jwtumbles.com
Suitable Sites: SC
Concentration: 3 in CA
   Expansion: All United States, Canada, Foreign
   Registered: CA,FL,IN,MD,MI,MN,ND,OR,SD,VA,WA,WI,DC
Field Support: SO, FC, H, N
   Training: 2-4 weeks San Diego, CA

Kinderdance International
268 N Babcock St
Melbourne, FL 32935
Developmental dance & gymnastics for children 2-8 yrs
   Phone: 407-242-0590   Accepts collect calls? N
   Toll Free: 800-554-2334   FAX: 407-254-3388
   Internet: vaxxine.com/franchise/kinderdance
Suitable Sites: HO
Concentration: 9 in CA, 4 in NY, 4 in FL
   Expansion: All United States, Canada, Foreign
   Registered: CA,FL,HI,IL,MD,MI,NY,OR,VA,WA,DC,AB
Field Support: DP, CP, EO, ST, SO, IC, FC, H, N
   Training: 6 days Melbourne, FL
             complete business overview
             opening & operating

The Little Gym International, Inc.
8160 N Hayden Rd #J-112
Scottsdale, AZ 85258
Gymnastics, sports, karate for children 4 mos to 12 yrs
   Phone: 602-948-2878   Accepts collect calls?
   Toll Free: 888-228-2878   FAX: 602-948-2765
   Internet: www.thelittlegymintl.com
Suitable Sites: SC, OTHER
Concentration: 10 in TX, 9 in NY, 8 in WA
   Expansion: All United States, Canada, Foreign
   Registered: FL,IL,IN,MD,MI,MN,NY,OR,WA
Field Support: CP, EO, ST, SO, $FC, H, N
   Training: 3-4 days business
             5 days curriculum
             7-14 days existing gym

Pee Wee Workout
34976 Aspenwood Ln
Willoughby, OH 44094

   Phone: 440-946-7888   Accepts collect calls?
   Toll Free: FAX: 440-946-7888
   Internet: www.members.alo.com/peeweework
Suitable Sites: HO
Concentration:
   Expansion: All United States, Canada, Foreign
   Registered:
Field Support: CP, H, N
   Training: video based

Child Development Industry

Child Fitness (Spread 2 of 2)

	Pre-Fit	Stretch-N-Grow of America	Tenniskids				
Startup Cost	2.5K-4.5K	8.3K-13.3K	10K-14K				
Franchise Fee	8.5K-24.5K	7.6K-12.6K	10K+				
Royalty	8-10%	$100/MO.	6%				
Advertising Fee	2%	$100/YR.	2%				
Financing Provided	Y	N	Y				
Experience Required	N						
Passive Ownership	D	D	A				
In Business Since	1987	1992	1991				
Franchised Since	1992	1994	1994				
Franchised Units 1996							
1997	48	68	12				
1998							
Company Owned 1996							
1997	1	0	8				
1998	2						
Number of Units U.S.	48	67	20				
Canada	1	1	0				
Foreign	0	0	0				
Projected New U.S.	10						
Canada							
Foreign							
Corporate Employees	5	2	2				
Contract Length	10/10	N/A	10/5				
Expand in Territory	Y	N	Y				
Full-Time Employees	1	1	1				
Part-Time Employees	2-4	1-2	1				
Conversions			N				
Site Selection Assist.	Y	N	Y				
Lease Negotiation Assist.							
Site Space Required	2000-4000						
Development Agreement	N	N	Y				
Develop. Agree. Term							
Sub-franchising	N	N	N				

Child Development Industry

Child Fitness (Spread 2 of 2)

Pre-Fit
    10926 S Western Ave
    Chicago, IL 60643
Mobile preschool fitness program/health club for children
        Phone: 773-233-7771   Accepts collect calls?
    Toll Free: FAX: 773-233-7121
    Internet: prefit@ameritech.net
Suitable Sites: HO, M, SC
Concentration: 13 in IL, 5 in PA, 3 in IA
    Expansion: All United States, Canada, Foreign
    Registered: FL,IL,MI,CA,WA,MD,VA,MN
Field Support: ST, SO, $FC, H, N
        Training: 2 days Chicago, IL for mobile program
                5 days Chicago, IL for club program

Stretch-N-Grow of America
    PO Box 261397 3501 Seltzer Dr
    Plano, TX 75023

        Phone: 972-519-1635   Accepts collect calls?
    Toll Free: 800-348-0166   FAX: 972-612-5819
    Internet: www.stretch-n-grow.com
Suitable Sites: HO
Concentration: 10 in TX, 5 in NY, 5 in PA
    Expansion: All United States, Foreign
    Registered: CA,FL,NY
Field Support: $CP, ST, $FC, H, N
    Training: 3 days Dallas, TX

Tenniskids
    322 S. Orchard
    Burbank, CA 91506
Teaching tennis to children ages 2-10
        Phone: Accepts collect calls? N
    Toll Free: 800-959-1322   FAX:
    Internet: www.tenniskids.com
Suitable Sites: AC, DA, FB, RM, SC, OTHER
Concentration: 9 in CA, 2 in NJ
    Expansion: All United States
    Registered: CA
Field Support: $DP, CP, EO, ST, IC, $FC, N
    Training: 2 weeks

Child Development Industry

Other Child Development (Spread 1 of 2)

	Baby News Childrens Stores	Building Blocks Franchise Corp	Children's Orchard	The Fourth R	High Touch-High Tech	Kid To Kid	Kiddie Kobbler	Kids Team
Startup Cost	150K-250K	155K-255K	55.6K-114.3K	50K-80K	28K-42K	88K-116K	100K	75K
Franchise Fee	15K	25K	15.5K-19.5K	7K-22K	20K-35K	20K	20K	10K
Royalty	1%	5%	4.5-6%	$120/MO+5%	7%	4.75%	4%	4%
Advertising Fee	0%		1.5%	0%	0%	.5%	.5%	1%
Financing Provided	N	N	Y	Y	Y	N	N	N
Experience Required						N		
Passive Ownership	N		N	A		D	N	A
In Business Since	1950	1986	1980	1991	1992	1992	1951	1972
Franchised Since	1961	1995	1985	1992	1994	1994	1968	1995
Franchised Units 1996		0						
1997	41	3	70	174	19	26	31	9
1998						27		
Company Owned 1996		12						
1997	1	1	4	0	2	0	0	2
1998						1		
Number of Units U.S.	42		74	78	21	28	0	11
Canada	0		0	6	0	0	31	0
Foreign	0		0	90	1	0	0	0
Projected New U.S.						6		
Canada								
Foreign								
Corporate Employees	14		8	9	4	6	6	3
Contract Length	5/5		10/5	10/10	10/10	10/5	10/5/5	10/10
Expand in Territory	Y		N	Y	Y	N	Y	Y
Full-Time Employees	3		1	2		3	2	1
Part-Time Employees	4		2-4	4	2-3	2	2	3
Conversions	Y		Y	Y		Y	Y	
Site Selection Assist.	Y		Y	Y	Y	Y	Y	Y
Lease Negotiation Assist.	Y		Y	Y		Y	Y	Y
Site Space Required	5000		1200-2500	800		2400	1000	750
Development Agreement	N		Y	Y	N	Y	Y	Y
Develop. Agree. Term				10		VAR.		5
Sub-franchising	N		Y	N	Y	N	Y	N

Child Development Industry   Other Child Development (Spread 1 of 2)

Baby News Childrens Stores
23521 Foley St
Hayward, CA 94545

    Phone: 510-786-3460   Accepts collect calls?
Toll Free: FAX: 510-785-1580
Internet:
Suitable Sites: FB, RM, SC
Concentration: CA
    Expansion: All United States, Canada, Foreign
    Registered: CA
Field Support: DP, CP, EO, $ST, SO, IC, FC, N
    Training: 1-2 weeks various locations

Building Blocks Franchise Corp
6465 Permiter Dr
Dublin, OH 43016
Educational toy store
    Phone: Accepts collect calls?
Toll Free: 888-654-8697   FAX:
Internet:
Suitable Sites:
Concentration:
    Expansion: Canada
    Registered:
Field Support:
    Training:

Children's Orchard
315 E Eisenhower Pkwy #316
Ann Arbor, MI 48108

    Phone: 313-994-9199   Accepts collect calls?
Toll Free: 800-999-5437   FAX: 313-994-9323
Internet: www.childorch.com
Suitable Sites: SC
Concentration: 18 in CA, 14 in MA, 8 in MI
    Expansion: All United States, Canada, Foreign
    Registered: CA,FL,IL,IN,MD,MI,NY,VA
Field Support: $CP, EO, ST, SO, IC, FC, H, N
    Training: 10 days Ann Arbor, MI +5 onsite
                10 days Newburyport, MA +5 onsite

The Fourth R
1715 Market St #103
Kirkland, WA 98033

    Phone: 425-828-0336   Accepts collect calls?
Toll Free: 800-821-8653   FAX: 425-828-0192
Internet: www.fourthr.com
Suitable Sites: HO, OC, SC, SF
Concentration: 9 in CA, 8 in PA, 7 in WA
    Expansion: All United States, Canada, Foreign
    Registered: CA,FL,HI,IL,IN,MD,MI,MN,NY,OR,VA,WA,WI,DC,AB
Field Support: CP, EO, FC, H, N
    Training: 5 days Seattle, WA

High Touch-High Tech
7908 Wiles Rd
Coral Springs, FL 33067

    Phone: 954-755-2900   Accepts collect calls?
Toll Free: 800-444-4968   FAX: 954-755-1242
Internet: www.handsonscience.com
Suitable Sites: HO
Concentration: 5 in FL, 2 in NJ
    Expansion: All United States, Canada, Foreign
    Registered: CA,FL,IL,NY,VA,WI
Field Support: EO, ST, FC, H, N
    Training: 5 days national programming off.

Kid To Kid
406 W South Jordan Pkwy #160
South Jordan, UT 84095
Upscale childrens' resale store, parents buy/sell kids used item
    Phone: 801-553-8799   Accepts collect calls?
Toll Free: 888-543-2543   FAX: 801-553-8793
Internet:
Suitable Sites: FB, SC, SF
Concentration: 12 in UT, 4 in TX, 2 in PA
    Expansion: All United States, Canada
    Registered: CA,FL,HI,IL,IN,MD,MI,MN,ND,NY,OR,RI,SD,VA,WA,WI,DC
Field Support: CP, EO, $ST, SO, $IC, FC, H, N
    Training: 10 days Salt Lake City UT

Kiddie Kobbler
68 Robertson Rd #106
Nepean, ON K2H-8P5 CANADA

    Phone: 613-820-0505   Accepts collect calls?
Toll Free: 800-561-9762   FAX: 613-820-8250
Internet:
Suitable Sites: RM, SC
Concentration: 25 in ON, 2 in NS
    Expansion: Area & Master Franchise Terr, Canada
    Registered:
Field Support: EO, ST, SO, FC, H, N
    Training: 4 weeks on-site
                6 weeks supervised home study

Kids Team
135 N Penn St #1700
Indianapolis, IN 46204

    Phone: 317-229-3339   Accepts collect calls?
Toll Free: 800-875-5439   FAX: 317-229-3330
Internet:
Suitable Sites: RM
Concentration: 3 in IN
    Expansion: All United States
    Registered: AS REQUIRED
Field Support: EO, ST, SO, IC, FC, N
    Training: 5 days corp ofc, Merrillville NJ

Child Development Industry

Other Child Development (Spread 2 of 2)

	The Mad Science Group	Once Upon A Child	Patty-Cakes International, Inc.	The Peanut Club	Safe-T-Child	Stork News of America	USA Baby	
Startup Cost	55K	85K-145K	8K-10K	50K	15K-30K	7K-12K	250K-300K	
Franchise Fee	23.5K	20K	7K	25K	12.5K	7K-10K	7.5K-16.5K	
Royalty	8%	5%	5%	5%	6%	$0.5-1K	3%	
Advertising Fee	0%	$500/YR.	0%	1%	0%	N/A	5%	
Financing Provided	Y	Y	N	N	N	N	N	
Experience Required			N	N				
Passive Ownership	N	D	N	A	A	A	D	
In Business Since	1985	1985	1947	1990	1986	1983	1975	
Franchised Since	1995	1993	1988		1992	1985	1986	
Franchised Units 1996								
1997	66	200	59		71	178	46	
1998			58	1				
Company Owned 1996								
1997	0	4	0		1	1	10	
1998			0'	2				
Number of Units U.S.	50	204	58		67	174	56	
Canada	10	0	1	3	4	2	0	
Foreign	6	0	0		1	3	0	
Projected New U.S.			10					
Canada			0					
Foreign			0					
Corporate Employees	30	200	4	2	9	14	8	
Contract Length	10/5	10/10	10/10	5	10/20	INDEFIN.	10/10	
Expand in Territory	Y	Y	Y		N	Y	Y	
Full-Time Employees	1	3	1	2	2	1	4	
Part-Time Employees	3-5	2	1	6-8	2	1	2-3	
Conversions		Y		Y			Y	
Site Selection Assist.	N	Y	N		N	N	Y	
Lease Negotiation Assist.		Y	N				Y	
Site Space Required		2000-3000		2000-3000			7000-9000	
Development Agreement	N	N	N	Y	Y	N	Y	
Develop. Agree. Term				5				
Sub-franchising	N	N	N	N	N	N	Y	

Child Development Industry

Other Child Development (Spread 2 of 2)

The Mad Science Group
3400 Jen Talon W #101
Montreal, QC H3R-2E8   CANADA

    Phone: 514-344-4181   Accepts collect calls?
Toll Free: 800-586-5231   FAX: 514-344-6695
Internet: www.madscience.org
Suitable Sites: HO
Concentration: 9 in CA, 5 in NJ, 4 in BC
    Expansion: All United States, Canada, Foreign
    Registered: CA,FL,HI,IL,IN,MD,MI,MN,ND,NY,OR,RI,SD,VA,WA,WI,DC
Field Support: DP, $CP, EO, ST, SO, IC, $FC, $H, N
    Training: 2 weeks Montreal, PQ

Once Upon A Child
4200 Dahlberg Dr
Minneapolis, MN 55422-4837

    Phone: 612-520-8500   Accepts collect calls?
Toll Free: 800-445-1006   FAX: 612-520-8510
Internet: www.ouac.com
Suitable Sites: FB, SC
Concentration: 15 in OH
    Expansion: All United States, Canada
    Registered: CA,FL,HI,IL,IN,MD,MI,MN,ND,NY,OR,RI,SD,VA,WA,WI,DC
Field Support: CP, EO, ST, SO, IC, FC, H, N
    Training: 12 days Minneapolis, MN

Patty-Cakes International, Inc.
1726 W Third St
Montgomery, AL 36106
Provide parents w/ unique, bronzed keepsake of child hand & foot
    Phone: 334-272-2826   Accepts collect calls? Y
Toll Free: 888-847-7244   FAX: 334-264-9062
Internet: www.patty-cakes.com
Suitable Sites: HO, K, SF
Concentration: 7 in AL, 7 in FL, 7 in CA
    Expansion: All United States
    Registered: FL,IL,IN
Field Support: CP, EO, H, N
    Training: 2-3 hours training via videotape

The Peanut Club
36 Cranfield Rd
Toronto, ON M4B-3H3   CANADA
Catering to children's parties, children's indoor playground
    Phone: 416-693-1048   Accepts collect calls? N
Toll Free: FAX: 416-751-5608
Internet:
Suitable Sites: DA, FB, IP, LI, RM, SC, SF, OTHER
Concentration: 3 in ONT
    Expansion:
    Registered:
Field Support: ST, SO, FC
    Training: full training
        2 weeks existing site

Safe-T-Child
203 Barsana Ave
Austin, TX 78737
Child protection & security
    Phone: 512-288-2882   Accepts collect calls?
Toll Free: 800-828-0098   FAX: 512-288-2898
Internet: www.yellodyno.com
Suitable Sites:
Concentration: 8 in CA, 6 in TX, 4 in NY
    Expansion: All United States, Canada
    Registered: CA,FL,HI,MI,MN,NY,OR
Field Support: EO, $ST, $FC, $N
    Training:

Stork News of America
5075 Morganton Rd #12a
Fayetteville, NC 28314

    Phone: 910-868-3065   Accepts collect calls?
Toll Free: 800-633-6395   FAX: 910-868-1029
Internet: www.quikpage.com/s/storknews
Suitable Sites: HO
Concentration: 20 in FL, 17 in VA, 13 in CA
    Expansion: All United States, Canada
    Registered: CA,FL,HI,IL,IN,MD,MI,MN,ND,NY,OR,RI,SD,VA,WA,WI,DC
Field Support: CP, IC, H, N
    Training: home office at discretion

USA Baby
857 N Larch Ave
Elmhurst, IL 60126

    Phone: 630-832-9880   Accepts collect calls?
Toll Free: 800-323-4108   FAX: 630-832-0139
Internet:
Suitable Sites: FB, SC, SF
Concentration: 9 in IL, 9 in NY, 5 in MI
    Expansion: All United States, Canada, Foreign
    Registered: CA,FL,HI,IL,IN,MD,MI,MN,ND,NY,OR,RI,SD,VA,WA,WI,DC
Field Support: EO, ST, SO, $IC, FC, N
    Training: 2 weeks corporate HQ
        1 week on-site

Cleaning and Repair Industry
Carpet, Upholstery, Drapery (Spread 1 of 2)

	Capital Carpet Cleaning	CarpetMate	Carpet/Drapery/Upholstery Chem-Dry	Carpet/Upholstery (Canada) Chem-Dry	Fabri-Zone Cleaning Systems	Heaven's Best	Joy Carpet Dry Cleaning	Langenwalter Carpet Dyeing
Startup Cost	35K-45K	3.95K	6.9K-27.6K	16K-32K	15K-30K	4.6K-16K	21.2K-88K	30K
Franchise Fee	1K-10K	8.55K	18.9K	16K	5K	2.9K	20K	18K
Royalty	0%	$105/MO	$192/MO	$290/MO	6%	$80/MO	5%	$110/MO
Advertising Fee	0%		0%	$0	0%	0	1%	0%
Financing Provided	Y	Y	Y	Y	Y	Y	N	N
Experience Required			N			N	N	
Passive Ownership	A		A	D	N	A	A	N
In Business Since	1983	1995	1977	1977	1981	1983	1983	1975
Franchised Since	1990	1996	1978	1978	1984	1983	1997	1981
Franchised Units 1996		6	4141			183	0	
1997	12	7	4017	130	39	221	0	170
1998			3912			280	1	
Company Owned 1996		0	0			4	0	
1997	2	0	0	0	1	4	1	3
1998			0			2	1	
Number of Units U.S.	14		2652	0	7	271	2	152
Canada	0		130	130	30	3	0	19
Foreign	0		1235	0	3	6	0	2
Projected New U.S.			150			350	15	
Canada			10			6		
Foreign			30			12		
Corporate Employees	2		57	12	20	6	15	10
Contract Length	5/5		5/5	5/5	3/3	5/5/5	10/10/10	3/3
Expand in Territory	Y		Y	N		Y		Y
Full-Time Employees	1		2	3	2			
Part-Time Employees	1				4		1-2	1
Conversions	Y				Y	Y	N	N
Site Selection Assist.	Y		N	N	N		Y	N
Lease Negotiation Assist.	Y		N				Y	
Site Space Required				500				
Development Agreement	N		N	N	Y	Y		N
Develop. Agree. Term						5		
Sub-franchising	N		N	N		Y	Y	N

Cleaning and Repair Industry

Carpet, Upholstery, Drapery (Spread 1 of 2)

Capital Carpet Cleaning
1306 Coral Park Ln
Vero Beach, FL 32963

Phone: 561-234-3707   Accepts collect calls?
Toll Free: FAX: 561-234-3707
Internet:
Suitable Sites: HO
Concentration: 7 in FL, 4 in MN, 3 in CA
    Expansion: All United States, Canada, Foreign
    Registered: CA,FL,MN
Field Support: EO, ST, SO, FC, N
    Training: 2 weeks Florida

CarpetMate
PO Box 445
Kulpsville, PA 19443
Carpet cleaning service
    Phone: Accepts collect calls?
Toll Free: 800-962-5010   FAX:
Internet:
Suitable Sites:
Concentration:
    Expansion: CA,IN,VA
    Registered:
Field Support:
    Training:

Chem-Dry Carpet/Drapery/Upholstery
1530 North 1000 West
Logan, UT 84321
Patented, hot carbonating carpet & upholstery cleaning
    Phone: 435-755-0099   Accepts collect calls? N
Toll Free: 800-841-6583   FAX: 435-755-0021
Internet: www.chemdry.com
Suitable Sites: FB, HO, IP, OC, OS
Concentration: 450 in CA, 185 in TX, 163 in FL
    Expansion: All United States, Canada, Foreign
    Registered: CA,FL,HI,IL,IN,MD,MI,MN,ND,NY,OR,RI,SD,VA,WA,WI,DC
Field Support: CP, EO, ST, FC, H, N
    Training: 5 days Logan UT
       8 hours home study with video

Chem-Dry Carpet/Upholstery (Canada)
8361 B Noble Rd
Chilliwack, BC V2P-7X7 CANADA

Phone: 604-795-9918   Accepts collect calls?
Toll Free: 888-243-6379   FAX: 604-795-7071
Internet: www.chemdry.com
Suitable Sites: HO
Concentration: 48 in ON, 31 in BC, 14 in PQ
    Expansion: N, Canada
    Registered: AB
Field Support: CP, EO, ST, FC, H, N
    Training: 5 days Chilliwack BC
       5 days Ottawa ON
       5 days Montreal PQ

Fabri-Zone Cleaning Systems
3135 Universal Dr #6
Mississauga, ON L4X-2E2 CANADA

Phone: 905-602-7691   Accepts collect calls?
Toll Free: FAX: 905-602-7821
Internet:
Suitable Sites:
Concentration:
    Expansion: Canada, Foreign
    Registered:
Field Support: CP, EO, $ST, $SO, FC, H, N
    Training: 8 days Toronto on

Heaven's Best
247 N First East
Rexburg, ID 83440
Chemical carpet & upholstery cleaning
    Phone: 208-359-1106   Accepts collect calls? Y
Toll Free: 800-359-2095   FAX: 208-359-1236
Internet: heavensbest.com
Suitable Sites: HO
Concentration: ID, CA
    Expansion: All United States, Canada, Foreign
    Registered: CA,FL,IN,MD,MI,MN,OR,WA
Field Support: DP, EO, ST, IC, FC, H, N
    Training: 4 days corporate HQ

Joy Carpet Dry Cleaning
3209 Premier Dr #115
Plano, TX 75075
Carpet dry extraction cleaning, upholstery & drapery cleaning
    Phone: 972-867-4185   Accepts collect calls? N
Toll Free: 800-959-5136   FAX: 972-379-6444
Internet: joycarpt@flash.net
Suitable Sites: AC, DA, FB, HO, IP, LI, M, OC, OS, RM, SC, SF, WR, OTHER
Concentration: 2 in TX
    Expansion: TX,OK,LA,AK,TN,MS,MO,NM,CO,KS,AZ, Canada, Foreign
    Registered:
Field Support: CP, EO, ST, SO, IC, H, N
    Training: 2 weeks initial field & classroom
       ongoing field & seminars

Langenwalter Carpet Dyeing
1111 S Richfield Rd
Placentia, CA 92870-6790

Phone: 714-528-7610   Accepts collect calls?
Toll Free: 800-422-4370   FAX: 714-528-7620
Internet: www.home.navisoft.com/langenwalter
Suitable Sites: HO
Concentration: 75 in CA, 10 in BC, 9 in MA
    Expansion: All United States, Canada, Foreign
    Registered: CA,FL,IN,MD,MI,MN,NY,OR,RI,VA,WA,WI,AB
Field Support: $FC, H, N
    Training: 5 days Placentia CA

Cleaning and Repair Industry   Carpet, Upholstery, Drapery (Spread 2 of 2)

	Professional Carpet Systems	Rainbow International Carpet Care & Restoration Specialist	Roto-Static International	Steam Brothers Professional Cleaning & Restoration	Steamatic	Carpet Dyeing And Cleaning Tri-Color		
Startup Cost	19.7K+	28.9K-86K	38.5K	11K-55K	25K-75K	30K-60K		
Franchise Fee	14.7K	15K	14.5K	9K-33K	5K-18K	17.5K		
Royalty	6%	7%	5%	5-6.5%	5-8%	$350/MO		
Advertising Fee	0%	2%	0%	1.5%	0%	0%		
Financing Provided	N	Y	N	Y	Y	Y		
Experience Required		N	N					
Passive Ownership	D	D	D	N	D	N		
In Business Since	1978	1980	1977	1977	1946	1984		
Franchised Since	1979	1981	1977	1983	1968	1996		
Franchised Units 1996								
1997	165	573	141	21	294	2		
1998								
Company Owned 1996								
1997	1	0	0	0	10	4		
1998								
Number of Units U.S.	158	350	0	21	193	6		
Canada	8	25	141	0	72	0		
Foreign	N	130	0	0	10	0		
Projected New U.S.		20						
Canada		10						
Foreign		30						
Corporate Employees	8	14	8	2	32	5		
Contract Length	10/10	10/5	25/25	7/7	10/5	10/5		
Expand in Territory	Y	Y	N	Y	N	Y		
Full-Time Employees	1	2	1-2	1	5-40	2		
Part-Time Employees		1			3-10			
Conversions	N	Y	N	Y	Y	Y		
Site Selection Assist.	Y	N	N	Y	N	Y		
Lease Negotiation Assist.		N	N	N		Y		
Site Space Required			300	1000		500		
Development Agreement	N	N	N	Y	N	Y		
Develop. Agree. Term				20		10		
Sub-franchising	N	N	N	Y	N	N		

Cleaning and Repair Industry

Carpet, Upholstery, Drapery (Spread 2 of 2)

Professional Carpet Systems
5182 Old Dixie Hwy
Forest Park, GA 30050

Phone: 404-362-2300	Accepts collect calls?
Toll Free: 800-925-5055	FAX: 404-362-2888
Internet:	

Suitable Sites: HO
Concentration: 24 in CA, 12 in FL, 9 in NC
    Expansion: All United States, Canada, Foreign
    Registered: CA,FL,HI,IL,IN,MD,MI,MN,ND,NY,OR,RI,SD,VA,WA,WI,DC
Field Support: DP, CP, EO, ST, IC, FC, H, N
    Training: 2 weeks HQ

Rainbow International Carpet Care & Restoration Specialist
1010 N University Parks Dr
Waco, TX 76707
Expert carpet care & restoration services, water/smoke/fire dam.

Phone: 254-745-2444	Accepts collect calls? Y
Toll Free: 800-280-9963	FAX: 254-745-2592
Internet: www.rainbowintl.com	

Suitable Sites: DA, FB, HO, IP, LI, OS
Concentration: 63 in TX, 27 in CA, 27 in FL
    Expansion: All United States, Canada, Foreign
    Registered: CA,FL,HI,IL,IN,MD,MI,MN,ND,NY,OR,RI,SD,VA,WA,WI,DC
Field Support: DP, $CP, EO, ST, SO, FC, H, N
    Training: 2 weeks corporate HQ
        field mentoring & seminars
        ongoing support

Roto-Static International
90 Delta Park Blvd Bldg A
Brampton, ON L6T-5E7   CANADA
Carpet, upholstery, ceiling, wall & hard floor cleaning

Phone: 905-458-7002	Accepts collect calls? N
Toll Free:	FAX: 905-458-8650
Internet:	

Suitable Sites: HO, IP, LI, OS
Concentration: ON, PQ, BC
    Expansion: Y, Canada, Foreign
    Registered: AB
Field Support: EO, ST, SO, IC, FC, H, N
    Training: 4 days Toronto on

Steam Brothers Professional Cleaning & Restoration
933 1/2 Basin Ave
Bismarck, ND 58504

Phone: 701-222-1263	Accepts collect calls?
Toll Free: 800-767-5064	FAX: 701-222-1372
Internet:	

Suitable Sites: HO, WR
Concentration: 9 in MN, 7 in ND, 3 in SD
    Expansion: Midwest, NW, West
    Registered: MN,SD
Field Support: EO, ST, SO, FC, H, N
    Training: 5 days franchisor's HQ

Steamatic
303 Arthur St
Fort Worth, TX 76107

Phone: 817-332-1575	Accepts collect calls?
Toll Free: 800-527-1295	FAX: 817-332-5349
Internet: www.steamatic.com	

Suitable Sites: WR
Concentration: 19 in TX, 15 in FL, 8 in IL
    Expansion: All United States, Canada, Foreign
    Registered: CA,FL,HI,IL,IN,MD,MI,MN,ND,NY,OR,RI,SD,VA,WA,WI,DC
Field Support: DP, CP, EO, ST, SO, IC, FC, H, N
    Training: 2 weeks Fort Worth TX

Tri-Color Carpet Dyeing And Cleaning
3805 C Abbott Martin Rd
Nashville, TN 37215

Phone: 615-383-6650	Accepts collect calls?
Toll Free: 800-452-9065	FAX: 615-385-7140
Internet:	

Suitable Sites: HO
Concentration: 4 in TN, 2 in KY
    Expansion: S,SE
    Registered: FL
Field Support: DP, CP, EO, ST, $SO, IC, FC, H, N
    Training: 2 weeks Nashville TN home office
        3 days regional meetings

Cleaning and Repair Industry

Commercial Cleaning (Spread 1 of 6)

	AeroWest & WestAir Sanitation Services	Aire-Master of America	Aqua Bio Technologies	Arodal	Biologix	Brite Site	Building Services of America	Chemstation International
Startup Cost	3K-40K	25K-75K	7K-12K	100K		15K	7.5K-20K	500K
Franchise Fee	2K	12K+	1.35K	50K	12.5K	5K	1.5K-15K	25K
Royalty	35%	5%	0	7	4%	10%	8%	4%
Advertising Fee	0%	0%	0	0	N/A	0-2%	0%	2%
Financing Provided	Y	Y	N	Y	N	Y	N	N
Experience Required		N		N	N	N	Y	
Passive Ownership	D	D	N		D	N	N	D
In Business Since	1983	1958	1987	1971	1989	1971	1992	1983
Franchised Since	1983	1976	1995	1980	1995	1993	1992	1984
Franchised Units 1996								
1997	38	40	16		19	6	31	33
1998		41		3	23			
Company Owned 1996								
1997	37	5	1		2	1	1	5
1998		4		2	2			
Number of Units U.S.	75	44	15	1	2	7	32	38
Canada	0	1	0	3	0	0	0	0
Foreign	0	0	1	0	0	0	0	0
Projected New U.S.				0	24			
Canada				0				
Foreign				0				
Corporate Employees	12	52	3	10	30	6	7	25
Contract Length	5/1	20/3	1/1	5/5	5/5	10	10/10	10/5
Expand in Territory	Y	Y	Y	Y	Y	Y	Y	Y
Full-Time Employees	1	2	5	5-6	2		VAR.	6
Part-Time Employees				1	2		VAR.	
Conversions		Y		Y	N	N	Y	
Site Selection Assist.	N	N	N	Y	N	Y	N	Y
Lease Negotiation Assist.		N		Y		Y	N	Y
Site Space Required								6000
Development Agreement		N	N	Y	N	Y	N	N
Develop. Agree. Term				5		10/10		
Sub-franchising	N	N	Y	Y	N	N	N	N

Cleaning and Repair Industry

Commercial Cleaning (Spread 1 of 6)

AeroWest & WestAir Sanitation Services
3882 Del Amo Blvd #602
Torrance, CA 90503

Phone: 310-793-4242   Accepts collect calls?
Toll Free: FAX: 310-793-4250
Internet:
Suitable Sites: HO
Concentration: 13 in CA, 9 in NY, 7 in IL
Expansion: All United States, Foreign
Registered: CA,KY,MD,IL,NY,WA,MI
Field Support: DP, CP, EO, ST, FC, N
Training: 1-2 weeks local, near fnchees home

Aire-Master of America
1821 N Highway Cc PO Box 2310
Nixa, MO 65714
Deodorizing & restroom sanitation, products + service
Phone: 417-725-2691   Accepts collect calls? N
Toll Free: 800-525-0957   FAX: 417-725-8227
Internet:
Suitable Sites: HO
Concentration: 4 in MO, 3 in CA, 3 in NJ
Expansion: Canada
Registered: CA,IL,NY
Field Support: ST, SO, FC, H, N
Training: 1 week HQ
1 week territory

Aqua Bio Technologies
3955 Shell Rd
Sarasota, FL 34242

Phone: 941-312-9100   Accepts collect calls?
Toll Free: FAX: 941-312-9300
Internet: www.aquabiotech.com
Suitable Sites: HO
Concentration: 3 in FL, 2 in TX, 1 in AZ
Expansion: All United States, Canada, Foreign
Registered: CA,FL,IL,NY,WI
Field Support: $ST, SO, IC, FC, $H
Training: 1 week Sarasota FL

Arodal
6171 Conin Dr
Mississauga, ON L4V-1N8   CANADA

Phone: 905-678-6888   Accepts collect calls?
Toll Free: FAX: 905-678-6967
Internet:
Suitable Sites: IP, LI, OS
Concentration:
Expansion:
Registered: WA
Field Support: DP, ST, SO, IC, FC, H
Training: 3 months home office
ongoing

Biologix
8503 Mid-County Industrial Dr
Saint Louis, MO 63114
Environmental services to the food service & hospitality indust.
Phone: 314-423-1945   Accepts collect calls? N
Toll Free: 800-747-1885   FAX: 314-423-4394
Internet:
Suitable Sites: HO
Concentration: 4 in MO, 2 in OH, 2 in TX
Expansion: All United States
Registered: IL,IN,MD,MI,RI,VA,WI,FL,HI
Field Support: DP, CP, EO, ST, IC, FC, H, N
Training: 1 week St Louis MO

Brite Site
4616 W Fullerton Ave
Chicago, IL 60639-1816
Cleaning services to retailers
Phone: 773-772-7300   Accepts collect calls? N
Toll Free: FAX: 773-772-7631
Internet:
Suitable Sites: HO, IP, SF
Concentration: 6 in IL, 1 in IN, 1 in WI
Expansion: Midwest
Registered: IL,IN
Field Support: DP, CP, EO, ST, SO, FC, H, N
Training: 3-14 days extensive classroom & field

Building Services of America
11900 W 87th Pkwy #135
Lenexa, KS 66215

Phone: 913-599-6200   Accepts collect calls? N
Toll Free: FAX: 913-599-4441
Internet:
Suitable Sites:
Concentration: 14 in KS, 18 in MO
Expansion: All United States
Registered:
Field Support: DP, EO, ST, FC, N
Training: 1-2 weeks corporate office

Chemstation International
3400 Encrete Ln
Dayton, OH 45439

Phone: 937-294-8265   Accepts collect calls?
Toll Free: 800-554-8265   FAX: 937-294-5360
Internet:
Suitable Sites: LI, OC
Concentration: 5 in OH, 3 in MI, 3 in IN
Expansion: West, NY,NE, Canada, Foreign
Registered:
Field Support: DP, CP, EO, ST, SO, IC, FC, H, N
Training: 1 week Dayton OH

Cleaning and Repair Industry

Commercial Cleaning (Spread 2 of 6)

	Cleaning Consultant Services	CleanNet USA	Coit Services	Coverall Cleaning Concepts	DuraClean International	E.P.I.C. Systems, Inc.	Energy Wise	Envirobate
Startup Cost	5K	3.5K-350K	30K-100K	7.8K-76.8K	11K-30K	6.5K-60K	23.5K-44.3K	90K-130K
Franchise Fee	2.5K	3K-200K	10.5K	7.5K-71.9K	6.4K	6.5K	12.5K	25K
Royalty	0%	3%	2-6%	15%	2-8%	4-10%	5%	6%
Advertising Fee	0%	0%	0%	0%	0%	N/A	0%	.5%
Financing Provided	N	Y	Y	Y	Y	Y	N	N
Experience Required		N					n	
Passive Ownership	N	D	D	D	D	D	D	N
In Business Since	1976	1987	1950	1985	1930	1993	1990	1988
Franchised Since	1979	1988	1963	1985	1945	1994	1996	1991
Franchised Units 1996								
1997	5	1718	57	4331	521	9	2	6
1998		2042						
Company Owned 1996								
1997	4	7	12	18	1	0	1	0
1998								
Number of Units U.S.	8	1725	65	4184	441	9	3	6
Canada	1	0	3	69	22	0	0	0
Foreign	0	0	1	96	59	0	0	0
Projected New U.S.		2500				12		
Canada								
Foreign								
Corporate Employees	3	75	19	175	25	4		5
Contract Length	3/2	20/20	10/10	20/20	3/3	10/10	10/5	10/5
Expand in Territory	N	Y	Y	Y	Y	Y	Y	Y
Full-Time Employees	1	2-8	2	3+	2	1	1	VAR
Part-Time Employees		10	1	1	1	5		
Conversions	N	Y	Y	Y	Y	Y	N	N
Site Selection Assist.	N	Y	Y	N	N	Y	N	N
Lease Negotiation Assist.	N	Y	Y			N		N
Site Space Required		2000	1000			250-700		900
Development Agreement	N	Y	N	N	Y	Y	N	Y
Develop. Agree. Term		20			10	10		
Sub-franchising	N	Y	N	N	N	Y	N	Y

Cleaning and Repair Industry

Commercial Cleaning (Spread 2 of 6)

Cleaning Consultant Services
3693 Marginal Wy S
Seattle, WA 98134

Phone: 206-682-9748   Accepts collect calls?
Toll Free: FAX: 206-622-6876
Internet: www.cleaningconsultants.com
Suitable Sites:
Concentration:
   Expansion: All United States, Canada, Foreign
   Registered:
Field Support: $ST
   Training: 3 days seattl6 WA
         3 days on-site

CleanNet USA
9861 Broken Land Pkwy #208
Columbia, MD 21046
Commercial cleaning services for single to multi-story buildings
Phone: 410-720-6444   Accepts collect calls? N
Toll Free: 800-735-8838   FAX: 410-720-5307
Internet:
Suitable Sites: HO, OC
Concentration: 366 in MD, 308 in NJ, 195 in PA
   Expansion: All United States, Canada, Foreign
   Registered: CA,FL,IL,MD,MI,VA,NY,DC
Field Support: DP, CP, EO, ST, SO, FC, H, N
   Training: up to 4 weeks company offices
         up to 3 weeks master office

Coit Services
897 Hinckley Rd
Burlingame, CA 94010

Phone: 650-697-5471   Accepts collect calls?
Toll Free: 800-243-8797   FAX: 650-697-6117
Internet:
Suitable Sites: LI
Concentration: 16 in CA, 4 in WA, 4 in OH
   Expansion: NE,SE, Midwest, Canada
   Registered: CA,FL,HI,IL,IN,MD,MI,MN,ND,NY,OR,RI,SD,VA,WA,WI,DC
Field Support: DP, CP, EO, ST, SO, FC, H, N
   Training: 7 days corporate HQ
         1-2 weeks in-field

Coverall Cleaning Concepts
3111 Camino Del Rio N 9th Fl
San Diego, CA 92108

Phone: 619-584-1911   Accepts collect calls?
Toll Free: 800-537-3371   FAX: 619-584-4923
Internet: www.coverall.com
Suitable Sites:
Concentration: 620 in FL, 333 in VA, 443 in CA
   Expansion: All United States, Canada, Foreign
   Registered: CA,FL,IL,IN,MD,MI,MN,NY,OR,RI,VA,WA,WI,DC
Field Support: DP, CP, EO, ST, FC, H, N
   Training: 10 sessions regional office

DuraClean International
2151 Waukegan Rd
Deerfield, IL 60015

Phone: 847-945-2000   Accepts collect calls?
Toll Free: 800-251-7070   FAX: 847-945-2023
Internet:
Suitable Sites: HO
Concentration: 38 in FL, 34 in IL, 30 in CA
   Expansion: All United States, Canada, Foreign
   Registered: CA,FL,HI,IL,IN,MD,MI,MN,ND,NY,OR,RI,SD,VA,WA,WI,DC
Field Support: EO, ST, FC, H, N
   Training: 6 days success institute corp of
         2 days on-site cleaning
         home study program

E.P.I.C. Systems, Inc.
402 East Maryland
Evansville, IN 47711
Professional cleaning services for commercial, offices, medical
Phone: 812-428-7750   Accepts collect calls? N
Toll Free: 800-230-3742   FAX: 812-428-4162
Internet:
Suitable Sites: HO, OC
Concentration: 3 in IN, 6 in KY
   Expansion: Midwest
   Registered: FL,IN,MI
Field Support: $EO, ST, H
   Training: 2 weeks HQ

Energy Wise
708 Gravenstein Hwy North #101
Sebastopol, CA 95472

Phone: 707-824-8775   Accepts collect calls?
Toll Free: 800-553-6800   FAX: 707-824-8775
Internet: www.energywiseinc.com
Suitable Sites: HO
Concentration: 3 in CA
   Expansion: California and West
   Registered: CA
Field Support: EO, IC, FC, H, N
   Training: 1 week Sonoma county CA

Envirobate
401 N Third St #490
Minneapolis, MN 55401

Phone: 612-349-9211   Accepts collect calls?
Toll Free: 800-944-8095   FAX: 612-349-9167
Internet:
Suitable Sites: WR
Concentration: 3 in MN, 1 in GA, 1 in VA
   Expansion: All United States
   Registered: MN,VA,WI
Field Support: DP, CP, EO, ST, SO, $FC, H
   Training: 10 days HQ
         5 days on-site

Cleaning and Repair Industry   Commercial Cleaning (Spread 3 of 6)

	Environmental Biotech	Hydro Physics Pipe Inspection	Jan-Pro Franchising Int'l Inc	Jani-King International	Jantize America	JDI Cleaning Systems	Kwik Dry International	Laser Chem "White Glove" Commercial Cleaning
Startup Cost	120K	65K-80K	TO 500	2.9K-40K	20K	18.5K	11.7K	9.5K
Franchise Fee	29K	19.5K	1K-44K	8K-33K	3.5K-16K	10.5K	6K	8.3K
Royalty	3%	7.5%	8%	10%	9%	13%	$175/MO	7%
Advertising Fee	1%	2%		1%	0%	2%	0%	0%
Financing Provided	N	Y	Y	Y	Y	Y	Y	Y
Experience Required		N		N				N
Passive Ownership	N	N		A	D	D	A	A
In Business Since	1991	1991	1991	1969	1985	1992	1967	1993
Franchised Since	1991	1996	1992	1974	1988	1992	1995	1994
Franchised Units 1996			515					4
1997	101	2	516	7000	21	26	12	21
1998		3		7000				40
Company Owned 1996			0					1
1997	1	1	0	35	1	1	0	1
1998				35				1
Number of Units U.S.	72	4		4724	23	0	12	41
Canada	1	0		351	0	27	0	0
Foreign	29	0		528	0	0	0	0
Projected New U.S.								17
Canada								0
Foreign								0
Corporate Employees	26	3		80	8	4		9
Contract Length	5/5	10/10		20/20	10/10	5/5	5/5	10/10
Expand in Territory	N	Y		Y	N	Y	Y	Y
Full-Time Employees	5	1				1	1	0
Part-Time Employees					3-20	2		0
Conversions	N				Y	Y		Y
Site Selection Assist.	Y	N		N	Y	N	N	N
Lease Negotiation Assist.	N	Y		N	N			N
Site Space Required	1000							
Development Agreement	N	N		Y	N	Y	N	N
Develop. Agree. Term				20		10		
Sub-franchising	N	N		Y	Y	N	N	N

Cleaning and Repair Industry

Commercial Cleaning (Spread 3 of 6)

Environmental Biotech
4404 N Tamiami Trail
Sarasota, FL 34234

        Phone: 941-358-9112   Accepts collect calls?
    Toll Free: 800-314-6263   FAX: 941-359-9744
    Internet:
Suitable Sites: OC, WR
Concentration: 12 in FL, 5 in TX, 7 in PA
    Expansion: All United States, Canada, Foreign
    Registered: CA,FL,HI,IL,IN,MD,MI,MN,NY,ND,OR,SD,VA,WA,WI,DC,AB
Field Support: CP, EO, ST, SO, $FC, N
    Training: 3 weeks EBI HQ
               1 week franchise location

Hydro Physics Pipe Inspection
1855 W Union Ave #N
Englewood, CO 80110

        Phone: 303-781-2474   Accepts collect calls? N
    Toll Free: 800-781-3164   FAX: 303-781-0477
    Internet:
Suitable Sites: HO, IP, LI, OS
Concentration: 1 in CO, 1 in TX, 1 in MO
    Expansion: All United States
    Registered: CA,VA
Field Support: CP, EO, ST, SO, IC, FC, H, N
    Training: 2 weeks Denver CO
               5 days on-site in Denver

Jan-Pro Franchising Int'l Inc
500 E Washington St
North Attleboro, MA 02760
Commercial cleaning services
        Phone: 508-695-3993   Accepts collect calls?
    Toll Free: 800-668-1001   FAX:
    Internet:
Suitable Sites:
Concentration:
    Expansion: IL,RI, Canada, Foreign
    Registered:
Field Support:
    Training:

Jani-King International
16885 Dallas Parkway
Addison, TX 75001

        Phone: 972-991-0900   Accepts collect calls? N
    Toll Free: 800-552-5264   FAX: 972-239-7706
    Internet: www.janiking.com
Suitable Sites: HO
Concentration: 880 in TX, 737 in CA, 307 in FL
    Expansion: All United States, Canada, Foreign
    Registered: CA,FL,HI,IL,IN,MI,MN,NY,OR,SD,VA,WA,WI,DC
Field Support: DP, CP, EO, ST, FC, H, N
    Training: 2 weeks local regional office

Jantize America
15449 Middlebelt
Livonia, MI 48154

        Phone: 734-421-4733   Accepts collect calls?
    Toll Free: 800-968-9182   FAX: 734-421-4936
    Internet:
Suitable Sites:
Concentration: 22 in MI, 1 in VA
    Expansion: All United States, Canada
    Registered: MI,VA
Field Support: $DP, ST, SO, FC, H, N
    Training: 3-6 days HQ
               3 days franchisse location

JDI Cleaning Systems
3390 South Service Rd
Burlington, ON L7N-3J5   CANADA

        Phone: 905-634-5228   Accepts collect calls?
    Toll Free: 800-567-5091   FAX: 905-634-8790
    Internet:
Suitable Sites:
Concentration: 27 in ON
    Expansion: Northeastern United States, Canada
    Registered:
Field Support: DP, CP, EO, ST, FC, $H, N
    Training: 2 days head office
               30 days on-site

Kwik Dry International
25665 Caton Farm Rd
Plainfield, IL 60544

        Phone: 815-436-0333   Accepts collect calls?
    Toll Free: FAX: 815-436-7519
    Internet:
Suitable Sites: HO
Concentration: 6 in IL, 3 in MO
    Expansion: All United States
    Registered: IL
Field Support: CP, $FC, N
    Training: 5 days Plainsfield IL

Laser Chem "White Glove" Commercial Cleaning
7022 South 400 West
Midvale, UT 84047
Professional janitorial services
        Phone: 801-569-9500   Accepts collect calls? Y
    Toll Free: 888-569-9533   FAX: 801-569-8400
    Internet:
Suitable Sites: HO
Concentration: 41 in UT
    Expansion: All United States, Canada, Foreign
    Registered:
Field Support: CP, IC, $FC, H, N
    Training: 12-24 hours classroom
               hands-on & video in Midvale, UT

Cleaning and Repair Industry   Commercial Cleaning (Spread 4 of 6)

	Maintain Cleaning Systems	Professional Cleaning Systems / Master Care	Environmental Services / MaxCare	National Homecraft / Millicare	National Hygiene/Lien	National Maintenance Contractors	O.P.E.N. Cleaning Systems
Startup Cost	8.5K-25K	5K-200K	22.5K-89.2K	70K-170K	50K-150K	15.9K-92.3K	2K-22K	7K-80.5K
Franchise Fee	7K	4.5K-125K	12.5K+	16K	25K-75K	9.5K-50K	1K-20K	6K-67.5K
Royalty	5%	5-15%	6%	6%	5%	VAR	6%	15%
Advertising Fee	N/A	1%	2%	2%	10% GROSS	N/A	0	
Financing Provided	Y	Y	Y	N	N	N	Y	Y
Experience Required		N		N				
Passive Ownership	N	D	D	A	D	D	D	D
In Business Since	1993	1960	1989	1982	1997	1964	1975	1983
Franchised Since	1993	1987	1997	1996	1997	1968	1978	1983
Franchised Units 1996				34				
1997	49	107	25	51	0	15	409	438
1998				70				
Company Owned 1996				0				
1997	0	1	3	0	1	2	0	3
1998				0				
Number of Units U.S.	49	0	28	65	1	17	409	441
Canada	0	108	0	5	0	0	0	0
Foreign	0	0	0	0	0	0	0	0
Projected New U.S.				30				
Canada				2				
Foreign				7				
Corporate Employees	10	4	15	22	4	7	32	38
Contract Length	5/2	5/5	10/10	5	10/10	10/10	5/5	10/10/10
Expand in Territory		Y	N	Y	N	Y	Y	Y
Full-Time Employees		2	3		3	1	1-4	4
Part-Time Employees	1							
Conversions	Y	Y		N	Y	Y	Y	Y
Site Selection Assist.	N	Y	N	N	Y	N	N	N
Lease Negotiation Assist.				N	Y			
Site Space Required					1500			
Development Agreement	N	Y	Y	N	Y	Y	N	N
Develop. Agree. Term		10	1		10	10		
Sub-franchising	N	Y	N	N	N	N	N	Y

Cleaning and Repair Industry

Commercial Cleaning (Spread 4 of 6)

Maintain Cleaning Systems
931 State Rte 28
Milford, OH 45150

Phone: 513-576-6622   Accepts collect calls?
Toll Free: 800-861-4168   FAX: 800-867-0056
Internet:
Suitable Sites:
Concentration: 40 in OH, 9 in KY
  Expansion: Midwest Only
  Registered:
Field Support: DP, EO, ST, SO, FC, H
  Training: 2 days Cincinnati OH

Master Care
#327 555 6th St
New Westminster, BC V3L-4Y4   CANADA
Provide commercial contract cleaning for buildings & offices
  Phone: 604-525-8221   Accepts collect calls? N
Toll Free: 800-889-2799   FAX: 604-526-2235
  Internet: www.mastercare.com
Suitable Sites:
Concentration: 108 in BC
  Expansion: Master Franchises Only, Canada
  Registered:
Field Support: DP, CP, EO, ST, SO, $FC, H, N
  Training: 1-6 weeks head office

MaxCare Professional Cleaning Systems
210 Townpark Dr
Kennesaw, GA 30144

Phone: 770-590-9369   Accepts collect calls?
Toll Free: 800-707-4332   FAX: 770-426-9681
Internet: www.maxcare.com
Suitable Sites:
Concentration: 5 in GA, 3 in NC, 3 in FL
  Expansion: All United States, Canada
  Registered: CA,FL,HI,IL,IN,MD,MI,MN,ND,NY,OR,RI,SD,VA,WA,WI,DC
Field Support: CP, EO, $ST, IC, $FC, H, N
  Training: 10 days Atlanta GA

Millicare Environmental Services
201 Lukken Industrial Dr W
La Grange, GA 30240

  Phone: Accepts collect calls? N
Toll Free: 888-886-2273   FAX: 706-880-3279
  Internet: carol_brewton@millicare.com
Suitable Sites: IP, LI, WR
Concentration:
  Expansion: All United States, Canada, Foreign
  Registered:
Field Support: EO, ST, SO, FC, H, N
  Training:

National Homecraft
4441 SE 53rd Ave
Ocala, FL 34480-7401

Phone: 352-694-2580   Accepts collect calls?
Toll Free: FAX:
Internet:
Suitable Sites:
Concentration: 1 in FL
  Expansion: All United States
  Registered: FL
Field Support: EO, ST, SO, IC, FC, H, N
  Training: 10 days corporate HQ Ocala FL
            4 days franchisee territory

National Hygiene/Lien
950 N Rand Rd #119
Wauconda, IL 60084

  Phone: 847-487-9400   Accepts collect calls?
Toll Free: 800-888-8407   FAX: 847-487-9404
  Internet:
Suitable Sites:
Concentration: IL, WI, MI
  Expansion: All United States, Canada, Foreign
  Registered: IL,IN,WI
Field Support: DP, CP, EO, ST, SO, IC, FC, H, N
  Training: 2 weeks home office

National Maintenance Contractors
1801 130th Ave NE
Bellevue, WA 98005

Phone: 206-881-0500   Accepts collect calls?
Toll Free: 800-347-7844   FAX: 206-883-4785
Internet:
Suitable Sites:
Concentration: 275 in WA, 139 in OR
  Expansion: Washington and Oregon Only
  Registered: OR,WA
Field Support: DP, EO, ST, FC, H, N
  Training: 5 days HQ

O.P.E.N. Cleaning Systems
2398 E Camelback Rd
Phoenix, AZ 85016

  Phone: 602-224-0440   Accepts collect calls?
Toll Free: 800-777-6736   FAX: 602-468-3788
  Internet: www.opencs.com
Suitable Sites: HO
Concentration: 162 in AZ, 136 in WA, 130 in CA
  Expansion: All United States, Canada, Foreign
  Registered: CA,WA
Field Support: DP, $CP, EO, ST, SO, FC, H, N
  Training: 28 hours office of open
            11 hours off-site

Cleaning and Repair Industry

Commercial Cleaning (Spread 5 of 6)

	Professional Polish	ProForce USA	PuroFirst International	RACS International	SaniBrite	SealMaster	Serv U-1st	Service One
Startup Cost	50K	780-2.5K	50K-100K	4.4K-43.1K	2K-20K	200K-400K	6.5K-13.5K	6.1K-19.3K
Franchise Fee	25K	2.7K-29.5K	30K	3K-31.5K	.95K-15K	35K	2.3K	6K-18.3K
Royalty	5%	3%	2-7%	5%	9.5%	5%	6-15%	$175/MO
Advertising Fee	0%		0%	1%	4%	1.5%	0%	0
Financing Provided	Y	Y	N	Y	Y	N	Y	Y
Experience Required								
Passive Ownership	D		D	N	N	D	N	N
In Business Since	1981	1992	1985	1989	1987	1969	1988	1965
Franchised Since	1986	1992	1991	1991	1989	1993	1988	1985
Franchised Units 1996		247						
1997	42	469	98	11	45	17	11	140
1998								
Company Owned 1996		3						
1997	1	3	0	31	1	1	0	0
1998								
Number of Units U.S.	36		98	42	0	18	11	140
Canada	0		0	0	45	0	0	0
Foreign	0		0	0	1	0	0	0
Projected New U.S.								
Canada								
Foreign								
Corporate Employees	7		16	11	5	27	2	6
Contract Length	25/25		5/5	20/20	10/5/5	10/5/5/5	10/10	10/10
Expand in Territory	Y		N	Y	N		Y	N
Full-Time Employees	2		2	5	2	3	1-2	
Part-Time Employees	1		2		1	3		
Conversions	Y		Y	Y	Y	Y	Y	
Site Selection Assist.	Y		N	Y	Y	Y	N	N
Lease Negotiation Assist.	Y		N	Y	Y			
Site Space Required	1000			1500	700-1000	7000-10000		
Development Agreement	Y		N	Y	Y		N	N
Develop. Agree. Term	25			10	10/5			
Sub-franchising	N		N	Y	Y		N	N

Cleaning and Repair Industry

Commercial Cleaning (Spread 5 of 6)

Professional Polish
5450 East Loop 820 South
Fort Worth, TX 76119

Phone: 817-572-7353   Accepts collect calls?
Toll Free: 800-255-0488   FAX: 817-561-6193
Internet:
Suitable Sites:
Concentration: 30 in TX, 5 in NC, 1 in AL
Expansion: SE and SE Only, Foreign
Registered: FL
Field Support: DP, CP, EO, ST, SO, IC, FC, H, N
Training: 10 days Fort Worth TX
30 days franchise city
7 days follow-up franchise city

ProForce USA
621 NW 53rd St #240
Boca Raton, FL 33487
Commercial cleaning
Phone: 561-995-1473   Accepts collect calls?
Toll Free: FAX:
Internet:
Suitable Sites:
Concentration:
Expansion: MD,VA
Registered:
Field Support:
Training:

PuroFirst International
5610 NW 12th Ave #209
Fort Lauderdale, FL 33309

Phone: 954-771-3121   Accepts collect calls?
Toll Free: 800-247-9047   FAX: 954-938-8807
Internet: www.purofirst.com
Suitable Sites:
Concentration: 24 in CA, 12 in PA, 10 in NY
Expansion: All United States
Registered: CA,FL,IL,IN,MD,MI,MN,NY,VA,WA,WI
Field Support: DP, CP, EO, ST, SO, IC, FC, H, N
Training: 11 days Fort Lauderdale FL
5 days franchisee's own office

RACS International
10333 N Meridian St #170
Indianapolis, IN 46290

Phone: 317-844-8152   Accepts collect calls?
Toll Free: 800-949-7227   FAX: 317-844-2270
Internet:
Suitable Sites: HO, OTHER
Concentration: 23 in FL, 11 in IN, 8 in GA
Expansion: All United States
Registered: FL,IN
Field Support: DP, $CP, EO, ST, H, N
Training: 18 hours RACS office
12 hours on-the-job

SaniBrite
3045 Southcreek Rd #19
Mississauga, ON L4X-2X7   CANADA

Phone: 905-624-4290   Accepts collect calls?
Toll Free: FAX: 905-602-5383
Internet:
Suitable Sites: DA
Concentration: 44 in ON, 1 in PQ
Expansion: All United States, Canada, Foreign
Registered:
Field Support: DP, CP, EO, ST, SO, FC, H, N
Training: 3 hours head office
5 days on-site

SealMaster
2520 S Campbell St
Sandusky, OH 44870

Phone: 419-626-4375   Accepts collect calls?
Toll Free: 800-395-7325   FAX: 419-626-5477
Internet:
Suitable Sites: FB
Concentration:
Expansion: All United States, Canada, Foreign
Registered: CA,FL,HI,IL,IN,MD,MI,MN,NY,OR,RI,VA,WA,WI,DC
Field Support: DP, CP, EO, ST, SO, H, N
Training: 2 weeks corporate HQ OH

Serv U-1st
10175 SW Barbur Blvd Bldg B-100ba
Portland, OR 97219

Phone: 503-244-7628   Accepts collect calls?
Toll Free: FAX: 503-244-0287
Internet:
Suitable Sites: HO
Concentration: 11 in OR
Expansion: Oregon Only
Registered: OR
Field Support: EO, ST, SO, FC
Training: 20x2 hours sessions Portland or

Service One
5104 N Orange Blossom Tr #114
Orlando, FL 32810

Phone: 407-293-7645   Accepts collect calls?
Toll Free: 800-522-7111   FAX: 407-299-4306
Internet:
Suitable Sites:
Concentration: 87 in FL, 5 in AZ, 13 in NC
Expansion: Non-Registration States
Registered: FL
Field Support: DP, SO, H, N
Training: 2 days where convenient

Cleaning and Repair Industry

Commercial Cleaning (Spread 6 of 6)

	Service-Tech Corporation	ServPro	Sparkle Wash	Swisher Hygiene	Tower Cleaning Systems	Value Line Maintenance Systems	Window Gang	
Startup Cost	59K-89K	31.3K-59.9K	50K	50K-100K	3.4K-34K	50K	5K-15K	
Franchise Fee	19K	25K	15K	15K-85K	4K-33.6K	30K	5K-20K	
Royalty	4-6%	3-10%	3-5%	6%	3%	10%	6%	
Advertising Fee	1%	0	0%	2%	0%	0%	0	
Financing Provided	Y	Y	Y	Y	Y	Y	Y	
Experience Required		N				N	N	
Passive Ownership	N	D	A	D	A	D	N	
In Business Since	1960	1967	1965	1981	1988	1959	1986	
Franchised Since	1988	1969	1967	1990	1990	1982	1996	
Franchised Units 1996			178				2	
1997	3	929	177	102	1270	22	10	
1998			171			22	30	
Company Owned 1996			1				4	
1997	4	0	1	5	0	3	2	
1998			1			3	4	
Number of Units U.S.	8	929	91	100	1270	25	10	
Canada	0	0	1	7	0	0		
Foreign	0	0	79	6	0	0		
Projected New U.S.		60	8				30	
Canada		0	0					
Foreign		0	4					
Corporate Employees	35	85	15	53	50+	12	10	
Contract Length	10/10+	5/5	CONTINUAL	5/5	10/10	10/10	10	
Expand in Territory	Y	Y	Y	Y	Y	Y	Y	
Full-Time Employees	4	4	2	5	1-5	2	2+	
Part-Time Employees	2	VAR.	2					
Conversions		Y	Y		Y		Y	
Site Selection Assist.	N	N	N	N	N	Y	Y	
Lease Negotiation Assist.		N		N			N	
Site Space Required	2000			900-1200			500-1500	
Development Agreement	N	N	N	N	Y	N	Y	
Develop. Agree. Term					10		1	
Sub-franchising	N	N	N	N	N	N	N	

Cleaning and Repair Industry

Commercial Cleaning (Spread 6 of 6)

Service-Tech Corporation
21012 Aurora Rd
Warrensville Hts, OH 44146-1010

Phone: 216-663-2600   Accepts collect calls?
Toll Free: 800-992-9302   FAX: 216-663-8804
Internet: www.servicetechcorp.cpm
Suitable Sites: HO
Concentration: 4 in OH, 1 in MI, 1 in FL
    Expansion: All United States
    Registered: FL,IL,MI
Field Support: CP, EO, ST, SO, FC, H
    Training: 2 weeks HQ
       1 week franchisee location

ServPro
575 Airport Blvd
Gallatin, TN 37066
Professional residential & commercial cleaning & restoration
    Phone: 615-451-0200   Accepts collect calls? N
    Toll Free: 800-826-9586   FAX: 615-451-4861
    Internet: www.servpro.com
Suitable Sites: FB, IP, LI, OS, WR
Concentration: 93 in CA, 77 in FL, 51 in OH
    Expansion: All United States
    Registered: CA,FL,HI,IL,IN,MD,MI,MN,ND,NY,OR,RI,SD,VA,WA,WI,DC
Field Support: CP, EO, ST, SO, FC, N
    Training: 2 weeks home study
       2 weeks national training center Gallatin, TN
       1 week franchise location

Sparkle Wash
26851 Richmond Rd
Bedford Heights, OH 44146
Safe, on-site cleaning, restoration & preservation of surfaces
    Phone: 216-464-4212   Accepts collect calls? N
    Toll Free: 800-321-0770   FAX: 216-464-8869
    Internet: www.sparklewash.com
Suitable Sites: HO
Concentration: 14 in PA, 13 in OH, 8 in NY
    Expansion: All United States, Canada, Foreign
    Registered: CA,FL,HI,IL,IN,MD,MI,MN,NY,OR,RI,SD,VA,WA,WI,DC,ND
Field Support: CP, EO, ST, FC, H, N
    Training: 1 week HQ
       3 days franchisee location
       3 days national/regional meeting

Swisher Hygiene
6849 Fairview Rd
Charlotte, NC 28210

    Phone: 704-364-7707   Accepts collect calls?
    Toll Free: 800-444-4138   FAX: 704-364-1202
    Internet:
Suitable Sites:
Concentration: 8 in CA, 7 in FL, 5 in TX
    Expansion: All United States, Canada, Foreign
    Registered: CA,FL,HI,IL,IN,MD,MI,MN,ND,NY,OR,RI,SD,VA,WA,WI,DC
Field Support: DP, CP, EO, ST, SO, IC, FC, H, N
    Training: 1 week on-site
       1 week charlotte NC

Tower Cleaning Systems
PO Box 80642
Valley Forge, PA 19484

Phone: 800-678-6937   Accepts collect calls?
Toll Free: 800-355-4000   FAX: 610-650-8268
Internet:
Suitable Sites:
Concentration: 480 in PA, 235 in NJ, 225 in WA
    Expansion: All United States, Canada
    Registered: CA,FL,HI,IL,IN,MD,MI,MN,ND,NY,OR,RI,SD,VA,WA,WI,DC
Field Support: DP, CP, EO, ST, FC, H, N
    Training: 1 week local office
       2-3 days on-site

Value Line Maintenance Systems
PO Box 6450
Great Falls, MT 59406

    Phone: 406-761-4471   Accepts collect calls? N
    Toll Free: 800-824-4838   FAX: 406-761-4486
    Internet: wmci@valcom.net
Suitable Sites:
Concentration: MT, CA, WY
    Expansion: California
    Registered: CA
Field Support: DP, CP, EO, ST, SO, IC, H
    Training: 1 week corporate
       2 weeks on-location

Window Gang
6509 Aviation Parkway
Morrisville, NC 27560
Window, gutter, blind & pressure cleaning service
    Phone: 919-571-3888   Accepts collect calls? N
    Toll Free: 800-849-2308   FAX: 919-571-3884
    Internet: www.windowgang.com
Suitable Sites: HO, LI, OS
Concentration: 18 in NC, 20 in SC, 4 in VA
    Expansion: All United States, Canada, Foreign
    Registered:
Field Support:
    Training: 14 days extensive training at HQ
       includes technical, sales, marketing
       and business procedures

Cleaning and Repair Industry   Lawn Care, Landscaping (Spread 1 of 2)

	Groundskeeping Services Clintar	Emerald Green Lawn Care	Enviro Masters Lawn Care	Home & Garden Showplace	Lawn Doctor	Liqui-Green Lawn & Tree Care	Naturalawn of America	Nitro-Green Professional Lawn & Tree Care
Startup Cost	150K-200K	49.6K-84.8K	20K-30K	500K-2M	41K		50K+CREDI	35K-50K
Franchise Fee	30K	18K	15K	0	0		29.5K	19.5K
Royalty	8%	6.5-8.5%	5%	0%	10%		7-9%	7-8.5%
Advertising Fee	0%	N/A	2%	$400/MO	10%		0%	
Financing Provided	Y	Y	Y	N	Y	Y	Y	Y
Experience Required	N						N	N
Passive Ownership	N	A	A	D	D		D	A
In Business Since	1973	1984	1987	1910	1967		1987	1977
Franchised Since	1984	1984	1991	1910	1967		1989	1979
Franchised Units 1996	9				326			
1997	9	25	16	250	330	31	43	42
1998	9			300	360		48	
Company Owned 1996	0				0			
1997	0	6	2	0	0	1	3	53
1998	1			0	0		3	
Number of Units U.S.	0	31	1	248	330	31	46	93
Canada	15	0	17	1	0	1	0	0
Foreign	0	0	0	1	0	32	0	0
Projected New U.S.	0			50			8	96
Canada	2			1			1	
Foreign	0			1				
Corporate Employees	9	8	2	9	50		12	20
Contract Length	10/5	12/6	10/10	N/A	20/5/5	10/5-10	5/10	20/10
Expand in Territory	Y	Y	Y	N	Y	Y	Y	Y
Full-Time Employees	10	1-3	1	6			2	1
Part-Time Employees	15	1-3	2	12	2	1	4	1-2
Conversions	Y	Y	Y	Y	N		Y	Y
Site Selection Assist.	Y	N	Y	Y	N	Y	Y	Y
Lease Negotiation Assist.	Y		Y	Y	N		N	Y
Site Space Required	3000			10000			1200-1500	100
Development Agreement	N	N	Y		N		N	N
Develop. Agree. Term			10					
Sub-franchising	N	N	N	N	N	Y	N	N

Cleaning and Repair Industry

Lawn Care, Landscaping (Spread 1 of 2)

Clintar Groundskeeping Services
70 Esna Park Dr Unit 1
Markham, ON L3R-1E3   CANADA
Grounds care svc provider for fortune 500 industrial companies
    Phone: 416-291-1611   Accepts collect calls? Y
    Toll Free: 800-361-3542   FAX: 416-291-6792
    Internet: www.clintar.com
Suitable Sites: FB, IP
Concentration: 15 in ON
    Expansion: Great Lakes Area, Canada
    Registered:
Field Support: $DP, CP, EO, ST, SO, IC, FC, H, N
    Training: 4 weeks Toronto

Emerald Green Lawn Care
14111 Scotts Lawn Rd
Marysville, OH 43041

    Phone: 937-644-7377   Accepts collect calls?
    Toll Free: 800-783-0981   FAX: 937-644-7422
    Internet:
Suitable Sites: FB, HO
Concentration: 6 in OH, 5 in IN, 2 in TX
    Expansion: All United States
    Registered: IN,MD,MI,ND,VA
Field Support: CP, EO, ST, IC, FC, H, N
    Training: 1 week Anderson IN
            1 week franchisee location

Enviro Masters Lawn Care
Box 178
Caledon East, ON L0N-1E0 CANADA
Organic & enviro considerate lawn care
    Phone: 905-584-9592   Accepts collect calls?
    Toll Free: FAX:
    Internet:
Suitable Sites: HO
Concentration: 13 in ON, 2 in AB, 2 in PQ
    Expansion: All United States, Canada
    Registered:
Field Support: CP, EO, ST, SO, IC, FC, $H, N
    Training: 2-3 weeks head office
            organic turf mgmnt, sales
            marketing, applications, admin

Home & Garden Showplace
8600 W Bryn Mawr Ave
Chicago, IL 60631-3505
Garden center support, merchandise, store develop, ads, training
    Phone: 773-695-5379   Accepts collect calls? N
    Toll Free: 888-474-9752   FAX: 773-695-7049
    Internet: www.h-g-showplace.com
Suitable Sites: FB
Concentration: 18 in NY, 16 in PA, 14 in WI
    Expansion: All United States, Canada
    Registered: CA,FL,HI,IL,IN,MD,MI,MN,ND,NY,OR,RI,SD,VA,WA,WI,DC
Field Support: $DP, CP, EO, ST, $SO, $IC, FC, H, N
    Training: 3 days Chicago IL

Lawn Doctor
142 State Route 34
Holmdel, NJ 07733-2092
Innovative & high-tech automated lawn/tree/shrub care equipment
    Phone: 732-946-0029   Accepts collect calls?
    Toll Free: 800-631-5660   FAX: 732-946-9089
    Internet:
Suitable Sites: HO
Concentration: 63 in NJ, 37 in NY, 35 in PA
    Expansion: All United States, Canada
    Registered: FL,IL,IN,MD,MI,MN,NY,RI,SD,VA,WI,DC
Field Support: CP, EO, ST, FC, H, N
    Training: 2 weeks New Jersey

Liqui-Green Lawn & Tree Care
9601 N Allen Rd
Peoria, IL 61615

    Phone: 309-243-5815   Accepts collect calls?
    Toll Free: 800-747-5211   FAX: 309-243-5247
    Internet:
Suitable Sites:
Concentration:
    Expansion: NW, SE
    Registered: IL,IN,VA,WA
Field Support: $CP, EO, FC, H, N
    Training:

Naturalawn of America
5 W Church St
Frederick, MD 21701
Natural organic-based fertilization, weed/insect/disease control
    Phone: 301-694-5440   Accepts collect calls? N
    Toll Free: 800-989-5444   FAX: 301-846-0320
    Internet: www.nl-amer.com
Suitable Sites: LI, WR
Concentration: 5 in MD, 5 in VA, 5 in CO
    Expansion: All United States, Canada, Foreign
    Registered: CA,FL,IL,IN,MD,MI,MN,NY,OR,RI,VA,WA,DC,WI
Field Support: CP, EO, ST, SO, IC, $FC, H, N
    Training: 1 week Frederick MD
            2 weeks franchisee location
            1 week regional location

Nitro-Green Professional Lawn & Tree Care
1335 Canyon Hwy Ste G
Marietta, GA 30066
Lawn fertilization/weed control/tree/shrub care
    Phone: 970-204-9681   Accepts collect calls? N
    Toll Free: 800-982-5296   FAX: 970-204-9020
    Internet: www.nitrogreen.com
Suitable Sites: FB, HO, LI, WR
Concentration: 8 in MT, 5 in ND, 5 in CA
    Expansion: All United States
    Registered: CA,MI,MN
Field Support: EO, ST, SO, FC, H, N
    Training: 6 days

Cleaning and Repair Industry

Lawn Care, Landscaping (Spread 2 of 2)

	Ecology-Friendly Lawn Care	Nutri-Lawn, Nutrite	Super Lawns	Terra Systems	U.S. Lawns	Weed Man		
Startup Cost	50K-100K	40K	60K	40K-50K	40K-70K	75K		
Franchise Fee	25K	10K	17.5K	19K-22K	29K	25K-34K		
Royalty	6%	$3.5K/YR	10% MAX	5%	4%	$800/VEHCL		
Advertising Fee	1%	0%	0%	0%	1%	8% ROYALTY		
Financing Provided	Y	N	Y	N	Y	N		
Experience Required	N				N			
Passive Ownership	N	A	D	N	D	D		
In Business Since	1985	1967	1975	1992	1986	1970		
Franchised Since	1987	1984	1979	1994	1987	1976		
Franchised Units 1996								
1997	43	44	22	0	22	130		
1998	38				36			
Company Owned 1996								
1997	0	0	2	1	2	2		
1998	0				4			
Number of Units U.S.	3	0	24	1	36	6		
Canada	35	44	0	0	0	126		
Foreign	0	0	0	0	0	0		
Projected New U.S.	2			2	24			
Canada	2				0			
Foreign					0			
Corporate Employees	4	30	3	2	14	9		
Contract Length	5/10	5/5	20/5	10/5	5/5	10/10		
Expand in Territory	Y	N	Y	Y	Y	Y		
Full-Time Employees	0	2	1	2	8-10			
Part-Time Employees	7		1	1		5		
Conversions	Y	Y		Y	Y	Y		
Site Selection Assist.	Y	Y	Y	Y	Y	Y		
Lease Negotiation Assist.	Y	N		N	Y	N		
Site Space Required				4000				
Development Agreement	Y	N	N	N	Y	Y		
Develop. Agree. Term								
Sub-franchising	N	N	N	N	N	N		

Cleaning and Repair Industry

Lawn Care, Landscaping (Spread 2 of 2)

Nutri-Lawn, Ecology-Friendly Lawn Care
5397 Eglinton Ave W #110
Toronto, ON M9C-5K6 CANADA
Minimize pesticide usage, create beautiful lawn, turn ipm pract.

Phone: 416-620-7100	Accepts collect calls? N
Toll Free: 800-396-6096	FAX: 416-620-7771
Internet: nli@iscar.ca	

Suitable Sites: HO, LI
Concentration: 20 in ON, 7 in BC, 3 in NS
  Expansion: PA,NY,DE,OH,OR,DC,MN, Canada
  Registered: FL,IL,WA
Field Support: CP, EO, ST, SO, FC, N
  Training: 1 week Toronto on
    1 week on-site
    2 days computer

Nutrite
PO Box 1000
Brossard, PQ J4Z-3N2 CANADA

Phone: 514-462-2555	Accepts collect calls?
Toll Free: 800-561-7449	FAX: 514-462-3634
Internet:	

Suitable Sites:
Concentration: 37 in PQ, 5 in ON, 2 in NB
  Expansion: N, Canada
  Registered: CA
Field Support: DP, CP, EO, ST, IC, $FC, $H, N
  Training: n limit on location

Super Lawns
PO Box 5677
Rockville, MD 20855

Phone: 301-948-8181	Accepts collect calls?
Toll Free: 800-445-2961	FAX: 301-948-8461
Internet:	

Suitable Sites:
Concentration: 9 in MD, 5 in VA, 3 in DE
  Expansion: East Of Mississippi
  Registered: MD,VA
Field Support: EO, ST, IC, FC, H
  Training: 7-10 days Rockville MD

Terra Systems
1515 Cliffwood Pl
Charlotte, NC 28203

Phone: 704-342-0310	Accepts collect calls?
Toll Free:	FAX: 704-342-0317
Internet: terrasys@bellsouth.net	

Suitable Sites: FB, HO, LI, SC
Concentration: 2 in NC
  Expansion: East Coast/Midwest
  Registered:
Field Support: CP, EO, ST, IC, $FC, N
  Training: 2 weeks HQ (charlotte NC)
    1 week franchise location

U.S. Lawns
4777 Old Winter Garden Rd
Orlando, FL 32811
Commercial landscape maintenance services

Phone: 407-522-1630	Accepts collect calls? N
Toll Free: 800-875-2967	FAX: 407-522-1669
Internet: uslawns@aol.com	

Suitable Sites: HO, IP, OC, OS
Concentration: FL, AL, TX
  Expansion: All United States, Canada
  Registered: CA,FL,IN,MD,MI,MN,VA,WI,DC
Field Support: DP, $CP, EO, ST, FC, H, N
  Training: 5 days Florida
    5 days your location

Weed Man
2399 Royal Windsor Dr
Mississauga, ON L5J-1K9 CANADA

Phone: 905-823-8550	Accepts collect calls?
Toll Free:	FAX: 905-823-4594
Internet: www.weed-man.com	

Suitable Sites: HO, SC
Concentration:
  Expansion: NW, Central and East, Canada, Foreign
  Registered: IL,IN,MI,MN,ND,OR,WA,WI
Field Support: CP, EO, ST, IC, FC, N
  Training: 1 week Mississauga on

Cleaning and Repair Industry
Residential Cleaning (Spread 1 of 2)

	Classy Maids USA	The Cleaning Authority	CottageCare	Home Cleaning Centers	Hour Hands	Maid Brigade Services	Maid To Perfection	MaidPro
Startup Cost	12K	27.8K-52.6K	55K-60K	30K-50K	9K-23K	35K-40K	25K-42K	12K-18K
Franchise Fee	9.9K	9K-16.8K	16.5K-19.5K	16.5K	19.5K	16.9K	9K	7.9K
Royalty	6%	5-7%	5.50%	4.5-5%	5%/MO	7-3%	3-7%	3-6%
Advertising Fee	0%	2%	4-10%	0%		2%/$6K MAX	0%	N/A
Financing Provided	Y	Y	Y	N	Y	Y	Y	Y
Experience Required			N					N
Passive Ownership	N	N	A	D		D	D	N
In Business Since	1980	1977	1988	1981	1992	1982	1980	1991
Franchised Since	1985	1996	1989	1984	1996	1984	1990	1997
Franchised Units 1996					0			
1997	8	10	44	28	0	255	121	7
1998			50				146	9
Company Owned 1996					1			
1997	0	1	2	0	1	5	2	1
1998		1					0	3
Number of Units U.S.	8	12	46	28		172	121	12
Canada	0	0	5	0		88	2	0
Foreign	0	0	0	0		0	0	0
Projected New U.S.			12				40	7
Canada			4				10	
Foreign								
Corporate Employees	3	5	14	2		10	6	5
Contract Length	10/10	10/5	10/10	10/10		10/10	5/5	10/5
Expand in Territory	Y	N	Y	N		Y	Y	Y
Full-Time Employees	1	VAR	1	12		12	15	15
Part-Time Employees	5-8		25-30				5	3
Conversions	Y		Y	N		N	Y	Y
Site Selection Assist.	N	Y	Y	Y		Y	Y	Y
Lease Negotiation Assist.		N	Y	Y		N	Y	Y
Site Space Required		500	700-800	500-700		500-1000	500	500-1500
Development Agreement	N	N	N	N		Y	Y	N
Develop. Agree. Term						5	5	
Sub-franchising	N	N	Y	N		Y	N	N

Cleaning and Repair Industry

Residential Cleaning (Spread 1 of 2)

Classy Maids USA
PO Box 160879
Altamonte Springs, FL 32716-0879

Phone: 407-862-0493   Accepts collect calls?
Toll Free: 800-445-5238   FAX: 407-862-4221
Internet:
Suitable Sites: HO
Concentration: 2 in MN, 2 in WI, 2 in FL
   Expansion: All United States
   Registered: FL
Field Support: $DP, $CP, $EO, $ST, $SO, $FC, H, N
   Training: 2 days Altamonte Springs FL or
      2-3 days franchisee location

The Cleaning Authority
9009 Mendenhall Ct #G
Columbia, MD 21045

Phone: 410-290-3880   Accepts collect calls?
Toll Free: 800-783-6243   FAX: 410-290-3885
Internet: www.thecleaningauthority.com
Suitable Sites:
Concentration: 6 in MD, 2 in OH, 2 in TN
   Expansion: All United States
   Registered: CA,FL,MD,VA
Field Support: EO, ST, SO, IC, $FC, H, N
   Training: 2 weeks home office
      3 days new location
      2 days follow-up new location

CottageCare
6323 W 110th St
Overland Park, KS 66211
General housecleaning services
Phone: 913-469-8778   Accepts collect calls? N
Toll Free: 800-469-6303   FAX: 913-469-0822
Internet: www.cottagecare.com
Suitable Sites: SC, SF
Concentration: 5 in TX, 3 in FL, 3 in KS
   Expansion: All United States, Canada, Foreign
   Registered: CA,FL,HI,IL,IN,MD,MI,MN,ND,NY,OR,RI,SD,VA,WA,WI,DC
Field Support: EO, ST, SO, IC, FC, N
   Training: 2 weeks Kansas City HQ

Home Cleaning Centers
PO Box 14070
Palm Desert, CA 92255

Phone: 760-360-0202   Accepts collect calls?
Toll Free: 800-767-1118   FAX: 760-360-2661
Internet:
Suitable Sites:
Concentration: 7 in MO, 4 in KS, 4 in CO
   Expansion: All United States
   Registered: CA,IL,IN,MN,NY,OR
Field Support: CP, EO, ST, SO, IC, FC, H, N
   Training: 5 days Denver CO or St Louis MO

Hour Hands
4701 Central Ave
Saint Petersburg, FL 33713
Resid. Cleaning, yard work, chores, minor repairs
Phone: Accepts collect calls?
Toll Free: 800-268-8077   FAX:
Internet:
Suitable Sites:
Concentration:
   Expansion: Canada
   Registered:
Field Support:
   Training:

Maid Brigade Services
850 Indian Trail Rd
Lilburn, GA 30047

Phone: 770-564-2400   Accepts collect calls?
Toll Free: 800-722-6243   FAX: 770-279-9668
Internet: www.maidbrigade.com
Suitable Sites: HO
Concentration: 35 in VA, 18 in WA, 17 in MD
   Expansion: All United States, Canada
   Registered: CA,FL,IL,MD,MI,MN,NY,OR,VA,WA,WI,DC
Field Support: CP, EO, ST, SO, FC, H, N
   Training: 1 week Atlanta GA
      days on-site

Maid To Perfection
7133 Rutherford Rd Ste 105
Baltimore, MD 21244
Upscale residential maid service, window clean, carpet clean
Phone: 410-944-6466   Accepts collect calls? N
Toll Free: 800-648-6243   FAX: 410-944-6469
Internet: www.maidtoperfectioncorp.com
Suitable Sites: FB, IP, LI, OS
Concentration: 50 in MD, 28 in PA, 12 in CA
   Expansion: All United States, Canada
   Registered: CA,FL,IL,IN,MD,MI,MN,NY,OR,VA,WA,WI,DC
Field Support: CP, EO, ST, $FC, H, N
   Training: 5 days Baltimore MD
      labor mgmt, business operations
      estimating, sales, etc.

MaidPro
180 Canal St
Boston, MA 02114

Phone: 617-742-8787   Accepts collect calls?
Toll Free: 888-624-3776   FAX: 617-720-0700
Internet: www.maidpro.com
Suitable Sites: OC, SF
Concentration: 5 in MA, 1 in AZ, 1 in FL
   Expansion: All United States
   Registered: CA,FL,HI,IL,IN,MD,MI,MN,ND,NY,OR,RI,SD,VA,WA,WI,DC
Field Support: EO, $ST, SO, $FC, H, N
   Training: 1-2 weeks Boston MA

Cleaning and Repair Industry — Residential Cleaning (Spread 2 of 2)

	The Maids	Merry Maids	Service Systems Of Canada	Mini Maid	Molly Maid	ServiceMaster Residential/Commercial (Canada)	ServiceMaster Residential/Commercial	Window Butler	Workenders
Startup Cost	50K-60K	24.9K-41.4K	14K	50K-60K	20K-49K		33.6K-67.1K	7.5K-27K	<50K
Franchise Fee	17.5K	13.5K-21.5K	10K	16.9K	11.5K-28.5K		14.7K-26.5K	9.9K-16.9K	22.5K
Royalty	3.3-7%	5-7%	6%	3-6%	4-9%		4-10%	7%	3-6%
Advertising Fee	1%	.25-1%	2%	0-2%	1%		.5-1%	3%	0
Financing Provided	Y	Y	N	N	Y		Y	Y	N
Experience Required		N					N	N	N
Passive Ownership	D	D	N	N	N		D	N	N
In Business Since	1979	1979	1979	1979		1947	1947	1997	1991
Franchised Since	1980	1980	1979	1979		1947	1952	1997	1992
Franchised Units 1996									26
1997	329	1083	80	526	160		4277	2	22
1998	361	1160						16	21
Company Owned 1996									0
1997	0	59	21	0	0		0	0	0
1998	3	62						0	0
Number of Units U.S.	346	782	0	249	0		2952	16	
Canada	15	38	101	161	160	158		0	
Foreign	0	340	0	116	0		1167	0	
Projected New U.S.	15							30	
Canada	5							0	
Foreign	0							0	
Corporate Employees	35	55	5	31	100		200	7	2
Contract Length	20/20	5/5	10/10	10	5/5		5/5	10/10	20
Expand in Territory	Y	Y	Y	Y	Y		Y	Y	Y
Full-Time Employees	1-2	2	6	12	VAR.		3	0-6	6-30
Part-Time Employees	8-12	12					2	0-2	
Conversions	Y	Y	N	Y	Y		Y	Y	N
Site Selection Assist.	Y	N	Y	N	N		N	N	N
Lease Negotiation Assist.	N	N		N			N	N	Y
Site Space Required	200	800		400					500-1000
Development Agreement	Y	N	Y	N	N		N	Y	N
Develop. Agree. Term	10		5					NEG.	
Sub-franchising	Y	N	Y	N	N		Y	N	N

Cleaning and Repair Industry

Residential Cleaning (Spread 2 of 2)

The Maids
4820 Dodge St
Omaha, NE 68132

Phone: 402-558-5555   Accepts collect calls?
Toll Free: 800-843-6243   FAX: 402-558-4112
Internet: www.maids.com
Suitable Sites: FB, SC, SF
Concentration: 46 in CA, 23 in NY, 22 in IL
Expansion: All United States, Canada, Foreign
Registered: CA,FL,HI,IL,IN,MD,MI,MN,ND,NY,OR,RI,SD,VA,WA,WI,DC,AB
Field Support: DP, CP, EO, ST, SO, IC, FC, H, N
Training: 8 days managerial training HQ
8 days technical training HQ
90 days on-site

Merry Maids
860 Ridge Lake Blvd
Memphis, TN 38120
Top quality house cleaning on a scheduled or one-time basis
Phone: 901-537-8100   Accepts collect calls? N
Toll Free: 800-798-8000   FAX: 901-537-8140
Internet: www.merrymaids.com
Suitable Sites: DA, FB, SC
Concentration: 114 in CA, 40 in TX, 42 in IL
Expansion: All United States, Canada, Foreign
Registered: CA,FL,HI,IL,IN,MD,MI,MN,ND,NY,OR,RI,SD,VA,WA,WI,DC,AB
Field Support: EO, ST, FC, H, N
Training: 8 days HQ
regular scheduled regional meeting
on-site visits

Mini Maid Service Systems Of Canada
192 Shorting Rd
Scarborough, ON M1S-3S7 CANADA

Phone: 416-298-7288   Accepts collect calls?
Toll Free: 800-363-6243   FAX: 416-298-8445
Internet:
Suitable Sites:
Concentration: 20 in ON, 16 in BC, 9 in PQ
Expansion: N, Canada
Registered: AB
Field Support: CP, EO, ST, FC, H, N
Training: 1 week HQ
annual seminars

Molly Maid
1340 Eisenhower Pl
Ann Arbor, MI 48108

Phone: 734-975-1000   Accepts collect calls?
Toll Free: 800-665-5962   FAX: 734-975-9000
Internet: www.mollymaid.com
Suitable Sites:
Concentration: 146 in ON, 37 in CA, 31 in MI
Expansion: All United States, Canada, Foreign
Registered: CA,FL,IL,IN,MD,MI,MN,NY,OR,RI,VA,WA,WI,DC
Field Support: EO, ST, IC, FC, N
Training: 5 days home office
6 months right start program
2 days franchise location

ServiceMaster Residential/ Commercial (Canada)
6540 Tomken Rd
Mississauga, ON L5T-2E9 CANADA
Clean-up & reconstruction after fire & flood, janitorial svcs
Phone: 905-670-0000   Accepts collect calls? Y
Toll Free: 800-263-5928   FAX: 905-670-0077
Internet: www.svm.com
Suitable Sites: HO, OS
Concentration: 80 in ON, 19 in BC, 11 in AB
Expansion: N, Canada
Registered: AB
Field Support: CP, EO, ST, $FC, H, N
Training: 2 weeks Memphis TN

ServiceMaster Residential/Commercial
860 Ridge Lake Rd
Memphis, TN 38120-9792

Phone: 901-684-7500   Accepts collect calls?
Toll Free: 800-230-2360   FAX: 901-685-7600
Internet: www.svm.com
Suitable Sites:
Concentration: 212 in IL, 168 in CA, 150 in OH
Expansion: All United States, Canada, Foreign
Registered: CA,FL,HI,IL,IN,MD,MI,MN,ND,NY,OR,RI,SD,VA,WA,WI,DC
Field Support: DP, CP, EO, ST, IC, FC, H, N
Training: 2 weeks Memphis TN
1 week on location

Window Butler
6355 E Kemper Rd #250
Cincinnati, OH 45241
Provides busy homeowners w/ window cleaning & maintenance
Phone: 513-489-4000   Accepts collect calls? N
Toll Free: 800-808-6470   FAX: 513-469-2226
Internet: www.windowbutlet.com
Suitable Sites: HO
Concentration: 4 in OH, 2 in TN, 2 in KS
Expansion: All United States
Registered: CA,FL,IL,IN,MD,MN,MI,NY,OR,DC
Field Support: EO, ST, SO, FC, H, N
Training: 1 week Cincinnati OH
field training as needed

Workenders
4400 N Federal Hwy #210
Boca Raton, FL 33431
Residential cleaning service
Phone: 561-347-2591   Accepts collect calls? N
Toll Free: 888-249-0074   FAX: 561-477-5321
Internet: www.workenders.com
Suitable Sites:
Concentration: 3 in OR
Expansion: All United States
Registered: CA,FL,NY,OR,WA
Field Support: EO, ST, SO, FC, H, N
Training: 3 weeks mentor franchise location
1 week on-site opening assistance

Cleaning and Repair Industry

Surface Restoration (Spread 1 of 2)

	Bathcrest	BMR Bath Master Reglazing Ltd.	Color-Glo International	KCS Applications	Marble Renewal	MarbleLife	Perma Glaze	Profusion Systems
Startup Cost	26.9K-34K	13K-20K	15K-40K	450	50K-75K	90K-125K	19.5K+	35K-120K
Franchise Fee	3.5K	3.9K	5K	9.5K	5K-25K	25K AVG	19.5K+	25K
Royalty	$100/MO	5%/$200/MO	4%	$350/YR	5-8%	6%	N/A	6%
Advertising Fee	0%	2%			0%	2%	$1800/YR	1%
Financing Provided	Y	N	N	N	Y	Y	N	Y
Experience Required		N					N	
Passive Ownership	A	D	A		D	A	N	D
In Business Since	1979	1989	1970	1992	1988	1987	1978	1984
Franchised Since	1985	1992	1988	1994	1989	1993	1981	1984
Franchised Units 1996				14				
1997	152	10	199	15	27	40	177	43
1998		10					177	
Company Owned 1996				0				
1997	1	0	1	0	1	0	1	1
1998		1					1	
Number of Units U.S.	146	0	160		20	32	124	30
Canada	6	10	20		1	2	2	5
Foreign	1	0	20		7	6	51	8
Projected New U.S.								
Canada		4						
Foreign								
Corporate Employees	10	2	12		7	10	6	4
Contract Length	15/15	5/5	10/5		10/10	10/10	10/10	10/5
Expand in Territory	Y	Y	Y		Y	Y	Y	Y
Full-Time Employees	3	1	1		2	5	1	3
Part-Time Employees		0			1	1	1	1
Conversions		Y			Y	Y	N	Y
Site Selection Assist.	N	N	N		N	N	Y	Y
Lease Negotiation Assist.	N	N				N	N	Y
Site Space Required	300-1000	300						
Development Agreement	N	N	Y		Y	N	Y	Y
Develop. Agree. Term			10		5-7		10	10
Sub-franchising	N	Y	Y		Y	N	N	Y

Cleaning and Repair Industry

Surface Restoration (Spread 1 of 2)

Bathcrest
2425 S Progress Dr
Salt Lake City, UT 84119

Phone: 801-972-1110   Accepts collect calls?
Toll Free: 800-826-6790   FAX: 801-977-0328
Internet:
Suitable Sites: HO, IP
Concentration: 19 in CA, 10 in PA, 10 in OH
  Expansion: All United States, Canada
  Registered:
Field Support: CP, ST, FC, H, N
  Training: 5 days HQ
            3 days HQ 30-60 after init tr

BMR Bath Master Reglazing Ltd.
Rr2 Ste 27b Comp 13
Peachland, BC V0H-1X0 CANADA
Bathtub, sink, tile, cupboard & countertop resurfacing
  Phone: 250-767-2336   Accepts collect calls? Y
Toll Free: 800-808-9666   FAX: 250-767-2336
Internet:
Suitable Sites: HO
Concentration: 3 in BC, 3 in SK, 2 in ONT
  Expansion: NW, Canada, Foreign
  Registered:
Field Support: CP, EO, ST, IC, FC, H, N
  Training: 10 days minimum Peachland BC

Color-Glo International
7111-7115 Ohms Ln
Minneapolis, MN 55439-2158

Phone: 612-835-1338   Accepts collect calls?
Toll Free: 800-333-8523   FAX: 612-835-1395
Internet: cgi-online.com
Suitable Sites:
Concentration: 15 in FL, 12 in GA, 12 in OR
  Expansion: All United States, Canada, Foreign
  Registered: CA,FL,HI,IL,IN,MD,MI,MN,ND,NY,OR,RI,SD,VA,WA,WI,DC
Field Support: EO, ST, SO, IC, FC, H, N
  Training: 1 week CO, OR, FL

KCS Applications
61 Howard St
Hastings, NY 13076
Acrylic asphalt sealing
  Phone: 315-668-2370   Accepts collect calls?
Toll Free: FAX:
Internet:
Suitable Sites:
Concentration:
  Expansion: NE,SE
  Registered:
Field Support:
  Training:

Marble Renewal
6805 W 12th St #H
Little Rock, AR 72204

Phone: 501-663-2080   Accepts collect calls?
Toll Free: 888-664-7866   FAX: 501-663-2401
Internet:
Suitable Sites: HO
Concentration: 2 in FL, 2 in TX, 1 in ON
  Expansion: All United States, Canada, Foreign
  Registered: FL,IL,DC
Field Support: DP, CP, $EO, $ST, SO, IC, FC, H, N
  Training: 10 days little rock AR

MarbleLife
805 W North Carrier Pkwy #220
Grand Prairie, TX 75050

Phone: 972-623-0500   Accepts collect calls?
Toll Free: 800-627-4569   FAX: 972-623-0220
Internet: marblelife.com
Suitable Sites: HO, SF
Concentration: 3 in FL, 4 in CA, 3 in TX
  Expansion: All United States, Canada, Foreign
  Registered: CA,FL,HI,IL,IN,MD,MI,MN,ND,NY,OR,RI,SD,VA,WA,WI,DC
Field Support: EO, ST, SO, FC, H, N
  Training: 2 weeks Grand Prairie TX

Perma Glaze
1638 S Research Loop Rd #160
Tucson, AZ 85710
Restoration/refinishing of bath/kitchen fixtures, wall tile, etc
  Phone: 520-722-9718   Accepts collect calls?
Toll Free: 800-332-7397   FAX: 520-296-4393
Internet: www.permaglaze.com
Suitable Sites:
Concentration: 6 in AZ, 6 in FL, 2 in HI
  Expansion: All United States, Canada, Foreign
  Registered: CA,IL,IN,MD,MI,MN,NY,ND,OR,SD,VA,WA,WI
Field Support: EO, ST, FC, H, N
  Training: 1 week Tucson AZ

Profusion Systems
8201 East Pacific Pl #605
Denver, CO 80231

Phone: 303-337-4208   Accepts collect calls?
Toll Free: 800-770-3873   FAX: 303-337-0790
Internet: www.profusionsystems.com
Suitable Sites: HO, LI, WR
Concentration: 2 in IL, 2 in GA, 2 in MI
  Expansion: All United States, Canada, Foreign
  Registered: RE-FILING
Field Support: DP, CP, EO, ST, SO, $FC, H, N
  Training: 80 hours home study
            80 hours home office
            40 hours fielding trng frnchee loc

Cleaning and Repair Industry

Surface Restoration (Spread 2 of 2)

	Re-Bath	Surface Specialists Systems						
Startup Cost	38.4K-78.6K	13.9K-42K						
Franchise Fee	15K-30K	9.5K-30K						
Royalty	$25/LINER	5%						
Advertising Fee	0%	N/A						
Financing Provided	Y	Y						
Experience Required								
Passive Ownership	N	D						
In Business Since	1978	1981						
Franchised Since	1991	1982						
Franchised Units 1996								
1997	76	26						
1998								
Company Owned 1996								
1997	1	0						
1998								
Number of Units U.S.	74	26						
Canada	1	0						
Foreign	2	0						
Projected New U.S.								
Canada								
Foreign								
Corporate Employees	10	4						
Contract Length	7/7	10/10						
Expand in Territory	Y	Y						
Full-Time Employees	1	2						
Part-Time Employees	2	2						
Conversions		Y						
Site Selection Assist.	Y	N						
Lease Negotiation Assist.	N							
Site Space Required	200	300						
Development Agreement	N	Y						
Develop. Agree. Term								
Sub-franchising	N	N						

Cleaning and Repair Industry

Re-Bath

1055 S Country Club Dr Bldg #2
Mesa, AZ 85210-4613

Phone: 602-844-1575　　Accepts collect calls?
Toll Free: 800-426-4573　　FAX: 602-833-7199
Internet:
Suitable Sites: SF
Concentration: 7 in CA, 7 in NY, 6 in FL
　Expansion: All United States, Canada
　Registered: CA,FL,HI,IL,IN,MD,MI,MN,NY,OR,RI,VA,WA,WI,DC,AB
Field Support: $FC, H, N
　Training: 1 week mesa AZ, corp HQ

Surface Specialists Systems

5168 Country Club Dr
High Ridge, MO 63049

Phone: 314-677-6008　　Accepts collect calls?
Toll Free: 888-376-4468　　FAX: 314-376-8889
Internet:
Suitable Sites: HO
Concentration: 5 in MI, 4 in WI, 2 in FL
　Expansion: All United States
　Registered: FL,IL,MI,DC
Field Support: CP, $EO, ST, $FC, H, N
　Training: 3 weeks high ridge MO

Cleaning and Repair Industry   Vinyl Repair

	Creative Colors Int'l Inc	Dr. Vinyl & Assoc.						
Startup Cost	25.3K-37.6K	35K-40K						
Franchise Fee	27.5K	19.5K						
Royalty	6%	4-7%						
Advertising Fee		1%						
Financing Provided	Y	Y						
Experience Required	N	N						
Passive Ownership		D						
In Business Since	1980	1972						
Franchised Since	1991	1980						
Franchised Units 1996	28							
1997	39	115						
1998	42	125						
Company Owned 1996	1							
1997	1	3						
1998	2	2						
Number of Units U.S.		123						
Canada		2						
Foreign		0						
Projected New U.S.		15						
Canada		4						
Foreign		2						
Corporate Employees	8	15						
Contract Length	10/10/10/10	10/10						
Expand in Territory	Y	Y						
Full-Time Employees	1-8	1						
Part-Time Employees								
Conversions								
Site Selection Assist.	Y	N						
Lease Negotiation Assist.	Y	N						
Site Space Required								
Development Agreement		Y						
Develop. Agree. Term		10						
Sub-franchising		Y						

Cleaning and Repair Industry

Vinyl Repair

Creative Colors Int'l Inc
5550 W 175th St
Tinley Park, IL 60477
Mobile plastic/vinyl/leather/restor/rpr
    Phone: 708-614-7786   Accepts collect calls? N
    Toll Free: 800-933-2656   FAX: 708-614-9685
    Internet: creativecolorsintl.com
Suitable Sites:
Concentration: 6 in IL, 4 in OH, 5 in FL
    Expansion: All United States, Canada, Foreign
    Registered: CA,FL,IL,IN,MI,MN,NY,WI,AB
Field Support: DP, CP, EO, ST, SO, IC, $FC, H, N
    Training: 3 weeks intensive hands-on at HQ
        1 week in field

Dr. Vinyl & Assoc.
9501 E 350 Hwy
Raytown, MO 64133
Auto, furniture & marine repair & appearance conditioning
    Phone: 816-356-3312   Accepts collect calls? N
    Toll Free: 800-531-6600   FAX: 816-356-9049
    Internet: www.drvinyl.com
Suitable Sites: HO
Concentration: 18 in MO, 7 in OH, 6 in CA
    Expansion: All United States, Canada, Foreign
    Registered: CA,FL,IL,IN,MI,OR,WI
Field Support: $CP, EO, ST, IC, $FC, H, N
    Training: 2 weeks Raytown corp office
        2 weeks field training

Cleaning and Repair Industry — Other Cleaning and Repair (Spread 1 of 2)

	American Leak Detection	BladeRunner Mobile Sharpening	Ceiling Doctor	Deckare Services	DuctBusters / Buster Enterprises Inc	Furniture Medic	Glass Magnum	House Doctors Handyman Service
Startup Cost	75K-100K	6K-35K	35K	45K	20K-60K	10K-15K	6K-8K	18.5K-38.5K
Franchise Fee	49.5K	1K	12.5K	14.5K	7.5K-24K	16.4K	5K	10.9K-22.9K
Royalty	8-10%	0	8%	5%	5.5-7%	7%/$200 MIN	5%	6%
Advertising Fee	NA		2%	N/A	0	1%/$30 MIN	1%	3%
Financing Provided	Y	Y	N	N	Y	Y	Y	Y
Experience Required				N	Y			N
Passive Ownership	D		D	A	D	N	N	A
In Business Since	1974	1988	1984	1995	1985	1992	1982	1994
Franchised Since	1985	1994	1985	1997	1992	1992	1990	1995
Franchised Units 1996		536			6			
1997	278	580	110	6	15	539	21	145
1998				33	23			183
Company Owned 1996		2			1			
1997	3	1	1	1	1	0	1	0
1998				0	1			
Number of Units U.S.	215		52	7	21	506	21	145
Canada	7		20	0		30	0	0
Foreign	59		39	0	3	3	0	0
Projected New U.S.				40	5			50
Canada								
Foreign					3			
Corporate Employees	27		4	6	6	18	1	12
Contract Length	10/5		5/45	5/25	10/5/5	5/5	5/5	10/10/10
Expand in Territory	Y		Y	Y	Y	Y	Y	N
Full-Time Employees	1-3		1	1	2	1	1	2-8
Part-Time Employees	1		2	1	0	1		
Conversions			Y	N	Y		Y	Y
Site Selection Assist.	N		N	N	N	Y	N	N
Lease Negotiation Assist.				N	N	N		N
Site Space Required			150					
Development Agreement	Y		Y	N	N	N	Y	Y
Develop. Agree. Term	10		50				5	
Sub-franchising	Y		N	N	Y	N	Y	N

Cleaning and Repair Industry

Other Cleaning and Repair (Spread 1 of 2)

American Leak Detection
888 Research Dr #100 PO Box 1701
Palm Springs, CA 92263

Phone: 760-320-9991   Accepts collect calls?
Toll Free: 800-755-6697   FAX: 760-320-1288
Internet: www.leakbusters.com
Suitable Sites:
Concentration: 63 in CA, 28 in FL, 16 in TX
    Expansion: NE,SE,S,MW, Canada, Foreign
    Registered: CA,FL,HI,IL,IN,MD,MI,MN,NY,OR,RI,VA,WA,WI,DC
Field Support: $DP, CP, EO, ST, $IC, FC, H, N
    Training: 6 weeks palm springs CA

BladeRunner Mobile Sharpening
6431 Orr Rd
Charlotte, NC 28213
Mobile sharpening system
    Phone: 704-597-8266   Accepts collect calls?
Toll Free: 800-742-7754   FAX:
Internet:
Suitable Sites:
Concentration:
    Expansion: Foreign
    Registered:
Field Support:
    Training:

Ceiling Doctor
17810 Davenport Rd #108
Dallas, TX 75252

Phone: 972-250-3311   Accepts collect calls?
Toll Free: 800-992-6299   FAX: 972-250-3929
Internet:
Suitable Sites: HO
Concentration: 7 in ON, 5 in OH, 4 in PA
    Expansion: All United States, Canada, Foreign
    Registered: CA,FL,HI,IL,IN,MI,NY,VA,WA
Field Support: EO, ST, SO, IC, FC, H, N
    Training: 7 days Dallas TX

Deckare Services
1501 Raff Rd S W
Canton, OH 44710
Cleaning, protecting & maintenance of all natural exterior wood
    Phone: 330-478-3665   Accepts collect calls? N
Toll Free: 800-711-3325   FAX: 330-478-0311
    Internet: www.deckcare.com
Suitable Sites: HO
Concentration: 4 in OH, 3 in KY, 4 in NC
    Expansion: All United States, Canada, Foreign
    Registered: CA,FL,IL,IN,MD,MI,MN,NY,VA
Field Support: EO, ST, FC, H, N
    Training: 5 days corporate office
       4 days franchisee's location

DuctBusters / Buster Enterprises Inc
29160 U S Hwy 19 N
Clearwater, FL 33761-2400
Duct & hvac-system cleaning, indoor air quality testing
    Phone: 727-787-7087   Accepts collect calls? Y
Toll Free: 800-786-3828   FAX: 727-789-0060
    Internet: www.ductbusters.com
Suitable Sites: FB, HO, IP, LI, OC, OS, SC, WR
Concentration: 14 in FL, 2 in LA
    Expansion: All United States, Canada, Foreign
    Registered: CA,FL,IL,IN,MD,NY,OR
Field Support: DP, CP, EO, ST, IC, $FC, H, N
    Training: 5 days corporate HQ
       2 days franchise location
       2 site visits per year

Furniture Medic
860 Ridge Lake Blvd 3rd Fl
Memphis, TN 38120

Phone: 901-820-8600   Accepts collect calls?
Toll Free: 800-877-9933   FAX: 901-820-8660
    Internet: www.furnituremedic.com
Suitable Sites:
Concentration: 41 in CA, 28 in NY, 16 in NJ
    Expansion: All United States, Canada, Foreign
    Registered: CA,FL,HI,IL,MD,MI,MN,ND,RI,SD,VA,WA,WI
Field Support: DP, CP, ST, $FC, H, N
    Training: 2 weeks Memphis TN

Glass Magnum
5855 SW 152nd Ave
Beaverton, OR 97007
Repair crystal, plate-glass, auto-glass
    Phone: 503-641-6926   Accepts collect calls?
Toll Free: FAX: 503-641-9393
Internet:
Suitable Sites:
Concentration: 14 in OR, 2 in WA, 2 in HI
    Expansion: All United States, Canada
    Registered: HI, OR, WA
Field Support: CP, ST, IC, H, N
    Training: 300 hours Beaverton, OR

House Doctors Handyman Service
6355 E Kemper Rd #250
Cincinnati, OH 45241

Phone: 513-409-2443   Accepts collect calls? N
Toll Free: 800-319-3359   FAX: 513-469-2226
    Internet: www.housedoctors.com
Suitable Sites:
Concentration:
    Expansion: All United States, Canada, Foreign
    Registered: CA,FL,IL,MD,MI,MN,ND,NY,OR,RI,SD,VA,WA,WI,DC
Field Support: DP, EO, ST, SO, FC, H, N
    Training: 7 days Cincinnati, OH HQ
       as required in field

Cleaning and Repair Industry   Other Cleaning and Repair (Spread 2 of 2)

	Jet-Black Sealcoating & Repair	Mr. Rooter Corp.	Property Damage Appraisers	Roto-Rooter	The Screen Machine	Slats Blind Cleaning	Truly Nolen	
Startup Cost	20K-40K		9.2K-23K	25K-99K	47.6K-63.7K	25K-87K	7.5K-1M	
Franchise Fee	7.5K	17.5K	0	5K	25K	17.5K	15K	
Royalty	8%	6-3%	15%	VAR	5%	5%	7%	
Advertising Fee	NA	2%	0%	VAR	3%	0%	0%	
Financing Provided	Y	Y	N	N	N	Y	Y	
Experience Required					N	N		
Passive Ownership	N	N	N	D	D	A	A	
In Business Since	1988	1968	1963	1935	1986	1995	1938	
Franchised Since	1993	1972	1963	1935	1988	1995	1996	
Franchised Units 1996					15			
1997	23	270	263	535	18	2	0	
1998					20			
Company Owned 1996					1			
1997	0	0	0	90	1	2	63	
1998					1			
Number of Units U.S.	23	191	263	600	21	4	63	
Canada	0	24	0	25	0	0	0	
Foreign	0	55	0	35	0	0	0	
Projected New U.S.					3			
Canada					0			
Foreign					0			
Corporate Employees	3	13	36	6	2	3	50	
Contract Length	15/15	10/5	3/5	10/10	10/10	10/5	5/5	
Expand in Territory	Y	Y	Y	N	Y	Y	Y	
Full-Time Employees	2		2		1	2	5	
Part-Time Employees								
Conversions	N	Y	Y		N	Y	Y	
Site Selection Assist.	Y	N	Y	N	N	Y	N	
Lease Negotiation Assist.				N	N	N		
Site Space Required						1000		
Development Agreement	N	Y	N	N	N	N	N	
Develop. Agree. Term		10						
Sub-franchising	N	Y	N	N	N	N	N	

Cleaning and Repair Industry

Jet-Black Sealcoating & Repair
680 W 92nd St
Bloomington, MN 55420

Phone: 612-888-4444   Accepts collect calls?
Toll Free: FAX: 612-888-7050
Internet:
Suitable Sites: HO
Concentration: 17 in MN, 1 in WI
   Expansion: All United States, Canada
   Registered: IL,MI,MN,WI
Field Support: DP, CP, EO, ST, SO, IC, FC, N
   Training: 1 week Bloomington, MN

Mr. Rooter Corp.
1020 N University Parks Dr
Waco, TX 76707

Phone: 254-745-2500   Accepts collect calls?
Toll Free: 800-583-8003   FAX: 254-745-2501
Internet:
Suitable Sites:
Concentration: 33 in CA, 15 in TX, 13 in ON
   Expansion: Uncovered Areas, Canada, Foreign
   Registered: CA,FL,HI,IL,IN,MD,MI,MN,ND,NY,OR,RI,SD,VA,WA,WI,DC
Field Support: EO, ST, SO, IC, FC, H, N
   Training: 1 week Waco TX

Property Damage Appraisers
6100 SW Blvd #200
Fort Worth, TX 76109-3964

Phone: 817-731-5555   Accepts collect calls?
Toll Free: 800-749-7324   FAX: 817-731-5550
Internet: www.pdahomeoffice.com
Suitable Sites:
Concentration: 25 in TX, 21 in CA, 15 in FL
   Expansion: All United States
   Registered: CA,FL,HI,IL,IN,MD,MI,MN,ND,NY,OR,RI,SD,VA,WA,WI,DC
Field Support: DP, EO, ST, FC, H, N
   Training: 1 week corporate HQ
      4 days on-site

Roto-Rooter
300 Ashworth Rd
West Des Moines, IA 50265
Sewer cleaning and residential plumbing
Phone: 515-223-1343   Accepts collect calls? N
Toll Free: 800-575-7737   FAX: 515-223-6109
Internet:
Suitable Sites:
Concentration: 44 in CA, 24 in FL, 28 in TX
   Expansion: N, Foreign
   Registered: CA,FL,HI,IL,IN,MD,MI,MN,ND,NY,OR,RI,SD,VA,WA,WI,DC
Field Support: EO, $FC, H, N
   Training:

The Screen Machine
19636 8th St East
Sonoma, CA 95476
Mobile screening service. Window & door screens. New or re-screen
Phone: 707-996-5551   Accepts collect calls? N
Toll Free: FAX: 707-996-0139
Internet: www.screenmachine.com
Suitable Sites: HO, IP
Concentration: 21 in CA
   Expansion: West
   Registered: CA
Field Support: DP, EO, ST, $FC, N
   Training: 6 days Sonoma, CA

Slats Blind Cleaning
3119 Porter Gulch Rd
Aptos, CA 95003

Phone: 408-476-1667   Accepts collect calls?
Toll Free: 800-667-5287   FAX: 408-476-2480
Internet:
Suitable Sites: HO, LI
Concentration: 4 in CA
   Expansion: Western United States
   Registered: CA
Field Support: $CP, EO, $ST, SO, $FC, H, N
   Training: 1 week CA

Truly Nolen
3620 E Speedway Blvd
Tucson, AZ 85715

Phone: 520-546-9132   Accepts collect calls?
Toll Free: 800-458-3664   FAX: 520-546-2511
Internet:
Suitable Sites:
Concentration: 34 in FL, 15 in AZ, 6 in CA
   Expansion: All United States, Canada, Foreign
   Registered: CA,FL
Field Support: $CP, EO, ST, SO, IC, FC, H, N
   Training: 4 weeks Tucson AZ or Orlando FL

Construction Industry   Closet Systems

	California Closet Company	The Closet Factory	Closettec					
Startup Cost	75K-225K	99.5K-185K	128K-240K					
Franchise Fee	9K-39.5K	28.5K-39.5K	30K					
Royalty	6%	5.80%	4.50%					
Advertising Fee	5%	1%						
Financing Provided	N	Y	N					
Experience Required								
Passive Ownership	D	A	D					
In Business Since	1979	1983	1985					
Franchised Since	1982	1985	1986					
Franchised Units 1996								
1997	152	89	35					
1998								
Company Owned 1996								
1997	0	1	0					
1998								
Number of Units U.S.	128	79	35					
Canada	9	4	0					
Foreign	15	7	0					
Projected New U.S.								
Canada								
Foreign								
Corporate Employees	22	110	9					
Contract Length	10/10	5/5	15/15					
Expand in Territory	Y	N	Y					
Full-Time Employees	6	5-6	3-5					
Part-Time Employees								
Conversions		Y	Y					
Site Selection Assist.	Y	Y	Y					
Lease Negotiation Assist.	Y	Y	Y					
Site Space Required	2000-6000	3500-4000	2500-3000					
Development Agreement	N	N	N					
Develop. Agree. Term								
Sub-franchising	N	N	N					

Construction Industry   Closet Systems

California Closet Company
1000 Fourth St #800
San Rafael, CA 94901

    Phone: 415-256-8500   Accepts collect calls?
    Toll Free: 800-241-3222   FAX: 415-256-8501
    Internet: www.calclosets.com
Suitable Sites: LI
Concentration: 14 in CA, 10 in NY, 10 in FL
    Expansion: Various U.S. Locations, Canada, Foreign
    Registered: CA,IL,IN,MD,MI,MN,NY,RI,VA,WA,WI
Field Support: CP, EO, ST, SO, IC, FC, H, N
    Training: 2 weeks HQ
           1 week on-site

The Closet Factory
12800 S Broadway
Los Angeles, CA 90061-1116

    Phone: 310-516-7000   Accepts collect calls?
    Toll Free: 800-692-5673   FAX: 310-538-2676
    Internet:
Suitable Sites: WR
Concentration: 8 in CA, 6 in TX, 5 in FL
    Expansion: All United States, Canada, Foreign
    Registered: CA,FL,IL,IN,MD,MI,MN,NY,OR,VA,WA,WI,DC,AB
Field Support: CP, EO, ST, SO, $FC, N
    Training: 2 weeks corporate HQ
           4 weeks on-site

Closettec
55 Carnegie Row
Norwood, MA 02062

    Phone: 781-769-9997   Accepts collect calls?
    Toll Free: 800-365-2021   FAX: 781-769-9996
    Internet: www.closettec.com
Suitable Sites: LI
Concentration: 4 in MA, 2 in NY, 2 in OH
    Expansion: All United States
    Registered:
Field Support: EO, ST, SO, FC, H
    Training: 2 weeks Norwood, MA

Construction Industry   Kitchens, Baths, Cabinets

	Bath Fitter	Kitchen Solvers	Kitchen Tune-Up	Kitchen Wizards	Miracle Method	Perma Ceram Enterprises	Reface It Kitchen Systems	Worldwide Refinishing Systems, Inc.
Startup Cost	30K-50K	10.8K	10K-25K	125K-175K	5K-20K	24.5K	75K-140K	25K-50K
Franchise Fee	12.5K	8K-14K	6K-12.5K	12.5K	16.5K	0	15K-27.5K	12.5K
Royalty	0%	6%	4.5-7%	7-3%	5-7.5%	0	4%	3-6%
Advertising Fee	1%	0	0%	2%	3%	0	1%	2%
Financing Provided	N	Y	Y	Y	Y	N	N	Y
Experience Required	N	N			N	N		N
Passive Ownership	N	D	D	A	D		N	D
In Business Since	1984	1982	1975	1991	1979	1974	1989	1970
Franchised Since	1992	1984	1989	1994	1980	1975	1990	1971
Franchised Units 1996								347
1997	45	0	330	26	101		13	397
1998	59	0				186		408
Company Owned 1996								0
1997	2	72	1	0	0		0	0
1998	3	95				1		0
Number of Units U.S.	46	95	330	25	50	172	13	215
Canada	13	0	3	0	0	10	0	13
Foreign	0	0	0	1	51	4	0	180
Projected New U.S.	18	20	20		10			
Canada	6	10						
Foreign		0			5			
Corporate Employees	9	8	10	4	2	25	4	25
Contract Length	5/5	10	10/10	10/10	5		5/5/5	10/5
Expand in Territory	Y	N	Y	Y	N	Y	Y	Y
Full-Time Employees	2-3		1	2	1		1-10	VAR.
Part-Time Employees	1-2		2	2	0			
Conversions	Y	Y	Y	Y	Y		Y	Y
Site Selection Assist.	Y	N	N	Y	N		Y	Y
Lease Negotiation Assist.		N		N	N		N	Y
Site Space Required	500			1800			3500	
Development Agreement	N	N	N	Y	N		N	Y
Develop. Agree. Term				5				
Sub-franchising	N	N	N	Y	N	Y	N	N

Construction Industry

Kitchens, Baths, Cabinets

Bath Fitter

27 Berard Dr #2701
South Burlington, VT 05403
Sell & install custom molded acrylic tub liners, shower bases
    Phone: 802-860-2919   Accepts collect calls?
    Toll Free: 800-892-2847   FAX: 802-862-7976
    Internet: www.bathfitter.com
Suitable Sites: DA, HO, IP, LI, OS
Concentration: 7 in ON, 7 in NY, 6 in PA
    Expansion: NE, Midwest, SE, Canada
    Registered: FL,IL,IN,MD,MI,MN,NY,OR,RI,VA,WA,WI,DC CA AL
Field Support: CP, EO, ST, SO, FC, H, N
    Training: 5 days HQ
            5 days franchisee site

Kitchen Solvers

401 Jay St
La Crosse, WI 54601
Kitchen remodeling services, resurfacing of cabinets & counters
    Phone: 608-791-5520   Accepts collect calls? N
    Toll Free: 800-845-6779   FAX: 608-784-2917
    Internet: www.kitchensolvers.com
Suitable Sites: FB, HO, OS, SC, SF
Concentration: 15 in WI, 12 in IA, 10 in IL
    Expansion: All United States, Canada
    Registered: FL,IL,IN,MD,MI,MN,ND,OR,SD,VA,WA,WI
Field Support: DP, CP, EO, ST, FC, H, N
    Training: 6 days corporate HQ sales & marketing
            hands-on installation
            videos & manuals

Kitchen Tune-Up

813 Circle Dr
Aberdeen, SD 57401-3349
Cabinet & nook restoration, new cabinet doors, custom cabinets
    Phone: 605-225-4049   Accepts collect calls?
    Toll Free: 800-333-6385   FAX: 605-225-1371
    Internet: www.ncrtv.com/~kituneup
Suitable Sites:
Concentration: 17 in CA, 12 in IL, 12 in CO
    Expansion: All United States, Canada
    Registered: CA,FL,HI,IL,IN,MD,MI,MN,ND,NY,OR,SD,VA,WA,WI
Field Support: DP, CP, EO, ST, IC, $FC, H, N
    Training: 6 days home office
            5 days on-site

Kitchen Wizards

1020 N University Park Dr
Waco, TX 76707

    Phone: 254-745-2488   Accepts collect calls?
    Toll Free: 800-893-6777   FAX: 254-745-2573
    Internet:
Suitable Sites: FB, SC, SF
Concentration: 6 in TX, 3 in WA, 2 in IL
    Expansion: All United States, Canada, Foreign
    Registered: CA,FL,HI,IL,IN,MD,MI,MN,ND,NY,OR,RI,SD,VA,WA,WI,DC
Field Support: DP, EO, $ST, SO, FC, H, N
    Training: 3 days corporate training
            5 days model locations
            3 days owner's location

Miracle Method

4239 N Nevada #110
Colorado Springs, CO 80907
Bath & kitchen refinishing, bathtubs, tile, showers, countertops
    Phone: 719-594-9196   Accepts collect calls? Y
    Toll Free: 800-444-8827   FAX: 719-594-9282
    Internet: www.miraclemethodusa.com
Suitable Sites: FB, HO, IP, LI, SF, WR
Concentration: 13 in CA, 4 in TX, 2 in CT
    Expansion: All United States, Canada, Foreign
    Registered: CA,FL,RI,WA
Field Support: EO, ST, FC, H, N
    Training: 10 days on-site
            1 week regional location

Perma Ceram Enterprises

65 Smithtown Blvd
Smithtown, NY 11788
Bathroom & kitchen reglazing
    Phone: 516-724-1205   Accepts collect calls? Y
    Toll Free: 800-645-5039   FAX: 516-724-9626
    Internet:
Suitable Sites: HO, OC, SF
Concentration:
    Expansion: All United States, Canada, Foreign
    Registered: CA,FL,HI,IL,IN,MD,MI,MN,ND,NY,OR,RI,SD,VA,WA,WI,DC
Field Support:
    Training:

Reface It Kitchen Systems

5506-C Nielson Rd
Ferndale, WA 98248

    Phone: 360-384-3546   Accepts collect calls?
    Toll Free: FAX: 360-384-0246
    Internet:
Suitable Sites: HO, WR
Concentration: 5 in WA, 5 in CO, 3 in OR
    Expansion: NW, SE, Mountain States, TX
    Registered: CA,HI,OR,WA
Field Support: ST, FC, N
    Training: 1-2 weeks Ferndale, WA

Worldwide Refinishing Systems, Inc.

1020 N University Parks Dr
Waco, TX 76707
Bath & kitchen-remodeling options, refinish & recolor tub/wall
    Phone: 254-745-2477   Accepts collect calls? N
    Toll Free: 800-253-9153   FAX: 254-745-2588
    Internet: www.wwrefinishing.com
Suitable Sites: DA, HO, LI, OC, OS, SC
Concentration: 11 in FL, 23 in TX, 13 in IL
    Expansion: All United States, Canada, Foreign
    Registered: CA,FL,HI,IL,IN,MD,MI,MN,ND,NY,OR,RI,SD,VA,WA,WI,DC
Field Support: CP, EO, ST, FC, H, N
    Training: 2 weeks orientation manual
            1 week business
            2 weeks hands-on at HQ

Construction Industry   Repair, Reconstruction

	Guardsman WoodPro	Rich's Chimney Fix-It	The Screenmobile						
Startup Cost	12K-25K	17.1K-52.9K	56.3K						
Franchise Fee	12K-18K	15K-17.5K	25K						
Royalty	6-8%	1K/MO	5%						
Advertising Fee	1%		0%						
Financing Provided	Y	Y	Y						
Experience Required									
Passive Ownership	D		D						
In Business Since	1900	1977	1980						
Franchised Since	1984	1997	1982						
Franchised Units 1996									
1997	80	0	50						
1998									
Company Owned 1996		1							
1997	0	1	2						
1998									
Number of Units U.S.	72		52						
Canada	8		0						
Foreign	0		0						
Projected New U.S.									
Canada									
Foreign									
Corporate Employees	60		6						
Contract Length	10/10		5/5						
Expand in Territory	Y		Y						
Full-Time Employees	2		1						
Part-Time Employees									
Conversions	Y								
Site Selection Assist.	N		Y						
Lease Negotiation Assist.			N						
Site Space Required			1000						
Development Agreement	Y		N						
Develop. Agree. Term	VAR								
Sub-franchising	Y		N						

Construction Industry

Repair, Reconstruction

Guardsman WoodPro
4999 36th St SE
Grand Rapids, MI 49512

Phone: 616-285-7877   Accepts collect calls?
Toll Free: 800-496-6377   FAX: 616-285-7882
Internet: www.guardsmanwoodpro.com
Suitable Sites:
Concentration: MI, PA, VA
   Expansion: All United States, Canada
   Registered: CA,FL,HI,IL,IN,MD,MI,MN,ND,NY,OR,RI,SD,VA,WA,WI,DC
Field Support: DP, CP, EO, ST, FC, H, N
   Training: 2 weeks Grand Rapids MI

Rich's Chimney Fix-It
15965 Jeanette St
Southfield, MI 48075
Masonry repair/chimney & fireplace maint
   Phone: 248-559-1415   Accepts collect calls?
   Toll Free: FAX:
   Internet:
Suitable Sites:
Concentration:
   Expansion: MI
   Registered: MI
Field Support:
   Training:

The Screenmobile
457 W Allen Ave #107
San Dimas, CA 91773

Phone: 909-394-4581   Accepts collect calls?
Toll Free: FAX: 909-394-0273
   Internet: www.screenmobile.com
Suitable Sites: HO
Concentration: CA, AZ, CO
   Expansion: All United States, Canada
   Registered: CA,OR
Field Support: ST, SO, IC, FC, N
   Training: 6 days palm springs, CA
             2 days on-site

Construction Industry   Windows, Doors, Siding

	ABC Seamless	Garage Door Franchise	United States Seamless, Inc. Schumacher					
Startup Cost	73.8K-212K	30K-70K	49K-97K					
Franchise Fee	12K	15K	8.5K					
Royalty	2-5%	5%						
Advertising Fee	.05%	0%	.5-.125%					
Financing Provided	Y	Y	Y					
Experience Required	Y	N	N					
Passive Ownership	D	A	N					
In Business Since	1973	1987	1992					
Franchised Since	1978	1997	1992					
Franchised Units 1996			73					
1997	126	0	82					
1998		0	93					
Company Owned 1996			9					
1997	6	1	10					
1998		1	10					
Number of Units U.S.	132	1	92					
Canada	0	0	0					
Foreign	0	0	0					
Projected New U.S.		1	15					
Canada			0					
Foreign			0					
Corporate Employees	50	2	10					
Contract Length	10/10	15/15	15/15					
Expand in Territory	Y	Y	Y					
Full-Time Employees	4	1	3					
Part-Time Employees								
Conversions	Y	Y	Y					
Site Selection Assist.	N	N	N					
Lease Negotiation Assist.	Y	N	N					
Site Space Required			2000					
Development Agreement	Y	Y	N					
Develop. Agree. Term		15						
Sub-franchising	N	N	N					

Construction Industry   Windows, Doors, Siding

ABC Seamless
> 3001 Fiechtner Dr
> Fargo, ND 58103
> Seamless steel siding, seamless steel gutters
>> Phone: 701-293-5952   Accepts collect calls? N
>> Toll Free: 800-732-6577   FAX: 701-293-3107
>> Internet: www.abcseamless.com
> Suitable Sites:
> Concentration: 22 in MN, 16 in WI, 12 in IL
>> Expansion: All United States
>> Registered: CA,FL,HI,IL,IN,MD,MI,MN,ND,NY,OR,RI,SD,VA,WA,WI,DC
> Field Support: EO, ST, SO, FC, H, N
>> Training: 2 weeks franchisee's site

Schumacher Garage Door Franchise
> PO Box 891780
> Temecula, CA 92589
> Repair & sales of residential garage door openers, door repair
>> Phone: Accepts collect calls? N
>> Toll Free: 800-671-0977   FAX: 909-678-9880
>> Internet: www.pe.net/~shoe
> Suitable Sites: HO
> Concentration: 1 in CA
>> Expansion: All United States, Canada, Foreign
>> Registered: CA
> Field Support: DP, EO, ST, SO, IC, FC, H
>> Training: 2 weeks riverside, CA

United States Seamless, Inc.
> 2001 1st Ave N
> Fargo, ND 58102-2426
> Home improvement specializing in seamless steel siding
>> Phone: 701-241-8888   Accepts collect calls?
>> Toll Free: FAX: 701-241-9999
>> Internet: www.usseamless.com
> Suitable Sites: HO, K, OS, WR
> Concentration: 9 in ND, 33 in MN, 17 in WI
>> Expansion: All United States
>> Registered: IL,IN,MI,MN,ND,OR,SD,WA,WI
> Field Support: CP, ST, IC, FC, H, N
>> Training: 1 week Fargo, ND

Construction Industry   Other Construction (Spread 1 of 2)

	American Concrete Raising	Archadeck	Arthur Rutenberg Homes	B-Dry System	Castart	Certa Propainters Ltd	Dec-K-ing	Decorating Den Painting & Home Imp
Startup Cost	50K-75K	39.5K-93.3K	350K-600K	40K-74K	12.7K-50.6K	21K-35K		4.35K-8.9K
Franchise Fee	15K	16.5K-30K	60K	15K-60K	12.8K-48K	15K		3.9K-7.9K
Royalty	6%	4-7%	3.50%	6%	VAR.	TO 1K/MO	0	$400-1K/MO
Advertising Fee	0%	1%	0%	0%				
Financing Provided	N	Y	N	Y	N	N	N	N
Experience Required							N	
Passive Ownership	D	D	A	D				
In Business Since	1983	1980	1980	1958	1995	1992	1978	1994
Franchised Since	1989	1985	1980	1978	1997	1992	1985	1996
Franchised Units 1996						167		4
1997	3	60	29	63	0	189		9
1998								
Company Owned 1996					0	1	2	0
1997	1	0	0	5	1	1	2	0
1998							2	
Number of Units U.S.	4	60	29	68				
Canada	0	0	0	0				
Foreign	0	0	0	0				
Projected New U.S.		7						
Canada								
Foreign		1						
Corporate Employees	4	23	80	10			5	
Contract Length	10/10	10/20	10	5/5				
Expand in Territory	Y	Y		Y			Y	
Full-Time Employees	4	1	VAR	6				
Part-Time Employees	3	1		1				
Conversions		N	N	N				
Site Selection Assist.	N	N	Y	N			N	
Lease Negotiation Assist.	N			N			N	
Site Space Required				4000				
Development Agreement	N	N	N	N				
Develop. Agree. Term								
Sub-franchising	N	N	N	N			N	

Construction Industry

Other Construction (Spread 1 of 2)

American Concrete Raising
916 Westwood Ave
Addison, IL 60101

Phone: 630-543-5775	Accepts collect calls?
Toll Free:	FAX: 630-543-5930
Internet:	

Suitable Sites:
Concentration: 2 in IL, 2 in OH
   Expansion: Eastern United States, Canada
   Registered: IL
Field Support: CP, EO, ST, FC
   Training: 2-3 weeks Chicago, IL
      1-2 weeks on-site

Archadeck
2112 W Laburnam Ave #100
Richmond, VA 23227

Phone: 804-353-6999	Accepts collect calls? N
Toll Free: 800-722-4668	FAX: 804-358-1878
Internet: www.archadeck.com	

Suitable Sites:
Concentration: 8 in GA, 8 in PA, 6 in OH
   Expansion: All United States, Canada
   Registered: CA,FL,IL,IN,MD,MI,MN,NY,OR,RI,VA,WA,WI
Field Support: $CP, EO, ST, FC, H, N
   Training: 4 weeks Richmond, VA

Arthur Rutenberg Homes
13922 58th St N
Clearwater, FL 34760

Phone: 813-536-5900	Accepts collect calls?
Toll Free: 800-274-6637	FAX: 813-538-9089
Internet:	

Suitable Sites:
Concentration: 28 in FL, 1 in AL
   Expansion: Florida
   Registered:
Field Support: DP, CP, EO, ST, FC, H
   Training: y

B-Dry System
1341 Copley Rd
Akron, OH 44320

Phone: 330-867-2576	Accepts collect calls?
Toll Free: 800-321-0985	FAX: 330-867-7693
Internet:	

Suitable Sites: FB, HO
Concentration: 10 in OH, 8 in PA, 7 in NY
   Expansion: NE, NW
   Registered:
Field Support: CP, EO, ST, IC, $FC, H, N
   Training: 2 weeks national office Akron, OH
      2 weeks on-site
      1-2 days on-going regional seminar

Castart
1041 E Miles St
Tucson, AZ 85719
Decorative rock install for pools/waterfalls

Phone:	Accepts collect calls?
Toll Free: 800-871-8838	FAX:
Internet:	

Suitable Sites:
Concentration:
   Expansion: All United States, Canada, Foreign
   Registered:
Field Support:
   Training:

Certa Propainters Ltd
1140 Valley Forge Rd
Valley Forge, PA 19482
Residential & commercial painting

Phone: 610-983-9411	Accepts collect calls?
Toll Free: 800-452-3782	FAX:
Internet:	

Suitable Sites:
Concentration:
   Expansion: All United States, Canada, Foreign
   Registered:
Field Support:
   Training:

Dec-K-ing
19292 60th Ave #119
Surrey, BC V3S-8E5 CANADA
Deck products, waterproofing membranes & railings for deck/patio

Phone: 604-530-0050	Accepts collect calls?
Toll Free: 800-804-6288	FAX: 604-530-4466
Internet: www.dec-k-ing.com	

Suitable Sites: HO, LI
Concentration: BC, ALTA, QUE
   Expansion: All United States, Canada, Foreign
   Registered:
Field Support:
   Training:

Decorating Den Painting & Home Imp
19100 Montgomery Ave
Burtonsville, MD 20866
Painting & home-improvement services

Phone: 301-272-1500	Accepts collect calls?
Toll Free:	FAX:
Internet:	

Suitable Sites:
Concentration:
   Expansion: MD,VA, Canada
   Registered:
Field Support:
   Training:

Construction Industry　　　　　　　　　　Other Construction (Spread 2 of 2)

	Diamond Seal Inc	ElDorado Stone	Four Seasons Sunrooms	Handyman Connection	Insulated Dry Roof Systems	Permacrete Systems	Superior Walls of America	United Energy Partners
Startup Cost	6.8K	80K-149K	13.3K-82.5K	45K-100K	35K-65K	18.5K-35K	250K-750K	75K-80K
Franchise Fee	7.5K+	50K	7.5K-15K	25K-75K	25K-50K	18.5K	30K	36K
Royalty	6%	5%/10C/SF	0%	4-5%	3%/$300	5%	4%	2-8.5%
Advertising Fee	3%	$0	0%	0%	N/A	0%	0%	1.5%
Financing Provided	Y	N	N	Y	Y	Y	Y	Y
Experience Required	N		N					
Passive Ownership	A	D	D	D	A	D	D	D
In Business Since	1994	1969	1974	1990	1986	1980	1981	1991
Franchised Since	1997	1969	1985	1993	1989	1990	1985	1995
Franchised Units 1996	0							
1997	4	26	232	62	28	19	16	7
1998	22							
Company Owned 1996	1							
1997	1	0	2	1	0	2	0	2
1998	0							
Number of Units U.S.	22	14	175	48	27	4	15	9
Canada		1	12	15	1	16	0	0
Foreign		11	47	0	0	1	1	0
Projected New U.S.	25							
Canada								
Foreign								
Corporate Employees	5	8	240	4	20	7	10	5
Contract Length	8/7	10/10	10/10	10/10/10	5/5	5/5	10/10	10/10
Expand in Territory		Y	Y	Y	N	Y	Y	Y
Full-Time Employees	1	6+	2	2	5	1	8	1
Part-Time Employees	1		2			1	2	1
Conversions			Y				N	
Site Selection Assist.		Y	Y	Y	Y	N	Y	N
Lease Negotiation Assist.		N	N		N	N		
Site Space Required		5000-8000	750	500-600	1000		10000	100
Development Agreement		Y	N	Y	N	N	N	N
Develop. Agree. Term		10		7				
Sub-franchising	N	N	N	Y	N	N	N	N

Construction Industry   Other Construction (Spread 2 of 2)

Diamond Seal Inc
1290 W 2320 South #B
Salt Lake City, UT 84119
Glass/tile/granite sealant system
    Phone: 801-975-9988   Accepts collect calls? N
    Toll Free: 800-599-9401   FAX: 801-975-9989
    Internet: www.diamondseal.com
Suitable Sites:
Concentration: 6 in UT, 4 in CA
    Expansion: All United States, Canada, Foreign
    Registered: CA,FL,HI,MI,MN,OR,WA
Field Support: EO, ST, $FC, H, N
    Training: 1 week Salt Lake City, UT

ElDorado Stone
PO Box 489 4190 Tolt Ave N E
Carnation, WA 98014

    Phone: 425-333-6722   Accepts collect calls?
    Toll Free: 800-925-1491   FAX: 425-333-4755
    Internet: www.eldoradostone.com
Suitable Sites: FB
Concentration: 2 in PA, 1 in OH, 1 in CA
    Expansion: All United States, Canada, Foreign
    Registered: CA,FL,IL,MN,WA,WI,DC
Field Support: CP, EO, ST, FC, H, N
    Training: 4-5 days training facility WA
             4-5 days franchisee's facility

Four Seasons Sunrooms
5005 Veterans Memorial Hwy
Holbrook, NY 11741
Sunrooms, solariums, conservatories and porch enclosures
    Phone: 516-563-4000   Accepts collect calls?
    Toll Free: 800-521-0179   FAX: 516-563-4010
    Internet: www.four-seasons-sunrooms.com
Suitable Sites: SF
Concentration: 17 in CA, 21 in NY, 16 in PA
    Expansion: All United States, Canada, Foreign
    Registered: CA,FL,HI,IL,IN,MD,MI,MN,ND,NY,OR,RI,SD,VA,WA,WI,DC
Field Support: EO, ST, SO, IC, FC, H, N
    Training: 5 days Holbrook, NY
             5 days Hayward, CA
             5 days regionally

Handyman Connection
227 Northland Blvd
Cincinnati, OH 45246

    Phone: 513-771-1122   Accepts collect calls?
    Toll Free: 800-466-5530   FAX: 513-771-6439
    Internet: www.handymanconnection.com
Suitable Sites: FB
Concentration: 7 in OH, 4 in TX, 4 in MI
    Expansion: All United States, Canada, Foreign
    Registered:
Field Support: DP, EO, ST, SO, FC, H, N
    Training: 2 weeks flagship Cincinnati, OH
             1 week franchisee location

Insulated Dry Roof Systems
152 SE 5th Ave
Hillsboro, OR 97123

    Phone: 503-693-1619   Accepts collect calls? N
    Toll Free: 800-779-1357   FAX: 503-693-1993
    Internet: www.dryroof.com
Suitable Sites:
Concentration: 6 in WA, 3 in OR, 2 in ID
    Expansion: All United States
    Registered: IL,IN,MN,ND,OR,SD,WA
Field Support: DP, $CP, EO, ST, $FC, H, N
    Training: 4 days HQ
             4-7 days on-site

Permacrete Systems
21 Williams Ave
Dartmouth, NS B3B-1X3 CANADA

    Phone: 902-468-1700   Accepts collect calls?
    Toll Free: 800-565-5325   FAX: 902-468-7474
    Internet:
Suitable Sites: HO
Concentration: 7 in NS, 4 in NB, 2 in AB
    Expansion: All United States, Foreign
    Registered: AB
Field Support: DP, EO, ST, FC, H, N
    Training: 2 weeks head office Dartmouth, NS

Superior Walls of America
PO Box 427
Ephrata, PA 17522

    Phone: 717-626-9255   Accepts collect calls?
    Toll Free: 800-452-9255   FAX: 717-626-7319
    Internet: www.superiorwalls.com
Suitable Sites:
Concentration: 8 in PA, 2 in NY, 1 in IA
    Expansion: All United States, Canada, Foreign
    Registered: IN,NY
Field Support: CP, $EO, $ST, FC, N
    Training: 1 week corporate office
             2 weeks field location

United Energy Partners
461 Sovereign Ct
St Louis, MO 63011

    Phone: 314-230-9900   Accepts collect calls?
    Toll Free: 800-467-8887   FAX: 314-230-3020
    Internet: www.unitedenergy.com
Suitable Sites: HO
Concentration: 3 in MO, 2 in IL, 2 in IN
    Expansion: All United States
    Registered: CA,FL,HI,IL,IN,MD,MI,MN,ND,NY,OR,RI,SD,VA,WA,WI,DC
Field Support: DP, CP, EO, ST, SO, IC, FC, H, N
    Training: 2 weeks St. Louis, MO
             1 week home

Consumer Service Industry   Consumer Finance

	Ace America's Cash Express	Cash Plus	Cash Converters USA	Checkcare Systems	Fast Bucks Development LLC	United Capital Mortgage Assistance	United Check Cashing	X-Bankers Check Cashing
Startup Cost	129.6K-187.3K	75K-100K	N/A	110K-169K	26.65K-63K	6.5K-13.6K	110K-135K	65K
Franchise Fee	15K-30K	17.5K	N/A	12.5K-45K	20K	6.99K	19.5K	14.5K
Royalty	5%/$750 MIN	6%	N/A	5%	5%	5%	.2% VOLUME	3%
Advertising Fee	3%	3%	N/A	.5%				0
Financing Provided	Y	Y	N	Y	N	N	Y	Y
Experience Required		N						N
Passive Ownership	D	A	A	D			D	A
In Business Since	1968	1985	1995	1982	1986	1996	1977	1992
Franchised Since	1996	1988	1995	1984	1994	1997	1991	1992
Franchised Units 1996					9			3
1997	95	21	11	71	15	0	70	2
1998		32						2
Company Owned 1996					0	0		4
1997	645	1	0	0	2	1	5	5
1998		2						6
Number of Units U.S.	740	33	10	71			75	6
Canada	0	1	38	0			0	0
Foreign	0	0	385	0			0	0
Projected New U.S.		60						8
Canada		15						0
Foreign								0
Corporate Employees		5	10	20			15	4
Contract Length	10/5	5/5	10/10	7/7			15/15	10/5/5
Expand in Territory	Y	Y	Y	N			Y	Y
Full-Time Employees	2	1	5-8	13			2	1
Part-Time Employees	1	2	1-2	2				0
Conversions	Y	Y	N	Y			Y	Y
Site Selection Assist.	Y	Y	Y	Y			Y	Y
Lease Negotiation Assist.	Y	Y	Y	N			Y	Y
Site Space Required	1500	1200	3000-6000	2000			1000	1000
Development Agreement	Y	Y	Y	Y			Y	N
Develop. Agree. Term		5	10	1				
Sub-franchising	N	N	Y	N			N	Y

Consumer Service Industry   ## Consumer Finance

Ace America's Cash Express
1231 Greenway Dr #800
Irving, TX 75038

Phone: 972-753-2307   Accepts collect calls?
Toll Free: 800-713-3338   FAX: 972-582-1406
Internet: www.aceashexpress.com
Suitable Sites: SC
Concentration: 237 in TX, 53 in AZ, 44 in MD
Expansion: Canada
Registered: CA,MI,NY,ND,RI,SD,WA,WI
Field Support: SO, FC, H, N
Training: 1 day corp HQ in Dallas
2 weeks Dallas

Ca$h Plus
3002 Dow Ave #510
Tustin, CA 92780
Retail financial centers; small loans, check cashing, wire xfers
Phone: 714-731-2274   Accepts collect calls? Y
Toll Free: 888-707-2274   FAX: 714-731-2099
Internet: www.cashplusinc.com
Suitable Sites: AC, FB, PC, SC, SF
Concentration: 30 in CA, 3 in NV, 1 in FL
Expansion: West, SE, NW, Midwest, SE, Canada
Registered: CA,WA
Field Support: $DP, $CP, EO, ST, SO, IC, $FC, H, N
Training: 1 week Anaheim, CA
3 days franchisee store

Cash Converters USA
Zurich Towers #1350 1450 E American Ln
Schaumburg, IL 60173-4989

Phone: 847-330-1122   Accepts collect calls?
Toll Free: 888-910-2274   FAX: 847-330-1660
Internet: www.cashconverters.com
Suitable Sites: RM, SC, SF
Concentration: 4 in IL, 4 in MA, 1 in WA
Expansion: All United States, Canada, Foreign
Registered: CA,FL,HI,IL,IN,MI,MN,NY,OR,RI,VA,WA
Field Support: EO, ST, SO, IC, $FC, H, N
Training: 200 hours in-store & at corp office

Checkcare Systems
PO Box 9636
Columbus, GA 31908

Phone: 706-596-1306   Accepts collect calls?
Toll Free: FAX: 706-596-0337
Internet:
Suitable Sites: OC
Concentration: 7 in GA, 6 in FL, 5 in TX
Expansion: West Coast, NE, Canada
Registered: CA,FL,IL,IN,MD,MI,MN,VA,DC
Field Support: $CP, $EO, $ST, $SO, $FC, N
Training: 2 weeks Columbus, GA

Fast Bucks Development LLC
4408 N 70th St
Lincoln, NE 68507
Check cashing services
Phone: Accepts collect calls?
Toll Free: 800-814-9660   FAX:
Internet:
Suitable Sites:
Concentration:
Expansion: IN,SD,WA
Registered:
Field Support:
Training:

United Capital Mortgage Assistance
1300 Mercantile Ln, #126c
Largo, MD 20774
Foreclosure prevention services
Phone: 301-386-8803   Accepts collect calls?
Toll Free: FAX:
Internet:
Suitable Sites:
Concentration:
Expansion: All United States
Registered:
Field Support:
Training:

United Check Cashing
325 Chestnut St #1005
Philadelphia, PA 19106

Phone: 215-238-0300   Accepts collect calls?
Toll Free: 800-626-0787   FAX: 215-238-9056
Internet:
Suitable Sites: FB, RM, SC, SF
Concentration: 42 in PA, 23 in NJ, 3 in DE
Expansion: NJ, OH, MD, VA, FL, GA, NW
Registered: CA,FL,HI,IL,IN,MD,MI,MN,ND,NY,OR,RI,SD,VA,WA,WI,DC
Field Support: DP, EO, ST, SO, FC, H, N
Training: 1 week corporate HQ
1 week on-site

X-Bankers Check Cashing
1155 Main St
Bridgeport, CT 06604
Check cashing and related services
Phone: 203-374-1377   Accepts collect calls? N
Toll Free: 800-873-9226   FAX: 203-336-3075
Internet: xbankers@compuserve.com
Suitable Sites: K, SF
Concentration: 6 in CT
Expansion: All United States
Registered:
Field Support: EO, ST, SO, N
Training: 5 days hands on training in Conn.

Consumer Service Industry   Dating Services

	Calculated Couples	Successful Introduction						
Startup Cost	5.1K-10K	37.7K						
Franchise Fee	5K	19.5K						
Royalty	0	6%						
Advertising Fee	0							
Financing Provided	Y	N						
Experience Required	N							
Passive Ownership	A							
In Business Since	1983	1989						
Franchised Since	1987	1997						
Franchised Units 1996								
1997	9	0						
1998								
Company Owned 1996		1						
1997	6	1						
1998								
Number of Units U.S.	14							
Canada	0							
Foreign	0							
Projected New U.S.								
Canada								
Foreign								
Corporate Employees	2							
Contract Length	2/2							
Expand in Territory	Y							
Full-Time Employees	0							
Part-Time Employees	4							
Conversions	Y							
Site Selection Assist.	Y							
Lease Negotiation Assist.	N							
Site Space Required								
Development Agreement	Y							
Develop. Agree. Term	2							
Sub-franchising	N							

Consumer Service Industry

Calculated Couples
4839 E Greenway Rd
Scottsdale, AZ 85254

    Phone: Accepts collect calls? N
Toll Free: 800-446-2824   FAX:
    Internet: lovedoctor@juno.com
Suitable Sites:
Concentration: 5 in NY, 1 in AZ, 1 in NE
    Expansion: All United States
    Registered: CA,NY
Field Support: $CP, $EO, $ST, $SO, $FC, H, N
    Training: video w/manuals

Successful Introduction
PO Box 165
Scarborough, ME 04070
Professional dating service
    Phone: 207-883-1003   Accepts collect calls?
    Toll Free: FAX:
    Internet:
Suitable Sites:
Concentration:
    Expansion: NE
    Registered:
Field Support:
    Training:

Consumer Service Industry   Dry Cleaning, Laundry (Spread 1 of 2)

	ApparelMaster USA	Cleaners Franchise Inc.	Champion Clean 'N' Press America	Comet One-Hour Cleaners	Dry Cleaning Station	Eagle Cleaners	Ecomat	Harvey Washbangers
Startup Cost	5K-30K	315K-341K	20K-400K	200K-300K	190K-270K	88K-227K	200K-250K	250K-425K
Franchise Fee	15K	25K	9.5K-40K	20K	22.5K	19.95K	18K	20K
Royalty	4%/$200	4%	5%	N/A	2-5%	5% OR $175/WK	6%	5%
Advertising Fee	0%		VAR	N/A	0%	3%	3%	2%
Financing Provided	Y	Y	Y	Y	Y	N	Y	Y
Experience Required						N	N	N
Passive Ownership	D		D	D	D	D	A	D
In Business Since	1971	1993	1991	1960	1987	1991	1992	1986
Franchised Since	1971	1995	1991	1967	1993	1993	1995	1996
Franchised Units 1996		1						
1997	119	9	40	330	11	92	2	2
1998						97	5	
Company Owned 1996		1						
1997	9	2	0	12	3	0	4	1
1998						0	2	
Number of Units U.S.	125		40	329	14	97	7	3
Canada	20		0	0	0	0	0	0
Foreign	3		0	13	0	0	2	0
Projected New U.S.							12	3
Canada							2	0
Foreign							1	0
Corporate Employees	50		6	12	5	16	10	2
Contract Length	10/5-10		10/10	5/5/5	15/2-5	15/10	SELF RENEW	10/10
Expand in Territory	Y		Y	Y	Y	Y	Y	Y
Full-Time Employees	4		VAR	6	4	3	3	4
Part-Time Employees	D		VAR	2-3	2	1	3	6
Conversions	Y		Y	N	N	N	Y	N
Site Selection Assist.	N		Y	Y	Y	Y	Y	Y
Lease Negotiation Assist.	N		Y	Y	Y	Y	Y	Y
Site Space Required	1800		850-3500	1800-2000	2200-4000	1800-2200	1500	4500
Development Agreement	N		Y	N	Y	Y	Y	N
Develop. Agree. Term			VAR		OPEN	10		
Sub-franchising	N		Y	N	N	N	Y	N

Consumer Service Industry

Dry Cleaning, Laundry (Spread 1 of 2)

ApparelMaster USA
PO Box 62687
Cincinnati, OH 45262

Phone: 513-772-7721   Accepts collect calls?
Toll Free: 800-543-1678   FAX: 513-772-5616
Internet:
Suitable Sites: FB, SC, SF
Concentration:
   Expansion: All United States, Canada, Foreign
   Registered: FL,IL,IN,MD,MI,MN,NY,VA,WA,WI
Field Support: $DP, CP, $EO, ST, SO, IC, FC, H, N
   Training: 3 weeks licensee's location

Champion Cleaners Franchise Inc.
5959 Shallowford Rd #215
Chattanooga, TN 37421
Dry cleaning & laundry services
   Phone: 423-899-4185   Accepts collect calls?
Toll Free: 800-357-0797   FAX:
Internet:
Suitable Sites:
Concentration:
   Expansion: Canada, Foreign
   Registered:
Field Support:
   Training:

Clean 'N' Press America
500 Airport Blvd #100
Burlingame, CA 94010

Phone: 650-344-2377   Accepts collect calls?
Toll Free: 800-237-1711   FAX: 650-344-2545
Internet:
Suitable Sites: HO, SC, SF
Concentration: 40 in MN
   Expansion: All United States, Canada
   Registered: CA,MN
Field Support: EO, ST, SO, IC, H
   Training: 3 weeks phoenix AZ or other loc

Comet One-Hour Cleaners
406 W Division St
Arlington, TX 76011

Phone: 817-461-3555   Accepts collect calls?
Toll Free: FAX: 817-861-4779
Internet:
Suitable Sites: SC
Concentration: 212 in TX, 21 in AR, 16 in TN
   Expansion: All United States
   Registered: CA
Field Support: $EO, $ST, SO, N
   Training: 1 week Waco TX
       1 week in store

Dry Cleaning Station
1000 Shelard Pkwy #320
Minneapolis, MN 55426-1053

Phone: 612-541-0832   Accepts collect calls?
Toll Free: 800-655-8134   FAX: 612-542-2246
Internet:
Suitable Sites: FB, SC, SF
Concentration: 5 in MN, 4 in NE
   Expansion: All United States, Canada, Foreign
   Registered: FL,IL,MI,MN
Field Support: CP, EO, ST, SO, FC, H, N
   Training: 10-15 days store and HQ

Eagle Cleaners
1750 University Dr #111
Coral Springs, FL 33071
Providing highest levels of quality drycleaning & superior svc
   Phone: 954-346-9501   Accepts collect calls?
Toll Free: 800-275-9751   FAX: 954-346-9505
Internet:
Suitable Sites: AC, FB, SC
Concentration: CT, NY, FL
   Expansion: East, Midwest, Foreign
   Registered: FL,IL,MI,NY,MD
Field Support: DP, EO, ST, SO, IC, FC, H, N
   Training: 3 weeks coral springs FL
       1 week opening

Ecomat
147 Palmer Ave
Mamaroneck, NY 10543-3632

Phone: 914-777-3600   Accepts collect calls? Y
Toll Free: 800-299-2309   FAX: 914-777-3502
Internet: www.ecomat.com
Suitable Sites: AC, DA, FB, IP, PC, RM, SC, SF
Concentration: NJ, 4 in NY, 1 in TX
   Expansion: All United States, Canada, Foreign
   Registered: CA,FL,IL,MI,NY,VA,WA,DC
Field Support: CP, EO, ST, SO, IC, H
   Training: 2 weeks Mamaroneck NY
       1 week site of franchise

Harvey Washbangers
106 29th Ave N
Nashville, TN 37203

Phone: 615-322-1270   Accepts collect calls?
Toll Free: FAX: 615-322-9930
Internet: www.harveywashbangers.com
Suitable Sites: FB, SC
Concentration: 1 in TN, 1 in CA, 1 in TX
   Expansion: All United States
   Registered: CA,FL
Field Support: DP, EO, ST, SO, IC, $FC, $H, N
   Training: 2 weeks home office
       1 week your store

Consumer Service Industry   Dry Cleaning, Laundry (Spread 2 of 2)

	London Cleaners	Nu-Look 1-Hr. Cleaners	One Hour Martinizing	Pressed 4 Time	Valet Express	Wedding Gown Specialists/Restoration		
Startup Cost	25K	125K-200K+	191K-267K	15K-20K	6K	2.5K+		
Franchise Fee	25K	20K	25K	12.5K	12.5K	N/A		
Royalty	5%	2%	4%	3.5/$300/MO	3.5%	20% FEE		
Advertising Fee	3%	3%	.5%	1%/$30/MO		0%		
Financing Provided	N	Y	Y	N	Y	N		
Experience Required	N							
Passive Ownership	N	D	D	D		D		
In Business Since	1929	1967	1949	1987	1988	1987		
Franchised Since	1983	1967	1949	1990	1993	1987		
Franchised Units 1996	20				12			
1997	21	53	804	90	15	119		
1998	24							
Company Owned 1996	1				1			
1997	2	1	0	0	2	1		
1998	2							
Number of Units U.S.		52	581	66		100		
Canada	26	0	40	0		10		
Foreign		2	183	24		10		
Projected New U.S.								
Canada	4							
Foreign								
Corporate Employees	5	4	17	4		3		
Contract Length	10	20/10	10/10	10/10		1-IND/1		
Expand in Territory	Y	Y	Y	Y		Y		
Full-Time Employees	1	2	2	1		1		
Part-Time Employees	1	2	4			1		
Conversions	Y	Y	Y	Y		N		
Site Selection Assist.	Y	Y	Y	Y		N		
Lease Negotiation Assist.	Y	Y	Y			N		
Site Space Required	500	1200-1400	1200-2000			500-1000		
Development Agreement	N	Y	Y	N		Y		
Develop. Agree. Term			3-20			1-INDE		
Sub-franchising	N	Y	Y	N		N		

Consumer Service Industry   **Dry Cleaning, Laundry (Spread 2 of 2)**

London Cleaners
21 Amber St #12
Markham, ON L3R-4Z3   CANADA

Phone: 905-475-1350   Accepts collect calls?
Toll Free: FAX: 905-475-7249
Internet:
Suitable Sites: AC, DA, M, SC
Concentration: 26 in ONT
 Expansion: Canada
 Registered:
Field Support: CP, ST, SO, IC, FC, N
 Training:

One Hour Martinizing
2005 Ross Ave
Cincinnati, OH 45212-2009

Phone: 513-351-6211   Accepts collect calls?
Toll Free: 800-827-0345   FAX: 513-731-5513
Internet: www.martinizing.com
Suitable Sites: FB, SC
Concentration: 99 in MI, 88 in CA, 48 in TX
 Expansion: All United States, Canada, Foreign
 Registered: CA,FL,HI,IL,IN,MD,MI,MN,ND,NY,OR,RI,SD,VA,WA,WI,DC
Field Support: EO, $ST, SO, FC, H, N
 Training: 1 week classroom
                2 weeks in-store

Valet Express
10151 University Blvd, #224
Orlando, FL 32817
Dry cleaning delivery service
Phone: Accepts collect calls?
Toll Free: 800-788-1107   FAX:
Internet:
Suitable Sites:
Concentration:
 Expansion: All United States, Canada, Foreign
 Registered:
Field Support:
 Training:

Nu-Look 1-Hr. Cleaners
15 NE Second Ave
Deerfield Beach, FL 33441-3503

Phone: 954-426-1111   Accepts collect calls?
Toll Free: 800-413-7881   FAX: 954-570-6248
Internet:
Suitable Sites: FB, SC
Concentration: 24 in FL, 12 in MD, 10 in VA
 Expansion: All United States, Canada, Foreign
 Registered: FL,MD,VA
Field Support: EO, ST, SO, FC, N
 Training: 4 weeks Deerfield Beach FL

Pressed 4 Time
124 Boston Post Rd
Sudbury, MA 01776

Phone: 978-443-9200   Accepts collect calls?
Toll Free: 800-423-8711   FAX: 978-443-0709
Internet:
Suitable Sites: HO
Concentration: 9 in PA, 5 in CT, 4 in CO
 Expansion: All United States, Canada
 Registered: CA,FL,IL,IN,MD,MI,MN,NY,OR,RI,VA,DC
Field Support: CP, ST, FC, H, N
 Training: 2 days corporate office
                2 days territory

Wedding Gown Specialists/Restoration
48-D King St
Roswell, GA 30075

Phone: 770-998-3111   Accepts collect calls?
Toll Free: 800-543-8987   FAX: 770-682-8736
Internet:
Suitable Sites: FB, HO, RM, SC, SF
Concentration: 7 in OH, 5 in CA, 5 in NC
 Expansion: All United States, Canada
 Registered:
Field Support: $CP, $EO, $ST, $FC, H, N
 Training: not required

Consumer Service Industry   Income Tax

	EconoTax	Electronic Tax Filers	H & R Block	Jackson Hewitt Tax Service	Peyron Tax Service	Triple Check Income Tax Service		
Startup Cost	15K-25K	14.5K		30K-48K	3K-150K	5K-8K		
Franchise Fee	10K	7.5K		25K	3K	0		
Royalty	14%	8%		12%	5%	VAR.		
Advertising Fee	4%	4%		6%				
Financing Provided	Y	Y	Y	Y	Y	Y		
Experience Required		N	N	N				
Passive Ownership	D	D	D	A	A	D		
In Business Since	1965	1990	1955	1986	1960	1941		
Franchised Since	1968	1991	1956	1986	1968	1979		
Franchised Units 1996			4000	1062				
1997	52	31	4000	1296	500	279		
1998		39	4000	2698				
Company Owned 1996			4400	145				
1997	0	1	4600	76	2	2		
1998		1	4800	164				
Number of Units U.S.	52	40		3000	502	281		
Canada	0	0			0	0		
Foreign	0	0			0	1		
Projected New U.S.		10		1000				
Canada								
Foreign								
Corporate Employees	6	VAR		203		35		
Contract Length	5/1	3/17	5	5	VAR./11	5/5		
Expand in Territory	Y	Y	Y	Y	Y	Y		
Full-Time Employees	2	2	1	0	0-2			
Part-Time Employees	2	4	VAR.	10	1			
Conversions		N	N	Y	Y	Y		
Site Selection Assist.	Y	Y	Y	Y	Y	Y		
Lease Negotiation Assist.	N	Y	Y	Y	Y	N		
Site Space Required	800	1000		400	50-200			
Development Agreement	N	N	N	N	Y	N		
Develop. Agree. Term								
Sub-franchising	N	N	N	N	Y	N		

Consumer Service Industry   Income Tax

EconoTax
PO Box 13829
Jackson, MS 38236

    Phone: 601-956-0500   Accepts collect calls?
    Toll Free: 800-748-9106   FAX: 601-956-0583
    Internet: www.econotax.com
Suitable Sites: SC
Concentration: 33 in MI, 8 in AL, 4 in LA
    Expansion: All United States
    Registered: FL
Field Support: CP, ST, FC, H, N
    Training: 1 week Jackson, MI
             1 week on-site

Electronic Tax Filers
PO Box 2077
Cary, NC 27512-2077
Electronic filing to IRS/state & refund anticipation loans
    Phone: 919-469-0651   Accepts collect calls? N
    Toll Free: 800-945-9277   FAX: 919-467-2094
    Internet:
Suitable Sites: FB, RM, SC, SF
Concentration: 8 in NC, 4 in GA, 4 in MI
    Expansion: Eastern United States
    Registered: CA,FL,HI,IL,IN,MD,MI,MN,ND,NY,OR,RI,SD,VA.WA,WI,DC
Field Support: DP, EO, ST, SO, FC, H
    Training: 1 week Cary, NC

H & R Block
4400 Main St
Kansas City, MO 64111
Tax preparation, electronic filing
    Phone: 816-932-7558   Accepts collect calls? N
    Toll Free: FAX: 816-932-8489
    Internet: vhall@hrblock.com
Suitable Sites: AC, DA, FB, K, M, OC, RM, SC, SF
Concentration: ALL US
    Expansion: Planned, Foreign
    Registered: CA,FL,HI,IL,IN,MD,MI,MN,ND,NY,OR,RI,SD,VA,WA,WI,DC,AB
Field Support: CP, EO, ST, FC, H, N
    Training: initial tax training
             ongoing management & operations

Jackson Hewitt Tax Service
4575 Bonney Rd
Virginia Beach, VA 23462
Tax return preparation features custom software, electronic file
    Phone: 757-473-3300   Accepts collect calls? N
    Toll Free: 800-277-3278   FAX: 757-490-7117
    Internet: www.jacksonhewitt.com
Suitable Sites: AC, DA, FB, K, M, RM, SC, SF, OTHER
Concentration: 274 in TX, 227 in FL, 204 in IL
    Expansion: All United States, Canada, Foreign
    Registered: CA,FL,HI,IL,IN,MD,MI,MN,ND,NY,OR,RI,SD,VA,WA,WI,DC
Field Support: DP, CP, EO, ST, SO, FC, H, N
    Training: business mgmt & processing
             advance bus. mgmt
             annual update

Peyron Tax Service
3212 Preston St
Louisville, KY 40213

    Phone: 502-637-7483   Accepts collect calls?
    Toll Free: FAX:
    Internet:
Suitable Sites: FB, HO, RM, SC, SF
Concentration:
    Expansion: All United States
    Registered: CA,FL,HI,IL,IN,MD,MI,MN,ND,NY,OR,RI,SD,VA,WA,WI,DC
Field Support: EO, ST, SO, FC, H, N
    Training: 2 days to 2 weeks on-site

Triple Check Income Tax Service
2441 Honolulu Ave
Montrose, CA 91020

    Phone: 818-236-2944   Accepts collect calls?
    Toll Free: 800-283-1040   FAX: 818-236-2946
    Internet:
Suitable Sites: ES, DA, HO, SC, SF
Concentration: 92 in CA, 24 in FL, 9 in NY
    Expansion: All United States
    Registered: CA,FL,HI,IL,IN,MD,MI,MN,NY,OR,RI,VA,WA,WI,DC
Field Support: $DP, $CP, EO, $FC, H, N
    Training: 80 hours on tape

Consumer Service Industry

Packaging, Mailing, Shipping (Spread 1 of 2)

	Aim Mail Centers	Craters & Freighters	Express One	Handle With Care Packaging Store	Mail Boxes Etc.	Mail Boxes Etc. (Canada)	Pack Mart	Packaging And Shipping Specialist
Startup Cost	70K-90K	54K-76K	20K-250K	48.5K-51K	108.6K-163.7K	110K-135K	5K-75K	56K-85K
Franchise Fee	21.5K	24.8K	20K-250K	21.5K	29.9K	29.9K	1.5K-15K	24.5K
Royalty	1-5%	5%	6%	5%	5%	6%	5%	0%
Advertising Fee	2%	1%		3%	3.5%	2%	1%	0%
Financing Provided	Y	Y	Y	Y	Y	Y	Y	Y
Experience Required	N	N	N					N
Passive Ownership	D	D		N	A	D	D	A
In Business Since	1985	1990	1995	1980	1980	1990	1993	1981
Franchised Since	1989	1991	1996	1984	1980	1990	1995	1988
Franchised Units 1996		17	4					
1997	40	46	14	325	3466	215	1	397
1998	51	54	30					447
Company Owned 1996		1	8					
1997	3	1	4	0	1	1	3	7
1998	1	1	6					7
Number of Units U.S.	52	54	36	315	2903	0	4	447
Canada	0	0		1	197	216	0	10
Foreign	0	0		9	367	0	0	34
Projected New U.S.	24		21					65
Canada								
Foreign								
Corporate Employees	7	12	14	20	275	20		20
Contract Length	15	10/10		PERPETUAL	10/10	10/10	5/5	5/5/5
Expand in Territory	Y	Y	Y	N	Y	Y	Y	Y
Full-Time Employees	1	3		1-2	2	2	1	2
Part-Time Employees	2			1-2	2	1	1	2
Conversions	Y	Y	Y	Y	Y	Y	Y	Y
Site Selection Assist.	Y	Y	Y	Y	Y	Y	Y	Y
Lease Negotiation Assist.	Y	Y	N	N	Y	Y	Y	Y
Site Space Required	1200	1800-2000		1200-1500	1800-2000	1200	100-1000	1000-2000
Development Agreement	Y	N	N	Y	Y	Y	Y	Y
Develop. Agree. Term	5			OPEN	10	10	5	10
Sub-franchising	N	N		N	N	N	Y	N

Consumer Service Industry

Packaging, Mailing, Shipping (Spread 1 of 2)

Aim Mail Centers
20381 Lake Forest Dr #B-2
Lake Forest, CA 92630
Business services
    Phone: 949-837-4151   Accepts collect calls? N
Toll Free: 800-669-4246   FAX: 949-837-4537
Internet: www.aimmailcenters.com
Suitable Sites: AC, IP, OC, PC, SC, SF
Concentration: 47 in CA, 1 in NV, 2 in WA
    Expansion: All United States, Canada
    Registered: CA,FL,WA,IL
Field Support: EO, ST, SO, IC, FC, H, N
    Training: 2 weeks corp HQ
        3 days in store

Craters & Freighters
7000 E 47th Ave Dr #100
Denver, CO 80216
Specialty freight handling services
    Phone: 303-399-8190   Accepts collect calls?
Toll Free: 800-949-9931   FAX: 303-393-7644
Internet: www.cratersandfreighters.com
Suitable Sites: IP, LI, WR
Concentration: 5 in TX, 5 in CA, 5 in FL
    Expansion: All United States
    Registered: CA,FL,IL,NY
Field Support: DP, CP, EO, ST, SO, $FC, H, N
    Training: 7 days home office in Denver CO

Express One
8160 S Highland Dr #A-3
Sandy, UT 84093
Resale of overnight freight services (DHL) w/ other trans. Modes
    Phone: 801-944-1661   Accepts collect calls?
Toll Free: 800-399-3971   FAX: 800-944-4448
Internet:
Suitable Sites: ES, HO, OC
Concentration: 8 in FL, 5 in TX, 5 in CA
    Expansion: All United States, Canada, Foreign
    Registered: CA,FL,IL,OR
Field Support:
    Training: 1 week corp office
        1 week sales in field
        follow up as needed

Handle With Care Packaging Store
5675 Dtc Blvd #280
Englewood, CO 80111

    Phone: 303-741-6626   Accepts collect calls?
Toll Free: 800-525-6309   FAX: 303-741-6653
Internet:
Suitable Sites: SC
Concentration: 57 in CA, 25 in FL, 20 in VA
    Expansion: All United States, Canada
    Registered: CA,FL,HI,IL,IN,MD,MI,MN,ND,NY,OR,RI,SD,VA,WA,WI,DC
Field Support: EO, ST, SO, FC, H, N
    Training: 2 weeks Denver CO
        3 days on-site at opening

Mail Boxes Etc.
6060 Cornerstone Court West
San Diego, CA 92121-3795

    Phone: 619-455-8800   Accepts collect calls?
Toll Free: 800-456-0414   FAX: 619-546-7488
Internet: www.mbe.com
Suitable Sites: FB, SC, OTHER
Concentration: 524 in CA, 245 in FL, 154 in TX
    Expansion: All United States, Canada, Foreign
    Registered: CA,FL,HI,IL,IN,MD,MI,MN,ND,NY,OR,RI,SD,VA,WA,WI,DC
Field Support: $CP, EO, ST, $SO, $FC, $H, N
    Training: 2 weeks San Diego CA
        1 week franchisee's pilot center

Mail Boxes Etc. (Canada)
505 Iroquois Shore Rd #4
Oakville, ON L6H-2R3 CANADA

    Phone: 905-338-9754   Accepts collect calls?
Toll Free: 800-661-6232   FAX: 905-338-7491
Internet: www.mbe.com
Suitable Sites: FB, SC, SF
Concentration:
    Expansion: All United States, Canada, Foreign
    Registered: AB
Field Support: $DP, CP, EO, ST, $SO, $FC, N
    Training: 1 1|2 week centre
        2 weeks corporate office

Pack Mart
13529 Us Hwy #1
Sebastian, FL 32958

    Phone: 407-589-6007   Accepts collect calls?
Toll Free: 800-234-7411   FAX: 561-589-0680
Internet:
Suitable Sites: FB, RM, SC, SF
Concentration: 4 in FL
    Expansion: SE and SE
    Registered: FL
Field Support: EO, $ST, SO, $IC, $FC, H
    Training: 3 weeks Sebastian FL

Packaging And Shipping Specialist
5211 85th St #104
Lubbock, TX 79424
Complete postal shipping & copy center w/ latest technology
    Phone: 806-794-0202   Accepts collect calls? N
Toll Free: 800-877-8884   FAX: 806-794-9997
Internet: www.packship.com
Suitable Sites: AC, DA, FB, K, M, PC, RM, SC, SF
Concentration: 110 in TX, 25 in NY, 20 in IL
    Expansion: All United States, Canada, Foreign
    Registered: CA,FL,HI,IL,IN,MD,MI,MN,ND,NY,OR,RI,SD,VA,WA,WI,DC
Field Support: CP, EO, ST, SO, $FC, H, N
    Training: 7-14 days Chicago IL
        7-14 days Lubbock TX

Consumer Service Industry — Packaging, Mailing, Shipping (Spread 2 of 2)

	Pak Mail Centers (Canada)	Pak Mail Centers of America	Parcel Plus	Mailbox & Business Centers / Pony	Postal Annex+	Postal & Business Centers / Postnet	Unishippers Association
Startup Cost	90K-115K	58K-103K	70K-90K	65K-75K	89K-125K	85K-120K	10K-100K
Franchise Fee	25K	24K	21.5K	3K	23.9K	24.9K	10K-50K
Royalty	6%	5%	4%	$3K/YR	5%	3%	16.50%
Advertising Fee	2%	2%	1%	N/A	2%	2%	1% GROSS
Financing Provided	Y	Y	Y	Y	Y	Y	Y
Experience Required		N					
Passive Ownership	N	A	D	N	A	N	A
In Business Since	1995	1983	1986	1982	1985	1985	1987
Franchised Since	1996	1984	1988	1986	1986	1993	1987
Franchised Units 1996		300					
1997	15	320	136	46	200	430	295
1998		350					
Company Owned 1996		0					
1997	0	0	0	1	2	2	2
1998		0					
Number of Units U.S.	0	320	136	47	201	275	296
Canada	15	8	0	0	0	15	0
Foreign	0	22	0	0	1	142	1
Projected New U.S.		54					
Canada		5					
Foreign		10					
Corporate Employees	4	18	11	5	18	35	35
Contract Length	10/10	10/10	10/10	6/5	15/15	10/10	5/5
Expand in Territory	Y	Y	Y	Y	Y	N	N
Full-Time Employees	2	1	1	1	1	3	1
Part-Time Employees	2	1	2	1	2		
Conversions	Y	Y	Y	N	Y	Y	
Site Selection Assist.	Y	Y	Y	Y	Y	Y	N
Lease Negotiation Assist.	Y	Y	Y	Y	Y	Y	N
Site Space Required	1000	1200	1000	1200	1200	1000	
Development Agreement	Y	Y	Y	Y	Y	Y	N
Develop. Agree. Term	5	5	10	5	15		
Sub-franchising	N	N	N	N	Y	Y	Y

Consumer Service Industry

Packaging, Mailing, Shipping (Spread 2 of 2)

Pak Mail Centers (Canada)
4699 Keele St #4
North York, ON M3J-2N8 CANADA

    Phone: 416-663-5995   Accepts collect calls?
  Toll Free: 800-387-8335   FAX: 416-663-4939
    Internet: www.pakmail.com
Suitable Sites: FB, SC, SF
Concentration: 10 in ON, 2 in AB, 2 in SK
  Expansion: N/A, Canada
  Registered: AB
Field Support: CP, EO, ST, SO, $FC, N
  Training: 10 days Denver CO
       1 week on-site

Pak Mail Centers of America
3033 S Parker Rd #1200
Aurora, CO 80014-2934
One stop packaging, shipping & business support svcs, internet
    Phone: 303-752-3500   Accepts collect calls? N
  Toll Free: 800-833-2821   FAX: 303-755-9721
    Internet: www.pakmail.com
Suitable Sites: AC, DA, FB, IP, LI, OC, SC, SF, WR
Concentration: 78 in FL, 37 in GA, 20 in CA
  Expansion: All United States, Canada, Foreign
  Registered: CA,FL,HI,IL,IN,MD,MI,MN,ND,NY,OR,RI,SD,VA,WA,WI,DC
Field Support: DP, CP, EO, ST, SO, FC, H, N
  Training: 10 days aurora CO
       3 days existing store
       3 days in-store

Parcel Plus
2661 Riva Rd Bldg 1000 Ste 1022
Annapolis, MD 21401-8405

    Phone: 410-266-3200   Accepts collect calls?
  Toll Free: 800-662-5553   FAX: 410-266-3266
    Internet: www.parcelplus.com
Suitable Sites: SC
Concentration: 30 in VA, 29 in MD, 15 in TX
  Expansion: All United States
  Registered: CA,FL,IL,MD,MI,NY,VA,WA,WI,DC
Field Support: EO, ST, SO, FC, H, N
  Training: 1 week orientation @ nat sup ctr
       2 weeks cargo training
       2 weeks stores

Pony Mailbox & Business Centers
13110 NE 177th Place
Woodinville, WA 98072

    Phone: 425-483-0360   Accepts collect calls?
  Toll Free: 800-767-7668   FAX: 425-486-6495
    Internet:
Suitable Sites: FB, RM, SC, SF
Concentration: TN
  Expansion: All United States
  Registered: FL,IL,MD,MN,OR,WA
Field Support: EO, ST, $SO, H, N
  Training: 5-8 days home office

Postal Annex+
9050 Friars Rd #400
San Diego, CA 92108

    Phone: 619-563-4800   Accepts collect calls?
  Toll Free: 800-456-1525   FAX: 619-563-9850
    Internet:
Suitable Sites: SC, SF
Concentration: 120 in CA, 15 in OR, 15 in MI
  Expansion: All United States, Canada, Foreign
  Registered: CA,FL,IL,MD,MI,NY,OR,WA,WI,DC
Field Support: DP, CP, EO, ST, SO, IC, $FC, H, N
  Training: 2 weeks San Diego CA

Postnet Postal & Business Centers
2501 N Green Valley Pkwy #101
Henderson, NV 89014

    Phone: 702-792-7100   Accepts collect calls?
  Toll Free: 800-841-7171   FAX: 702-792-7115
    Internet: www.postnet.net
Suitable Sites: SC
Concentration: 16 in CA, 14 in IL, 10 in NY
  Expansion: All United States, Canada, Foreign
  Registered: CA,FL,HI,IL,IN,MD,MI,MN,ND,NY,OR,RI,SD,VA,WA,WI,DC
Field Support: EO, ST, SO, IC, FC, H, N
  Training: 3-5 days training center
       1 week on-site
       1-2 days follow-up on-site

Unishippers Association
2595 E 3300 S
Salt Lake City, UT 84109

    Phone: 801-487-0600   Accepts collect calls?
  Toll Free: 800-999-8721   FAX: 801-487-0920
    Internet: www.unishippers.com
Suitable Sites:
Concentration: 27 in CA, 20 in NY, 20 in TX
  Expansion: N, Canada, Foreign
  Registered: CA,FL,HI,IN,MD,MI,MN,NY,ND,OR,RI,SD,VA,WA,WI,DC
Field Support: EO, ST, $FC, H, N
  Training: 1 week Salt Lake City UT
       2 days franchisee's location

Consumer Service Industry   Personal Services

	A Quicki Services	English Butler Canada	Home Helpers	Homewatch Caregivers			
Startup Cost	5K-150K	250K	7.6K-15.7K	15K-30K			
Franchise Fee	7.5K-17.5K	25K	13.9K-23.9K	21.5K			
Royalty	4%	6%	4-7%	5%			
Advertising Fee	2%	.5%	3%	0%			
Financing Provided	Y	Y	Y	N			
Experience Required	N		N	N			
Passive Ownership	A	D		A			
In Business Since	1984	1984	1997	1973			
Franchised Since	1989	1994	1997	1986			
Franchised Units 1996							
1997		14	0	22			
1998			45	6			
Company Owned 1996			0				
1997		6	0	4			
1998			1	1			
Number of Units U.S.		0	1	25			
Canada		20		1			
Foreign		0		0			
Projected New U.S.			50	40			
Canada				0			
Foreign				2			
Corporate Employees	10	7	20	6			
Contract Length	20/10/10	10/5		10/5/5			
Expand in Territory	Y	Y	Y	Y			
Full-Time Employees	1+	2		5			
Part-Time Employees		3-5		40			
Conversions	Y	N	Y	Y			
Site Selection Assist.	Y	Y	N	N			
Lease Negotiation Assist.	Y	Y	N	N			
Site Space Required		2000		300			
Development Agreement	Y	N	Y	Y			
Develop. Agree. Term	15			10+			
Sub-franchising	N	N	N	N			

Consumer Service Industry   Personal Services

A Quicki Services
1730 Cumberland Point Dr #5
Marietta, GA 30067
Variety of personal svcs incl dry clean, alterations, maid, hair
    Phone: 770-951-9440   Accepts collect calls? N
    Toll Free: 800-255-8145   FAX: 770-933-8268
    Internet: hqcorp@bellsouth.net
Suitable Sites: AC, HO, K, M, OC, PC, RM, SC, SF
Concentration: 19 in GA
    Expansion: All United States, Canada, Foreign
    Registered:
Field Support: EO, ST, SO, FC, H, N
    Training: corp HQ Atlanta, GA
        ongoing in field

English Butler Canada
39 King St
Saint John, NB E2L-4W3 CANADA

    Phone: 506-652-4110   Accepts collect calls?
    Toll Free: FAX: 506-634-6980
    Internet:
Suitable Sites: RM
Concentration: 15 in ON, 3 in NB, 2 in NS
    Expansion: N, Canada
    Registered:
Field Support: CP, ST, SO, IC, $FC
    Training: 3 weeks corporate stores

Home Helpers
4010 Executive Park Dr #100
Cincinnati, OH 45241
Non-medical in-home elder care
    Phone: Accepts collect calls? N
    Toll Free: 800-216-4196   FAX: 513-563-2961
    Internet: www.bison1.com/homehelpers
Suitable Sites:
Concentration: 4 in PA, 3 in TX, 3 in OH
    Expansion: All United States, Canada
    Registered: CA,FL,IL,IN,MI,MN,NY,OR,RI,VA,WA,WI,DC
Field Support:
    Training: 5 days intensive train at Cincinnati HQ
        marketing, technical & business

Homewatch Caregivers
2865 S Colorado Blvd
Denver, CO 80222
Nonmedical personal care services to the elderly
    Phone: 303-758-7290   Accepts collect calls? Y
    Toll Free: 800-777-9770   FAX: 303-758-1724
    Internet: homewatch-intl.com
Suitable Sites: HO, OC
Concentration: 3 in CO, 2 in MN
    Expansion: All United States, Canada, Foreign
    Registered: CA,FL,MD,MN,OR
Field Support: CP, EO, SO, FC, H, N
    Training: 5 days Denver, CO
        2 days franchisee location

Consumer Service Industry   Special Event Services

	American Mobile Sound	Complete Music						
Startup Cost	10K-87K	15.5K-35K						
Franchise Fee	6K-15K	15.5K						
Royalty	7%/$150	8%						
Advertising Fee	0%	2%						
Financing Provided	Y	Y						
Experience Required		N						
Passive Ownership	A	D						
In Business Since	1991	1972						
Franchised Since	1994	1982						
Franchised Units 1996								
1997	28	143						
1998								
Company Owned 1996								
1997	0	1						
1998								
Number of Units U.S.	28	140						
Canada	0	4						
Foreign	0	0						
Projected New U.S.								
Canada								
Foreign								
Corporate Employees	2	5						
Contract Length	10/10	LIFETIME						
Expand in Territory	Y	Y						
Full-Time Employees		2						
Part-Time Employees	5	5-40						
Conversions		Y						
Site Selection Assist.	Y	Y						
Lease Negotiation Assist.	Y	Y						
Site Space Required	250							
Development Agreement	N	N						
Develop. Agree. Term								
Sub-franchising	N	N						

Consumer Service Industry

Special Event Services

American Mobile Sound
600 Ward Dr #A-1
Santa Barbara, CA 93111

Phone: 805-681-8132   Accepts collect calls?
Toll Free: 800-788-9007   FAX: 805-681-8134
Internet:
Suitable Sites: HO, OC
Concentration: 9 in CA, 5 in CO, 3 in TX
Expansion: All United States
Registered: CA
Field Support: $CP, EO, ST, SO, FC, H, N
Training: 9 days Santa Barbara CA

Complete Music
7877 L St
Omaha, NE 68127
Mobile disc jockey entertainment service
Phone: 402-339-0001   Accepts collect calls?
Toll Free: 800-843-3866   FAX: 402-339-1285
Internet: www.cmusic.com
Suitable Sites: AC, FB, HO, IP, OC, OS, RM, SC, SF
Concentration: 21 in TX, 11 in NE, 8 in CO
Expansion: All United States, Canada
Registered: CA,FL,IL,IN,MD,MI,MN,OR,SD,WA,WI
Field Support: CP, $EO, ST, SO, IC, FC, $H, N
Training: 9 days Omaha NE
4 days on-site

Consumer Service Industry

Other Consumer Service

	A Wonderful Wedding	Air Brook Limousine	Critter Control Inc	Two Men And A Truck	United Consumers Club			
Startup Cost	11.45K-25.4K	150K-500K	6.25K-25.75K	62.8K-168.6K	60K-120K			
Franchise Fee	20K	24.5K	12K-18K	20K	55K			
Royalty	10%	5%	6-18%	6%	22%			
Advertising Fee		2%		1%				
Financing Provided	N	Y	N	Y	Y			
Experience Required					N			
Passive Ownership				D	D			
In Business Since	1993		1983	1985	1971			
Franchised Since	1997		1987	1989	1972			
Franchised Units 1996			54		82			
1997	0		54	48	74			
1998					72			
Company Owned 1996	1		42		11			
1997	1	.	33	1	14			
1998					18			
Number of Units U.S.				49	81			
Canada				0	9			
Foreign				0	0			
Projected New U.S.								
Canada								
Foreign								
Corporate Employees		30		9	130			
Contract Length		10/10		7/7	12/12			
Expand in Territory		Y		Y	N			
Full-Time Employees		4		6	12			
Part-Time Employees		2		3	2			
Conversions		N						
Site Selection Assist.		Y		Y	Y			
Lease Negotiation Assist.		N		N	Y			
Site Space Required		1500		800-1000	4000-6000			
Development Agreement				N	N			
Develop. Agree. Term		N						
Sub-franchising		N		Y	N			

Consumer Service Industry

Other Consumer Service

A Wonderful Wedding
2011-B Bee's Ferry Rd
Charleston, SC 29414
Bridal guides & shows
     Phone: 803-556-1500   Accepts collect calls?
     Toll Free: FAX:
     Internet:
Suitable Sites:
Concentration:
     Expansion:
     Registered:
Field Support:
     Training:

Air Brook Limousine
PO Box 123
Rochelle Park, NJ 07662

     Phone: Accepts collect calls?
     Toll Free: FAX:
     Internet:
Suitable Sites: WR
Concentration:
     Expansion: All United States, Foreign
     Registered: CA,FL,IL,IN,MD,MI,MN,NY,OR,RI,VA,WA
Field Support: DP, CP, EO, ST, SO, IC, FC, H, N
     Training: 2 weeks Westwood, MA
                 4 weeks on-site

Critter Control Inc
10244 E San Remo Blvd
Traverse City, MI 49684
Urban/rural wildlife management
     Phone: 616-929-0370   Accepts collect calls?
     Toll Free: FAX:
     Internet:
Suitable Sites:
Concentration:
     Expansion: CA,IN,MI,NY,WI, Canada
     Registered:
Field Support:
     Training:

Two Men And A Truck
1915 E Michigan Ave
Lansing, MI 48912
Residential local moving
     Phone: 517-482-6683   Accepts collect calls?
     Toll Free: 800-345-1070   FAX: 800-278-6114
     Internet: www.twomen.com
Suitable Sites: FB, IP, SC, SF
Concentration: 14 in MI, 5 in OH, 5 in FL
     Expansion: All United States, Canada
     Registered: CA, FL, MI, NY, WA, WI
Field Support: EO, FC, H, N
     Training: 5 days Lansing, MI

United Consumers Club
8450 Broadway, PO Box 13006
Merrillville, IN 46443006
Private buying service; our members purchase goods at wholesale
     Phone: 219-736-1100   Accepts collect calls? N
     Toll Free: 800-827-6400   FAX: 219-755-6208
     Internet: www.shopucc.com
Suitable Sites: LI, SC
Concentration: 10 in MI, 8 in NY, 7 in OH
     Expansion: All United States, Canada, Foreign
     Registered: CA,FL,HI,IL,IN,MD,MI,MN,ND,NY,OR,RI,SD,VA,WA,DC,AB
Field Support: DP, CP, EO, ST, SO, FC, N
     Training: 4 weeks corporate support center
                4 weeks at operating franchise
                hands-on internship

Education Industry   Computer Training

	Interactive Multimedia C.B.S.	Computer U Learning Centers	CTI Computer Training Institutes	ExecuTrain Corp.	New Horizons Computer Learning Center	PC Professor		
Startup Cost	250K	15K-20K	90K-250K	200K-500K	249K-435K	175K		
Franchise Fee	40K	20K	30K	30K-50K	29K-60K	40K		
Royalty	10%	6%	6%	6-9%	6%	8%		
Advertising Fee	2%	1%	0%		1%	0		
Financing Provided	N	N	N	Y	Y	Y		
Experience Required	N	N				N		
Passive Ownership	N	N	A		D	N		
In Business Since	1992	1992	1996	1984	1982	1989		
Franchised Since	1995	1997	1997	1986	1992	1996		
Franchised Units 1996	1			138		0		
1997	1	0	1	141	202	1		
1998	1	10				2		
Company Owned 1996	3			2		2		
1997	3	2	1	20	7	2		
1998	3	4						
Number of Units U.S.		14	2		131			
Canada	4	0	0		4			
Foreign		0	0		67			
Projected New U.S.		10						
Canada	1	0						
Foreign		0						
Corporate Employees	35	3	5		75	34		
Contract Length	10	10/5	10/10		10/5	7		
Expand in Territory	Y	Y	Y		Y	Y		
Full-Time Employees	3		2		15	5		
Part-Time Employees	2		1-2			0		
Conversions	N		Y		Y	Y		
Site Selection Assist.	Y	Y	Y		Y	Y		
Lease Negotiation Assist.	Y	Y	Y		Y	Y		
Site Space Required	2000-5000	400	800-1500		4000-5000	2000		
Development Agreement	N	N	N		Y	Y		
Develop. Agree. Term					10			
Sub-franchising	N	N	N		Y	Y		

Education Industry   Computer Training

C. B. S. Interactive Multimedia
#2 Bloor St W #1001
Toronto, ON M4W-3E2 CANADA
New media, information technology & business computer training
    Phone: 416-925-9929   Accepts collect calls? N
    Toll Free: 888-925-9929   FAX: 416-925-9220
    Internet: www.cbstraining.com
Suitable Sites: ES, DA, FB, M, OC, OS
Concentration: 4 in ONT
    Expansion: Canada
    Registered:
Field Support: DP, CP, EO, $ST, SO, $IC, $FC, H, N
    Training: 2 weeks administrative
             2 weeks computer
             2 weeks on-site

Computer U Learning Centers
75-850 Osage Trl
Indian Wells, CA 92210
Classroom & private instruction of PC's for mature adults
    Phone: 760-340-2453   Accepts collect calls? N
    Toll Free: 888-708-7877   FAX: 760-340-0306
    Internet: www.computeru.com
Suitable Sites: AC, ES, FB, LI, M, OC, PC, RM, SC, SF
Concentration: 4 in CA, 5 in NV, 4 in FL
    Expansion:
    Registered: CA,FL,MI,OR,WI,DC
Field Support: EO, $ST, SO, $FC
    Training: 6 days palm springs, CA
             3 days on-site

CTI Computer Training Institutes
3401 E Saginam St #201
Lansing, MI 48912

    Phone: 517-332-5600   Accepts collect calls?
    Toll Free: FAX: 517-332-5651
    Internet:
Suitable Sites: FB, IP, OC, SC, SF
Concentration: 2 in MI
    Expansion: 43 States, Canada
    Registered: FL,MI,MN,OR,DC
Field Support: EO, ST, SO, FC
    Training: 10 days corporate office
             4-6 weeks informal prior to opening
             3 days on-site

ExecuTrain Corp.
4800 N Point Pkwy
Alpharetta, GA 30202
Computer software training & support
    Phone: Accepts collect calls?
    Toll Free: 800-843-6984   FAX:
    Internet:
Suitable Sites:
Concentration:
    Expansion: All United States, Canada, Foreign
    Registered:
Field Support:
    Training:

New Horizons Computer Learning Center
1231 E Dyer Rd #110
Santa Ana, CA 92705-5643

    Phone: 714-438-9491   Accepts collect calls?
    Toll Free: FAX: 714-432-7676
    Internet: www.newhorizons.com
Suitable Sites: FB, IP, OC
Concentration: 18 in CA, 6 in NY, 6 in TX
    Expansion: All United States, Canada, Foreign
    Registered: CA,FL,HI,IL,IN,MD,MI,MN,ND,NY,OR,RI,SD,VA,WA,WI,DC
Field Support: CP, EO, ST, FC, H, N
    Training: 2 weeks HQ
             1 week franchise location
             2 days regional

PC Professor
7056 Beracasa Way
Boca Raton, FL 33433
Computer training/repair centers
    Phone: 561-684-3333   Accepts collect calls? N
    Toll Free: 888-PC1-2345   FAX: 561-684-0882
    Internet: www.pcprofessor.com
Suitable Sites: AC, SF
Concentration: 4 in FL
    Expansion: All United States, Canada, Foreign
    Registered:
Field Support: CP, ST, SO, H, N
    Training: 2 weeks hands-on in south FL

Education Industry   Other Education (Spread 1 of 2)

	Academy for Mathematics & Science	American Institute of Small Business	Berlitz Franchising Corp.	Citizens Against Crime	Crestcom International, Ltd.	ELS Language Centers	Gwynne Learning Academy	Hammett's Learning World
Startup Cost	50K-70K	10K	120K-270K	10K-40K	44.4K-72K	100K-300K	45K-65K	200K-250K
Franchise Fee	29.5K	5K	30K+	12.5K-25K	35K-52.5K	30K+	25K	25K
Royalty	5-8%	0%	10%	0%	1.50%	5%	7%	6%
Advertising Fee	2%	0%		3-6%		0%	2%	3%
Financing Provided	Y	Y	N	Y	Y	N	Y	N
Experience Required					N	N		
Passive Ownership	N	A		A	D	D	A	N
In Business Since	1992	1985	1978	1980	1987	1956	1991	1900
Franchised Since	1993	1988	1996	1986	1992	1978	1991	1986
Franchised Units 1996			2					
1997	36	5	6	25	102	54	14	4
1998				26				
Company Owned 1996		1	323					
1997	4	2	325	1	0	25	1	58
1998		2		4		27		
Number of Units U.S.	0	6		29	27	26	2	62
Canada	40	1		0	4	1	0	0
Foreign	0	1		0	71	53	12	0
Projected New U.S.		7		8	10			
Canada		1		1	2			
Foreign		1		1	24			
Corporate Employees	13	8		5	12	25	2	11
Contract Length	5/5	2/VAR.		10/10	7/7/7	10	10/10	10
Expand in Territory	Y	Y		N	Y	Y	Y	Y
Full-Time Employees	2			5	2-5	6-20	2	2-3
Part-Time Employees	6	1						3-7
Conversions				Y		Y		N
Site Selection Assist.	Y	Y		Y	N	Y	Y	Y
Lease Negotiation Assist.	Y			Y		N	Y	N
Site Space Required	1000	600					600	3000
Development Agreement	Y	N		N	N	Y	N	N
Develop. Agree. Term	10					10-20		
Sub-franchising	Y	N		N	N	N	N	N

Education Industry   Other Education (Spread 1 of 2)

Academy for Mathematics & Science
30 Glen Cameron Rd #200
Thornhill, ON L3T-1N7   CANADA

Phone: 905-709-3233   Accepts collect calls?
Toll Free: 800-809-5555   FAX: 905-709-3045
Internet: www.acadfor.com
Suitable Sites: RM, SC
Concentration: 35 in ON, 4 in BC, 1 in AB
  Expansion: Not Yet, Canada
  Registered: AB
Field Support: EO, ST, SO, FC, H, N
  Training: 1 week corporate office
            1 week training center

American Institute of Small Business
7515 Wayzata Blvd #201
Minneapolis, MN 55426
Books, video, software, seminars on how to set up & run business
Phone: 612-545-7001   Accepts collect calls?
Toll Free: 800-328-2906   FAX: 612-545-7020
Internet: www.accessil.com/aisb
Suitable Sites:
Concentration: 1 in MN, 1 in CO, 1 in IL
  Expansion: All United States, Canada, Foreign
  Registered: MN
Field Support: CP, ST, SO, $FC, H
  Training: 2 days HQ

Berlitz Franchising Corp.
400 Alexander Park
Princeton, NJ 08540
Language instruction,publications,translations
Phone: 609-514-3046   Accepts collect calls?
Toll Free: 800-626-6419   FAX:
Internet:
Suitable Sites:
Concentration:
  Expansion: All United States, Canada, Foreign
  Registered:
Field Support:
  Training:

Citizens Against Crime
1111 Jupiter Rd #C-101
Plano, TX 75074
Crime safety seminars and safety products, resolving conflict
Phone: 972-578-2287   Accepts collect calls?
Toll Free: 800-466-1010   FAX: 972-509-0054
Internet: www.trainingexperience.com
Suitable Sites: AC, ES, FB, HO, IP, OC, SC
Concentration:
  Expansion: All United States, Canada, Foreign
  Registered:
Field Support: DP, EO, ST, SO, IC, FC, H, N
  Training: 1 week Dallas
            1 week franchise

Crestcom International, Ltd.
6900 E Belleview Ave
Englewood, CO 80111

Phone: 303-267-8200   Accepts collect calls? N
Toll Free: 800-276-5439   FAX: 303-267-8207
Internet: crestcom@ix.netcom.com
Suitable Sites: HO
Concentration:
  Expansion: All United States, Canada, Foreign
  Registered: CA,FL,HI,IL,IN,MD,MI,MN,ND,NY,OR,RI,SD,VA,WA,WI,DC
Field Support: ST, FC, N
  Training: 7-10 days Denver/Phoenix/Sacramento
            prior to any commitment

ELS Language Centers
400 Alexander Park
Princeton, NJ 08540
English language training courses for academic/professional dev.
Phone: 609-750-3500   Accepts collect calls? N
Toll Free: 800-468-8978   FAX: 609-750-3596
Internet: www.els.com
Suitable Sites: FB, OC, OTHER
Concentration:
  Expansion: N, Canada, Foreign
  Registered: CA
Field Support: EO, ST, FC, N
  Training: 2 weeks management academy Princeton, NJ

Gwynne Learning Academy
1432 W Emerald #735
Mesa, AZ 85202

Phone: 602-644-1434   Accepts collect calls?
Toll Free: FAX: 602-644-1434
Internet:
Suitable Sites: FB, RM, SC, SF
Concentration: 2 in AZ
  Expansion: All United States, Canada, Foreign
  Registered:
Field Support: $CP, ST, $SO, H
  Training: 7 days phoenix, AZ

Hammett's Learning World
PO Box 859057
Braintree, MA 02185-9057

Phone: 781-848-1000   Accepts collect calls?
Toll Free: 800-955-2200   FAX: 781-848-3970
Internet: www.hammett.com
Suitable Sites: SC
Concentration: 8 in TX, 7 in NY, 6 in MA
  Expansion: Y
  Registered: FL,IL,NY
Field Support: $ST, SO, $FC, H
  Training: 5 days MA corporate office
            10 days retail store

Education Industry

Other Education (Spread 2 of 2)

	The Honors Learning Center	Huntington Learning Center	Kumon Math & Reading Center	Sears Driver Training	The Sleeping Giant Within Inc.	Sylvan Learning Centers		
Startup Cost	65K-132K	118.5K-175.6K	4.62K	36K-45K	10K	89K-162K		
Franchise Fee	15K	33K	$500	20K	25K	34K-42K		
Royalty	8%	8%	$29/STUDENT	6%	8%	8-9%		
Advertising Fee	0%	2%		5%		1.5%		
Financing Provided	N	Y	N	N	Y	Y		
Experience Required								
Passive Ownership	N	N		D		N		
In Business Since	1987	1977	1958	1978	1990	1979		
Franchised Since	1992	1985	1958	1994	1995	1980		
Franchised Units 1996			1303		0			
1997	2	137	1296	8	1	619		
1998					2			
Company Owned 1996			0		9			
1997	0	22	0	8	2	41		
1998					2			
Number of Units U.S.	2	159		0		607		
Canada	0	0		16		50		
Foreign	0	0		0		3		
Projected New U.S.					3			
Canada								
Foreign								
Corporate Employees	2	42		17		350		
Contract Length	10/10	10/10		5/5/5		10/10		
Expand in Territory	Y	N		Y	Y	Y		
Full-Time Employees	2	2-4		2		2		
Part-Time Employees	8			1-2		5		
Conversions	Y	N		Y		N		
Site Selection Assist.	Y	Y		Y	Y	Y		
Lease Negotiation Assist.	N	Y		Y		N		
Site Space Required	1100-1300	1800-2000		700		2400-3200		
Development Agreement	N	Y			Y	Y		
Develop. Agree. Term								
Sub-franchising	N	N		Y		N		

Education Industry

The Honors Learning Center
5959 Shallowford Rd #517
Chattanooga, TN 37421

Phone: 423-892-1800   Accepts collect calls?
Toll Free: FAX: 423-892-1800
Internet:
Suitable Sites: OC, SC
Concentration: 1 in TN, 1 in FL
    Expansion: All United States
    Registered: FL
Field Support: EO, $ST, SO, $FC, N
    Training: 2-3 weeks corporate office

Huntington Learning Center
496 Kinderkamack Rd
Oradell, NJ 07649

Phone: 201-261-8400   Accepts collect calls?
Toll Free: 800-653-8400   FAX: 201-261-3233
Internet:
Suitable Sites: RM, SC
Concentration: 13 in NY, 11 in NJ, 10 in IL
    Expansion: All United States
    Registered: CA,FL,IL,IN,MD,MI,MN,NY,RI,VA,WA,WI
Field Support: CP, EO, ST, SO, IC, $FC, H, N
    Training: 2 1/2 weeks Oradell, NJ

Kumon Math & Reading Center
300 Frank Burr Blvd, 2nd Fl
Teaneck, NJ 07666
Supplemental education
    Phone: Accepts collect calls?
Toll Free: 800-222-6284   FAX:
Internet:
Suitable Sites:
Concentration:
    Expansion: All United States, Canada, Foreign
    Registered:
Field Support:
    Training:

Sears Driver Training
247 N Service Rd W #301
Oakville, ON L6M-3E6 CANADA

Phone: 416-363-7483   Accepts collect calls?
Toll Free: FAX: 905-842-4251
Internet:
Suitable Sites:
Concentration: 15 in ON
    Expansion: N, Canada
    Registered: AB
Field Support: $DP, $CP, EO, $ST, $SO, $FC
    Training: 2 weeks Oakville, ON

The Sleeping Giant Within Inc.
3697 Hwy C
Leslie, MO 63056
Motivational/human development training
    Phone: Accepts collect calls?
Toll Free: 800-205-7439   FAX:
Internet:
Suitable Sites: HO, OTHER
Concentration: 1 in IL, 1 in NY, 1 in CA
    Expansion: All United States, Canada, Foreign
    Registered:
Field Support: DP, CP, EO, ST
    Training:

Sylvan Learning Centers
1000 Lancaster St
Baltimore, MD 21202

Phone: 410-843-8000   Accepts collect calls? N
Toll Free: 800-284-8214   FAX: 410-843-8717
Internet: www.educate.com
Suitable Sites: FB, SC, SF
Concentration: CA, TX, NY
    Expansion: All United States, Canada, Foreign
    Registered: CA,FL,HI,IL,IN,MD,MI,MN,ND,NY,OR,RI,SD,VA,WA,WI,DC
Field Support: CP, EO, ST, SO, FC, H, N
    Training: 8 days Baltimore, MD
         7 days various locations

Food Industry

Candy

	Bourbon Street Candy Company	Candy Bouquet International	Candy Express	Candy HQ/Sweets From Heaven	Fudge Co.	Kilwin's Chocolates Franchise	Rocky Mountain Chocolate Factory
Startup Cost	170K-210K	7K-29K	75K-175K	125K-232K	28K-35K	75K-160K	113K-213K
Franchise Fee	20K	3.5K-20.5K	25K-35K	30K	12.5K-15K	20K	19.5K
Royalty	5%	0%	6%	6%	3%	5%	5%
Advertising Fee	0	0%	1%	0%	0%		1%
Financing Provided	Y	Y	Y	Y	N	N	Y
Experience Required	N			N			
Passive Ownership		A	A	A	D		D
In Business Since	1990	1989	1989	1992	1978	1946	1981
Franchised Since	1990	1994	1989	1993	1981	1982	1982
Franchised Units 1996		52				27	
1997		201	43	160	8	31	183
1998		320					
Company Owned 1996	1					1	
1997	1	1	5	16	1	0	37
1998	4						
Number of Units U.S.	24	180	40	48	7		202
Canada	0	42	0	0	0		17
Foreign	0	6	8	124	2		1
Projected New U.S.	10	245					
Canada	2	42					
Foreign	0	7					
Corporate Employees	4	13	10	13			12
Contract Length		5/5	10/10	10/5	10/10		5/5
Expand in Territory	Y	Y	Y	Y	Y		Y
Full-Time Employees		2	1	4	2		2
Part-Time Employees		3	3	3	2		4
Conversions	Y		Y	Y			
Site Selection Assist.	Y	Y	Y	Y	Y		Y
Lease Negotiation Assist.	Y	Y	Y	Y	N		Y
Site Space Required	600-1500	900	150-1000	800	300-600		800-1200
Development Agreement	Y	Y	Y	Y	Y		N
Develop. Agree. Term		10	20	10			
Sub-franchising	N	Y	Y	Y			N

Food Industry   Candy

Bourbon Street Candy Company
287-266 Elmwood Avenue
Buffalo, NY 14222
In-house construction company
      Phone: 905-894-4819   Accepts collect calls? N
      Toll Free: 888-568-2722   FAX: 905-894-3072
      Internet:
Suitable Sites: M
Concentration:
      Expansion: All United States, Canada
      Registered: CA,IL,NY,VA
Field Support:
      Training: corporate store
              operations manual

Candy Express
10480 Little Patuxent Pkwy #320
Columbia, MD 21044

      Phone: 410-964-5500   Accepts collect calls?
      Toll Free: FAX: 410-964-6404
      Internet:
Suitable Sites: AC, FB, FC, K, RM, SF
Concentration: 6 in MD, 5 in GA, 4 in VA
      Expansion: All United States, Canada, Foreign
      Registered: CA, MD, VA, DC
Field Support: DP, CP, EO, ST, SO, IC, FC, N
      Training: 2 weeks Maryland

Fudge Co.
103 Belvedere Ave
Charlevoix, MI 49720

      Phone: 616-547-4612   Accepts collect calls?
      Toll Free: FAX: 616-547-4612
      Internet:
Suitable Sites: FB, RM, OTHER
Concentration: 2 in AZ, 2 in AL, 2 in VA
      Expansion: All United States, Canada, Foreign
      Registered: FL,HI,MI,OR
Field Support: $CP, $EO, ST, SO
      Training: 10-14 days AZ or MI.

Rocky Mountain Chocolate Factory
265 Turner Dr
Durango, CO 81301

      Phone: 970-259-0554   Accepts collect calls?
      Toll Free: 800-438-7623   FAX: 888-259-5895
      Internet:
Suitable Sites: OTHER
Concentration: 36 in CA, 22 in CO, 12 in BC
      Expansion: All United States, Foreign
      Registered: CA,FL,HI,IL,IN,MD,MI,MN,NY,OR,SD,VA,WA,WI
Field Support: CP, EO, ST, SO, IC, FC, H, N
      Training: 7 days Durango, CO.
              5 days store site

Candy Bouquet International
2326 Cantrell Rd
Little Rock, AR 72202

      Phone: 501-375-9990   Accepts collect calls?
      Toll Free: FAX: 501-375-9998
      Internet: www.candybouquet.com
Suitable Sites: HO, SF
Concentration: 37 in AR, 23 in CA, 23 in TX
      Expansion: All United States, Canada, Foreign
      Registered: CA,FL,HI,IL,IN,MD,MI,MN,ND,NY,OR,RI,VA,WA,WI,DC,AB
Field Support: CP, $EO, ST, $SO, $IC, FC, H, N
      Training: 5 days little rock, AR
              9 days Kuala Lumpur, Malaysia

Candy HQ/Sweets From Heaven
1830 Forbes Ave
Pittsburgh, PA 15219

      Phone: 412-434-6711   Accepts collect calls?
      Toll Free: FAX: 412-434-6718
      Internet: www.sweetsfromheaven.com
Suitable Sites: K, M, RM, SF
Concentration: 6 in TX, 5 in FL, 6 in PA
      Expansion: All United States, Canada, Foreign
      Registered: CA,FL,IL,NY,VA,MD
Field Support: CP, EO, ST, SO, IC, N
      Training: 1 week corporate office
              1 week company store
              1 week franchisee's store

Kilwin's Chocolates Franchise
355 N Division Rd
Petoskey, MI 49770
Chocolate, fudge, ice cream
      Phone: 616-347-3800   Accepts collect calls?
      Toll Free: FAX:
      Internet:
Suitable Sites:
Concentration:
      Expansion: NE,SE,S,MW
      Registered:
Field Support:
      Training:

Food Industry

Coffees, Teas (Spread 1 of 2)

	Barnie's Coffee & Tea Company	Blenz Coffee	Brew Thru	Caffe Appassionato	The Coffee Beanery	Gloria Jean's Gourmet Coffees	The Gourmet Cup	Lisa's Tea Treasures
Startup Cost	250K-500K	135K-190K	90K-410K	230K-275K	44K-204K	132.8K-307.6K	90K-180K	70K-300K
Franchise Fee	25K	25K	100K	25K	5K-25K	15K-25K	25K	$0
Royalty	6%	8%	0%	4.50%	6%	6%	8%	0%
Advertising Fee	1%	2%	0%	1%	2%	2%	2%	0%
Financing Provided	N	Y	Y	Y	Y	Y	N	N
Experience Required	N					N	N	
Passive Ownership	D	N	A	D	A	D	D	D
In Business Since	80	1990	1977	1991	1976	1979	1985	1988
Franchised Since	85	1991	1997	1993	1985	1986	1986	1992
Franchised Units 1996	28							
1997	26	16	5	5	157	241	63	12
1998	29					248	39	
Company Owned 1996	18							
1997	80	0	1	12	25	36	2	0
1998	84					32	2	
Number of Units U.S.	113	0	6	17	193	250	0	10
Canada		15	0	0	0	0	41	0
Foreign		1	0	0	0	30	0	2
Projected New U.S.	10					40		
Canada							2	
Foreign						4		
Corporate Employees	35	4	1	4	100	60	9	6
Contract Length	10/10	10	10/10	10/5/5	lease	lease	5/5	3/3
Expand in Territory	Y	Y	Y	Y	Y	Y	Y	Y
Full-Time Employees	2-6	4	3	5	1	2	2	3
Part-Time Employees	3-6	10	1	7	8-10	8	2	2
Conversions	N	N	Y	Y	Y	Y	Y	Y
Site Selection Assist.	Y	Y	N	Y	Y	Y	Y	N
Lease Negotiation Assist.	Y	Y	Y	Y	Y	Y	Y	N
Site Space Required	1000-1800	750-2000	2000	1200	2000	700	400-800	1000
Development Agreement	Y	Y	Y	Y	Y	N	N	N
Develop. Agree. Term	10	20	10	5/5				
Sub-franchising	N	Y	Y	N	N	N	N	N

Food Industry

Barnie's Coffee & Tea Company
340 N Primrose Dr
Orlando, FL 32803
Specialty coffees, teas & related products - national brand
Phone: 407-894-1416   Accepts collect calls? N
Toll Free: 800-456-1416   FAX: 407-898-5341
Internet: www.barniescoffee.com
Suitable Sites: AC, FB, PC, RM, SC, SF, WF
Concentration: 11 in FL, 3 in AL, 3 in IN
Expansion: Primary East Coast
Registered: FL,IL,IN,MI,NY,VA
Field Support: CP, ST, SO, FC, N
Training: 1 week Orlando, FL
10 days assistance at location
on call

Blenz Coffee
535 Thurlow St #300
Vancouver, BC V6E-3L2   CANADA

Phone: 604-682-2995   Accepts collect calls?
Toll Free: FAX: 604-684-2542
Internet:
Suitable Sites: FB, RM, SC, SF
Concentration: 15 in BC
Expansion: Y, Canada, Foreign
Registered:
Field Support: DP, CP, EO, ST, SO, FC
Training: 2 weeks exisiting operation
2 weeks new location

Brew Thru
PO Box 3158
Virginia Beach, VA 23454

Phone: 757-631-3040   Accepts collect calls?
Toll Free: 888-256-2739   FAX: 757-496-3686
Internet: www.brewthru.com
Suitable Sites: FB, SC
Concentration: 5 in NC, 1 in VA
Expansion: All United States
Registered: VA
Field Support: CP, EO, ST, SO, IC, FC, H, N
Training: 2 weeks Virginia Beach, VA

Caffe Appassionato
4001 21st Ave W
Seattle, WA 98199

Phone: 206-281-8040   Accepts collect calls?
Toll Free: 888-502-2333   FAX: 213-655-6207
Internet:
Suitable Sites: FB, SF
Concentration: 13 in WA, 3 in MA, 1 in MD
Expansion: All United States, Canada, Foreign
Registered: CA,FL,HI,IL,MD,MI,MN,ND,OR,RI,SD,VA,WA,WI
Field Support: CP, EO, ST, SO, IC, $FC, H, N
Training: 7-10 days franchisee site
2-3 weeks corp HQ in Seattle

The Coffee Beanery
3429 Pierson Place Rd
Flushing, MI 48433

Phone: 810-728-2326   Accepts collect calls?
Toll Free: 800-728-2326   FAX: 810-733-6847
Internet:
Suitable Sites: FB, SC, SF
Concentration: 34 in MI, 15 in NY, 14 in PA
Expansion: NW, SE, Midwest
Registered: CA,FL,IN,MD,MI,NY,VA
Field Support: CP, EO, ST, SO, IC, FC, H, N
Training: 5 days corp office Flushing, MI
3 weeks flint or Birmingham store

Gloria Jean's Gourmet Coffees
11480 Commercial Parkway
Castroville, CA 95012
Specialty coffee & tea store specialize in beverages, whole bean
Phone: 831-633-6300   Accepts collect calls? N
Toll Free: 800-333-0050   FAX: 831-633-3276
Internet: www.greatbeans.com
Suitable Sites: AC, FB, FC, K, M, OC, RM, SC, SF, WF, OTHER
Concentration: 40 in CA, 32 in IL, 10 in WI
Expansion: All United States
Registered: CA,FL,HI,IL,IN,MD,MI,MN,ND,NY,OR,RI,SD,VA,WA,WI,DC
Field Support: CP, EO, ST, SO, IC, FC, H, N
Training: 3 weeks coffee university Castroville HQ
on-site pre-opening

The Gourmet Cup
2265 W Railway St Box 490
Abbotsford, BC V2S-5Z5   CANADA
Gourmet coffee bar specialize in coffee & tea/complimentary menu
Phone: 604-852-8771   Accepts collect calls? N
Toll Free: FAX: 604-859-1711
Internet: www.shefieldgourmet.com
Suitable Sites: AC, DA, FC, K, M, OC, PC, RM, SC, WF
Concentration: 11 in BC, 12 in ON, 6 in AB
Expansion: N
Registered: AB
Field Support: EO, ST, SO, H, N
Training: intensive

Lisa's Tea Treasures
645 Mc Glincey Ln #B
Campbell, CA 95008

Phone: 408-559-1832   Accepts collect calls?
Toll Free: 800-500-4832   FAX: 408-371-1875
Internet: www.lisasteas.com
Suitable Sites: FB, HO, RM, SC, SF
Concentration: 8 in CA, 1 in WA, 1 in NH
Expansion: CO,AZ,NV,TX(Non-Reg States), Canada, Foreign
Registered: CA,WA
Field Support: $H
Training: consulting train at site

Food Industry

Coffees, Teas (Spread 2 of 2)

	McBeans	Moxie Java	P.A.M.'s Coffee & Tea Co.	P.J.'s Coffee & Tea	Coffees By Chock Full O' Nuts	Quikava - The Second Cup	Shefield Gourmet	
Startup Cost	135K-185K	100K-175K	165K-200K	100K-190K	86K-380K	250K-300K	95K-180K	
Franchise Fee	25K	10K	25K	20K	3K-20K	20K	25K	
Royalty	7%	0	8%	5%	5%	9%	8%	
Advertising Fee	0%	0	2%	1%	4%	2%	2%	
Financing Provided	Y	N	Y	N	N	N	N	
Experience Required	N				N		N	
Passive Ownership	A	D	N	A	D	N	D	
In Business Since	1983	1987	1981	1978	1990	1975	1996	
Franchised Since	1985	1989	1991	1987	1993	1975	1996	
Franchised Units 1996					6			
1997	16	37	19	18	12	300	63	
1998			20		39		11	
Company Owned 1996					8			
1997	1	1	1	4	9	10	2	
1998			1		8		1	
Number of Units U.S.	0	36	0	22	47	0	0	
Canada	17	0	20	0	0	310	12	
Foreign	0	2	0	0	0	1	0	
Projected New U.S.					25			
Canada			10				6	
Foreign								
Corporate Employees	7	50	6	74	11	50	9	
Contract Length	lease	3/3/3	10/VAR.	10/10	3/3 OR 10/10	lease	5/5	
Expand in Territory	Y	Y	Y	Y	N	Y	Y	
Full-Time Employees	1-3	4	2	1	2	5	2	
Part-Time Employees	3-5	4	2	6	12	10	2	
Conversions	Y	Y	Y	Y	Y	N	Y	
Site Selection Assist.	Y	Y	Y	Y	Y	Y	Y	
Lease Negotiation Assist.	Y	Y	Y	Y	Y	Y	Y	
Site Space Required	600	120-1500	500-1200	1200	150-20000	300-3000	500-1000	
Development Agreement	N	N	N	Y	Y	N	N	
Develop. Agree. Term					5			
Sub-franchising	N	N	N	N	N	N	N	

Food Industry

McBeans
1560 Church Ave #6
Victoria, BC V8P-2H1   CANADA

Phone: 604-721-2411   Accepts collect calls?
Toll Free: FAX: 604-721-3213
Internet:
Suitable Sites: FB, FC, OC, PC, RM, SC, SF
Concentration: 8 in BC, 9 in AB
   Expansion: N, Canada
   Registered: AB
Field Support: EO, ST, SO, IC
   Training: 2 weeks on-site

Moxie Java
199 E 52nd St
Boise, ID 83714

Phone: 208-322-7773   Accepts collect calls?
Toll Free: 800-659-6963   FAX: 208-322-6226
Internet: www.moxiejava.com
Suitable Sites: FB, SC, SF, OTHER
Concentration: ID, ND, WI
   Expansion: All United States
   Registered: ND
Field Support: EO, $ST, $SO, $IC, FC, H, N
   Training: 3-4 days Boise, id
          3-4 days owner's location

P.A.M.'S Coffee & Tea Co.
2900 John St #202
Markham, ON L3R-5G3   CANADA

Phone: 905-305-9595   Accepts collect calls? N
Toll Free: FAX: 905-305-9597
Internet:
Suitable Sites: FB, FC, K, M, PC, RM, SC, SF
Concentration: 20 in ON
   Expansion: Canada
   Registered:
Field Support: CP, EO, ST, SO, N
   Training: 1 week head office
          2 weeks in store

P.J.'S Coffee & Tea
500 N Hagan Ave
New Orleans, LA 70119

Phone: 504-486-2827   Accepts collect calls?
Toll Free: FAX: 504-486-2345
Internet: www.pjscoffee.com
Suitable Sites: SC, SF
Concentration: 17 in LA, 2 in MS, 2 in FL
   Expansion: SE
   Registered: FL
Field Support: CP, EO, ST, SO, $FC, H, N
   Training: 2 days corporate office
          10 days corporate store
          3 days on-location sites

Quikava - Coffees By Chock Full O' Nuts
190 Old Derby St #304
Hingham, MA 02043
Chock full o' nuts (NYSE:CHF) drive-thru coffee cafe
Phone: 781-749-4242   Accepts collect calls? N
Toll Free: 800-381-6303   FAX: 781-749-7222
Internet: quickava.com
Suitable Sites: AC, FB, PC, SC, OTHER
Concentration: 15 in MA, 4 in NH, 9 in NY
   Expansion: NE
   Registered: MD,NY,RI,VA,DC
Field Support: DP, CP, EO, ST, SO, IC, FC, H, N
   Training: 4 days classroom at HQ in MA
          6 days in store

The Second Cup
175 Bloor St E S Tower #801
Toronto, ON M4W-3R8   CANADA

Phone: 416-975-5541   Accepts collect calls?
Toll Free: 800-569-6318   FAX: 416-975-5207
Internet:
Suitable Sites: FB, PC, RM, SC, SF
Concentration: 150 in ON, 40 in AB, 30 in PQ
   Expansion: N, Canada
   Registered: AB
Field Support: DP, CP, EO, ST, SO, IC, $FC, H, N
   Training: 3 weeks Toronto, ON

Shefield Gourmet
2265 W Railway St Box 490
Abbotsford, BC V2S-5Z5   CANADA
Gourmet coffee bar, specialty beverages, traditional smoke-shop
Phone: 604-859-1014   Accepts collect calls? N
Toll Free: FAX: 604-859-1711
Internet: www.shefieldgourmet.com
Suitable Sites: AC, DA, FB, K, M, OC, PC, RM, SC, SF, WF
Concentration: 3 in BC, 3 in ON, 4 in AB
   Expansion: N
   Registered: AB
Field Support: EO, ST, SO, H, N
   Training: intensive

Food Industry   Convenience Stores

	7-Eleven Convenience Stores	Convenient Food Mart	Express Mart Convenient Store	Jackpot Convenience Stores	UncleSam's Convenient Store			
Startup Cost	12.5K+	197K-298K	136K-460K	75K-250K	100K-1.5M			
Franchise Fee	VAR.	18K	15K	5K-10K	25K			
Royalty	VAR.	5%	4%	0.50%	5%			
Advertising Fee	0	INCLUDED	1%	1%	1%			
Financing Provided	Y	N	N	N	Y			
Experience Required	N		N	N	N			
Passive Ownership	N	D	A	N	D			
In Business Since	1927	1958	1975	1981	1969			
Franchised Since	1964	1959	1990	1990	1996			
Franchised Units 1996	12857							
1997	14549	256	12	104	0			
1998			22	100				
Company Owned 1996	2528							
1997	2535	50	47	10	52			
1998			50	2				
Number of Units U.S.		306	72	102	52			
Canada		0	0	0	0			
Foreign		0	0	0	0			
Projected New U.S.			20	2	10			
Canada								
Foreign								
Corporate Employees	30,000	50	300		6			
Contract Length	10	20/20	5/5/5/5	5/5 OR 2/2	5/5/5/5			
Expand in Territory	Y	Y	Y	N	Y			
Full-Time Employees		6	7		6			
Part-Time Employees		4	4		2			
Conversions		Y	Y		Y			
Site Selection Assist.	Y	Y	Y	N	Y			
Lease Negotiation Assist.	N	Y	Y	N	Y			
Site Space Required		3000	800-5000		2500			
Development Agreement	N	N	Y	N	Y			
Develop. Agree. Term			10					
Sub-franchising	N	Y	Y	N	N			

Food Industry   Convenience Stores

7-Eleven Convenience Stores
2711 N Haskell Ave
Dallas, TX 75204
Convenience store
Phone: Accepts collect calls? N
Toll Free: 800-255-0711   FAX: 214-841-6776
Internet: www.7-eleven.com
Suitable Sites:
Concentration: 1165 in CA, 235 in NY, 218 in WA
Expansion: NE,MW,SE,W,NW, Canada
Registered: CA,IL,IN,MD,MI,NY,OR,RI,VA,WA,DC
Field Support: DP, CP, EO, ST, SO, IC, FC, H, N
Training: 4 weeks in-store

Convenient Food Mart
467 North State St
Painesville, OH 44077

Phone: 440-639-6515   Accepts collect calls?
Toll Free: 800-860-4844   FAX: 440-639-6526
Internet: www.convenientfoodmart.com
Suitable Sites: FB, SC, SF
Concentration: 121 in OH, 47 in NY, 40 in IL
Expansion: Ohio and New York
Registered: PENDING IN IL,IN,NY
Field Support: DP, EO, ST, SO, FC, H
Training: 2 weeks training center
1 week actual store

Express Mart Convenient Store
6567 Kinne Rd PO Box 46
Dewitt, NY 13214
Retail convenience store, co-brand w/ subway, mcds, burger king
Phone: 315-446-0125   Accepts collect calls? N
Toll Free: FAX: 315-446-1355
Internet:
Suitable Sites: FB
Concentration: 65 in NY, 6 in MA, 1 in CT
Expansion: All United States, Canada, Foreign
Registered: NY
Field Support: DP, CP, EO, ST, SO, IC, N
Training: 1 week corp. HQ.
1 week store training

Jackpot Convenience Stores
2737 W Commorde Wy
Seattle, WA 98199
Convenience store with adjoining gasoline operation
Phone: Accepts collect calls? N
Toll Free: 800-772-5765   FAX: 425-776-2129
Internet: jackpotstores.com
Suitable Sites: FB, SC
Concentration: 60 in WA, 15 in CA, 13 in OR
Expansion: WA,OR,CA,NV,ID
Registered: CA,OR,WA
Field Support: DP, EO, ST, SO, IC, $FC, H, N
Training: 4 weeks Seattle, WA
ongoing

UncleSam's Convenient Store
PO Box 870
Elsa, TX 78543-0870

Phone: 956-262-7273   Accepts collect calls? N
Toll Free: 888-786-7373   FAX: 956-262-7290
Internet: www.unclesamscstore.com
Suitable Sites: FB
Concentration: 52 in TX
Expansion: All United States
Registered: CA,FL
Field Support: DP, CP, EO, ST, SO, IC, FC, H, N
Training: 4 weeks corp. office

Food Industry   **Health Food, Vitamins**

	General Nutrition Centers	Great Earth Vitamins	L. A. Smoothie Healthmart & Cafe	Bulk And Natural Foods	Nutter's	Sangsters Health Centres			
Startup Cost	112.4K-197.9K	75K-135K	30K-100K	150K-250K	95K-120K				
Franchise Fee	27.5K	30K	9K-15K	30K	25K				
Royalty	6%	6%	5%	4%	5%				
Advertising Fee	3%	$150/MO	3%	0%	1%				
Financing Provided	Y	Y	Y	Y	Y				
Experience Required					N				
Passive Ownership	N	D	A	N	D				
In Business Since	1935	1971	1991	1982	1971				
Franchised Since	1988	1979	1992	1983	1978				
Franchised Units 1996									
1997	1252	130	15	31	39				
1998					43				
Company Owned 1996									
1997	1947	1	0	3	1				
1998					4				
Number of Units U.S.	2947	130	14	1	0				
Canada	18	6	0	33	47				
Foreign	234	1	1	0	0				
Projected New U.S.									
Canada					8				
Foreign									
Corporate Employees	7000	18	4	11	11				
Contract Length	10/5	10/5	10/10	10/10	5/5				
Expand in Territory	Y	Y	Y	Y	Y				
Full-Time Employees		2	2-4	3	1				
Part-Time Employees	3+	2	2-6	3	2				
Conversions	Y	Y	N	Y	Y				
Site Selection Assist.	Y	Y	Y	Y	Y				
Lease Negotiation Assist.	Y	Y	Y	Y	Y				
Site Space Required	1200-1600	650-1400	300-1200	3500	600-800				
Development Agreement	N	Y	Y	N	Y				
Develop. Agree. Term			10						
Sub-franchising	N	Y	N	N	Y				

Food Industry   # Health Food, Vitamins

General Nutrition Centers
300 Sixth Ave
Pittsburgh, PA 15222

Phone: 412-288-2043   Accepts collect calls?
Toll Free: 800-766-7099   FAX: 412-288-2033
Internet: www.bison1.com/gnc
Suitable Sites: RM, SC, SF
Concentration:
  Expansion: All United States, Canada, Foreign
  Registered: CA,FL,HI,IL,IN,MD,MI,MN,ND,NY,OR,RI,SD,VA,WA,WI,DC
Field Support: CP, EO, ST, SO, IC, FC, H, N
  Training: 2 weeks on-site
          1 week Pittsburgh, PA

Great Earth Vitamins
11478 Mission Vista Dr
Rancho Cucamonga, CA 91730
Full line vitamin, mineral, herbal & nutritional supplements
Phone: 909-987-8892   Accepts collect calls?
Toll Free: 800-284-8243   FAX: 909-941-3472
Internet: www.greatearth.com
Suitable Sites: AC, DA, M, PC, RM, SC
Concentration: 77 in CA, 16 in TX, 5 in NV
  Expansion: All United States, Canada
  Registered: CA,FL,HI,IL,IN,MD,MI,MN,ND,NY,OR,RI,SD,VA,WA,WI,DC
Field Support: CP, EO, ST, SO, $FC, H, N
  Training: 4 weeks Cerritos CA

L. A. Smoothie Healthmart & Cafe
701 Edwards Ave #B
Harahan, LA 70123

Phone: 504-734-5849   Accepts collect calls?
Toll Free: FAX: 504-734-5849
Internet:
Suitable Sites: FB, RM, SC, OTHER
Concentration: 12 in LA, 1 in IL, 1 in NJ
  Expansion: All United States, Canada, Foreign
  Registered: CA,FL
Field Support: CP, EO, ST, SO, IC, N
  Training: 1 week franchisee's unit

Nutter's Bulk And Natural Foods
1601 Dunmore Rd SE #107
Medicine Hat, AB T1A-1Z8 CANADA

Phone: 403-529-1664   Accepts collect calls?
Toll Free: 800-665-5122   FAX: 403-529-6507
Internet:
Suitable Sites: SC
Concentration: 17 in AB, 12 in SK, 3 in BC
  Expansion: NW, Canada
  Registered: AB
Field Support: $CP, EO, ST, SO, $IC, $FC, H, N
  Training: 2 weeks head office
          2 weeks on-site

Sangsters Health Centres
2218 Hanselman Ave
Saskatoon, SK S7L-6A4 CANADA

Phone: 306-653-4481   Accepts collect calls? Y
Toll Free: FAX: 306-653-4688
Internet: www.sangsters.ca
Suitable Sites: RM
Concentration: 14 in SK, 11 in ON, 8 in AB
  Expansion: All United States, Canada, Foreign
  Registered: AB
Field Support: EO, ST, SO, IC, $FC, N
  Training: 5 days head office
         1-2 weeks franchisee location

Food Industry   Snack Foods

	Bw-3 Franchise Systems Inc	I.B. Nuts & Fruit Too	Kernels	Stuckey's Express	Tom's Foods	Tropik Sun Fruit & Nut		
Startup Cost	425K-750K	12K-20K	100K+	28K-135K	30K-250K	86K-171K		
Franchise Fee	25K	5K	25K	2.5K		20K		
Royalty	5%	0%	8%	$250/MO	2.5%	6%		
Advertising Fee		NA	1%	0.5%		0%		
Financing Provided	N	N	N	N	N	Y		
Experience Required			N		N			
Passive Ownership		N	D	A	A	A		
In Business Since	1982	1990	1983	1930	1925	1980		
Franchised Since	1991	1993	1984	1960	1977	1980		
Franchised Units 1996	61		60					
1997	64	11	59	120		75		
1998					770			
Company Owned 1996	10		10					
1997	10	1	8	2		5		
1998					66			
Number of Units U.S.		12		122	770	80		
Canada		0	66	0		0		
Foreign		0	14	0		0		
Projected New U.S.			3		50			
Canada			1					
Foreign			4					
Corporate Employees		8	10	12	2000	9		
Contract Length		5/5		20/10	7	lease		
Expand in Territory		Y	Y	Y	Y	N		
Full-Time Employees		1		VAR		1		
Part-Time Employees		1				4-8		
Conversions		N		Y		Y		
Site Selection Assist.		Y	Y	Y	Y	Y		
Lease Negotiation Assist.		Y	Y	Y	N	Y		
Site Space Required		750			1000-10000	200-1000		
Development Agreement		N		N		N		
Develop. Agree. Term								
Sub-franchising		N		N	N	N		

Food Industry   Snack Foods

Bw-3 Franchise Systems Inc
617 W Ohio Pike
Cincinnati, OH 45245
Buffalo wings
    Phone: 513-943-9293   Accepts collect calls?
    Toll Free: FAX:
    Internet:
Suitable Sites:
Concentration:
    Expansion: NE,S,SE,MW, Canada, Foreign
    Registered:
Field Support:
    Training:

I.B. Nuts & Fruit Too
1206 Business Loop 70 W
Columbia, MO 65202

    Phone: 573-875-2998   Accepts collect calls?
    Toll Free: FAX: 573-449-8971
    Internet:
Suitable Sites: HO, SF
Concentration: 8 in MO, 2 in IA, 1 in KS
    Expansion: Midwest
    Registered: AS REQUIRED
Field Support: EO, ST, SO, IC, FC, N
    Training: 2 days Columbia MO
              2-3 days franchise location

Kernels
40 Eglinton Ave E #250
Toronto, ON M4P-3A2 CANADA
Flavored popcorn
    Phone: 416-487-4194   Accepts collect calls?
    Toll Free: 888-COR-NCOB   FAX: 416-487-3920
    Internet: www.kernelspopcorn.com
Suitable Sites: AC, M
Concentration: ONT, BC, ALB
    Expansion: All United States, Canada, Foreign
    Registered: CA
Field Support:
    Training: 2-6 weeks store operations, marketing
              inventory, accounting

Stuckey's Express
4601 Willard Ave
Chevy Chase, MD 20815

    Phone: 301-913-9800   Accepts collect calls?
    Toll Free: 800-423-6171   FAX: 301-913-5424
    Internet:
Suitable Sites: ES, DA
Concentration: 10 in MS, 6 in SC, 5 in TN
    Expansion: All United States
    Registered: CA,IL,IN,MD,MI,VA,DC
Field Support: CP, EO, ST, SO, IC, FC, H
    Training: 1 week in-store

Tom's Foods
PO Box 60 900 8th St
Columbus, GA 31902
Manufacturer and marketer of snack foods
    Phone: 706-323-2721   Accepts collect calls?
    Toll Free: 800-704-1983   FAX: 706-323-9502
    Internet:
Suitable Sites: LI
Concentration:
    Expansion:
    Registered:
Field Support:
    Training: training & support provided by field staff

Tropik Sun Fruit & Nut
37 Sherwood Terrace #101
Lake Bluff, IL 60044

    Phone: 847-234-3407   Accepts collect calls?
    Toll Free: FAX: 847-234-3856
    Internet:
Suitable Sites: RM
Concentration: 15 in TX, 4 in AZ, 4 in LA
    Expansion: All United States
    Registered: CA,FL,HI,IL,IN,MD,MI,MN,ND,NY,OR,RI,SD,VA,WA,WI,DC
Field Support: EO, ST, SO, IC, $FC, N
    Training: 60 hours on-site

Food Industry

Other Food (Spread 1 of 2)

	Borvin Beverage	Chili Chompers	Heavenly Ham	Juice World	M & M Meat Shops	Open Pantry Food Marts	The Potato Sack	Star Mart
Startup Cost	37.75K	50K-95K	91K-216K	90K-295K	300K		200K-275K	70K-2.75M
Franchise Fee	25K	25K	30K	20K	30K	10K	20K	15K
Royalty	5%	5%	5%	4%	3%		5%	40%
Advertising Fee			1%	2%	1.5%		1%	2%
Financing Provided	Y	N	Y	Y	Y	Y	N	Y
Experience Required								
Passive Ownership			N	D	N	N	N	D
In Business Since	1993	1994	1984	1995	1980	1966	1980	1904
Franchised Since	1994	1996	1984	1995	1981	1966	1992	1992
Franchised Units 1996	1	0						
1997	1	2	151	3	211	39	4	112
1998					257			
Company Owned 1996	1	4						
1997	1	4	2	5	1	15	2	247
1998					1			
Number of Units U.S.			153	8	0	54	6	359
Canada			0	0	212	0	0	0
Foreign			0	0	0	0	0	0
Projected New U.S.					0			
Canada					30			
Foreign					0			
Corporate Employees			25	7	69	18	3	40
Contract Length			10/10	15/15	10/10		10/5	3/3
Expand in Territory			Y	Y	Y		N	Y
Full-Time Employees			2	3	2	3	3	4
Part-Time Employees			2	20	1	3	10	5
Conversions			N	N	Y	N	Y	Y
Site Selection Assist.			Y	Y	Y	N	Y	Y
Lease Negotiation Assist.			Y	Y	Y		Y	N
Site Space Required			2000	1100	1400			
Development Agreement			N	Y	N	N	N	N
Develop. Agree. Term				15				
Sub-franchising			N	Y	N	N	N	N

Food Industry

Borvin Beverage
1022 King St
Alexandria, VA 22314
Wholesale wines & distribution
     Phone: 703-683-9463   Accepts collect calls?
  Toll Free: FAX:
   Internet:
Suitable Sites:
Concentration:
  Expansion:
  Registered:
Field Support:
   Training:
	Chili Chompers
	PO Box 1128
	Stone Mountain, GA 30086
	Hot & spicy foods, chili-themed clothing & gifts
	     Phone: 770-465-7111 Accepts collect calls?
	  Toll Free: FAX:
	   Internet:
	Suitable Sites:
	Concentration:
	  Expansion: CA,MI,ND,VA,WI, Canada, Foreign
	  Registered:
	Field Support:
	   Training:

Heavenly Ham
20 Mansell Ct E #500
Roswell, GA 30076
 	
     Phone: 770-993-2232   Accepts collect calls?
  Toll Free: 800-899-2228   FAX: 770-587-3529
   Internet: www.heavenlyham.com
Suitable Sites: FB, SC
Concentration: 15 in FL, 10 in SC, 12 in MD
  Expansion: All United States
  Registered: CA,FL,IL,IN,MD,MI,MN,NY,OR,RI,VA,WA,WI,DC
Field Support: EO, ST, SO, IC, FC, H, N
   Training: 5 days Atlanta GA
	Juice World
	1238 Grand Ave
	Arroyo Grande, CA 93420
	
	     Phone: 805-481-9596 Accepts collect calls?
	  Toll Free: 800-658-4237 FAX: 805-481-8993
	   Internet: www.juiceworld.com
	Suitable Sites: SC, SF
	Concentration: 7 in CA, 1 in UT
	  Expansion: All United States, Canada, Foreign
	  Registered: CA,FL,OR,WA
	Field Support: $DP, EO, ST, SO, IC, FC, H, N
	   Training: 1 week office
	              1 week jw
	              1 week franchise store

M & M Meat Shops
640 Trillium Dr PO Box 2488
Kitchener, ON N2H-6M3 CANADA
 	
     Phone: 519-895-1075   Accepts collect calls? N
  Toll Free: FAX: 519-895-0762
   Internet:
Suitable Sites: SC
Concentration: 156 in ON, 28 in AB, 33 in PQ
  Expansion: N, Canada
  Registered: AB
Field Support: DP, CP, EO, ST, SO, IC, FC, H, N
   Training: 2 weeks head office or regional
              2 weeks franchisee store
              ongoing
	Open Pantry Food Marts
	817 S Main St
	Racine, WI 53403
	
	     Phone: 414-632-3161 Accepts collect calls?
	  Toll Free: 800-242-1018 FAX: 414-632-1463
	   Internet:
	Suitable Sites: FB, SC, SF
	Concentration: 53 in WI, 1 in IL
	  Expansion:
	  Registered: WI
	Field Support: EO, ST, SO, FC, H, N
	   Training:

The Potato Sack
201 Monroeville Mall
Monroeville, PA 15146
 	
     Phone: 412-373-0850   Accepts collect calls?
  Toll Free: 800-828-3770   FAX: 412-373-4497
   Internet:
Suitable Sites: RM
Concentration: 4 in PA, 2 in FL
  Expansion: PA, FL
  Registered: FL,NY,VA
Field Support: EO, ST, SO, IC, $FC, H, N
   Training: 10 days corp store in PA or FL
	Star Mart
	10 Universal City Plz #1039
	Universal City, CA 91608
	
	     Phone: 818-505-3795 Accepts collect calls?
	  Toll Free: 888-629-6919 FAX: 818-505-2497
	   Internet:
	Suitable Sites: FB
	Concentration: 84 in CA, 62 in AZ, 57 in WA
	  Expansion: Western United States
	  Registered: CA,MN,OR,SD,WA
	Field Support: EO, ST, FC, N
	   Training: 3 weeks phoenix, AZ

Food Industry

Other Food (Spread 2 of 2)

	Steak-Out	White Hen Pantry					
Startup Cost	207K-280K						
Franchise Fee	24.5K	25K					
Royalty	5%	7%+					
Advertising Fee	2%	0%					
Financing Provided	Y	Y					
Experience Required							
Passive Ownership	A	N					
In Business Since	1986	1965					
Franchised Since	1987	1965					
Franchised Units 1996							
1997	82	285					
1998							
Company Owned 1996							
1997	2	23					
1998							
Number of Units U.S.	84	308					
Canada	0	0					
Foreign	0	0					
Projected New U.S.							
Canada							
Foreign							
Corporate Employees	25	260					
Contract Length	10/10	10/10					
Expand in Territory	Y	N					
Full-Time Employees	2	2					
Part-Time Employees	35	12					
Conversions	Y						
Site Selection Assist.	Y	N					
Lease Negotiation Assist.	Y						
Site Space Required	1500	2500					
Development Agreement	Y	N					
Develop. Agree. Term							
Sub-franchising	N	N					

Food Industry

Other Food (Spread 2 of 2)

Steak-Out
1967 Lakeside Pkwy #420
Norcross, GA 30092

Phone: 770-493-6110   Accepts collect calls?
Toll Free: FAX: 770-493-6093
Internet:
Suitable Sites: FB, SC, SF
Concentration: 18 in AL, 15 in TN, 9 in GA
Expansion: SE, Midwest, Mid-Atlantic
Registered: FL,IL,IN,MD,MI,MN,OR,VA,WI,DC
Field Support: CP, EO, ST, SO, FC, N
Training: 4 weeks Columbia SC
1 week home study
1-2 weeks on-site

White Hen Pantry
660 Industrial Dr
Elmhurst, IL 60126

Phone: 630-833-3100   Accepts collect calls?
Toll Free: 800-726-8791   FAX: 630-833-0292
Internet:
Suitable Sites: SC
Concentration: 246 in IL, 55 in MA, 7 in IN
Expansion: IL,IN,MA,NH Only
Registered: IL,IN,MA
Field Support: DP, EO, ST, SO, FC, H, N
Training: 1 week corp. office
2 weeks on-site

Health Industry   **Adult Fitness**

	East Shore Athletic Club	Golds Gym	Jazzercise Inc	Lady of America	Madame Et Monsieur	World Gym		
Startup Cost	330K-565K	475K-1.8M	1.36K-16.85K	20K-40K	160K	208K-619K		
Franchise Fee	25K	12K	325-650	12.5K		12.75K		
Royalty	VAR.	VAR.	TO 20%	10%	$300/MO	$6.5K/YR		
Advertising Fee			0	0%	NEG.	0%		
Financing Provided	Y	Y	N	Y	Y	N		
Experience Required			N	N		N		
Passive Ownership			N	A	D	A		
In Business Since	1982	1979	1977	1984	1983	1977		
Franchised Since	1997	1987	1982	1986	1983	1985		
Franchised Units 1996		473	4458			231		
1997	0	498	4786	135	81	272		
1998			5078	175		264		
Company Owned 1996	0	1	2			1		
1997	3	1	2	10	2	1		
1998			2	0		1		
Number of Units U.S.			4119	170	9	249		
Canada			96	0	0	3		
Foreign			863	5	74	12		
Projected New U.S.			575	50		45		
Canada			25	20		2		
Foreign			100	10		5		
Corporate Employees			125	20	40	11		
Contract Length			5	10/5	5-10/5-10	3/3		
Expand in Territory			Y	Y	Y	Y		
Full-Time Employees				4	3	3-4		
Part-Time Employees				6		3		
Conversions				Y	N	Y		
Site Selection Assist.			Y	Y	Y	Y		
Lease Negotiation Assist.			Y	Y	Y	Y		
Site Space Required				1500-5000	1000	10000-15000		
Development Agreement			N	Y	N	Y		
Develop. Agree. Term				10		6		
Sub-franchising			N	Y		Y		

Health Industry   ## Adult Fitness

East Shore Athletic Club
709 Johnnie Dodds Blvd
Mount Pleasant, SC 29464
Coed fitness centers
    Phone: 803-849-3000   Accepts collect calls?
    Toll Free: FAX:
    Internet:
Suitable Sites:
Concentration:
    Expansion: IN,MI, Canada
    Registered:
Field Support:
    Training:

Golds Gym
358 Hampton Dr
Venice, CA 90291
Gym & fitness centers
    Phone: 310-392-3005   Accepts collect calls?
    Toll Free: FAX:
    Internet:
Suitable Sites:
Concentration:
    Expansion: All United States, Canada, Foreign
    Registered:
Field Support:
    Training:

Jazzercise Inc
2808 Roosevelt St
Carlsbad, CA 92008
Dance/exercise classes
    Phone: 760-434-2101   Accepts collect calls? N
    Toll Free: 800-FIT-ISIT   FAX: 760-434-8958
    Internet: www.jazzercise.com
Suitable Sites: AC, DA, FB, HO, IP, LI, M, OC, RM, SC, SF, WF, WR, OTHER
Concentration: 607 in CA, 315 in OH, 309 in TX
    Expansion: All United States, Canada, Foreign
    Registered: CA,FL,HI,IL,IN,MD,MI,MN,ND,NY,OR,RI,SD,VA,WA,WI,DC,AB
Field Support: FC, H, N
    Training: video + manual home study
    2-3 days on-site seminars

Lady of America
2400 E Commercial Blvd #808
Fort Lauderdale, FL 33308
Ladies only fitness centers specializing in aerobics, weight trn
    Phone: 954-492-1201   Accepts collect calls? N
    Toll Free: 800-833-5239   FAX: 954-492-1187
    Internet: www.ladyofamerica.com
Suitable Sites: AC, FB, M, PC, RM, SC, SF
Concentration: 42 in TX, 29 in FL, 8 in PA
    Expansion: All United States, Canada, Foreign
    Registered: CA,FL,IL,IN,MN,NY
Field Support: CP, $EO, ST, SO, $FC, H, N
    Training: 3 weeks on-site

Madame Et Monsieur
9669 Wilshire Blvd
Beverly Hills, CA 90210

    Phone: 310-275-8901   Accepts collect calls?
    Toll Free: FAX: 310-275-8906
    Internet:
Suitable Sites: RM, SF
Concentration:
    Expansion: All United States, Canada, Foreign
    Registered: CA,NY
Field Support: CP, ST, SO, FC, $H
    Training: 60 hours Beverly Hills CA
    3 weeks Beverly Hills CA

World Gym
2210 Main St
Santa Monica, CA 90405
Gym/fitness center, sell memberships, clothing, accessories
    Phone: 310-450-0080   Accepts collect calls? N
    Toll Free: 800-544-7441   FAX: 310-450-3455
    Internet: www.worldgym.com
Suitable Sites: DA, FB, M, RM, SC
Concentration: 32 in FL, 24 in CA, 18 in NY
    Expansion: All United States, Canada, Foreign
    Registered: CA,FL,HI,IL,IN,MD,MI,MN,NY,ND,RI,SD,VA,WA,WI
Field Support: ST, FC, H, N
    Training:

Health Industry   Medical Supplies (Spread 1 of 2)

	Amigo Mobility Center	Arrow Prescription Center	The Better Back Store	CPR+	Diversified Dental Services	Hayes Handpiece Franchises Inc	Health Mart	Medicap Pharmacy
Startup Cost	65K-89K	VAR.	139.5K-213.5K	7.5K	8.2K	5.5K	150K-300K	22.5K-285K
Franchise Fee	20K AVG	15K	22K	7.5K	18.5K	17K	500	8.5K-15K
Royalty	2-5%	6%	5%/$9K/YR.	5%	5%	3.5-5%	0%	2-4%
Advertising Fee	1%		1%	3%			150/MO	1%
Financing Provided	Y	Y	N	N	Y	N	N	Y
Experience Required								Y
Passive Ownership	D	D	D	D			A	A
In Business Since	1968	1989	1981	1993	1995	1989	1981	1971
Franchised Since	1984	1990	1993	1996	1995	1995	1983	1974
Franchised Units 1996					13	7		
1997	42	56	15	43	46	20	600	163
1998								
Company Owned 1996					0	6		
1997	5	3	0	1	9	7	0	8
1998								
Number of Units U.S.	47	59	15	44			600	168
Canada	0	0	0	0			0	0
Foreign	0	0	0	0			0	0
Projected New U.S.								
Canada								
Foreign								
Corporate Employees	9	30	5	3			5	47
Contract Length	10/5	20/10	10/10	5/5			5/5	20/20
Expand in Territory	Y	N	Y	Y			Y	Y
Full-Time Employees	2	2	2	1			2	2
Part-Time Employees	2	1-6	1				1	
Conversions	Y	Y		Y			Y	Y
Site Selection Assist.	Y	Y	Y	Y			N	Y
Lease Negotiation Assist.	Y	N	Y	N			N	Y
Site Space Required	1600	1500	2000	800			500	1500
Development Agreement	Y	Y	Y	Y			N	N
Develop. Agree. Term		5		10				
Sub-franchising	N	N	N	N			N	N

Health Industry

Amigo Mobility Center
6693 Dixie Hwy
Bridgeport, MI 48722-0402

Phone: 517-777-6537   Accepts collect calls?
Toll Free: 800-821-2710   FAX: 517-777-8184
Internet:
Suitable Sites: IP
Concentration: 9 in MI, 5 in FL, 5 in OH
Expansion: Midwest, SE,NE and Sunbelt, Foreign
Registered: FL,IL,IN,MI,NY,MN
Field Support: DP, CP, EO, ST, SO, IC, FC, H, N
Training: 14 days corporate HQ
18 days franchise center

Arrow Prescription Center
312 Farmington Ave
Farmington, CT 06032

Phone: 860-676-1222   Accepts collect calls?
Toll Free: 800-203-2776   FAX: 860-676-1499
Internet:
Suitable Sites: FB, SC
Concentration: 42 in CT, 5 in MI, 5 in MA
Expansion: All United States
Registered:
Field Support: DP, EO, ST, SO, IC, FC, H, N
Training: 1-2 weeks corporate training ctr

The Better Back Store
7636 E Arapahoe Ct #2100
Englewood, CO 80112

Phone: 303-721-1369   Accepts collect calls?
Toll Free: 800-501-2225   FAX: 303-721-1091
Internet: www.betterback.com
Suitable Sites: SC, SF
Concentration: 5 in CO
Expansion: All United States, Canada
Registered: CA,FL,HI,IL,IN,MD,MI,MN,ND,NY,OR,RI,SD,VA,WI,DC,AB
Field Support: ST, SO, $FC, N
Training: 40 hours Denver, CO
40 hours your site

CPR+
1044 Manhattan Beach Blvd
Manhattan Beach, CA 90266

Phone: 310-545-4191   Accepts collect calls?
Toll Free: 800-277-3333   FAX: 310-545-1712
Internet: www.cprplusnet.com
Suitable Sites: ES, DA
Concentration: 42 in CA, 1 in WA, 1 in LA
Expansion: All United States, Canada
Registered: CA,WA
Field Support: CP, EO, ST, SO, IC, FC, H, N
Training: 1 week home office in CA

Diversified Dental Services
10641 1st St E #204
Treasure Island, FL 33706
Dental handpiece repairs & sales
Phone: 813-367-6801   Accepts collect calls?
Toll Free: 800-365-4189   FAX:
Internet:
Suitable Sites:
Concentration:
Expansion: MI, Canada, Foreign
Registered:
Field Support:
Training:

Hayes Handpiece Franchises Inc
171 Saxony Rd #B
Encinitas, CA 92024
Dental handpiece repairs
Phone: 619-632-0911   Accepts collect calls?
Toll Free: FAX:
Internet:
Suitable Sites:
Concentration:
Expansion: All United States, Canada, Foreign
Registered:
Field Support:
Training:

Health Mart
1220 Senlac Dr
Carrollton, TX 75006

Phone: 972-446-4581   Accepts collect calls?
Toll Free: FAX: 972-446-5359
Internet:
Suitable Sites: FB, RM, SC, SF
Concentration: 83 in IL, 64 in MO, 59 in LA
Expansion: All United States
Registered: CA,FL,HI,IL,IN,MD,MI,MN,ND,NY,OR,RI,SD,VA,WA,WI,DC
Field Support: $CP, EO, ST, $SO, $FC, H, N
Training: 1-3 days on-site

Medicap Pharmacy
4700 Westown Pkwy #300
West Des Moines, IA 50266-6730
Pharmacy franchise company
Phone: 515-224-8400   Accepts collect calls? Y
Toll Free: 800-445-2244   FAX: 515-224-8415
Internet: www.medicaprx.com
Suitable Sites: FB, SC, SF
Concentration: 50 in IA, 10 in IL, 12 in NC
Expansion: All United States, Canada, Foreign
Registered: CA,FL,IL,IN,MD,MN,ND,OR,SD,WA,WI,MI,NY,RI,VA
Field Support: CP, EO, ST, SO, IC, FC, H, N
Training: 5 days HQ
3 days on-site
3 days computer

Health Industry   Medical Supplies (Spread 2 of 2)

	Medichair	The Medicine Shoppe	Miracle-Ear	Option Care	Relax The Back Franchising Co	Sutton Homes Franchising Corp	Total Medical Compliance	Women's Health Boutique
Startup Cost	80K-150K	54.6K-99K	100K-200K		130K-235K	220K-395K	50K-100K	214K-235K
Franchise Fee	25K	10K-18K	28K-60K	15K-35K	25K	33.3K-66.6K	35K-80K	20.8K
Royalty	5%	5.50%	$46.50/UNIT	VAR	4%	4-8%	2%	4-7%
Advertising Fee	0%	.6%	$26/INQUIRY	1.5%			.25%	0
Financing Provided	Y	Y	N	N	N	N	N	Y
Experience Required	N							N
Passive Ownership	D	A	N	A			A	N
In Business Since	1985	1970	1948	1979	1984	1985	1993	1988
Franchised Since	1988	1970	1983	1984	1989	1993	1995	1993
Franchised Units 1996					56	28		
1997	30	1250	1179	147	74	27	5	
1998	39	1238						14
Company Owned 1996					2	0		
1997	0	7	108	31	8	7	2	1
1998	2	10						2
Number of Units U.S.	0	1052	1267	178			7	16
Canada	41	37	0	0			0	0
Foreign	0	159	20	0			0	0
Projected New U.S.		23						10
Canada	50	7						0
Foreign		17						0
Corporate Employees	20	261	3	64			5	
Contract Length	5/5	20/10	5/5	20/10			5/5	10/10
Expand in Territory	Y	Y	Y	Y			Y	Y
Full-Time Employees	4	1	2				2	1
Part-Time Employees	1	2	1				1	1
Conversions	Y	Y		Y				N
Site Selection Assist.	Y	Y	N	N			N	Y
Lease Negotiation Assist.	Y	Y	N	N				Y
Site Space Required	2500	1200	750	1500				1500-2000
Development Agreement	Y	Y	Y	N			N	N
Develop. Agree. Term	10	3/20	1-1.5					
Sub-franchising	N	N	N	N			N	N

Health Industry

Medical Supplies (Spread 2 of 2)

Medichair

2506 Southern Ave
Brandon, MB R7B-0S4   CANADA
Provides all forms of home medical equipment and supplies

Phone: 204-726-1245   Accepts collect calls? Y
Toll Free: 800-667-0087   FAX: 204-726-5716
Internet: www.medichair.com
Suitable Sites: LI, SC
Concentration: 9 in BC, 15 in ON, 5 in AB
Expansion: Canada
Registered: AB
Field Support: DP, CP, EO, ST, SO, FC, H, N
Training: product, protocol, sales, admin.
MIS system
1 week corp store

The Medicine Shoppe

1100 N Lindbergh Blvd
Saint Louis, MO 63132
Professional pharmacies specialize in prescription & health-care

Phone: 314-993-6000   Accepts collect calls? N
Toll Free: 800-325-1397   FAX: 314-872-5500
Internet:
Suitable Sites: FB, SC, SF
Concentration: 122 in PA, 74 in OH, 74 in CA
Expansion: All United States, Canada, Foreign
Registered: CA,FL,HI,IL,IN,MD,MI,MN,ND,NY,OR,RI,SD,VA,WA,WI,DC,AB
Field Support: CP, EO, ST, SO, FC, H, N
Training: 6 days St. Louis, MO

Miracle-Ear

4101 Dahlberg Dr
Golden Valley, MN 55422

Phone: 612-520-9637   Accepts collect calls?
Toll Free: 800-234-7714   FAX: 612-520-9529
Internet: www.miracle-ear.com
Suitable Sites: FB, RM, SC, SF
Concentration: 96 in CA, 39 in TX, 74 in FL
Expansion: West and Midwest, Foreign
Registered: CA,FL,HI,IL,IN,MD,MI,MN,ND,NY,OR,RI,SD,VA,WA,WI,DC
Field Support: DP, EO, ST, SO, $FC, H, N
Training: 2 weeks corporate HQ
10 weeks on-site

Option Care

100 Corporate North #212
Bannockburn, IL 60015

Phone: 847-615-1690   Accepts collect calls?
Toll Free: 800-879-6137   FAX: 847-615-1755
Internet:
Suitable Sites: FB, SC, SF
Concentration: 16 in CA, 13 in FL, 13 in OH
Expansion: All United States
Registered: CA,HI,IL,IN,MD,MI,MN,NY,ND,RI,SD,VA,WA,WI
Field Support: CP, FC, H, N
Training: 4 days clinical ops Chicago IL
4 days sales/bus devel Chicago

Relax The Back Franchising Co

5910 Courtyard Dr #260
Austin, TX 78731
Products for back pain relief/prevention

Phone: Accepts collect calls?
Toll Free: 800-451-5168   FAX:
Internet:
Suitable Sites:
Concentration:
Expansion: All United States, Canada
Registered:
Field Support:
Training:

Sutton Homes Franchising Corp

5690 Dtc Blvd #270 W
Englewood, CO 80111
Alzheimer/personal care homes

Phone: 303-220-7989   Accepts collect calls?
Toll Free: FAX:
Internet:
Suitable Sites:
Concentration:
Expansion: MI, Canada
Registered:
Field Support:
Training:

Total Medical Compliance

11077 Biscayne Blvd #302
North Miami, FL 33161

Phone: 305-893-8767   Accepts collect calls?
Toll Free: 800-840-6742   FAX: 305-893-9340
Internet: www.centercourt.com/tmc
Suitable Sites:
Concentration: 4 in FL, 1 in NC, 1 in SC
Expansion: All United States
Registered: CA,FL,HI,IL,IN,MD,MI,MN,ND,NY,OR,RI,SD,VA,WA,WI,DC
Field Support: $CP, EO, ST, $FC, H, N
Training: 1 week home office
1 week franchisee territory

Women's Health Boutique

12715 Telge Rd
Cypress, TX 77429
Products & services for post breast surgery, pre/post natal etc.

Phone: 281-256-4100   Accepts collect calls? N
Toll Free: 888-280-2053   FAX: 281-256-4178
Internet: www.w-h-b.com
Suitable Sites: FB, M, SC, SF
Concentration: 5 in TX, 2 in MI, 2 in GA
Expansion: All United States
Registered: CA,FL,IL,IN,MD,MI,MN,NY,OR,RI,VA,WA,WI,DC
Field Support: CP, EO, ST, SO, $FC, H, N
Training: 3 week certification, operation, marketing
1 week existing boutique
3 on-site visits

Health Industry   Optical Supplies

	First Optometry Eye Care Centers	Pearle Vision Center	Sterling Optical					
Startup Cost	150K-250K	135K-2.5M	50K-100K					
Franchise Fee	10K	30K	20K					
Royalty	8%	7%	8%					
Advertising Fee	5%	9%	6%					
Financing Provided	Y	Y	Y					
Experience Required								
Passive Ownership	N	N	D					
In Business Since	1980	1961	1992					
Franchised Since	1981	1980	1992					
Franchised Units 1996								
1997	18	323	280					
1998								
Company Owned 1996								
1997	42	368	70					
1998								
Number of Units U.S.	50	637	341					
Canada	0	18	9					
Foreign	0	36	0					
Projected New U.S.								
Canada								
Foreign								
Corporate Employees	25	250	100					
Contract Length	10/5	10/10	10/10					
Expand in Territory	Y	Y	Y					
Full-Time Employees	5	VAR	3					
Part-Time Employees	2		2					
Conversions	Y	Y	Y					
Site Selection Assist.	Y		Y					
Lease Negotiation Assist.	Y	N	Y					
Site Space Required	2000	2000-2500	1200					
Development Agreement	Y	N	N					
Develop. Agree. Term	10							
Sub-franchising	Y	N	N					

Health Industry

Optical Supplies

First Optometry Eye Care Centers
32600 Grattiot Ave PO Box 710
Roseville, MI 48066

Phone: 810-296-7800   Accepts collect calls?
Toll Free: 800-792-3262   FAX: 810-294-2623
Internet: www.opimeyes.com
Suitable Sites: FB, RM, SC
Concentration:
    Expansion: Michigan Only
    Registered: MI
Field Support: DP, CP, EO, ST, SO, FC, H, N
    Training: 2 weeks Roseville MI
       on-going field training

Pearle Vision Center
2534 Royal Ln
Dallas, TX 75229

Phone: 972-277-5000   Accepts collect calls?
Toll Free: 800-732-7531   FAX: 972-277-5979
Internet:
Suitable Sites: FB, RM, SC
Concentration: 65 in PA, 53 in IL, 49 in TX
    Expansion: All United States
    Registered: CA,FL,HI,IL,IN,MD,MI,MN,NY,ND,OR,RI,SD,VA,WI,DC
Field Support: $DP, CP, EO, ST, SO, IC, FC, H, N
    Training: var w/skill assessment

Sterling Optical
1500 Hempstead Turnpike
East Meadow, NY 11577

Phone: 516-390-2100   Accepts collect calls?
Toll Free: FAX: 516-390-2111
Internet:
Suitable Sites: RM
Concentration: NY, CA, WI
    Expansion: All United States, Canada, Foreign
    Registered: CA,FL,IL,IN,MD,MI,MN,NY,OR,RI,VA,WA,WI,DC
Field Support: CP, EO, ST, SO, IC, FC, N
    Training: on-site

Health Industry   Weight Loss and Control

	Beverly Hills Weight Loss & Wellness	Diet Center Worldwide	Diet Light Weight Loss System	Hollywood Weight Loss Centre	Jenny Craig Weight Loss Centres	L A Weight Loss Centers Inc	Our Weigh	Slimmer Image Weight Loss Clinics
Startup Cost	50K-55K	16.4K-34.9K	25K-30K	1K-7.5K	150K-600K	35K-50K	3K	33.5K-100K
Franchise Fee	15K	4.9K	5K	1.5K-7.5K	50K	35K-20K	0	5K
Royalty	6%	8%/$75/WK	0%	4%/$100/WK	7%	7%	0%	4%
Advertising Fee	SUGG 2-4%	4%	0%	0%	0%	0	0%	
Financing Provided	Y	N	N	Y	N	N	N	Y
Experience Required						N		
Passive Ownership	D	N	D	N	D		D	
In Business Since	1986	1972	1983	1990	1983	1989	1974	1986
Franchised Since	1989	1972	1988	1990	1986	1997	1974	1996
Franchised Units 1996						0		0
1997	53	321	7	9	124	0	1	0
1998						13		
Company Owned 1996						35		9
1997	0	0	11	3	597	54	13	9
1998						123		
Number of Units U.S.	53	289	24	12	651	123	14	
Canada	0	31	0	0	30		0	
Foreign	0	1	0	0	40		0	
Projected New U.S.						60		
Canada								
Foreign								
Corporate Employees	5	19	3	3	200	700	1	
Contract Length	5/5-20	5/5/5	20/5	3/3	10/10	10/10		
Expand in Territory	Y	N	Y	Y	Y	Y	Y	
Full-Time Employees	2	2-3	1	1	4	2	1	
Part-Time Employees	1-2		2	1		4	1	
Conversions	Y	Y		Y			N	
Site Selection Assist.	Y	Y	Y	Y	Y	Y	N	
Lease Negotiation Assist.	Y	Y	Y	Y	Y	Y	N	
Site Space Required	2000	700-1200	600	250	1800	1000-1500	1500	
Development Agreement	Y	N	N	Y	Y	Y	Y	
Develop. Agree. Term	5			1	VAR	NEG.		
Sub-franchising	Y	N	N	N	N	Y	Y	

Health Industry   Weight Loss and Control

Beverly Hills Weight Loss & Wellness
200 Highpoint Ave #B-5
Portsmouth, RI 02871

   Phone: 401-683-6620   Accepts collect calls?
Toll Free: 800-825-4500   FAX: 401-683-6885
   Internet: www.beverlyhillsintl.com
Suitable Sites: SC, SF
Concentration:
   Expansion: All United States, Canada
   Registered: CA,FL,IN,MN,NY,RI,VA
Field Support: CP, EO, ST, SO, IC, FC, H, N
   Training: 2 weeks regional location

Diet Center Worldwide
395 Springside Dr
Akron, OH 44333-2496

   Phone: 330-665-5861   Accepts collect calls?
Toll Free: 800-656-3294   FAX: 330-666-2197
   Internet: www.dietcenterworldwide.com
Suitable Sites:
Concentration: 29 in NY, 25 in CA, 21 in NC
   Expansion: All United States, Canada
   Registered: CA,FL,HI,IL,IN,MD,MI,MN,ND,NY,OR,RI,SD,VA,WA,WI,DC
Field Support: DP, CP, $EO, $ST, SO, $FC, N
   Training: 1 week Akron OH

Diet Light Weight Loss System
300 Market St #101
Lebanon, OR 97355

   Phone: 541-259-3573   Accepts collect calls?
Toll Free: 800-248-7712   FAX: 541-259-3506
   Internet:
Suitable Sites: FB, RM, SC, SF
Concentration: 11 in OR, 4 in CA, 2 in TN
   Expansion: All United States
   Registered: CA,FL,HI,IL,IN,MD,MI,MN,ND,NY,OR,RI,SD,VA,WA,WI,DC
Field Support: CP, $EO, $ST, $SO, FC, H, N
   Training: 3 days Lebanon, OR

Hollywood Weight Loss Centre
PO Box 1070 College Station
Fredericksburg, VA 22402

   Phone: 540-891-7494   Accepts collect calls?
Toll Free: 888-477-5673   FAX: 540-891-7492
   Internet:
Suitable Sites: FB, SC, SF
Concentration: 10 in PA, 2 in WV, 1 in NC
   Expansion: SE, NE
   Registered:
Field Support: $EO, $ST, $SO, $FC, N
   Training: 2 days Fredericksburg VA
            2 days Uniontown PA

Jenny Craig Weight Loss Centres
11355 N Torrey Pines Rd
La Jolla, CA 92038-7910

   Phone: 619-812-7000   Accepts collect calls?
Toll Free: 800-583-6151   FAX: 619-812-2711
   Internet: www.jennycraig.com
Suitable Sites: SC
Concentration: 115 in CA, 42 in TX, 40 in IL
   Expansion: All United States, Canada, Foreign
   Registered: CA,IL,MI,MN,NY,ND,SD,VA,WA,WI,DC
Field Support: EO, ST, SO, IC, FC, H, N
   Training: 2 weeks San Diego CA
            1 week on-site
            2 weeks in field

L A Weight Loss Centers Inc
255 Business Center Dr #150
Horsham, PA 19044
Health services/weight loss counseling
   Phone: 215-328-9250   Accepts collect calls?
Toll Free: 888-411-8446   FAX: 215-328-9251
   Internet: www.laweightloss.com
Suitable Sites: AC, FB, OC, SF
Concentration: 37 in PA, 18 in NJ, 21 in NY
   Expansion: All United States, Canada, Foreign
   Registered: CA FL HI IL IN MD MI MN ND NY OR RI SD WA WI DC
Field Support: DP, CP, EO, ST, SO, IC, FC, H, N
   Training: 3 weeks for main operators
            3 days owner orientation

Our Weigh
3637 Park #201
Memphis, TN 38111

   Phone: 901-458-7546   Accepts collect calls?
Toll Free: FAX:
   Internet:
Suitable Sites: ES, DA
Concentration: 8 in TN, 4 in MS, 1 in AR
   Expansion: South
   Registered:
Field Support: $CP, $ST, $FC
   Training: 0

Slimmer Image Weight Loss Clinics
4240 Blue Ridge Blvd #350
Kansas City, MO 64133
Weight-loss centers
   Phone: 816-356-4000   Accepts collect calls?
Toll Free: 800-723-6258   FAX:
   Internet:
Suitable Sites:
Concentration:
   Expansion: IL
   Registered:
Field Support:
   Training:

Human Resources Industry   Executive-search Personnel

	Fortune Personnel Consultants	Management Recruiters	Sanford Rose Associates					
Startup Cost	28.6K-50.8K	89K-122K	51K-83K					
Franchise Fee	40K	65K	40K					
Royalty	7%	7%	3-7%					
Advertising Fee		0.5%	0%					
Financing Provided	Y	Y	Y					
Experience Required			N					
Passive Ownership		D	N					
In Business Since	1959	1957	1959					
Franchised Since	1973	1965	1970					
Franchised Units 1996	75							
1997	92	530	55					
1998								
Company Owned 1996	0							
1997	0	28	0					
1998								
Number of Units U.S.		558	50					
Canada		0	0					
Foreign		1	3					
Projected New U.S.			12					
Canada			1					
Foreign			1					
Corporate Employees		91	6					
Contract Length		5-20/10	7/1					
Expand in Territory		Y	N					
Full-Time Employees		3-4	1-10					
Part-Time Employees			1					
Conversions		Y	Y					
Site Selection Assist.		Y	Y					
Lease Negotiation Assist.		Y	Y					
Site Space Required		600-1000	300-1000					
Development Agreement		N	Y					
Develop. Agree. Term			7					
Sub-franchising		N	N					

Human Resources Industry

Executive-search Personnel

Fortune Personnel Consultants

1155 Ave Of The Americas
New York, NY 10036
Middle-management & executive recruiting
  Phone: 212-302-1141 Accepts collect calls?
  Toll Free: 800-886-7839 FAX:
  Internet:
Suitable Sites:
Concentration:
  Expansion: All United States, Canada, Foreign
  Registered:
Field Support:
  Training:

Management Recruiters

200 Public Sq 31st Fl
Cleveland, OH 44114-2301

  Phone: 216-696-1122 Accepts collect calls?
  Toll Free: 800-875-4000 FAX: 216-696-3221
  Internet: www.mrinet.com
Suitable Sites: FB
Concentration: 50 in FL, 49 in NC, 46 in CA
  Expansion: All United States
  Registered: CA,FL,HI,IL,IN,MD,MI,MN,ND,NY,OR,RI,SD,VA,WA,WI,DC
Field Support: EO, ST, SO, FC, H, N
  Training: 3 weeks HQ, Cleveland, OH
      3 weeks franchisee's location

Sanford Rose Associates

3737 Embassy Parkway Ste 200
Akron, OH 44333
Executive search services thru global network w/ specialists
  Phone: 330-670-9797 Accepts collect calls? N
  Toll Free: 800-731-7724 FAX: 330-670-9798
  Internet: www.sanfordrose.com
Suitable Sites: FB, OC
Concentration: 7 in OH, 4 in CA, 6 in IL
  Expansion: All United States, Canada, Foreign
  Registered: CA,IL,MD,MI,NY,VA,WA
Field Support: DP, CP, EO, ST, SO, IC, FC, H, N
  Training: 10 days corporate HQ
      5 days on-site
      6-9 months on-going basic support

Human Resources Industry   General Personnel

	ATS Personnel	Atwork Personnel Services	Dunhill Staffing Systems, Inc.	Express Personnel Services	Labor Force	Link Staffing Services	Snelling Personnel Services	
Startup Cost	75K-110K	35K-75K	60K-150K	100K-150K	111K-127K	95K-150K	97K-142K	
Franchise Fee	12.5K	$1	15K-38K	14.5K-17.5K	15K-25K	15K	9K	
Royalty	6.90%	8%	7%	6-9%	6%	VAR.	4.5-7%	
Advertising Fee	0.5%	0%	1%	.6-2%	0%	.05%	0.5-1%	
Financing Provided	Y	Y	Y	Y	N	Y	Y	
Experience Required			N			N		
Passive Ownership	N	D	D	N	D	D	D	
In Business Since	1978	1990	1952	1983	1970	1980	1951	
Franchised Since	1991	1992	1961	1985	1992	1994	1955	
Franchised Units 1996			157					
1997	5	40	164	350	23	26	280	
1998			171					
Company Owned 1996			17					
1997	9	0	19	0	16	13	28	
1998			26					
Number of Units U.S.	14	40	161	330	39	39	302	
Canada	0	0	4	7	0	0	0	
Foreign	0	0	0	13	0	0	6	
Projected New U.S.			10			11		
Canada			2					
Foreign			0					
Corporate Employees	17	15	38	140	20	40	100	
Contract Length	10/5	10/5	10/10	5/5	10/10	10/5/5/5	LIFETIME	
Expand in Territory	Y	Y	Y	Y	Y	Y	N	
Full-Time Employees	2	3	4	2	3	3	4-6	
Part-Time Employees	1	1	1	1				
Conversions	N	Y	Y	N	Y	Y	Y	
Site Selection Assist.	Y	Y	Y	Y	Y	Y	Y	
Lease Negotiation Assist.	Y	N	Y	Y	Y	Y	Y	
Site Space Required	1000	800	1000	1200	800-1200	1600-1800	600-800	
Development Agreement	N	N	N	N	N	N	Y	
Develop. Agree. Term								
Sub-franchising	N	N	N	N	N	N	N	

Human Resources Industry   General Personnel

ATS Personnel
10407 Centurian Pkwy N #101
Jacksonville, FL 32256

Phone: 904-645-9505   Accepts collect calls?
Toll Free: 800-346-5574   FAX: 904-645-0390
Internet: www.ats-services.com
Suitable Sites: SC
Concentration: 7 in GA, 2 in SC, 2 in LA
Expansion: FL, NC
Registered: FL,NY
Field Support: DP, CP, EO, ST, SO, IC, $FC, H, N
Training: 2 weeks corporate office
2 weeks on-site

Atwork Personnel Services
1470 Main St PO Box 989
White Pine, TN 37821

Phone: 423-674-7666   Accepts collect calls?
Toll Free: 800-233-6846   FAX: 423-674-8780
Internet:
Suitable Sites: FB, RM, SC, SF
Concentration: 15 in TN, 3 in NC, 2 in ME
Expansion: All United States
Registered: CA,FL,HI,IL,IN,MD,MI,MN,ND,NY,OR,RI,SD,VA,WA,WI,DC
Field Support: DP, EO, ST, FC, H
Training: 4-5 days corporate office

Dunhill Staffing Systems, Inc.
150 Motor Pkwy
Hauppauge, NY 11788
Professional & temporary staffing, executive, technical
Phone: 516-952-3000   Accepts collect calls? N
Toll Free: 800-386-7823   FAX: 516-952-3500
Internet: www.dunhillstaff.com/dun18.htm
Suitable Sites: ES, FB, IP, OC, RM, SC, SF
Concentration: 8 in IN, 7 in CT, 10 in TX
Expansion: All United States, Canada
Registered: CA,FL,IL,IN,MD,MI,MN,ND,NY,OR,RI,SD,VA,WA,WI,DC
Field Support: $DP, $CP, EO, ST, $SO, IC, $FC, H, N
Training: 3 weeks HQ & franchisee locat.

Express Personnel Services
6300 NW Expy
Oklahoma City, OK 73132

Phone: 405-840-5000   Accepts collect calls?
Toll Free: 800-652-6400   FAX: 405-720-1040
Internet: www.monster.com/expresspersonnel
Suitable Sites: RM, SC, SF
Concentration: 28 in TX, 22 in OK, 17 in WA
Expansion: All United States, Canada, Foreign
Registered: CA,FL,HI,IL,IN,MD,MI,MN,ND,NY,OR,RI,SD,VA,WA,WI,DC
Field Support: DP, CP, EO, ST, SO, IC, FC, H, N
Training: 3 weeks Oklahoma City, OK
1 week on-site

Labor Force
5225 Katy Fwy #600
Houston, TX 77007

Phone: 713-802-1284   Accepts collect calls?
Toll Free: 800-299-4312   FAX: 713-864-9897
Internet: www.laborforce.com
Suitable Sites: SC
Concentration: 17 in TX, 5 in GA, 3 in AZ
Expansion: All United States, Canada, Foreign
Registered:
Field Support: CP, EO, ST, SO, FC, H, N
Training: 2 weeks national training center
1 week on-site

Link Staffing Services
1800 Bering Dr #801
Houston, TX 77057-3129

Phone: 713-784-4400   Accepts collect calls? N
Toll Free: 800-848-5465   FAX: 713-784-4454
Internet:
Suitable Sites: IP, SC
Concentration: 16 in TX, 9 in FL, 3 in GA
Expansion: All United States, Canada
Registered: CA,FL,IN,MD,MN,NY,OR,RI,VA,WA,WI,DC,IL,MI,ND,SD
Field Support: DP, CP, EO, ST, SO, FC, H, N
Training: 2 weeks Houston, TX
1 week field

Snelling Personnel Services
12801 N Central Expy #700
Dallas, TX 75243

Phone: 972-239-7575   Accepts collect calls?
Toll Free: 800-766-5556   FAX: 972-239-6881
Internet: www.snelling.com
Suitable Sites: FB, SC, SF
Concentration: 31 in TX, 20 in MI, 18 in IL
Expansion: All United States
Registered: CA,FL,HI,IL,IN,MD,MI,MN,ND,NY,OR,RI,SD,VA,WA,WI,DC
Field Support: DP, $CP, EO, ST, SO, FC, H, N
Training: 2 weeks Snelling university

Human Resources Industry

Medical Personnel

	Firstat Nursing Services	Health Force	Home Instead Senior Care	Interim Healthcare	NurseFinders	Staff Builders Home Health Care	We Care Home Health Services	Western Medical Services
Startup Cost	200K	100K-120K	20K-25.7K	150K-200K	110K-145K	110K-150K	100K-150K	200K-250K
Franchise Fee	25K	19.5K	14.5K	10K	19.6K	29.5K	25K	30K-40K
Royalty	0.3-0.5%	VAR.	5%	7%	7%	VAR.	5%	8%
Advertising Fee	N/A	.5%	0%	.0025%	0%	N/A	2%	INCLUDED
Financing Provided	Y	Y	N	Y	Y	Y	Y	N
Experience Required		N			N			
Passive Ownership	N	D	D	D	D	A	N	N
In Business Since	1989	1976	1994	1946	1974	1967	1984	1967
Franchised Since	1990	1982	1995	1966	1978	1967	1988	1975
Franchised Units 1996								
1997	33	56	92	277	54	202	64	16
1998		49			52			
Company Owned 1996								
1997	2	24	1	117	60	48	0	38
1998		24			60			
Number of Units U.S.	34	73	93	378	112	248	0	54
Canada	1	0	0	13	0	0	64	0
Foreign	0	0	0	3	0	2	0	0
Projected New U.S.		80			15			
Canada								
Foreign								
Corporate Employees	15		8	500	118	350	15	250
Contract Length	5/10	10/10	5/5	5/5	10/5/5	10/5	10/10	INDEFIN.
Expand in Territory	Y	Y	Y	Y	Y	Y	N	Y
Full-Time Employees	5	3	1	3	5	4	2	3
Part-Time Employees	1		30-40		100	2	2	
Conversions	Y	Y	N	Y	Y	Y	Y	Y
Site Selection Assist.	Y	Y	Y	Y	Y	Y	Y	Y
Lease Negotiation Assist.	Y	Y	Y	Y	Y	N	Y	N
Site Space Required	1500	800-1000		1000-1200	1500-2000	1000	850-1000	500-750
Development Agreement	N	N	N	N	Y	N	Y	N
Develop. Agree. Term					5/5		10	
Sub-franchising	N	N	N	N	N	N	N	N

Human Resources Industry   Medical Personnel

Firstat Nursing Services
801 Village Blvd #303
West Palm Beach, FL 33409

    Phone: 561-689-7100   Accepts collect calls?
Toll Free: 800-845-7828   FAX: 561-689-4057
Internet: www.firstatnursingservices.com
Suitable Sites: OC, SC, SF
Concentration: 4 in FL, 4 in MN, 4 in OH
    Expansion: All United States, Canada
    Registered: CA,FL,HI,IL,IN,MD,MI,MN,ND,NY,OR,RI,SD,VA,WA,WI,DC
Field Support: EO, ST, SO, FC, H, N
    Training: 5 days home office
        5 days franchisee location

Health Force
185 Crossways Park Dr
Woodbury, NY 11797-2047
Home health care & health staffing services
    Phone: 516-682-1441   Accepts collect calls? N
Toll Free: FAX: 516-496-3283
Internet:
Suitable Sites:
Concentration: 12 in NY, 10 in FL, 6 in CA
    Expansion: All United States, Canada, Foreign
    Registered: CA,FL,IL,IN,MD,MI,MN,NY,OR,WA,WI,DC,RI,VA
Field Support: DP, CP, EO, ST, SO, IC, FC, N
    Training: training at operation center
        and on-site

Home Instead Senior Care
1104 S 76th Ave #A
Omaha, NE 68124

    Phone: 402-391-2555   Accepts collect calls?
Toll Free: 888-484-5759   FAX: 402-391-2491
Internet: homeinstead@aol.com
Suitable Sites: SF
Concentration: 10 in FL, 10 in CA, 5 in MO
    Expansion: All United States, Canada, Foreign
    Registered: CA,FL,HI,IL,IN,MD,MI,MN,ND,NY,OR,RI,SD,VA,WA,WI,DC
Field Support: DP, CP, EO, $ST, SO, IC, FC, H, N
    Training: 1 week Omaha, NE
        48 hours local office visit

Interim Healthcare
2050 Spectrum Blvd
Fort Lauderdale, FL 33309

    Phone: 954-938-7600   Accepts collect calls?
Toll Free: 800-840-6568   FAX: 954-938-7750
Internet: www.interim.com
Suitable Sites: OC, SC
Concentration: 36 in FL, 32 in NC, 29 in CA
    Expansion: ID, IN, MI, ND Only, Foreign
    Registered: CA,FL,HI,IL,IN,MD,MI,MN,ND,NY,OR,RI,SD,VA,WA,WI,DC
Field Support: DP, EO, ST, SO, FC, H, N
    Training: 2 weeks HQ
        1 week on-site

NurseFinders
1200 Copeland Rd #200
Arlington, TX 76011

    Phone: 817-460-1181   Accepts collect calls?
Toll Free: 800-445-0459   FAX: 817-460-1969
Internet: www.nursefinders.com
Suitable Sites: ES, OC
Concentration: 11 in FL, 7 in NJ, 5 in IN
    Expansion: All United States
    Registered: CA,FL,HI,IL,IN,MD,MI,MN,ND,NY,OR,RI,SD,VA,WA,WI,DC
Field Support: DP, CP, EO, ST, SO, $FC, H, N
    Training: 1 week Arlington, TX
        1 week company office
        2 weeks on-site

Staff Builders Home Health Care
1983 Marcus Ave
Lake Success, NY 11042-7011

    Phone: 516-358-1000   Accepts collect calls?
Toll Free: 800-444-4633   FAX: 516-358-3678
Internet:
Suitable Sites: FB, SC, SF
Concentration: 20 in PA, 19 in NY, 18 in OH
    Expansion: All United States, Canada, Foreign
    Registered: CA,FL,HI,IL,IN,MD,MI,MN,ND,NY,OR,RI,SD,VA,WA,WI,DC
Field Support: DP, CP, EO, ST, SO, FC, N
    Training: 5 days corporate office in NY
        5 days regional location

We Care Home Health Services
201 City Centre Dr #606
Mississauga, ON L5B-2T4   CANADA

    Phone: 905-949-9488   Accepts collect calls?
Toll Free: 800-316-2212   FAX: 905-949-9717
Internet: www.docker.com/~wecare.home.html
Suitable Sites:
Concentration: 23 in ON, 14 in BC, 8 in AB
    Expansion: Canada
    Registered: CA,AB
Field Support: EO, ST, SO, FC, H, N
    Training: 3 weeks Mississauga, ON
        1 week franchisee's location

Western Medical Services
220 N Wiget Ln
Walnut Creek, CA 94598

    Phone: 925-256-1561   Accepts collect calls?
Toll Free: 800-872-8367   FAX: 925-952-2591
Internet: www.westaff.com
Suitable Sites: FB, SC, SF
Concentration: 10 in IN, 8 in CA, 5 in OH
    Expansion: All United States
    Registered: CA,FL,IL,IN,MD,MI,MN,NY,OR,SD,VA,WA,WI
Field Support: DP, CP, EO, ST, SO, FC, H, N
    Training: 5 days corporate HQ
        5 days on-site

Human Resources Industry　　　　　　　Temporary Personnel (Spread 1 of 2)

	AccuStaff Inc	Checkmate	CompuTemp Inc	Legal Staffing Services	LawCorps	PrideStaff	Remedy Intelligent Staffing	Talent Tree Staffing Services	TechStaff
Startup Cost	75K-100K	25K-50K	136.7K-202K	81K-106K	86.5K-135.8K	95K-150K		100K-125K
Franchise Fee	12.5K	23.5K	30K	25K	0	17K	10K-20K	25K
Royalty	30%	7.50%	7%	8%	VAR.	VAR.	40%-$2M	6.9-3.9%
Advertising Fee		0%		N/A		0%	0	N/A
Financing Provided	N	N	Y	Y	Y	Y	N	Y
Experience Required				N	N			
Passive Ownership		N		D	N	D	A	D
In Business Since	1960	1992	1984	1988	1978	1965	1976	1985
Franchised Since	1975	1993	1991	1995	1996	1988	1991	1987
Franchised Units 1996	29		19		1			
1997	37	15	26	1	5	118	18	10
1998				3	9			
Company Owned 1996	10		7		10			
1997	0	0	7	1	11	80	150	0
1998				3	13			
Number of Units U.S.		15		6	22	198	168	10
Canada		0		0	0	0	0	0
Foreign		0		0	0	0	0	0
Projected New U.S.				4	10			
Canada								
Foreign								
Corporate Employees		5		5	50	140	110	7
Contract Length		10/5		7/7	10/5/5	10/5	10/5	20/20
Expand in Territory		Y		N	Y	Y	Y	Y
Full-Time Employees		3		2	2	5	4	2
Part-Time Employees		1-2		1	0	1	1	
Conversions		Y		Y	N	Y	Y	
Site Selection Assist.		N		Y	Y	Y	Y	Y
Lease Negotiation Assist.				N	Y	Y	Y	Y
Site Space Required				200-500	1000-1200	1200	1000	1500
Development Agreement		N		N	N	Y	N	Y
Develop. Agree. Term						10		2-3
Sub-franchising		N		N	N	N	N	Y

Human Resources Industry

AccuStaff Inc
177 Crossways Park Dr
Woodbury, NY 11797
Employment services

Phone: 516-682-1432   Accepts collect calls?
Toll Free: FAX:
Internet:
Suitable Sites:
Concentration:
Expansion:
Registered:
Field Support:
Training:

Checkmate
PO Box 32034
Charleston, SC 29417
Employee leasing

Phone: 803-763-9393   Accepts collect calls? N
Toll Free: 800-964-6298   FAX: 803-571-1851
Internet: www.checkmatepeo.com
Suitable Sites: HO, OC
Concentration: 4 in LA, 3 in SC, 2 in FL
Expansion: All United States
Registered:
Field Support: $FC, H, N
Training: 1 week New Orleans, LA

CompuTemp Inc
4401 N Federal Hwy #202
Boca Raton, FL 33431
Info tech staffing services

Phone: 561-362-9104   Accepts collect calls?
Toll Free: 800-275-2667   FAX:
Internet:
Suitable Sites:
Concentration:
Expansion: All United States
Registered:
Field Support:
Training:

LawCorps Legal Staffing Services
1899 L St NW 5th Fl
Washington, DC 20036
Provides law firms and corp legal depts w/ temp legal staff

Phone: 202-785-5996   Accepts collect calls?
Toll Free: 800-437-8809   FAX: 202-785-1118
Internet: www.lawcorps.com
Suitable Sites: AC, ES
Concentration: 1 in DC, 1 in IL
Expansion: All United States, Canada, Foreign
Registered: CA,FL,IL,MI,MN,NY
Field Support: $DP, $CP, EO, ST, SO, FC, H, $N
Training: 2 weeks HQ
    1 week franchise offices

PrideStaff
6780 N West Ave #103
Fresno, CA 93711-1393
Staffing services

Phone: 559-432-7780   Accepts collect calls? N
Toll Free: 800-774-3316   FAX: 559-432-4371
Internet: www.pridestaff.com
Suitable Sites: FB, OC
Concentration: 4 in CA, 2 in AZ
Expansion: All United States, Canada
Registered:
Field Support: DP, CP, EO, ST, SO, IC, FC, H, N
Training: pre-opening
    on-site
    ongoing courses

Remedy Intelligent Staffing
32122 Camino Capistrano
San Juan Capistrano, CA 92675

Phone: 714-661-1211   Accepts collect calls?
Toll Free: 800-722-8367   FAX: 714-248-0813
Internet: www.remedystaff.com
Suitable Sites: OC
Concentration: 68 in CA, 14 in FL, 10 in TX
Expansion: All United States
Registered: CA,FL,HI,IL,IN,MD,MI,MN,NY,OR,RI,VA,WA,WI,DC,AB
Field Support: DP, EO, ST, SO, FC, H, N
Training: 2 weeks home office
    1 week on-site

Talent Tree Staffing Services
9703 Richmond Ave
Houston, TX 77042

Phone: 713-789-1818   Accepts collect calls?
Toll Free: 800-827-8733   FAX: 713-974-6507
Internet: www.ttree.com
Suitable Sites: OC
Concentration: 32 in CA, 14 in TX, 14 in GA
Expansion: All United States
Registered:
Field Support: DP, $CP, EO, ST, SO, $FC, H, N
Training: 3-4 weeks Houston, TX

TechStaff
11270 W Park Pl #111
Milwaukee, WI 53224

Phone: 414-359-4444   Accepts collect calls?
Toll Free: 800-515-4440   FAX: 414-359-4949
Internet: www.techstaff.com
Suitable Sites: OC, SF
Concentration: 3 in CA, 2 in WI, 2 in MI
Expansion: All United States
Registered: CA,FL,IL,IN,MD,MI,WI,DC
Field Support: DP, CP, EO, ST, SO, FC, N
Training: 1 week corporate office
    13 weeks franchise office

Human Resources Industry

Temporary Personnel (Spread 2 of 2)

	Today's Temporary	TRC Staffing Services					
Startup Cost	90K-145K	25K					
Franchise Fee	20K	$0					
Royalty	VAR.	9.50%					
Advertising Fee	0%	0%					
Financing Provided	N	Y					
Experience Required							
Passive Ownership	N	N					
In Business Since	1982	1980					
Franchised Since	1983	1984					
Franchised Units 1996							
1997	16	42					
1998							
Company Owned 1996							
1997	104	27					
1998							
Number of Units U.S.	108	69					
Canada	11	0					
Foreign	0	0					
Projected New U.S.							
Canada							
Foreign							
Corporate Employees	85	117					
Contract Length	5/5/5	5/5					
Expand in Territory	Y	Y					
Full-Time Employees	3	2					
Part-Time Employees							
Conversions	Y	Y					
Site Selection Assist.	Y	Y					
Lease Negotiation Assist.	N	Y					
Site Space Required	1200	800					
Development Agreement	Y	N					
Develop. Agree. Term							
Sub-franchising	N	N					

Human Resources Industry

Temporary Personnel (Spread 2 of 2)

Today's Temporary

18111 Preston Rd #700
Dallas, TX 75252-4383

Phone: 972-380-9380   Accepts collect calls? N
Toll Free: 800-822-7868   FAX: 972-713-4198
Internet:
Suitable Sites: OC
Concentration: 4 in TX, 2 in FL
Expansion: All United States
Registered: CA,IN,MI,NY
Field Support: DP, EO, ST, SO, FC, H, N
Training: 2 weeks Dallas, TX
2 weeks field

TRC Staffing Services

100 Ashford Center N #500
Atlanta, GA 30338

Phone: 770-392-1411   Accepts collect calls?
Toll Free: 800-488-8008   FAX: 770-698-7885
Internet: www.trcstaff.com
Suitable Sites: OC
Concentration: 21 in GA, 10 in TX, 7 in CA
Expansion: All United States
Registered: CA,FL,HI,IL,IN,MD,MN,NY,OR,RI,VA,WA,WI,DC
Field Support: DP, $CP, EO, ST, SO, $FC, H, N
Training: 1 week Atlanta, GA
1 week on-site

Human Resources Industry   Other Human Resources

	Norrell Services	PersoNet-The Personnel Network	The Resume Hut	Seniors for Seniors/ Seniors for Business				
Startup Cost	75.7K-176.4K	15K+	25K-625K	50K-100K				
Franchise Fee	$0	15K	12.5K	15K-30K				
Royalty	VAR.	VAR.	FIXED	5%				
Advertising Fee	0%	0	FIXED	3%				
Financing Provided	Y	Y	N	N				
Experience Required		N	N					
Passive Ownership	N	A	N	N				
In Business Since	1961	1994	1986	1985				
Franchised Since	1966	1994	1993	1990				
Franchised Units 1996		3						
1997	114	4	0	4				
1998		5	0					
Company Owned 1996		0						
1997	161	0	1	2				
1998		0						
Number of Units U.S.	270	5	0	0				
Canada	5	0	1	6				
Foreign	0	0	0	0				
Projected New U.S.		7						
Canada		0	5					
Foreign		0						
Corporate Employees	450	4	0	5				
Contract Length	10/15	10	5/5	5/5				
Expand in Territory	Y	Y	Y	Y				
Full-Time Employees	VAR	2	1	5				
Part-Time Employees		0	1					
Conversions		Y	Y					
Site Selection Assist.	Y	Y	Y	Y				
Lease Negotiation Assist.	N	N	Y	Y				
Site Space Required	1000	600	500	1000				
Development Agreement	N	Y	N	Y				
Develop. Agree. Term		10		5				
Sub-franchising	N	N	N	N				

Human Resources Industry

Other Human Resources

Norrell Services
3535 Piedmont Rd NE
Atlanta, GA 30305

Phone: 404-240-3687   Accepts collect calls?
Toll Free: 800-765-6342   FAX: 404-240-3084
Internet: www.norrell.com
Suitable Sites:
Concentration: 32 in CA, 29 in FL, 21 in GA
Expansion: All United States, Canada
Registered: CA,FL,IL,IN,MD,MI,MN,NY,OR,SD,VA,WA,WI
Field Support: DP, CP, EO, ST, SO, FC, H
Training: 135 hours classroom Atlanta
40+ weeks pre-open. in-field
120 hours pre-post-opening

PersoNet-The Personnel Network
PO Box 3436
Holiday, FL 34690
Staffing/human resource consulting/payroll svcs/employee leasing
Phone: 727-372-2996   Accepts collect calls? N
Toll Free: 800-628-3777   FAX: 727-372-3608
Internet: www.personet.com
Suitable Sites: ES, DA, IP, OC, SC, SF
Concentration: 3 in FL, 1 in MI, 1 in IN
Expansion:
Registered: FL,IN,MI
Field Support: DP, $ST, FC, N
Training: depends on experience - customized

The Resume Hut
743 View St
Victoria, BC V8W-1J9 CANADA
Career consultancy providing resumes, career assessment, etc
Phone: 250-383-3983   Accepts collect calls?
Toll Free: 800-441-6488   FAX: 250-383-1580
Internet: www.resumehut.com
Suitable Sites: FB, HO, M, OC, RM, SC, SF
Concentration: 1 in BC
Expansion: All United States, Canada
Registered:
Field Support: SO
Training: 1 week Victoria, Vancouver Island

Seniors for Seniors/ Seniors for Business
55 Eglinton Ave E #311
Toronto, ON M4P-1G8 CANADA

Phone: 416-481-4579   Accepts collect calls?
Toll Free: FAX: 416-481-6752
Internet:
Suitable Sites:
Concentration: 4 in ON, 1 in NS, 1 in PQ
Expansion: SE, Canada
Registered:
Field Support: EO, ST, FC, N
Training: 3 weeks Toronto, ON

Interior Design Industry   Carpet

	Carpet Master	Carpet Network	Floor Coverings International	GCO Carpet Outlet	Mobile Carpet Showroom	Floor & Window Coverings Lifestyle	Nationwide Coverings		
Startup Cost	62K-97K	26K	18.5K-35K	260K-522K	15K-20K	5K		
Franchise Fee	25K	15.5K	14K	25K	12K	11.9K+		
Royalty	5%	5%	5%/$45/WK	3-5%	5%	5%		
Advertising Fee	2%	0%	2%/$15/WK	500/MO	0%	0		
Financing Provided	Y	Y	Y	Y	N	Y		
Experience Required		N	N			N		
Passive Ownership	D	D	D	D	D	A		
In Business Since	1994	1991	1988	1988	1991	1992		
Franchised Since	1995	1992	1989	1989	1992	1995		
Franchised Units 1996						11		
1997	12	55	394	102	5	14		
1998						17		
Company Owned 1996						0		
1997	0	1	0	6	0	0		
1998						0		
Number of Units U.S.	12	56	220	108	5	17		
Canada	0	0	16	0	0	0		
Foreign	0	0	158	0	0	0		
Projected New U.S.						12		
Canada						1		
Foreign						0		
Corporate Employees	12	4	20	33	8	3		
Contract Length	10/5	5/5/5/5	10/10	10/5/5	10/10	10		
Expand in Territory	Y	Y	Y	Y	Y	Y		
Full-Time Employees	2	1	1	4	1	0		
Part-Time Employees		0		1		0		
Conversions	Y		Y	Y	Y	Y		
Site Selection Assist.	Y	Y	Y	Y	N	N		
Lease Negotiation Assist.	Y	N		Y		N		
Site Space Required	1000			10000				
Development Agreement	Y	N	Y	N	N	N		
Develop. Agree. Term	3		10/20					
Sub-franchising	Y	N	N	N	N	N		

Interior Design Industry   Carpet

Carpet Master
5066 Sunrise Hwy
Massapequa Park, NY 11762

Phone: 516-798-7000   Accepts collect calls?
Toll Free: 800-596-7847   FAX: 516-795-3545
Internet:
Suitable Sites: FB, SC, SF
Concentration: 10 in NY, 2 in NJ
Expansion: All United States, Canada, Foreign
Registered: FL,MD,NY,VA
Field Support: DP, CP, EO, ST, SO, $FC, H, N
Training: 2 weeks long island
1 week store set-up
2 weeks after grand opening

Carpet Network
109 Gaither Dr #302
Mount Laurel, NJ 08054
Mobile floor-covering and window treatment business
Phone: 609-273-2877   Accepts collect calls? N
Toll Free: 800-428-1067   FAX: 609-273-0160
Internet: www.carpetnetwork.com
Suitable Sites: HO
Concentration: PA, NY, IA
Expansion: All United States
Registered: CA,FL,IN,MD,MI,NY,VA,WI
Field Support: $FC, H, N
Training: 2 weeks in home
2 days corp. office

Floor Coverings International
5182 Old Dixie Hwy
Forest Park, GA 30297
Mobile retail floor covering business, soft & hard flooring
Phone: 404-361-5047   Accepts collect calls? N
Toll Free: 800-955-4324   FAX: 404-366-4606
Internet: www.carpetvan.com
Suitable Sites: HO, OC
Concentration: 17 in PA, 13 in OH, 10 in NC
Expansion: All United States, Canada, Foreign
Registered: CA,FL,HI,IL,IN,MD,MI,MN,ND,NY,OR,RI,SD,VA,WA,WI,DC
Field Support: EO, ST, FC, H, N
Training: 2 weeks home study
2 weeks Atlanta, GA
1 week in field

GCO Carpet Outlet
7061 Halcyon Summit Dr
Montgomery, AL 36117-6927

Phone: 334-279-8345   Accepts collect calls?
Toll Free: 800-279-8345   FAX: 334-279-0536
Internet:
Suitable Sites: FB, SC, SF
Concentration: 19 in FL, 9 in MN, 8 in WI
Expansion: All United States
Registered: CA,FL,HI,IL,IN,MD,MI,MN,ND,NY,OR,RI,SD,VA,WA,WI
Field Support: DP, CP, EO, ST, SO, $IC, FC, H, N
Training: 2 weeks Montgomery, AL

Lifestyle Mobile Carpet Showroom
PO Box 3876
Dalton, GA 30721

Phone: 706-278-7919   Accepts collect calls?
Toll Free: 800-346-4531   FAX: 706-278-7711
Internet:
Suitable Sites:
Concentration: 2 in GA, 1 in TN, 1 in AL
Expansion: SE
Registered:
Field Support: DP, CP, EO, ST, SO, IC, FC, H, N
Training: 1 week Dalton, GA

Nationwide Floor & Window Coverings
828 N Broadway #800
Milwaukee, WI 53202
Mobile floor & window coverings. Carpet, vinyl, hardwood, etc
Phone: Accepts collect calls? N
Toll Free: 800-366-8088   FAX:
Internet:
Suitable Sites: HO, OC
Concentration: 8 in WI, 6 in MI, 1 in IL
Expansion: All United States, Canada, Foreign
Registered: FL,IL,MI,WI
Field Support: CP, EO, ST, SO, IC, FC, H, N
Training: 4 weeks home based w/ video, audio, manuals
1 week hands-on at HQ Milwaukee, WI
ongoing support

Interior Design Industry

Furnishings (Spread 1 of 2)

	Decor-At-Your-Door International	Expressions In Fabrics	Living Lighting	Naked Furniture	Norwalk - The Furniture Idea	SlumberLand International	Soft Touch Interiors	Consign & Design Furnishings	Terri's
Startup Cost	5K	296K-449K	200K-225K	143K-245K	225K-355K	100K-200K	30.8K-36.3K	70K-167K
Franchise Fee	4K	30K	30K	19.5K	35K	10K	18K	24K
Royalty	1%	3.50%	4%	4%	0%	3%	6%	2.50%
Advertising Fee	1%	2%	1%	0%	0%	0%	2%	1%
Financing Provided	N	Y	N	Y	Y	N	N	Y
Experience Required	N				N			
Passive Ownership	A	A		A	A	D	A	D
In Business Since	1983	1978	1968	1972	1902	1967	1995	1979
Franchised Since	1995	1983	1970	1979	1987	1978	1996	1993
Franchised Units 1996								
1997	25	49	28	40	83	35	1	5
1998								
Company Owned 1996								
1997	0	4	0	2	9	17	1	6
1998								
Number of Units U.S.	23	53	0	42	86	52	2	11
Canada	2	0	28	0	6	0	0	0
Foreign	0	0	0		0	0	0	0
Projected New U.S.					15			
Canada					2			
Foreign								
Corporate Employees	5	35	18	19	825		3	6
Contract Length	8	10/10		10/10	20/5	10/10	3/3	10/5/5
Expand in Territory	Y	Y		Y	Y	Y	N	Y
Full-Time Employees	1	7		3	7	4	VAR	8
Part-Time Employees	0			2	2	2		2
Conversions	N	Y		Y	N	Y		Y
Site Selection Assist.	N	Y	Y	Y	Y	N	N	Y
Lease Negotiation Assist.	N	Y	Y	Y	Y	Y		Y
Site Space Required		5000		6500	5000	10000		12000
Development Agreement	N	Y		Y	Y	N	N	N
Develop. Agree. Term		3						
Sub-franchising	N	N		N	N	N	N	N

Interior Design Industry

Furnishings (Spread 1 of 2)

Decor-At-Your-Door International
PO Box 2290
Pollock Pines, CA 95726

Phone: 916-644-6056   Accepts collect calls? N
Toll Free: 800-936-3326   FAX: 916-644-3326
Internet: decor-at-your-door.com
Suitable Sites: HO, K, M, RM
Concentration: 4 in CA, 2 in HI
Expansion: All United States, Canada
Registered: CA,FL,MI,NY,OR,SD,WA,DC
Field Support: DP, $CP, SO, IC, FC, H, N
Training: 1 week corp. office

Expressions In Fabrics
1040 N Tustin Ave
Anaheim, CA 92807-1724

Phone: 714-688-4000   Accepts collect calls?
Toll Free: 888-222-6076   FAX: 714-688-4050
Internet: www.expressions-furniture.com
Suitable Sites: FB, SC, SF
Concentration: 5 in CA, 5 in TX, 4 in MI
Expansion: All United States
Registered: CA,FL,HI,IL,IN,MD,MI,MN,ND,NY,OR,RI,SD,VA,WA,WI,DC
Field Support: $DP, CP, EO, ST, SO, FC
Training: 10 days corp. store

Living Lighting
4699 Keele St #1
Downsview, ON M3J-2N8 CANADA

Phone: 416-661-9916   Accepts collect calls?
Toll Free: FAX: 416-661-9706
Internet:
Suitable Sites:
Concentration: 27 in ON, 1 in BC
Expansion: Canada
Registered: AB
Field Support:
Training:

Naked Furniture
1157 Lackawanna Trl PO Box F
Clarks Summit, PA 18411

Phone: 717-587-7800   Accepts collect calls?
Toll Free: 800-352-2522   FAX: 717-586-8587
Internet:
Suitable Sites: FB, RM, SC, SF
Concentration: 9 in MI, 8 in IL, 4 in IN
Expansion: East Of Mississippi
Registered: FL,IL,IN,MD,MI,MN,NY,RI,VA,WI
Field Support: $DP, EO, ST, SO, IC, $FC, H, N
Training: 1 week HQ
         1 week on-site

Norwalk - The Furniture Idea
815 Crocker Rd N 5
Westlake, OH 44145
Upscale custom living room furniture retail storewide selection

Phone: 419-668-4461   Accepts collect calls? N
Toll Free: 888-667-9255   FAX: 440-871-6057
Internet: www.norwalkfurniture.com
Suitable Sites: AC, FB, PC, SC, SF
Concentration: 13 in FL, 6 in TX, 5 in GA
Expansion: All United States, Canada
Registered: CA,FL,HI,IL,IN,MD,MI,MN,NY,OR,RI,VA,WA,WI,DC,ND,SD
Field Support: EO, ST, SO, FC, H, N
Training: 1 week Cleveland
         1 week kansas city
         2 weeks another store opening & on-site

SlumberLand International
3060 Centerville Rd
Little Canada, MN 55117

Phone: 612-482-7500   Accepts collect calls?
Toll Free: FAX: 612-490-0479
Internet:
Suitable Sites: FB, SC
Concentration: 25 in MN, 13 in IA
Expansion: Central Midwest
Registered: IL,MN,ND,SD,WI
Field Support: CP, $EO, $ST, FC, $H, N
Training: 3-4 weeks HQ

Soft Touch Interiors
550 N Brand Blvd 7th Fl
Glendale, CA 91203

Phone: 818-246-9979   Accepts collect calls?
Toll Free: 800-276-3886   FAX: 818-952-8649
Internet:
Suitable Sites:
Concentration: 1 in AZ, 1 in TX
Expansion: All United States
Registered: CA
Field Support: EO, ST, $FC, H, N
Training: 2 weeks Scottsdale, AZ

Terri's Consign & Design Furnishings
1826 W Broadway Rd #3
Mesa, AZ 85202

Phone: 602-969-1121   Accepts collect calls?
Toll Free: 800-455-0400   FAX: 602-969-5052
Internet:
Suitable Sites: FB, PC, SC, WR
Concentration: 2 in NV, 1 in CA, 1 in AZ
Expansion: All United States
Registered: CA,OR,WA
Field Support: $DP, $CP, EO, $ST, SO, IC, FC, H, N
Training: 1 week mesa, AZ

Interior Design Industry

Furnishings (Spread 2 of 2)

	Verlo Mattress Factory Stores	Furniture & Country Store	Yesterday's						
Startup Cost	140K	118K							
Franchise Fee	30K	27.5K							
Royalty	5%	5%							
Advertising Fee	1%								
Financing Provided	N	N							
Experience Required	N								
Passive Ownership	D								
In Business Since	1958	1994							
Franchised Since	1989	1997							
Franchised Units 1996	54								
1997	59	0							
1998	67								
Company Owned 1996	3	1							
1997	1	1							
1998	2								
Number of Units U.S.									
Canada									
Foreign									
Projected New U.S.	12								
Canada									
Foreign									
Corporate Employees									
Contract Length	5/5								
Expand in Territory	Y								
Full-Time Employees	2-5								
Part-Time Employees	3-5								
Conversions	Y								
Site Selection Assist.	Y								
Lease Negotiation Assist.	Y								
Site Space Required	3000-10000								
Development Agreement									
Develop. Agree. Term									
Sub-franchising	N								

Interior Design Industry

Verlo Mattress Factory Stores
PO Box 298
Whitewater, WI 53190
Hand crafted quality mattresses at a comfortable price
Phone: 414-473-8957   Accepts collect calls? N
Toll Free: 800-229-8957   FAX:
Internet: www.verlo.com
Suitable Sites: AC, DA, FB, SC
Concentration: IL, WI
Expansion: NE,SE,S, Canada
Registered: FL,IL,IN,MD,MI,MN,NY,VA,WI,DC
Field Support: EO, ST, SO, FC, H, N
Training: store appearance & presentation
marketing, operations,
employee education, customer service

Yesterday's Furniture & Country Store
2000 S 7 Hwy
Blue Springs, MO 64014
Furniture & country merchandise
Phone: Accepts collect calls?
Toll Free: 888-228-0800   FAX:
Internet:
Suitable Sites:
Concentration:
Expansion: NE,S,SE,MW,SE
Registered:
Field Support:
Training:

Interior Design Industry   Window Coverings

	AWC Commercial Window Coverings	Budget Blinds	Decorating Den Interiors	Drapery Works Systems	KitchenPro	Spring Crest Drapery Centers	Window Perfect	Window & Wall Creations
Startup Cost	122.5K-181.4K	7K-34K	4K-15K	25K-53K	110K-227.7K	58K-65K	20K-50K	4.9K-7.7K
Franchise Fee	25K	14.9K	15.9K	14.5K	25K	15K	15K	7.9K
Royalty	5-12.5%	4-5%	7-11%	6%	5%	3-5%	3%	6-9%
Advertising Fee	2.5%			2%		2%	$200/MO	
Financing Provided	Y	N	Y	Y	N	Y	Y	Y
Experience Required		N						
Passive Ownership	N	D		N		D	D	
In Business Since	1963	1992	1969	1978	1993	1965	1995	1996
Franchised Since	1992	1994	1970	1993	1993	1968	1996	1996
Franchised Units 1996			865		0			12
1997	6	144	831	6	0	139	3	24
1998		153						
Company Owned 1996			1		0			0
1997	4	2	1	1	0	1	0	0
1998		3						
Number of Units U.S.	10	156		7		116	3	
Canada	0	0		0		9	0	
Foreign	0	0		0		15	0	
Projected New U.S.		200						
Canada								
Foreign								
Corporate Employees	8	9		4		8	2	
Contract Length	10/10	5/5		10/10		10/10	5/5	
Expand in Territory	Y	Y		Y		Y	Y	
Full-Time Employees	1	1		1		2	2	
Part-Time Employees	AS ND					2		
Conversions	Y	Y		N		Y	Y	
Site Selection Assist.	N	N		Y		Y	Y	
Lease Negotiation Assist.	Y	N				Y		
Site Space Required						1200		
Development Agreement	N	N		Y		Y	Y	
Develop. Agree. Term				10		20	5	
Sub-franchising	N	N		Y		N	N	

Interior Design Industry   Window Coverings

AWC Commercial Window Coverings
825 W Williamson Wy
Fullerton, CA 92832

Phone: 714-879-3880 — Accepts collect calls?
Toll Free: 800-252-2280 — FAX: 714-879-8419
Internet: www.ibos.com/pub/ibos/awc
Suitable Sites: HO
Concentration: 4 in CA, 1 in MD, 1 in NV
Expansion: All United States, Canada, Foreign
Registered: CA,MD,DC
Field Support: DP, CP, EO, ST, IC, $FC, H
Training: 1 week Fullerton plant
1 week their location
on-going as necessary

Budget Blinds
1570 Corporate Dr #B
Costa Mesa, CA 92626
Sales of name brand window coverings
Phone: 714-708-3338 — Accepts collect calls? N
Toll Free: 800-420-5374 — FAX: 714-708-3339
Internet: www.budgetblinds.com
Suitable Sites: ES, DA, HO, OC
Concentration:
Expansion: All United States, Canada, Foreign
Registered: CA,FL,HI,IL,IN,MD,MI,MN,ND,NY,OR,RI,SD,VA,WA,WI,DC
Field Support: EO, ST, FC, H, N
Training: 2 weeks southern CA
13 week accelerated start-up program

Decorating Den Interiors
19100 Montgomery Ave
Burtonsville, MD 20866
Full-service interior decorating services
Phone: 301-272-1500 — Accepts collect calls?
Toll Free: 800-428-1366 — FAX:
Internet:
Suitable Sites:
Concentration:
Expansion: All United States, Canada, Foreign
Registered:
Field Support:
Training:

Drapery Works Systems
4640 Western Ave
Lisle, IL 60532

Phone: 630-963-2820 — Accepts collect calls?
Toll Free: 800-353-7273 — FAX: 630-963-1370
Internet:
Suitable Sites: OC
Concentration: 6 in IL, 1 in NC
Expansion: All United States
Registered: FL,IL,KY,TX,WI
Field Support: EO, ST, $SO, FC, H, N
Training: 2 weeks lisle, IL
6 weeks field

KitchenPro
10451 Mill Run Cir #400
Owings Mills, MD 21117
Kitchen & bath design showrooms
Phone: 410-356-8889 — Accepts collect calls?
Toll Free: — FAX:
Internet:
Suitable Sites:
Concentration:
Expansion: MD
Registered:
Field Support:
Training:

Spring Crest Drapery Centers
190 Arovista Cir
Brea, CA 92821

Phone: 714-529-9993 — Accepts collect calls?
Toll Free: 800-552-5523 — FAX: 714-529-2093
Internet:
Suitable Sites: SC
Concentration: 15 in CA, 10 in OK, 8 in FL
Expansion: Canada, Foreign
Registered: CA,FL,MI,MN,OR,AB
Field Support: EO, ST, SO, $FC, H, N
Training: 2 weeks HQ
2 weeks on-site

Window Perfect
PO Box 62254
San Angelo, TX 76906

Phone: — Accepts collect calls?
Toll Free: 800-758-2646 — FAX: 610-366-9524
Internet: www.windowperfect.com
Suitable Sites: HO
Concentration: 2 in CA, 1 in GA
Expansion: All United States
Registered: CA
Field Support: EO, ST, SO, FC, H
Training: 2 weeks California
1 week in-field

Window & Wall Creations
5650 Greenwood Plaza Bl #207
Englewood, CO 80111
Custom window coverings/wallpaper/decorative access
Phone: 303-741-5073 — Accepts collect calls?
Toll Free: 800-461-5180 — FAX:
Internet:
Suitable Sites:
Concentration:
Expansion: All United States
Registered:
Field Support:
Training:

Interior Design Industry   Other Interior Design

	A Shade Better	The More Space Place	Wallpapers To Go					
Startup Cost	105.5K-147K	108.25-153.8K	139K-194K					
Franchise Fee	35K	22.5K	15K					
Royalty	6%	4.5%/$250/W	6%					
Advertising Fee	1%	2.5%/$500/M	5%					
Financing Provided	N	N	N					
Experience Required								
Passive Ownership	D	D	N					
In Business Since	1988	1989	1973					
Franchised Since	1993	1993	1986					
Franchised Units 1996								
1997	8	14	40					
1998								
Company Owned 1996								
1997	7	0	16					
1998								
Number of Units U.S.	15	14	56					
Canada	0	0	0					
Foreign	0	0	0					
Projected New U.S.								
Canada								
Foreign								
Corporate Employees	6	12	81					
Contract Length	5/5/5/5	10/10	10/10					
Expand in Territory	Y	Y	Y					
Full-Time Employees	2	3	3					
Part-Time Employees	2	1	3					
Conversions	Y	Y	Y					
Site Selection Assist.	Y	Y	Y					
Lease Negotiation Assist.	Y	Y	Y					
Site Space Required	1800	2500	3500					
Development Agreement	Y	Y	N					
Develop. Agree. Term		10						
Sub-franchising	N	N	N					

Interior Design Industry

Other Interior Design

A Shade Better
3615 Superior Ave
Cleveland, OH 44114

Phone: 216-391-5267	Accepts collect calls?
Toll Free: 800-722-8676	FAX: 216-391-8118

Internet:
Suitable Sites: SC
Concentration: 5 in OH, 3 in IL, 2 in AZ
Expansion: Midwest and SE
Registered: CA,FL,IL,IN,MD,MI,WI
Field Support: CP, EO, ST, SO, $FC, H
Training: 6 days Cleveland or phoenix
6 days on-site

The More Space Place
7301 124th Ave N
Largo, FL 33773

Phone: 813-539-1611	Accepts collect calls?
Toll Free: 888-731-3051	FAX: 813-524-6382

Internet:
Suitable Sites: FB, SC, SF
Concentration: 13 in FL, 1 in MI
Expansion: All United States
Registered: FL,IL,MI,VA,WI
Field Support: CP, EO, ST, SO, IC, FC
Training: 2 weeks HQ largo, FL
3 days on-site

Wallpapers To Go
PO Box 801069
Dallas, TX 75380-1069

Phone: 972-503-8688	Accepts collect calls?
Toll Free: 800-843-7094	FAX: 972-503-8737

Internet: www.wallpapertogo.com
Suitable Sites: FB, SC
Concentration: 14 in CA, 13 in TX, 4 in WA
Expansion: TX,AZ,CA,WA,OR,CO,MI,OH,IN
Registered:
Field Support: EO, ST, SO, $FC, H, N
Training: 8 days corporate offices
5 days corporate store

Lodging Industry

Campgrounds

	Kampgrounds of America/KOA	Yogi Bear Jellystone Park Camp-Resorts						
Startup Cost	250K+	28K+						
Franchise Fee	25K	18K-28K						
Royalty	8%	6%						
Advertising Fee	2%	1%						
Financing Provided	N	Y						
Experience Required	N	N						
Passive Ownership	D	D						
In Business Since	1961	1969						
Franchised Since	1962	1970						
Franchised Units 1996								
1997	520	76						
1998	510	72						
Company Owned 1996								
1997	10	0						
1998	10	0						
Number of Units U.S.	466	69						
Canada	34	3						
Foreign	10	0						
Projected New U.S.		3						
Canada		2						
Foreign								
Corporate Employees	72	6						
Contract Length	5/5	5-20/5-10						
Expand in Territory	Y	N						
Full-Time Employees	2	3						
Part-Time Employees	1	25						
Conversions	Y	Y						
Site Selection Assist.	Y	Y						
Lease Negotiation Assist.	N	Y						
Site Space Required	7-15 acres							
Development Agreement	N	N						
Develop. Agree. Term								
Sub-franchising	Y	N						

Lodging Industry   Campgrounds

Kampgrounds of America/KOA
PO Box 30558
Billings, MT 59114

Phone: 406-248-7444   Accepts collect calls?
Toll Free: 800-548-7239   FAX: 406-248-7414
Internet: www.koakampgrounds.com
Suitable Sites:
Concentration: 30 in CA, 29 in FL, 30 in CO
Expansion: All United States, Canada, Foreign
Registered: CA,FL,HI,IL,IN,MD,MI,MN,ND,NY,OR,RI,SD,VA,WA,WI,DC
Field Support: DP, CP, EO, ST, SO, IC, $FC, H, N
Training: 3 days new campground training at HQ
5 days orientation for existing campgrounds
3 days management school

Yogi Bear Jellystone Park Camp-Resorts
6201 Kellogg Ave
Cincinnati, OH 45228-1118
North american franchiser of family oriented campgrounds
Phone: 513-232-6800   Accepts collect calls?
Toll Free: 800-626-3720   FAX: 513-231-1191
Internet:
Suitable Sites: DA
Concentration: 8 in IN, 7 in MI, 7 in WI
Expansion: All United States, Canada
Registered: CA,FL,IL,IN,MD,MI,MN,NY,VA,WI,ND,OR,SD,WA
Field Support: CP, EO, ST, SO, FC, H, N
Training: 2-3 days site
3-4 days HQ
1-3 days year on-site

Lodging Industry   Hotels, Motels (Spread 1 of 3)

	AmericInn International	Ashbury Suites & Inns	Choice Hotels Intl	Country Inns & Suites by Carlson	Days Inns of America Inc	Doubletree Hotel Systems	Hawthorn Suites/ Hawthorn Suites Ltd	Hilton Inns
Startup Cost	1.5M-2.5M	1.5M-3M	VAR.	1.5M-3M	336K-6.1M	20M-38M	4M-5M	15M-25M
Franchise Fee	25K	25K	25K-50K	30K	VAR.	25K-50K	40K	20K+
Royalty	5%	4%	3-5.25%	3-4%	6.5%	2-4%	5%	5%
Advertising Fee	2%	2%		2-3%		3.5%		1%
Financing Provided	Y	Y	N	Y	Y	N	Y	N
Experience Required		N						Y
Passive Ownership	D			A		A		A
In Business Since	1984	1996	1939	1987	1970	1989	1986	1919
Franchised Since	1984	1996	1962	1987	1972	1989	1986	1967
Franchised Units 1996		0	3124		1693		18	
1997	93	1	3348	111	1778	128	20	177
1998								
Company Owned 1996		0	67		0		0	
1997	5	0	71	4	0	127	0	68
1998								
Number of Units U.S.	98	1		98		251		228
Canada	0			12		1		0
Foreign	0			5		3		17
Projected New U.S.		25						70
Canada		1						2
Foreign		0						0
Corporate Employees	35	8		15		300		600
Contract Length	20/20	15		15/0		10/10		15-20
Expand in Territory	Y	Y				Y		Y
Full-Time Employees	9	10-12		8		100		150
Part-Time Employees		Y		8				
Conversions		Y		Y		Y		Y
Site Selection Assist.	Y	Y		Y		N		Y
Lease Negotiation Assist.	Y	N		N		N		N
Site Space Required	60000	60000		43560		5-10 acres		135000
Development Agreement	N	Y		N		Y		N
Develop. Agree. Term						VAR		
Sub-franchising	N	Y		N		N		N

Lodging Industry

AmericInn International
18202 Minnetonka Blvd
Deephaven, MN 55391

Phone: 612-476-9020   Accepts collect calls?
Toll Free: 800-634-3444   FAX: 612-476-7601
Internet: www.americinn.com
Suitable Sites: FB
Concentration: 48 in MN, 28 in WI, 7 in IA
Expansion: All United States, Canada, Foreign
Registered: CA,FL,HI,IL,IN,MD,MI,MN,ND,NY,OR,RI,SD,VA,WA,WI,DC
Field Support: $DP, $CP, $EO, ST, SO, $IC, FC, H, N
Training: 1 week 3 sites

Ashbury Suites & Inns
2400 W Michigan Ave #16
Pensacola, FL 32526-2102
Hotels/suites & inns
Phone: 850-457-3469   Accepts collect calls? N
Toll Free: 888-ASHBURY   FAX: 850-453-1121
Internet: www.ashburysuites.com
Suitable Sites: ES, DA, FB, FC, IP, LI, M, OS, RM, SC, WF
Concentration: 5 in FL, 10 in TX, 5 in AL
Expansion: All United States, Canada, Foreign
Registered: FL
Field Support: DP, CP, EO, ST, SO, IC, FC, H, N
Training: operation & mgmt of hotels
      housekeeping, front desk, maintenance
      bookkeeping, general admin

Choice Hotels Intl
10750 Columbia Pike
Silver Spring, MD 20901
Hotels inns suites & resorts
Phone: Accepts collect calls?
Toll Free: 800-547-0007   FAX:
Internet:
Suitable Sites:
Concentration:
Expansion: All United States, Canada, Foreign
Registered:
Field Support:
Training:

Country Inns & Suites by Carlson
PO Box 59159 Carlson Pkwy
Minneapolis, MN 55459-8203

Phone: 612-449-1326   Accepts collect calls?
Toll Free: 800-477-4200   FAX: 612-449-1338
Internet:
Suitable Sites: FB
Concentration: 25 in MN, 10 in WI, 5 in TN
Expansion: All United States, Canada, Foreign
Registered: CA,FL,HI,IL,IN,MD,MI,MN,ND,NY,OR,RI,SD,VA,WA,WI,DC
Field Support: CP, EO, ST, SO, IC, $FC, H, N
Training: 2 weeks Minneapolis MN

Days Inns of America Inc
339 Jefferson Rd
Parsippany, NJ 07054
Hotels & inns
Phone: 973-428-9700   Accepts collect calls?
Toll Free: FAX:
Internet:
Suitable Sites:
Concentration:
Expansion: All United States, Canada, Foreign
Registered:
Field Support:
Training:

Doubletree Hotel Systems
410 N 44th St #700
Phoenix, AZ 85008

Phone: 602-220-6666   Accepts collect calls?
Toll Free: 800-222-8733   FAX: 602-681-3516
Internet: www.doubletreehotels.com
Suitable Sites: AC, ES, FB
Concentration: 25 in CA, 18 in FL, 11 in TX
Expansion: All United States, Canada
Registered: CA,FL,HI,IL,IN,MD,MI,MN,ND,NY,OR,RI,SD,VA,WA,WI,DC
Field Support: DP, $CP, $EO, $ST, $FC
Training:

Hawthorn Suites/ Hawthorn Suites Ltd
13 Corporate Sq #250
Atlanta, GA 30329
Extended-stay suite hotels
Phone: 404-321-4045   Accepts collect calls?
Toll Free: FAX:
Internet:
Suitable Sites:
Concentration:
Expansion: All United States, Canada, Foreign
Registered:
Field Support:
Training:

Hilton Inns
9336 Civic Center Dr
Beverly Hills, CA 90210

Phone: 310-278-4321   Accepts collect calls? N
Toll Free: 800-286-0645   FAX: 310-205-7655
Internet: www.hilton.com
Suitable Sites:
Concentration: 33 in CA, 23 in FL, 20 in TX
Expansion: All United States, Canada
Registered: CA,FL,IN,MD,MI,NY,ND,OR,RI,WA,WI,DC,IL,MN,SD,VA,AB
Field Support: $CP, EO, ST, FC, N
Training: 4 days Dallas TX
      3 days Beverly Hills
      3 days regional office

Lodging Industry

Hotels, Motels (Spread 2 of 3)

	Holiday Hospitality	Holiday Inn Worldwide	Hospitality International	Howard Johnson Intl Inc	InnSuites Hotels	Knights Franchise Systems Inc	Motel 6	Radisson Hotels International
Startup Cost		VAR.		372K-6.2M	10K	196K-5.6M	1M-3M	14M-40M
Franchise Fee	50K+	VAR.	10K	VAR.	10K	15K	25K	35K
Royalty	5%	5%	4%	4%	3%	4.5%	4%	4%
Advertising Fee	1.5-2%		1%		1%		3%	3.75%
Financing Provided	Y	Y	N	Y	N	Y	N	N
Experience Required					N			N
Passive Ownership	A		D		A		A	N
In Business Since	1952	1952	1982	1925	1980	1972	1962	1962
Franchised Since	1954	1954	1982	1954	1980	1991	1996	1983
Franchised Units 1996		2031		520	1	175		346
1997	2264	2257	268	517	0	191	36	350
1998			266		0			379
Company Owned 1996		177		0	7	0		1
1997	110	117	0	0	9	0	723	1
1998			0		10			1
Number of Units U.S.	1876		266		1665		759	222
Canada	73		0		0		0	16
Foreign	425		0		0		0	142
Projected New U.S.					900			40
Canada					0			
Foreign					0			
Corporate Employees	85		42		12		284	210
Contract Length	10/10		10/5		1		10-15	
Expand in Territory	Y		Y		Y		N	N
Full-Time Employees	VAR				20+		2-4	
Part-Time Employees					0		4-10	
Conversions	Y		Y		Y		Y	Y
Site Selection Assist.	N		Y		N		N	N
Lease Negotiation Assist.			N		N		N	N
Site Space Required					120000		14-40000	
Development Agreement	N		N		N		Y	N
Develop. Agree. Term							2-5	
Sub-franchising	N		N		N		N	N

Lodging Industry   Hotels, Motels (Spread 2 of 3)

Holiday Hospitality
3 Ravinia Dr #2900
Atlanta, GA 30346-2149

    Phone: 770-604-2166   Accepts collect calls?
    Toll Free: FAX: 770-604-2107
    Internet: www.holiday-inn.com
Suitable Sites: ES, DA
Concentration: 142 in CA, 142 in FL, 121 in TX
    Expansion: All United States, Canada, Foreign
    Registered: CA,FL,HI,IL,IN,MD,MI,MN,ND,NY,OR,RI,SD,VA,WA,WI,DC
Field Support:
    Training: on-site at new hotel opng

Holiday Inn Worldwide
3 Ravinia Dr #2000
Atlanta, GA 30346
Hotels
    Phone: 770-604-2000   Accepts collect calls?
    Toll Free: FAX:
    Internet:
Suitable Sites:
Concentration:
    Expansion: All United States, Canada, Foreign
    Registered:
Field Support:
    Training:

Hospitality International
1726 Montreal Circle
Tucker, GA 30084
Franchisor of limited service motels in the economy/budget markt
    Phone: 770-270-1180   Accepts collect calls? N
    Toll Free: 800-247-4677   FAX: 777-270-1077
    Internet: www.reservahost.com
Suitable Sites:
Concentration: 39 in FL, 42 in GA, 26 in TN
    Expansion: All United States, Foreign
    Registered: CA,FL,HI,IN,MI,MN,NY,ND,RI,SD,VA,WI,DC,IL,MD,OR
Field Support: EO, ST, SO, FC, H, N
    Training: 2-5 days Atlanta annually

Howard Johnson Intl Inc
339 Jefferson Rd
Parsippany, NJ 07054
Hotels
    Phone: 201-428-9700   Accepts collect calls?
    Toll Free: FAX:
    Internet:
Suitable Sites:
Concentration:
    Expansion: All United States, Canada, Foreign
    Registered:
Field Support:
    Training:

InnSuites Hotels
1625 E. Northern #201
Phoenix, AZ 85020

    Phone: 602-820-2030   Accepts collect calls? N
    Toll Free: 800-842-4242   FAX: 602-491-1008
    Internet: stay@innsuites.com
Suitable Sites: FB, IP, WF
Concentration: 1165 in AZ, 465 in CA
    Expansion: NM,CO,CA,TX, Canada, Foreign
    Registered:
Field Support: $DP, CP, EO, ST, SO, $IC, FC, H, N
    Training: on-site & phoenix, AZ

Knights Franchise Systems Inc
339 Jefferson Rd
Parsippany, NJ 07054
Hotels
    Phone: 973-428-9700   Accepts collect calls?
    Toll Free: FAX:
    Internet:
Suitable Sites:
Concentration:
    Expansion: All United States, Canada, Foreign
    Registered:
Field Support:
    Training:

Motel 6
14651 Dallas Pkwy #500
Dallas, TX 75240

    Phone: 972-702-6809   Accepts collect calls?
    Toll Free: 888-688-3503   FAX: 972-702-3610
    Internet:
Suitable Sites: FB
Concentration: 193 in CA, 96 in TX, 37 in AZ
    Expansion: All United States, Canada
    Registered: CA,FL,HI,IL,IN,MD,MI,MN,ND,NY,OR,RI,SD,VA,WA,WI,DC
Field Support: $CP, EO, ST, SO, FC, H, N
    Training: 1 week Dallas TX

Radisson Hotels International
PO Box 59159 Carlson Pkwy
Minneapolis, MN 55459-8204
Upscale plaza hotels, suite hotels, hotels, resorts, cruise ship
    Phone: 612-212-5526   Accepts collect calls? N
    Toll Free: FAX: 612-212-3400
    Internet:
Suitable Sites: DA, FB
Concentration: 30 in FL, 28 in CA, 15 in TX
    Expansion: All United States, Canada, Foreign
    Registered: CA,FL,HI,IL,IN,MD,MI,MN,ND,NY,OR,RI,SD,VA,WA,WI,DC,AB
Field Support:
    Training: new hotel orientation to Radisson system
              operations manuals provided

Lodging Industry   Hotels, Motels (Spread 3 of 3)

	Radisson Hotels Worldwide	Ramada Franchise Canada, Inc.	Ramada Franchise Systems Inc	Super 8 Motels Inc	U.S. Franchise Systems			
Startup Cost	VAR.	2M-20M	337.2K-2.9M	218K-2.2M	1.2M-7M			
Franchise Fee	30K	35K+	VAR.	20K+	35K-40K			
Royalty	4%	4%	4%	5%	5-6%			
Advertising Fee		4%			2-2.5%			
Financing Provided	N	N	Y	Y	Y			
Experience Required		N						
Passive Ownership		A			A			
In Business Since	1962	1992	1954	1974	1995			
Franchised Since	1983	1992	1990	1976	1995			
Franchised Units 1996	307		829	1427				
1997	342	48	906	1582	80			
1998								
Company Owned 1996	22		0	0				
1997	1	0	0	0	0			
1998								
Number of Units U.S.		0			80			
Canada		48			0			
Foreign		0			0			
Projected New U.S.								
Canada		11						
Foreign								
Corporate Employees		15			80			
Contract Length		5/5/5/5			10-20/10			
Expand in Territory		Y			Y			
Full-Time Employees		80			12-30			
Part-Time Employees		20						
Conversions		Y			Y			
Site Selection Assist.		Y			Y			
Lease Negotiation Assist.		Y			N			
Site Space Required					65000			
Development Agreement		Y			N			
Develop. Agree. Term		5						
Sub-franchising		N			Y			

Lodging Industry   Hotels, Motels (Spread 3 of 3)

Radisson Hotels Worldwide
Carlson Pkwy PO Box 59159
Minneapolis, MN 55459-8204
Hotels/inns/resorts/cruise ships
    Phone: 612-540-5526   Accepts collect calls?
    Toll Free: FAX:
    Internet:
Suitable Sites:
Concentration:
    Expansion: All United States, Canada, Foreign
    Registered:
Field Support:
    Training:

Ramada Franchise Canada, Inc.
36 Toronto Street Ste 750
Toronto, ON M5C-2C5 CANADA

    Phone: 416-361-1010   Accepts collect calls? N
    Toll Free: 800-361-4173   FAX: 416-361-9050
    Internet: www.ramada.ca
Suitable Sites: AC, ES, FB, IP, LI, OC, SC
Concentration: 20 in ON, 12 in BC, 6 in AB
    Expansion: N, Canada
    Registered: AB
Field Support: DP, CP, EO, ST, SO, FC, H, N
    Training: 3-5 days on-site

Ramada Franchise Systems Inc
339 Jefferson Rd
Parsippany, NJ 07054
Inns/plaza hotels
    Phone: 973-428-9700   Accepts collect calls?
    Toll Free: FAX:
    Internet:
Suitable Sites:
Concentration:
    Expansion: All United States, Canada, Foreign
    Registered:
Field Support:
    Training:

Super 8 Motels Inc
339 Jefferson Rd
Parsippany, NJ 07054
Economy motels
    Phone: 973-428-9700   Accepts collect calls?
    Toll Free: 800-889-8847   FAX:
    Internet:
Suitable Sites:
Concentration:
    Expansion: All United States, Canada, Foreign
    Registered:
Field Support:
    Training:

U.S. Franchise Systems
13 Corporate Square #250
Atlanta, GA 30329

    Phone: 404-235-7410   Accepts collect calls?
    Toll Free: FAX: 404-235-7460
    Internet:
Suitable Sites:
Concentration: TN, NY, NC
    Expansion: All United States
    Registered: CA,FL,HI,IL,IN,MD,MI,MN,ND,NY,OR,RI,SD,VA,WA,WI,DC
Field Support: $CP, EO, ST, SO, $FC, H, N
    Training: 4 days Atlanta GA
              10 days on-site

Pets Industry   Pet Care

	Canine Counselors	Critter Care of America	Hawkeye's Home Sitters	Pet Centre Franchising Inc	Haynes	Laund-Ur-Mutt	U-Wash Doggie		
Startup Cost	15K-20K	25K-40K	1.5K-3K	44.8K-68.2K		100K	67K		
Franchise Fee	9.5K	12.5K	3.5K-7K	15K		25K	12.5K		
Royalty	7%	5%	4%	$140/WK.		5%	6%		
Advertising Fee	2-5%	2%				$50/MO	2%		
Financing Provided	N	Y	N	N		Y	Y		
Experience Required						N	N		
Passive Ownership	N	D				A			
In Business Since	1975	1984	1987	1988		1992	1992		
Franchised Since	1987	1987	1997	1996		1994	1997		
Franchised Units 1996				0		4	0		
1997	1	18	3	2		3	0		
1998						3	0		
Company Owned 1996			4	4		0	5		
1997	3	2	3	2		0	5		
1998						0	5		
Number of Units U.S.	4	18				4	5		
Canada	0	0							
Foreign	0	0							
Projected New U.S.						3			
Canada									
Foreign									
Corporate Employees	5	4				0			
Contract Length	10/10	10/5/5				10	10		
Expand in Territory	N	Y				Y	Y		
Full-Time Employees	6	3				0	2		
Part-Time Employees		5-10				2	1		
Conversions	Y	Y				Y	Y		
Site Selection Assist.	Y	N				Y	Y		
Lease Negotiation Assist.	Y					Y	Y		
Site Space Required							1200		
Development Agreement	Y	Y				Y			
Develop. Agree. Term	10	5				10			
Sub-franchising	N	N				Y	N		

Pets Industry   Pet Care

Canine Counselors
1660 Southern Blvd A
West Palm Beach, FL 33406

Phone: 561-640-3970   Accepts collect calls?
Toll Free: 800-456-3647   FAX: 561-640-3973
Internet: www.caninecounselors.com
Suitable Sites: ES
Concentration: 4 in FL
  Expansion: SE and NE
  Registered: FL
Field Support: $DP, CP, $EO, $ST, SO, FC, H, $N
  Training: 2 weeks palm beach or Miami, FL

Critter Care of America
8261 Summa Ave #F
Baton Rouge, LA 70809

Phone: 504-769-4160   Accepts collect calls?
Toll Free: 800-256-3014   FAX: 504-769-4268
Internet: www.crittercare.com
Suitable Sites:
Concentration: 3 in NY, 2 in CA, 2 in TX
  Expansion: All United States
  Registered: CA,FL,NY,OR
Field Support: CP, EO, ST, FC, H, N
  Training: 6 days home office
           2 days field

Hawkeye's Home Sitters
14920-95 A St
Edmonton, AB T5E-4A6 CANADA
In-home pet care/house-sitting services
Phone: Accepts collect calls?
Toll Free: 888-247-2787   FAX:
Internet:
Suitable Sites:
Concentration:
  Expansion: N, Canada
  Registered:
Field Support:
  Training:

Haynes Pet Centre Franchising Inc
10515 Wynbridge Dr
Alpharetta, GA 30022
Pet shop & grooming service
Phone: 404-570-4200   Accepts collect calls?
Toll Free: FAX:
Internet:
Suitable Sites:
Concentration:
  Expansion: SE
  Registered:
Field Support:
  Training:

Laund-Ur-Mutt
8854 S Edgewood St
Highlands Ranch, CO 80126
Full-service, self-service pet grooming & retail supplies
Phone: 303-470-1540   Accepts collect calls? N
Toll Free: FAX: 303-470-8869
Internet: www.laundurmutt.com
Suitable Sites: AC, FB, SC, SF
Concentration: 3 in CO
  Expansion: CO,PA,NH
  Registered:
Field Support: ST, SO, N
  Training: 1 week corporate HQ
            1 week on-site

U-Wash Doggie
1056 W Alameda
Burbank, CA 91506
Self-service/full-service pet grooming
Phone: 818-846-9600   Accepts collect calls? N
Toll Free: 888-820-7900   FAX: 805-297-2029
Internet:
Suitable Sites: AC, DA, SC, SF
Concentration:
  Expansion: All United States, Canada, Foreign
  Registered: CA
Field Support:
  Training: 15 days classroom/HQ
            ongoing

Pets Industry   **Pet Supplies (Spread 1 of 2)**

	The Bone Appetit Bakery	IncrediPet	Pet Habitat	The Pet Pantry International	Pet Valu	Petland	Pets Are Inn	Ruffin's Pet Centres
Startup Cost	11.7K-50.5K	161.2K-522.5K	150K-500K	65K	85K-170K	175K-450K	20K-25K	65K-85K
Franchise Fee	17.5K	25K	10K+	20K	20K	25K	15K	20K
Royalty	6%	3%	5%	0%	0%	4.50%	5-10%	4%
Advertising Fee	1%		2%	0%	0%	NA		1%
Financing Provided	N	N	Y	N	N	Y	Y	N
Experience Required	N							
Passive Ownership	D		D	A	N	D	D	N
In Business Since	1996	1986	1979	1995	1977	1967	1982	1981
Franchised Since	1997	1997		1995	1987	1972	1992	1986
Franchised Units 1996	0							
1997	1	0	8	38	211	166	20	14
1998	18							
Company Owned 1996	1	3						
1997	1	3	2	1	89	4	1	0
1998	1							
Number of Units U.S.	19		0	39	64	111	24	0
Canada			10	0	236	49	0	14
Foreign			5	0	0	10	0	0
Projected New U.S.	20							
Canada								
Foreign								
Corporate Employees	6		6	13	29	47	2	3
Contract Length	10/5/5		5/5	7/7	10/5/5	20/20		5/5
Expand in Territory	Y		Y	Y	N	Y	Y	N
Full-Time Employees	1		3	1	2	5	2	1
Part-Time Employees	2		3		3	7		3
Conversions	Y		Y	N	Y	Y	Y	Y
Site Selection Assist.	Y		Y	Y	Y	Y	N	Y
Lease Negotiation Assist.	Y		Y	N	Y	Y		Y
Site Space Required	750		1500	600	2500-3000	3000		1500
Development Agreement	N		N	N	N	N		N
Develop. Agree. Term								
Sub-franchising	N		Y	N	N	N	Y	N

Pets Industry   ## Pet Supplies (Spread 1 of 2)

The Bone Appetit Bakery
1919 S 40th St #202
Lincoln, NE 68506
Gourmet bakery & boutique for dogs and cats
    Phone: 402-434-5620   Accepts collect calls? N
    Toll Free: 800-865-2378   FAX: 402-434-5624
    Internet: www.boneappetitbakery.com
Suitable Sites: FB, M, RM, SC, SF
Concentration: 4 in TX, 2 in IN, 2 in NE
    Expansion: All United States
    Registered: CA,FL,HI,IL,IN,MD,MN,NY,RI,SD,VA,WA
Field Support: CP, EO, ST, SO, H, N
    Training: 1 week HQ
            1 week on-site

IncrediPet
3080 Richmond Rd
Lexington, KY 40509
Pet supplies superstore
    Phone: 606-269-7377   Accepts collect calls?
    Toll Free: FAX:
    Internet:
Suitable Sites:
Concentration:
    Expansion: SE,S,MW
    Registered:
Field Support:
    Training:

Pet Habitat
6921 Heather St
Vancouver, BC V6P-3P5   CANADA

    Phone: 604-266-2721   Accepts collect calls?
    Toll Free: FAX: 604-266-5880
    Internet:
Suitable Sites: RM
Concentration: 10 in BC
    Expansion: N, Canada, Foreign
    Registered: N
Field Support: $DP, $CP, EO, ST, $SO, IC, FC
    Training: 1 week head office
            2 weeks corp store

The Pet Pantry International
2221 Meridian Blvd Unit B
Minden, NV 89423

    Phone: 702-783-9722   Accepts collect calls?
    Toll Free: 800-381-7387   FAX: 702-783-9513
    Internet:
Suitable Sites: HO
Concentration: 8 in CA, 4 in WA, 2 in PA
    Expansion: All United States, Canada, Foreign
    Registered: CA,FL,HI,IL,IN,MD,MI,MN,ND,NY,OR,RI,SD,VA,WA,WI,DC
Field Support: CP, EO, ST, IC, FC, H
    Training: 5 days Minden, NV at corp office

Pet Valu
2 Devon Square 744 Lancaster Ave #200
Wayne, PA 19087

    Phone: 610-225-0800   Accepts collect calls?
    Toll Free: 888-564-6784   FAX: 610-225-0822
    Internet:
Suitable Sites: SC
Concentration: 219 in ON, 17 in MB, 26 in PA
    Expansion: NE, Canada
    Registered:
Field Support: DP, CP, EO, ST, SO, IC
    Training: 2 weeks classroom at Denvon, PA
            2 weeks in-store

Petland
195 N Hickory St PO Box 1606
Chillicothe, OH 45601-5606

    Phone: 614-775-2464   Accepts collect calls?
    Toll Free: 800-221-5935   FAX: 614-775-2575
    Internet:
Suitable Sites: FB, RM, SC
Concentration: 19 in OH, 14 in FL, 11 in IL
    Expansion: All United States, Canada, Foreign
    Registered: AB
Field Support: CP, EO, ST, SO, IC, FC, H, N
    Training: 1.5 weeks store Chillicothe, OH
            1 week classroom
            2 weeks new store location

Pets Are Inn
15965 Jeanette
Southfield, MI 48075

    Phone: 248-557-2784   Accepts collect calls?
    Toll Free: 800-745-1415   FAX: 248-557-7931
    Internet: www.wfcnet.com
Suitable Sites: HO
Concentration:
    Expansion: All United States, Canada, Foreign
    Registered:
Field Support: ST, H
    Training: 4 days HQ

Ruffin's Pet Centres
109 Industrial Dr
Dunnville, ON N1A-2X5   CANADA

    Phone: 905-774-7079   Accepts collect calls?
    Toll Free: FAX: 905-774-1096
    Internet:
Suitable Sites: RM, SC
Concentration: 14 in ON
    Expansion: N, Canada
    Registered:
Field Support: CP, EO, ST, SO, $IC, FC, N
    Training: 1 week operating store
            1-2 weeks head office
            1-2 weeks on-site

Pets Industry   **Pet Supplies (Spread 2 of 2)**

	True Friends	Wild Bird Centers of America, Inc.	Wild Bird Marketplace	Wild Birds Unlimited				
Startup Cost	140K-190K	75K-131K	90K-150K	85K-135K				
Franchise Fee	25K	19.5K	15K	18K				
Royalty	6%	3-4.5%	4%	4%/$8K MIN.				
Advertising Fee	1%	2.1-2.7K	0%					
Financing Provided	N	Y	Y	Y				
Experience Required	N							
Passive Ownership	D	D	D	N				
In Business Since	1983	1985	1988	1981				
Franchised Since	1996	1988	1990	1983				
Franchised Units 1996								
1997	1	100	30	244				
1998	1							
Company Owned 1996								
1997	2	3	0	0				
1998	3							
Number of Units U.S.	4	100	29	229				
Canada	0	3	1	15				
Foreign	0	0	0	0				
Projected New U.S.	2	6						
Canada								
Foreign		0						
Corporate Employees	6	11	3	40				
Contract Length	5/5/5/5	5/5/5	10/10	10/5				
Expand in Territory	Y	Y	Y	Y				
Full-Time Employees	1	1	1	2				
Part-Time Employees	4	2	2	4				
Conversions	Y	N	Y					
Site Selection Assist.	Y	Y	Y	Y				
Lease Negotiation Assist.	Y	Y	Y	Y				
Site Space Required	1000	1500-2400	2000	2000				
Development Agreement	N	N	Y	N				
Develop. Agree. Term								
Sub-franchising	N	N	N	N				

Pets Industry

True Friends
318 N Carson St #214
Carson City, NV 89701
Collectibles depicting your favorite pet
Phone: 702-882-1963   Accepts collect calls?
Toll Free: 800-654-5156   FAX: 800-654-5161
Internet:
Suitable Sites: DA, RM, SF
Concentration: 2 in HI, 1 in OH, 1 in CA
Expansion: All United States, Foreign
Registered: CA,FL,HI,IL,WA
Field Support: EO, ST, SO, IC, FC, H, N
Training: 10 days IEL univ in Honolulu, HI

Wild Bird Centers of America, Inc.
7370 Macarthur Blvd
Glen Echo, MD 20812
Franchising the ultimate wild bird specialty shops
Phone: 301-229-9585   Accepts collect calls? N
Toll Free: 800-945-3247   FAX: 301-320-6154
Internet: www.wildbirdcenter.com
Suitable Sites: DA, SC
Concentration: 10 in MD, 7 in VA, 8 in PA
Expansion: All United States, Canada, Foreign
Registered: CA,FL,IL,IN,MD,MI,MN,NY,OR,RI,SD,VA,WA,WI,DC,AB
Field Support: EO, $ST, SO, IC, $FC, N
Training: 10 days home office

Wild Bird Marketplace
1891 Santa Barbara Dr #106
Lancaster, PA 17601

Phone: 717-581-5310   Accepts collect calls?
Toll Free: 800-851-2711   FAX: 717-581-5312
Internet: www.wildbird.com
Suitable Sites: FB, SC, SF
Concentration: 8 in PA, 3 in OH, 3 in NJ
Expansion: NE, SE, Canada
Registered: FL,IL,IN,MD,MI,NY,RI,WI,AB
Field Support: EO, ST, SO, IC, FC, H, N
Training: 5 days corporate HQ
3 days at store

Wild Birds Unlimited
11711 N College Ave #146
Carmel, IN 46032-5601

Phone: 317-571-7100   Accepts collect calls?
Toll Free: 888-302-2473   FAX: 317-571-7110
Internet: www.wbu.com
Suitable Sites: FB, SC
Concentration: 19 in MI, 18 in TX, 13 in IL
Expansion: All United States, Canada
Registered: CA,FL,IL,IN,MD,MI,MN,NY,OR,VA,WA,WI,DC
Field Support: EO, ST, SO, IC, FC, H, N
Training: 5 days Indianapolis, IN
1 day store site

Photography Industry   Photography (Spread 1 of 2)

	Glamour Shots	I N V U Portraits	Infinity Video Productions Inc	Lindelle Studios	Motophoto & Portrait Studio	One Hour Portrait Studio	One Hour Motophoto & Portrait Studio (Canada)	Picture Hits	Special Delivery Photos Inc
Startup Cost	133K	18K-44.5K	1.5K-10K	15K-20K	55K		225K-250K	60K-130K	6.75K-12.85K
Franchise Fee	15K	12K	18.5K	9.9K	35K		35K	20K	10K
Royalty		6%	2%	10%	6%		6%	6%	6%
Advertising Fee	$357/MO	1%		0	0.5%		6%		
Financing Provided	Y	N	N	Y	Y		Y	Y	N
Experience Required		N			N	N	N		
Passive Ownership	N	N			D	A	N		
In Business Since	1988	1995	1983	1946	1981		1986	1993	1984
Franchised Since	1992	1997	1995	1998	1982		1987	1996	1991
Franchised Units 1996		0	4					0	7
1997	210	0	4	2	383		53	1	8
1998		35			343		42		
Company Owned 1996		3	8					3	1
1997	2	11	8	5			3	2	1
1998		0			37		10		
Number of Units U.S.	195	30		7	329		0		
Canada	9	0		0	51		56		
Foreign	8	0		0	43		26		
Projected New U.S.		80			15		80		
Canada		4					10		
Foreign		1							
Corporate Employees		45			30	100	70		
Contract Length		10/5			5	10/5/5	10/2-5		
Expand in Territory	Y	N			N	Y	Y		
Full-Time Employees					1	3	3		
Part-Time Employees					VAR	3	2		
Conversions	Y	N			Y	Y	Y		
Site Selection Assist.	Y	N			Y	Y	Y		
Lease Negotiation Assist.	Y	N			Y	Y	Y		
Site Space Required	800-1200				300	1200-1400	800-1200		
Development Agreement	Y	N			Y	Y	N		
Develop. Agree. Term					5	10			
Sub-franchising	N	N			Y	N	N		

Photography Industry

Glamour Shots
1300 Metropolitan Ave
Oklahoma City, OK 73108

Phone: 405-947-8747   Accepts collect calls?
Toll Free: 800-336-4550   FAX: 405-951-7343
Internet: www.glamourshots.com
Suitable Sites: RM
Concentration: 25 in TX, 21 in FL, 14 in CA
Expansion: All United States, Canada, Foreign
Registered: CA,FL,HI,IL,IN,MD,MI,MN,NY,OR,RI,SD,VA,WA,WI,DC
Field Support: DP, CP, EO, ST, SO, FC, N
Training: 1 week national training center
4 weeks training store

I N V U Portraits
563 W 500 South #250
Bountiful, UT 84010
Unique portraits in creative settings, sepia, B&W, hand colored
Phone: 801-292-4688   Accepts collect calls?
Toll Free: FAX:
Internet:
Suitable Sites: HO
Concentration: 4 in CA, 4 in FL, 5 in TX
Expansion: All United States
Registered: CA,IL,IN,MD,MI,MN,NY,OR,RI,VA,WA,WI
Field Support: DP, CP, EO, ST, FC, N
Training: 5 days corp. office
2 days in field

Infinity Video Productions Inc
1028 W Maude Ave #403
Sunnyvale, CA 94086
Video production services
Phone: 408-720-0281   Accepts collect calls?
Toll Free: FAX:
Internet:
Suitable Sites:
Concentration:
Expansion: All United States, Canada, Foreign
Registered:
Field Support:
Training:

Lindelle Studios
724 Old York Rd
Jenkintown, PA 19046
Wedding/bar mitzvah/social photography and video
Phone: 215-572-8900   Accepts collect calls? N
Toll Free: 800-925-6657   FAX: 215-572-7054
Internet: www.lindelle.com
Suitable Sites: AC, ES, DA, FB, HO, IP, K, M, OC, PC, RM, SC, SF, OTHER
Concentration: 5 in PA, 2 in NJ
Expansion: All United States, Canada, Foreign
Registered:
Field Support: CP, EO, $ST, $SO, $FC, H
Training: 2 weeks sales & management

One Hour Motophoto & Portrait Studio
4444 Lake Center Dr
Dayton, OH 45426
One hour photo finishing & other related imaging services
Phone: 937-854-6686   Accepts collect calls?
Toll Free: 800-733-6686   FAX: 937-854-0140
Internet: www.motophoto.com
Suitable Sites: AC, FB, RM, SC, SF
Concentration: 51 in ON, 48 in NJ, 27 in IL
Expansion: All United States, Canada, Foreign
Registered: CA,FL,HI,IL,IN,MD,MI,MN,NY,RI,VA,WA,WI,DC
Field Support: CP, EO, ST, SO, FC, H, N
Training: 3 weeks Dayton, OH
3 weeks local market

One Hour Motophoto & Portrait Studio (Canada)
1315 Lawrence Ave E #509
Toronto, ON M3A-3R3 CANADA
Photo-finishing & digital imaging svcs, sell cameras, film, etc
Phone: 416-443-1900   Accepts collect calls? Y
Toll Free: FAX: 416-443-1653
Internet: www.motophoto.com
Suitable Sites: K, RM, SC, SF
Concentration: 52 in ON
Expansion: Canada
Registered: CA,FL,HI,IL,IN,MD,MI,MN,ND,NY,OR,RI,SD,VA,WA,WI,DC
Field Support: DP, CP, EO, ST, SO, IC, FC, N
Training: 3 weeks corporate HQ
on-site

Picture Hits
1028 Oakhaven #101
Memphis, TN 38119
Portrait photography studio
Phone: 901-682-8493   Accepts collect calls?
Toll Free: FAX:
Internet:
Suitable Sites:
Concentration:
Expansion: NE,SE,S,MW,SE
Registered:
Field Support:
Training:

Special Delivery Photos Inc
PO Box 34905
Bartlett, TN 38134
In-hospital newborn photography
Phone: 901-829-3555   Accepts collect calls?
Toll Free: FAX:
Internet:
Suitable Sites:
Concentration:
Expansion: Canada, Foreign
Registered:
Field Support:
Training:

Photography Industry

	The Sports Section	The Visual Image						
Startup Cost	9.9K+	35K						
Franchise Fee	9.9K+	73.5K						
Royalty	0%	0%						
Advertising Fee	0%	0%						
Financing Provided	N	Y						
Experience Required		N						
Passive Ownership	D	D						
In Business Since	1983	1984						
Franchised Since	1985	1994						
Franchised Units 1996		7						
1997	135	8						
1998		17						
Company Owned 1996		2						
1997	2	4						
1998		4						
Number of Units U.S.	134	17						
Canada	3	0						
Foreign	0	0						
Projected New U.S.		5						
Canada								
Foreign								
Corporate Employees	20	3						
Contract Length	5/5	2/5						
Expand in Territory	Y	Y						
Full-Time Employees	2	1						
Part-Time Employees	2	1						
Conversions	Y	Y						
Site Selection Assist.	N	N						
Lease Negotiation Assist.		N						
Site Space Required								
Development Agreement	Y	N						
Develop. Agree. Term	INT'L							
Sub-franchising	Y	N						

Photography Industry

The Sports Section
3871 Lakefield Dr #100
Suwanee, GA 30024

Phone: 770-622-4900   Accepts collect calls?
Toll Free: 800-321-9127   FAX: 770-622-4949
Internet: www.sports-section.com
Suitable Sites: HO
Concentration: 12 in GA, 10 in FL, 9 in CA
Expansion: All United States, Canada, Foreign
Registered: CA,FL,HI,IL,IN,MD,MI,MN,ND,NY,OR,RI,SD,VA,WA,WI,DC
Field Support: DP, $CP, EO, ST, $FC, H, N
Training: 4-6 days franchisees territory

The Visual Image
523 Highland Ave
Maryville, TN 37803
Train to take photographs on-site for preschools & pet shops
Phone: 423-981-1270   Accepts collect calls?
Toll Free: 800-344-0323   FAX: 423-681-0279
Internet:
Suitable Sites: HO
Concentration: 4 in FL, 3 in TN, 2 in GA
Expansion: All United States
Registered: FL,IN,MI
Field Support: CP, EO, ST, $FC, H, N
Training: 1 week home office
2 weeks on location

Printing and Copying Industry   Printing and Copying (Spread 1 of 3)

	Printshops Of The Future	Alphagraphics Printing Centers	American Speed	Wholesale Thermographers American	BCT	Copy Club	Copy Copy	Kwik Kopy Printing	Kwik-Kopy Printing (Canada)
Startup Cost	256.4K-447.9K	250K	340K-352K	354K-441K	361K-495K	159.9K-233.9K	296K-358K	120K-220K
Franchise Fee	25.9K	19.5K	30K	35K	30K	25K	25K	20K
Royalty	6%	3.6-6%	5%	6%	7%	5%	4-8%	6%
Advertising Fee	2.5%	1%	0	N/A	0	0%	0%	3%
Financing Provided	Y	Y	Y	Y	Y	N	Y	N
Experience Required			N				N	
Passive Ownership	N	D	N	N	N	N	N	N
In Business Since	1970	1976	1980	1975	1992	1989	1967	1978
Franchised Since	1980	1977	1981	1977	1994	1996	1967	1979
Franchised Units 1996								
1997	329	450	0	92	14	0	848	77
1998			20				783	
Company Owned 1996								
1997	1	0	0	2	0	4	0	0
1998			0		0		0	
Number of Units U.S.	249	370	16	87	14	4	374	0
Canada	1	66	4	7	0	0	98	77
Foreign	80	14	0	0	0	0	409	0
Projected New U.S.								
Canada								
Foreign								
Corporate Employees	99	60		32		2	125+	14
Contract Length	20/20	20/20	25/25	25/10	25/25	10/5	25/25	25
Expand in Territory	Y	Y	Y	N	Y	N	Y	Y
Full-Time Employees	5	3	2	10	5	6	3-7	4
Part-Time Employees		1	1	6	2		1	
Conversions	Y	Y	N	Y	N		N	
Site Selection Assist.	Y	Y	Y	Y	Y	Y	Y	Y
Lease Negotiation Assist.	N	Y	Y	Y	Y	Y	Y	Y
Site Space Required	2000-2400	1500	2500-3000	4000	3000-4000	2000	1500-2000	800-1500
Development Agreement	Y	N	N	N	N	N	N	Y
Develop. Agree. Term	N/A							25
Sub-franchising	N	Y	N	N	N	N	N	N

Printing and Copying Industry

Alphagraphics Printshops Of The Future
3760 N Commerce Dr Ste 100
Tucson, AZ 85705

Phone: 520-293-9200	Accepts collect calls?
Toll Free: 800-528-4885	FAX: 520-887-2850

Internet: www.alphagraphics.com
Suitable Sites: FB, SC
Concentration: 33 in AZ, 27 in TX, 22 in IL
Expansion: All United States, Canada, Foreign
Registered: CA,FL,IL,IN,MD,MI,MN,NY,OR,RI,VA,WA,WI
Field Support: CP, EO, ST, SO, $FC, H, N
Training: 4 weeks Tucson service center
1 week field location

American Speedy Printing Centers
1800 W Maple Rd
Troy, MI 48084

Phone: 810-614-3700	Accepts collect calls?
Toll Free: 800-726-9050	FAX: 248-614-3719

Internet:
Suitable Sites: FB, IP, RM, SC, SF
Concentration: 92 in MI, 36 in CA, 32 in IL
Expansion: All United States, Canada
Registered: CA,FL,HI,IL,IN,MD,MI,NY,ND,OR,RI,SD,VA,WA,WI,DC
Field Support: DP, CP, EO, ST, SO, IC, FC, H, N
Training: 2-2.5 weeks home office
1-2 weeks on-site

American Wholesale Thermographers
12715 Telge Rd
Cypress, TX 77429
Wholesale printing, raised-letter printing for retailers

Phone: 281-256-4100	Accepts collect calls? N
Toll Free: 888-280-2053	FAX: 281-256-4178

Internet: www.awt.com
Suitable Sites: LI, OS, SC, SF, WR
Concentration: 2 in CA, 2 in VA, 1 in OH
Expansion: All United States, Canada
Registered: FL,IL,IN,NY
Field Support: CP, EO, ST, SO, H, N
Training: 2 weeks classroom
2 weeks existing awt
2 on-site visits

BCT
3000 NE 30th Place 5th Flr
Fort Lauderdale, FL 33306

Phone: 954-563-1224	Accepts collect calls?
Toll Free: 800-627-9998	FAX: 954-565-0742

Internet: www.bct-net.com
Suitable Sites: FB, OC, SC
Concentration: 16 in CA, 7 in FL, 5 in NY
Expansion: NJ,NE
Registered: CA,FL,HI,IL,IN,MD,MI,MN,ND,NY,OR,RI,SD,VA,WA,WI,DC
Field Support: $DP, CP, EO, $ST, SO, $FC, H, N
Training: 2 weeks Ft Lauderdale FL
1 week pre-opening at new site
2 weeks after and on-going

Copy Club
12715 Telge Rd
Cypress, TX 77429
24hr retail digital imaging to high speed copying, fast paced

Phone: 281-256-4100	Accepts collect calls? N
Toll Free: 888-280-2053	FAX: 281-256-4178

Internet: www.copyclub.com
Suitable Sites: FB, PC, SC, SF
Concentration: 10 in TX, 3 in CA, 1 in FL
Expansion: All United States, Foreign
Registered: CA,FL,IL,IN,MD,NY,OR,RI,VA,WA,DC
Field Support: CP, EO, ST, SO, $FC, H, N
Training: 1 week in field
4 weeks classroom
5 on-site visits

Copy Copy
101 W Main St #107 PO Box 2732
Frisco, CO 80443

Phone: 970-668-0494	Accepts collect calls?
Toll Free: 888-289-2679	FAX: 970-668-0496

Internet:
Suitable Sites: SC
Concentration: 4 in CO
Expansion: CO,AZ,NM,TX,KS,NE,LA,AR,MO
Registered:
Field Support: $DP, CP, EO, $ST, SO, IC, FC, H
Training: 3 weeks corporate HQ
1 week franchise location

Kwik Kopy Printing
12715 Telge Rd
Cypress, TX 77429
Traditional printing, digital imaging, high speed color copying

Phone: 281-256-4100	Accepts collect calls? N
Toll Free: 888-280-2053	FAX: 281-256-4178

Internet: www.kwikkopy.com
Suitable Sites: FB, IP, OC, SC, SF
Concentration: 147 in TX, 32 in IL, 27 in CA
Expansion: All United States, Canada, Foreign
Registered: CA,FL,IL,IN,MD,MI,MN,NY,OR,RI,VA,WA,WI,DC,AB
Field Support: CP, EO, ST, SO, $FC, H, N
Training: 4 weeks 2 people lodging included
3 trainer visits on-site
outside sales rep train

Kwik-Kopy Printing (Canada)
15900 Yonge St
Aurora, ON L4G-3G8 CANADA

Phone: 905-798-7007	Accepts collect calls?
Toll Free: 800-387-9725	FAX: 905-727-1952

Internet: www.ca.kwikkopy.com
Suitable Sites: SC, OTHER
Concentration: 54 in ON, 5 in BC, 5 in AB
Expansion: N, Canada
Registered: CA,FL,HI,IL,IN,MD,MI,MN,ND,NY,OR,RI,SD,VA,WA,WI,DC
Field Support: $EO, ST, SO, $FC, $H, $N
Training: 3.5 weeks Houston TX
2 weeks on-site

Printing and Copying Industry

	LazerQuick	Le Print Express	Minuteman Press International	Proforma	Screen Printing USA	Signal Graphics Printing	Sir Speedy	Sir Speedy (Canada)
Startup Cost	172.5K-275K	170K-190K	-120K	22K-27K	40K-60K	190K-230K	200K-300K	150K-220K
Franchise Fee	25K	0	44.5K	19.5K	25K	18K	20K	20K
Royalty	5%/$500	$1K/MO	6%	9%	6%	0-5%	4-6%	6%
Advertising Fee	0	$350/MO	0%	1%	2%	$100/MO	1-2%	3%
Financing Provided	Y	Y	Y	Y	Y	Y	Y	Y
Experience Required	N							
Passive Ownership	N	D	D	N	D	D	D	D
In Business Since	1968	1991	1975	1978	1988	1974	1968	1968
Franchised Since	1990	1993	1975	1985	1988	1982	1968	1983
Franchised Units 1996								
1997	17	45	860	280	32	47	863	7
1998	21							
Company Owned 1996								
1997	36	10	0	0	0	2	19	0
1998	31							
Number of Units U.S.	52	21	743	260	30	46	752	752
Canada	1	33	70	20	2	0	5	5
Foreign	0	1	47	0	0	3	125	0
Projected New U.S.	6							
Canada	2							
Foreign								
Corporate Employees	60	20	150	140	4		75	
Contract Length	7/7/7	10/10	35/35	10/10	10/10	25/25	20/20	20/20
Expand in Territory	N	Y	Y		Y	Y	Y	Y
Full-Time Employees	2	1	3	1	2	4	6	3
Part-Time Employees	2	2			1	1	1	
Conversions	Y		Y	Y	N	Y	Y	Y
Site Selection Assist.	Y	Y	Y	N	Y	Y	Y	Y
Lease Negotiation Assist.	Y	Y	Y		Y	Y	Y	Y
Site Space Required	1400-1800	400	1200		1500	1500	1500-2000	1500
Development Agreement	Y	Y	N	N	Y	N	Y	N
Develop. Agree. Term		10			10		20	
Sub-franchising	N	Y	N	N	Y	N	Y	N

Printing and Copying Industry

Printing and Copying (Spread 2 of 3)

LazerQuick
27375 SW Parkway Ave #200
Wilsonville, OR 97070
One-stop printing & copying centers, computer svcs, offset print

Phone: 503-682-1322	Accepts collect calls?
Toll Free: 800-477-2679	FAX: 503-682-7816

Internet: www.lazerquick.com
Suitable Sites: SC
Concentration: 35 in OR, 13 in WA, 2 in CA
Expansion: All United States, Canada
Registered: CA,FL,IL,MD,MI,OR,WA,WI,IN,MN,NY,VA
Field Support: CP, EO, ST, SO, FC, H
Training: 5-6 weeks corporate HQ

Le Print Express
151 Nashdene Rd #53
Toronto, ON M1V-4C4   CANADA

Phone: 416-754-8440	Accepts collect calls?
Toll Free: 800-263-1723	FAX: 416-754-2200

Internet: www.leprint.com/beta
Suitable Sites: RM
Concentration: 21 in ON, 6 in BC, 4 in PQ
Expansion: All United States, Canada, Foreign
Registered: FL,IL,IN,VA,DC
Field Support: CP, EO, ST, SO, IC, FC, H, N
Training: 2 weeks training ctr Toronto on

Minuteman Press International
1640 New Highway
Farmingdale, NY 11735

Phone: 516-249-1370	Accepts collect calls?
Toll Free: 800-645-3006	FAX: 516-249-5618

Internet:
Suitable Sites: SC, SF
Concentration: 70 in CA, 65 in NY, 55 in TX
Expansion: All United States, Canada, Foreign
Registered: ALL STATES,AB
Field Support: CP, EO, ST, SO, IC, $FC, H, N
Training: 3 weeks corporate HQ
2 weeks on-site as needed

Proforma
8800 E Pleasant Valley Rd
Cleveland, OH 44131

Phone: 216-520-8400	Accepts collect calls?
Toll Free: 800-825-1525	FAX: 216-520-8474

Internet: www.proforma.com
Suitable Sites: HO
Concentration: 18 in CA, 10 in OH, 10 in NY
Expansion: All United States, Canada
Registered: CA,FL,HI,IL,IN,MD,MI,MN,ND,NY,OR,RI,SD,VA,WA,WI,DC
Field Support: DP, EO, ST, IC, FC, H, N
Training: 1 week HQ
2 days regional
2 days national

Screen Printing USA
534 W Shawnee Ave
Plymouth, PA 18651

Phone: 717-779-5175	Accepts collect calls?
Toll Free:	FAX:

Internet:
Suitable Sites: FB, HO, SF
Concentration: PA, NY
Expansion: All United States, Canada
Registered: FL,MN,NY,VA
Field Support: CP, EO, ST, SO, FC, N
Training: 2 weeks Plymouth PA

Signal Graphics Printing
6789 S Yosemite St
Englewood, CO 80112

Phone: 303-779-6789	Accepts collect calls?
Toll Free: 800-852-6336	FAX: 303-779-8445

Internet: www.signalgraphics.com
Suitable Sites: SC
Concentration: 18 in CO, 3 in CA, 5 in TX
Expansion: All United States, Canada, Foreign
Registered: CA,FL,HI,IL,IN,MD,MI,MN,NY,OR,RI,VA,WA,WI,DC
Field Support: CP, EO, $ST, SO, FC, H, N
Training: 3 weeks HQ
2 weeks on-site

Sir Speedy
26722 Plaza Dr
Mission Viejo, CA 92691

Phone: 714-348-5000	Accepts collect calls?
Toll Free: 800-854-3321	FAX: 714-348-5068

Internet: www.sirspeedy.com
Suitable Sites: SC, SF
Concentration: 100 in CA, 70 in CA, 50 in IL
Expansion: All United States, Canada, Foreign
Registered: CA,FL,HI,IL,IN,MD,MI,MN,ND,NY,OR,RI,SD,VA,WA,WI,DC
Field Support: CP, EO, ST, SO, IC, FC, H, N
Training: 2 weeks classroom at HQ
2 weeks on-site
1+ week another center

Sir Speedy (Canada)
2800 14th Ave #24
Markham, ON L3R-0E4   CANADA

Phone: 905-475-9394	Accepts collect calls?
Toll Free: 800-263-2308	FAX: 905-475-7628

Internet:
Suitable Sites: SC, SF
Concentration: 5 in ON
Expansion: N, Canada
Registered:
Field Support: EO, ST, SO, IC, FC, H, N
Training: 2 weeks California
2 weeks on-site

Printing and Copying Industry

Printing and Copying (Spread 3 of 3)

	Speedy Printing Centers	United Printing Unlimited					
Startup Cost	140K-150K	120K					
Franchise Fee	19.5K	18K					
Royalty	6%	5% GROSS					
Advertising Fee	1-1.5%	1%					
Financing Provided	Y	Y					
Experience Required							
Passive Ownership	D	A					
In Business Since	1986	1985					
Franchised Since	1987	1996					
Franchised Units 1996							
1997	457	13					
1998							
Company Owned 1996							
1997	0	2					
1998							
Number of Units U.S.	403	15					
Canada	33	0					
Foreign	21	0					
Projected New U.S.							
Canada							
Foreign							
Corporate Employees	1	4					
Contract Length	20/20	20/20					
Expand in Territory	Y	Y					
Full-Time Employees	3	3					
Part-Time Employees		1					
Conversions	Y	Y					
Site Selection Assist.	Y	Y					
Lease Negotiation Assist.	Y	Y					
Site Space Required	1500	1200					
Development Agreement	Y	Y					
Develop. Agree. Term		5					
Sub-franchising	N	N					

Printing and Copying Industry

Printing and Copying (Spread 3 of 3)

Speedy Printing Centers
1357 Point Mercer Dr
Qualicum Beach, BC V9K-2K5 CANADA

Phone: 250-752-7539
Accepts collect calls?
Toll Free: 888-522-4567
FAX: 250-752-5397
Internet:
Suitable Sites: FB, SC, SF
Concentration: 17 in BC
Expansion: N, Canada
Registered:
Field Support: CP, EO, ST, SO, FC, H, N
Training: 2 weeks troy MI
3 weeks BC

United Printing Unlimited
PO Box 2020
Davenport, IA 52809

Phone: 407-246-0160
Accepts collect calls?
Toll Free:
FAX: 407-246-0207
Internet:
Suitable Sites: FB, SC, SF
Concentration: FL, IA, IL
Expansion: All United States, Canada
Registered: FL,IL,IN
Field Support: DP, CP, EO, ST, SO, $IC, N
Training: 4 weeks

Publishing Industry   **Publishing**

	Bingo Bugle Newspaper	Home Guide Magazine	The Homesteader	International News	Rental Guide	Street Corner News		
Startup Cost	5K	9.25K-38K	3.31K-22K	40K-150K	19K-55K	90K-150K		
Franchise Fee	5K	8K	5K	30K	35K	17.5K		
Royalty	10%	VAR.	10%	3%	VAR.	4.5K		
Advertising Fee	0			0%		0%		
Financing Provided	N	Y	N	Y	Y	N		
Experience Required				N				
Passive Ownership	N			D		A		
In Business Since	1981	1973	1989	1993	1973	1988		
Franchised Since	1983	1984	1993	1994	1988	1995		
Franchised Units 1996		28	12		21			
1997	71	24	10	70	20	8		
1998	71			26				
Company Owned 1996		0	6		6			
1997	0	0	5	4	5	7		
1998	0							
Number of Units U.S.	66			0		17		
Canada	5			74		0		
Foreign	0			0		0		
Projected New U.S.	10							
Canada	2			35				
Foreign	0							
Corporate Employees				10		3		
Contract Length	5			5/5		10/5		
Expand in Territory	Y			Y		Y		
Full-Time Employees	1			2		2		
Part-Time Employees	1			2		4		
Conversions	Y			Y		N		
Site Selection Assist.	N			Y		Y		
Lease Negotiation Assist.	N			Y		Y		
Site Space Required				500		450		
Development Agreement	N			Y		Y		
Develop. Agree. Term				5/5		10		
Sub-franchising	Y			N		N		

Publishing Industry

Bingo Bugle Newspaper
PO Box 527
Vashon Island, WA 98070
Bingo & gambling news
    Phone: 206-463-5656   Accepts collect calls?
    Toll Free: 800-327-6437   FAX: 206-463-5630
    Internet: www.bingobugle.com
Suitable Sites: HO
Concentration: 12 in CA, 6 in NY, 5 in FL
    Expansion: Canada, Foreign
    Registered:
Field Support:
    Training: 3 days

Home Guide Magazine
PO Box 5018
Tallahassee, FL 32314
Pictorial community real estate adv magazine
    Phone: 904-574-2111   Accepts collect calls?
    Toll Free: FAX:
    Internet:
Suitable Sites:
Concentration:
    Expansion: All United States
    Registered:
Field Support:
    Training:

The Homesteader
PO Box 2824
Framingham, MA 01703
Newspaper for new homeowners
    Phone: Accepts collect calls?
    Toll Free: 800-941-9907   FAX:
    Internet:
Suitable Sites:
Concentration:
    Expansion: NY, Canada
    Registered:
Field Support:
    Training:

International News
2000 Argentina Rd Plaza 1 #270
Mississauga, ON L5N-1P7 CANADA

    Phone: 905-826-0862   Accepts collect calls? N
    Toll Free: 800-319-5666   FAX: 905-826-2105
    Internet:
Suitable Sites: FB, FC, K, M, OC, RM, SC, SF
Concentration: 65 in ON, 10 in BC, 15 in AB
    Expansion: Canada
    Registered: AB
Field Support: CP, EO, ST, SO, IC, FC, H, N
    Training: 2 days office
                1 week store

Rental Guide
PO Box 5018
Tallahassee, FL 32314
Pictorial rental property magazine
    Phone: 904-574-2111   Accepts collect calls?
    Toll Free: FAX:
    Internet:
Suitable Sites:
Concentration:
    Expansion: All United States
    Registered:
Field Support:
    Training:

Street Corner News
800 W 47th St #420
Kansas City, MO 64112

    Phone: 816-531-8898   Accepts collect calls?
    Toll Free: 800-783-4854   FAX: 816-531-8818
    Internet:
Suitable Sites: RM
Concentration: 4 in KS, 2 in NY, 2 in CA
    Expansion: All United States, Canada
    Registered: CA,FL,MI,MN,NY,WI
Field Support: EO, ST, SO, IC, $FC, H, N
    Training: 1 week various locations

Quick-service Industry

Bakery: Bagels (Spread 1 of 2)

	Bagelsmith Restaurants & Food Stores	Bagelz-The Bagel Bakery	Between Rounds Bagel Deli & Bakery	Big City Bagels Inc	Chesapeake Bagel Bakery	Goldberg's New York Bagels	The Great American Bagel	The Great Canadian Bagel
Startup Cost	213K-303K	140K	145K-188K	220K-300K	400K-500K	175K-225K	230K-280K	260K-300K
Franchise Fee	25K	10K	18K	30K	25K	25K	20K	30K
Royalty	1-4%	8%	4%	4%	5%	5%	4%	6%
Advertising Fee	3%		2%		4%	1%	2%	1.5%
Financing Provided	N	Y	N	Y	Y	Y	N	Y
Experience Required			N					
Passive Ownership	D		D		A	D	N	D
In Business Since	1979	1990	1990	1992	1981	1938	1987	1993
Franchised Since	1983	1994	1993	1993	1983	1995	1994	1994
Franchised Units 1996		19		11				
1997	21	24	7	12	165	21	35	153
1998			3					151
Company Owned 1996		3		3				
1997	1	3	3	6	0	10	5	11
1998			4					10
Number of Units U.S.	23		7		164	31	40	0
Canada	0		0		1	0	0	161
Foreign	0		0		0	0	0	2
Projected New U.S.			3					
Canada								
Foreign								3
Corporate Employees	5		4		35	35		200
Contract Length	10		10/5/5/5		20/10	10/10	20/5	10/5
Expand in Territory	Y		Y		Y	Y	Y	Y
Full-Time Employees	8		3		3	4	3	7
Part-Time Employees	4		5		21	10	9	5
Conversions			Y		Y	Y		N
Site Selection Assist.	Y		Y		Y	Y	Y	Y
Lease Negotiation Assist.	Y		Y		Y	Y	Y	Y
Site Space Required	2000		1600		1800-2400	1500	2000	1800-2000
Development Agreement	N		Y		N	Y	N	N
Develop. Agree. Term			NEG.					
Sub-franchising	N		N		N	N	N	Y

Quick-service Industry

Bagelsmith Restaurants & Food Stores
37 Van Syckel Rd
Hampton, NJ 08827

Phone: 908-730-8600   Accepts collect calls?
Toll Free: FAX: 908-730-8165
Internet:
Suitable Sites: FB, SC
Concentration: 20 in NJ, 3 in PA
Expansion: NE
Registered:
Field Support: EO, $ST, N
Training: 180 hours Hampton, NJ

Bagelz-The Bagel Bakery
95 Oak St
Glastonbury, CT 06033
Bagels, sandwiches, soups & salads
Phone: 860-657-4400   Accepts collect calls?
Toll Free: FAX:
Internet:
Suitable Sites:
Concentration:
Expansion: IN,RI
Registered:
Field Support:
Training:

Between Rounds Bagel Deli & Bakery
19a John Fitch Blvd
South Windsor, CT 06074
Upscale bagel deli bakery - catering svcs - delivery
Phone: 860-291-0323   Accepts collect calls?
Toll Free: FAX: 860-289-2732
Internet:
Suitable Sites: AC, AM, DA, FB, IP, LI, PC, RM, SC, SF, WF
Concentration: 4 in CT, 2 in MA, 1 in WV
Expansion: Mid-Atlantic and NE
Registered:
Field Support: $DP, EO, ST, SO, IC, N
Training: 2 weeks CO stores in CT
1-2 weeks own unit

Big City Bagels Inc
151 Kalmus Dr #C0001
Costa Mesa, CA 92626
Upscale bagel bakery cafe & deli
Phone: 714-434-3500   Accepts collect calls?
Toll Free: 800-882-2435   FAX:
Internet:
Suitable Sites:
Concentration:
Expansion: All United States, Canada, Foreign
Registered:
Field Support:
Training:

Chesapeake Bagel Bakery
6 Concourse Pkwy #1700
Atlanta, GA 30328

Phone: 770-353-3182   Accepts collect calls?
Toll Free: 800-848-8248   FAX: 770-350-3652
Internet:
Suitable Sites: SC, SF
Concentration: 31 in VA, 10 in MD, 9 in DC
Expansion: All United States, Canada, Foreign
Registered: CA,FL,HI,IL,IN,MD,MI,MN,ND,NY,OR,RI,SD,VA,WA,WI,DC
Field Support: CP, EO, ST, SO, IC, FC, H, N
Training: 4 weeks HQ, Atlanta, GA

Goldberg's New York Bagels
104 New Era Dr
South Plainfield, NJ 07080

Phone: 908-757-3022   Accepts collect calls?
Toll Free: 800-922-4350   FAX: 908-757-8857
Internet:
Suitable Sites: FB, SC, SF
Concentration: 6 in NY, 6 in FL, 4 in CT
Expansion: NE and SE
Registered: CA,FL,IL,MD,NY
Field Support: CP, EO, ST, SO, FC, H, N
Training: 1 week HQ
2 weeks store

The Great American Bagel
519 N Cass Ave #1w
Westmont, IL 60559

Phone: 630-963-3393   Accepts collect calls?
Toll Free: 888-224-3563   FAX: 630-963-7799
Internet:
Suitable Sites: FB, RM, SC, SF
Concentration: 25 in IL, 3 in WA, 2 in IN
Expansion: All United States
Registered: FL,IL,IN,MI,MN,ND,WA,WI
Field Support: CP, EO, ST, SO, $FC, $N
Training: 4 weeks Western Springs, IL.

The Great Canadian Bagel
8 Beamish Dr
Etobicoke, ON M9B-3P3 CANADA
24 varieties of fresh baked bagels, 21 flavours of cream cheese
Phone: 416-234-2800   Accepts collect calls? N
Toll Free: FAX: 416-234-5744
Internet: www.greatcanadianbagel.com
Suitable Sites: FB, K, M, PC, SC, SF
Concentration: 90 in ON, 29 in BC, 18 in AB
Expansion: See The Great American Bagel, Canada, Foreign
Registered: AB
Field Support: DP, CP, EO, ST, SO, IC, $FC, H, N
Training: 4-6 weeks Toronto, ON.

Quick-service Industry

	Lox of Bagels	Manhattan Bagel Co Inc	Manhattan Bagel Company				
Startup Cost	145K-185K	161.75K-404.5K	150K-337K				
Franchise Fee	24.5K	30K	30K				
Royalty	0%	5%	5%				
Advertising Fee	0%		2.5-4.0%				
Financing Provided	N	Y	N				
Experience Required	N						
Passive Ownership	A		D				
In Business Since	1986	1987	1987				
Franchised Since	1995	1988	1988				
Franchised Units 1996		219					
1997	8	310	300				
1998							
Company Owned 1996		38					
1997	3	31	11				
1998							
Number of Units U.S.	11		311				
Canada	0		0				
Foreign	0		0				
Projected New U.S.							
Canada							
Foreign							
Corporate Employees	4		313				
Contract Length	5/5		10/10				
Expand in Territory	Y		Y				
Full-Time Employees	3		3				
Part-Time Employees	3		9				
Conversions	Y		Y				
Site Selection Assist.	Y		Y				
Lease Negotiation Assist.	Y		Y				
Site Space Required	900-1200		1200-1600				
Development Agreement	Y		Y				
Develop. Agree. Term	20						
Sub-franchising	N		Y				

Quick-service Industry

Bakery: Bagels (Spread 2 of 2)

Lox of Bagels
24412 Hawthorne Blvd
Torrance, CA 90505

Phone: 310-373-6550 Accepts collect calls? N
Toll Free: 800-879-6927 FAX: 310-539-7494
Internet:
Suitable Sites: FB, FC, M, PC, SC, SF
Concentration:
Expansion: All United States, Canada, Foreign
Registered: CA,FL,HI,IL,IN,MD,MI,MN,ND,NY,OR,RI,SD,VA,WA,WI,DC
Field Support: EO, ST, SO, IC, H
Training: 5 days on-site

Manhattan Bagel Co Inc
246 Industrial Wy
Eatontown, NJ 07724-2242
Bagel bakery & deli
Phone: 908-544-0155 Accepts collect calls?
Toll Free: FAX:
Internet:
Suitable Sites:
Concentration:
Expansion: All United States, Canada
Registered:
Field Support:
Training:

Manhattan Bagel Company
246 Industrial Wy W
Eatontown, NJ 07724-9886

Phone: 732-544-0155 Accepts collect calls?
Toll Free: 800-872-2243 FAX: 732-544-1315
Internet: www.manhattanbagel.com
Suitable Sites: FB, SC
Concentration: 33 in NJ, 18 in PA, 17 in CA
Expansion: All United States
Registered: CA,FL,HI,IL,IN,MD,MI,MN,ND,NY,OR,RI,SD,VA,WA,WI,DC
Field Support: CP, EO, ST, SO, IC, $FC, N
Training: 2 weeks corporate office
1 week in-store

Quick-service Industry   **Bakery: Cinnamon Rolls**

	Cindy's Cinnamon Rolls	Saint Cinnamon Bake Shoppe							
Startup Cost	130K	80K-150K							
Franchise Fee	25K	25K							
Royalty	5%	6%							
Advertising Fee	0%	3%							
Financing Provided	N	N							
Experience Required									
Passive Ownership	A	N							
In Business Since	1985	1986							
Franchised Since	1986	1986							
Franchised Units 1996									
1997	35	127							
1998									
Company Owned 1996									
1997	0	1							
1998									
Number of Units U.S.	29	1							
Canada	0	70							
Foreign	3	57							
Projected New U.S.									
Canada									
Foreign									
Corporate Employees	3	7							
Contract Length	10/10	10/5							
Expand in Territory	Y	Y							
Full-Time Employees	8	2							
Part-Time Employees		5							
Conversions	Y								
Site Selection Assist.	Y	Y							
Lease Negotiation Assist.	Y	Y							
Site Space Required	800	300-600							
Development Agreement	N	Y							
Develop. Agree. Term		10							
Sub-franchising	N	Y							

Quick-service Industry

Bakery: Cinnamon Rolls

Cindy's Cinnamon Rolls
1432 S Mission Rd
Fallbrook, CA 92028

Phone: 760-723-1121   Accepts collect calls?
Toll Free: 800-468-7655   FAX: 760-723-4143
Internet:
Suitable Sites: RM
Concentration: 8 in NY, 3 in CA, 2 in NJ
Expansion: All United States, Canada, Foreign
Registered: NY,CA
Field Support: CP, EO, ST, SO, IC, FC, H, N
Training: 1 week New York
4 days in-store

Saint Cinnamon Bake Shoppe
7181 Woodbine Ave #222
Markham, ON L3R-1A3 CANADA

Phone: 905-470-1517   Accepts collect calls?
Toll Free: FAX: 905-470-8112
Internet:
Suitable Sites: RM
Concentration: 44 in ON, 17 in PQ, 4 in MB
Expansion: All United States, Canada, Foreign
Registered:
Field Support: DP, CP, EO, ST, $SO, IC, $FC, N
Training: 2 weeks Ontario

Quick-service Industry

Bakery: Cookies

	Blue Chip Cookies	Cafe By George/ Cookies By George	Cookie Bouquet/ Cookies By Design	Cookies In Bloom	Great American Cookie Company, Inc.	Monsieur Felix & Mr. Norton Cookies	Mrs. Fields Cookies	
Startup Cost	117K-200K	100K-125K	75K-140K	49.5K-81K	119.5K-501K	135K-175K	146K-245K	
Franchise Fee	29.5K	25K	20K	12.5K	25K	25K	25K	
Royalty	4%	6%	6%	5%	7%	5%	6%	
Advertising Fee	2%	1.5%	1%	2%	NA	6%	0-2%	
Financing Provided	Y	N	N	N	N	N	N	
Experience Required		N	N					
Passive Ownership	D	D	D	A	A	N	N	
In Business Since	1983	1983	1983	1988	1977	1985	1977	
Franchised Since	1986	1985	1987	1992	1977	1990	1990	
Franchised Units 1996								
1997	35	16	166	14	246	18	426	
1998			180					
Company Owned 1996								
1997	7	2	1	0	83	8	147	
1998			1					
Number of Units U.S.	42	0	180	14	327	0	528	
Canada	0	18	0	0	0	26	11	
Foreign	0	0	0	0	2	0	34	
Projected New U.S.			25					
Canada								
Foreign								
Corporate Employees		20	10	2	65	18	60	
Contract Length	10/10	5/5	5/5	5/5		10/5/5	7/5/5	
Expand in Territory	Y	Y	Y		Y	Y	Y	
Full-Time Employees	4-5	2	3	3	VARY	1	3	
Part-Time Employees	1-2	3	2	2		6	4	
Conversions		Y	N		Y	N	Y	
Site Selection Assist.	Y	Y	Y	Y	Y	Y	Y	
Lease Negotiation Assist.	Y	Y	Y	Y	Y	Y	Y	
Site Space Required	550	350-1200	1200-1500	1200	625	600-800	650-800	
Development Agreement	Y	Y	Y	Y	N	Y	Y	
Develop. Agree. Term	15	10	VAR.					
Sub-franchising	N	Y	N	N	N	Y	N	

Quick-service Industry

Bakery: Cookies

Blue Chip Cookies
100 First St #2030
San Francisco, CA 94105

Phone: 415-546-3840 Accepts collect calls?
Toll Free: 800-888-9866 FAX: 415-546-9717
Internet: www.bluechipcookies.com
Suitable Sites: RM, SF
Concentration: 11 in OH, 12 in CA, 4 in NJ
Expansion: All United States
Registered: CA,FL,HI,IN,MI,NY,WA
Field Support: CP, EO, ST, SO, IC, $FC, H, N
Training: 2-3 weeks San Francisco, CA

Cafe By George/ Cookies By George
650 Bath Rd
Kingston, ON K7M-4X6 CANADA
Bakery cafe specialize in gourmet cookies & specialty gifts
Phone: 613-634-1069 Accepts collect calls? N
Toll Free: FAX: 613-634-1556
Internet: www.kin.igs.net/~bygeorge
Suitable Sites: FB, OC, RM, SC, SF
Concentration: 9 in AB, 5 in ON, 2 in BC
Expansion: Canada
Registered: AB
Field Support: CP, EO, $ST, SO, $FC, N
Training: 3 weeks Toronto, ON

Cookie Bouquet/ Cookies By Design
1865 Summit Ave #605
Plano, TX 75074

Phone: 972-398-9536 Accepts collect calls?
Toll Free: 800-945-2665 FAX: 972-398-9542
Internet: www.cookiebouquet.com
Suitable Sites: AC, FB, SC, SF
Concentration: 28 in TX, 16 in FL, 15 in CA
Expansion: All United States
Registered: CA,FL,HI,IL,IN,MD,MI,MN,NY,OR,SD,VA,WA,WI,ND
Field Support: EO, $ST, SO, $FC, H, N
Training: 2 weeks Dallas, TX

Cookies In Bloom
5429 N Macarthur Blvd
Irving, TX 75038

Phone: 972-518-1749 Accepts collect calls?
Toll Free: 800-222-3104 FAX: 972-580-1831
Internet:
Suitable Sites: SC
Concentration: 6 in TX, 1 in AZ, 1 in WA
Expansion: All United States, Canada, Foreign
Registered: CA,IL,FL,MI,NY,VA,WA
Field Support: CP, EO, ST, SO, FC, H, N
Training: 10 days in irving, TX

Great American Cookie Company, Inc.
4685 Frederick Dr S.W.
Atlanta, GA 30336

Phone: 404-505-3534 Accepts collect calls?
Toll Free: 800-336-2447 FAX: 404-505-3533
Internet: www.greatamericancookies.com
Suitable Sites: RM
Concentration: 47 in TX, 24 in GA, 24 in FL
Expansion: All United States
Registered: CA,FL,HI,IL,IN,MD,MI,MN,ND,NY,OR,RI,SD,VA,WA,WI,DC
Field Support: CP, EO, ST, SO, FC, H, N
Training: 6 days Atlanta, GA.

Monsieur Felix & Mr. Norton Cookies
4100 Thimens Blvd
Saint Laurent, QC H4R-1X4 CANADA

Phone: 514-333-4118 Accepts collect calls?
Toll Free: 800-463-7055 FAX: 514-333-7277
Internet:
Suitable Sites: RM, SC, SF
Concentration: 22 in PQ, 4 in ON
Expansion: N/A, Canada
Registered:
Field Support: CP, EO, ST, SO, IC, FC, H, N
Training: 2 weeks home office Montreal, PQ
1 week on-site

Mrs. Fields Cookies
462 W Bearcat Dr
Salt Lake City, UT 84115-2520

Phone: 801-463-2000 Accepts collect calls?
Toll Free: 800-348-6311 FAX: 801-463-2176
Internet:
Suitable Sites: RM, SC, SF, OTHER
Concentration: 86 in CA, 27 in IL, 19 in NY
Expansion: All United States, Canada, Foreign
Registered: CA,FL,HI,IL,IN,MD,MI,MN,ND,NY,OR,RI,SD,VA,WA,WI,DC
Field Support: DP, CP, EO, ST, SO, IC, FC, H, N
Training: 5-10 days field training
10 days park city, UT

Quick-service Industry

Bakery: Doughnuts (Spread 1 of 2)

	Baker's Dozen Donuts	Coffee Time Donuts	Donut Delite Cafe	Donut Inn	Dunkin' Donuts	Krispy Kreme Doughnuts	Lamar's Donuts	Robin's Donuts
Startup Cost	65K-350K	160K-250K	110K-150K	200K	350K-3M	1.3M	190K-240K	240K-260K
Franchise Fee	INCLUDED		20K	12.5K	10K-40K	25K	24.5K	25K
Royalty	5%	4.5%	6%	5.95%	4.90%	4.5%	5%	4%
Advertising Fee	2%	2%	2%	3%	5%	1%	2%	3%
Financing Provided	Y	N	Y	Y	Y	N	N	N
Experience Required				N		Y	N	N
Passive Ownership	A	N	D		D	N	D	N
In Business Since	1977	1982	1984	1975	1950	1937	1960	1975
Franchised Since	1984	1987	1986	1975	1955	1994	1993	1977
Franchised Units 1996							13	217
1997	112	304	22		4736		13	212
1998				14			21	214
Company Owned 1996							1	25
1997	3	20	0		0		1	24
1998				1			2	25
Number of Units U.S.	0	0	0	15	3384			0
Canada	113	324	22		242			236
Foreign	2	0	0		1110			0
Projected New U.S.				5			25	
Canada								15
Foreign				2				
Corporate Employees	28	50	10	5	700	150	11	286
Contract Length	10/5		10/5	15	10-20/NA	15	10/10	10/5/5
Expand in Territory	Y	Y	Y	Y	Y	Y	Y	Y
Full-Time Employees	3	6	3	4		25	8-10	12
Part-Time Employees	6	4	7	2-3			5-10	6
Conversions		Y	Y		Y	N	Y	Y
Site Selection Assist.	Y		Y	Y	Y	Y	Y	Y
Lease Negotiation Assist.	Y		Y	Y	N	N	Y	Y
Site Space Required	1800-2500		1500-2000	1200	800-2000	3500	2000	2250
Development Agreement	N		Y	Y	Y	Y	Y	Y
Develop. Agree. Term			10		3	VAR.	NEG.	NEG.
Sub-franchising	N	N	Y	Y	N	N	Y	N

Quick-service Industry

Bakery: Doughnuts (Spread 1 of 2)

Baker's Dozen Donuts
1224 Dundas St E #15
Mississauga, ON L4Y-4A2   CANADA
Bakery goods & light lunches
    Phone: 905-272-1825   Accepts collect calls?
    Toll Free: 800-265-6298   FAX: 905-272-0140
    Internet:
Suitable Sites: FB, K, RM, SC
Concentration: 113 in ON
    Expansion: Eastern and Midwest, Canada, Foreign
    Registered: CA,FL,HI,IL,IN,MD,MI,MN,ND,NY,OR,RI,SD,VA,WA,WI,DC
Field Support: CP, EO, ST, SO, IC, FC, H
    Training: 3 weeks Toronto, ON

Coffee Time Donuts
477 Ellesmere Rd
Toronto, ON M1R-4E5   CANADA

    Phone: 416-288-8515   Accepts collect calls?
    Toll Free: FAX: 416-288-8895
    Internet:
Suitable Sites: FB, RM, SF
Concentration: 319 in ON, 3 in MB, 1 in AB
    Expansion: All United States, Canada, Foreign
    Registered:
Field Support: $CP, EO, ST, SO, IC, FC, N
    Training: 3-6 weeks Scarborough, ON

Donut Delite Cafe
3380 S Service Rd
Burlington, ON L7N-3J5   CANADA

    Phone: 905-681-8448   Accepts collect calls?
    Toll Free: FAX: 905-637-7745
    Internet:
Suitable Sites: FB, SC, SF
Concentration: 22 in ON
    Expansion: All United States, Canada
    Registered:
Field Support: CP, EO, ST, SO, IC, FC, N
    Training: 1 week classroom
            2 weeks training store
            1 week own store

Donut Inn
22120 Clarendon St #110
Woodland Hills, CA 91367
Donuts, pastries, croissants, muffins, bagels, catering
    Phone: 818-888-2220   Accepts collect calls? N
    Toll Free: 800-422-5379   FAX: 818-888-2893
    Internet: donut@ix.netcom.com
Suitable Sites: AC, DA, FC, K, M, SC, SF, OTHER
Concentration: 14 in CA, 1 in NV
    Expansion: TX,FL,MI,WA,WI, Foreign
    Registered: CA,FL,MI,WA,WI
Field Support: DP, CP, EO, ST, SO, IC, FC, H, N
    Training: 2-7 weeks system, operations
            on-site employee orientation
            5 days on-site assistance

Dunkin' Donuts
14 Pacella Park Dr,PO Box 317
Randolph, MA 02368

    Phone: 781-961-4000   Accepts collect calls?
    Toll Free: 800-777-9983   FAX: 781-963-3942
    Internet:
Suitable Sites: FB, RM, SC, SF
Concentration: 490 in MA, 359 in NY, 237 in IL
    Expansion: NY,MD,DC,GA,PA,FL,MI,IN,IL, Canada, Foreign
    Registered: CA,FL,IL,IN,MD,MI,MN,NY,OR,RI,VA,WA,WI,DC
Field Support: CP, EO, ST, SO, IC, FC, N
    Training: 5 weeks Dunkin' Donuts Univ

Krispy Kreme Doughnuts
PO Box 83
Winston Salem, NC 27102

    Phone: 910-725-2981   Accepts collect calls? N
    Toll Free: 800-242-8880   FAX:
    Internet:
Suitable Sites: FB
Concentration:
    Expansion: All United States, Canada, Foreign
    Registered: CA,FL,HI,IL,IN,MD,MI,MN,ND,NY,OR,RI,SD,VA,WA,WI,DC
Field Support: SO, FC
    Training:

Lamar's Donuts
245 S 84th St #210
Lincoln, NE 68510
Donuts & baked goods
    Phone: 402-484-5900   Accepts collect calls? N
    Toll Free: 800-533-7489   FAX:
    Internet:
Suitable Sites: DA, FB, SC, SF
Concentration: 9 in MO, 7 in KS, 3 in VA
    Expansion: All United States
    Registered: FL IN VA
Field Support: $DP, CP, EO, ST, SO, IC, FC, H, N
    Training:

Robin's Donuts
725 Hewitson St
Thunder Bay, ON P7B-6B5   CANADA
7 days, 24 hrs coffee, donut, deli restaurant, pastries, soups
    Phone: 807-623-4453   Accepts collect calls? N
    Toll Free: FAX: 807-623-4682
    Internet: robinsdonuts.com
Suitable Sites: FB, FC, K, M, OC, RM, SC
Concentration: 65 in ON, 42 in MB, 36 in AB
    Expansion: N, Canada
    Registered: MN,WA,AB
Field Support: CP, EO, ST, SO, IC, FC, N
    Training: 4 weeks thunder bay, ON
            2 weeks store opening

Quick-service Industry

Bakery: Doughnuts (Spread 2 of 2)

	Southern Maid Donuts							
Startup Cost	40K-75K							
Franchise Fee	5K							
Royalty	0%							
Advertising Fee	0%							
Financing Provided	N							
Experience Required								
Passive Ownership	A							
In Business Since	1937							
Franchised Since	1941							
Franchised Units 1996								
1997	87							
1998								
Company Owned 1996								
1997	0							
1998								
Number of Units U.S.	87							
Canada	0							
Foreign	0							
Projected New U.S.								
Canada								
Foreign								
Corporate Employees	6							
Contract Length	10/10							
Expand in Territory	Y							
Full-Time Employees	3							
Part-Time Employees	3							
Conversions	Y							
Site Selection Assist.	Y							
Lease Negotiation Assist.	Y							
Site Space Required	1200-1500							
Development Agreement	Y							
Develop. Agree. Term	10							
Sub-franchising	Y							

Quick-service Industry

Bakery: Doughnuts (Spread 2 of 2)

Southern Maid Donuts
3615 Cavalier Dr
Garland, TX 75042-7599

Phone: 972-272-6425   Accepts collect calls?
Toll Free: 800-936-6887   FAX: 972-276-3549
Internet:
Suitable Sites: FB, SC
Concentration: 67 in TX, 7 in LA, 3 in AR
Expansion: All United States, Canada, Foreign
Registered: CA,OR
Field Support: EO, ST, SO, IC, H
Training: 3-7 days on-site

Quick-service Industry

Bakery: Muffins

	Mmmarvellous Mmmuffins	My Favorite Muffin					
Startup Cost	180K-200K	234K-382.3K					
Franchise Fee	25K	25K					
Royalty	7%	5%					
Advertising Fee	1-1.5%	2%					
Financing Provided	Y	Y					
Experience Required							
Passive Ownership	N	D					
In Business Since	1979	1987					
Franchised Since	1980	1988					
Franchised Units 1996							
1997	117	63					
1998							
Company Owned 1996							
1997	8	8					
1998							
Number of Units U.S.	0	71					
Canada	119	0					
Foreign	6	0					
Projected New U.S.							
Canada							
Foreign							
Corporate Employees	35	28					
Contract Length	10/10	10/10					
Expand in Territory	N	Y					
Full-Time Employees	2-3	3					
Part-Time Employees	4-7	15					
Conversions	N						
Site Selection Assist.	Y	Y					
Lease Negotiation Assist.	Y	Y					
Site Space Required	300	1800-2200					
Development Agreement	N	Y					
Develop. Agree. Term		NEG.					
Sub-franchising	Y	N					

Quick-service Industry   **Bakery: Muffins**

Mmmarvellous Mmmuffins
  3300 Bloor St W #2900 Box 54
  Etobicoke, ON M8X-2X3   CANADA

  Phone: 416-236-0055   Accepts collect calls?
  Toll Free: FAX: 416-236-0054
  Internet: www.mmmuffins.com
Suitable Sites: RM, SF
Concentration: 44 in ON, 30 in PQ, 11 in AB
  Expansion: N, Canada, Foreign
  Registered: AB
Field Support: DP, CP, EO, ST, SO, IC, $FC, N
  Training: 17 days Toronto, ON.

My Favorite Muffin
  8501 W Higgins Rd #320
  Chicago, IL 60631

  Phone: 773-380-6100   Accepts collect calls?
  Toll Free: 800-251-6101   FAX: 773-380-6100
  Internet:
Suitable Sites: FB, RM, SC
Concentration: 18 in NJ, 10 in PA, 8 in FL
  Expansion: All United States, Canada, Foreign
  Registered: CA,FL,HI,IL,IN,MD,MI,MN,ND,NY,OR,RI,SD,VA,WA,WI,DC
Field Support: EO, ST, SO, H, N
  Training: 12 days New Jersey

Quick-service Industry

Bakery: Pretzels

	Auntie Anne's Hand-Rolled Soft Pretzels	The Different Twist Pretzel Co.	Pretzel Time	The Pretzel Twister	PretzelMaker	Pretzels Plus	Wetzel's Pretzels
Startup Cost	151.2K-240K	40K-80K	175K-250K	82.7K-140.2K	90K-160K	60K-80K	116.8K
Franchise Fee	30K	5K	25K	17.5K	22.5K	12K	20K
Royalty	6%	5%	9%	5%	5%	4%	6%
Advertising Fee	1%		1%		1.5%	0%	
Financing Provided	N	Y	N	Y	Y	N	Y
Experience Required						N	
Passive Ownership	D	A	A		D	A	
In Business Since	1988	1992	1991	1992	1991	1990	1994
Franchised Since	1989	1992	1992	1993	1992	1991	1996
Franchised Units 1996				24			11
1997	396	20	140	27	191	28	51
1998						23	
Company Owned 1996				0			4
1997	16	0	80	0	14	0	4
1998							
Number of Units U.S.	395	20	218		191	23	
Canada	0	0	2		14	0	
Foreign	17	0	0		0	0	
Projected New U.S.							
Canada							
Foreign							
Corporate Employees	66	6	26		37	3	
Contract Length	5/5	10/10	20/5		10/10	5	
Expand in Territory		Y	Y		Y	Y	
Full-Time Employees	3	3	3		5	5	
Part-Time Employees	12	3	9		7	4	
Conversions		Y	Y		Y	Y	
Site Selection Assist.	Y	Y	Y		Y	Y	
Lease Negotiation Assist.	Y	Y	Y		Y	N	
Site Space Required	400-800	150-400	400-1000		500-700	1000	
Development Agreement	N	Y	Y		Y	N	
Develop. Agree. Term					3		
Sub-franchising	N	Y	N		N	N	

Quick-service Industry   ## Bakery: Pretzels

Auntie Anne's Hand-Rolled Soft Pretzels
PO Box 529 160-A Rt 41
Gap, PA 17527

Phone: 717-442-4766	Accepts collect calls?
Toll Free:	FAX: 717-442-4139
Internet:	

Suitable Sites: RM, OTHER
Concentration: 74 in PA, 27 in CA, 25 in NY
Expansion: All United States, Canada, Foreign
Registered: CA,FL,HI,IL,IN,MD,MI,MN,ND,NY,OR,RI,SD,VA,WA,WI,DC
Field Support: CP, $EO, $ST, SO, $FC, N
Training: 8-11 days pretzel univ., Gap, PA
7 days on-site at store opening

The Different Twist Pretzel Co.
PO Box 334 6052 Rte 8
Bakerstown, PA 15007

Phone: 412-443-8010	Accepts collect calls?
Toll Free:	FAX: 412-443-7287
Internet:	

Suitable Sites: RM, SF, OTHER
Concentration: 2 in WV, 1 in FL, 1 in MA
Expansion: All United States, Canada
Registered: FL
Field Support: $CP, ST, $SO
Training: 1 week on-site

Pretzel Time
462 Bearcat Dr
Salt Lake City, UT 84115

Phone: 801-463-2390	Accepts collect calls?
Toll Free: 800-348-6311	FAX: 801-463-2176
Internet: www.pretzel-time.com	

Suitable Sites: RM
Concentration: 29 in CA, 20 in NY, 19 in TX
Expansion: All United States, Canada, Foreign
Registered: CA,FL,HI,IL,IN,MD,MI,MN,ND,NY,OR,RI,SD,VA,WA,WI,DC
Field Support: CP, EO, ST, SO, IC, FC, H, N
Training: 5 days corporate training center
5 days on-site

The Pretzel Twister
2706 S Horseshoe Dr #112
Naples, FL 34104
Hand-twisted soft pretzels & fruit shakes

Phone: 941-643-2075	Accepts collect calls?
Toll Free:	FAX:
Internet:	

Suitable Sites:
Concentration:
Expansion:
Registered:
Field Support:
Training:

PretzelMaker
1050 17th St Ste 1400
Denver, CO 80265

Phone: 303-573-4800	Accepts collect calls?
Toll Free:	FAX: 303-573-0004
Internet:	

Suitable Sites: FB, RM, SC
Concentration: 21 in CA, 13 in UT, 11 in CO
Expansion: All United States, Canada, Foreign
Registered: CA,FL,HI,IL,IN,MD,MI,MN,ND,NY,OR,RI,SD,VA,WA,WI,DC
Field Support: CP, EO, ST, SO, IC, FC, N
Training: 5 days Denver, CO

Pretzels Plus
639 Frederick St
Hanover, PA 17331
Hand rolled soft pretzels & sandwiches on pretzel roll

Phone: 717-633-7927	Accepts collect calls? N
Toll Free: 800-559-7927	FAX: 717-633-5078
Internet:	

Suitable Sites: RM
Concentration: 8 in PA, 4 in NC, 3 in VA
Expansion: Eastern United States, Canada, Foreign
Registered: MD,VA
Field Support: CP, ST, SO, H
Training: 3 days before opening
7 days after

Wetzel's Pretzels
65 N Raymond Ave #310
Pasadena, CA 91103
Hand-rolled soft pretzels

Phone: 818-432-6900	Accepts collect calls?
Toll Free:	FAX:
Internet:	

Suitable Sites:
Concentration:
Expansion: CA,MD,MI,NY,WA, Canada, Foreign
Registered:
Field Support:
Training:

Quick-service Industry   Bakery: Other (Spread 1 of 2)

	Atlanta Bread Co	Baker Street Artisan Breads & Cafe	Breadsmith	Buns Master Bakery Systems	Creative Cakery	Croissant + Plus	Grandma Lee's Bakery Cafe	Great Harvest Bread Co.
Startup Cost	320K	300K-600K	200K-260K	275K	150K-350K	100K-200K	125K-225K	106K-308K
Franchise Fee	40K	30K	25K	25K	22.5K	10K-30K	25K	24K
Royalty	5%	4%	7%	5%	5%	5%	6.5%	5-7%
Advertising Fee		2%	0%	1%	0%	3%	1.5%	0%
Financing Provided	Y	Y	Y	Y	Y	Y	Y	N
Experience Required					N			N
Passive Ownership		A	N	N	A	D	A	N
In Business Since	1993	1992	1993	1970	1983	1980	1971	1976
Franchised Since	1995	1992	1994	1977	1997	1981	1971	1978
Franchised Units 1996	12							116
1997	25	3	39	106	0	32	67	117
1998					1			130
Company Owned 1996	1							0
1997	2	7	3	0	0	8	1	1
1998								1
Number of Units U.S.		10	42	1	2	0	4	130
Canada		0	0	105	0	0	57	0
Foreign		0	0	0	0	0	7	0
Projected New U.S.					6			20
Canada								
Foreign								
Corporate Employees		10	8	44	3	10	6	32
Contract Length		10/10	15/15	20	15/10	10/5	10/10	10
Expand in Territory		Y	Y	Y	Y	Y	Y	Y
Full-Time Employees		5	2	6	6	2	4	6
Part-Time Employees		10	12	12		3-5	4	2
Conversions		Y		Y	Y		Y	Y
Site Selection Assist.		Y	Y	Y	Y	Y	Y	Y
Lease Negotiation Assist.		Y	Y	Y	Y	Y	Y	Y
Site Space Required		2000	1500		1200	300-1000		1500
Development Agreement		Y	Y	N	Y	Y	Y	Y
Develop. Agree. Term					15	10/10	20	2
Sub-franchising		N	N	N	Y	Y	Y	N

Quick-service Industry

Atlanta Bread Co
115-D Davis Cir
Marietta, GA 30060
Bakery/cafe
    Phone: 770-425-1073   Accepts collect calls?
    Toll Free: FAX:
    Internet:
Suitable Sites:
Concentration:
    Expansion: All United States, Canada, Foreign
    Registered:
Field Support:
    Training:

Baker Street Artisan Breads & Cafe
847 W Lancaster Ave
Bryn Mawr, PA 19010

    Phone: 610-520-2920   Accepts collect calls?
    Toll Free: 888-213-2375   FAX: 610-520-3199
    Internet:
Suitable Sites: FB, SC, SF
Concentration:
    Expansion: All United States, Canada, Foreign
    Registered: CA,FL,HI,IL,IN,MD,MI,MN,ND,NY,OR,RI,SD,VA,WA,WI,DC
Field Support: EO, ST, SO, IC, FC, H, N
    Training: 3 weeks Philadelphia PA
            7 days store location

Breadsmith
3510 N Oakland Ave #212
Shorewood, WI 53211

    Phone: 414-962-1965   Accepts collect calls?
    Toll Free: FAX: 414-962-5888
    Internet:
Suitable Sites: FB, SC, SF
Concentration: 8 in IL, 5 in WI, 4 in MN
    Expansion: All United States, Canada
    Registered: CA,FL,IL,IN,MI,MN,NY,OR,SD,VA,WA,WI
Field Support: EO, ST, SO, IC, H, N
    Training: 2 weeks corporate store
            10 days franchisee store

Buns Master Bakery Systems
2 E Beaver Creek Rd Bldg #1
Richmond Hill, ON L4B-2N3 CANADA

    Phone: 905-764-7066   Accepts collect calls?
    Toll Free: FAX: 905-764-7634
    Internet:
Suitable Sites: SC
Concentration: 50 in ON, 30 in BC, 9 in SK
    Expansion: Y, Canada
    Registered: AB
Field Support: DP, CP, EO, ST, SO, IC, $FC, H, N
    Training: 7 days head office
            14 days on-site

Creative Cakery
636 Redondo Ave
Long Beach, CA 90814

    Phone: 562-438-2301   Accepts collect calls? N
    Toll Free: 800-224-4261   FAX: 562-433-2423
    Internet:
Suitable Sites: AC, SC
Concentration: 2 in CA
    Expansion: All United States, Canada, Foreign
    Registered: CA
Field Support: EO, ST, SO, IC, FC, H, N
    Training: 20-30 days CA & local

Croissant + Plus
2020 St Patrick
Montreal, PQ H3K-1A9 CANADA

    Phone: 514-931-5550   Accepts collect calls?
    Toll Free: 800-267-4896   FAX: 514-931-3749
    Internet:
Suitable Sites: FB, OC, RM, SC, SF
Concentration: 37 in PQ, 2 in ON, 1 in BC
    Expansion: All United States, Canada
    Registered:
Field Support: CP, EO, ST, SO, IC, FC, H
    Training: 2-6 weeks Montreal, PQ
            2-6 weeks Quebec City, PQ

Grandma Lee's Bakery Cafe
2059 Lakeshore Blvd
Burlington, ON L7R-1E1 CANADA

    Phone: 905-634-4111   Accepts collect calls?
    Toll Free: 800-894-7063   FAX: 905-634-1101
    Internet: www.heritageconcepts.com
Suitable Sites: FB, SF
Concentration: 21 in ON, 16 in AB, 6 in BC
    Expansion: All United States, Canada, Foreign
    Registered: AB
Field Support: CP, EO, ST, SO, IC, FC, H, N
    Training: 6 weeks closest approved store

Great Harvest Bread Co.
28 S Montana St
Dillon, MT 59725-2434
Neighborhood bakery specialize in whole-wheat breads
    Phone: 406-683-6842   Accepts collect calls?
    Toll Free: 800-442-0424   FAX: 406-683-5537
    Internet: www.greatharvest.com
Suitable Sites: FB, SC, OTHER
Concentration: 10 in UT, 7 in OR, 8 in IL
    Expansion: All United States, Canada
    Registered: CA,FL,HI,IL,IN,MD,MI,MN,ND,NY,OR,RI,SD,VA,WA,WI,DC,AB
Field Support: CP, EO, ST, SO, FC, H, N
    Training: 2 weeks at host bakeries
            1 week HQ
            trainers at opening

Quick-service Industry   Bakery: Other (Spread 2 of 2)

	Le Croissant Shop	McCoy's Cake & Pie Shop	Paradise Bakery & Cafe	Bread Company, Inc. Saint Louis	Tim Hortons	Treats		
Startup Cost	200K-300K	104.3K-133K	222K-439K	550K-800K	300K-360K	100K-150K		
Franchise Fee	22.5K	15K	35K	35K	35K-50K	25K		
Royalty	5%	5%	6%	5%	3-4.5%	7%		
Advertising Fee			2%	2.4-5%	4%	1%		
Financing Provided	N	Y	Y	N	N	N		
Experience Required								
Passive Ownership	A		A	N	N	D		
In Business Since	1981	1983	1976	1987	1964	1977		
Franchised Since	1984	1996	1987	1993	1965	1979		
Franchised Units 1996		0						
1997	44	0	36	14	1405	142		
1998				46				
Company Owned 1996		1						
1997	3	1	16	58	100	3		
1998				67				
Number of Units U.S.	21		52	72	58	5		
Canada	0		0	0	1447	140		
Foreign	26		0	0	0			
Projected New U.S.				93				
Canada								
Foreign								
Corporate Employees	6		17	54	580	15		
Contract Length	10/5/5		10/5	20/AGRMT	20/10/10	lease		
Expand in Territory	Y		Y	N	Y	Y		
Full-Time Employees	10		5	17	22-25	3		
Part-Time Employees			11	17		2		
Conversions	N		N	N	Y	Y		
Site Selection Assist.	Y		Y	Y	Y	Y		
Lease Negotiation Assist.	Y		Y	N	Y	Y		
Site Space Required	1000		1000-2000	3500	2650	500-1500		
Development Agreement	Y		Y	Y	N	Y		
Develop. Agree. Term	10		10	3-13		15		
Sub-franchising	N		N	N	N	Y		

Quick-service Industry   Bakery: Other (Spread 2 of 2)

Le Croissant Shop
227 W 40th St
New York, NY 10018

Phone: 212-719-5940   Accepts collect calls?
Toll Free: FAX: 212-944-0269
Internet:
Suitable Sites: FB, RM, SC, SF
Concentration: 19 in NY, 1 in PA, 1 in FL
Expansion: East Coast, Foreign
Registered: FL,IL,MD,NY,VA
Field Support: EO, ST, SO
Training: 4 weeks HQ in New York

McCoy's Cake & Pie Shop
4925 W Fond Du Lac Ave
Milwaukee, WI 53216
Cakes & pies
Phone: 414-871-9363   Accepts collect calls?
Toll Free: FAX:
Internet:
Suitable Sites:
Concentration:
Expansion: MW
Registered:
Field Support:
Training:

Paradise Bakery & Cafe
1610 Arden Wy #145
Sacramento, CA 95815

Phone: 916-568-2310   Accepts collect calls?
Toll Free: 800-951-9582   FAX: 916-568-1240
Internet:
Suitable Sites:
Concentration: 20 in CA, 8 in TX, 7 in AZ
Expansion: All United States, Canada
Registered: CA,HI
Field Support: CP, EO, ST, SO, IC, H, N
Training: 5 weeks

Saint Louis Bread Company, Inc.
7930 Big Bend Blvd
Webster Groves, MO 63119
More than 25 varieties of sourdough-based breads and bagels, etc
Phone: 314-918-7779   Accepts collect calls?
Toll Free: 800-301-5566   FAX: 314-918-7773
Internet:
Suitable Sites: FB, RM, SC, SF
Concentration: 38 in MO, 26 in IL, 8 in GA
Expansion: All United States
Registered: CA,FL,HI,IL,IN,MD,MI,MN,ND,NY,OR,RI,SD,VA,WA,WI,DC
Field Support: CP, EO, ST, SO, IC, FC, H, N
Training: 10 weeks St. Louis, MO

Tim Hortons
874 Sinclair Rd
Oakville, ON L6K-2Y1 CANADA

Phone: 905-845-6511   Accepts collect calls?
Toll Free: FAX: 905-845-0265
Internet:
Suitable Sites: FB, RM, SC, SF
Concentration: ON, PQ, NS
Expansion: NY,MI,OH, North Central U.S., Canada
Registered: IN,MI,MN,NY,RI,WI,AB
Field Support: CP, EO, SO, FC, N
Training: 8 weeks Oakville, ON

Treats
418 Preston St
Ottawa, ON K1S-4N2 CANADA

Phone: 613-563-4073   Accepts collect calls?
Toll Free: 800-461-4003   FAX: 613-563-1982
Internet: www.treats.com
Suitable Sites: RM, SC, SF
Concentration: 75 in ON, 25 in PQ, 10 in AB
Expansion: East Coast, Canada, Foreign
Registered: CA,FL,IL,IN,MD,MI,MN,NY,OR,RI,VA,WA,WI,DC,AB
Field Support: CP, EO, ST, SO, FC, H, N
Training: 2 weeks training center
1 week on-site

Quick-service Industry   Frozen: Ice Cream (Spread 1 of 2)

	2001 Flavors Plus Potatoes	Baskin-Robbins Canada	Baskin-Robbins USA Co	Ben & Jerry's	Bruster's Old-Fashioned Ice Cream & Yogurt	Carvel Ice Cream Bakery	Cold Stone Creamery	Emack & Bolio's Ice Cream & Yogurt
Startup Cost	85K-150K	150K-175K	47.3K-351.7K	150K-250K	150K-761K	185K-240K	121K-172K	60K-80K
Franchise Fee	2.5K-15K	25K	TO 15K	30K	30K	10K	18K	$0
Royalty	5%	1%	0.5-1%	0%	5%	$1.55/GAL.	6%	0%
Advertising Fee	0-2%	6%		4%	UP TO 3%	$1.33/GAL.		0%
Financing Provided	Y	N	Y	N	Y	Y	N	N
Experience Required					N			N
Passive Ownership	D	D		D	D	N		A
In Business Since	1993	1940	1945	1978	1989	1934	1992	1975
Franchised Since	1993	1971	1948	1981	1993	1947	1994	1977
Franchised Units 1996			3843				29	
1997	19	276	4425	165	15	437	37	40
1998					25			
Company Owned 1996			5				0	
1997	1	0	0	3	2	4	0	4
1998					3			
Number of Units U.S.	14	0		150	28	409		41
Canada	1	276		4	0	3		0
Foreign	5	0		14	0	29		1
Projected New U.S.					35			
Canada								
Foreign								
Corporate Employees	2	30		14	7	100		3
Contract Length	20/10	10/5		10/10	20/10	10/10		10/10
Expand in Territory	Y	Y			Y	Y		Y
Full-Time Employees	3	1		2	2-3	2		2
Part-Time Employees	4	5		6-10	25	6		8
Conversions	Y	Y		Y	N	Y		Y
Site Selection Assist.	Y	Y		Y	Y	Y		N
Lease Negotiation Assist.	Y	Y		N	Y	Y		Y
Site Space Required	800-1400	300-900		1000	22000	1200-1500		200-1500
Development Agreement	Y	N			Y	N		Y
Develop. Agree. Term	10							10/10
Sub-franchising	N	N			N	N		N

Quick-service Industry

2001 Flavors Plus Potatoes
PO Box 4223
Chatsworth, CA 91313

Phone: 818-341-9910	Accepts collect calls?
Toll Free: 800-200-1352	FAX: 818-341-9923

Internet:
Suitable Sites: FB, RM, SC, SF
Concentration: 13 in CA, 1 in FL
    Expansion: All United States, Canada, Foreign
    Registered: CA,FL,MI
Field Support: CP, EO, ST, SO, IC, $FC, H, N
    Training: 1 week Los Angeles, CA or Tampa

Baskin-Robbins Canada
50 Ronson Dr #131
Etobicoke, ON M9W-1B3 CANADA

Phone: 416-245-3131	Accepts collect calls?
Toll Free: 800-268-4933	FAX: 416-245-3040

Internet:
Suitable Sites: RM, SC
Concentration: 112 in ON, 26 in BC, 13 in AL
    Expansion: N, Canada
    Registered: AB
Field Support: CP, EO, SO, FC, H, N
    Training: 3 weeks Burbank, CA

Baskin-Robbins USA Co
14 Pacella Park Dr
Randolph, MA 02368
Ice cream & yogurt

Phone:	Accepts collect calls?
Toll Free: 800-777-9983	FAX:

Internet:
Suitable Sites:
Concentration:
    Expansion: SE,W,NW, Canada, Foreign
    Registered:
Field Support:
    Training:

Ben & Jerry's
30 Community Dr
S Burlington, VT 05404

Phone: 802-651-9600	Accepts collect calls?
Toll Free:	FAX: 802-651-9624

Internet:
Suitable Sites: RM, SC, SF
Concentration: 34 in CA, 19 in NY, 11 in MA
    Expansion: Varied, Foreign
    Registered: CA,FL,IL,IN,MD,MI,NY,OR,RI,VA,WA
Field Support: EO, ST, SO, $FC, H, N
    Training: 12 days Vermont

Bruster's Old-Fashioned Ice Cream & Yogurt
730 Mulberry St
Bridgewater, PA 15009
Homemade ice cream, yogurt, sherbet, waffle cones, cakes

Phone: 724-774-4250	Accepts collect calls? Y
Toll Free:	FAX: 724-774-0666

Internet: www.brustersicecream.baweb.com
Suitable Sites: FB
Concentration: 14 in PA, 8 in GA, 2 in OH
    Expansion: Eastern United States, Canada, Foreign
    Registered: NY,VA,FL,IN
Field Support: CP, EO, ST, SO, FC, N
    Training: 2-4 weeks western PA

Carvel Ice Cream Bakery
20 Batterson Park Rd
Farmington, CT 06032

Phone: 860-677-6811	Accepts collect calls?
Toll Free: 800-322-4848	FAX: 860-677-8211

Internet:
Suitable Sites: FB, RM, SF
Concentration: 220 in NY, 70 in NJ, 40 in FL
    Expansion: East Coast, Foreign
    Registered: MD,NY,RI
Field Support: DP, CP, EO, ST, SO, FC, H, N
    Training: 17 days Farmington, CT

Cold Stone Creamery
16101 N 82nd St #A4
Scottsdale, AZ 85260
Ice cream & frozen yogurt

Phone: 602-348-1704	Accepts collect calls?
Toll Free:	FAX:

Internet:
Suitable Sites:
Concentration:
    Expansion: CA,HI, Canada, Foreign
    Registered:
Field Support:
    Training:

Emack & Bolio's Ice Cream & Yogurt
PO Box 703
Brookline Village, MA 02447
Super premium ice cream + yogurt

Phone: 617-739-7995	Accepts collect calls? N
Toll Free:	FAX: 617-232-1102

Internet: enbic@aol.com
Suitable Sites: AC, FB, FC, K, M, RM, SC, SF, WF
Concentration: 11 in MA, 6 in NJ, 3 in NY
    Expansion: All United States, Canada, Foreign
    Registered: CA,FL,HI,IL,IN,MD,MI,MN,ND,NY,OR,RI,SD,VA,WA,WI,DC
Field Support: CP, EO, ST, SO, IC, H, N
    Training: 1 week Boston, MA or New York, NY

Quick-service Industry   Frozen: Ice Cream (Spread 2 of 2)

	Gelato Amare	Ice Cream Parlour/Rest.	High Wheeler Marble Slab Creamery	Morrone's Italian Ices	Petrucci's Ice Cream Co.	Scoopers Ice Cream		
Startup Cost	90K-225K	500K-1.5M	158K-174K	79K-134K	94.8K-176K	50K-80K		
Franchise Fee	18.9K	25K	19K-25K	20K	20K	15K		
Royalty	5%	4%	6%	5%	5%	5%		
Advertising Fee	2%	2%	2%	3%	2%	0%		
Financing Provided	Y	N	N	Y	Y	N		
Experience Required	N			N	N	N		
Passive Ownership	A	D	D	D	A	A		
In Business Since	1983	1975	1983	1925	1983	1981		
Franchised Since	1986	1985	1984	1995	1996	1991		
Franchised Units 1996					8			
1997	4	2	80	13	22	8		
1998	3			13	35			
Company Owned 1996					1			
1997	1	1	1	2	0	2		
1998	1			2	0			
Number of Units U.S.	4	4	81	15	35	10		
Canada	0	0	0	0	0	0		
Foreign	0	0	0	0	0	0		
Projected New U.S.				20	20			
Canada				0	0			
Foreign				0	0			
Corporate Employees	4		10	5	7	5		
Contract Length	10/5/5	20/10	10/10	10/15	10	20		
Expand in Territory	Y	Y	N	N	Y	Y		
Full-Time Employees	1	6	2	1-2	4	2		
Part-Time Employees	6	50	8	2-4	3	20		
Conversions	Y	N	Y		Y	Y		
Site Selection Assist.	Y	Y	Y	Y	Y	Y		
Lease Negotiation Assist.	Y	Y	Y	Y	Y	Y		
Site Space Required	500-1100	5000	500-1300	500-1000	1000	700-1200		
Development Agreement	Y	Y	Y	Y	Y	Y		
Develop. Agree. Term		20		10	10	10		
Sub-franchising	Y	N	N	N	Y	N		

Quick-service Industry   Frozen: Ice Cream (Spread 2 of 2)

Gelato Amare
11504 Hyde Pl
Raleigh, NC 27614
Homemade super-premium ice cream, yogurt, smoothies, coffee, etc
    Phone: 919-847-4435   Accepts collect calls? N
    Toll Free: FAX:
    Internet:
Suitable Sites: AC, FB, FC, K, M, PC, RM, SC, SF, WF
Concentration: 4 in NC
    Expansion: All United States, Canada, Foreign
    Registered: CA,FL,IL,MI,NY
Field Support: CP, EO, ST, SO, $FC, N
    Training: 2 weeks HQ

High Wheeler Ice Cream Parlour/Rest.
PO Box 141
Kalamazoo, MI 49004

    Phone: 616-345-0950   Accepts collect calls?
    Toll Free: FAX: 616-345-0950
    Internet:
Suitable Sites: FB, SC
Concentration:
    Expansion: All United States, Canada, Foreign
    Registered:
Field Support: EO, ST, SO, IC
    Training: 5 weeks on-site

Marble Slab Creamery
3100 S Gessner Dr #305
Houston, TX 77063

    Phone: 713-780-3601   Accepts collect calls?
    Toll Free: FAX: 713-780-0264
    Internet:
Suitable Sites: RM, SC
Concentration: 52 in TX, 8 in LA, 7 in AZ
    Expansion: SE, South, SE
    Registered: FL,CA
Field Support: CP, EO, ST, SO, FC
    Training: 10 days franchisor location
        6 days franchisee site

Morrone's Italian Ices
117 S 69th St
Upper Darby, PA 19082
Homemade Italian ices, ice-cream, ice-cream cakes
    Phone: 888-MOR-RONE   Accepts collect calls? N
    Toll Free: 800-871-2975   FAX: 610-446-8381
    Internet:
Suitable Sites: FB, SC
Concentration: 13 in PA, 1 in DE, 1 in DC
    Expansion: NE
    Registered: 0
Field Support: CP, EO, ST, SO, IC, FC, H, N
    Training: 2 weeks Upper Darby, PA or on
        location for out-of-state

Petrucci's Ice Cream Co.
507 W Corporate Dr
Langhorne, PA 19047
Ice cream, water ice, yogurt, cakes
    Phone: 215-860-4848   Accepts collect calls?
    Toll Free: FAX: 215-860-6123
    Internet: www.petruccis.com
Suitable Sites:
Concentration:
    Expansion: NE
    Registered: MD, DC
Field Support: CP, EO, ST, SO, IC, FC, H, N
    Training: corp. HQ training
        in-store setup & train
        ongoing assistance

Scoopers Ice Cream
22 Woodrow Ave
Youngstown, OH 44512-3306
Fresh made daily ice cream store
    Phone: 330-793-9049   Accepts collect calls? N
    Toll Free: FAX:
    Internet:
Suitable Sites: FB, RM, SC, SF
Concentration: 7 in PA, 2 in OH, 1 in FL
    Expansion: All United States, Canada
    Registered:
Field Support: SO
    Training: 2-4 days main store location
        1 day store opening

Quick-service Industry   Frozen: Soft-serve

	Dairy Queen	Dairy Queen Canada Inc.	Fosters Freeze, Incorporated	Interstate Dairy Queen				
Startup Cost		400K-1.2M	VAR.	175K-550K				
Franchise Fee	15K-30K	35K	25K	25K				
Royalty	4-5%	4%	4%	4-7%				
Advertising Fee	3-6%	3-6%	3%	3-6%				
Financing Provided	N	Y	N	Y				
Experience Required		N	N					
Passive Ownership	D	D	D	A				
In Business Since	1940	1940	1946	1977				
Franchised Since	1940	1950		1977				
Franchised Units 1996			128					
1997	5649	512	127	145				
1998			127	151				
Company Owned 1996			1					
1997	44	0	1	2				
1998			3	2				
Number of Units U.S.	5027	0	130	151				
Canada	474	505		0				
Foreign	192	0		0				
Projected New U.S.			2					
Canada		16						
Foreign								
Corporate Employees	500	70	105	14				
Contract Length	10		20	FOREVER				
Expand in Territory	N	Y	Y	Y				
Full-Time Employees	VAR	20	5	2				
Part-Time Employees		40	30	15-20				
Conversions	Y	Y	N	Y				
Site Selection Assist.	Y	Y	N	Y				
Lease Negotiation Assist.	Y	Y	N	Y				
Site Space Required	20000	2000-3000						
Development Agreement	N	N	Y	N				
Develop. Agree. Term			NEG.					
Sub-franchising	Y	N	Y	N				

Quick-service Industry   Frozen: Soft-serve

Dairy Queen
PO Box 39286-0286
Minneapolis, MN 55439-0286

Phone: 612-830-0200   Accepts collect calls?
Toll Free: FAX: 612-830-0450
Internet:
Suitable Sites: FB, RM, SC
Concentration: 786 in TX, 284 in IL, 273 in OH
Expansion: All United States, Canada, Foreign
Registered: CA,FL,IL,IN,MD,MI,MN,NY,OR,RI,WA,WI,DC
Field Support: EO, ST, SO, FC, N
Training: 3 weeks Minneapolis, MN
on-going on-site

Dairy Queen Canada Inc.
5245 Harvester Rd PO Box 430
Burlington, ON L7R-3Y3 CANADA
Quick service restaurants, multiple concepts
Phone: 905-639-1492   Accepts collect calls?
Toll Free: 800-285-8515   FAX: 905-681-3623
Internet:
Suitable Sites: FB
Concentration: 172 in ON, 99 in AB, 94 in BC
Expansion: All United States, Canada, Foreign
Registered: AB
Field Support: DP, CP, EO, ST, SO, IC, FC, H, N
Training: 3 weeks Minneapolis, MN
in-store/opening team

Fosters Freeze, Incorporated
3701 S Higuera St #102
San Luis Obispo, CA 93401

Phone: 805-781-6100   Accepts collect calls? N
Toll Free: FAX: 805-781-6106
Internet:
Suitable Sites: AC, FB, M, SC, SF, OTHER
Concentration: 130 in CA
Expansion: CA,AZ
Registered: CA
Field Support: $DP, CP, EO, ST, SO, $IC, FC, N
Training:

Interstate Dairy Queen
4601 Willard Ave
Chevy Chase, MD 20815

Phone: 301-913-9800x23   Accepts collect calls? N
Toll Free: FAX: 301-913-5424
Internet:
Suitable Sites: ES, DA, SC, SF
Concentration: 31 in GA, 21 in FL, 12 in SC
Expansion: Most Interstate Highways
Registered: CA,FL,IL,IN,MD,MI,NY,DC
Field Support: CP, EO, ST, $SO, IC, FC, H, N
Training: 3 weeks Minneapolis, MN

Quick-service Industry   Frozen: Yogurt

	Frozen Yogurt/Ice Cream	All American Everything Yogurt & Salad Cafe	Good For You! Fruit & Yogurt Ltd.	I Can't Believe It's Yogurt	TCBY Treats	Yogen Fruz Worldwide		
Startup Cost	81K-153K	169K-214K	70K-110K	110K-203K	150K-350K	75K-150K		
Franchise Fee	7.5K-20K	25K	25K	15K	2.5K-20K	25K		
Royalty	5%	5%	6%	0%	4%	6%		
Advertising Fee	1%	1%	2%	2.3%	3%	2%		
Financing Provided	N	Y	Y	N	N	Y		
Experience Required			N					
Passive Ownership	D		D	D	D	N		
In Business Since	1986	1976	1983	1977	1981	1986		
Franchised Since	1988	1981	1983	1983	1982	1987		
Franchised Units 1996		90						
1997	19	93	16	400	2765	3551		
1998		90	15			4920		
Company Owned 1996		3						
1997	1	2	0	940	1	9		
1998		3	1					
Number of Units U.S.	20	231	0	1025	2541	3500		
Canada	0		16	0	25	320		
Foreign	0	2	0	317	200	1100		
Projected New U.S.		28	2			500		
Canada						10		
Foreign						200		
Corporate Employees	3	30	3	60	350	65		
Contract Length	10/0	10	5/5	10/10	5/10/5/10	10/10		
Expand in Territory	Y		Y	Y	Y	Y		
Full-Time Employees	1	4	1	2	2	2		
Part-Time Employees	6	8	1	6	8	4		
Conversions	Y		Y	Y	Y	Y		
Site Selection Assist.	Y	Y	Y	Y	Y	Y		
Lease Negotiation Assist.	Y	Y	Y	Y	N	Y		
Site Space Required	600-800	400-1200	250-500	1200	100-2000	100-1500		
Development Agreement	Y		Y	Y	N	Y		
Develop. Agree. Term	2		5			10+10		
Sub-franchising	N		N	Y	N	Y		

Quick-service Industry   **Frozen: Yogurt**

All American Frozen Yogurt/Ice Cream
812 SW Washington St Ste 1110
Portland, OR 97205

Phone: 503-224-6199   Accepts collect calls?
Toll Free: FAX: 503-224-5042
Internet:
Suitable Sites: RM, SC
Concentration: 11 in OR, 6 in WA, 2 in ID
Expansion: West, Inter-Mountain, and SE
Registered: CA,HI,OR,WA
Field Support: CP, EO, ST, SO, IC, N
Training: 1 week head office, Portland, OR
1 week franchisee location

Everything Yogurt & Salad Cafe
1000 South Ave
Staten Island, NY 10314
Frozen yogurt, salads, smoothies, pretzels, sandwiches, fries
Phone: 718-494-8888   Accepts collect calls? N
Toll Free: FAX: 718-494-8776
Internet:
Suitable Sites: FB, FC, K, M, RM, SC
Concentration:
Expansion: All United States, Foreign
Registered: NY
Field Support: CP, EO, ST, SO, FC, H, N
Training: 10 days Staten Island, NY

Good For You! Fruit & Yogurt Ltd.
24-4567 Lougheed Hwy
Burnaby, BC V5C-3Z6 CANADA
Frozen yogurt w/ fresh frozen fruit, yogurt drinks, sandwiches
Phone: 604-570-0570   Accepts collect calls? N
Toll Free: FAX: 604-299-2797
Internet: www.goodforyouyogurt.com
Suitable Sites: AC, M, RM
Concentration: 9 in AB, 7 in BC
Expansion: N, Canada, Foreign
Registered: AB
Field Support: EO, ST, SO, $FC, H, N
Training: 5 days Alberta

I Can't Believe It's Yogurt
3361 Boyington Dr #160
Carrollton, TX 75006

Phone: 972-788-4788   Accepts collect calls?
Toll Free: 800-269-4374   FAX: 972-233-4129
Internet: www.yogenfruz.com
Suitable Sites: RM, SC
Concentration: 33 in TX, 16 in NC, 15 in FL
Expansion: All United States, Foreign
Registered: CA,IL,IN,MN,OR,RI,WA,WI,DC
Field Support: SO, N
Training: 10 days corporate HQ
1 week store

TCBY Treats
425 W Capitol Ave
Little Rock, AR 72201

Phone: 501-688-8229   Accepts collect calls?
Toll Free: 800-900-8229   FAX: 501-688-8549
Internet: www.tcby.com
Suitable Sites: FB, RM, SC, SF, OTHER
Concentration:
Expansion: All United States, Canada, Foreign
Registered: CA,FL,HI,IL,IN,MD,MI,MN,ND,NY,OR,RI,SD,VA,WA,WI,DC
Field Support: $CP, EO, ST, SO, $FC, H, N
Training: 8 days little rock, AR

Yogen Fruz Worldwide
8300 Woodbine Ave 5th Fl
Markham, ON L3R-9Y7 CANADA

Phone: 905-479-8762   Accepts collect calls? N
Toll Free: FAX: 905-479-5235
Internet: www.yogenfruz.com
Suitable Sites: FB, K, M, OC, RM, SC, SF
Concentration: 135 in TX, 120 in IL, 147 in ON
Expansion: All United States, Canada, Foreign
Registered: FL,IL,VA,DC,MI,AB
Field Support: CP, EO, $ST, SO, IC, FC, H, N
Training: 2 weeks Dallas, TX
1.5 weeks Toronto, ON

Quick-service Industry

Frozen: Other (Spread 1 of 2)

	Arctic Circle	Bahama Buck's Original Shaved Ice Co.	Culver Franchising System Inc	Dairy Belle Freeze	Frozen Fusion Fruit Smoothies	Happy & Healthy Products	Kohr Bros. Frozen Custard	Oh Mighty Ices Franchise Corp
Startup Cost	550K-750K	55K-138K	784.58K-1.5M	50K-250K	180K-280K	18K-40K	145.9K-277.5K	44K-60K
Franchise Fee	20K	15K	35K	12.5K	20K	12.8K-17.8K	27.5K	15K
Royalty	3%	5%	4%	4.50%	5%	0%	5%	0
Advertising Fee	3.5%	1%		2%	3%	$500/YR.	.5%	
Financing Provided	N	Y	N	N	Y	N	N	N
Experience Required		N					N	
Passive Ownership	N	A		N	D	A	D	
In Business Since	1953	1989	1984	1957	1995	1991	1919	1965
Franchised Since	1956	1992	1988	1981	1996	1993	1994	1995
Franchised Units 1996			41				5	0
1997	64	4	48	15	7	101	16	0
1998		7					24	
Company Owned 1996			3				9	3
1997	23	3	4	0	11	0	9	3
1998		3					11	
Number of Units U.S.	87	10		15	18	101	35	
Canada	0	0		0	0	0	0	
Foreign	0	0		0	0	1	0	
Projected New U.S.		10					24	
Canada							0	
Foreign							0	
Corporate Employees	25	5		4	12	7	14	
Contract Length	15/15	10/10		10/10	10/VAR.	10/5	5/5/5/5	
Expand in Territory	Y	Y		Y	Y	Y	Y	
Full-Time Employees	6	1		4	5	1-2	4	
Part-Time Employees	25	12		10	7		4	
Conversions	Y	Y		Y	N	N	Y	
Site Selection Assist.	Y	Y		Y	Y	Y	Y	
Lease Negotiation Assist.	N	Y		Y	Y	N	Y	
Site Space Required	35000	300-1200		1600	500-750		500	
Development Agreement	N	Y		N	Y	N	Y	
Develop. Agree. Term		10			10			
Sub-franchising	N	Y		N	N	N	N	

Quick-service Industry   **Frozen: Other (Spread 1 of 2)**

Arctic Circle
411 W 7200 S #200 PO Box 339
Midvale, UT 84047

Phone: 801-561-3620   Accepts collect calls?
Toll Free: FAX: 801-561-9646
Internet:
Suitable Sites: FB
Concentration: 45 in UT, 16 in ID, 9 in OR
Expansion: ID,WY,MT,WA,OR,UT
Registered: OR,WA
Field Support: CP, EO, ST, SO, FC, N
Training: 4-6 weeks Salt Lake City, UT

Bahama Buck's Original Shaved Ice Co.
1741 W University Dr #148
Tempe, AZ 85281
Tropical theme frozen dessert specialize gourmet shaved ice
Phone: 602-894-4408   Accepts collect calls?
Toll Free: FAX: 602-894-4409
Internet:
Suitable Sites: FB, K, RM, SC, SF
Concentration: 7 in AZ, 3 in TX
Expansion: SE, South
Registered:
Field Support: CP, EO, ST, SO, IC, FC, H
Training: 10 days Tempe AZ

Culver Franchising System Inc
827 Water St
Sauk City, WI 53583
Butter burgers/frozen custard
Phone: 608-643-7980   Accepts collect calls?
Toll Free: FAX:
Internet:
Suitable Sites:
Concentration:
Expansion: MW,SE
Registered:
Field Support:
Training:

Dairy Belle Freeze
832 N Hillview Dr
Milpitas, CA 95035

Phone: 408-263-2612   Accepts collect calls?
Toll Free: FAX: 408-263-2797
Internet: www.dairybelle.com
Suitable Sites: FB
Concentration: 15 in CA
Expansion: CA
Registered: CA
Field Support: CP, EO, ST, SO, IC, FC, N
Training: 10 days franchised location
         5 days office
         10 days purchased franchise loca.

Frozen Fusion Fruit Smoothies
15020 N 74th St #B
Scottsdale, AZ 85260

Phone: 602-948-5604   Accepts collect calls?
Toll Free: 800-386-3765   FAX: 602-948-6203
Internet: www.frozenfusion.com
Suitable Sites: RM, SF
Concentration: 3 in AZ, 2 in PA, 2 in DC
Expansion: 2 Major Markets Only, Canada, Foreign
Registered: CA,FL,HI,IL,IN,MD,MI,MN,NY,VA,WA,WI,DC
Field Support: DP, CP, EO, ST, SO, IC, $FC, H, N
Training: 1 week Scottsdale AZ
         1 week store opening

Happy & Healthy Products
1600 S Dixie Hwy #2ab
Boca Raton, FL 33432

Phone: 561-367-0739   Accepts collect calls?
Toll Free: FAX: 561-368-5267
Internet: www.fruitfullcom
Suitable Sites: HO
Concentration:
Expansion: All United States
Registered: CA,FL,HI,IL,IN,MD,MI,MN,NY,OR,VA,WI,DC,AB
Field Support: EO, ST, FC, N
Training: 1 week franchise MSA

Kohr Bros. Frozen Custard
2115 Berkmar Dr
Charlottesville, VA 22901
The original frozen custard since 1919 simple and unique concept
Phone: 804-975-1500   Accepts collect calls? N
Toll Free: 888-KBS-YSTE   FAX: 804-975-1505
Internet: www.kohrbros.com
Suitable Sites: AC, DA, FB, K, M, PC, RM, SC, SF, WF
Concentration: 10 in NJ, 6 in VA, 5 in PA
Expansion: East Coast, TX, AZ
Registered: FL,MD,NY,VA,DC
Field Support: CP, EO, $ST, SO, FC, H, N
Training: 6 days corporate HQ or designated location
         3 days at unit

Oh Mighty Ices Franchise Corp
13023 Bustleton Ave
Philadelphia, PA 19116
Italian ices, ice cream, gelati, fresh-baked pretzels
Phone: 215-969-5055   Accepts collect calls?
Toll Free: FAX:
Internet:
Suitable Sites:
Concentration:
Expansion: All United States, Canada, Foreign
Registered:
Field Support:
Training:

Quick-service Industry

Frozen: Other (Spread 2 of 2)

	Orange Julius Canada Inc.	Power Smoothie	Rita's Italian Ice	Smoothie King			
Startup Cost	175K-300K	64.4K-123.9K	100K-150K	90.5K-198.5K			
Franchise Fee	20K	20K	22.5K	20K			
Royalty	6%	5%	6.50%	5%			
Advertising Fee	3-5%	1.5-3%	2.5%	1%			
Financing Provided	Y	Y	Y	N			
Experience Required	N	N					
Passive Ownership	D	A	D				
In Business Since	1940	1991	1984	1987			
Franchised Since	1950	1994	1989	1987			
Franchised Units 1996							
1997	106	5	154	120			
1998		13					
Company Owned 1996							
1997	0	2	3	5			
1998		0					
Number of Units U.S.	0	13	157	125			
Canada	106	0	0	0			
Foreign	0	0	0	0			
Projected New U.S.		25					
Canada	4						
Foreign							
Corporate Employees	70	5	33	15			
Contract Length	15 MAX	10/10	10/10	10/10			
Expand in Territory	Y	Y	Y	Y			
Full-Time Employees		2	1	3			
Part-Time Employees		5	9	5			
Conversions	Y	Y	Y	N			
Site Selection Assist.	Y	Y	Y	Y			
Lease Negotiation Assist.	Y	Y	Y	Y			
Site Space Required	100-400	800-1500	600-1500	1000			
Development Agreement	N	Y	Y	Y			
Develop. Agree. Term		NEG.					
Sub-franchising	N	N	N	N			

Quick-service Industry   **Frozen: Other (Spread 2 of 2)**

Orange Julius Canada Inc.
5245 Harvester Rd PO Box 430
Burlington, ON L7R-3Y3 CANADA
Quick service restaurants, multiple concepts
  Phone: 905-639-1492 Accepts collect calls?
  Toll Free: 800-285-8515 FAX: 905-681-3623
  Internet:
Suitable Sites: DA, FC, M, RM
Concentration: 12 in ON, 29 in AB, 49 in BC
 Expansion: All United States, Canada, Foreign
 Registered: AB
Field Support: DP, CP, EO, ST, SO, IC, FC, H, N
 Training: 1 week Minneapolis, MN
    in-store/opening team

Power Smoothie
160 S University Dr Ste B
Plantation, FL 33324
Offers delicious fruit smoothies, fresh squeeze juices, sandwich
  Phone: 954-370-3913 Accepts collect calls?
  Toll Free: 888-818-7693 FAX: 954-370-3913
  Internet: www.powersmoothie.com
Suitable Sites: FC, K, M, PC, RM, SC, SF
Concentration: 10 in FL, 2 in NV, 1 in TX
 Expansion: All United States, Foreign
 Registered: FL
Field Support: EO, ST, SO, IC, H
 Training: 2 weeks plantation FL

Rita's Italian Ice
1525 Ford Rd
Bensalem, PA 19020

  Phone: 215-633-9899 Accepts collect calls?
  Toll Free: 800-677-7482 FAX: 215-633-9922
  Internet:
Suitable Sites: FB
Concentration: 89 in PA, 38 in NJ, 8 in DE
 Expansion: FL, MD, OH, VA, PA
 Registered: CA,MD,NY,VA
Field Support: CP, EO, ST, SO, $FC, N
 Training: 5 days corporate office
    2-4 days on-site

Smoothie King
2400 Veterans Blvd #110
Kenner, LA 70062

  Phone: 504-467-4006 Accepts collect calls?
  Toll Free: 800-577-4200 FAX: 504-469-1274
  Internet: www.smoothieking.com
Suitable Sites: FB, RM, SC, SF
Concentration: 37 in LA, 28 in TX, 14 in FL
 Expansion: All United States
 Registered: CA,FL,WA,MD,VA,IL,IN,NY
Field Support: EO, ST, SO
 Training: 8 days corporate office
    9 days at store location

Quick-service Industry

Juices, Smoothies

	Fresh Juice & Smoothie Bar	Juice Connection Bunnies	La Smoothie Franchises Inc	Zuka Juice				
Startup Cost	33.75K-188.5K	83.5K-165.3K	26K-69.5K	177.5K-236.9K				
Franchise Fee	24.5K	20K	9K-15K	20K				
Royalty	5%	5%	TO 5%	5%				
Advertising Fee				2%				
Financing Provided	N	Y	Y	N				
Experience Required				N				
Passive Ownership				A				
In Business Since	1993	1994	1991	1995				
Franchised Since	1995	1995	1992	1997				
Franchised Units 1996	0	2	17	0				
1997	0	2	15	7				
1998				69				
Company Owned 1996	1	2	0	0				
1997	1	2	3	11				
1998				21				
Number of Units U.S.				90				
Canada								
Foreign								
Projected New U.S.				50				
Canada								
Foreign								
Corporate Employees				30				
Contract Length				10/5/5				
Expand in Territory								
Full-Time Employees				2-3				
Part-Time Employees				5-15				
Conversions				Y				
Site Selection Assist.				Y				
Lease Negotiation Assist.				Y				
Site Space Required				500-1500				
Development Agreement				Y				
Develop. Agree. Term				VAR.				
Sub-franchising				N				

Quick-service Industry

Juices, Smoothies

Bunnies Fresh Juice & Smoothie Bar
PO Box 880
Mandeville, LA 70470
Health beverages & products
    Phone:
    Toll Free: 800-240-0002
    Internet:
Suitable Sites:
Concentration:
    Expansion:
    Registered:
Field Support:
    Training:

Accepts collect calls?
FAX:

Juice Connection
1160 N Blue Gum
Anaheim, CA 92806
Juice & smoothies
    Phone: 714-632-1012
    Toll Free:
    Internet:
Suitable Sites:
Concentration:
    Expansion: CA, Foreign
    Registered:
Field Support:
    Training:

Accepts collect calls?
FAX:

La Smoothie Franchises Inc
701 Edwards Ave
Harahan, LA 70123
Smoothies, health foods, vitamins, activewear
    Phone: 504-734-5848
    Toll Free:
    Internet:
Suitable Sites:
Concentration:
    Expansion: CA, Canada, Foreign
    Registered:
Field Support:
    Training:

Accepts collect calls?
FAX:

Zuka Juice
488 E 6400 South #200
Salt Lake City, UT 84107
Fresh-squeezed juices & smoothies
    Phone: 801-265-8423
    Toll Free: 888-GET-ZUKA
    Internet: www.zukajuice.com
Suitable Sites: AC, FB, FC, K, M, PC, SC, WF
Concentration: 32 in UT, 12 in OR, 10 in TX
    Expansion: All United States, Canada
    Registered: WA
Field Support: DP, EO, ST, SO, IC, FC, N
    Training: comprehensive
             ongoing

Accepts collect calls? N
FAX: 801-265-3932

Quick-service Industry

Meals: Cheese-steak

	Great Steak & Potato Company	Philly Connection							
Startup Cost	165K	150K-199K							
Franchise Fee	20K	20K							
Royalty	5%	5%							
Advertising Fee	0	5%							
Financing Provided	N	Y							
Experience Required	N	N							
Passive Ownership	A	A							
In Business Since	1983	1987							
Franchised Since	1986	1988							
Franchised Units 1996	195	59							
1997	201	69							
1998	216	80							
Company Owned 1996	21	3							
1997	20	4							
1998	23	1							
Number of Units U.S.	200	81							
Canada	13								
Foreign	3								
Projected New U.S.	25								
Canada	3								
Foreign	3								
Corporate Employees	250	7							
Contract Length	10	10							
Expand in Territory	Y								
Full-Time Employees	2								
Part-Time Employees	10								
Conversions	Y	N							
Site Selection Assist.	Y	Y							
Lease Negotiation Assist.	Y	Y							
Site Space Required		1700							
Development Agreement	Y	Y							
Develop. Agree. Term	NEG.	3							
Sub-franchising	Y	N							

Quick-service Industry

Meals: Cheese-steak

Great Steak & Potato Company
222 High St #300
Hamilton, OH 45011
Cheesesteaks, grilled sandwiches, salads, frys
Phone: 513-896-9695   Accepts collect calls? N
Toll Free: FAX: 513-896-3750
Internet: thegreatsteak.com
Suitable Sites: AC, FB, FC, M, OC, PC, RM, SC, SF
Concentration: 24 in IL, 28 in OH, 17 in CA
Expansion: All United States, Canada, Foreign
Registered: CA,FL,HI,IL,IN,MD,MI,MN,ND,NY,OR,RI,SD,VA,WA,WI,DC,AB
Field Support: CP, EO, ST, SO, IC, N
Training: 2 weeks comprehensive in Cincinnati, OH

Philly Connection
120 Interstate N Pkwy E #112
Atlanta, GA 30339
Philly cheesesteaks, specialty sandwiches & premium ice cream
Phone: Accepts collect calls? N
Toll Free: 800-886-8826   FAX: 770-952-3168
Internet: phillycon@mindspring.com
Suitable Sites: AC, FB, SC
Concentration: 42 in GA, 10 in FL, NC
Expansion: GA,TN,KY,AL,FL,NC,SC, Foreign
Registered: FL,WA
Field Support: $DP, EO, ST, SO, IC, H, N
Training: comprehensive franchisee training
initial start-up staff
marketing

Quick-service Industry

Meals: Chicken, Turkey (Spread 1 of 2)

	Bassett's Original Turkey	Bojangles' Restaurants Inc	Brown's Chicken & Pasta	Bw-3 Buffalo Wild Wings	Chef's Fried Chicken	Chicken Delight	Churchs Chicken	Cluck-U Chicken
Startup Cost	100K-275K	175K-1.2M	150K-160K	450K-750K	100K-300K	200K-300K	214.8K-290.8K	125K-225K
Franchise Fee	25K	15K-20K	25K	25K	25K	20K	15K	2.5K
Royalty	5%	4%	5%	5%	6%	5%	5%	5%
Advertising Fee	1%	1%	4%	3%	3%	2%	4%	2%
Financing Provided	Y	N	N	N	N	N	Y	Y
Experience Required								
Passive Ownership	A		N	D	N	D	D	N
In Business Since	1983	1977	1965	1982	1970	1952	1952	1985
Franchised Since	1989	1978	1965	1991	1974	1952	1972	1991
Franchised Units 1996		118						
1997	14	115	63	65	5	40	859	34
1998		106						
Company Owned 1996		113						
1997	3	128	11	10	0	16	475	1
1998		153						
Number of Units U.S.	17	249	74	74	5	17	1056	35
Canada	0		0	0	0	37	104	0
Foreign	0	4	0	1	0	2	174	0
Projected New U.S.		30						
Canada								
Foreign		2						
Corporate Employees	10	80+	12			25	350	5
Contract Length	10/5		15/5	10/5	15/15	10/10	20/10	20/10
Expand in Territory	Y		N	Y	N	Y	Y	Y
Full-Time Employees	3		3	6	6	6	30-35	8
Part-Time Employees	5		12	40	4	6		
Conversions	Y		Y	Y	Y	Y	Y	Y
Site Selection Assist.	Y	Y	Y	Y	Y	Y	Y	Y
Lease Negotiation Assist.	Y	N	Y	N	Y	Y	Y	Y
Site Space Required	600-800		1500	5000-7000	1600	1800	22000	1500
Development Agreement	Y	Y	Y	Y	Y	Y	Y	N
Develop. Agree. Term	10		15		2	10		
Sub-franchising	N	N	N	N	N	N	N	Y

Quick-service Industry

Meals: Chicken, Turkey (Spread 1 of 2)

Bassett's Original Turkey
228 Lakeside Dr
Horsham, PA 19044

Phone: 215-675-9670   Accepts collect calls?
Toll Free: 800-282-8875   FAX: 215-675-9690
Internet: www.bassetts.com
Suitable Sites: SC
Concentration: 10 in PA, 2 in NJ, 2 in NY
   Expansion: All United States
   Registered: CA,FL,IL,IN,MD,MI,MN,NY,RI,VA,WI,DC
Field Support: DP, CP, EO, ST, SO, IC, FC, N
   Training: 2 weeks corporate store
       1 week corporate office

Bojangles' Restaurants Inc
PO Box 240239
Charlotte, NC 28224
Chicken & biscuits, wide variety of breakfast biscuits/side item
Phone: 704-527-2675   Accepts collect calls? N
Toll Free: FAX: 704-523-6676
Internet:
Suitable Sites: DA, FB, OTHER
Concentration: 48 in NC, 30 in SC, 10 in GA
   Expansion: IL,MD,VA,WV,AL,TN,GA,FL
   Registered: FL,IL,VA
Field Support: CP, EO, ST, SO, IC, FC, H, N
   Training: 5 weeks extensive in-store and classroom training

Brown's Chicken & Pasta
1200 Jorie Blvd
Oak Brook, IL 60523

Phone: 630-571-5300   Accepts collect calls?
Toll Free: FAX: 630-571-5378
Internet:
Suitable Sites: FB, SC
Concentration: 80 in IL, 5 in FL
   Expansion: FL, IL, IN, Foreign
   Registered: FL,IL,IN
Field Support: CP, EO, ST, SO, IC, FC, H, N
   Training: 6 weeks corporate office

Bw-3 Buffalo Wild Wings
600 S Hwy 169 1919 Interchange Tower
Minneapolis, MN 55426

Phone: 612-593-9943   Accepts collect calls?
Toll Free: FAX: 612-593-9787
Internet:
Suitable Sites: FB, RM, SC, SF
Concentration: 28 in OH, 6 in MI, 5 in IN
   Expansion: All United States
   Registered: CA,FL,HI,IL,IN,MD,MI,MN,ND,NY,OR,RI,SD,VA,WA,WI,DC
Field Support: DP, CP, EO, ST, SO, IC, FC, N
   Training: 3 weeks Cincinnati, OH

Chef's Fried Chicken
20 Audubon Oaks Blvd
Lafayette, LA 70506

Phone: 318-233-1621   Accepts collect calls?
Toll Free: FAX: 318-233-9038
Internet:
Suitable Sites: FB, RM
Concentration: 1 in LA
   Expansion: All United States
   Registered:
Field Support: $ST, SO, IC, FC, H, N
   Training: 2 weeks Carencro, LA

Chicken Delight
395 Berry St
Winnipeg, MB R3J-1N6 CANADA

Phone: 204-885-7570   Accepts collect calls?
Toll Free: FAX: 204-831-6176
Internet:
Suitable Sites: FB, RM, SC, SF
Concentration: 33 in MB, 3 in SK, 1 in ON
   Expansion: All United States, Canada, Foreign
   Registered: MI,MN,ND,AB
Field Support: $DP, CP, EO, ST, SO, IC, $FC, N
   Training: 4 weeks Winnipeg, MB

Churchs Chicken
Six Concourse Pkwy #1700
Atlanta, GA 30328

Phone: 770-353-3048   Accepts collect calls?
Toll Free: 800-848-8248   FAX: 770-353-3306
Internet: www.afc-online.com
Suitable Sites: FB
Concentration: 400 in TX, 100 in GA, 50 in CA
   Expansion: All United States, Canada, Foreign
   Registered: CA,FL,HI,IL,IN,MD,MI,MN,ND,NY,OR,RI,SD,VA,WA,WI,DC
Field Support: DP, EO, ST, SO, IC, FC, H, N
   Training: 6 weeks regional

Cluck-U Chicken
261 Raymond Rd
Princeton, NJ 08540

Phone: 732-438-1900   Accepts collect calls?
Toll Free: FAX: 732-438-0055
Internet: www.clucku.com
Suitable Sites: FB, SC, SF
Concentration: NJ, MO, PA
   Expansion: All United States
   Registered: CA,MD
Field Support: CP, EO, ST, SO, IC, FC, H, N
   Training: 6 weeks Delaware, CA or NJ

Quick-service Industry

Meals: Chicken, Turkey (Spread 2 of 2)

	Golden Chick	Hartz Chicken	KFC	Popeyes Chicken & Biscuits	Wing Machine	Yaya's Flame Broiled Chicken		
Startup Cost	400K-750K	300K-1M	700K-1.2M	209.8K-320.6K	102K-204K	233K-336K		
Franchise Fee	15K	20K	25K	15K	10K	15K		
Royalty	4%	4%	4%	5%	6%	4%		
Advertising Fee	1%	2-3%	4.5%	3%	3%	4%		
Financing Provided	N	N	N	Y	Y	N		
Experience Required								
Passive Ownership	N	D	N	D	D	N		
In Business Since	1967	1972	1954	1972	1965	1985		
Franchised Since	1972	1975	1959	1976	1987	1988		
Franchised Units 1996								
1997	84	50	6671	1013	11	11		
1998								
Company Owned 1996								
1997	7	1	3198	119	1	9		
1998								
Number of Units U.S.	80	42	3122	945	0	20		
Canada	0	0	3555	6	12	0		
Foreign	4	9	3192	181	0	0		
Projected New U.S.								
Canada								
Foreign								
Corporate Employees	22	10	820		25	6		
Contract Length	20/N/A	20/5	20/10	20/10	5/5	10/10		
Expand in Territory	N	Y	Y	Y	Y	Y		
Full-Time Employees		7	2	30-35	4	7		
Part-Time Employees		6	22		2	7		
Conversions	N	Y	N	Y				
Site Selection Assist.	Y	Y	Y	Y	Y	N		
Lease Negotiation Assist.	N	Y	N	Y	Y			
Site Space Required	1800	3000	2000-3000	22000	1000	2800		
Development Agreement	N	Y	N		Y	Y		
Develop. Agree. Term						10		
Sub-franchising	N	Y	N	N	Y	N		

Quick-service Industry   **Meals: Chicken, Turkey (Spread 2 of 2)**

Golden Chick
11488 Luna Rd
Dallas, TX 75234

Phone: 972-831-0911   Accepts collect calls?
Toll Free: FAX: 972-831-0401
Internet:
Suitable Sites: FB
Concentration: 76 in TX, 3 in OK, 4 in MX
Expansion: South, SE
Registered:
Field Support: EO, $ST, SO, IC, FC, N
Training: 6 weeks Dallas, TX

Hartz Chicken
14451 Cornerstone Village Dr #250
Houston, TX 77014

Phone: 281-583-0020   Accepts collect calls?
Toll Free: FAX: 281-580-3752
Internet: www.hartz-chicken.com
Suitable Sites: FB
Concentration: 41 in TX, 1 in MS
Expansion: South, Foreign
Registered:
Field Support: CP, EO, ST, SO, H, N
Training: 6 weeks Houston, TX

KFC
1441 Gardiner Ln
Louisville, KY 40232-2070

Phone: 502-454-2070   Accepts collect calls?
Toll Free: FAX: 502-456-8732
Internet: www.kentuckyfriedchicken.com
Suitable Sites: FB
Concentration: CA, TX, IL
Expansion: All United States, Canada, Foreign
Registered: CA,FL,HI,IL,IN,MD,MI,MN,ND,NY,OR,RI,SD,VA,WA,WI,DC
Field Support: EO, $ST, SO, $FC, H, N
Training: 14 weeks varied sites

Popeyes Chicken & Biscuits
6 Concourse Pkwy #1700
Atlanta, GA 30328

Phone: 770-391-9500   Accepts collect calls?
Toll Free: 800-848-8248   FAX: 770-353-3170
Internet: www.popeyes.com
Suitable Sites: FB, RM, SC, OTHER
Concentration:
Expansion: All United States, Canada, Foreign
Registered: CA,HI,IL,IN,MD,MI,MN,ND,NY,OR,RI,SD,VA,WA,WI
Field Support: CP, EO, ST, SO, IC, FC, H, N
Training: 4 weeks Atlanta, GA

Wing Machine
156 Willowdale Ave
Willowdale, ON M2N-4Y6 CANADA

Phone: 416-961-1000   Accepts collect calls?
Toll Free: FAX: 416-362-8217
Internet:
Suitable Sites: SF
Concentration: 12 in ON
Expansion: All United States, Canada, Foreign
Registered:
Field Support: DP, CP, EO, ST, SO, IC, FC, N
Training: 6 weeks corporate store

Yaya's Flame Broiled Chicken
521 S Dort Hwy
Flint, MI 48503

Phone: 810-235-6550   Accepts collect calls?
Toll Free: 800-754-1242   FAX: 810-235-5210
Internet:
Suitable Sites: FB, SC, SF
Concentration: 14 in MI, 6 in FL
Expansion: All United States, Canada
Registered: FL,MI,MN
Field Support: EO, ST, SO, IC, FC, H
Training: 3 weeks flint, MI

Quick-service Industry   Meals: Hamburgers (Spread 1 of 2)

	Back Yard Burgers	Bullets Corporation of America, Inc.	Burger King (Canada)	Cheeburger Cheeburger	Farmer Boys Hamburgers	FatBurger	Flamers Charbroiled Hamburgers & Chicken	Hardee's Food Systems
Startup Cost	339K-832K		300K-1.1M	180K-280K	216K-644.5K	300K-600K	180K-210K	1.19M-1.25M
Franchise Fee	25K		40K	17.5K	30K	30K	25K	35K
Royalty	4%		4%	4.5%	5%	5%	5%	4%
Advertising Fee	3%		4%	1%	2%	2%	1%	5%
Financing Provided	N	N	N	N	N	N	Y	N
Experience Required	N	Y		N	N			N
Passive Ownership	D	A	A	D	D	A	D	A
In Business Since	1987	1990	1954	1986	1981	1952	1987	1960
Franchised Since	1988	1993	1969	1990	1997	1980	1988	1961
Franchised Units 1996		19						
1997	44	31	141	6	0	17	72	2401
1998	49	33		15	0			1317
Company Owned 1996		6						
1997	32	7	115	2	8	12	10	793
1998	33	5		3	10			1369
Number of Units U.S.	82	12	0	18	10	29	81	3113
Canada	0	0	256	0	0	0	0	0
Foreign	0	0	0	0	0	0	1	96
Projected New U.S.	12	100		10	7			57
Canada		0						
Foreign		0						
Corporate Employees	30	120	60	5	6	12	11	500
Contract Length	10/5		20/20	10/5	20/10/10	15/10/10	10/10/10	20/5
Expand in Territory	Y	Y	Y	Y	N	N	Y	Y
Full-Time Employees	8	3	15	5	7-10	8	3-4	40
Part-Time Employees	22	15	25	10	10-15	8	7-10	
Conversions	Y	N	Y	Y	N	Y	Y	N
Site Selection Assist.	Y	N	Y	Y	Y	Y	Y	Y
Lease Negotiation Assist.	Y	N	Y	Y	Y	N	Y	N
Site Space Required	30000	1000-1600	3600	2000	2500-3000	1800-2000	500-2000	2000
Development Agreement	Y	N	Y	Y	Y	Y	Y	Y
Develop. Agree. Term	10		1-5	5	VAR.	5	20	NEG.
Sub-franchising	N	N	N	N	N	N	Y	N

Quick-service Industry   **Meals: Hamburgers (Spread 1 of 2)**

Back Yard Burgers
2768 Colony Park Dr
Memphis, TN 30117
Quick, casual restaurant serving 1/3lb gourmet burgers & chicken
Phone: 901-367-0888   Accepts collect calls? N
Toll Free: 800-292-6939   FAX: 901-367-0997
Internet: www.backyardburgers.com
Suitable Sites: FB
Concentration: 30 in TN, 13 in AR, 7 in NC
Expansion: SE, MW, Mid-Atlantic, SE
Registered: FL,IL,IN,MI,VA
Field Support: CP, EO, ST, SO, IC, FC, N
Training: 8 weeks corporate HQ

Bullets Corporation of America, Inc.
9201 Forest Hill Ave Ste 109
Richmond, VA 23235
QSR solution for G&C and other markets, flame broiled burger/BBQ
Phone: 804-330-0837   Accepts collect calls? N
Toll Free: FAX: 804-330-5405
Internet: www.bulletsnet.com
Suitable Sites: FB, FC, OTHER
Concentration: 15 in VA, 5 in GA, 4 in AL
Expansion: VA, NC, TN, KY, SC, AL, MS, GA, PA, SD, WY, UT, FL, LA
Registered: FL, IL, IN, SD, VA
Field Support: ST, SO
Training:

Burger King (Canada)
401 The West Mall 7th Fl
Etobicoke, ON M9C-5J4   CANADA

Phone: 416-626-7444   Accepts collect calls?
Toll Free: FAX: 416-626-6691
Internet:
Suitable Sites: FB, RM, SC, SF
Concentration: 125 in ON, 45 in PQ, 25 in BC
Expansion: Canada
Registered: AB
Field Support: CP, EO, ST, SO, IC, FC
Training: 14 weeks classroom/restaurant

Cheeburger Cheeburger
15951 Mc Gregor Blvd
Fort Myers, FL 33908
Gourmet cheeseburgers, french fries, onion rings & milk shakes
Phone: 941-437-1611   Accepts collect calls? N
Toll Free: 800-487-6211   FAX: 941-437-1512
Internet:
Suitable Sites: FB, SC, SF
Concentration: 9 in FL, 1 in AL, 2 in TN
Expansion: East Of Mississippi
Registered: IL,MI,NY,FL,WI
Field Support: EO, ST, SO, IC, FC, H
Training: 17 days

Farmer Boys Hamburgers
3890 11th St #203
Riverside, CA 92501
Over 100 breakfst/lunch/dinner items dine-in/take-out/drive-thru
Phone: 909-275-9900   Accepts collect calls?
Toll Free: 888-930-3276   FAX: 909-275-9930
Internet:
Suitable Sites: FB
Concentration: 10 in CA
Expansion: CA
Registered: CA
Field Support: CP, EO, ST, SO, IC, H
Training: 6 months company-operated unit

FatBurger
1218 Third St Promenade
Santa Monica, CA 90401-1308

Phone: 310-914-1850   Accepts collect calls?
Toll Free: FAX: 310-319-1863
Internet:
Suitable Sites: FB, SC, SF
Concentration: 24 in CA, 5 in NV
Expansion: All United States, Canada
Registered: CA,IL,MD,NY,WA
Field Support: EO, ST, SO, FC
Training: 5 weeks Los Angeles, CA
10 days on-site

Flamers Charbroiled Hamburgers & Chicken
500 S 3rd St
Jacksonville, FL 32233

Phone: 904-241-3737   Accepts collect calls?
Toll Free: 800-952-7645   FAX: 904-241-1301
Internet: www.flamersgrill.com
Suitable Sites: RM, SC, SF
Concentration: 21 in FL, 11 in DC, 7 in PA
Expansion: All United States, Foreign
Registered: CA,FL,HI,IL,IN,MD,MI,NY,OR,RI,VA,WA,WI,DC
Field Support: $DP, CP, EO, ST, SO, IC, FC, H, N
Training: 2 weeks company unit Boston, MA
2 weeks franchisee's store

Hardee's Food Systems
1233 Hardee's Blvd
Rocky Mount, NC 27804-2815
Quick service hamburger restaurants
Phone: 252-450-8821   Accepts collect calls? N
Toll Free: FAX: 252-450-8491
Internet: www.hardees.com
Suitable Sites: FB, FC, M, RM, SC, OTHER
Concentration: 353 in NC, 209 in GA, 203 in VA
Expansion: SE and Midwest, Foreign
Registered: CA,FL,HI,IL,IN,MD,MI,MN,ND,NY,OR,RI,SD,VA,WA,WI,DC
Field Support: DP, CP, EO, ST, SO, $IC, $FC, H
Training: 3 days local restaurant
360 hours formal training

Quick-service Industry

Meals: Hamburgers (Spread 2 of 2)

	The Krystal Company	McDonald's	Restaurants of Canada Limited McDonald's	Sonic Drive-In	Restaurants of Canada Inc. Wendy's			
Startup Cost	800K-1.5M	407.6K-646.4K		500K-900K	600K-1.477			
Franchise Fee	32.5K	45K	45K	30K	40K			
Royalty	4.5%	12.50%	17%	1-5%	4%			
Advertising Fee	4%	4%		4%	4%			
Financing Provided	N	N	N	Y	N			
Experience Required	Y		N	N	Y			
Passive Ownership	N	N		N	N			
In Business Since	1932	1955	1967	1953	1969			
Franchised Since	1989	1956	1968	1959	1975			
Franchised Units 1996			387					
1997	94	15394	421	1428	126			
1998	111		739	1602				
Company Owned 1996			156					
1997	249	4205	142	256	114			
1998	243		340	299				
Number of Units U.S.	354	11016		1901	0			
Canada	0	819	1084	0	270			
Foreign	0	7764		0	0			
Projected New U.S.	35			200				
Canada					315			
Foreign								
Corporate Employees	150			170	101			
Contract Length	10/10	20/20	20	20/10	20			
Expand in Territory	Y	N	N	Y	Y			
Full-Time Employees	10			35	4			
Part-Time Employees	65			15	60			
Conversions	Y		N	N	Y			
Site Selection Assist.	Y	N	Y	Y	Y			
Lease Negotiation Assist.	Y		N	N	Y			
Site Space Required	35000-40000	2000		1300	45000			
Development Agreement	Y	N	N	Y	N			
Develop. Agree. Term	10							
Sub-franchising	N	N	N	N	N			

Quick-service Industry

Meals: Hamburgers (Spread 2 of 2)

The Krystal Company
One Union Square 10th Fl
Chattanooga, TN 37402
Hamburger, Krystal chik, french fries, etc.
    Phone: 423-757-5601   Accepts collect calls? N
    Toll Free: 800-458-5912   FAX: 423-757-1590
    Internet: csherlin@krystalco.com
Suitable Sites: FB
Concentration: 109 in GA, 95 in TN, 53 in AL
    Expansion: SE, SE
    Registered: CA,FL,IL,IN,VA
Field Support: DP, CP, EO, ST, SO, IC, FC, H
    Training: 5 weeks on-site

McDonald's
One Mcdonald's Plaza Kroc Dr
Oak Brook, IL 60521

    Phone: 630-623-6196   Accepts collect calls?
    Toll Free: FAX: 630-623-5645
    Internet: www.mcdonalds.com
Suitable Sites: FB
Concentration: 1039 in CA, 692 in TX, 655 in FL
    Expansion: All United States, Canada, Foreign
    Registered: CA,FL,HI,IL,IN,MD,MI,MN,ND,NY,OR,RI,SD,VA,WA,WI,DC
Field Support: $CP, EO, $ST, SO, $FC, N
    Training:

McDonald's Restaurants of Canada Limited
Mc Donald's Place
Toronto, ON M3C-3L4 CANADA

    Phone: 416-443-1000   Accepts collect calls? N
    Toll Free: FAX: 416-446-3600
    Internet:
Suitable Sites:
Concentration: 270 in ONT, 178 in PQ, 77 in BC
    Expansion: Canada, Foreign
    Registered:
Field Support:
    Training: 1600 hours over min. of 2 yrs

Sonic Drive-In
101 Park Ave #1400
Oklahoma City, OK 73102
Drive-in featuring hamburgers, Coneys, ice-cream & spec. Drinks
    Phone: 405-280-7526   Accepts collect calls? N
    Toll Free: 800-569-6656   FAX: 405-290-7404
    Internet: www.sonicdrivein.com
Suitable Sites: FB, FC, M
Concentration: 539 in TX, 200 in OK, 152 in TN
    Expansion: SE, SE, West
    Registered: CA,FL,IN,OR,VA,WA,DC,MI
Field Support: CP, EO, ST, SO, IC, FC, H, N
    Training: 1 week Oklahoma City, OK
            9 weeks local market

Wendy's Restaurants of Canada Inc.
6715 Airport Rd #301
Mississauga, ON L4V-1X2 CANADA

    Phone: 905-677-7023   Accepts collect calls? N
    Toll Free: FAX: 905-677-5297
    Internet:
Suitable Sites: AM, ES, FB, FC, IP, LI, OC, PC, RM
Concentration: 125 in ON, 47 in AB, 36 in BC
    Expansion: Canada
    Registered: AB
Field Support: CP, EO, ST, SO, IC, $FC, N
    Training: 16 weeks in-store & classroom

Quick-service Industry

Meals: Hot Dogs

	AJ Texas Hots	Boardwalk Fries	Boz Hot Dogs	Potts Doggie Shop	Wienerschnitzel			
Startup Cost	75K	69K-192K	50K	60K	450K-1M			
Franchise Fee	25K	25K		15K	20K			
Royalty	$500/MO.	5-7%	5%	4%	5%			
Advertising Fee				2%	4-6%			
Financing Provided	Y	N	N	N	Y			
Experience Required			N					
Passive Ownership			N	A	D			
In Business Since	1968	1981	1969	1971	1961			
Franchised Since	1994	1983	1993	1985	1965			
Franchised Units 1996	0	50	28					
1997	1	42	26	2	312			
1998			24					
Company Owned 1996	1	6	4					
1997	1	7	4	5	0			
1998			4					
Number of Units U.S.			28	7	312			
Canada				0	0			
Foreign				0	0			
Projected New U.S.			2					
Canada								
Foreign								
Corporate Employees				1	40			
Contract Length			OPEN	5/5	20/5			
Expand in Territory			Y	Y				
Full-Time Employees			1	4	1-2			
Part-Time Employees			4	5	10-20			
Conversions								
Site Selection Assist.			Y	Y				
Lease Negotiation Assist.			Y	Y	N			
Site Space Required			800-1000	1400	680-2000			
Development Agreement			N	Y	Y			
Develop. Agree. Term				5	2			
Sub-franchising			N	N	N			

Quick-service Industry   Meals: Hot Dogs

AJ Texas Hots
824 Foote Ave
Jamestown, NY 14701
Hot dogs & hamburgers
  Phone: 716-484-9646 Accepts collect calls?
  Toll Free: 800-223-7365 FAX:
  Internet:
Suitable Sites:
Concentration:
  Expansion: NE,SE,S
  Registered:
Field Support:
  Training:

Boardwalk Fries
9110 Red Branch Rd
Columbia, MD 21045
French fries, hot dogs, burgers
  Phone: 410-720-0020 Accepts collect calls?
  Toll Free: FAX:
  Internet:
Suitable Sites:
Concentration:
  Expansion: MD
  Registered:
Field Support:
  Training:

Boz Hot Dogs
770 E 142nd St
Dolton, IL 60419

  Phone: 708-841-3747 Accepts collect calls?
  Toll Free: FAX:
  Internet:
Suitable Sites: FB, LI, SF
Concentration: 25 in IL
  Expansion: IL,IN
  Registered: IL
Field Support: EO, ST, SO, FC, N
  Training: in-store
     our store

Potts Doggie Shop
16305 San Carlos Blvd
Fort Myers, FL 33908

  Phone: 941-466-7747 Accepts collect calls?
  Toll Free: FAX: 941-466-1769
  Internet:
Suitable Sites: FB, RM, SC, SF
Concentration: 3 in FL, 3 in PA, 1 in NJ
  Expansion: Eastern Seaboard
  Registered: FL
Field Support:
  Training: 2-3 weeks Ft Myers, FL

Wienerschnitzel
4440 Von Karman Ave #222
Newport Beach, CA 92660

  Phone: 714-851-2609 Accepts collect calls?
  Toll Free: 800-764-9353 FAX: 714-851-2615
  Internet: www.bizopnet.com/wiener
Suitable Sites: FB
Concentration: 223 in CA, 22 in TX, 8 in NM
  Expansion: CA, HI, SE, Foreign
  Registered: CA,FL,HI,IL,IN,OR,WA
Field Support: $DP, CP, EO, $ST, SO, IC, FC, H
  Training: 6 weeks CA or SW

Quick-service Industry

Meals: Italian

	Antonello's	EB's Express	Figaro's Italian Kitchen	Mamma Ilardo's	Sbarro, The Italian Eatery			
Startup Cost	126K-209K	100K-134K	154.5K-181.5K	175K-320K				
Franchise Fee	20K	25K	18.5K	25K	45K			
Royalty	5%	5%	5%	4-5%	7%			
Advertising Fee			2%	1-2%	0			
Financing Provided	N	N	Y	Y	N			
Experience Required					Y			
Passive Ownership			D	D	D			
In Business Since	1957	1986	1981	1976	1959			
Franchised Since	1997	1996	1986	1984	1979			
Franchised Units 1996		0			219			
1997	0	0	80	48	239			
1998					266			
Company Owned 1996	0	0			597			
1997	1	0	0	1	623			
1998					623			
Number of Units U.S.			80	49				
Canada			0	0				
Foreign			0	0				
Projected New U.S.					50			
Canada					3			
Foreign					50			
Corporate Employees			23	8	7000+			
Contract Length			5/5/5/5	10/10	5 OR 10			
Expand in Territory			Y	Y	Y			
Full-Time Employees			2	8	5+			
Part-Time Employees			10-12	10	3+			
Conversions			Y	Y	Y			
Site Selection Assist.			Y	Y	Y			
Lease Negotiation Assist.			Y	Y	N			
Site Space Required			950-1500	200-1500	720			
Development Agreement			Y	Y	N			
Develop. Agree. Term				10				
Sub-franchising			N	Y	N			

Quick-service Industry   Meals: Italian

Antonello's
2886 Brooklyn Rd
Jackson, MI 49203
Italian food
  Phone: 517-768-1100   Accepts collect calls?
  Toll Free: FAX:
  Internet:
Suitable Sites:
Concentration:
  Expansion: Canada, Foreign
  Registered:
Field Support:
  Training:

EB's Express
385 Walnut St Extension
Agawam, MA 01001
Italian take out/delivery
  Phone: Accepts collect calls?
  Toll Free: 800-241-7040   FAX:
  Internet:
Suitable Sites:
Concentration:
  Expansion: NE
  Registered:
Field Support:
  Training:

Figaro's Italian Kitchen
1500 Liberty St S E #160
Salem, OR 97302

  Phone: 503-371-9318   Accepts collect calls?
  Toll Free: 888-344-2767   FAX: 503-363-5364
  Internet:
Suitable Sites: FB, SC, SF
Concentration: 55 in OR, 15 in WA, 4 in ID
  Expansion: 14 Western States
  Registered: CA,FL,IN,MN,ND,OR,SD,TX,UT,WA
Field Support: CP, EO, ST, SO, IC, FC, H, N
  Training: 12 days Salem training stores

Mamma Ilardo's
3600 Clipper Mill Rd #260
Baltimore, MD 21211

  Phone: 410-662-1930   Accepts collect calls?
  Toll Free: FAX: 410-662-1936
  Internet:
Suitable Sites: RM, SF
Concentration: 17 in MD, 4 in NV, 3 in TX
  Expansion: All United States, Canada, Foreign
  Registered: CA,FL,HI,IL,MD,MI,NY,OR,DC
Field Support: CP, EO, ST, SO, IC, FC, N
  Training: 3 weeks corporate office

Sbarro, The Italian Eatery
401 Broadhollow Rd
Melville, NY 11747
Italian quick-service restaurant, full menu concept >250 items
  Phone: 516-715-4148   Accepts collect calls? N
  Toll Free: 800-955-7227   FAX: 516-715-4183
  Internet: www.sbarroinc.com
Suitable Sites: DA, FB, FC, K, M, RM, SC, SF
Concentration: IL, NY, FL
  Expansion: All United States, Canada, Foreign
  Registered: CA FL HI IL IN MD MI MN ND NY OR SD VA WA WI DC AB
Field Support: $DP, CP, EO, ST, SO, IC, FC, H, N
  Training: 4 weeks in-depth management
          certification course
          Long Island, NY

Quick-service Industry

Meals: Mexican (Spread 1 of 3)

	Cap'n Taco	Del Taco	Diamond Dave's Taco Company	El Pollo Loco	La Salsa Fresh Mexican Grill	Nach-O Fast	Nacho Nana's Worldwide Inc	New York Burrito-Gourmet Wraps
Startup Cost	80K-175K	466K-679K	150K-250K	315.5K-630.5K	222K-371K	75K-160K	176K-199.95K	32.5K-62.5K
Franchise Fee	15K	25K	15K	35K	29.5K	15K	25K	12.5K
Royalty	5%	5%	4%	4%	5%	5%	6%	7%
Advertising Fee	2%	4%	1%	4%	1%	.5-2%		4%
Financing Provided	N	N	N	Y	N	N	Y	Y
Experience Required								N
Passive Ownership	D	N	D	A	N			A
In Business Since	1976	1964	1980	1975	1979	1995	1993	1995
Franchised Since	1986	1967	1982		1988	1996	1993	1996
Franchised Units 1996							8	2
1997	2	97	32	150	64	21	6	20
1998								41
Company Owned 1996							0	1
1997	2	204	4	95	32	1	0	0
1998								2
Number of Units U.S.	4	301	36	235	96	22		
Canada	0	0	0	0	0	0		
Foreign	0	0	0	10	0	0		
Projected New U.S.								83
Canada								
Foreign								
Corporate Employees	2	120	4	50				7
Contract Length	10/5/5	20/15	10/10	20/10/20	10/10			
Expand in Territory	Y	Y	Y	Y	N			
Full-Time Employees	2	2	5	3	12			
Part-Time Employees	4	24	15	10-20	4			
Conversions	Y	N	Y	Y	Y			N
Site Selection Assist.	Y	N	Y	Y	N			Y
Lease Negotiation Assist.	Y	N	Y	Y	N			Y
Site Space Required	1000	2100	2000-3000	2663	1800-2000			750-1500
Development Agreement	N	Y	Y	Y	Y			Y
Develop. Agree. Term								OPEN
Sub-franchising	N	N	N	N	N			

Quick-service Industry   Meals: Mexican (Spread 1 of 3)

Cap'n Taco
16099 Brookpark Rd
Brookpark, OH 44142

Phone: 216-676-9100   Accepts collect calls?
Toll Free: FAX:
Internet:
Suitable Sites: SC
Concentration: 4 in OH
Expansion: All United States, Canada, Foreign
Registered:
Field Support: CP, EO, ST, SO, IC, $FC, N
Training: 2 weeks brook park, OH

Del Taco
23041 Avenida De La Carlota
Laguna Hills, CA 92653

Phone: 714-462-9300   Accepts collect calls?
Toll Free: FAX: 714-462-7444
Internet:
Suitable Sites: FB
Concentration: 265 in CA, 15 in NV, 9 in GA
Expansion: SE, SE, NE, NW
Registered: CA,IL,NY
Field Support: EO, ST, SO, $IC, FC, H, N
Training: 5 days Laguna Hills, CA
6 weeks in-restaurant, CA

Diamond Dave's Taco Company
201 S Clinton St #281
Iowa City, IA 52240

Phone: 319-337-7690   Accepts collect calls?
Toll Free: FAX: 319-337-4707
Internet:
Suitable Sites: RM, SC
Concentration: 14 in IA, 9 in IL, 9 in WI
Expansion: Midwest Only
Registered: IL,MN,SD,WI
Field Support: EO, ST, SO, IC, FC, N
Training: 2-4 weeks local restaurant

El Pollo Loco
3333 Michelson Dr #550
Irvine, CA 92612

Phone: 714-251-5400   Accepts collect calls?
Toll Free: FAX: 714-251-5371
Internet:
Suitable Sites: FB, RM
Concentration: 218 in CA, 6 in NV, 4 in TX
Expansion: SE, CA, TX, NM
Registered: CA
Field Support: CP, EO, ST, SO, FC, H
Training: 5 weeks southern CA

La Salsa Fresh Mexican Grill
10474 Santa Monica Blvd #300
Los Angeles, CA 90025

Phone: 310-446-8744   Accepts collect calls?
Toll Free: 800-527-2572   FAX: 310-446-8733
Internet: www.lasalsa.com
Suitable Sites: RM, SC, SF
Concentration: 62 in CA, 7 in AZ, 6 in UT
Expansion: All United States, Canada
Registered: CA,FL,IL,IN,MD,MI,MN,NY,VA,WA,WI
Field Support: CP, EO, ST, SO, FC, H, N
Training: 5-8 weeks Los Angeles, CA

Nach-O Fast
563 W 500 S #200
Bountiful, UT 84010

Phone: 801-298-0199   Accepts collect calls?
Toll Free: 888-462-2467   FAX: 801-298-0299
Internet: www.nachofast.com
Suitable Sites:
Concentration: 6 in UT, 4 in CA, 4 in WA
Expansion:
Registered: CA,FL,HI,IL,IN,MD,MI,MN,ND,NY,OR,RI,SD,VA,WA,WI,DC
Field Support:
Training:

Nacho Nana's Worldwide Inc
1220 S Alma School Rd #101
Mesa, AZ 85210
Mexican quick-service restaurant
Phone: 602-644-1340   Accepts collect calls?
Toll Free: 800-316-2627   FAX:
Internet:
Suitable Sites:
Concentration:
Expansion: CA,MI
Registered:
Field Support:
Training:

New York Burrito-Gourmet Wraps
955 E Javelina Ave #110
Mesa, AZ 85204
Quick-service gourmet wraps & fresh fruit smoothies, beer & wine
Phone: Accepts collect calls? N
Toll Free: 800-711-4036   FAX: 602-503-1850
Internet: newyorkburrito.com
Suitable Sites: AC, FB, M, RM, SC, SF
Concentration:
Expansion: CA, Canada, Foreign
Registered: CA,FL,MI,OR
Field Support: CP, EO, ST, SO, FC, H, N
Training: 1 week HQ
1 week on-site

Quick-service Industry

Meals: Mexican (Spread 2 of 3)

	Panchero's Mexican Grill	Taco Bell Corp	Taco John's Int'l Inc	The Taco Maker	Taco Mayo	Taco Villa	Tacotime	Tippy's Taco House
Startup Cost	200K-350K	191.4K-470.2K	160K-535.5K	65K-350K	99K-499K	140K-150K	167.5K-295K	150K+
Franchise Fee	15K-25K	45K	19.5K	5K-30K	15K	20K	18K	20K
Royalty	5%	5.5%	4%	5-7%	4%	6%	5%	3%
Advertising Fee	3%				3%	3%	2%	4%	.03%
Financing Provided	N	N	N	Y	Y	Y	N	N
Experience Required				N	N	N		
Passive Ownership	D			D	N	N	N	D
In Business Since	1992	1962	1968	1978	1978	1983	1959	1958
Franchised Since	1995	1964	1969	1978	1980	1985	1960	1968
Franchised Units 1996		2193	414	110				
1997	1	2563	436	125	87	16	327	15
1998				143	86			
Company Owned 1996		2846	15	2				
1997	8	2392	18	2	34	1	4	0
1998				3	34			
Number of Units U.S.	9			135	120	0	208	15
Canada	0			0	0	17	112	0
Foreign	0			8	0	0	11	0
Projected New U.S.				30				
Canada				2				
Foreign				10				
Corporate Employees	6				23	7	27	2
Contract Length	5/5			15	10/10	10/10	15/10	20/20
Expand in Territory	N			Y	Y	Y	Y	Y
Full-Time Employees	2				5	3	5	5
Part-Time Employees	12				16	5	30	3
Conversions	Y			Y	Y	Y	Y	Y
Site Selection Assist.	Y			Y	Y	Y	Y	Y
Lease Negotiation Assist.	Y			Y	Y	Y	Y	Y
Site Space Required	2000			200-3000	900-2200	350-400	1500-2160	1500-2000
Development Agreement	Y			Y	Y	N	Y	Y
Develop. Agree. Term				15	10			
Sub-franchising	N			Y	N	Y	Y	Y

Quick-service Industry   **Meals: Mexican (Spread 2 of 3)**

Panchero's Mexican Grill
PO Box 1786
Iowa City, IA 52244

    Phone: 319-351-4551   Accepts collect calls?
    Toll Free: 888-639-2378   FAX: 319-358-6435
    Internet: www.pancheros.com
Suitable Sites: FB, SC, SF
Concentration: 3 in IA, 2 in MI
    Expansion: Midwest
    Registered: FL,IL,IN,MI,MN,WI
Field Support: CP, EO, ST, SO, IC, FC
    Training: 1 week Iowa City
        7 weeks on-site

Taco Bell Corp
17901 Von Karman
Irvine, CA 92614
Mexican quick-service restaurant
    Phone: 714-863-4500   Accepts collect calls?
    Toll Free: FAX:
    Internet:
Suitable Sites:
Concentration:
    Expansion: All United States, Canada, Foreign
    Registered:
Field Support:
    Training:

Taco John's Int'l Inc
808 W 20th
Cheyenne, WY 82001
Mexican food
    Phone: 307-635-0101   Accepts collect calls?
    Toll Free: FAX:
    Internet:
Suitable Sites:
Concentration:
    Expansion: MW,W,NW
    Registered:
Field Support:
    Training:

The Taco Maker
PO Box 150650
Ogden, UT 84415
Mexican fast food, 50's diner style burgers, fries, shakes
    Phone: 801-476-9780   Accepts collect calls? N
    Toll Free: 800-207-5804   FAX: 801-476-9788
    Internet: www.tacomaker.com
Suitable Sites: AC, FB, FC, M, RM, SC, OTHER
Concentration: 13 in UT, 11 in WA, 72 in PR
    Expansion: All United States, Canada, Foreign
    Registered: CA,FL,HI,IL,IN,MD,MI,MN,ND,NY,OR,RI,SD,VA,WA,WI,DC
Field Support: EO, ST, SO, H, N
    Training: 2 weeks comprehensive at HQ, UT

Taco Mayo
10405 Greenbriar Pl #B
Oklahoma City, OK 73159

    Phone: 405-691-8226   Accepts collect calls?
    Toll Free: 800-291-8226   FAX: 405-691-2572
    Internet:
Suitable Sites: FB, FC, M, RM, OTHER
Concentration: 91 in OK, 15 in TX, 4 in KS
    Expansion: OK,KS,AR,MO,IA,MS,N.TX
    Registered:
Field Support: $DP, CP, EO, ST, SO, FC, H, N
    Training: 3 weeks Tulsa or Oklahoma City, OK
        2 weeks franchise store

Taco Villa
3710 Chesswood Dr #220
North York, ON M3J-2W4 CANADA

    Phone: 416-636-9348   Accepts collect calls?
    Toll Free: 800-608-8226   FAX: 416-636-9162
    Internet:
Suitable Sites: FC, RM
Concentration: 17 in ON
    Expansion: NE, Canada
    Registered:
Field Support: DP, CP, EO, ST, SO, FC, H, N
    Training: 1 week head office
        3 weeks in store

Tacotime
3880 W 11th Ave
Eugene, OR 97402

    Phone: 541-687-8222   Accepts collect calls?
    Toll Free: 800-547-8907   FAX: 541-343-5208
    Internet: www.tacotime.com
Suitable Sites: FB
Concentration: 77 in OR, 47 in AB, 43 in UT
    Expansion: All United States, Canada, Foreign
    Registered: CA,FL,HI,IL,IN,MI,MN,ND,NY,OR,SD,VA,WA,WI,DC
Field Support: CP, EO, ST, SO, IC, $FC, H, N
    Training: 2-4 weeks corp office/regional trng

Tippy's Taco House
5025 Falcon Hollow
Mckinney, TX 75070

    Phone: 972-547-0888   Accepts collect calls?
    Toll Free: FAX: 972-529-1973
    Internet:
Suitable Sites: FB, SC, SF
Concentration: VA, NC
    Expansion: SE, SE, North
    Registered:
Field Support: CP, ST, SO, IC, FC, N
    Training: 1 week closest approved unit

Quick-service Industry

Meals: Mexican (Spread 3 of 3)

	Z-Teca						
Startup Cost	208K-403K						
Franchise Fee	25K						
Royalty	5%						
Advertising Fee							
Financing Provided	Y						
Experience Required							
Passive Ownership							
In Business Since	1995						
Franchised Since	1996						
Franchised Units 1996	0						
1997	0						
1998							
Company Owned 1996	1						
1997	5						
1998							
Number of Units U.S.							
Canada							
Foreign							
Projected New U.S.							
Canada							
Foreign							
Corporate Employees							
Contract Length							
Expand in Territory							
Full-Time Employees							
Part-Time Employees							
Conversions							
Site Selection Assist.							
Lease Negotiation Assist.							
Site Space Required							
Development Agreement							
Develop. Agree. Term							
Sub-franchising							

Quick-service Industry

Z-Teca
1531 Market St
Denver, CO 80202
Fresh Mexican grill
Phone: Accepts collect calls?
Toll Free: 888-349-7277   FAX:
Internet:
Suitable Sites:
Concentration:
Expansion: CA,IL
Registered:
Field Support:
Training:

Quick-service Industry   **Meals: Oriental**

	Ho-Lee-Chow	Made In Japan, Teriyaki Experience	Magic Wok	Manchu Wok (U.S.)				
Startup Cost	150K-175K	90K-135K	95K-150K	150K-750K				
Franchise Fee	INCLUDED	25K	12.5K	20K				
Royalty	6%	6%	5%	7%				
Advertising Fee	3%	2%	3%	1%				
Financing Provided	Y	Y	N	Y				
Experience Required		N						
Passive Ownership	D	D	D	D				
In Business Since	1989	1986	1983	1980				
Franchised Since	1989	1987	1991	1989				
Franchised Units 1996		43						
1997	18	44	12	135				
1998		43						
Company Owned 1996		0						
1997	5	0	10	62				
1998		0						
Number of Units U.S.	0		11	120				
Canada	23	43	0	77				
Foreign	0	5	2	0				
Projected New U.S.		4						
Canada		10						
Foreign		14						
Corporate Employees	20	23	7	20				
Contract Length	5/15	8-15	10/10	5/5				
Expand in Territory	Y	Y	Y	Y				
Full-Time Employees	4		2	3				
Part-Time Employees	1		8	7				
Conversions	Y	Y	Y	Y				
Site Selection Assist.	Y	Y	Y	Y				
Lease Negotiation Assist.	Y	Y	Y	Y				
Site Space Required	900	380-1200	1600	550				
Development Agreement	Y	Y	N	N				
Develop. Agree. Term	20	VAR.						
Sub-franchising	Y	Y	N	N				

Quick-service Industry

Meals: Oriental

Ho-Lee-Chow

658 Danforth Ave #201
Toronto, ON M4J-5B9 CANADA

Phone: 416-778-6660   Accepts collect calls?
Toll Free: 800-465-9924   FAX: 416-778-6818
Internet:
Suitable Sites: FB, SC, SF
Concentration: 19 in ON, 4 in AB
Expansion: All United States, Canada
Registered:
Field Support: DP, CP, EO, ST, SO, IC, FC, H, N
Training: 1 week Toronto, OR
4 weeks on-site

Made In Japan, Teriyaki Experience

2133 Royal Windsor Dr #23
Mississauga, ON L5J-1K5 CANADA
Japanese fast food
Phone: 905-823-8883   Accepts collect calls?
Toll Free: 800-555-5726   FAX: 905-823-8883
Internet: info@donatogroup.com
Suitable Sites:
Concentration: 29 in ONT
Expansion: Y, Canada, Foreign
Registered: IL
Field Support: DP, CP, EO, ST, SO, IC, FC, H, N
Training: initial & ongoing

Magic Wok

2060 Laskey Rd
Toledo, OH 43613

Phone: 419-471-0696   Accepts collect calls?
Toll Free: 800-447-8998   FAX: 419-471-0405
Internet:
Suitable Sites: FB
Concentration: 12 in OH, 6 in MI
Expansion: Midwest, Foreign
Registered: FL,IL,IN,MD,MI,VA
Field Support: EO, ST, SO, IC, FC, H
Training: 3-4 weeks Toledo, OH

Manchu Wok (U.S.)

Quorum Ctr 816 S Military Trl Bldg #6
Deerfield Beach, FL 33432

Phone: 954-481-9555   Accepts collect calls?
Toll Free: 800-423-4009   FAX: 954-481-9670
Internet:
Suitable Sites: RM
Concentration: 20 in FL, ON, IL
Expansion: NE, TX, SC, OH
Registered: CA,FL,IL,IN,MD,MI,MN,NY,ND,VA,WA,WI,DC,AB
Field Support: CP, EO, ST, SO, IC, FC, H, N
Training: 3 weeks

Quick-service Industry

Meals: Sandwiches, Soups, Salad (Spread 1 of 2)

	Brown Baggers	Edelweiss Deli Express / Sub Express	Frullati Cafe	Sandwiches & Frozen Yogurt / Hogi Yogi Franchise Systems, Inc.	Jersey Mike's Franchise Systems, Inc.	Gourmet Sandwich Shops / Jimmy John's	Moe's Italian Sandwiches	The Sandwich Board
Startup Cost	54.8K-122.7K	85K	150K-275K	76.4K-246.8K	150K	178.4K	50K-70K	125K-175K
Franchise Fee	20K	20K	20K	15K	18.5K	12.5K-25K	12.5K	25K
Royalty	6%	6%	6%	6%	5.5%	6%	5%	5%
Advertising Fee	1%	2%	.25%		1%	2%	1%	2%
Financing Provided	N	N	N	Y	Y	N	Y	N
Experience Required	N	N	N		N			
Passive Ownership	A	A	D		A	D	D	D
In Business Since	1988	1973	1985	1989	1956	1983	1959	1981
Franchised Since	1993	1986	1994	1992	1986	1993	1993	1985
Franchised Units 1996	1	15		67				
1997	1	18	45	79		38	15	17
1998	1	20	57					
Company Owned 1996	2			1				
1997	2		30	1		8	0	1
1998	2		37					
Number of Units U.S.	3		94		150	39	15	0
Canada			0			0	0	18
Foreign			0			7	0	0
Projected New U.S.	6	4	30		100			
Canada		4						
Foreign		6						
Corporate Employees	6	6	25		20	10	2	6
Contract Length	10/5/5	20	10/5/5		20	10/5/5	10/10	10/5-10
Expand in Territory	Y	Y	Y		Y	Y	Y	Y
Full-Time Employees	2-3	2	2		2	2	1	3
Part-Time Employees	4-5	3	6		5-15	20	2	
Conversions	Y	Y	Y		N			Y
Site Selection Assist.	Y	Y	Y		Y	Y	Y	Y
Lease Negotiation Assist.	Y	Y	Y		Y	N	Y	Y
Site Space Required	1800	1000	600		1200-1800	1200	900	600-800
Development Agreement	N	Y	Y		Y	Y	N	N
Develop. Agree. Term		20	NEG.		10			
Sub-franchising	N	N	N		N	N	N	N

Quick-service Industry

Meals: Sandwiches, Soups, Salad (Spread 1 of 2)

Brown Baggers
1919 S 40th #202
Lincoln, NE 68506
Sandwich shop/bakery & delivery
Phone: 402-434-5620   Accepts collect calls? N
Toll Free: 800-865-2378   FAX: 402-434-5624
Internet: www.franchisedevelopers.com
Suitable Sites: FB, RM, SF
Concentration: 6 in NE
Expansion: All United States
Registered: CA,FL
Field Support: $CP, EO, ST, SO, H, N
Training: 1 week Nebraska
1 week on-site

Edelweiss Deli Express / Sub Express
Unit 7 3331 Viking Wy
Richmond, BC V6V-1X7   CANADA
Gourmet sandwiches, subs, salads, soup,philly's,breakfast
Phone: 604-270-2360   Accepts collect calls? Y
Toll Free: FAX: 604-270-6560
Internet:
Suitable Sites: AC, FB, FC, IP, K, LI, M, OC, PC, RM, SC, SF, WF, OTHER
Concentration:
Expansion: WA,VA,WV, Foreign
Registered: OR,VA,WV
Field Support: CP, EO, ST, SO, IC, N
Training: 2 weeks
1 week grand opening

Frullati Cafe
5720 Lbj Fwy #370
Dallas, TX 75240

Phone: 972-490-8700   Accepts collect calls? N
Toll Free: 800-289-8291   FAX: 972-490-8787
Internet: www.frulatti.com
Suitable Sites: AC, FC, M, PC, RM, SC
Concentration: 30 in TX, 13 in IL, 8 in FL
Expansion: All United States
Registered: CA,FL,HI,IL,IN,MD,MI,MN,ND,NY,OR,RI,SD,VA,WA,WI,DC
Field Support: EO, ST, SO, FC, H, N
Training: 21 days Dallas, TX
7 days on site

Hogi Yogi Sandwiches & Frozen Yogurt
4833 N Edgewood Dr
Provo, UT 84604
Sandwiches, frozen yogurt & fruit smoothies
Phone: Accepts collect calls?
Toll Free: 800-653-4581   FAX:
Internet:
Suitable Sites:
Concentration:
Expansion: SE,W,NW
Registered:
Field Support:
Training:

Jersey Mike's Franchise Systems, Inc.
2517 Hwy 35 #K201
Manasquan, NJ 08736
Giant size submarine sandwiches, fresh salads & soups
Phone: 732-528-7676   Accepts collect calls? Y
Toll Free: 800-321-7676   FAX: 732-528-7818
Internet: jmikes@injersey.com
Suitable Sites: AC, FB, FC, M, RM, SC, SF
Concentration: 20 in NJ, 60 in NC, 24 in OH
Expansion: All United States, Canada, Foreign
Registered: CA FL HI IL IN MD MI MN ND NY OR RI VA WA WI DC
Field Support: DP, CP, EO, ST, SO, IC, FC, H, N
Training: store operations
marketing

Jimmy John's Gourmet Sandwich Shops
600 Tollgate Rd
Elgin, IL 60123

Phone: 847-888-7206   Accepts collect calls?
Toll Free: 800-594-6904   FAX: 847-888-7070
Internet: www.jimmyjohns.com
Suitable Sites: FB, SC, SF
Concentration: 21 in IL, 6 in MI, 3 in WI
Expansion: All United States, Canada, Foreign
Registered: FL,IL,IN,MI,MN,RI,VA,WI,DC
Field Support: EO, ST, SO, IC, FC, H, N
Training: 3 weeks Champaign, IL

Moe's Italian Sandwiches
95 Court St #200
Portsmouth, NH 03801

Phone: 603-431-0005   Accepts collect calls?
Toll Free: 800-588-6637   FAX: 603-431-5845
Internet: www.moesitaliansandwiches.com
Suitable Sites: FB, SC, SF
Concentration: NH, ME, MA
Expansion: New England & New York
Registered: N
Field Support: EO, ST, SO, IC, FC, H, N
Training: 3 weeks in-store
4 days corporate office

The Sandwich Board
10 Plastics Ave
Etobicoke, ON M8Z-4B7   CANADA

Phone: 416-255-0898   Accepts collect calls?
Toll Free: FAX: 416-255-8086
Internet: www.novacor.net
Suitable Sites: RM, SF
Concentration: 18 in ON
Expansion: N, Canada
Registered:
Field Support: DP, CP, EO, ST, SO, IC, FC, N
Training: 4-6 weeks designated corp store

Quick-service Industry

Meals: Sandwiches, Soups, Salad (Spread 2 of 2)

	Sandwich Tree Restaurants	Schlotzsky's Deli	Select Sandwich					
Startup Cost	50K-150K	300K-1.6M	240K					
Franchise Fee	17.5K	20K	30K					
Royalty	5%	6%	6%					
Advertising Fee	3%	1%	2%					
Financing Provided	Y	Y	Y					
Experience Required	N							
Passive Ownership	D	N	N					
In Business Since	1978	1971	1979					
Franchised Since	1979	1977	1980					
Franchised Units 1996								
1997	43	615	34					
1998								
Company Owned 1996								
1997	0	4	1					
1998								
Number of Units U.S.	0	507	0					
Canada	43	1	35					
Foreign	0	12	0					
Projected New U.S.								
Canada								
Foreign								
Corporate Employees	15	102	8					
Contract Length	5/5/5	20/10	10/10					
Expand in Territory	Y	Y	Y					
Full-Time Employees	4	2	4					
Part-Time Employees	7	12	2					
Conversions	Y	N	Y					
Site Selection Assist.	Y	Y	Y					
Lease Negotiation Assist.	Y	Y	Y					
Site Space Required	1800	3000						
Development Agreement	Y	Y	Y					
Develop. Agree. Term	10	50	10					
Sub-franchising	Y	Y	Y					

Quick-service Industry

Meals: Sandwiches, Soups, Salad (Spread 2 of 2)

Sandwich Tree Restaurants
535 Thurlow St #300
Vancouver, BC V6E-3L2   CANADA
Soup: sandwich franchise
      Phone: 604-684-3314   Accepts collect calls? N
      Toll Free: 800-663-8733   FAX: 604-684-2542
      Internet: phelme@towncore.com
Suitable Sites: FB, FC, IP, LI, M, OS, RM, SF
Concentration: 25 in BC, 7 in NS, 5 in ON
    Expansion: N, Canada, Foreign
    Registered: AB
Field Support: $DP, CP, EO, ST, SO, IC, FC, H, N
    Training: 3 weeks HQ
           1 week Toronto
           1 week Halifax, NS

Select Sandwich
1090 Don Mills Rd #401
Toronto, ON M3B-1P9   CANADA

      Phone: 416-391-1244   Accepts collect calls?
      Toll Free: FAX: 416-391-5244
      Internet:
Suitable Sites: RM, SF
Concentration:
    Expansion: N, Canada
    Registered:
Field Support: $DP, CP, EO, ST, SO, IC, FC, H, N
    Training: 6 weeks location to be determined

Schlotzsky's Deli
200 W Fourth St
Austin, TX 78701

      Phone: 512-469-7500   Accepts collect calls?
      Toll Free: 800-846-2867   FAX: 512-469-7571
      Internet:
Suitable Sites: FB
Concentration: 192 in TX, 28 in CA, 28 in GA
    Expansion: All United States, Canada, Foreign
    Registered: CA,FL,HI,IL,IN,MD,MI,MN,ND,NY,OR,RI,SD,VA,WA,WI,DC
Field Support: CP, EO, ST, SO, IC, FC, H, N
    Training: 3 weeks Austin TX

Quick-service Industry   **Meals: Seafood**

	Arthur Treacher's Fish & Chips	Captain D's Seafood	Chowderhead's Seafood Restaurants	Long John Silver's				
Startup Cost	80K-210K	833.5K-1M	46K-82K	500K-800K				
Franchise Fee	19.5K	20K	11.5K	20K				
Royalty	6%	3%	6%	4%				
Advertising Fee	3%	5.25%	2%	5%				
Financing Provided	N	N	N	N				
Experience Required			N					
Passive Ownership	D	D	N					
In Business Since	1969	1969	1990	1969				
Franchised Since	1970	1969	1997	1970				
Franchised Units 1996								
1997	59	215	0	501				
1998			3					
Company Owned 1996			1					
1997	61	378	1	922				
1998			1					
Number of Units U.S.	111	593	4	1408				
Canada	9	0		0				
Foreign	0	0		15				
Projected New U.S.			4					
Canada								
Foreign								
Corporate Employees	25		6	200				
Contract Length	20/20	20/20	20	15/5/5				
Expand in Territory	Y	Y	Y	Y				
Full-Time Employees	3	5						
Part-Time Employees	12	15						
Conversions	Y	N	Y					
Site Selection Assist.	Y	Y	Y	Y				
Lease Negotiation Assist.	Y	N	N					
Site Space Required	500-2000	2424-2757	1600					
Development Agreement	Y	Y	Y	Y				
Develop. Agree. Term			5-50					
Sub-franchising	Y	N	Y	N				

Quick-service Industry

Meals: Seafood

Arthur Treacher's Fish & Chips
7400 Baymeadows Wy #300
Jacksonville, FL 32256

Phone: 904-739-1200   Accepts collect calls?
Toll Free: 800-321-3113   FAX: 904-739-2500
Internet:
Suitable Sites: FB, RM, SC, SF
Concentration: 51 in OH, 27 in PA, 25 in FL
Expansion: NE & SE
Registered: FL,MI,NY
Field Support: CP, EO, ST, SO, IC, FC, H, N
Training: 3 weeks Jacksonville, FL

Captain D's Seafood
1717 Elm Hill Pike #A-10
Nashville, TN 37210

Phone: 615-231-2616   Accepts collect calls?
Toll Free: 800-346-9637   FAX: 615-231-2790
Internet:
Suitable Sites: FB
Concentration: 97 in GA, 83 in TN, 67 in AL
Expansion: S & SE
Registered: IL,IN,MD,MN,NY,VA
Field Support: CP, EO, ST, SO, $FC, H, N
Training: 6 weeks Nashville, TN

Chowderhead's Seafood Restaurants
430 E. Bridge St.
Westbrook, ME 04092
Quick serve eat in/take-out specialize in chowder & seafood
Phone: 207-854-5052   Accepts collect calls? N
Toll Free: 888-883-8330   FAX: 207-854-5052
Internet:
Suitable Sites: AC, FB, FC, M, RM, SC, SF, WF
Concentration: 3 in ME, 1 in MA
Expansion: ME NH MA RI CN
Registered: RI
Field Support: EO, ST, SO
Training: 2 week two people hands on
cooking, ordering, service
bookkeeping, ads + mktg

Long John Silver's
PO Box 11988
Lexington, KY 40579

Phone: 606-388-6000   Accepts collect calls?
Toll Free: 800-545-8360   FAX: 606-388-6190
Internet:
Suitable Sites: FB, SC, OTHER
Concentration: 185 in TX, 114 in OH, 101 in IN
Expansion: All United States
Registered:
Field Support: EO, ST, SO, $FC, N
Training: 5 weeks closest training shop

Quick-service Industry

Meals: Steak, BBQ

	Arby's	Buddy's Bar-B-Q	The Steak Escape	Steak 'N Shake	Steaks To Go			
Startup Cost	902.9K-1.95M	300K-1M	189K-223K	1.1M-2.4M	85K			
Franchise Fee	37.5K	30K	20K	30K	19.5K			
Royalty	4%	4%	6%	4%	3%			
Advertising Fee	.7-2%	0.25%	.05%	5%				
Financing Provided	N	N	Y	N	N			
Experience Required								
Passive Ownership	A	A	A					
In Business Since	1964	1972	1982	1934	1990			
Franchised Since	1965	1992	1982	1939	1995			
Franchised Units 1996					4			
1997	3057	6	122	55	7			
1998								
Company Owned 1996				1				
1997	0	9	13	194	1			
1998								
Number of Units U.S.	2889	15	132	249				
Canada	116	0	0	0				
Foreign	52	0	3	0				
Projected New U.S.								
Canada								
Foreign								
Corporate Employees	133	9	28	60				
Contract Length	20/VAR.	15/15	10/10	20/20				
Expand in Territory	Y	Y	Y	Y				
Full-Time Employees	10	12	4	20-25				
Part-Time Employees	15-22	10-15	12	30-40				
Conversions	Y	Y	Y	N				
Site Selection Assist.	N	Y	Y	N				
Lease Negotiation Assist.	N	Y	Y	N				
Site Space Required	28000-40000	900-3400	600-1500	3630				
Development Agreement	Y	Y	Y	Y				
Develop. Agree. Term				3-6				
Sub-franchising	N	N	Y	N				

Quick-service Industry   Meals: Steak, BBQ

Arby's
1000 Corporate Dr
Fort Lauderdale, FL 33332

Phone: 954-351-5155   Accepts collect calls?
Toll Free: 800-487-2729   FAX: 954-351-6822
Internet:
Suitable Sites: FB
Concentration: 234 in OH, 162 in CA, 154 in MI
Expansion: All United States, Canada
Registered: CA,FL,HI,IL,IN,MD,MI,MN,ND,NY,OR,RI,SD,VA,WA,WI,DC
Field Support: $CP, EO, $ST, SO, IC, $FC, H, N
Training: 2-3 days specified by Arbys
5 weeks mtp-certified trn loc

Buddy's Bar-B-Q
5806 Kingston Pike
Knoxville, TN 37919

Phone: 423-558-9253   Accepts collect calls?
Toll Free: 800-368-9208   FAX: 423-588-7211
Internet:
Suitable Sites: FB, RM
Concentration: 11 in TN, 4 in KY
Expansion: SE
Registered:
Field Support: CP, EO, ST, SO, IC, H
Training: 60 days gm
30 days managers
7 days on-site

The Steak Escape
222 Neilston St
Columbus, OH 43215

Phone: 614-224-0300   Accepts collect calls?
Toll Free: FAX: 614-224-6460
Internet: www.steakescape.com
Suitable Sites: FB, RM, SC, SF
Concentration: 10 in OH, 10 in CA, 8 in TN
Expansion: All United States, Canada, Foreign
Registered: CA,FL,HI,IL,IN,MD,MI,MN,ND,NY,OR,RI,SD,VA,WA,WI,DC
Field Support: DP, CP, EO, ST, $SO, IC, FC, H, N
Training: 3 weeks Columbus, OH

Steak 'N Shake
36 S Pennsylvania St #500
Indianapolis, IN 46204

Phone: 317-633-4100   Accepts collect calls?
Toll Free: FAX: 317-656-4500
Internet:
Suitable Sites: FB
Concentration: 60 in MO, 51 in IN, 46 in IL
Expansion: Midwest and SE
Registered: FL,IL,IN,MI,VA
Field Support:
Training: 6-8 weeks operating steak n' shake

Steaks To Go
1029 Franklin Rd #33-I
Marietta, GA 30067
Steak/chicken/sandwich delivery
Phone: 770-929-6024   Accepts collect calls?
Toll Free: FAX:
Internet:
Suitable Sites:
Concentration:
Expansion: IL,IN,MN, Canada, Foreign
Registered:
Field Support:
Training:

Quick-service Industry   Meals: Submarine Sandwiches (Spread 1 of 3)

	Admiral Subs	Baldinos Giant Jersey Subs	Blimpie Subs And Salads	Cousins Subs	Erbert & Gerbert's Subs & Clubs	Great Outdoor Sub Shops	Jerry's Subs & Pizza	Larry's Giant Subs
Startup Cost	100K	100K-200K	100K-200K	165K-240K	94.6K-183.8K	75K-265K	150K-225K	110K
Franchise Fee	10K	10K	18K	12.5K	9.5K	25K	10K-25K	15K
Royalty	5%	4.50%	6%	4-6%	6.50%	4%	5%	5%
Advertising Fee	2%	.5%	4%	2%	2%	3%	4%	2%
Financing Provided	Y	N	N	Y	Y	N	Y	Y
Experience Required			N	N				
Passive Ownership	D	N	A	N	D	N	D	N
In Business Since	1980	1975	1964	1972	1987	1973	1954	1982
Franchised Since	1986	1984	1977	1985	1992	1996	1980	1985
Franchised Units 1996								
1997	52	15	1755	102	15	1	97	64
1998			2025					
Company Owned 1996								
1997	1	6	0	35	1	8	3	2
1998								
Number of Units U.S.	53	21	1980	137	16	9	100	65
Canada	0	0	20	0	0	0	0	0
Foreign	0	0	25	0	0	0	0	1
Projected New U.S.			300	32				
Canada			25					
Foreign			25					
Corporate Employees	4	4	95	600	5	8	20	6
Contract Length	10/10	15/10	20	10/10	15/5	10/10	20/OPEN	10/10
Expand in Territory	Y	Y	Y	Y		Y	Y	Y
Full-Time Employees	2	8	3-4	3	2-3	6		3
Part-Time Employees	4	12	8-10	17	10	5		8
Conversions	Y	Y	N	Y	Y	Y	Y	Y
Site Selection Assist.	Y	Y	Y	Y	Y	Y	Y	Y
Lease Negotiation Assist.	Y	Y	Y	Y	Y	Y	Y	Y
Site Space Required	1000	1800-2400	1600	500-2300	1000-2000	2000	2000	1200-1800
Development Agreement	Y	Y	N	Y	Y	Y	Y	Y
Develop. Agree. Term	10	15+		10+		10	20	20
Sub-franchising	N	Y	Y	N	N	N	N	Y

Quick-service Industry

Meals: Submarine Sandwiches (Spread 1 of 3)

Admiral Subs
One Lake Bellevue Dr #201
Bellevue, WA 98005

Phone: 425-453-5216   Accepts collect calls?
Toll Free: 800-453-5216   FAX: 425-454-7951
Internet:
Suitable Sites: SC
Concentration: 47 in WA, 4 in OR, 1 in CA
Expansion: NW, Canada, Foreign
Registered: OR,WA
Field Support: CP, EO, ST, SO, $FC, H, N
Training: 2 weeks Bellevue, WA

Baldinos Giant Jersey Subs
760 Elaine St
Hinesville, GA 31313

Phone: 912-368-2822   Accepts collect calls?
Toll Free: FAX: 912-369-3923
Internet:
Suitable Sites: FB
Concentration: 13 in GA, 5 in NC, 3 in SC
Expansion: GA, SC, NC
Registered: FL
Field Support: CP, EO, ST, SO, IC, FC, H, N
Training: 4 weeks HQ

Blimpie Subs And Salads
1775 The Exchange #600
Atlanta, GA 30339
Subs & salads
Phone: 770-984-2707   Accepts collect calls? N
Toll Free: 800-447-6256   FAX: 770-980-9176
Internet: www.blimpie.com
Suitable Sites: AC, DA, FB, FC, IP, K, LI, M, OC, PC, RM, SC, SF
Concentration: 199 in GA, 179 in FL, 150 in TX
Expansion: All United States, Canada, Foreign
Registered:
Field Support: CP, EO, ST, SO, IC, FC, N
Training: 120 hours on job training
1 week classroom

Cousins Subs
N83 W 13400 Leon Rd
Menomonee Falls, WI 53051
Better bread, better subs, provided by better people
Phone: 414-253-7700   Accepts collect calls?
Toll Free: 800-238-9736   FAX: 414-253-7705
Internet: www.cousinssubs.com
Suitable Sites: AC, DA, FB, FC, IP, K, LI, PC, RM, SC, SF
Concentration: 78 in WI, 16 in MN, 18 in AZ
Expansion: Midwest, SE, West, Canada
Registered: IL,IN,MI,MN,ND,SD,WI,CA,AB
Field Support: CP, EO, ST, SO, IC, FC, H, N
Training: 1 week corporate HQ
4 weeks training store
10 days franchisee's new store

Erbert & Gerbert's Subs & Clubs
320 Graham Ave
Eau Claire, WI 54703

Phone: 715-833-1375   Accepts collect calls?
Toll Free: 800-283-5241   FAX: 715-833-8523
Internet:
Suitable Sites: SC, SF
Concentration: 7 in WI, 5 in MN, 1 in ND
Expansion: All United States
Registered: FL,IL,MI,MN,ND,WI
Field Support: EO, $ST, SO, FC, H, N
Training: 2 weeks home office
1 week on-site during opening

Great Outdoor Sub Shops
900 E Parker Rd
Plano, TX 75074

Phone: 972-424-7823   Accepts collect calls?
Toll Free: FAX: 972-424-7798
Internet:
Suitable Sites: FB, SC
Concentration: 9 in TX
Expansion: All United States
Registered:
Field Support: EO, $ST, $SO
Training: 6 weeks Dallas, TX

Jerry's Subs & Pizza
15942 Shady Grove Rd
Gaithersburg, MD 20877

Phone: 301-921-8777   Accepts collect calls?
Toll Free: FAX: 301-948-3508
Internet:
Suitable Sites: FB, RM, SC
Concentration: MD, VA, DC
Expansion: All United States
Registered: CA,FL,MD,NY,VA,WI,DC
Field Support: CP, EO, ST, SO, IC, FC, H, N
Training: 10 weeks aspen hill, MD

Larry's Giant Subs
8616 Baymeadows Rd
Jacksonville, FL 32256

Phone: 904-739-9069   Accepts collect calls?
Toll Free: 800-358-6870   FAX: 904-739-2502
Internet: www.gentech.net/larrys
Suitable Sites: FB, SC, SF
Concentration: 65 in FL
Expansion: All United States, Canada, Foreign
Registered: FL
Field Support: CP, EO, ST, SO, IC, FC, H, N
Training: 30 days home office
on-site as needed

Quick-service Industry   Meals: Submarine Sandwiches (Spread 2 of 3)

	Mr. GoodCents Subs & Pasta	Mr. Hero	Penn Stations East Coast Subs	Port of Subs	Quizno's Classic Subs	Sobik's Subs	Sub Station Ii	Submarina
Startup Cost	73.8K-160K	111.1K-265K	153.2K-283.2K	134K-200K	129K-199K	44K-126K	75K-150K	142K-182K
Franchise Fee	12.5K	16.5K	25K	16K	20K	10K	10.5K	20K
Royalty	5%	5.5%	4.3-7.5%	5.50%	6%	5%	4%	6%
Advertising Fee	2.5%	4.5%	1-2%	1%	1%	4%	2%	2%
Financing Provided	Y	N	N	Y	Y	N	Y	Y
Experience Required		N						
Passive Ownership	N	A	A	D	D	D	A	N
In Business Since	1989	1969	1985	1972	1981	1969	1975	1977
Franchised Since	1990	1969	1988	1986	1984	1972	1976	1988
Franchised Units 1996								
1997	95	102	62	78	240	50	89	22
1998		117						
Company Owned 1996								
1997	7	13	3	9	12	2	1	1
1998		15						
Number of Units U.S.	101	117	65	87	248	52	90	23
Canada	0	0	0	0	4	0	0	0
Foreign	0	0	0	0	0	0	0	0
Projected New U.S.		25	20					
Canada								
Foreign								
Corporate Employees	40	30	9	17	46	3	8	10
Contract Length	10/10	10/10	5/5/5/5	10/10	15	10/10	10/10	10/10
Expand in Territory	Y	N	Y	Y	Y	Y	Y	Y
Full-Time Employees	1-3	1	11	2	2	2	4	1
Part-Time Employees	10-20	12	10	4-6	6	2	8	6
Conversions	Y	Y	N	Y	Y	N	Y	Y
Site Selection Assist.	Y	Y	Y	Y	Y	Y	Y	Y
Lease Negotiation Assist.	Y	Y	Y	Y	Y	N	Y	Y
Site Space Required	1700	1200-2000	1600-1800	1200	1200	1800-2000	1500	1200
Development Agreement	N	Y	N	Y	Y	Y	N	Y
Develop. Agree. Term		5			10	10		10
Sub-franchising	N	N	N	N	Y	Y	Y	N

Quick-service Industry ·   ## Meals: Submarine Sandwiches (Spread 2 of 3)

Mr. GoodCents Subs & Pasta
16210 W 110th St
Lenexa, KS 66219

Phone: 913-888-9800   Accepts collect calls?
Toll Free: 800-648-2368   FAX: 913-888-8477
Internet: www.mrgoodcents.com
Suitable Sites: FB, SC
Concentration: 38 in KS, 35 in MO, 4 in AZ
Expansion: All United States, Canada, Foreign
Registered: CA,FL,HI,IL,IN,MD,MI,MN,ND,NY,OR,RI,SD,VA,WA,WI,DC
Field Support: EO, $ST, $SO, $FC, H, N
Training: 30 days Kansas City, MO

Mr. Hero
5755 Granger Rd #200
Independence, OH 44131-1410
Adult fast food, hot subs, feature romanburger, Philly-steak etc
Phone: 216-398-1101   Accepts collect calls? N
Toll Free: 800-837-9599   FAX: 216-398-0707
Internet: mrhero@prodigy.net
Suitable Sites: DA, FB, FC, K, M, OC, RM, SC, SF, WF, OTHER
Concentration: 115 in OH, 4 in VA, 1 in NY
Expansion: Midwest, Mid-Atlantic, SE, Canada, Foreign
Registered: FL,IL,IN,KY,MD,MI,VA,WI,DC
Field Support: CP, EO, ST, SO, IC, FC, H, N
Training: 4 weeks independence, OH

Penn Stations East Coast Subs
8276 Beechmont Ave
Cincinnati, OH 45255-3153
Authentic east coast style subs incl Philly cheesesteak
Phone: 513-474-5957   Accepts collect calls? N
Toll Free: FAX: 513-474-7116
Internet:
Suitable Sites: AC, SC, SF
Concentration: 38 in OH, 13 in IN, 12 in KY
Expansion: Midwest, SE, South
Registered: IN
Field Support: EO, ST, SO, IC, FC, N
Training: 6-14 days company restaurant

Port of Subs
5365 Mae Anne Ave #A-29
Reno, NV 89523

Phone: 702-747-0555   Accepts collect calls?
Toll Free: FAX: 702-747-1510
Internet:
Suitable Sites: FB, SC, SF
Concentration: 44 in NV, 33 in CA, 8 in WA
Expansion: NW, Southwest
Registered: CA,HI,WA
Field Support: CP, EO, ST, SO, IC, FC, H, N
Training: 2 weeks HQ
      2 weeks in-store

Quizno's Classic Subs
1099 18th St #2850
Denver, CO 80202

Phone: 303-291-0999   Accepts collect calls?
Toll Free: 800-335-4782   FAX: 303-291-0909
Internet:
Suitable Sites: RM, SC
Concentration: CO, IL, TX
Expansion: All United States, Canada
Registered: CA,FL,HI,IL,IN,MD,MI,MN,ND,NY,OR,RI,SD,VA,WA,WI,DC
Field Support: EO, ST, SO, IC, FC, H, N
Training: 11 days regional mkt
      11 days corp office Denver CO

Sobik's Subs
9400 S Dadeland Blvd #720
Miami, FL 33156

Phone: 305-670-0746   Accepts collect calls?
Toll Free: 800-323-4636   FAX: 305-670-0767
Internet:
Suitable Sites: FB, SC
Concentration: 52 in FL
Expansion: SE
Registered:
Field Support: EO, $ST, $SO, FC, H, N
Training: 2-3 weeks Orlando, FL

Sub Station Ii
425 N Main St
Sumter, SC 29150

Phone: 803-773-4711   Accepts collect calls?
Toll Free: 800-779-2970   FAX: 803-775-2220
Internet:
Suitable Sites: FB, RM, SC, SF
Concentration: 40 in SC, 20 in NC, 15 in CA
Expansion: SE, Southern CA
Registered: CA,FL,VA
Field Support: CP, EO, ST, SO, $FC, N
Training: 7-10 days corp store
      10 days franchisee location

Submarina
10225 Barnes Canyon Rd #A-202
San Diego, CA 92121

Phone: 619-784-0760   Accepts collect calls?
Toll Free: FAX: 619-784-0765
Internet:
Suitable Sites: FB, RM, SC, SF
Concentration: 23 in CA
Expansion: Southern CA, AZ, NV
Registered: CA
Field Support: DP, CP, EO, ST, SO, IC, FC, N
Training: 2 weeks corp office/training
      2 weeks their store

Quick-service Industry

Meals: Submarine Sandwiches (Spread 3 of 3)

	Subs Plus	Subway	Thundercloud Subs	Tubby's Submarines	Zero's Subs			
Startup Cost	150K	66.2K-175K	60K-100K	110K-300K	100K-150K			
Franchise Fee	12K	10K	10K	15K	12.5K			
Royalty	3.5%	8%	4%	6%	5.5%			
Advertising Fee	2%	3.5%		3.5%	2%			
Financing Provided	Y	Y	N	Y	Y			
Experience Required	N							
Passive Ownership	N	N	D	D	D			
In Business Since	1985	1965	1975	1968	1967			
Franchised Since	1991	1974	1989	1978	1990			
Franchised Units 1996								
1997	3	12956	30	83	52			
1998		13537						
Company Owned 1996								
1997	1		8	5	6			
1998		2						
Number of Units U.S.	0	11533	38	87	45			
Canada	4	1278	0	1	0			
Foreign	0	726	0	0	0			
Projected New U.S.					50			
Canada	3							
Foreign								
Corporate Employees	2	550	5	13	15			
Contract Length	10/10	20/20	10+8/4/4	10/10	5/5/5/5/5			
Expand in Territory	Y	Y	Y	Y	Y			
Full-Time Employees	1	2-3	2	2	4			
Part-Time Employees	6-10	6-10	6-12	3	3			
Conversions	Y		Y	Y	Y			
Site Selection Assist.	Y	Y	Y	Y	Y			
Lease Negotiation Assist.	Y	Y	Y	Y	Y			
Site Space Required	1500	500-1500	1000-1500	1200	1600			
Development Agreement	Y	Y	Y	Y	Y			
Develop. Agree. Term	10	20						
Sub-franchising	N	N	N	N	Y			

Quick-service Industry   Meals: Submarine Sandwiches (Spread 3 of 3)

Subs Plus
173 Queenston St
St Catharines, ON L2R-3A2 CANADA
Submarine sandwiches, cakes & pastries baked on-site
    Phone: 905-641-3696   Accepts collect calls? N
    Toll Free: 888-549-7777   FAX: 905-641-3696
    Internet:
Suitable Sites: DA, FB, RM, SC, SF
Concentration: 4 in ON
    Expansion: Canada
    Registered:
Field Support: EO, ST, SO, IC, FC
    Training: 8 weeks head office
        3-4 weeks on-site
        ongoing

Subway
325 Bic Dr
Milford, CT 06460-3059
Submarine sandwiches and salads
    Phone: 203-877-4281   Accepts collect calls?
    Toll Free: 800-888-4848   FAX: 203-876-6688
    Internet: www.subway.com
Suitable Sites: FB, FC, RM, SC, SF, OTHER
Concentration: CA, TX, FL
    Expansion: All United States, Canada, Foreign
    Registered: CA,FL,HI,IL,IN,MD,MI,MN,ND,NY,OR,RI,SD,VA,WA,WI,DC
Field Support: DP, CP, EO, ST, SO, IC, FC, H, N
    Training: 2 weeks Milford, CT
        Costa Rica
        Sydney, Australia

Thundercloud Subs
1102 W 6th St
Austin, TX 78703

    Phone: 512-479-8805   Accepts collect calls?
    Toll Free: 800-256-7895   FAX: 512-479-8806
    Internet: www.thundercloud.com
Suitable Sites: FB, SC, SF
Concentration: 37 in TX
    Expansion: Primarily SE
    Registered:
Field Support: EO, ST, SO, IC, $FC, H, N
    Training: 1-2 weeks corp. HQ Austin, TX
        5-10 days franchisee's store

Tubby's Submarines
6029 East 14 Mile Rd
Sterling Heights, MI 48312-5801

    Phone: 810-978-8829   Accepts collect calls?
    Toll Free: 800-752-0644   FAX: 810-977-8083
    Internet: www.tubby.com
Suitable Sites: SC, SF
Concentration: 77 in MI, 4 in OH, 3 in NJ
    Expansion: All United States, Canada
    Registered: FL,IL,MI,WI,DC
Field Support: EO, ST, SO, FC, N
    Training: 4 weeks HQ/training store
        6 days on-site

Zero's Subs
2106 Pacific Ave
Virginia Beach, VA 23451
Specialize in hot-oven baked subs, pizzas, grilled Philly style
    Phone: 757-425-8306   Accepts collect calls?
    Toll Free: 800-588-0782   FAX: 757-422-9157
    Internet: zeros@norfolk.infi.net
Suitable Sites: SC
Concentration: 51 in VA, 5 in NC, 2 in AZ
    Expansion: Mid-Atlantic, AZ, Foreign
    Registered: FL,VA
Field Support: CP, EO, ST, SO, IC, FC, H, N
    Training: 3-6 weeks Virginia Beach, VA
        2 weeks site assistance

Quick-service Industry

Pizza: Dine-in or Delivery (Spread 1 of 6)

	Ameci Pizza & Pasta	Boston Pizza	Buck's Pizza Franchising, Inc.	Pizza & Pasta Emporium Captain Tony's	Chicago's Pizza	Cici's Pizza	Domino's Pizza Inc	Donatos Pizza
Startup Cost	135K-235K	800K-950K	75K-95K	65K-250K	100K-300K	233K-375K	76.5K-187K	350K-900K
Franchise Fee	25K	65K	10K	10K-20K	10K	25K	0	35K
Royalty	4%	7%	3%	$200-400/WK	4%	4%	5.5%	4%
Advertising Fee	2%	4%	0	0%	2%	3%/2.3K		4%
Financing Provided	N	Y	Y	Y	N	N	N	Y
Experience Required			N		N	N		Y
Passive Ownership	D	D	D	D	N	N		D
In Business Since	1979	1963	1994	1985	1979	1985	1960	1963
Franchised Since	1987	1968	1994	1985	1981	1987	1967	1991
Franchised Units 1996							4790	
1997	41	102	31	10	12	201	4990	42
1998			52			257		52
Company Owned 1996							710	
1997	2	1	0	0	0	24	710	72
1998						24		83
Number of Units U.S.	43	0	31	8	12	281		135
Canada	0	103	0	0	0	0		0
Foreign	0	0	0	2	0	0		0
Projected New U.S.			25		2	331		30
Canada						0		
Foreign						0		
Corporate Employees	7	48	6		3			90
Contract Length	10/10	10/10	10/10	20	10/10	10/10		20/5
Expand in Territory	Y	Y	Y		Y	Y		Y
Full-Time Employees	4	20	2		3	8		15
Part-Time Employees	5	30	8		12	15		20
Conversions	Y	N	N	Y	N	N		Y
Site Selection Assist.	Y	Y	Y	Y	Y	Y		Y
Lease Negotiation Assist.	Y	Y	Y	Y	Y	Y		Y
Site Space Required	1200	5000	1000	1200	1800-3000	3600-4000		2500
Development Agreement	Y	Y	Y		Y	N		Y
Develop. Agree. Term	10/10	10	VAR.		OPEN			20
Sub-franchising	N	N	N		N	N		N

Quick-service Industry

Ameci Pizza & Pasta
6603 B Independence Ave
Canoga Park, CA 91303

Phone: 818-712-0110   Accepts collect calls?
Toll Free: FAX: 818-712-0792
Internet: www.imal.com
Suitable Sites: SC
Concentration: 43 in CA
Expansion: Foreign
Registered: CA
Field Support: DP, CP, EO, ST, SO, IC, FC, H, N
Training: 4 weeks school at home
2 weeks unit location

Boston Pizza
5500 Parkwood Way #200
Richmond, BC V6V-2M4   CANADA
Full service restaurants
Phone: 604-270-1108   Accepts collect calls?
Toll Free: 800-887-7757   FAX: 604-270-4168
Internet:
Suitable Sites: FB
Concentration: 52 in AB, 39 in BC, 5 in SK
Expansion: Pacific NW, Canada, Foreign
Registered: FL,MI,MN,WI,DC,AB
Field Support: CP, EO, ST, SO, IC, FC, N
Training: 8 weeks Richmond, BC

Buck's Pizza Franchising, Inc.
PO Box 405 / 12 Industrial Dr
Du Bois, PA 15801
Pizza, hoagies, stromboli & cheese stix
Phone: 814-371-3076   Accepts collect calls? N
Toll Free: 800-310-8848   FAX: 814-371-4214
Internet: www.buckspizza.com
Suitable Sites: AC, FB, SC, SF
Concentration: 7 in SC, 9 in GA, 6 in TX
Expansion: All United States
Registered: VA,MN,FL,MD,NY,WA,WI
Field Support: EO, ST, SO, IC, $FC, H
Training: 10-14 days on-site
2 days HQ

Captain Tony's Pizza & Pasta Emporium
258 E Altamonte Dr
Altamonte Springs, FL 32701

Phone: 904-736-9855   Accepts collect calls?
Toll Free: 800-332-8669   FAX: 904-736-7237
Internet:
Suitable Sites:
Concentration: 4 in CA, 2 in OH
Expansion: All United States, Foreign
Registered: FL,NY
Field Support: ST, SO, H
Training: 3 weeks Orlando, FL

Chicago's Pizza
1111 N Broadway
Greenfield, IN 46140
Pizza/sandwiches/pasta/drinks
Phone: 317-462-9878   Accepts collect calls? N
Toll Free: FAX:
Internet:
Suitable Sites: FB, SC
Concentration: 10 in IN, 1 in OH, 1 in KY
Expansion: IN, OH, MI, KY, and IL
Registered: IN
Field Support: EO, ST, SO, IC, FC, H
Training: 2 weeks existing store

Cici's Pizza
1620 Rafe St #114
Carrollton, TX 75006-6658
Pizza, salad, dessert, pasta buffets + pizza take-out, family
Phone: 972-398-2424   Accepts collect calls? N
Toll Free: FAX: 972-389-2425
Internet: www.cicispizza.com
Suitable Sites: SC
Concentration:
Expansion: South, SE
Registered: IN,VA
Field Support: CP, EO, ST, SO, IC, FC, N
Training: 6 months Dallas, Houston, Atlanta, Orlando

Domino's Pizza Inc
30 Frank Lloyd Wright Dr
Ann Arbor, MI 48106
Pizza
Phone: 313-930-3030   Accepts collect calls?
Toll Free: FAX:
Internet:
Suitable Sites:
Concentration:
Expansion: All United States, Canada, Foreign
Registered:
Field Support:
Training:

Donatos Pizza
935 Taylor Station Rd
Columbus, OH 43230
Pizza, subs, salads thru delivery, dine-in, pickup window, cater
Phone: 614-864-2444   Accepts collect calls? N
Toll Free: 800-366-2867   FAX: 614-575-4480
Internet:
Suitable Sites: FB, SC, SF
Concentration: 103 in OH, 18 in IN, 5 in KY
Expansion: Midwest and SE
Registered: FL,IL,IN,MD,MI,MN,VA,DC
Field Support: CP, EO, ST, SO, FC, H, N
Training: 6-8 weeks Columbus, OH

Quick-service Industry   Pizza: Dine-in or Delivery (Spread 2 of 6)

	East of Chicago Pizza Company	Family Pizza	Faro's Franchise Systems	Four Star Pizza	Fox's Pizza Den	Godfather's Pizza	Greco Pizza Donair	Happy Joe's Pizza & Ice Cream Parlor
Startup Cost	150K	75K-100K	81K-124.5K	48K-70K	45K-65K	82.5K-358K	150K-180K	50K-1.5M
Franchise Fee	16K	15K	10K	2K	8K	20K	15K	20K
Royalty	5%	4%	4%	5%	$200/MO.	5%	5%	4.50%
Advertising Fee	2%	5%		0%	0%	0%	3%	1%
Financing Provided	Y	Y	Y	Y	Y	N	N	Y
Experience Required	N							
Passive Ownership	D	D		D	D	D	D	D
In Business Since	1990	1983	1991	1981	1971	1973	1977	1972
Franchised Since	1991	1987	1993	1985	1974	1974	1981	1973
Franchised Units 1996	76		9					
1997	89	12	9	38	168	372	52	46
1998	104							
Company Owned 1996	3		0					
1997	2	1	0	7	0	177	2	18
1998	7							
Number of Units U.S.	115	0		27	168	547	0	64
Canada		13		0	0	2	54	0
Foreign		0		18	0	0	0	0
Projected New U.S.	40							
Canada								
Foreign								
Corporate Employees	25	3		6	3	92	19	30
Contract Length	10	5/5		10/10	5/5	15/10	10/5/5	15/10
Expand in Territory	Y	Y		Y	Y	Y	Y	Y
Full-Time Employees		4		3-4	2-3	6	5	4
Part-Time Employees		6		8-10	8-10	20	10	30
Conversions		Y		Y	Y	Y	Y	Y
Site Selection Assist.	Y	Y		Y	Y	Y	Y	Y
Lease Negotiation Assist.	Y	Y		Y	N	N	Y	Y
Site Space Required				1000	1000-2000	3500	1200	3500
Development Agreement	N	Y		Y	Y	Y	Y	Y
Develop. Agree. Term		5		25		5		15
Sub-franchising	Y	N		N	Y	N	Y	N

Quick-service Industry   **Pizza: Dine-in or Delivery (Spread 2 of 6)**

East of Chicago Pizza Company
318 W Walton St
Willard, OH 44890
Pizza, subs & pasta
    Phone: 419-935-3033   Accepts collect calls? N
    Toll Free: FAX: 419-935-3278
    Internet:
Suitable Sites:
Concentration: OH, IN, PA
    Expansion: Canada
    Registered:
Field Support: DP, CP, EO, ST, SO, IC, FC, N
    Training: training programs at HQ
        mgmnt, operations, marketing
        accounting & systems
	Family Pizza
	Bay 10-318 105th St
	Saskatoon, SK S7N-1Z3 CANADA
	
	    Phone: 306-955-0215 Accepts collect calls?
	    Toll Free: FAX: 306-955-0215
	    Internet:
	Suitable Sites: FB, SC
	Concentration: 12 in SK, 1 in AB
	    Expansion: N, Canada
	    Registered: AB
	Field Support: DP, CP, EO, ST, SO, IC, FC, H, N
	    Training: 2-4 weeks in-store

Faro's Franchise Systems
PO Box 150200
Grand Rapids, MI 49515-0200
Pizza & subs
    Phone: 616-949-8187   Accepts collect calls?
    Toll Free: FAX:
    Internet:
Suitable Sites:
Concentration:
    Expansion: MI
    Registered:
Field Support:
    Training:
	Four Star Pizza
	PO Box W
	Claysville, PA 15323
	
	    Phone: 412-484-9235 Accepts collect calls?
	    Toll Free: 800-628-3398 FAX: 412-484-9267
	    Internet:
	Suitable Sites: FB, SC, SF
	Concentration: 15 in PA, 5 in MD, 2 in OH
	    Expansion: PA, VA, MD, WV, OH, NJ, NY
	    Registered: MD,NY,VA
	Field Support: CP, EO, ST, SO, IC, FC, N
	    Training: 2 weeks corporate stores

Fox's Pizza Den
3243 Old Frankstown Rd
Pittsburgh, PA 15239
 	
    Phone: 412-733-7888   Accepts collect calls?
    Toll Free: 800-899-3697   FAX: 412-325-5479
    Internet:
Suitable Sites: FB, SC, SF
Concentration: 101 in PA, 16 in WV, 10 in OH
    Expansion: All United States
    Registered: FL,MD,MI,NY,VA
Field Support: CP, EO, ST, SO, IC, FC, H, N
    Training: 7-10 days on-site
	Godfather's Pizza
	9140 W Dodge Rd #300
	Omaha, NE 68114
	
	    Phone: 402-391-1452 Accepts collect calls?
	    Toll Free: 800-456-8347 FAX: 402-255-2685
	    Internet:
	Suitable Sites: FB, SC
	Concentration: 72 in WA, 47 in IA, 45 in MN
	    Expansion: All United States
	    Registered: CA,FL,IL,IN,MD,MI,MN,OR,SD,WA
	Field Support: ST, H, N
	    Training: 35 days Omaha, NE

Greco Pizza Donair
PO Box 1040 105 Walker St
Truro, NS B2N-5G9 CANADA
 	
    Phone: 902-893-4141   Accepts collect calls?
    Toll Free: 800-565-4389   FAX: 902-895-7635
    Internet:
Suitable Sites: FB, RM, SC, SF
Concentration: 21 in NB, 23 in NS, 5 in NF
    Expansion: N, Canada
    Registered:
Field Support: $DP, $CP, EO, ST, SO, IC, $FC, H, N
    Training: 4 weeks correspondence
        2 days HQ
        3 weeks on-site
	Happy Joe's Pizza & Ice Cream Parlor
	2705 Commerce Dr
	Bettendorf, IA 52722
	
	    Phone: 319-332-8811 Accepts collect calls?
	    Toll Free: FAX: 319-332-5822
	    Internet: www.happyjoe.com
	Suitable Sites: FB, SC, SF
	Concentration: 34 in IA, 12 in IL, 7 in WI
	    Expansion: Midwest
	    Registered: IL,ND,WI
	Field Support: CP, EO, ST, SO, $FC, N
	    Training: 6-12 weeks Iowa

Quick-service Industry   Pizza: Dine-in or Delivery (Spread 3 of 6)

	Hungry Howie's Pizza & Subs	Johnny's New York Style Pizza	La Pizza Loca	Marco's Pizza	Mazzio's Pizza	Mountain Mike's Pizza	Mr. Jim's Pizza	Nancy's Pizzeria
Startup Cost	85K-125K	100K-150K	120K-145K	110K-150K	309K-976K	150K-250K	60K-100K	190K
Franchise Fee	9.5K	22K	10K	12K	25K	20K	10K	20K
Royalty	3-5K	4%	5%	3-5%	3%	5%/1K	5%	5%
Advertising Fee	3%	1%	5%	1%	1%	3%	0%	2%
Financing Provided	Y	N	N	Y	N	Y	Y	N
Experience Required	N	N			N		N	N
Passive Ownership	D	N	A	N	D	N	D	D
In Business Since	1973	1977	1986	1978	1961	1978	1975	1974
Franchised Since	1982	1995	1991	1979	1979	1978	1977	1993
Franchised Units 1996		8						14
1997	371	12	23	79	132	79	66	35
1998	390	17			145			56
Company Owned 1996		3						0
1997	0	3	30	32	97	0	0	0
1998	0	3			106			0
Number of Units U.S.	390	20	53	111	251	79	64	
Canada	1		0	0	0	0	0	
Foreign	0		0	0	0	0	0	
Projected New U.S.	50	7			25		8	
Canada	3							
Foreign	0							
Corporate Employees	20		25	40	75	10	5	12
Contract Length	20/20	10	10/10	10/10	20/5	15/15	15/15	10
Expand in Territory	Y	Y	N	Y	Y	Y	Y	Y
Full-Time Employees	4	4	2	6	2	2	5	3
Part-Time Employees	8	4	13	10	25-35	15	15	17
Conversions	Y		Y		Y	Y	Y	Y
Site Selection Assist.	Y	Y	Y	Y	Y	Y	Y	Y
Lease Negotiation Assist.	Y	Y	Y	Y	N	Y	Y	Y
Site Space Required	1200	2000	1000	1200-1400	3000	2500	1100	1200
Development Agreement	Y		Y	Y	Y	Y	Y	Y
Develop. Agree. Term	20		5	10	5	15	15	VAR.
Sub-franchising	Y	N	N	N	N	N	N	N

Quick-service Industry

Pizza: Dine-in or Delivery (Spread 3 of 6)

Hungry Howie's Pizza & Subs
30300 Stephenson Highway #200
Madison Heights, MI 48071

Phone: 248-414-3300   Accepts collect calls?
Toll Free: 800-624-8122   FAX: 248-414-3301
Internet: www.hungryhowies.com
Suitable Sites: SC
Concentration: 165 in MI, 172 in FL, 13 in CA
Expansion: All United States
Registered: CA,FL,IL,IN,MD,MI,MN,NY,OR,RI,VA,WA,WI,DC
Field Support: CP, EO, ST, SO, IC, $FC, N
Training: 5 weeks Madison Heights, MI

Johnny's New York Style Pizza
834 Virginia Ave
Hapeville, GA 30354

Phone: 404-766-3727   Accepts collect calls? N
Toll Free: FAX: 404-766-0260
Internet:
Suitable Sites: AC, FB, SC, SF
Concentration: 20 in GA
Expansion: SE/GA,FL,AL,NC,TN,SC
Registered:
Field Support:
Training: training in company stores
on-site training

La Pizza Loca
7920 Orangethorpe Ave #202
Buena Park, CA 90620

Phone: 714-670-0934   Accepts collect calls?
Toll Free: 800-676-5622   FAX: 714-670-7849
Internet:
Suitable Sites: FB, SC
Concentration:
Expansion: SE
Registered: CA,FL
Field Support: CP, EO, ST, $SO, FC, H
Training: 4 weeks Buena Park, CA
2 weeks on-site

Marco's Pizza
5252 Monroe St
Toledo, OH 43623
Pizza, hot subs, cheesebread & salad for carry-out & delivery
Phone: 419-885-7000   Accepts collect calls? N
Toll Free: 800-262-7267   FAX: 419-885-5215
Internet:
Suitable Sites: SC, SF
Concentration: 83 in OH, 22 in MI, 6 in IN
Expansion: Midwest
Registered: IN,MI
Field Support: CP, EO, ST, SO, IC, FC, H, N
Training: 7 weeks Toledo, OH
2 weeks in-store

Mazzio's Pizza
4441 S 72nd E Ave
Tulsa, OK 74145-4692
Up-scale Italian restaurant featuring pizza, pasta, calzone, etc
Phone: 918-663-8880   Accepts collect calls? N
Toll Free: 800-827-1910   FAX: 918-641-1236
Internet: www.mazzios.com
Suitable Sites: FB, SC, SF
Concentration: 116 in OK, 40 in AR, 29 in MO
Expansion: South, SE, SE, Midwest
Registered: CA,FL,IL,IN,MI,VA
Field Support: CP, EO, ST, SO, IC, FC, H, N
Training: 8 weeks corporate HQ
3.5 weeks on-site

Mountain Mike's Pizza
4212 N Freeway Blvd #6
Sacramento, CA 95834

Phone: 916-929-3946   Accepts collect calls?
Toll Free: FAX: 916-929-6018
Internet:
Suitable Sites: SC, SF
Concentration: 63 in CA, 1 in NV, 1 in OR
Expansion: All United States
Registered: CA,FL,IL,IN,MD,MI,MN,OR,VA,WI
Field Support: DP, CP, EO, ST, SO, IC, FC, H
Training: 3 weeks boulder, CO/northern CA
2 weeks on-site at opening

Mr. Jim's Pizza
4276 Kellway Cir
Dallas, TX 76244
Pizza, subs & salad delivery
Phone: 972-267-5467   Accepts collect calls? Y
Toll Free: 800-583-5960   FAX: 972-267-5463
Internet: mr.jim
Suitable Sites: AC, FB, SC
Concentration: 58 in TX, 2 in LA, 2 in VA
Expansion: All United States
Registered: OR,VA
Field Support: CP, EO, ST, SO, IC, FC, H, N
Training: 2 months nearby store

Nancy's Pizzeria
15000 S Cicero Ave
Oak Forest, IL 60452
Carry out & delivery thin pizza, stuffed pizza, sandwich, salads
Phone: 708-535-2222   Accepts collect calls?
Toll Free: 800-626-2977   FAX: 708-535-2323
Internet:
Suitable Sites: FB, FC, K, RM, SC, SF, WF
Concentration: 53 in IL, 1 in MD, 1 in IA
Expansion: All United States, Foreign
Registered: CA,FL,IL,IN,MD,MI,VA,WI
Field Support: EO, ST, SO, FC, H, N
Training: detailed & documented training
every aspect of pizza business

Quick-service Industry

Pizza: Dine-in or Delivery (Spread 4 of 6)

	Pizza Delight	Pizza Factory Inc.	Pizza Inn Inc	Pizza Man - He Delivers	Pizza Nova	Pizza Pit	Pizza Pizza Limited	The Pizza Ranch
Startup Cost	150K-350K	130K-226K	67K-429K	80K	120K	100K-230K	80K-150K	200K-500K
Franchise Fee	10K-30K	20K	3.5K-20K	25K		16K-17.5K	30K	10K
Royalty	6-4%	4%	4-5%	4%	6%	5.50%	6%	4%
Advertising Fee	4.5%	1%		4%	4%	1%	6%	1.7-2.2K
Financing Provided	N	N	N	Y	N	Y	Y	Y
Experience Required	N	N					N	N
Passive Ownership	D	D		A	N	D	N	D
In Business Since	1968	1979	1960	1964	1963	1969	1967	1981
Franchised Since	1970	1985	1963	1973	1969	1982	1975	1984
Franchised Units 1996			469					
1997	144	87	479	53	69	37	152	81
1998						33		82
Company Owned 1996			5					
1997	3	3	5	0	1	10	123	8
1998						10		7
Number of Units U.S.	0	90		53	0	47	0	89
Canada	145	0		0	65	0	275	0
Foreign	2	0		0	5	0	0	0
Projected New U.S.						4		
Canada						0	12	
Foreign						0		
Corporate Employees	25	7		8	15	99	830	13
Contract Length	10	20		1+/1+	5/5	10	5/5	10/10/10
Expand in Territory	N	Y		Y	Y	Y	N	Y
Full-Time Employees	5-10	3		6	4	6	3-5	2
Part-Time Employees	5-10	12-15		2	6	9	3-5	20
Conversions	Y	Y		Y	Y	Y	Y	Y
Site Selection Assist.	Y	Y		Y	Y	Y	Y	Y
Lease Negotiation Assist.	Y	Y		Y	Y	Y	Y	Y
Site Space Required	1000-4000	300-2400		1200	800-1100	1500	1200-1500	4000
Development Agreement	N	Y		Y	N	Y	N	Y
Develop. Agree. Term				2		10		
Sub-franchising	N	N		N	N	N	N	N

Quick-service Industry

Pizza: Dine-in or Delivery (Spread 4 of 6)

Pizza Delight
PO Box 23070 331 Elmwood Dr
Moncton, NB E1A-6S8 CANADA

Phone: 506-853-0990   Accepts collect calls?
Toll Free: FAX: 506-853-4131
Internet:
Suitable Sites: AC, ES, FB, RM, SC, SF
Concentration: NB, NF, NS
   Expansion: Maybe MA, ME, Upstate NY, Canada
   Registered: N
Field Support: $DP, CP, EO, ST, SO, IC, $FC, $H, N
   Training: 12 days head office
          10 days on-the-job
          3 days per yr continous

Pizza Inn Inc
5050 Quorum #500
Dallas, TX 75240
Pizza, pasta, salads
   Phone: Accepts collect calls?
Toll Free: 800-284-3466   FAX:
Internet:
Suitable Sites:
Concentration:
   Expansion: All United States, Canada, Foreign
   Registered:
Field Support:
   Training:

Pizza Nova
2247 Midland Ave
Scarborough, ON M1P-4R1 CANADA

Phone: 416-439-0051   Accepts collect calls? N
Toll Free: FAX: 416-299-3558
Internet:
Suitable Sites: FC, M, RM, SC, SF
Concentration: 65 in ON
   Expansion: Canada, Foreign
   Registered:
Field Support: DP, CP, EO, ST, SO, IC, FC, N
   Training: 3 weeks

Pizza Pizza Limited
580 Jarvis St
Toronto, ON M4Y-2H9 CANADA
Fast food takeout & delivery
   Phone: 416-967-1010   Accepts collect calls? N
Toll Free: 800-263-5556   FAX: 416-967-0891
Internet:
Suitable Sites: FB, FC, M, SC, SF
Concentration: 271 in ON, 4 in PQ
   Expansion: N, Canada
   Registered:
Field Support: DP, CP, EO, ST, SO, IC, $FC, H, N
   Training: 7 weeks teaching center
          4-6 weeks in-store

Pizza Factory Inc.
PO Box 989 49430 Road 426
Oakhurst, CA 93644

Phone: 559-683-3377   Accepts collect calls? N
Toll Free: 800-654-4840   FAX: 559-683-6879
Internet: pizzafactoryinc.com
Suitable Sites: SC
Concentration: 53 in CA, 16 in WA, 8 in ID
   Expansion: All United States, Canada, Foreign
   Registered: CA,FL,MN,OR,SD,WA
Field Support: EO, ST, SO, FC, H, N
   Training: 325 hours training stores

Pizza Man - He Delivers
6930 1/2 Tujunga Ave
North Hollywood, CA 91605

Phone: 818-766-4395   Accepts collect calls?
Toll Free: FAX: 818-766-1496
Internet:
Suitable Sites: SF
Concentration: 53 in CA
   Expansion: All United States, Canada, Foreign
   Registered: CA
Field Support: CP, EO, ST, SO, IC, FC
   Training: 2 weeks southern CA

Pizza Pit
4253 Argosy Ct
Madison, WI 53714

Phone: 608-221-6777   Accepts collect calls? N
Toll Free: FAX: 608-221-6771
Internet:
Suitable Sites: SC
Concentration: 40 in WI, 3 in IA
   Expansion: West and Midwest
   Registered: WI
Field Support: CP, EO, ST, SO, IC, FC; N
   Training: 4-6 weeks HQ

The Pizza Ranch
1112 Main St Box 823
Hull, IA 51239
Pizza & chicken
   Phone: 712-439-1150   Accepts collect calls? N
Toll Free: 800-321-3401   FAX: 712-439-1125
Internet: www.pizza-ranch.com
Suitable Sites:
Concentration: 43 in IA, 23 in MN, 15 in SD
   Expansion: Midwest
   Registered: IL,MI,MN,ND,SD,WI
Field Support: EO, ST, SO, IC, FC, H, N
   Training: 2 weeks NW IA
          1 week on-site

Quick-service Industry

Pizza: Dine-in or Delivery (Spread 5 of 6)

	Pizzas By Marchelloni	Pizzeria Uno / Chicago Bar & Grill	Ronzio Pizza	Round Table Franchise Corp	Snappy Tomato Pizza	Straw Hat Pizza	Stuft Pizza & Brewing	Famous Gourmet Pizza	Tony Maroni's
Startup Cost	45K-202K	1.0M-1.8M	80K-115K	400K-471.3K	85K-150K	50K-450K	150K-650K		106.3K-169.5K
Franchise Fee	18.5K	35K	10K	25K	15K	10K	25K		20K
Royalty	5%	5%	4%	4%	5%	2%	3%		5%
Advertising Fee	2%	1%	1.5%		2.5%	.75%	0%		1%
Financing Provided	N	Y	Y	Y	N	Y	N		Y
Experience Required		N				N	N		
Passive Ownership	D	A	A		D	D	D	D	D
In Business Since	1986	1943	1987	1959	1981	1969		1976	1988
Franchised Since	1989	1979	1992	1962	1981	1969		1985	1996
Franchised Units 1996				541		64			
1997	37	70	18	533	46	60		27	7
1998		68				60		27	
Company Owned 1996				20		0			
1997	1	93	0	19	4	0		1	5
1998		96						1	
Number of Units U.S.	38	160	18		40	60		28	12
Canada	0	0	0		1			0	0
Foreign	0	2	0		9			0	0
Projected New U.S.		15				6	5		
Canada		0							
Foreign		2							
Corporate Employees	6	110	2		4	5	2		12
Contract Length	10/10	15/5/5	10/10		15/15	10	20/10		10/10
Expand in Territory	Y	Y	Y		Y	Y	Y	Y	Y
Full-Time Employees	2	35	2		2-3	VAR.	3		2
Part-Time Employees	12	25	13		10	VAR.	8-20		12-15
Conversions	Y	Y	Y		Y	Y	Y	Y	N
Site Selection Assist.		Y	Y		Y	N	Y	Y	Y
Lease Negotiation Assist.	Y	Y	Y		Y	N	Y	Y	Y
Site Space Required	2000	5200-6400	1000		1000-1500	1000-6000	1800-5000		1200
Development Agreement	Y	Y	Y		Y	Y	Y	Y	N
Develop. Agree. Term	10	NEG.	10		15	VAR.			
Sub-franchising	Y	N	N		Y	Y	Y		N

Quick-service Industry

Pizzas By Marchelloni

1051 Essington Rd #270
Joliet, IL 60435

Phone: 815-729-4494   Accepts collect calls?
Toll Free: 800-468-7434   FAX: 815-729-4508
Internet:
Suitable Sites: FB, SC
Concentration: 30 in IL, 4 in WI, 2 in PA
Expansion: Central
Registered: IL,IN,WI
Field Support: EO, $ST, SO, FC, H, N
Training: 2 weeks crest hill, IL

Pizzeria Uno Chicago Bar & Grill

100 Charles Park Rd
West Roxbury, MA 02132-4985
Full service casual theme restaurant
Phone: 617-218-5325   Accepts collect calls? N
Toll Free: 800-449-8667   FAX: 617-218-5376
Internet: pizzeriauno.com
Suitable Sites: AC, FB, M, RM, SC
Concentration: 27 in MA, 21 in NY, 11 in PA
Expansion: All United States, Canada, Foreign
Registered: CA,FL,HI,IL,IN,MD,MI,MN,ND,NY,OR,RI,SD,VA,WA,WI,DC
Field Support: CP, EO, ST, SO, IC, $FC, H, N
Training: 8-12 weeks CO operated units 3 person

Ronzio Pizza

194 Waterman Street
Providence, RI 02906

Phone: 401-751-4470   Accepts collect calls?
Toll Free: FAX: 401-331-4720
Internet:
Suitable Sites: SC, SF
Concentration: 18 in RI
Expansion: RI, CT, MA
Registered: RI
Field Support: CP, EO, ST, SO, IC, FC, N
Training: 2 weeks Cumberland, RI

Round Table Franchise Corp

2175 N California Blvd #400
Walnut Creek, CA 94596
Pizza
Phone: 510-274-1700   Accepts collect calls?
Toll Free: FAX:
Internet:
Suitable Sites:
Concentration:
Expansion: SE,W,NW
Registered:
Field Support:
Training:

Snappy Tomato Pizza

PO Box 336 7230 Turfway Rd
Florence, KY 41042

Phone: 606-525-4680   Accepts collect calls?
Toll Free: 888-463-7627   FAX: 606-525-4686
Internet:
Suitable Sites: SC
Concentration: 12 in KY, 8 in OH, 3 in FL
Expansion: All United States, Canada, Foreign
Registered: FL,IN
Field Support: CP, EO, ST, SO, IC, FC, H, N
Training: var.

Straw Hat Pizza

6400 Village Pkwy
Dublin, CA 94568
Pizza, salads & sandwiches
Phone: 925-829-1500   Accepts collect calls?
Toll Free: FAX:
Internet: www.strawhatpizza.com
Suitable Sites: AC, FB, M, RM
Concentration: 57 in CA, 3 in NV
Expansion: CA,WA
Registered: CA,HI,WA
Field Support: EO, ST, SO, FC, H, N
Training: 4 weeks hands-on in operating unit

Stuft Pizza & Brewing

1040 Calle Cordillera #103
San Clemente, CA 92673
Pizza, pasta & microbrewery
Phone: 714-361-2522   Accepts collect calls?
Toll Free: FAX: 714-361-2501
Internet: jbertstuft@aol.com
Suitable Sites: DA, FB, FC, K, M, PC, RM, SC, SF
Concentration: 24 in CA, 4 in OR
Expansion: SE
Registered: CA,OR
Field Support: EO, ST, SO, FC, N
Training: 2 weeks San Clemente, CA

Tony Maroni's Famous Gourmet Pizza

222 112th Ave NE #L-105
Bellevue, WA 98004

Phone: 425-453-8561   Accepts collect calls?
Toll Free: 800-884-4534   FAX: 425-453-7367
Internet:
Suitable Sites: SC
Concentration: 3 in WA
Expansion: West Coast, Canada
Registered: CA,HI,OR,WA
Field Support: $CP, EO, ST, SO, IC, FC, H, N
Training: 3 weeks Bellevue, WA

Quick-service Industry   ## Pizza: Dine-in or Delivery (Spread 6 of 6)

	Villa Pizza						
Startup Cost	190K-400K						
Franchise Fee	29K						
Royalty	4.50%						
Advertising Fee	1.5%						
Financing Provided	N						
Experience Required	Y						
Passive Ownership	N						
In Business Since	1964						
Franchised Since	1995						
Franchised Units 1996							
1997	2						
1998							
Company Owned 1996							
1997	100						
1998							
Number of Units U.S.	99						
Canada	0						
Foreign	1						
Projected New U.S.	20						
Canada							
Foreign	2						
Corporate Employees	25						
Contract Length	10/10						
Expand in Territory	N						
Full-Time Employees	2						
Part-Time Employees	4-7						
Conversions	Y						
Site Selection Assist.	Y						
Lease Negotiation Assist.	Y						
Site Space Required	600-1200						
Development Agreement	N						
Develop. Agree. Term							
Sub-franchising	N						

Quick-service Industry   **Pizza: Dine-in or Delivery (Spread 6 of 6)**

Villa Pizza
17 Elm St
Morristown, NJ 07960
Quick-service pizza & Italian restaurant
Phone: 973-285-4800   Accepts collect calls? N
Toll Free: FAX: 973-285-5252
Internet:
Suitable Sites: FC, M, RM
Concentration: 10 in PA, 10 in TX, 7 in VA
Expansion: All United States, Canada, Foreign
Registered: FL,IN,NY,VA,WA
Field Support: CP, EO, ST, SO, IC, FC, H, N
Training: 2-3 weeks training

Quick-service Industry

Pizza: Take and Bake

	Mom's Bake At Home Pizza	Papa Murphy's						
Startup Cost	50K	115K-165K						
Franchise Fee	15K	25K						
Royalty	0%	5%						
Advertising Fee	0%	1%						
Financing Provided	N	Y						
Experience Required								
Passive Ownership	N	N						
In Business Since	1961	1981						
Franchised Since	1981	1982						
Franchised Units 1996								
1997	17	268						
1998								
Company Owned 1996								
1997	0	3						
1998								
Number of Units U.S.	18	271						
Canada	0	0						
Foreign	0	0						
Projected New U.S.								
Canada								
Foreign								
Corporate Employees	12	43						
Contract Length	ON-GOING	10/5						
Expand in Territory	N	N						
Full-Time Employees	1	2						
Part-Time Employees	2	8						
Conversions	N	Y						
Site Selection Assist.	Y	Y						
Lease Negotiation Assist.	Y	Y						
Site Space Required	800	1200						
Development Agreement	N	N						
Develop. Agree. Term								
Sub-franchising	N	N						

Quick-service Industry

Pizza: Take and Bake

Mom's Bake At Home Pizza
4457 Main St
Philadelphia, PA 19127

Phone: 215-482-1044   Accepts collect calls?
Toll Free: FAX: 215-482-0402
Internet:
Suitable Sites: SC
Concentration: 12 in PA, 6 in NJ
Expansion: PA, NJ
Registered:
Field Support: CP, EO, ST, SO
Training: 7 days existing franchise

Papa Murphy's
8000 NE Parkway Dr #350
Vancouver, WA 98662

Phone: 360-260-7272   Accepts collect calls?
Toll Free: 800-257-7272   FAX: 360-260-0500
Internet:
Suitable Sites: FB, SC, SF
Concentration: CA, OR, WA
Expansion: West, NW, Midwest
Registered: CA,ND,OR,SD,WA
Field Support: CP, EO, ST, SO, IC, FC, H, N
Training: 100 hours in store
2 weeks in-store
5 days corporate office

Quick-service Industry

Other Quick-service (Spread 1 of 3)

	1 Potato 2	A. L. Van Houtte	Buscemi's International	Caterina's	Checkers Drive-In Restaurants	Cultures Restaurants	Culvers Franchising System	Fast Eddie's
Startup Cost	90K-180K	200K-250K	250K-450K	149K-255K	382.1K-522.7K	230K-285K	800K-1.5M	200K-400K
Franchise Fee	20K	40K	15K	19K	30K	35K	35K	15K
Royalty	4.50%	5%	2%	5%	4%	5%	4%	4-6%
Advertising Fee	1.75%	2%	1%	1%	.25%+4.75%	3%	2%	2%
Financing Provided	Y	Y	Y	N	N	N	N	N
Experience Required						N		
Passive Ownership	D	D	D	D	N	D	N	N
In Business Since	1977	1919	1956	1990	1986	1977	1984	1989
Franchised Since	1984	1983	1975	1993	1989	1981	1987	1989
Franchised Units 1996								
1997	33	94	20	2	249	37	53	0
1998								
Company Owned 1996								
1997	6	14	0	2	232	6	3	6
1998								
Number of Units U.S.	39	0	20	4	481	0	56	0
Canada	0	108	0	0	0	43	0	6
Foreign	0	0	0	0	0	0	0	0
Projected New U.S.								
Canada								
Foreign								
Corporate Employees	9	35	4		~100	45	17	18
Contract Length	8-10/8-10	10/5	15/5	10/10	20/AGRMT	10	15/15	N/A
Expand in Territory	Y	N	Y	Y	Y	Y	Y	Y
Full-Time Employees	2-3	4	10	4	10	7	10	3
Part-Time Employees	6-8	8	10	3	20	6	35	15
Conversions	Y	Y	Y	N	Y	Y	Y	N
Site Selection Assist.	Y	Y	Y	Y	Y	Y	Y	Y
Lease Negotiation Assist.	Y	Y	Y	Y		Y	Y	Y
Site Space Required	450-700	1500	3000-4000	1000	15000	500-1800	44000	900
Development Agreement	Y	Y	Y	N	Y	Y	N	N
Develop. Agree. Term		10	5			5		
Sub-franchising	N	N	Y	N	Y	N	N	N

Quick-service Industry

Other Quick-service (Spread 1 of 3)

1 Potato 2

7000 Bass Lake Rd #200
Minneapolis, MN 55428

Phone: 612-537-3833   Accepts collect calls?
Toll Free: 800-333-8034   FAX: 612-537-4241
Internet: www.1potato2.com
Suitable Sites: RM
Concentration: 10 in MN, 8 in WI, 6 in CA
Expansion: West & Midwest
Registered: CA,IL,IN,MN,WI
Field Support: DP, CP, EO, ST, SO, IC, FC, H, N
Training: 2 weeks Minneapolis, MN

A. L. Van Houtte

8470 19th Ave
Montreal, PQ H1Z-4J3   CANADA

Phone: 514-593-7711   Accepts collect calls?
Toll Free: 800-361-5628   FAX: 514-593-8755
Internet:
Suitable Sites: FB, RM, SC, SF
Concentration: 104 in PQ, 4 in ON
Expansion: All United States, Canada, Foreign
Registered:
Field Support: CP, EO, ST, SO, FC, H, N
Training: 2 weeks training schools
3 weeks training store
10 days actual store

Buscemi's International

30362 Gratiot Ave
Roseville, MI 48066

Phone: 810-296-5560   Accepts collect calls?
Toll Free: FAX: 810-296-3366
Internet:
Suitable Sites: FB, SC
Concentration: 20 in MI
Expansion: NW, Canada, Foreign
Registered: MI
Field Support: CP, EO, ST, SO, $IC, FC, $H, N
Training: 4 weeks in-store
1 week corporate office

Caterina's

415 Avenida Pico #N2
San Clemente, CA 92672

Phone: 714-492-7431   Accepts collect calls?
Toll Free: 800-765-4311   FAX: 714-492-9585
Internet:
Suitable Sites: RM, SC, SF, OTHER
Concentration: 4 in CA
Expansion: W, SE, NW
Registered: CA
Field Support: EO, ST, SO, H
Training: 1 week corporate store
1 week on-site
1 day grand opening

Checkers Drive-In Restaurants

600 Cleveland St 8th Fl
Clearwater, FL 33755

Phone: 813-441-3500   Accepts collect calls?
Toll Free: 800-275-3628   FAX: 813-461-0136
Internet:
Suitable Sites: FB
Concentration: 191 in FL, 85 in GA, 32 in AL
Expansion: Eastern United States
Registered: FL,IL,IN,MD,MI,MN,NY,VA,WA,WI,DC
Field Support: DP, CP, EO, ST, SO, IC, FC, H, N
Training: 4-6 weeks Atlanta, GA
4-6 weeks clearwater, FL

Cultures Restaurants

20 Bay St #1605
Toronto, ON M5J-2N8   CANADA

Phone: 416-368-1440   Accepts collect calls?
Toll Free: FAX: 416-368-0804
Internet: srishikof@compuserve.com
Suitable Sites: RM, SF
Concentration: 41 in ON, 2 in PQ
Expansion: All United States, Canada, Foreign
Registered:
Field Support: CP, EO, SO, FC
Training: 4-6 weeks Toronto, ON

Culvers Franchising System

107 Berkley Blvd #A
Baraboo, WI 53913

Phone: 608-356-5938   Accepts collect calls?
Toll Free: FAX: 608-356-9017
Internet:
Suitable Sites: FB, RM, SC
Concentration: 49 in WI, 3 in IL, 2 in MN
Expansion: Midwest - WI To TX
Registered: MIDWEST STATES
Field Support: EO, ST, SO, FC, N
Training: 12 weeks Sauk City, WI

Fast Eddie's

129 Wellington St #102
Brantford, ON N3T-5Z9   CANADA

Phone: 519-758-0111   Accepts collect calls?
Toll Free: FAX: 519-758-1393
Internet:
Suitable Sites: FB
Concentration: 6 in ON
Expansion: N, Canada
Registered: N
Field Support: EO, ST, SO, IC
Training: 2 weeks Brantford, ON

Quick-service Industry

Other Quick-service (Spread 2 of 3)

	Great Wraps	Hard Times Cafe	Lindy - Gertie's	Little King	My Friend's Place	New York Fries	Old Fashioned Egg Cream Co Inc	Pasta To Go
Startup Cost	200K-250K	423.5K-568.5K		65K-85K	95K-175K	125K-175K	20K	85K-132K
Franchise Fee	25K	30K	9.5K	12.5K	17.5K	25K	10K-15K	25K
Royalty	6%	4%	6%	6%	FLAT	6%	5%	5%
Advertising Fee	2.5%	2%	2%	1%	FLAT	1.5%		2%
Financing Provided	Y	N	Y	Y	N	N	N	Y
Experience Required								
Passive Ownership	D	N	N	D	N	A		D
In Business Since	1974	1980	1986	1977	1980	1984	1994	1987
Franchised Since	1980	1988	1987	1978	1990	1984	1994	1992
Franchised Units 1996							1	
1997	40	2	9	41	10	104	1	98
1998								
Company Owned 1996							0	
1997	0	3	1	2	2	12	0	1
1998								
Number of Units U.S.	38	5	10	43	12	2		105
Canada	0	0	0	0	0	114		0
Foreign	2	0	0	0	0	0		0
Projected New U.S.								
Canada								
Foreign								
Corporate Employees	11	15	1	2	4	15		4
Contract Length	10/10	10/10	10/10	15/15	15/10	10/5/5		10/10
Expand in Territory	Y	Y	Y	Y	Y	Y		N
Full-Time Employees	5	3	1	2	2	2		3-4
Part-Time Employees	6	27	2	8	2	6		5
Conversions	Y		Y	Y	Y			Y
Site Selection Assist.	Y	Y	Y	Y	Y	Y		Y
Lease Negotiation Assist.	Y	Y	Y	Y	Y	Y		Y
Site Space Required	600-1500	3300-3500		1200-1500	400-1500	200-300		1500-2000
Development Agreement	Y	Y	N	Y	N	N		Y
Develop. Agree. Term				10				10
Sub-franchising	N	N	N	Y	Y	N		N

Quick-service Industry

Other Quick-service (Spread 2 of 3)

Great Wraps
57 Executive Park S #440
Atlanta, GA 30329

Phone: 404-248-9900   Accepts collect calls?
Toll Free: 888-489-7277   FAX: 404-248-0180
Internet:
Suitable Sites: OTHER
Concentration: 19 in GA, 9 in FL, 3 in NC
    Expansion: NE, SE, Midwest, Foreign
    Registered: CA,FL,VA
Field Support: CP, EO, ST, SO, FC, N
    Training: 3 weeks Atlanta, GA

Hard Times Cafe
310 Commerce St
Alexandria, VA 22314

Phone: 703-893-0167   Accepts collect calls?
Toll Free: 888-482-4454   FAX: 703-893-1068
Internet: www.hardtimescafe.com
Suitable Sites: FB, SC, SF
Concentration: 3 in VA, 2 in MD
    Expansion: Eastern United States
    Registered: MD,VA
Field Support: EO, ST, SO, FC, H, N
    Training: 6 weeks dc metro area

Lindy - Gertie's
8437 Park Ave
Burr Ridge, IL 60521

Phone: 630-323-8003   Accepts collect calls?
Toll Free: FAX: 630-323-5449
Internet:
Suitable Sites: FB, RM, SC, SF
Concentration: 10 in IL
    Expansion: Illinois
    Registered: IL
Field Support: ST, SO
    Training: 1 week Chicago, IL
       1 week Chicago, IL

Little King
11811 I St
Omaha, NE 68137

Phone: 402-330-8019   Accepts collect calls?
Toll Free: 800-788-9478   FAX: 402-330-3221
Internet:
Suitable Sites:
Concentration: 29 in NE, 3 in IA, 2 in SD
    Expansion: Midwest
    Registered:
Field Support: CP, EO, ST, SO, IC, FC, H, N
    Training: 15 days Omaha HQ
       8 days on-site
       follow up as needed

My Friend's Place
106 Hammond Dr
Atlanta, GA 30328

Phone: 404-843-2803   Accepts collect calls?
Toll Free: FAX:
Internet:
Suitable Sites: RM, SC
Concentration: 10 in GA
    Expansion: SE Only, GA, FL, AL, NC, TX
    Registered:
Field Support: $CP, EO, $ST, SO, $IC
    Training: 12 days HQ
       12 days franchisee site

New York Fries
1220 Yonge St #400
Toronto, ON M4T-1W1 CANADA

Phone: 416-963-5005   Accepts collect calls?
Toll Free: 800-922-4350   FAX: 416-963-4920
Internet:
Suitable Sites: RM
Concentration: 64 in ON, 18 in BC, 17 in AB
    Expansion: Y, Canada, Foreign
    Registered: AB
Field Support: CP, EO, $ST, SO, $FC, N
    Training: 1 week Toronto on
       1 week on-site

Old Fashioned Egg Cream Co Inc
4270 NW 19th Ave #D
Pompano Beach, FL 33064
Egg cream drinks & specialty confections
Phone: 954-969-1600   Accepts collect calls?
Toll Free: FAX:
Internet:
Suitable Sites:
Concentration:
    Expansion: NY
    Registered:
Field Support:
    Training:

Pasta To Go
15965 Jeanette
Southfield, MI 48075

Phone: 248-557-2784   Accepts collect calls?
Toll Free: 800-745-1415   FAX: 248-557-7931
Internet:
Suitable Sites: RM, SC, SF
Concentration: 31 in TX, 25 in TX, 8 in MI
    Expansion: All United States
    Registered: MI,WI
Field Support: $DP, CP, EO, ST, SO, IC, FC, N
    Training: 10 days home office
       10 days franchisee site

Quick-service Industry

Other Quick-service (Spread 3 of 3)

	Pastel's Cafe	Petro's Chili & Chips	Renzios	Roli Boli			
Startup Cost	160K-250K	180K-350K	130K-199K	130K-195K			
Franchise Fee	25K	17.5K	15K	20K			
Royalty	5%	5%	5%	5%			
Advertising Fee	0%	0	2%	0%			
Financing Provided	Y	Y	Y	N			
Experience Required		N					
Passive Ownership	D	D	D	N			
In Business Since	1980	1985	1986	1987			
Franchised Since	1982	1991	1993	1987			
Franchised Units 1996							
1997	20	11	15	11			
1998							
Company Owned 1996							
1997	0	4	10	3			
1998							
Number of Units U.S.	0	15	25	13			
Canada	20	0	0	0			
Foreign	0	0	0	0			
Projected New U.S.		20					
Canada		0					
Foreign		0					
Corporate Employees	12	75	8	6			
Contract Length	10/10	10/5	10/5/5	10/10			
Expand in Territory	Y	Y	Y	Y			
Full-Time Employees	2	4-7	3	2			
Part-Time Employees	5	5-15	5	4			
Conversions	Y	N	Y				
Site Selection Assist.	Y	Y	Y	Y			
Lease Negotiation Assist.	Y	Y	Y	Y			
Site Space Required	1100	600	500-800	600			
Development Agreement	N	Y	Y	Y			
Develop. Agree. Term		NEG.	10				
Sub-franchising	N	N	N	N			

Quick-service Industry

Other Quick-service (Spread 3 of 3)

Pastel's Cafe

1121 Centre St N #440
Calgary, AB T2E-7K6   CANADA

Phone: 403-230-1151   Accepts collect calls?
Toll Free: 800-361-1151   FAX: 403-230-2182
Internet:
Suitable Sites: RM, SC, SF
Concentration: 15 in BC
Expansion: N, Canada
Registered: AB
Field Support: EO, ST, SO, $IC, $FC, N
Training: 21 days comp hands-on training

Petro's Chili & Chips

5614 Kingston Pike 2nd Fl
Knoxville, TN 37919
SW theme, specialize in chips, chili & delicious toppings
Phone: 423-588-1076   Accepts collect calls? N
Toll Free: 800-738-7639   FAX: 423-588-0916
Internet: www.petros.com
Suitable Sites: AC, AM, DA, FB, FC, IP, K, M, OC, RM, SC, SF, WF, OTHER
Concentration: 13 in TN, 1 in KY, 1 in AL
Expansion: All United States, Canada, Foreign
Registered:
Field Support: CP, EO, ST, SO, IC, FC, H, N
Training: 2 weeks min in Knoxville, TN
ongoing support & training
regular visits to stores

Renzios

4690 S Yosemite St
Greenwood Village, CO 80111

Phone: 303-267-0300   Accepts collect calls?
Toll Free: 800-892-3441   FAX: 303-267-0088
Internet:
Suitable Sites: RM, SC
Concentration: 10 in CO, 2 in NV, 4 in TX
Expansion: All United States, Canada
Registered: N
Field Support: CP, EO, ST, SO, IC, FC, H, N
Training: 21 days corp training center
5 days on-location

Roli Boli

109 Main St
Sayreville, NJ 08872

Phone: 732-257-8100   Accepts collect calls?
Toll Free: FAX: 732-257-3255
Internet:
Suitable Sites: RM
Concentration: 8 in NJ, 1 in CA, 1 in NC
Expansion: All United States, Canada, Foreign
Registered: CA,FL,NY
Field Support: EO, ST, SO, IC, N
Training: 2 weeks company store
1 week franchisee location

Real Estate Industry   Property Inspection (Spread 1 of 2)

	AmBIC Building Inspection Consult	AmeriSpec Home Inspection Service	The Brickkicker	Building Systems Analysis Inc.	Criterium Engineers	Critter Control	EnviroFree Inspections	The Hometeam Inspection Service
Startup Cost	10K-16.5K	25K-65K	19.4K-39.9K	9.8K-23.4K	25K	5K-25K	25K-40K	17.5K-44.6K
Franchise Fee	10K-16.5K	13.9K-23.9K	6.9K-12.9K	12.5K-17.5K	21.5K	15K-24K	15K	10.9K-28.9K
Royalty	6%	7%/$250	6%	5-6%	6%	6%+	$100/WK	6%
Advertising Fee		3%/$125	2%		1%	1-2%	4%	3%
Financing Provided	Y	Y	Y	N	Y	N	Y	Y
Experience Required		N			Y			N
Passive Ownership		D	D		N	D	N	A
In Business Since	1987	1987	1989	1976	1957	1983	1997	1991
Franchised Since	1988	1988	1995	1996	1989	1988	1997	1993
Franchised Units 1996	30			0	64			
1997	29	281	77	4	66	55	5	230
1998		296			66			
Company Owned 1996	0			1	0			
1997	0	0	2	1	0	42	0	0
1998		0			0			
Number of Units U.S.		250	79		66	95	5	275
Canada		40	0		0	1	0	3
Foreign		0	0		0	0	0	0
Projected New U.S.		48			6			36
Canada		10			1			2
Foreign		0						1
Corporate Employees		31	7		10	7	9	30
Contract Length		5/5/5	7/20		15/5	10/10	10/5	10/10/10
Expand in Territory		Y	Y		Y	N	N	Y
Full-Time Employees		1-2	1		2	2	1	1
Part-Time Employees		1-2			2			
Conversions		Y	Y			N	Y	Y
Site Selection Assist.		Y	N		N	Y	N	N
Lease Negotiation Assist.		N			N			
Site Space Required		300-500			300			
Development Agreement		N	N		N	N	N	N
Develop. Agree. Term								
Sub-franchising		N	N		N	N	N	N

Real Estate Industry   **Property Inspection (Spread 1 of 2)**

Ambic Building Inspection Consult
1200 Rte 130
Robbinsville, NJ 08691
Home/building inspections
    Phone: 609-448-3900   Accepts collect calls?
    Toll Free: 800-882-6242   FAX:
    Internet:
Suitable Sites:
Concentration:
    Expansion: CA,IL
    Registered:
Field Support:
    Training:

Amerispec Home Inspection Service
860 Ridge Lake Blvd
Memphis, TN 38120
Residential and small commercial inspection services
    Phone: 901-820-8500   Accepts collect calls? N
    Toll Free: 800-426-2270   FAX: 901-820-8520
    Internet: www.amerispec.com
Suitable Sites: HO
Concentration: 33 in CA, 13 in IL, 15 in FL
    Expansion: All United States, Canada, Foreign
    Registered: CA,FL,HI,IL,IN,MD,MI,MN,ND,NY,OR,RI,SD,VA,WA,WI,DC
Field Support: DP, CP, EO, ST, SO, IC, $FC, $H, N
    Training: 2 weeks Memphis TN
                operations, marketing, risk-management
                technical

The BrickKicker
1200 Iroquois Dr
Naperville, IL 60563

    Phone: 630-420-9900   Accepts collect calls?
    Toll Free: 800-821-1820   FAX: 630-420-2270
    Internet:
Suitable Sites:
Concentration: 16 in MI, 8 in WI, 7 in IN
    Expansion: All United States, Canada
    Registered: CA,FL,HI,IL,IN,MD,MI,MN,ND,NY,OR,RI,SD,VA,WA,WI,DC
Field Support: CP, EO, ST, SO, FC, H, N
    Training: 10 days Naperville IL
              3 days on-site

Building Systems Analysis Inc.
1872 Independence Sq, #A
Atlanta, GA 30338
Property inspections
    Phone: 770-454-9333   Accepts collect calls?
    Toll Free: FAX:
    Internet:
Suitable Sites:
Concentration:
    Expansion: SE,S
    Registered:
Field Support:
    Training:

Criterium Engineers
650 Brighton Ave
Portland, ME 04102
Res. Comm. & ind. Building inspection & engineering consulting
    Phone: 207-828-1969   Accepts collect calls? N
    Toll Free: 800-242-1969   FAX: 207-775-4405
    Internet: criterium-engineers.com
Suitable Sites:
Concentration: 5 in CA, 2 in FL, 2 in NJ
    Expansion: All United States, Canada
    Registered: CA,FL,IN,NY,RI,IL MI MN
Field Support: CP, EO, ST, FC, H, N
    Training: 1 week HQ

Critter Control
10244 San Remo
Traverse City, MI 49684

    Phone: 616-947-8164   Accepts collect calls?
    Toll Free: 800-451-6544   FAX: 616-929-0373
    Internet: crittercontrol.com
Suitable Sites: HO
Concentration: 10 in MI, 7 in OJ, 6 in PA
    Expansion: NE,SE, Canada
    Registered: CA,IN,MI,NY,VA,WI
Field Support: $EO, ST, SO, FC, H, N
    Training: 1 week Lexington KY

EnviroFree Inspections
4763 S Old Us 23 #A
Brighton, MI 48116

    Phone: 810-220-3097   Accepts collect calls?
    Toll Free: 800-220-0013   FAX: 810-220-2772
    Internet: www.envirofree.com
Suitable Sites: HO
Concentration:
    Expansion: All United States
    Registered: CA,IL,IN,MD,MI,NY,VA,WI
Field Support: CP, EO, ST, SO, FC, H, N
    Training: 3 weeks Brighton MI

The Hometeam Inspection Service
6355 E Kemper Rd #250
Cincinnati, OH 45241
Professional home inspection services incl pest,radon,septic,etc
    Phone: 513-469-2100   Accepts collect calls? N
    Toll Free: 800-598-5297   FAX: 513-469-2226
    Internet: www.hmteam.com
Suitable Sites: HO, OC
Concentration: 35 in FL, 18 in MI, 17 in OH
    Expansion: All United States, Canada, Foreign
    Registered: CA,FL,IL,IN,MD,MI,MN,NY,OR,RI,SD,VA,WA,WI,DC,ND
Field Support: EO, ST, FC, H, N
    Training: 2 weeks inspections, marketing
              proprietary software
              business systems

Real Estate Industry

Property Inspection (Spread 2 of 2)

	HouseMaster, The Home Inspection Professionals	National Property Inspections, Inc.	PestMaster Services	Pillar To Post	Pro-Tect	House Doctors, Inc. Professional	Termite & Pest Control Terminix	World Inspection Network
Startup Cost	15K-40K	17.8K-25.8K	60.8K-109.8K	15.9K-32.7K	180K	20K	25K-50K	26K-37K
Franchise Fee	8.5K-24K	17.8K-25.8K	22.5K	10.9K-20.9K	17.5K	15K	25K-50K	19.9K
Royalty	7.50%	8%	9%	7%/$200	5%	6%	7%	7%/$300/MO
Advertising Fee	2.5%	0%	.5%	2%/$100	2.5%	2%	2%	2%/$75/MO
Financing Provided	N	Y	Y	Y	Y	Y	Y	Y
Experience Required		N				N		
Passive Ownership	N	D	N	N	A	N	D	N
In Business Since	1971	1987	1990	1994	1994	1982	1927	1993
Franchised Since	1979	1987	1997	1994	1994	1991	1927	1994
Franchised Units 1996								
1997	292	86	11	112	29	2	545	61
1998								
Company Owned 1996								
1997	0	0	15	0	0	1	305	1
1998								
Number of Units U.S.	279	85	26	64	29	3	504	60
Canada	13	1	0	48	0	0	0	1
Foreign	0	0	0	0	0	0	346	0
Projected New U.S.								
Canada								
Foreign								
Corporate Employees	42	18	15	8	8		7215	12
Contract Length	5/5	5/5	10/10	5/5	5/3	5/5	5-7/5	10/10
Expand in Territory	Y	Y	Y	N	Y	Y	Y	Y
Full-Time Employees	3	1	2	1	4	1	VAR	1-3
Part-Time Employees	2		1	1		1		
Conversions	Y	Y	Y		Y	Y	Y	Y
Site Selection Assist.	N	N	Y	N	Y	Y	N	N
Lease Negotiation Assist.		N			N			
Site Space Required	500				1500			
Development Agreement	N	Y		Y	N	N		N
Develop. Agree. Term				5				
Sub-franchising	N	N	N	Y	N	N	N	N

Real Estate Industry

Property Inspection (Spread 2 of 2)

HouseMaster, The Home Inspection Professionals
421 W Union Ave
Bound Brook, NJ 08805

Phone: 732-469-6565   Accepts collect calls?
Toll Free: 800-526-3939   FAX: 732-469-7405
Internet: www.housemaster.com
Suitable Sites: HO
Concentration: 14 in FL, 12 in NJ, 13 in NY
Expansion: All United States, Canada
Registered: CA,FL,HI,IL,IN,MD,MI,MN,ND,NY,OR,RI,SD,VA,WA,WI,DC
Field Support: $CP, EO, ST, SO, IC, $FC, H, N
Training: 3 weeks New Jersey training facil

National Property Inspections, Inc.
11620 Arbor St #100
Omaha, NE 68144-1935
Residential & commercial property inspections
Phone: 402-333-9807   Accepts collect calls? Y
Toll Free: 800-333-9807   FAX: 800-933-2508
Internet: www.npiweb.com
Suitable Sites:
Concentration: 7 in IL, 5 in WI, 5 in NY
Expansion: All United States, Canada
Registered: CA,FL,HI,IL,IN,MD,MI,MN,ND,NY,OR,RI,SD,VA,WA,WI,DC,AB
Field Support: ST, FC, H, N
Training: 2 weeks Omaha NE in NPI corp off
ongoing technical, marketing & admin
support

PestMaster Services
137 E South St
Bishop, CA 93514

Phone: 760-873-8100   Accepts collect calls?
Toll Free: 800-525-8866   FAX: 760-873-5618
Internet: www.pestmaster.com
Suitable Sites:
Concentration: 19 in CA, 2 in NV, 2 in FL
Expansion: All United States
Registered: N
Field Support:
Training: 2 weeks corporate office
2 weeks franchise location

Pillar To Post
14502 N Dale Mabry Hwy #200
Tampa, FL 33618

Phone: 813-962-4461   Accepts collect calls?
Toll Free: 800-294-5591   FAX: 813-968-7462
Internet: www.pillartopost.com
Suitable Sites:
Concentration: 26 in ON, 10 in AB, 3 in GA
Expansion: All United States, Canada
Registered: CA,FL,MD,MI,OR,RI,VA,WA,WI,DC,AB
Field Support: $CP, EO, ST, IC, $FC, H, N
Training: 2 weeks corporate head office

Pro-Tect
660 White Plains Rd
Tarrytown, NY 11771

Phone: 914-366-0800   Accepts collect calls?
Toll Free: 800-261-1218   FAX: 914-366-6405
Internet: www.uslead.com
Suitable Sites: OC
Concentration: 11 in CT, 8 in WA, 7 in NY
Expansion: All United States
Registered: CA,FL,HI,IL,IN,MD,MI,MN,ND,NY,OR,RI,SD,VA,WA,WI,DC
Field Support: EO, ST, SO, $FC, H
Training: 3 weeks Tarrytown NY

Professional House Doctors, Inc.
1406 E 14th St
Des Moines, IA 50316-2406
Environmental & building science services
Phone: 515-265-6667   Accepts collect calls? N
Toll Free: 800-288-7437   FAX: 515-278-2070
Internet: www.prohousedr.com
Suitable Sites: FB, HO, IP, OC, SF
Concentration: 3 in IA
Expansion: All United States
Registered:
Field Support: DP, CP, EO, ST, SO, IC, FC, H, N
Training: 2 weeks corporate office

Terminix Termite & Pest Control
860 Ridge Lake Blvd
Memphis, TN 38120

Phone: 901-766-1376   Accepts collect calls?
Toll Free: 800-654-7848   FAX: 901-766-1208
Internet: www.terminix.com
Suitable Sites:
Concentration: 57 in NC, 44 in AR, 27 in SC
Expansion: Limited Areas, Canada, Foreign
Registered: CA,IL,IN,MD,MI,MN,NY,ND,OR,RI,SD,VA,WA,WI
Field Support: CP, EO, ST, $FC, H, N
Training: 5-6 days Memphis TN (initial)
6 weeks on-location training

World Inspection Network
2701 First Ave #340
Seattle, WA 98121-1123

Phone: 206-728-8100   Accepts collect calls?
Toll Free: 800-967-8127   FAX: 206-441-3655
Internet: www.wini.com
Suitable Sites: HO
Concentration: 13 in WA, 10 in OR, 7 in CA
Expansion: All United States, Canada
Registered: CA,FL,HI,IL,IN,MI,MN,NY,OR,WA,WI,AB
Field Support: $CP, EO, ST, IC, $FC, H, N
Training: 2 weeks franchisee's mkt
2 weeks home office Seattle WA

Real Estate Industry

Other Real Estate (Spread 1 of 3)

	America's Choice Int'l Inc.	Apartment Selector	Assist-2-Sell	Better Homes & Gardens Real Estate Service	Better Homes Realty	The Buyer's Agent	Buyer's Resource	By Owner Reality Network
Startup Cost	2.93K-12.9K		15.5K-49.5K	VAR		25K-50K	25K-50K	35K-50K
Franchise Fee	7K-16K	2.5K-10K	7K	3.9K	9.9K	14.9K	5K-14K	16.5K
Royalty	7-10%	5%	5%	1-5%	6%/5K	5%	5%	7.50%
Advertising Fee		1%	0	2.2%	10%	1%	2%/$125/MO	INCLUDED
Financing Provided	N	N	N	Y	Y	Y	N	N
Experience Required			Y			N		
Passive Ownership		D	N	A	A	A	D	D
In Business Since	1992	1959	1987	1902	1964	1988	1989	1985
Franchised Since	1994	1983	1993	1978	1969	1988	1989	1986
Franchised Units 1996	51							
1997	70	21	50	1599	50	70	108	4
1998						65		
Company Owned 1996	0							
1997	0	0	1	0	1	0	0	1
1998								
Number of Units U.S.		21	51	1599	51	70	108	5
Canada		0	0	0	0	0	0	0
Foreign		0	0	0	0	0	0	0
Projected New U.S.						25		
Canada								
Foreign								
Corporate Employees		3	10	132	10	12	4	1
Contract Length		3/3	7/7/7	5/5	5/5	5/5	5/5	5/5
Expand in Territory		Y	Y	Y	Y	Y	Y	N
Full-Time Employees		3	2			2-12	VAR	1
Part-Time Employees		3	0					
Conversions		Y	Y	Y	Y	Y	Y	Y
Site Selection Assist.		Y	Y	N	N	Y	N	Y
Lease Negotiation Assist.		N	Y	N		Y	N	Y
Site Space Required		250	150			300		1000
Development Agreement		N	N	N	Y	Y	Y	Y
Develop. Agree. Term					5	5	5	5
Sub-franchising		N	N	N	Y	N	Y	Y

Real Estate Industry

Other Real Estate (Spread 1 of 3)

America's Choice Int'l Inc.
646 N French Rd, #10
Amherst, NY 14228
Owner-assisted real estate marketing
    Phone: 716-691-0596   Accepts collect calls?
    Toll Free: FAX:
    Internet:
Suitable Sites:
Concentration:
    Expansion: IN,MD,MI,NY,VA, Canada
    Registered:
Field Support:
    Training:

Apartment Selector
6060 N Central Exy #464
Dallas, TX 75205

    Phone: 214-361-4420   Accepts collect calls?
    Toll Free: 800-324-3733   FAX: 214-361-8677
    Internet: www.aptselector.com
Suitable Sites: SC
Concentration: 8 in TX
    Expansion:
    Registered:
Field Support: $EO, $ST, $SO, $FC, $H, N
    Training: 1 week Dallas TX

Assist-2-Sell
535 E Plumb Ln #102
Reno, NV 89502
Discount real estate company
    Phone: 702-688-6060   Accepts collect calls? N
    Toll Free: 800-528-7816   FAX: 702-688-6069
    Internet: www.assist2sell.com
Suitable Sites: ES, FB, OC
Concentration: 4 in FL, 4 in IN, 3 in NC
    Expansion: All United States, Canada, Foreign
    Registered: CA,FL,IL,IN,MN,NY,OR,WA
Field Support: FC, H, N
    Training: 5 days Reno NV

Better Homes & Gardens Real Estate Service
2000 Grand Ave
Des Moines, IA 50312-4996

    Phone: 515-284-2711   Accepts collect calls?
    Toll Free: 800-274-7653   FAX: 515-284-3801
    Internet: www.bhg-real-estate.com
Suitable Sites:
Concentration: 106 in CA, 48 in IL, 78 in NY
    Expansion: All United States, Canada, Foreign
    Registered: CA,FL,HI,IL,IN,MD,MI,MN,ND,NY,OR,RI,SD,VA,WA,WI,DC
Field Support: $CP, EO, $ST, $SO, $FC, H, N
    Training: 2 days Des Moines IA

Better Homes Realty
2140 N Broadway PO Box 8181
Walnut Creek, CA 94596

    Phone: 510-937-9001   Accepts collect calls?
    Toll Free: 800-642-4428   FAX: 510-974-5310
    Internet: www.bhr.com
Suitable Sites:
Concentration: 50 in CA
    Expansion: NW
    Registered: CA,OR,WA
Field Support:
    Training: n/a

The Buyer's Agent
1255 A Lynnfield #273
Memphis, TN 38119
Real estate brokerage specialize exclusive buyer representation
    Phone: 901-767-1077   Accepts collect calls?
    Toll Free: 800-766-8728   FAX: 901-767-3577
    Internet: www.forbuyers.com
Suitable Sites: FB
Concentration: 9 in FL, 8 in CA, 8 in AL
    Expansion: All United States, Canada
    Registered: CA,FL,HI,IN,MD,MI,MN,NY,OR,RI,VA,WA,WI
Field Support: DP, CP, EO, $FC, H, N
    Training: 5 Memphis TN

Buyer's Resource
393 Hanover Center Rd
Etna, NH 03750

    Phone: 603-643-9300   Accepts collect calls?
    Toll Free: 800-359-4092   FAX: 603-643-0404
    Internet: www.buyersresource.com
Suitable Sites: FB, RM, SC, SF
Concentration: 10 in FL, 6 in CO, 6 in TX
    Expansion: All United States
    Registered: CA,FL,HI,IL,IN,MD,MI,MN,ND,NY,OR,RI,SD,VA,WA,WI,DC
Field Support: $CP, $EO, ST, $SO, $FC, H, N
    Training: 3-4 days New Hampshire

By Owner Reality Network
2115 Sherman #101
Coeur D Alene, ID 83814

    Phone: 208-667-6184   Accepts collect calls?
    Toll Free: FAX: 208-664-4539
    Internet:
Suitable Sites: SF
Concentration: 4 in MT, 1 in ID
    Expansion: NW,SE
    Registered:
Field Support: $CP, EO, ST, SO, $FC, N
    Training: 5 days HQ
             5 days on-site

Real Estate Industry

Other Real Estate (Spread 2 of 3)

	Castles Unlimited	Century 21 Real Estate	Coldwell Banker Affiliates (Canada)	Coldwell Banker Residential Affiliates	Elliott & Company Appraisers	Era Franchise Systems	Group Trans-Action Brokerage Services	Help-U-Sell
Startup Cost	15K-30K	50K-200K	10K-200K	15.1K-56.8K	5.1K-17.1K		10K-50K	15K-45K
Franchise Fee	11K	12.5K-25K	7.5K-18K	7.5K-20K	9.9K	12.5K-20K	6K-17K	4.5K
Royalty	4.50%	6%	6%	6%	8%/$200 MIN	6%	FLAT	5.5-3%
Advertising Fee	1%	2%	$40/PERSON	2.5%	2%/$50 MIN	2%	FLAT	1%
Financing Provided	Y	N	N	Y	Y	N	Y	N
Experience Required					Y		N	
Passive Ownership	D	D	D	N	N		N	D
In Business Since	1985	1971	1989	1906	1985	1971	1979	1976
Franchised Since	1990	1972	1989	1982	1994	1972	1982	1976
Franchised Units 1996					5			
1997	4	6200	230	2565	6	2600	55	147
1998					9		57	
Company Owned 1996					4			
1997	1	0	0	0	4	0	0	0
1998					4		0	
Number of Units U.S.	5	4493	0	2341	13	1300	0	145
Canada	0	265	230	224	0	0	55	2
Foreign	0	1442	0	0	0	1300	0	0
Projected New U.S.					6		0	
Canada							10	
Foreign							0	
Corporate Employees	2	357	26	200	5		4	
Contract Length	10/10	5-10/5-10	5-10/5-10	10/10	5/5	10/10	5/1	5/5
Expand in Territory	Y	Y	Y	Y	Y		Y	N
Full-Time Employees	10	VAR	3		1		10	4-10
Part-Time Employees	5		1					
Conversions	Y	Y	Y	Y	Y		Y	Y
Site Selection Assist.	Y	Y	Y	N	Y		Y	Y
Lease Negotiation Assist.	Y	N	N		Y		Y	N
Site Space Required	1500						1000	1000
Development Agreement	Y	N	N	N	N	N	Y	N
Develop. Agree. Term							5	
Sub-franchising	Y	N	N	N	N		N	Y

Real Estate Industry   Other Real Estate (Spread 2 of 3)

Castles Unlimited
837 Beacon St
Newton Centre, MA 02159
Originator of 100% plus(r) commission program
    Phone: 617-964-3300   Accepts collect calls? N
    Toll Free: FAX: 617-244-5847
    Internet: www.castlesunltd.com
Suitable Sites: SF
Concentration: 5 in MA
    Expansion: New England, Canada, Foreign
    Registered:
Field Support: $CP, EO, $ST, $SO, $IC, FC, H, N
    Training: 2 days Newton MA

Century 21 Real Estate
6 Sylvan Way
Parsippany, NJ 07054

    Phone: 973-496-7221   Accepts collect calls?
    Toll Free: 800-826-8083   FAX: 973-496-5527
    Internet: www.century21.com
Suitable Sites: FB, SC, SF
Concentration: 520 in CA, 348 in FL, 314 in IL
    Expansion: All United States, Canada, Foreign
    Registered: CA,FL,HI,IL,IN,MD,MI,MN,ND,NY,OR,RI,SD,VA,WA,WI,DC
Field Support: EO, $ST, $FC, H, N
    Training: 4.5 days Irvine CA

Coldwell Banker Affiliates (Canada)
1 Richmond St W #701
Toronto, ON M5H-3W4 CANADA

    Phone: 416-947-9229   Accepts collect calls?
    Toll Free: 800-268-9599   FAX: 416-777-4604
    Internet: www.coldwellbanker.com
Suitable Sites: DA, OTHER
Concentration: 136 in ON, 36 in BC, 25 in AB
    Expansion: N, Canada
    Registered: AB
Field Support: DP, EO, $ST, SO, FC, H, N
    Training: var.

Coldwell Banker Residential Affiliates
6 Sylvan Way
Parsippany, NJ 07054

    Phone: 973-496-5757   Accepts collect calls?
    Toll Free: FAX: 973-496-5908
    Internet: www.coldwellbanker.com
Suitable Sites: FB, SC, SF
Concentration: 237 in CA, 138 in IL, 125 in FL
    Expansion: All United States, Canada, Foreign
    Registered: CA,FL,HI,IL,IN,MD,MI,MN,ND,NY,OR,RI,SD,VA,WA,WI,DC
Field Support: EO, $ST, $FC, H, N
    Training: 1 week Coldwell bnkr systems ORN

Elliott & Company Appraisers
7 C Oak Branch Dr
Greensboro, NC 27407
Comprehensive mgmt & marketing system w/ strong advertising
    Phone: 910-854-3075   Accepts collect calls? Y
    Toll Free: 800-854-5889   FAX: 910-854-7734
    Internet: www.elliottco.com
Suitable Sites: FB, OC
Concentration: 9 in NC, 3 in SC, 1 in GA
    Expansion: All United States, Canada, Foreign
    Registered: FL,VA
Field Support: EO, ST, SO, $FC, H, N
    Training: 2 days Greensboro NC
        any added support needed getting started

Era Franchise Systems
6 Sylvan Wy
Parsippany, NJ 07054

    Phone: 973-496-5828   Accepts collect calls?
    Toll Free: FAX: 973-496-5904
    Internet: www.eraonline.com
Suitable Sites:
Concentration:
    Expansion: All United States, Canada, Foreign
    Registered:
Field Support:
    Training:

Group Trans-Action Brokerage Services
550 Sherbrooke St W #775
Montreal, QC H3A-1B9 CANADA
Complete real estate services
    Phone: 514-288-6777   Accepts collect calls? N
    Toll Free: FAX: 514-288-7543
    Internet: trans.action@sympatico.ca
Suitable Sites: FB, SF
Concentration: 55 in PQ
    Expansion: N, Canada
    Registered: CA,AB
Field Support: $DP, $CP, $EO, ST, SO, $IC, FC, $H, N
    Training: 3 days HQ
        ongoing

Help-U-Sell
225 W Hospitality Ln #200
San Bernardino, CA 92408

    Phone: 909-890-0682   Accepts collect calls?
    Toll Free: 800-366-1177   FAX: 909-890-2624
    Internet: www.helpusell.net
Suitable Sites: ES, FB, RM, SC, SF
Concentration: 45 in CA, 19 in FL, 6 in MD
    Expansion: All United States, Canada, Foreign
    Registered: CA,FL,HI,IN,MD,MI,OR,RI,SD,WA,WI,DC,AB
Field Support: $EO, ST, $SO, $FC, H, N
    Training: 4 days san Bernardino CA HQ

Real Estate Industry

Other Real Estate (Spread 3 of 3)

	Her Real Estate	Homeowners Concept	National Tenant Network	Re/Max International	Referral Service Centers	Room-Mate Sale By Owner Systems	Showhomes of America	
Startup Cost	9.3K-103K	16K-20K	85K	20K-150K	10K-25K	25K-60K	25K-505	
Franchise Fee	2.5K-80K	4.5K	30K	7.5K-25K	7.5K-15K	15K	15K-25K	
Royalty	5%	3%	10%	VAR	5%	6%	10%	
Advertising Fee	1%		2%	VAR	1%	2%	1%	
Financing Provided	Y	N	Y	Y	Y	N	Y	
Experience Required			N					
Passive Ownership	N	N	D	N	D	D	D	
In Business Since	1976	1982	1980	1973	1979	1992	1986	
Franchised Since	1981	1984	1987	1975	1985	1994	1988	
Franchised Units 1996								
1997	11	39	19	2885	17	3	20	
1998	11		21					
Company Owned 1996								
1997	21	0	2	0	1	1	2	
1998	24		2					
Number of Units U.S.	32	38	21	2261	18	4	22	
Canada	0	1	0	491	0	0	0	
Foreign	0	0	0	133	0	0	0	
Projected New U.S.			24					
Canada			1					
Foreign			0					
Corporate Employees	22	2	15	190		2	5	
Contract Length	5/5	10/10	10/10	5/5	10/10	5/5	10/5/5	
Expand in Territory	Y	Y	Y	Y	Y	Y	Y	
Full-Time Employees		5	2	2-4		1	3-4	
Part-Time Employees			3	1	1	1		
Conversions	Y	Y	N	Y	Y			
Site Selection Assist.	N	Y	N	Y	Y	Y	Y	
Lease Negotiation Assist.	N	N	N		Y		N	
Site Space Required		700	500		350	800-1500		
Development Agreement	N	N	N	N	N	Y	N	
Develop. Agree. Term						5		
Sub-franchising	Y	N	N	Y	Y	N	N	

Real Estate Industry

Other Real Estate (Spread 3 of 3)

Her Real Estate
4656 Executive Dr
Columbus, OH 43220

Phone: 614-459-7400   Accepts collect calls?
Toll Free: 800-848-7400   FAX: 614-459-6807
Internet: www.herrealtors.com
Suitable Sites:
Concentration: 32 in OH
   Expansion: Ohio Only
   Registered:
Field Support: ST, SO, IC, FC, H, N
   Training: 2 weeks HQ

Homeowners Concept
611 N Mayfair Rd
Milwaukee, WI 53226

Phone: 414-258-7778   Accepts collect calls?
Toll Free: 800-800-9890   FAX: 414-258-8276
Internet:
Suitable Sites: OC
Concentration: 7 in WI, 6 in OH, 4 in TX
   Expansion: All United States, Canada
   Registered: IL,WI,NY,FL,WA
Field Support: $ST, FC, H, N
   Training: 1 week Milwaukee WI

National Tenant Network
PO Box 1664
Lake Grove, OR 97035
National network reporting of tenant performance data, screening
Phone: 503-635-1118   Accepts collect calls? Y
Toll Free: 800-228-0989   FAX: 503-635-9392
Internet: ntn8ntnnet.com
Suitable Sites: ES, FB, HO, OC
Concentration: 3 in CA, 2 in NC, 2 in FL
   Expansion: All United States, Canada
   Registered: CA,FL,HI,IL,IN,MD,MI,MN,ND,NY,OR,RI,SD,VA,WA,WI,DC
Field Support: $DP, CP, EO, ST, SO, IC, $FC, H, N
   Training: 1 week franchisee location
               opening seminars

Re/Max International
PO Box 3907
Englewood, CO 80155-3907

Phone: 303-770-5531   Accepts collect calls?
Toll Free: 800-525-7452   FAX: 303-796-3599
Internet: www.remax.com
Suitable Sites: FB, RM, SC, SF
Concentration: 230 in CA, 191 in ON, 177 in IL
   Expansion: All United States, Canada, Foreign
   Registered: CA,FL,HI,IL,IN,MD,MI,MN,ND,NY,OR,RI,SD,VA,WA,WI,DC
Field Support: EO, ST, $FC, H, N
   Training: 40+ hours HQ Englewood CO

Room-Mate Referral Service Centers
PO Box 890575
Oklahoma City, OK 73189

Phone: 405-692-0947   Accepts collect calls?
Toll Free: FAX: 405-634-3096
Internet:
Suitable Sites: SC
Concentration: 4 in PA, 4 in GA, 4 in TX
   Expansion: All United States, Canada, Foreign
   Registered:
Field Support: ST, $SO, FC, $H, N
   Training: 3-5 days franchisee area

Sale By Owner Systems
1777 S Harrison St #820
Denver, CO 80210

Phone: 303-758-1800   Accepts collect calls?
Toll Free: 888-531-1800   FAX: 303-758-3168
Internet:
Suitable Sites: SC, SF
Concentration:
   Expansion: All United States, Canada
   Registered:
Field Support: CP, EO, ST, SO, FC, H, N
   Training: 1 week Denver CO

Showhomes of America
3010 Lbj Fwy #720
Dallas, TX 75234

Phone: 972-243-1900   Accepts collect calls?
Toll Free: FAX: 972-243-3909
Internet: www.showhomes.com
Suitable Sites:
Concentration: 4 in TX, 4 in FL, 2 in IL
   Expansion: Most United States
   Registered: CA,IL,NY,VA
Field Support: CP, $EO, ST, SO, $FC, N
   Training: 5-6 days Dallas TX

Restaurant Industry   **Barbecue**

	Bennett's Bar-B-Que Inc	Bobby Rubino's Place for Ribs	Colter's Bar-B-Q	Dickey's Barbecue Pit Restaurants	St. Hubert Bar-B-Q			
Startup Cost	425.2K-962.5K	450K-650K	730K-1.03M	450K-1.3M	700K-1.3M			
Franchise Fee	35K	50K	30K	25K	60K			
Royalty	3.5%	4%	4%	4%	4%			
Advertising Fee		3%	5%	2%	3%			
Financing Provided	N	N	Y	Y	N			
Experience Required								
Passive Ownership		D	D	D	N			
In Business Since	1984	1978	1982	1941	1951			
Franchised Since	1989	1980	1994	1994	1967			
Franchised Units 1996	8							
1997	7	13	8	17	81			
1998					86			
Company Owned 1996	6							
1997	5	0	5	4	13			
1998					5			
Number of Units U.S.		10	13	21	0			
Canada		0	0	0	91			
Foreign		3	0	0	0			
Projected New U.S.								
Canada					2			
Foreign								
Corporate Employees		1	10	10				
Contract Length		15/10	20/10-20	10/20	10/10			
Expand in Territory		Y	Y	N	Y			
Full-Time Employees		20	3	10	35			
Part-Time Employees		20	25	8	35			
Conversions		Y	N	Y				
Site Selection Assist.		Y	Y	Y	Y			
Lease Negotiation Assist.		Y		Y	N			
Site Space Required		6000	4600	4000	8000			
Development Agreement		Y	Y	Y	N			
Develop. Agree. Term		NEG.	OPEN	5				
Sub-franchising		Y	N	N	N			

Restaurant Industry   ## Barbecue

Bennett's Bar-B-Que Inc
6551 S Revere Pkwy #285
Englewood, CO 80111
Barbecue restaurant
     Phone: 303-792-3088   Accepts collect calls?
    Toll Free: FAX:
    Internet:
Suitable Sites:
Concentration:
    Expansion: NE,S,MW,SE,W,NW, Canada, Foreign
    Registered:
Field Support:
    Training:

Bobby Rubino's Place for Ribs
1990 E Sunrise Blvd
Fort Lauderdale, FL 33304

    Phone: 954-763-9871   Accepts collect calls?
    Toll Free: 800-997-7427   FAX: 954-467-1192
    Internet:
Suitable Sites: FB, RM, SC, SF
Concentration: 6 in FL, 1 in CA, 1 in NY
    Expansion: All United States, Canada, Foreign
    Registered: CA,FL,MI,NY
Field Support: $DP, EO, $ST, SO, IC, $FC, H
    Training: 6-8 weeks Fort Lauderdale, FL

Colter's Bar-B-Q
5910 N Central Expressway #1355
Dallas, TX 75206

    Phone: 214-987-5910   Accepts collect calls?
    Toll Free: 888-265-8377   FAX: 214-987-5938
    Internet:
Suitable Sites: FB
Concentration: 13 in TX
    Expansion: SE, NE
    Registered:
Field Support: CP, EO, ST, SO, IC, FC, H
    Training: 8 weeks Dallas, TX

Dickey's Barbecue Pit Restaurants
17304 Preston Rd #235
Dallas, TX 75252

    Phone: 972-716-9931   Accepts collect calls?
    Toll Free: 800-460-9000   FAX: 972-716-9913
    Internet:
Suitable Sites: FB, RM, SC, OTHER
Concentration: 18 in TX, 2 in CO, 1 in CA
    Expansion: West and Tidewater, Foreign
    Registered: CA,FL,RI
Field Support: CP, EO, ST, SO, IC, $FC, H
    Training: 30 days Dallas, TX

St. Hubert Bar-B-Q
1515 Chomedey Blvd #250
Laval, QC H7V-3Y7 CANADA
Rotisserie chicken and ribs
    Phone: 450-688-6500   Accepts collect calls? N
    Toll Free: FAX: 450-688-3900
    Internet: st-hubert.com
Suitable Sites: FB, SC
Concentration: 80 in PQ, 9 in ON, 2 in NB
    Expansion: N, Canada
    Registered:
Field Support: $DP, $CP, EO, $ST, $SO, $IC, FC, H, N
    Training: 8 weeks Laval, PQ

Restaurant Industry

Burgers

	Chelsea Street Pub & Grill	The Ground Round	The Ground Round Restaurant					
Startup Cost	700K	880K-1.6M	815K-1.3M					
Franchise Fee	30K	40K	40K					
Royalty	5%	3.5%	3.50%					
Advertising Fee	0%		2.5%					
Financing Provided	N	N	N					
Experience Required								
Passive Ownership	N		N					
In Business Since	1973	1969	1969					
Franchised Since	1975	1970	1970					
Franchised Units 1996		46						
1997	7	41	41					
1998								
Company Owned 1996		145						
1997	17	124	124					
1998								
Number of Units U.S.	24		164					
Canada	0		1					
Foreign	0		0					
Projected New U.S.								
Canada								
Foreign								
Corporate Employees	19		60					
Contract Length	10/OPEN		20/20					
Expand in Territory	Y		Y					
Full-Time Employees	20		75					
Part-Time Employees	30		25					
Conversions	N		Y					
Site Selection Assist.	Y		Y					
Lease Negotiation Assist.	Y		N					
Site Space Required	5000		5500-6000					
Development Agreement	N		N					
Develop. Agree. Term								
Sub-franchising	N		N					

Restaurant Industry

Burgers

Chelsea Street Pub & Grill
PO Box 9989
Austin, TX 78766

Phone: 512-454-7739   Accepts collect calls?
Toll Free: FAX: 512-454-1801
Internet:
Suitable Sites: RM
Concentration: 19 in TX, 3 in NM, 2 in LA
Expansion: TX, NM, LA, CO
Registered:
Field Support: $DP, CP, EO, ST, SO, IC, $FC, H
Training: 4 weeks Austin, TX

The Ground Round
P.O. Box 9078
Braintree, MA 02184
Full-service family restaurant
Phone: 617-380-3116   Accepts collect calls?
Toll Free: FAX:
Internet:
Suitable Sites:
Concentration:
Expansion: All United States
Registered:
Field Support:
Training:

The Ground Round Restaurant
PO Box 9078 35 Braintree Hill Off Pk
Braintree, MA 02184-9078

Phone: 617-380-3100   Accepts collect calls?
Toll Free: FAX: 617-380-3168
Internet:
Suitable Sites: FB, RM, SC, SF
Concentration: 26 in NY, 23 in MA, 19 in OH
Expansion: All United States
Registered: CA,FL,IL,IN,MD,MI,MN,NY,ND,OR,RI,SD,VA,WI,DC
Field Support: CP, EO, ST, SO, $FC, H
Training: 8-12 weeks regional training unit

Restaurant Industry   **Diner Style**

	Huddle House	The Soda Fountain						
Startup Cost	51K-712K	56.8K-85.5K						
Franchise Fee	15K	15K						
Royalty	4%	5%						
Advertising Fee	.5%							
Financing Provided	N	N						
Experience Required	N							
Passive Ownership	A							
In Business Since	1964	1992						
Franchised Since	1966	1997						
Franchised Units 1996								
1997	300	2						
1998								
Company Owned 1996		0						
1997	25	0						
1998								
Number of Units U.S.	325							
Canada	0							
Foreign	0							
Projected New U.S.	40							
Canada								
Foreign								
Corporate Employees	104							
Contract Length	15/5X3							
Expand in Territory	Y							
Full-Time Employees	15							
Part-Time Employees	8							
Conversions	Y							
Site Selection Assist.	Y							
Lease Negotiation Assist.	Y							
Site Space Required								
Development Agreement	Y							
Develop. Agree. Term	NEG..							
Sub-franchising	N							

Restaurant Industry   Diner Style

Huddle House
2969 E Ponce De Leon Ave
Decatur, GA 30030
24hr diner-style restaurant- always open - always fresh
Phone: 404-377-5700   Accepts collect calls?
Toll Free: 800-868-5700   FAX: 404-377-0497
Internet: www.huddlehouse.com
Suitable Sites: FB, SC, SF
Concentration: 48 in SC, 145 in GA, 27 in AL
Expansion: SE and SE
Registered: FL,VA
Field Support: CP, EO, $ST, SO, FC, H, N
Training: 5 weeks Atlanta, GA area
10 days new unit

The Soda Fountain
1805 Oriole Rd
Gatlinburg, TN 37738
Sandwiches/fountain drinks/ice cream
Phone: 423-436-0108   Accepts collect calls?
Toll Free: FAX:
Internet:
Suitable Sites:
Concentration:
Expansion: Canada
Registered:
Field Support:
Training:

Restaurant Industry   Family Style (Spread 1 of 3)

	Banners Restaurants	Bennigan's	Big Boy Restaurant & Bakery	Bonanza	Bridgeman's Restaurants Inc	Buffalo Wings & Rings	Buffalo's Cafe	Damon's International
Startup Cost	350K-400K	1.1M-2.1M	600K-1.8M	635K-1.4M	21K-609K	180K-375K	450K-1.2M	1M+
Franchise Fee	30K	50K	40K	30K	750K-25K	25K	35K	50K
Royalty	4%	4%	4%	4%	2%	4%	5%	4%
Advertising Fee	2%	5%	3%	5%		3%	2%	2.5%
Financing Provided	N	Y	N	Y	N	N	Y	N
Experience Required			N			N	N	Y
Passive Ownership	N	D	D	D		D	A	N
In Business Since	1990	1976	1936	1963	1936	1988	1985	1979
Franchised Since	1990	1995	1952	1966	1967	1989	1991	1982
Franchised Units 1996					19			82
1997	5	10	429	137	32	26	40	93
1998						21	35	109
Company Owned 1996					4			23
1997	0	214	74	0	3	3	1	22
1998						4	6	20
Number of Units U.S.	0	218	410	116		25	41	127
Canada	5	0	0	9		0	0	0
Foreign	0	6	93	12		0	2	2
Projected New U.S.			34			10	12	24
Canada								
Foreign			3					1
Corporate Employees	3	147	165	380		12	20	55
Contract Length	10/10	20/20	20	20/20		10/10	10/10/10	10/5/5/5
Expand in Territory	Y	Y	Y	Y		Y	Y	Y
Full-Time Employees	10		25	VAR		6-10		30
Part-Time Employees	10		20			10-15		50
Conversions	Y	Y	Y	Y		Y	N	Y
Site Selection Assist.	Y	N	Y	N		Y	Y	Y
Lease Negotiation Assist.	Y	N	Y	N		Y	Y	Y
Site Space Required	3000	6500	5200	6275		2500-4500	3600-4500	6500-8200
Development Agreement	N	N	Y	Y		Y	Y	Y
Develop. Agree. Term			20			5-10	VAR.	VAR.
Sub-franchising	N		N	Y		N	N	N

Restaurant Industry

Banners Restaurants
1965 W Fourth Ave #203
Vancouver, BC V6J-1M8 CANADA

Phone: 604-737-7748   Accepts collect calls?
Toll Free: FAX: 604-737-7993
Internet:
Suitable Sites: SC
Concentration: 5 in BC
Expansion: N, Canada
Registered:
Field Support: EO, ST, SO, $FC, N
Training: 3-4 weeks Chilliwack, BC

Bennigan's
12404 Park Central Dr
Dallas, TX 75251-1899

Phone: 214-404-5747   Accepts collect calls?
Toll Free: 800-543-9670   FAX: 214-404-5806
Internet:
Suitable Sites: FB
Concentration: 46 in TX, 40 in FL
Expansion: All United States, Canada, Foreign
Registered: CA,FL,HI,IL,IN,MD,MI,MN,ND,NY,OR,RI,SD,VA,WA,WI,DC
Field Support: CP, EO, ST, SO, IC, $FC, H
Training: 1 week home ofc & 11 wks in unit
2-4 weeks in unit - employees

Big Boy Restaurant & Bakery
4199 Marcy Dr
Warren, MI 48091
Full service family restaurant & bakery w/ breakfast & salad bar
Phone: 810-755-8114   Accepts collect calls?
Toll Free: 800-837-3003   FAX: 810-757-4737
Internet:
Suitable Sites: DA, FB
Concentration: 142 in MI, 102 in OH, 25 in KY
Expansion: All United States, Foreign
Registered: CA,FL,HI,IL,IN,MD,MI,MN,ND,NY,OR,RI,SD,VA,WA,WI,DC
Field Support: DP, CP, EO, ST, SO, IC, FC, H, N
Training: 6-8 weeks in-unit
1-2 weeks corporate HQ

Bonanza
12404 Park Central Dr
Dallas, TX 75251-1899

Phone: 214-404-5745   Accepts collect calls?
Toll Free: 800-543-9670   FAX: 214-404-5806
Internet:
Suitable Sites: FB
Concentration: 20 in PA, 17 in AR
Expansion: All United States, Canada, Foreign
Registered: CA,FL,HI,IL,IN,MD,MI,MN,ND,NY,OR,RI,SD,VA,WA,WI,DC
Field Support: CP, EO, ST, SO, IC, FC, H, N
Training: at restaurant Dallas, TX

Bridgeman's Restaurants Inc
5700 Smetana Dr #110
Minnetonka, MN 55343
Family-style restaurant/soda fountain
Phone: 612-931-3099   Accepts collect calls?
Toll Free: FAX:
Internet:
Suitable Sites:
Concentration:
Expansion: MW
Registered:
Field Support:
Training:

Buffalo Wings & Rings
1109 Vine St
Cincinnati, OH 45210
Casual dining restaurant specialize in chicken wings & curly fry
Phone: 513-723-1886   Accepts collect calls? N
Toll Free: 800-501-2865   FAX: 513-723-0465
Internet: wingsandrings.com
Suitable Sites: FB, SC, SF
Concentration: 19 in OH, 5 in KY, 1 in IL
Expansion: All United States, Canada, Foreign
Registered: CA,FL,IL,MD,NY,VA,WA,WI
Field Support: EO, $ST, SO, IC, FC, H
Training: 278 hours Cincinnati, OH

Buffalo's Cafe
707 Whitlock Ave SW Bldg H #13
Marietta, GA 30064
Hot wings & southwestern food served in kick-back, old-west fun
Phone: 770-420-1800   Accepts collect calls? N
Toll Free: 800-459-4647   FAX: 770-420-1811
Internet: www.buffaloscafe.com
Suitable Sites: AC, FB, PC, RM
Concentration: 29 in GA, 6 in FL, 3 in SC
Expansion: All United States, Canada, Foreign
Registered: FL
Field Support: CP, EO, ST, SO, IC, FC, H, N
Training: 30 days corporate store
2 weeks franchisee's store

Damon's International
4645 Executive Dr
Columbus, OH 43220
Casual dining sports entertainment restaurant bbq ribs prime rib
Phone: 614-442-7900   Accepts collect calls? N
Toll Free: FAX: 614-538-2517
Internet: www.damons.com
Suitable Sites: FB, SC
Concentration: 34 in OH, 11 in IN, 9 in PA
Expansion: All United States, Canada, Foreign
Registered: CA,FL,IL,IN,MD,MI,MN,NY,RI,SD,VA,WI,WA
Field Support: CP, EO, ST, SO, IC, FC, N
Training: 8 weeks training restaurant
1 week home office

Restaurant Industry

Family Style (Spread 2 of 3)

	Denny's Inc	The Griddle Family Restaurants / Ice Cream Corporation	Friendly's / Harvey's Restaurants	Humpty's Family Restaurant	Jungle Jim's Restaurants	Kelsey's Restaurants	Mikes Restaurants
Startup Cost	VAR.	875K-1.5M	60K-170K	510K-600K	350K-450K	395K-500K	600K-750K	275K-550K
Franchise Fee	35K	30K	17.5K	50K-75K	25K	25K	40K	45K
Royalty	4%	4%	5%	5%	0-5%	4%	5%	8%
Advertising Fee		3%	3%	4%	2%	2%	.5%	0%
Financing Provided	Y	Y	N	N	N	N	Y	Y
Experience Required			N			N		
Passive Ownership		A	A	N	D	N	N	N
In Business Since	1953	1934	1964	1900	1977	1991	1978	1967
Franchised Since	1984	1997	1976		1983	1992	1983	1972
Franchised Units 1996	662							
1997	728	34	62	346	42	11	21	103
1998								
Company Owned 1996	933							
1997	891	662	0	4	5	0	33	24
1998								
Number of Units U.S.		696	2	0	0	0	0	0
Canada		0	60	350	47	11	54	127
Foreign		0	0	0	0	0	0	0
Projected New U.S.								
Canada						3		
Foreign								
Corporate Employees		10	20	200	10	4	30	36
Contract Length		20/10-20	10/10	20/5X4	10/5	10/10	10/5/5	20/20
Expand in Territory		Y	Y	Y	Y	Y	Y	Y
Full-Time Employees		40	3	3	12	18	70-90	25
Part-Time Employees		35	25-30	40	12	12		10
Conversions		Y	Y	Y	Y	Y	N	Y
Site Selection Assist.		Y	Y	Y	Y	Y	Y	Y
Lease Negotiation Assist.			Y	Y	Y	Y	Y	Y
Site Space Required		4000	3000	2600	3500	4500	5000	3500
Development Agreement		Y	Y	N	Y	N		Y
Develop. Agree. Term					10			20
Sub-franchising		N	N	N	N	Y	N	N

Restaurant Industry   **Family Style (Spread 2 of 3)**

Denny's Inc
203 E Main St
Spartanburg, SC 29301
Full-service family restaurant
    Phone: 864-597-8000   Accepts collect calls?
    Toll Free: FAX:
    Internet:
Suitable Sites:
Concentration:
    Expansion: All United States, Canada
    Registered:
Field Support:
    Training:
	Friendly's Ice Cream Corporation
	1855 Boston Rd
	Wilbraham, MA 01095
	
	    Phone: 413-543-2400 Accepts collect calls?
	    Toll Free: 888-342-7776 FAX: 413-543-1015
	    Internet: www.friendly's.com
	Suitable Sites: FB
	Concentration: 164 in NY, 153 in MA, 67 in CT
	    Expansion: SE, NE, Mid-Atlantic, Foreign
	    Registered: MD,NY,RI,VA
	Field Support: DP, $CP, EO, $ST, SO, IC, N
	    Training: 2 days corporate training center

The Griddle Family Restaurants
505 Consumers Rd #1000
North York, ON M2J-4V8 CANADA
 	
    Phone: 416-493-3800   Accepts collect calls? N
    Toll Free: FAX: 416-493-3889
    Internet: www.goldengriddlecorp.com
Suitable Sites: AC, FB, M, OC, RM, SC, SF
Concentration: 51 in ON, 5 in BC, 1 in MI
    Expansion: All United States, Canada
    Registered: CA,FL,HI,IL,IN,MD,MI,MN,ND,NY,OR,RI,SD,VA,WA,WI,DC,AB
Field Support: CP, EO, $ST, $SO, IC, FC, N
    Training: 3-6 weeks training store
            on-site as required
	Harvey's Restaurants
	230 Bloor St W
	Toronto, ON M1C-2M4 CANADA
	
	    Phone: 416-962-4571 Accepts collect calls?
	    Toll Free: FAX: 416-969-2544
	    Internet:
	Suitable Sites: FB
	Concentration: ON, PQ, AB
	    Expansion: N, Canada
	    Registered: AB
	Field Support: EO, ST, SO, $FC, H, N
	    Training: 6-8 weeks Toronto, ON

Humpty's Family Restaurant
2505 Mac Leod Trail S
Calgary, AB T2G-5J4 CANADA
 	
    Phone: 403-269-4675   Accepts collect calls?
    Toll Free: 800-661-7589   FAX: 403-266-1973
    Internet:
Suitable Sites: FB, SC
Concentration: 27 in AB, 9 in SK, 7 in BC
    Expansion: NW, Canada
    Registered:
Field Support: CP, EO, ST, SO, IC, FC, H, N
    Training: 3 weeks Calgary, AB head office
            2 weeks on-site
	Jungle Jim's Restaurants
	PO Box 71553 Hill Crest
	White Rock, BC V4B-5J5 CANADA
	Jungle themed family friendly eateries
	    Phone: 604-541-8559 Accepts collect calls? N
	    Toll Free: FAX: 604-541-8535
	    Internet:
	Suitable Sites: FB, RM, SC, SF
	Concentration: 7 in NF, 2 in NB, 1 in NS
	    Expansion: N/A, Canada
	    Registered: AB
	Field Support: EO, ST, SO, FC
	    Training: 3-4 weeks existing location

Kelsey's Restaurants
450 S Service Rd W
Oakville, ON L6K-2H4 CANADA
 	
    Phone: 905-842-5510   Accepts collect calls?
    Toll Free: 800-982-1682   FAX: 905-842-9048
    Internet:
Suitable Sites: FB
Concentration: 42 in ON, 8 in AB, 1 in SK
    Expansion: N/A, Canada, Foreign
    Registered: AB
Field Support: $DP, CP, EO, ST, SO, IC, H, N
    Training: 12 weeks in restaurant
            1 week office
	Mikes Restaurants
	8250 Decarie Blvd #310
	Montreal, QC H4P-2P5 CANADA
	
	    Phone: 514-341-5544 Accepts collect calls?
	    Toll Free: FAX: 514-341-5635
	    Internet: www.mikes.ca
	Suitable Sites: FB, SC
	Concentration: 125 in PQ, 1 in ON, 1 in NB
	    Expansion: NE
	    Registered:
	Field Support: CP, EO, ST, SO, IC, FC
	    Training: 6-8 weeks Montreal, PQ

Restaurant Industry   **Family Style (Spread 3 of 3)**

	Palace Entertainment & Bullwinkles Restaurant	Perkins Family Restaurants	Smitty's	St. Jerome Restaurant	Village Inn Restaurants			
Startup Cost	1.1M-5M	1.6M-2.5M	300K-500K	150K-400K	514K-2.4M			
Franchise Fee	25K-75K	40K	35K	29K	35K			
Royalty	4%	4%	5%	5%	4%			
Advertising Fee	3.5%	3%	0%	2%	0%			
Financing Provided	Y	N	Y	N	N			
Experience Required		N	N					
Passive Ownership	D	D	D	N	D			
In Business Since	1982	1958	1960	1982	1958			
Franchised Since	1994	1958	1960	1991	1961			
Franchised Units 1996								
1997	2	336	120	10	107			
1998	3	357			111			
Company Owned 1996								
1997	7	138	10	5	97			
1998	16	140			100			
Number of Units U.S.	18	481	1	0	211			
Canada	0	16	129	15	0			
Foreign	1	0	0	0	0			
Projected New U.S.	15	38			12			
Canada	0	2						
Foreign	1							
Corporate Employees	22	250	20	4	200			
Contract Length	15/15	20/5-20	20/10	10/10	25/10			
Expand in Territory	N	Y	Y	Y	Y			
Full-Time Employees	40	35	20	15	20			
Part-Time Employees	40	40	10		40			
Conversions	Y	Y	Y	Y	Y			
Site Selection Assist.	Y	Y	Y	Y	Y			
Lease Negotiation Assist.	Y	Y	Y	Y	N			
Site Space Required	10000	4000-5100	4200-5000	2600	5200			
Development Agreement	Y	Y	Y	Y	Y			
Develop. Agree. Term	15	VAR.	20+	20				
Sub-franchising	N	N	Y	Y	N			

Restaurant Industry

Family Style (Spread 3 of 3)

Palace Entertainment & Bullwinkles Restaurant
18300 Von Karman Ave Ste 900
Irvine, CA 92612
Restaurant & family entertainment centers
Phone: 949-261-0404   Accepts collect calls? N
Toll Free: FAX: 949-261-1414
Internet: www.bullwinkles.com
Suitable Sites: FB
Concentration: 14 in CA, 1 in OR, 2 in FL
Expansion: All United States, Canada, Foreign
Registered: CA,FL,NY,OR
Field Support: DP, EO, ST, SO, IC, FC, N
Training: 5 weeks upland, CA
3 weeks on-site

Perkins Family Restaurants
6075 Poplar Ave #800
Memphis, TN 38119-4709
Full service restaurant w/ breakfast, lunch, dinner, bakery item
Phone: 901-766-6400   Accepts collect calls? N
Toll Free: 800-877-7375   FAX: 901-766-6482
Internet: www.perkinsrestuarants.com
Suitable Sites: FB, RM, SC, SF, OTHER
Concentration: 58 in OH, 44 in PA, 35 in NY
Expansion: All United States, Canada
Registered: CA,FL,IL,IN,MD,MI,MN,ND,NY,OR,SD,VA,WA,WI,DC,AB
Field Support: $DP, CP, EO, ST, $SO, IC, FC, H, N
Training: 4-12 weeks various locations

Smitty's
501 18th Ave SW #600
Calgary, AB T2S-0C7   CANADA

Phone: 403-229-3838   Accepts collect calls? N
Toll Free: FAX: 403-229-3899
Internet:
Suitable Sites: FB, RM
Concentration: 26 in BC, 43 in AHA, 17 in SASK
Expansion: N, Canada
Registered: AB,HI
Field Support: $CP, EO, ST, SO, IC, FC, N
Training: 3-4 weeks Calgary, AB

St. Jerome Restaurant
313 Ornice Albert Rd
Dartmouth, NS B2Y-1N3   CANADA

Phone: 902-429-2872   Accepts collect calls?
Toll Free: FAX: 902-469-5859
Internet:
Suitable Sites:
Concentration: 11 in NS, 3 in NF, 1 in NB
Expansion: Canada
Registered:
Field Support: CP, EO, ST, SO, $IC, FC
Training: 4-6 weeks Halifax, NS

Village Inn Restaurants
400 W 48th Ave
Denver, CO 80216
Full-service, family-style restaurant w/ variety of menu items
Phone: 303-296-2121   Accepts collect calls? N
Toll Free: 800-891-9978   FAX: 303-672-2212
Internet: www.vicorpinc.com
Suitable Sites: AC, FB, RM, SC
Concentration: 28 in CO, 21 in AZ, 15 in FL
Expansion: AR,FL,IN,KS,KY,MO,NC,TX,VA
Registered: CA,FL,HI,IL,MD,MI,MN,ND,RI,SD,VA,WA,WI,NY
Field Support: EO, $ST, SO, IC, H, N
Training: 12-20 management Denver, CO

Restaurant Industry   Italian

	Pizzaworks Restaurant	Doubledave's	East Side Mario's	Strings Italian Cafe						
Startup Cost	200K-250K	915K-1.1M	325K							
Franchise Fee	22.5K	40K	37.5K							
Royalty	4%	5%	5%							
Advertising Fee		4%	2%							
Financing Provided	Y	N	N							
Experience Required										
Passive Ownership		N	D							
In Business Since	1984	1979	1987							
Franchised Since	1995	1982	1989							
Franchised Units 1996	1									
1997	3	59	17							
1998										
Company Owned 1996	13									
1997	14	4	3							
1998										
Number of Units U.S.		0	18							
Canada		63	2							
Foreign		0	0							
Projected New U.S.										
Canada										
Foreign										
Corporate Employees		55	12							
Contract Length		10/5/5	10/5							
Expand in Territory		N	Y							
Full-Time Employees		50	4-6							
Part-Time Employees		25	15							
Conversions		Y	Y							
Site Selection Assist.		Y	Y							
Lease Negotiation Assist.		Y	Y							
Site Space Required		6000	2500							
Development Agreement		Y	Y							
Develop. Agree. Term			5							
Sub-franchising		Y	N							

Restaurant Industry   Italian

Doubledave's Pizzaworks Restaurant
9000 Manchaca
Austin, TX 78748
Hand-rolled pizza buffet & delivery
      Phone: 972-716-9931   Accepts collect calls?
      Toll Free: FAX:
      Internet:
  Suitable Sites:
  Concentration:
     Expansion:
     Registered:
  Field Support:
      Training:

East Side Mario's
10 Kingsbridge Garden Circle #600
Mississauga, ON L5R-3K6 CANADA

      Phone: 905-568-0000   Accepts collect calls?
      Toll Free: FAX: 905-568-0080
      Internet:
  Suitable Sites: FB
  Concentration: 45 in ON, 13 in PQ, 2 in NS
     Expansion: N/A, Canada
     Registered:
  Field Support: EO, ST, SO, FC
      Training: 6 weeks in-store
                1 week head office

Strings Italian Cafe
11344 Coloma Rd #545
Gold River, CA 95670

      Phone: 916-635-3990   Accepts collect calls?
      Toll Free: FAX: 916-631-9775
      Internet:
  Suitable Sites: RM, SC
  Concentration: 24 in CA, 2 in PQ, 1 in NV
     Expansion: All United States
     Registered: CA,FL,OR,WA
  Field Support: EO, ST, SO, IC, FC, N
      Training: 6 weeks gold river, CA
                3 weeks on-site

Restaurant Industry   Mexican

	Pepe's Mexican Restaurant	Taco Hut America Inc	Zuzu Mexican Food				
Startup Cost	75K-300K	100K-137K	129K-267K				
Franchise Fee	15K	15K	25K				
Royalty	4%	3%	4.50%				
Advertising Fee	3%		4%				
Financing Provided	N	N	Y				
Experience Required							
Passive Ownership	D		D				
In Business Since	1967	1968	1989				
Franchised Since	1968	1991	1992				
Franchised Units 1996		3					
1997	56	3	17				
1998							
Company Owned 1996		4					
1997	1	4	4				
1998							
Number of Units U.S.	57		21				
Canada	0		0				
Foreign	0		0				
Projected New U.S.							
Canada							
Foreign							
Corporate Employees	15		15				
Contract Length	20		10/10				
Expand in Territory	N	Y	Y				
Full-Time Employees	8	4	5				
Part-Time Employees	5	5	6				
Conversions	Y		Y				
Site Selection Assist.	Y	Y	Y				
Lease Negotiation Assist.	Y		Y				
Site Space Required	3000	1800	1600				
Development Agreement	Y	Y	Y				
Develop. Agree. Term			3				
Sub-franchising	N		Y				

Restaurant Industry   Mexican

Pepe's Mexican Restaurant
1325 W 15th St
Chicago, IL 60608

Phone: 312-733-2500   Accepts collect calls?
Toll Free: FAX: 312-733-2564
Internet:
Suitable Sites: FB, SC, SF
Concentration: 43 in IL, 13 in IN, 1 in VA
Expansion: Midwest
Registered: IL,IN,VA
Field Support: CP, EO, ST, SO, IC, FC, N
Training: 4 weeks HQ

Taco Hut America Inc
2014 S Rangeline
Joplin, MO 64804
Mexican restaurant
Phone: 417-781-4781   Accepts collect calls?
Toll Free: FAX: 417-781-4782
Internet:
Suitable Sites: FB, FC
Concentration:
Expansion: Canada, Foreign
Registered:
Field Support:
Training: at Joplin HQ

Zuzu Mexican Food
4300 Alpha Rd #101
Dallas, TX 75244

Phone: 972-788-2022   Accepts collect calls?
Toll Free: FAX: 972-239-0942
Internet:
Suitable Sites: FB, RM, SC
Concentration: 11 in TX
Expansion: All United States
Registered: FL
Field Support: CP, EO, ST, SO, IC, FC, H, N
Training: 3 weeks Dallas, TX

Restaurant Industry

Oriental

	Benihana of Tokyo	EDO Japan						
Startup Cost	1.3K-1.8K	145.1K-250K						
Franchise Fee	50K	20K						
Royalty	6%	6%						
Advertising Fee	0.5%	N/A						
Financing Provided	N	Y						
Experience Required								
Passive Ownership	D	A						
In Business Since	1964	1977						
Franchised Since	1970	1986						
Franchised Units 1996								
1997	18	85						
1998								
Company Owned 1996								
1997	48	9						
1998								
Number of Units U.S.	57	39						
Canada	1	54						
Foreign	8	1						
Projected New U.S.								
Canada								
Foreign								
Corporate Employees	51	29						
Contract Length	15/VAR.	5-10						
Expand in Territory	N	Y						
Full-Time Employees	35	3						
Part-Time Employees	7	3						
Conversions	Y							
Site Selection Assist.	Y	Y						
Lease Negotiation Assist.		Y						
Site Space Required	6000	500-700						
Development Agreement	Y	Y						
Develop. Agree. Term	15	10						
Sub-franchising	N	N						

Restaurant Industry

Oriental

Benihana of Tokyo
8685 NW 53rd Terr
Miami, FL 33166
Japanese steakhouse
Phone: 305-593-0770   Accepts collect calls?
Toll Free: 800-327-3369   FAX: 305-592-6371
Internet:
Suitable Sites: FB
Concentration: 15 in CA, 6 in FL, 3 in IL
Expansion: PA, MD, MI, NC, OH, AZ, TX, NY, Canada, Foreign
Registered: CA,HI,NY
Field Support: $DP, EO, $ST, SO, IC, FC, H
Training: 12-15 weeks Miami, FL

EDO Japan
4838 32nd St S E
Calgary, AB T2B-2S6 CANADA

Phone: 403-215-8800   Accepts collect calls?
Toll Free: FAX: 403-215-8801
Internet: www.edojapan.com
Suitable Sites: FC, M
Concentration: 25 in AB, 15 in ON, 11 in CA
Expansion: All United States
Registered: CA,FL,HI,IL,MD,NY,OR,WA,AB
Field Support: CP, EO, ST, SO, IC, FC, H, N
Training: 2 weeks Calgary, AB

Restaurant Industry   Specialty Style

	Copeland's of New Orleans	Famous Sam's Inc	Swiss Chalet Plus Restaurants / Swiss Chalet					
Startup Cost	1.5M-2.67M	317K-522K	1M-1.2M					
Franchise Fee	100K	30K	75K-90K					
Royalty	3.5%	5%	5%					
Advertising Fee			4%					
Financing Provided	N	Y	N					
Experience Required								
Passive Ownership			N					
In Business Since	1983	1979	1900					
Franchised Since	1993	1989						
Franchised Units 1996	5	20						
1997	5	28	129					
1998								
Company Owned 1996	8	0						
1997	11	0	24					
1998								
Number of Units U.S.			7					
Canada			146					
Foreign			0					
Projected New U.S.								
Canada								
Foreign								
Corporate Employees			200					
Contract Length			20/5X4					
Expand in Territory			Y					
Full-Time Employees			6					
Part-Time Employees			80					
Conversions			Y					
Site Selection Assist.			Y					
Lease Negotiation Assist.			Y					
Site Space Required			6000					
Development Agreement			N					
Develop. Agree. Term								
Sub-franchising			N					

Restaurant Industry   Specialty Style

Copeland's of New Orleans
1405 Airline Hwy
Metairie, LA 70001
Full service Cajun/Creole restaurant
  Phone: 504-830-1000 Accepts collect calls?
  Toll Free: FAX:
  Internet:
 Suitable Sites:
 Concentration:
  Expansion: All United States, Canada, Foreign
  Registered:
 Field Support:
  Training:

Famous Sam's Inc
3225 S Hardy #104
Tempe, AZ 85282
Sports bar/restaurant
  Phone: 602-902-0822 Accepts collect calls?
  Toll Free: FAX:
  Internet:
 Suitable Sites:
 Concentration:
  Expansion: All United States
  Registered:
 Field Support:
  Training:

Swiss Chalet/ Swiss Chalet Plus Restaurants
230 Bloor St W
Toronto, ON M2G-2M4 CANADA

  Phone: 416-962-4571 Accepts collect calls?
  Toll Free: FAX: 416-969-2544
  Internet:
 Suitable Sites: FB
 Concentration: ON, PQ, AB
  Expansion: N, Canada
  Registered: AB
 Field Support: EO, ST, SO, $FC, H, N
  Training: 10-12 weeks Toronto, ON

Restaurant Industry   Steak Houses (Spread 1 of 2)

	Charley's Steakery	Elmer's Pancake & Steak House	Golden Corral Family Steakhouse	Golden Corral Franchising Systems Inc	K-Bob's Steakhouses	Longbranch Steakhouse & Saloon Inc	Ponderosa Steakhouse	Sirloin Stockade Family Steakhouse
Startup Cost	117.5K-280.5K	N/A	1.2M-3.3M	1.2M-3.3M	500K-750K	512.8K-659.7K	711K-1.6M	1.2M-2.3M
Franchise Fee	19.5K	35K	40K	40K	25K	50K	30K	15K
Royalty	5%	4%	4%	4%	3%	4%	4%	3%
Advertising Fee	3-5%	1%	2%	2%	1%		0.5%	
Financing Provided	N	N	N	N	Y	Y	Y	N
Experience Required				Y				
Passive Ownership	D	N	N	N	N		D	
In Business Since	1986	1960	1973	1973	1966	1990	1965	1984
Franchised Since	1991	1966	1986	1987	1992	1995	1966	1984
Franchised Units 1996				230		0		70
1997	48	18	265	263	33	0	351	65
1998				297				
Company Owned 1996				213		2		7
1997	9	11	179	180	7	2	203	6
1998				152				
Number of Units U.S.	52	29	444	60	40		506	
Canada	5	0	0		0		8	
Foreign	0	0	0		0		40	
Projected New U.S.				60				
Canada								
Foreign								
Corporate Employees	16	11	190		12		380	
Contract Length	10/10	25/VAR.	15/5	15	20/10		20/20	
Expand in Territory	Y	Y	Y	Y	Y		Y	
Full-Time Employees	8	15	80		26		VAR	
Part-Time Employees	15	35	40		200			
Conversions	Y	N	N	N	Y		Y	
Site Selection Assist.	Y	Y	Y	Y	Y		N	
Lease Negotiation Assist.	Y	N	N	Y	N		N	
Site Space Required	500-1500	6800	8500-11000	80000-120000	6300		5700	
Development Agreement	Y	Y	Y	Y	N		Y	
Develop. Agree. Term		5		1-5				
Sub-franchising	Y	N	N	N	N		Y	

Restaurant Industry

Charley's Steakery
6610 Busch Blvd Ste 100
Columbus, OH 43229

Phone: 614-847-8100   Accepts collect calls?
Toll Free: 800-437-8325   FAX: 614-847-8110
Internet: www.charleyssteakery.com
Suitable Sites: RM, SC
Concentration: 13 in OH, 5 in FL, 5 in ON
  Expansion: All United States, Canada, Foreign
  Registered: FL,IL,IN,MI,NY,VA,WI
Field Support: CP, EO, ST, SO, IC, FC, H, N
  Training: 3 weeks Columbus, OH

Elmer's Pancake & Steak House
PO Box 16938
Portland, OR 97292-0938

Phone: 503-252-1485   Accepts collect calls?
Toll Free: 800-325-5188   FAX: 503-257-7448
Internet:
Suitable Sites: FB
Concentration: 12 in OR, 5 in WA, 4 in ID
  Expansion: NW
  Registered: CA,OR,WA
Field Support: CP, EO, ST, SO, $FC, N
  Training: 8-12 weeks Portland, OR

Golden Corral Family Steakhouse
PO Box 29502 5151 Glenwood Ave
Raleigh, NC 27626

Phone: 919-881-4647   Accepts collect calls?
Toll Free: 800-284-5673   FAX: 919-881-4496
Internet:
Suitable Sites: FB
Concentration: TX, OK, NC
  Expansion: All United States, Canada, Foreign
  Registered: CA,FL,HI,IL,IN,MD,MI,MN,ND,NY,OR,RI,SD,VA,WA,WI,DC
Field Support: EO, ST, SO, N
  Training: 12 weeks HQ and field

Golden Corral Franchising Systems Inc
5151 Glenwood Ave
Raleigh, NC 27612
Family steakhouse/buffet & bakery
Phone: 919-781-9310   Accepts collect calls? N
Toll Free: 800-284-5673   FAX: 919-881-5252
Internet: goldencorralrest.com
Suitable Sites: FB, PC
Concentration:
  Expansion: All United States, Canada
  Registered:
Field Support: EO, ST, SO, FC, N
  Training: extensive 12 wk program
              ongoing advanced mgmt workshops

K-Bob's Steakhouses
1600 Randolph SE #200
Albuquerque, NM 87106

Phone: 505-242-8403   Accepts collect calls?
Toll Free: 800-225-8403   FAX: 505-764-0492
Internet:
Suitable Sites: FB
Concentration: 22 in TX, 11 in NM, 3 in OK
  Expansion: SE and Midwest, Foreign
  Registered:
Field Support: $DP, $CP, EO, ST, SO, $IC, FC, H, N
  Training: 8 weeks

Longbranch Steakhouse & Saloon Inc
105 Deercreek Rd #M-204
Deerfield Beach, FL 33442
Casual western family-style steakhouse
Phone: 305-360-9927   Accepts collect calls?
Toll Free: 800-416-5582   FAX:
Internet:
Suitable Sites:
Concentration:
  Expansion: IL,IN, Canada, Foreign
  Registered:
Field Support:
  Training:

Ponderosa Steakhouse
12404 Park Central Dr
Dallas, TX 75251-1899

Phone: 972-404-5745   Accepts collect calls?
Toll Free: 800-543-9670   FAX: 972-404-5806
Internet:
Suitable Sites: FB
Concentration: 108 in OH, 59 in IN, 55 in NY
  Expansion: All United States, Foreign
  Registered: CA,FL,HI,IL,IN,MD,MI,MN,ND,NY,OR,RI,SD,VA,WA,WI,DC
Field Support: CP, EO, ST, SO, IC, FC, H, N
  Training: home office Dallas, TX

Sirloin Stockade Family Steakhouse
2908 N Plum
Hutchinson, KS 67502
Steaks chicken fish & salad bar/bakery
Phone: 316-669-9372   Accepts collect calls?
Toll Free: FAX:
Internet:
Suitable Sites:
Concentration:
  Expansion: IL,IN,VA, Foreign
  Registered:
Field Support:
  Training:

Restaurant Industry

	Tumbleweed LLC	Western Sizzlin'	Family Steakhouse / WSMP	Western Steer					
Startup Cost	839K-1.6M	811K-2.3M	1.3M-1.7M						
Franchise Fee	35K	20K	25K						
Royalty	3%	2-3% GROSS	3%						
Advertising Fee		$190/MO	2%						
Financing Provided	N	N	N						
Experience Required									
Passive Ownership			D						
In Business Since	1975	1962	1967						
Franchised Since	1981	1976	1975						
Franchised Units 1996	10								
1997	11	240	65						
1998									
Company Owned 1996	15								
1997	15	11	25						
1998									
Number of Units U.S.		251	90						
Canada		0	0						
Foreign		0	0						
Projected New U.S.									
Canada									
Foreign									
Corporate Employees		40	80						
Contract Length		20/10	10/10						
Expand in Territory		Y	Y						
Full-Time Employees		25	25						
Part-Time Employees		50	40						
Conversions		Y	Y						
Site Selection Assist.		Y	Y						
Lease Negotiation Assist.		N	Y						
Site Space Required		7500-8500	85000						
Development Agreement		Y	Y						
Develop. Agree. Term		NEG.	5						
Sub-franchising			N						

Restaurant Industry

Tumbleweed LLC
1900 Mellwood Ave
Louisville, KY 40206
Southwestern-style restaurant
    Phone: 502-893-0323   Accepts collect calls?
    Toll Free: FAX:
    Internet:
Suitable Sites:
Concentration:
    Expansion: All United States, Canada, Foreign
    Registered:
Field Support:
    Training:

Western Sizzlin'
902 Kermit Dr
Knoxville, TN 37912

    Phone: 423-219-9000   Accepts collect calls?
    Toll Free: 800-247-8325   FAX: 423-219-9013
    Internet:
Suitable Sites: FB
Concentration: 30 in AR, 29 in VA, 26 in GA
    Expansion: All United States
    Registered: FL,IL,IN,MD,VA
Field Support: EO, ST, SO, IC, $FC, H, N
    Training: 6 weeks training center

Western Steer Family Steakhouse / WSMP
Wsmp Dr PO Box 399
Claremont, NC 28610-9771

    Phone: 704-459-7626   Accepts collect calls?
    Toll Free: FAX: 704-459-3114
    Internet:
Suitable Sites: FB, RM
Concentration: 47 in NC, 10 in SC, 9 in GA
    Expansion: All United States
    Registered: FL,MD,VA,WA
Field Support: $DP, CP, EO, ST, SO, IC, FC, H, N
    Training: 4 weeks CO-owned training unit
        1 week pre-opening

Restaurant Industry   Other Restaurant (Spread 1 of 2)

	Applebee's International	Cafe La France	Dog N' Suds Drive-In Restaurants	Fuddruckers	Gigglebees	Houlihan's Restaurant Group	Hubb's Pub	Hudson's Grill of America
Startup Cost	1.74M-3.17M	95K-125K	400K-1M	700K-1.6M	260K-370K		320K-450K	100K-1M
Franchise Fee	35K/UNIT	15K	15K-25K	50K	25K	40K	50K	25K
Royalty	4%	5%	2-5%	5%	4.50%	4%	2-4%	4%
Advertising Fee	3%	0%	CO-OP	0%	0%	1.5%		1%
Financing Provided	N	N	Y	N	N	Y	Y	Y
Experience Required			N					
Passive Ownership	N	A	D	D	D	A	D	A
In Business Since	1980	1989	1953	1980	1985	1972	1982	1985
Franchised Since	1988	1993	1958	1983	1994	1987	1992	1986
Franchised Units 1996								
1997	730	7	19	79	1	29	3	14
1998								
Company Owned 1996								
1997	172	10	3	115	1	62	3	3
1998								
Number of Units U.S.	889	17	22	194	2	89	6	17
Canada	5	0	0	2	0	0	0	0
Foreign	8	0	0	7	0	0	0	0
Projected New U.S.			20					
Canada			0					
Foreign			0					
Corporate Employees	300	100	10	50	2	120	6	7
Contract Length	20/5	10/10	15/5/5	10/10	10/10	20/10	20/5	20/20
Expand in Territory	Y	Y	N	Y	Y	Y	Y	Y
Full-Time Employees	75-100	3	10	15	5	40	6	12
Part-Time Employees		3	10	25	40	80	10	38
Conversions	N	Y	N	Y	Y	Y	N	N
Site Selection Assist.	Y	Y	Y	Y	Y	Y	Y	Y
Lease Negotiation Assist.	Y	Y	Y	N	N	Y		Y
Site Space Required	5000-5400	1200	45000	5000-6000	12000	5000	4000-5000	4500
Development Agreement	Y	Y	Y	N	N	Y	Y	Y
Develop. Agree. Term		10					20	5
Sub-franchising	N	N	N	N	N	N	Y	Y

Restaurant Industry   **Other Restaurant (Spread 1 of 2)**

Applebee's International
4551 W 107th St #100
Overland Park, KS 66207

Phone: 913-967-4000	Accepts collect calls?
Toll Free:	FAX: 913-967-4135
Internet:	

Suitable Sites: FB, RM, SC
Concentration: 62 in FL, 54 in CA, 48 in OH
Expansion: NY, LA, HI, and AK, Canada, Foreign
Registered: CA,FL,HI,IL,IN,MD,MI,MN,ND,NY,OR,RI,SD,VA,WA,WI,DC
Field Support: DP, CP, EO, ST, SO, FC, H, N
Training: 8-12 weeks certified training unit
3 days seminars at HQ

Cafe La France
370 Richmond St
Providence, RI 02903

Phone: 401-453-2233	Accepts collect calls?
Toll Free: 800-791-2233	FAX: 401-453-0319
Internet:	

Suitable Sites: SF
Concentration: 16 in RI, 1 in MD
Expansion: NE, Canada, Foreign
Registered: MD,RI
Field Support: EO, ST, SO, IC, FC, H
Training: 3 weeks providence, RI
1 week your store

Dog N' Suds Drive-In Restaurants
4945 Fairway Dr
Plainfield, IN 46168
Old fashion car hop curb service drive-in restaurant

Phone: 317-718-0772	Accepts collect calls? Y
Toll Free: 800-364-6783	FAX: 317-718-0773
Internet: www.dognsuds.net	

Suitable Sites: FB, FC, K, M, RM, SC
Concentration: 11 in IN, 5 in IL, 3 in MO
Expansion: Midwest and Mid-South
Registered: IL,IN,WI
Field Support: CP, EO, ST, SO, IC, FC, H
Training: 6 weeks Indianapolis, in

Fuddruckers
One Corporate Pl 55 Ferncroft Rd
Danvers, MA 01923-4001

Phone: 978-774-6606	Accepts collect calls?
Toll Free:	FAX: 978-774-2974
Internet:	

Suitable Sites: FB, SC
Concentration: 36 in TX, 14 in VA, 13 in OH
Expansion: All United States, Canada, Foreign
Registered: CA,FL,HI,IL,IN,MD,MI,MN,NY,ND,OR,RI,SD,VA,WA,DC,AB
Field Support: CP, EO, ST, SO, FC, N
Training: 6-8 weeks regional training locatio

Gigglebees
519 S Minnesota Ave
Sioux Falls, SD 57104

Phone: 605-331-4242	Accepts collect calls?
Toll Free:	FAX: 605-334-4514
Internet:	

Suitable Sites: FB, SC
Concentration: 2 in SD
Expansion: Midwest
Registered: SD
Field Support: $CP, EO, ST, SO
Training: 21 days HQ in Sioux Falls, SD

Houlihan's Restaurant Group
2 Brush Creek Blvd PO Box 16000
Kansas City, MO 64112

Phone: 816-756-2200	Accepts collect calls?
Toll Free:	FAX: 816-561-2842
Internet:	

Suitable Sites: FB, RM, SC, SF
Concentration: PA, NJ
Expansion: All United States, Canada, Foreign
Registered: CA,FL,HI,IL,IN,MD,MI,MN,ND,NY,OR,RI,SD,VA,WA,WI,DC
Field Support: CP, EO, ST, $SO, IC, $FC, H, N
Training: 120 days various locations in u.s.

Hubb's Pub
895 Barton Blvd #B
Rockledge, FL 32955

Phone: 407-639-5080	Accepts collect calls?
Toll Free:	FAX: 407-639-8050
Internet: www.hubbspub.com	

Suitable Sites: FB, SC, SF
Concentration: 4 in FL, 2 in WA
Expansion: All United States, Canada, Foreign
Registered: FL,WA
Field Support: DP, CP, EO, ST, SO, IC, FC, N
Training: 6-8 weeks HQ

Hudson's Grill of America
16970 Dallas Pkwy #402
Dallas, TX 75248-1928

Phone: 972-931-9237	Accepts collect calls?
Toll Free:	FAX: 972-931-1326
Internet: www.hudsongrill.com	

Suitable Sites: FB
Concentration: 10 in CA, 4 in TX, 2 in MI
Expansion: All United States, Foreign
Registered: CA,FL,HI,IL,IN,MD,MI,MN,ND,NY,OR,SD,VA,WA,WI,DC,AB
Field Support: CP, EO, ST, SO, IC, FC
Training: 5-6 weeks CA
5-6 weeks Texas

Restaurant Industry   Other Restaurant (Spread 2 of 2)

	Joey's Only Seafood Restaurant	Le Peep	Mickey Finn's Sports Cafe	Red Hot & Blue	Shooters International Inc	Sunshine Cafe	Hospitality Worldwide	TGI Friday's	Ward's Restaurants
Startup Cost	149K-202.5K	100K-250K	170K-249K	347.7K-868K	1.53M-1.56M	150K-1.0M	1.7M-4M	250K-400K
Franchise Fee	25K	0	17.5K	30K	75K	25K	75K	20K
Royalty	4.5%	2.50%	5%	5%	4%	4%	4%	4-5%
Advertising Fee	1%	1%	N/A			3%	2-4%	1%
Financing Provided	N	N	Y	N	N	Y	N	N
Experience Required								
Passive Ownership	D	N	D			A	D	D
In Business Since	1985	1992	1995	1988	1982	1965	1965	1985
Franchised Since	1992	1992	1995	1991	1985	1985	1970	1985
Franchised Units 1996					6			
1997	60	60	8	22	5	12	296	19
1998								
Company Owned 1996					1			
1997	1	6	1	3	1	2	161	3
1998								
Number of Units U.S.	6	66	8	24		14	363	22
Canada	55	0	1	0		0	1	0
Foreign	0	0	0	1		0	93	0
Projected New U.S.								
Canada								
Foreign								
Corporate Employees	11	10	5			16	300+	4
Contract Length	10/5	15/10	20/10			5/5	20/VAR.	10/10
Expand in Territory	Y	Y	N			Y	Y	Y
Full-Time Employees	5	10	8-10			50	100	8
Part-Time Employees	15	10	10-12			10	125	17
Conversions	Y	Y	Y			Y	Y	Y
Site Selection Assist.	Y	Y	Y			Y	N	Y
Lease Negotiation Assist.	Y	N	Y			Y	N	N
Site Space Required	2000-2400	2500-3500	3750			4400-5600	6800	2000
Development Agreement	Y	N	Y			Y	Y	Y
Develop. Agree. Term	20					5		
Sub-franchising	Y	N	N			N	N	N

Restaurant Industry

Other Restaurant (Spread 2 of 2)

Joey's Only Seafood Restaurant
514 42nd Ave SE
Calgary, AB T2G-1Y6   CANADA

Phone: 403-243-4584   Accepts collect calls?
Toll Free: 800-661-2123   FAX: 403-243-8989
Internet:
Suitable Sites: FB, SC, SF
Concentration: 20 in AB, 2 in MT, 2 in ND
Expansion: All United States, Canada
Registered: CA,FL,ND,AB
Field Support: EO, ST, SO, IC, FC, H, N
Training: 5 weeks franchise ofc/corp store

Le Peep
4 W Dry Crk Cir #201
Littleton, CO 80120

Phone: 303-730-6300   Accepts collect calls?
Toll Free: FAX: 303-730-7105
Internet:
Suitable Sites: FB, SC
Concentration: 23 in CO, 9 in TX, 7 in GA
Expansion: All United States, Canada
Registered:
Field Support: $EO, $ST, $SO
Training: 4 weeks new location or Denver, CO

Mickey Finn's Sports Cafe
207 Galvin Rd N
Bellevue, NE 68005

Phone: 402-341-2424   Accepts collect calls?
Toll Free: 888-478-8463   FAX: 402-291-2345
Internet:
Suitable Sites: SC
Concentration: 7 in NE, 1 in ON
Expansion: All United States, Canada
Registered: FL
Field Support: CP, EO, ST, SO, IC, FC, H, N
Training: 2 weeks Omaha, NE
3-6 weeks on-site

Red Hot & Blue
1600 Wilson Blvd
Arlington, VA 22209

Phone: 703-276-8833   Accepts collect calls?
Toll Free: 800-723-0745   FAX: 703-528-4789
Internet:
Suitable Sites:
Concentration: 5 in MD, 4 in NC, 3 in VA
Expansion:
Registered: CA,FL,HI,IL,IN,MD,MI,MN,ND,NY,OR,VA,WA,WI,DC
Field Support:
Training:

Shooters International Inc
3033 NE 32nd Ave
Fort Lauderdale, FL 33308
Full-service restaurant
Phone: 305-566-3044   Accepts collect calls?
Toll Free: FAX:
Internet:
Suitable Sites:
Concentration:
Expansion: CA,IL,IN, Canada, Foreign
Registered:
Field Support:
Training:

Sunshine Cafe
7112 Zionsville Rd
Indianapolis, IN 46268-4153

Phone: 317-299-3391   Accepts collect calls?
Toll Free: 800-808-4774   FAX: 317-299-3390
Internet:
Suitable Sites: FB, SC
Concentration: 13 in IN, 1 in OH
Expansion: Midwest, N. Central U.S.
Registered: IL,IN,MI,WI
Field Support: CP, EO, ST, SO, IC, FC, N
Training: 7 weeks Indianapolis, in

TGI Friday's Hospitality Worldwide
7540 Lbj Fwy #100
Dallas, TX 75251

Phone: 972-450-5400   Accepts collect calls?
Toll Free: 800-374-3297   FAX: 972-450-3642
Internet: www.tgifridays.com
Suitable Sites: FB
Concentration: 31 in CA, 30 in TX, 25 in OH
Expansion: All United States, Canada, Foreign
Registered: CA,FL,HI,IL,IN,MD,MI,MN,ND,NY,OR,RI,SD,VA,WA,WI,DC
Field Support: $CP, $EO, $ST, $SO, $FC, H
Training: 2 weeks Dallas, TX

Ward's Restaurants
7 Professional Pkwy #103
Hattiesburg, MS 39402

Phone: 601-268-9273   Accepts collect calls?
Toll Free: 800-748-9273   FAX: 601-268-9283
Internet:
Suitable Sites: FB
Concentration: 15 in MS, 7 in AL
Expansion: All United States
Registered:
Field Support: $DP, EO, ST, SO, $IC, $FC, H, N
Training: 4 weeks home office

Retail Industry

Art, Prints, Framing

	Appletree Art Publishers	Color Me Mine	Deck The Walls	FastFrame USA	Framing & Art Centres	The Great Frame Up	Malibu Gallery	
Startup Cost	29.9K	105K-160K	226K-281K	82K-116K	110K-160K	126K	34K-81K	
Franchise Fee	29.9K	20K	35K	19.5K	20K	25K	20K	
Royalty	0	5%	6%	7.50%	6%	6%	6%	
Advertising Fee	0	1%	2%	3%	1%	2%	2%	
Financing Provided	Y	N	Y	Y	Y	Y	Y	
Experience Required		N	N				N	
Passive Ownership	D	N	D	N	N	D	D	
In Business Since	1992	1992	1979	1984	1974	1971	1986	
Franchised Since	1995	1996	1979	1987	1977	1975	1994	
Franchised Units 1996			205				2	
1997	19		199	160	65	125	3	
1998			191		52		3	
Company Owned 1996			1				4	
1997	0		1	2	0	0	4	
1998			1		0		4	
Number of Units U.S.	15	44	191	160	0	125	7	
Canada	4	3	0	0	52	0		
Foreign	0	1	0	2	0	0		
Projected New U.S.		25	8				4	
Canada		5			62			
Foreign		5						
Corporate Employees	20	45	50	14	4	30	6	
Contract Length	7/7	5/5/5	10/10	10/10	10/10		10/5/5	
Expand in Territory	Y	Y	Y	Y	Y		Y	
Full-Time Employees		2	3	2		2	2	
Part-Time Employees	1	4	2			3-4	2	
Conversions		Y	Y	Y	Y		Y	
Site Selection Assist.	Y	Y	Y	Y		Y	Y	
Lease Negotiation Assist.		Y	Y	Y	Y	Y	Y	
Site Space Required		1300-2000	1800	1500	1000	1800	1200-1500	
Development Agreement	N	N	N	Y	N	N	N	
Develop. Agree. Term				10				
Sub-franchising	N	N	N	Y	N	N	N	

Retail Industry   **Art, Prints, Framing**

Appletree Art Publishers
85 W Nyack Rd
Nanuet, NY 10954

Phone: 914-623-0553   Accepts collect calls?
Toll Free: 800-233-0553   FAX: 914-623-6634
Internet:
Suitable Sites:
Concentration: 5 in CA, 4 in NY, 2 in NJ
    Expansion: All United States, Canada
    Registered: CA,FL,MD,MI,NY,OR,VA,DC,AB
Field Support: DP, CP, EO, ST, SO, IC, FC, H, N
    Training: 3 days home office

Color Me Mine
14721 Califa St
Van Nuys, CA 91411

Phone: 818-989-8404   Accepts collect calls?
Toll Free: 888-265-6764   FAX: 818-780-1442
Internet: www.colormemine.com
Suitable Sites: DA, RM, SC, SF, OTHER
Concentration: 21 in CA, 5 in NJ, 5 in PA
    Expansion: All United States
    Registered: CA,FL,HI,IL,IN,MD,MI,MN,NY,OR,VA,WA,WI,DC,AB
Field Support: DP, CP, EO, ST, SO, IC, FC, H, N
    Training: 2 weeks intensive
                design, technical, operations
                construction, marketing

Deck The Walls
100 Glenborough Dr 14th Fl
Houston, TX 77067
Custom framing retailer
Phone: 281-775-5200   Accepts collect calls? N
Toll Free: 800-543-3325   FAX: 281-775-5250
Internet: www.deckthewalls.com
Suitable Sites: RM
Concentration: 16 in PA, 25 in TX, 15 in FL
    Expansion: All United States, Foreign
    Registered: CA,IL,IN,MD,MI,MN,NY,OR,ND,RI,SD,VA,WA,WI
Field Support: EO, ST, SO, IC, FC, H, N
    Training: 10 days HQ

FastFrame U S A
1200 Lawrence Dr #300
Newbury Park, CA 91320

Phone: 805-498-4463   Accepts collect calls?
Toll Free: 800-333-3225   FAX: 805-498-8983
Internet: www.fastframe.com
Suitable Sites: FB, PC, SC
Concentration: 91 in CA, 16 in IL, 8 in MN
    Expansion: All United States, Foreign
    Registered: CA,FL,IL,IN,MD,MI,MN,NY,RI,WA
Field Support: DP, CP, EO, ST, SO, IC, $FC, H, N
    Training: 2 weeks corporate HQ
                1 week store location

Framing & Art Centres
1800 Appleby Line
Burlington, ON L7L-6A1   CANADA
Custom picture framing and art retailer
Phone: 905-332-6116   Accepts collect calls? N
Toll Free: 800-563-7263   FAX: 905-335-5377
Internet: www.framingandartcentre.com
Suitable Sites: SC
Concentration: 29 in ON, 11 in BC, 5 in AB
    Expansion: Canada
    Registered: AB
Field Support: CP, EO, ST, SO, FC, H, N
    Training: 10 days home office & field

The Great Frame Up
9335 Belmont Ave
Franklin Park, IL 60131

Phone: 847-671-2530   Accepts collect calls?
Toll Free: 800-553-7263   FAX: 847-671-2580
Internet:
Suitable Sites: SC
Concentration: 29 in IL, 20 in CA, 10 in GA
    Expansion: All United States, Canada, Foreign
    Registered: CA,FL,HI,IL,IN,MD,MI,MN,ND,NY,OR,RI,SD,VA,WA,WI,DC
Field Support: EO, ST, SO, IC, FC, H, N
    Training: 33 days Evanston, IL

Malibu Gallery
1919 South 40th St Ste 202
Lincoln, NE 68506
High quality framing and art gallery
Phone: 402-434-5620   Accepts collect calls? N
Toll Free: 800-865-2378   FAX: 402-434-5624
Internet: www.franchisedevelopers.com
Suitable Sites: FB, M, SC, SF
Concentration: 5 in NE, 1 in KS, 1 in FL
    Expansion: All United States
    Registered: FL
Field Support: $CP, EO, ST, SO, H, N
    Training: 1 week NE
           1 week on-site

Retail Industry   **Books, Audiobooks**

	The Book Rack	Lemstone Books	Little Professor Book Centers	Talking Book World				
Startup Cost	18K+	220K-260K	300K-2M	150K-225K				
Franchise Fee	6K	30K	37K-75K	25K				
Royalty	$75/MO.	4%	3%	5%				
Advertising Fee	0	1%	.5%	2%				
Financing Provided	N	N	Y	Y				
Experience Required		N	N	N				
Passive Ownership	A	D	D	D				
In Business Since	1963	1981	1964	1993				
Franchised Since	1966	1982	1969	1995				
Franchised Units 1996								
1997	283	76	91	5				
1998		72	79	14				
Company Owned 1996								
1997	1	1	0	7				
1998		2	0	14				
Number of Units U.S.	283	73	79	11				
Canada	1	0	0	2				
Foreign	0	0	0	0				
Projected New U.S.		80	10					
Canada		0						
Foreign		0						
Corporate Employees	8	16	10	60				
Contract Length	LIFE	10/10	10	15/15				
Expand in Territory	Y	Y	Y	Y				
Full-Time Employees	1	1	2	1				
Part-Time Employees	1	4	3	2				
Conversions	Y	N	Y	Y				
Site Selection Assist.	Y	Y	Y	Y				
Lease Negotiation Assist.	Y	Y	Y	Y				
Site Space Required	1200-6000	1700-2500	3000	2000				
Development Agreement	N	N	Y	Y				
Develop. Agree. Term			5	5				
Sub-franchising	N	N	N	N				

Retail Industry   **Books, Audiobooks**

The Book Rack
2715 E Commercial Blvd
Fort Lauderdale, FL 33308

   Phone: 954-267-0304   Accepts collect calls?
   Toll Free: FAX:
   Internet:
Suitable Sites: SC
Concentration: TX, FL, TN
   Expansion: All United States, Canada
   Registered: CA,FL,HI,IL,IN,MD,MI,MN,NY,OR,RI,VA,WA,WI,DC
Field Support: EO, ST, SO, IC, FC, N
   Training: 7-10 days Ft. Lauderdale, FL

Lemstone Books
1123 Wheaton Oaks Ct
Wheaton, IL 60187
Christian book, gift & music stores
   Phone: 630-682-1400   Accepts collect calls? N
   Toll Free: FAX: 630-682-1828
   Internet: phild@lemstone.com
Suitable Sites: RM
Concentration: 9 in TN, 6 in NC, 7 in IL
   Expansion: All United States
   Registered: CA,FL,IL,IN,MD,MI,MN,NY,OR,WA,WI,VA
Field Support: DP, CP, EO, ST, SO, IC, FC, N
   Training: 8 days HQ
            5 days on-site

Little Professor Book Centers
405 Little Lake Dr #C
Ann Arbor, MI 48103
Offers full-line, full-service community oriented book stores
   Phone: 734-994-1212   Accepts collect calls? N
   Toll Free: 800-899-6232   FAX: 734-994-9009
   Internet: www.littleprofessor.com
Suitable Sites: AC, FB, M, RM, SC, SF
Concentration: 17 in OH, 8 in PA, 8 in WI
   Expansion: All United States
   Registered: CA,FL,IL,IN,MD,MI,MN,OR,RI,SD,VA,WA,WI,DC,NY
Field Support: DP, CP, EO, ST, SO, IC, FC, H, N
   Training: 1-2 weeks home office
            1-4 weeks on-site

Talking Book World
26211 Central Park #415
Southfield, MI 48076
Rent audiobooks w/ no due dates & sell audiobooks at discount
   Phone: 248-945-9999   Accepts collect calls? N
   Toll Free: 800-403-2933   FAX: 248-945-9606
   Internet: www.talkingbookworld.com
Suitable Sites: FB, SC
Concentration: 8 in MI, 2 in AZ, 2 in CO
   Expansion: All United States, Canada
   Registered: CA,FL,IL,MI
Field Support: $DP, $CP, EO, ST, SO, IC, FC, H, N
   Training: 1 week corporate HQ
            2 weeks corporate store
            1 week your store

Retail Industry   Computer Sales and Service

	Computer Doctor	Computer Renaissance	Cyber Exchange Software And Computers	Full Circle Image	Worldwide Information Services			
Startup Cost	117.9K-170.7K	181K-275K	89K-139K	1K	10K-50K			
Franchise Fee	20K	25K	9K-18K	20K				
Royalty	3%	3%	1.5-5%	5%	0%			
Advertising Fee	0	$500/YR.	1%	3%	0%			
Financing Provided	Y	Y	Y	N	N			
Experience Required	N			N				
Passive Ownership	A	D	A	N	A			
In Business Since	1992	1988	1993	1991	1993			
Franchised Since	1996	1993	1994	1997	1997			
Franchised Units 1996				0				
1997	12	148	61	5	73			
1998	67			12				
Company Owned 1996				4				
1997	0	4	2	4	0			
1998				3				
Number of Units U.S.	67	147	63	15	73			
Canada	0	5	0		0			
Foreign	0	0	0		0			
Projected New U.S.	35			22				
Canada								
Foreign	2							
Corporate Employees	7	40	20	30	13			
Contract Length	5/5	10/10	5/5	10	1/1			
Expand in Territory	Y	N	Y	N				
Full-Time Employees	2-3	7	2	0	1			
Part-Time Employees	1-2	2	2	0				
Conversions	Y	Y	Y	Y				
Site Selection Assist.	Y	Y	Y	N	N			
Lease Negotiation Assist.	Y	Y	Y	N	N			
Site Space Required	1500	2000						
Development Agreement	Y	Y	Y		N			
Develop. Agree. Term	5				2			
Sub-franchising	Y	N	N	N	Y			

Retail Industry   Computer Sales and Service

Computer Doctor
PO Box 487
Aberdeen, SD 57401
Computer service + sales, in-store or mobile service
     Phone: 605-225-4122   Accepts collect calls? Y
     Toll Free: 888-297-2292   FAX: 605-225-5176
     Internet: www.cdfs.com
Suitable Sites: FB, PC, SC, SF
Concentration: 8 in SD, 4 in ND, 2 in VA
     Expansion: All United States
     Registered: FI,MN,ND,SD,VA,CA,FL,MI,OR,WI
Field Support: $DP, $CP, EO, $ST, SO, $IC, FC, H, N
     Training: 2 weeks Aberdeen, SD

Computer Renaissance
4200 Dahlberg Dr
Minneapolis, MN 55422-4837

     Phone: 612-520-8500   Accepts collect calls?
     Toll Free: 800-868-8978   FAX: 612-520-8501
     Internet: www.cr1.com
Suitable Sites: SC
Concentration: 12 in IL, 11 in WA, 10 in MN
     Expansion: All United States, Canada
     Registered: CA,FL,HI,IL,IN,MD,MI,MN,ND,NY,OR,RI,SD,VA,WA,WI,DC
Field Support: CP, EO, ST, SO, IC, FC, H, N
     Training: 2 weeks Minneapolis, MN
          2 days in store

Cyber Exchange Software And Computers
2686 E Main St
Saint Charles, IL 60174

     Phone: 888-289-2923   Accepts collect calls?
     Toll Free: 800-520-7311   FAX: 630-443-0398
     Internet: www.cyberexchange.com
Suitable Sites: SC
Concentration: 9 in IL, 6 in TX, 4 in FL
     Expansion: All United States, Canada, Foreign
     Registered: CA,FL,HI,IL,IN,MD,MI,MN,ND,NY,OR,RI,SD,VA,WA,WI,DC
Field Support: DP, CP, EO, ST, SO, IC, FC, H, N
     Training: 1 week Chicago, IL

Full Circle Image
6256 34th Ave NW
Rochester, MN 55901
Recycled office products - inkjet, laser toner cartridge, ribbon
     Phone: 800-548-7244   Accepts collect calls? Y
     Toll Free: 800-446-8269   FAX: 800-280-2076
     Internet: www.fullcircleimage.com
Suitable Sites: ES, HO, OC, OS
Concentration: 6 in MN, 3 in WI
     Expansion: All United States, Canada
     Registered: FL,IL,IN,MD,MI,MN,ND,NY,OR,SD,VA,WI
Field Support: DP, CP, EO, ST, IC, H, N
     Training: lead generation, ON-site assist, bookkeeping
          help desk, sales, business plan, classes
          periodicals, marketing

Worldwide Information Services
7040 W Palmetto Park Rd #4 Ste 271
Boca Raton, FL 34333

     Phone: Accepts collect calls?
     Toll Free: 800-581-4651   FAX: 561-416-2531
     Internet:
Suitable Sites: HO
Concentration: 33 in CA, 7 in FL
     Expansion: All United States, Canada, Foreign
     Registered: CA,FL,HI,IL,IN,MD,MI,MN,ND,NY,OR,RI,SD,VA,WA,WI,DC
Field Support: CP, IC, H
     Training:

Retail Industry   Discount Stores

	A Buck Or Two Stores	Dollar Discount Stores	Just-A-Buck	Pinch-A-Penny				
Startup Cost	160K	99K-163.5K	134K-257K	109K-394K				
Franchise Fee	50K	18K	25K	5K-50K				
Royalty	6%	3%	4%	6%				
Advertising Fee	1%	1%	2%	4%				
Financing Provided	Y	Y	Y	N				
Experience Required		N						
Passive Ownership	D	D	N	D				
In Business Since	1987	1982	1988	1974				
Franchised Since	1989	1987	1992	1976				
Franchised Units 1996								
1997	180	70	8	110				
1998								
Company Owned 1996								
1997	10	0	18	5				
1998								
Number of Units U.S.	0	98	26	115				
Canada	190	0	0	0				
Foreign	0	0	0	0				
Projected New U.S.		42						
Canada								
Foreign								
Corporate Employees	100	10	14					
Contract Length	5/5	10/15	10/10X2	5/20				
Expand in Territory	Y	N	Y	Y				
Full-Time Employees	VARIE	1-2	11					
Part-Time Employees		3-4	10					
Conversions		N	Y	N				
Site Selection Assist.	N	Y	Y	Y				
Lease Negotiation Assist.		Y	Y	Y				
Site Space Required	2500-4000	2000-3000	3500	3500				
Development Agreement	N	N	N	N				
Develop. Agree. Term								
Sub-franchising	N	N		N				

Retail Industry   **Discount Stores**

A Buck Or Two Stores
350 Creditstone Rd #201
Concord, ON L4K-3Z2 CANADA

Phone: 905-738-3180   Accepts collect calls?
Toll Free: FAX: 905-738-3176
Internet:
Suitable Sites: RM
Concentration: 80 in ON, 19 in BC, 17 in NS
Expansion: N, Canada, Foreign
Registered: AB
Field Support: $DP, EO, ST, SO, $FC, N
Training: 1 week Hamilton, ON
2 weeks site location

Dollar Discount Stores
1362 Naamans Creek Rd
Boothwyn, PA 19061
Dollar store
Phone: 888-365-5271   Accepts collect calls? N
Toll Free: 800-227-5314   FAX: 610-485-6439
Internet: www.dollardiscount.com
Suitable Sites: AC, FB, M, PC, SC
Concentration: 23 in PA, 12 in NJ, 9 in FL
Expansion: All United States
Registered: CA,FL,IL,IN,MD,MI,MN,ND,NY,OR,RI,SD,VA,WA,WI,DC
Field Support: CP, EO, ST, SO, IC, FC, H, N
Training: 1 week corp office Boothwyn, PA

Just-A-Buck
30 Matthews St
Goshen, NY 10924

Phone: 914-291-7018   Accepts collect calls?
Toll Free: 800-332-2229   FAX: 914-291-7037
Internet: www.justabuck.com
Suitable Sites: RM, SC
Concentration: 13 in NY, 6 in NJ, 2 in CT
Expansion: East Coast
Registered: FL,NY,VA
Field Support: $DP, CP, EO, ST, SO, IC, $FC, N
Training: 10 days NY state
10 days on-site

Pinch-A-Penny
PO Box 6025
Clearwater, FL 34618

Phone: 813-531-8913   Accepts collect calls?
Toll Free: FAX: 813-536-8066
Internet:
Suitable Sites: SC
Concentration: 113 in FL, 1 in GA, 1 in AL
Expansion: Y
Registered: FL
Field Support: DP, CP, EO, ST, SO, FC, H
Training: 4 weeks HQ

Retail Industry   Electronics (Spread 1 of 2)

	Aaron's Rental Purchase	The Car Phone Store	Colortyme	Grand Rental Station/ Taylor Rental	Radio Shack International	RadioShack	Totally Wireless	Video Data Services
Startup Cost	175.5K-385.9K	16.4K-102.8K	264K-475K	200K-250K	50K-60K	45K-63K	126.8K-225K	20K-23K
Franchise Fee	35K	7.5K-25K	25K	1.5K	7.5K	10K	25K-75K	20K
Royalty	5%	VAR.	4%	1.30%	0%	0	7%	750/YR
Advertising Fee	2.5%		$250/MO	0%	0%		3%	0%
Financing Provided	Y	Y	Y	N	Y	Y	Y	Y
Experience Required								
Passive Ownership	A		A	D	D		D	N
In Business Since	1955	1988	1979	1910	1921	1921	1988	1981
Franchised Since	1992	1989	1981	1985	1969	1968	1997	1984
Franchised Units 1996		55				1873		
1997	82	60	264	1144	1935	1888	0	235
1998								
Company Owned 1996		1				4832		
1997	140	1	0	0	4920	4884	20	1
1998								
Number of Units U.S.	222		264	1144	6855		20	230
Canada	0		0	0	0		0	6
Foreign	0		0	0	0		0	0
Projected New U.S.								
Canada								
Foreign								
Corporate Employees	59		18	15	150		21	4
Contract Length	10/10		5-10/5-10	10/10	10/ANNUAL		15/10	10/10
Expand in Territory	Y		Y	N	Y		Y	N
Full-Time Employees	5		6	3			3	1
Part-Time Employees				2			2-3	1
Conversions			Y	Y	N		Y	
Site Selection Assist.	Y		Y	Y	N		Y	N
Lease Negotiation Assist.	Y		Y	Y	N		Y	
Site Space Required	7500		3500	5000	1500		500-2000	200
Development Agreement	Y		Y	N	N		Y	N
Develop. Agree. Term			5					
Sub-franchising	N		N	N	N		N	N

Retail Industry

Aaron's Rental Purchase
309 E Paces Ferry Rd NE
Atlanta, GA 30305-2377

Phone: 404-237-4016   Accepts collect calls?
Toll Free: 800-551-6015   FAX: 404-240-6575
Internet:
Suitable Sites: SC
Concentration: 50 in OH, 10 in GA, 8 in NY
   Expansion: SE, Midwest
   Registered: CA,FL,IL,IN,MI,VA,WI
Field Support: DP, CP, EO, ST, SO, IC, FC, H
   Training: 3 weeks corporate HQ
     2 weeks franchise site

The Car Phone Store
1807 Berlin Turnpike
Wethersfield, CT 06109
Wireless communications stores
   Phone: 860-571-7600   Accepts collect calls?
   Toll Free: FAX:
   Internet:
Suitable Sites:
Concentration:
   Expansion: NE
   Registered:
Field Support:
   Training:

Colortyme
1231 Greenway Dr #900
Irving, TX 75038-2040

Phone: 972-751-1711   Accepts collect calls?
Toll Free: 800-411-8963   FAX: 972-714-5436
Internet: www.colortyme.com
Suitable Sites: FB, RM, SC, SF
Concentration: 55 in TX, 17 in IN, 17 in KS
   Expansion: All United States
   Registered: CA,FL,HI,IL,IN,MD,MI,NY,ND,OR,RI,SD,VA,WA,WI,DC
Field Support: CP, EO, ST, SO, IC, FC, N
   Training: 3 weeks varied training

Grand Rental Station/ Taylor Rental
PO Box 1221
Butler, PA 16003

Phone: 412-284-6676   Accepts collect calls?
Toll Free: 800-833-3004   FAX: 412-284-6320
Internet: www.grandrental.com
Suitable Sites: FB, SC
Concentration: NY, MA, PA
   Expansion: All United States, Canada, Foreign
   Registered: CA,FL,HI,IL,IN,MD,MI,MN,ND,NY,OR,RI,SD,VA,WA,WI,DC
Field Support: CP, EO, ST, SO, IC, FC, H, N
   Training: 1 week Gary IL

Radio Shack International
100 Thockmorton St #1000
Fort Worth, TX 76102

Phone: 817-415-2110   Accepts collect calls?
Toll Free: 800-843-7422   FAX: 817-415-6845
Internet: www.radioshack.com
Suitable Sites: FB, RM, SC, SF
Concentration: CA, NY, IL
   Expansion: All United States
   Registered: CA,FL,IL,IN,MD,MI,MN,NY,ND,OR,SD,VA,WA,WI,DC
Field Support: CP, ST, $SO, $IC, $FC, H, N
   Training: 2-3 days on-site

RadioShack
100 Throckmorton St #1000
Fort Worth, TX 76102
Consumer electronics
   Phone: 817-390-3011   Accepts collect calls?
   Toll Free: FAX:
   Internet:
Suitable Sites:
Concentration:
   Expansion: All United States, Foreign
   Registered:
Field Support:
   Training:

Totally Wireless
522 S Mathilda Ave
Sunnyvale, CA 94086

Phone: 408-522-5220   Accepts collect calls?
Toll Free: 800-969-4735   FAX: 408-522-8964
Internet: www.totallywireless.com
Suitable Sites: PC, RM, SF
Concentration: 7 in CA, 7 in WA, 6 in UT
   Expansion: All United States, Canada, Foreign
   Registered: CA,FL,HI,IL,IN,MD,MI,MN,NY,OR,VA,WA,WI,DC
Field Support: DP, CP, EO, ST, SO, IC, FC, H, N
   Training: 2 weeks corporate office

Video Data Services
3136 Winton Rd S #304
Rochester, NY 14623

Phone: 716-424-5320   Accepts collect calls?
Toll Free: 800-836-9461   FAX: 716-424-5324
Internet:
Suitable Sites: HO
Concentration: 24 in CA, 12 in VA, 8 in NY
   Expansion: All United States, Canada
   Registered: CA,IL,NY,VA,MI,WA
Field Support: CP, FC, H, N
   Training: 3 days San Diego, CA
     3 days Rochester, NY

Retail Industry   **Electronics (Spread 2 of 2)**

	Video Impact								
Startup Cost	170K-225K								
Franchise Fee	25K								
Royalty	6%								
Advertising Fee	NA								
Financing Provided	Y								
Experience Required									
Passive Ownership	N								
In Business Since	1985								
Franchised Since	1997								
Franchised Units 1996									
1997	0								
1998									
Company Owned 1996									
1997	1								
1998									
Number of Units U.S.	1								
Canada	0								
Foreign	0								
Projected New U.S.									
Canada									
Foreign									
Corporate Employees	15								
Contract Length	10/10								
Expand in Territory	Y								
Full-Time Employees	2								
Part-Time Employees	1								
Conversions									
Site Selection Assist.	Y								
Lease Negotiation Assist.	Y								
Site Space Required	1000								
Development Agreement	N								
Develop. Agree. Term									
Sub-franchising	N								

Retail Industry

Video Impact
5975 Roswell Rd NE #355
Atlanta, GA 30328

Phone: 404-256-4108   Accepts collect calls?
Toll Free: 800-544-6139   FAX: 404-843-0491
Internet: www.videoimpact.com
Suitable Sites: SC
Concentration: 1 in GA
Expansion: All United States
Registered: CA,FL,IL,NY
Field Support: EO, ST, SO, $FC, H, N
Training: 2 weeks Atlanta, GA
1 week franchisee site selection
1 week grand opening

Retail Industry   **Flowers**

	Conroys 1-800-Flowers	Foliage Design Systems	Grower Direct Fresh Cut Flowers					
Startup Cost	VAR.	35K-150K	35K-40K					
Franchise Fee	30K	20K-100K	25K					
Royalty	6%	6%	$240/WK.					
Advertising Fee	3%	0%	$15/WK.					
Financing Provided	N	N	N					
Experience Required	N	N						
Passive Ownership	A	D	D					
In Business Since	1960	1971	1991					
Franchised Since	1974	1980	1991					
Franchised Units 1996	81							
1997	90	46	121					
1998	95	44						
Company Owned 1996	25							
1997	20	3	1					
1998	32	3						
Number of Units U.S.	32	45	0					
Canada	0	1	122					
Foreign	0	1	0					
Projected New U.S.	45							
Canada	3							
Foreign	8							
Corporate Employees	2000+	6	14					
Contract Length	10/10	20/5	10/10					
Expand in Territory	Y	Y	Y					
Full-Time Employees	VAR	2	1					
Part-Time Employees	VAR	2	2					
Conversions	N	Y	Y					
Site Selection Assist.	Y	Y	Y					
Lease Negotiation Assist.	Y	N	Y					
Site Space Required	2500	200	400-1000					
Development Agreement	Y	N	N					
Develop. Agree. Term	VAR.							
Sub-franchising	N	Y	Y					

Retail Industry

Flowers

Conroys 1-800-Flowers
1600 Stewart Ave 7th Fl
Westbury, NY 11590
Flowers gifts & related products
　　Phone: 516-237-6033　　Accepts collect calls? N
　　Toll Free: 800-557-4770　　FAX: 516-237-6097
　　Internet: 1800flowers.com
Suitable Sites: AC, FB, SC, SF
Concentration: 90 in CA, 5 in NY, 3 in IL
　　Expansion: All United States, Canada, Foreign
　　Registered: CA FL IL IN MD MI MN ND NY OR RI SD VA WA WI
Field Support: CP, EO, ST, SO, H, N
　　Training: 8 weeks comprehensive training

Foliage Design Systems
4496 35th St
Orlando, FL 32811-6504

　　Phone: 407-245-7776　　Accepts collect calls? N
　　Toll Free: 800-933-7351　　FAX: 407-245-7533
　　Internet:
Suitable Sites: IP, WR
Concentration: 16 in FL, 4 in SC, 3 in MS
　　Expansion: All United States, Canada, Foreign
　　Registered: FL,HI,VA
Field Support: $DP, CP, EO, ST, IC, FC, H, N
　　Training: 8-10 days HQ
　　　　3-5 days in field

Grower Direct Fresh Cut Flowers
4220 - 98 St #301
Edmonton, AB T6E-6A1 CANADA

　　Phone: 403-436-7774　　Accepts collect calls?
　　Toll Free: 800-567-7258　　FAX: 403-436-3336
　　Internet:
Suitable Sites: SC
Concentration: 38 in AB, 22 in ON, 15 in BC
　　Expansion: N, Canada
　　Registered: AB
Field Support: $CP, EO, ST, SO, FC, H, N
　　Training: 5 days in-store
　　　　5 days in-classrooms
　　　　5 days industry tours

Retail Industry   Games, Hobby

	Boomerang GameWare	Dufferin Game Room Store	Game Force Franchising	Hobbytown USA	Its About Games	MicroPlay Video Games	Rider's Hobby Shops	
Startup Cost	60K	250K(CAN)	39K-79.5K	120K-250K	100K-150K	120K-180K	200K-300K	
Franchise Fee	20K	20K(CAN)	19.5K	19.5K	20K	29.5K	17.5K	
Royalty	3%	5%	$500/MO.	2.50%	4%	TO 6%	3.50%	
Advertising Fee		2%		NA	$500/YR	1%	1%	
Financing Provided	Y	N	N	Y	Y	Y	N	
Experience Required					N	N		
Passive Ownership		N		D	D	D	D	
In Business Since	1991	1986	1993	1969	1990	1987	1946	
Franchised Since	1996	1987	1994	1986	1997	1993	1996	
Franchised Units 1996	0		15		0	143		
1997	41	18	25	128	0	143	7	
1998					3	139		
Company Owned 1996	0		2		0	0		
1997	0	26	3	1	40	2	6	
1998					60	0		
Number of Units U.S.		0		129	63	52	13	
Canada		44		0		83	0	
Foreign		0		0		4	0	
Projected New U.S.					10	52		
Canada						115		
Foreign						7		
Corporate Employees		300		27		15	8	
Contract Length		10/5		10/10	10	10/5/5	10/5	
Expand in Territory		N		Y	N	N	N	
Full-Time Employees		3		1-2	1	1	3-4	
Part-Time Employees		6		2-3	2-4	2	6-10	
Conversions		N		Y	Y	Y	Y	
Site Selection Assist.		Y		Y	Y	Y	Y	
Lease Negotiation Assist.		Y		Y	Y	Y	Y	
Site Space Required		3000-3500		2500	1000	1200	3000-5000	
Development Agreement		N		N	Y	Y	N	
Develop. Agree. Term					VAR.	10/5/5		
Sub-franchising		N		N	N	Y	N	

Retail Industry   **Games, Hobby**

Boomerang GameWare
4986 Park Ave
Memphis, TN 38117
Video/computer game sales
  Phone: 901-683-1037   Accepts collect calls?
  Toll Free: FAX:
  Internet:
  Suitable Sites:
  Concentration:
    Expansion: Canada, Foreign
    Registered:
  Field Support:
    Training:

Dufferin Game Room Store
3770 Nashua Dr
Mississauga, ON L4V-1M6 CANADA

  Phone: 905-677-7665   Accepts collect calls?
  Toll Free: 800-268-2597   FAX: 800-387-3157
  Internet:
Suitable Sites: FB, RM, SC
Concentration: 20 in ON, 9 in AB, 6 in BC
  Expansion: N
  Registered: AB
Field Support: EO, ST, SO, IC, $FC, H, N
  Training: head office

Game Force Franchising
2323 S Troy St Bldg 1 #301
Aurora, CO 80014
New & used video games
  Phone: Accepts collect calls?
  Toll Free: 800-226-4037   FAX:
  Internet:
  Suitable Sites:
  Concentration:
    Expansion: CA,IL, Canada
    Registered:
  Field Support:
    Training:

Hobbytown USA
6301 S 58th St
Lincoln, NE 68516

  Phone: 402-434-5052   Accepts collect calls?
  Toll Free: FAX: 402-434-5055
  Internet: www.hobbytown.com
Suitable Sites: RM, SC
Concentration: 7 in AZ, 7 in TX, 6 in CA
  Expansion: All United States
  Registered: CA,FL,HI,IL,IN,MD,MI,MN,ND,NY,OR,RI,SD,VA,WA,WI,DC
Field Support: DP, EO, ST, SO, IC, FC, H, N
  Training: 1 week home office
           2 weeks on-site

Its About Games
4200 Dahlberg Dr
Minneapolis, MN 55422
New & used video games
  Phone: 612-520-8500   Accepts collect calls? N
  Toll Free: 800-645-7299   FAX: 612-520-8501
  Internet: akinker@growbiz.com
Suitable Sites: M, PC, RM, SC, SF
Concentration: 1 in WI, 1 in NC, 1 in OH
  Expansion: All United States, Canada
  Registered: CA,FL,HI,IL,IN,MD,MI,MN,ND,NY,OR,RI,SD,VA,WA,WI,DC,AB
Field Support: EO, ST, SO, IC, FC, H, N
  Training: 2 weeks comprehensive

MicroPlay Video Games
918 Dundas St E 5th Fl
Mississauga, ON L4Y-4M9 CANADA
Sell/rent new/used video game/PC CD-ROM hardware, software & acc
  Phone: 905-949-2580   Accepts collect calls? N
  Toll Free: 800-265-7529   FAX: 905-949-4516
  Internet: www.microplay.com
Suitable Sites: AC, DA, M, PC, RM, SC
Concentration: 50 in ONT, 10 in QUE, 8 in BC
  Expansion: All United States, Canada, Foreign
  Registered:
Field Support: DP, CP, EO, ST, SO, IC, FC, H
  Training: 3 weeks classroom & in-store

Rider's Hobby Shops
3200 Wildwood Ave
Jackson, MI 49202

  Phone: 517-796-0950   Accepts collect calls?
  Toll Free: 888-530-9780   FAX: 517-796-2679
  Internet: www.riders.com
Suitable Sites: SC
Concentration: 11 in MI, 1 in TX, 1 in VA
  Expansion: Focus On Midwest, Foreign
  Registered: IL,IN,MI
Field Support: DP, CP, EO, ST, SO, IC, FC, H, N
  Training: 5 days corporate HQ
           14 days franchisee's retail loca.

Retail Industry

Gifts

	Ashley Avery's Collectables	Balloons & Bears	Country Clutter	Elephant House Inc	Elephant Walk Gift Galleries	For Olde Times Sake	Last Flight Out	Tinder Box International
Startup Cost	96K-398K	49.8K-85K	170K-270K	6.3K-13K	140K-190K	150K-175K	20.95K-39.2K	175K-500K
Franchise Fee	30K	25K	25K	24K	25K	25K	12.5K	30K
Royalty	6%	6%	5.50%	0	6%	6%	5%	5%/4%
Advertising Fee	2%		1%		1%			3%
Financing Provided	Y	Y	N	N	N	N	N	Y
Experience Required	N		N					N
Passive Ownership	D		D		D			A
In Business Since	1975	1989	1991	1991	1983	1988	1983	1928
Franchised Since	1990	1993	1992	1991	1996	1997	1995	1965
Franchised Units 1996	23	36	20	125			9	
1997	31	29	31	158	1	0	11	127
1998	33		40		0			128
Company Owned 1996	0	5	0	1		1	0	
1997	0	10	0	1	2	1	0	2
1998	1		0		14			2
Number of Units U.S.	33		40		14			129
Canada	0		0		0			1
Foreign	0		0		0			0
Projected New U.S.	5		20		2			150
Canada			0					3
Foreign			0					5
Corporate Employees	12		10		6			9
Contract Length	10		5/5		5/5/5			10/5/5
Expand in Territory	Y		Y		Y			Y
Full-Time Employees	2		2		1			2
Part-Time Employees	2		5		4			2-3
Conversions	Y		Y		Y			Y
Site Selection Assist.	Y		Y		Y			Y
Lease Negotiation Assist.	Y		Y		Y			Y
Site Space Required	1000		1800-2400		1000			1000-3000
Development Agreement	Y		Y		N			Y
Develop. Agree. Term			OPEN					5
Sub-franchising	N		N		N			N

Retail Industry   Gifts

Ashley Avery's Collectables
100 Glenborough Dr 14th Fl
Houston, TX 77067
Fine collectibles
       Phone: 281-775-5290   Accepts collect calls? N
       Toll Free: 800-543-3325   FAX: 281-775-5250
       Internet: www.ashleyaverys.com
Suitable Sites: RM
Concentration: 16 in TX
    Expansion: All United States
    Registered: CA,FL,IL,IN,MD,MI,MN,NY,OR,RI,SD,VA,WA,WI,DC
Field Support: DP, EO, ST, SO, IC, FC, H, N
    Training: 7 days Houston, TX

Balloons & Bears
1437 Pinerow Ct
Saint Louis, MO 63146
Balloons bears flowers gift baskets cards
       Phone: Accepts collect calls?
       Toll Free: 800-330-2327   FAX:
       Internet:
Suitable Sites:
Concentration:
    Expansion: All United States, Canada
    Registered:
Field Support:
    Training:

Country Clutter
3333 Vaca Valley Pkwy #900
Vacaville, CA 95688

       Phone: 707-451-6890   Accepts collect calls? N
       Toll Free: 800-425-8883   FAX: 707-451-0410
       Internet: ctryvision@aol.com
Suitable Sites: AC, PC, RM, OTHER
Concentration: 14 in CA, 3 in TX, 3 in GA
    Expansion: All United States, Canada
    Registered: CA,FL,HI,IL,MI,NY,OR,VA,WA,IN,MD,RI,WI
Field Support: EO, ST, SO, IC, $FC, H, N
    Training: 3-5 days HQ
           3-5 days on-site
           20 hours home training w/computer

Elephant House Inc
12741 Research Blvd #300
Austin, TX 78759
Greeting card distribution
       Phone: Accepts collect calls?
       Toll Free: 800-729-2273   FAX:
       Internet:
Suitable Sites:
Concentration:
    Expansion: All United States, Canada, Foreign
    Registered:
Field Support:
    Training:

Elephant Walk Gift Galleries
318 N Carson St #214
Carson City, NV 89701
Unique hand-craft gift gallery
       Phone: 702-882-1963   Accepts collect calls?
       Toll Free: 800-654-5156   FAX: 800-654-5161
       Internet:
Suitable Sites: DA, RM, SF
Concentration: 14 in HI, 1 in CA
    Expansion: All United States
    Registered: CA,FL,HI,IL
Field Support: EO, ST, SO, IC, FC, H, N
    Training: 10 days IEL Univ Honolulu, HI

For Olde Times Sake
9494 E Redfield Rd #1001
Scottsdale, AZ 85260
Nostalgic memorabilia
       Phone: 602-860-1060   Accepts collect calls?
       Toll Free: 888-803-3717   FAX:
       Internet:
Suitable Sites:
Concentration:
    Expansion: Canada, Foreign
    Registered:
Field Support:
    Training:

Last Flight Out
PO Box 1903
Key West, FL 33041
Gifts specialty clothing hats
       Phone: Accepts collect calls?
       Toll Free: 800-294-8008   FAX:
       Internet:
Suitable Sites:
Concentration:
    Expansion: Canada, Foreign
    Registered:
Field Support:
    Training:

Tinder Box International
Three Bala Plaza East #102
Bala Cynwyd, PA 19004-2449
America's #1 cigar-gift franchise
       Phone: 610-668-4220   Accepts collect calls? Y
       Toll Free: 800-846-3372   FAX: 610-668-4266
       Internet: www.tinderbox.com
Suitable Sites: AC, FB, M, PC, RM, SC, SF
Concentration: 21 in CA, 10 in IL, 7 in OH
    Expansion: All United States, Canada, Foreign
    Registered: CA,FL,HI,IL,IN,MD,MI,MN,ND,NY,OR,RI,SD,VA,WA,WI,DC
Field Support: $DP, EO, ST, SO, IC, FC, H, N
    Training: 1 week corporate HQ
           1 week on-site

Retail Industry   Hardware

	Almost Heaven, Ltd.	Color Your World	Re Tool	Snap-On Tools	Tempaco			
Startup Cost	10K-20K	180K-300K	110K-161K	121.7K-200.6K	100K			
Franchise Fee	0	35K-80K	20K	5K	50K			
Royalty	0%	7%	4%	$50/MO	4%			
Advertising Fee	0%	4%	5%	0%	0%			
Financing Provided	Y	N	Y	Y	N			
Experience Required			N					
Passive Ownership	A	D	D	N	D			
In Business Since	1971	1912	1998	1920	1946			
Franchised Since	1975	1977	1998	1991	1972			
Franchised Units 1996								
1997	2137	132		4077	15			
1998			2					
Company Owned 1996								
1997	0	144	2	237	5			
1998			3					
Number of Units U.S.	1573	0	6	3200	20			
Canada	70	276		379	0			
Foreign	494	0		735	0			
Projected New U.S.			40					
Canada								
Foreign								
Corporate Employees	99		140	7000	15			
Contract Length	5/5	10/5	10/10	10/5	10/10			
Expand in Territory	Y	N	Y	Y	Y			
Full-Time Employees	3	4	1	1	2-3			
Part-Time Employees	2	3	3		1			
Conversions	Y		Y		Y			
Site Selection Assist.	Y	N	Y	N	Y			
Lease Negotiation Assist.	Y		Y		N			
Site Space Required	1000	3000	2200-3000		3500			
Development Agreement	Y	N	Y	N	N			
Develop. Agree. Term	5		3					
Sub-franchising	Y	N	N	N	N			

Retail Industry   Hardware

Almost Heaven, Ltd.
Rt. 5-Fs
Renick, WV 24966

Phone: 304-497-3163   Accepts collect calls?
Toll Free: FAX: 304-497-2698
Internet: www.almostheaven.net
Suitable Sites: FB
Concentration: 71 in MA, 49 in NY, 42 in MD
Expansion: All United States, Canada, Foreign
Registered: CA,FL,HI,IL,IN,MD,MI,MN,ND,NY,OR,RI,SD,VA,WA,WI,DC
Field Support: DP, CP, EO, ST, SO, IC, $FC, H, N
Training: 2 weeks factory
2 weeks on-site

Color Your World
2600 Steeles Ave W
Concord, ON L4K-3C8   CANADA

Phone: 905-738-0080   Accepts collect calls?
Toll Free: 800-387-7311   FAX: 905-738-9723
Internet:
Suitable Sites: FB
Concentration: ON, BC, AB
Expansion: N, Canada
Registered: AB
Field Support: DP, CP, EO, ST, IC, $FC, H, N
Training: 8 weeks various locations

Re Tool
4200 Dahlberg Dr
Minneapolis, MN 55422-4837
Retail store that buys & sells new & used tools & accessories
Phone: 612-520-4500   Accepts collect calls? N
Toll Free: 800-269-4075   FAX: 612-520-8601
Internet:
Suitable Sites: SC, SF
Concentration: 3 in MN, 2 in MI, 1 in ND
Expansion: All United States, Canada
Registered: CA,FL,HI,IL,IN,MD,MI,MN,ND,NY,OR,RI,SD,VA,WA,WI,DC,AB
Field Support: EO, ST, SO, FC, H
Training: 10 days Minneapolis, MN

Snap-On Tools
2801 80th St
Kenosha, WI 53141

Phone: 414-656-5376   Accepts collect calls?
Toll Free: 800-775-7630   FAX: 414-656-5088
Internet:
Suitable Sites:
Concentration:
Expansion: All United States, Canada, Foreign
Registered: CA,FL,HI,IL,IN,MD,MI,MN,ND,NY,OR,RI,SD,VA,WA,WI,DC
Field Support: DP, CP, EO, ST, FC, H, N
Training: 5 weeks branch/field

Tempaco
PO Box 547667
Orlando, FL 32854-7667
heating & cooling parts & supplies for industrial & commercial
Phone: 407-898-3456   Accepts collect calls?
Toll Free: 800-868-7838   FAX: 407-898-7316
Internet: www.tempaco.com
Suitable Sites: FB, SF
Concentration: 16 in FL, 2 in GA, 2 in TN
Expansion: SE, TX
Registered: FL
Field Support: $DP, $CP, EO, ST, SO, $FC, H
Training: 2 weeks corporate HQ
10+ days store location
on-going

Retail Industry

Music, Video

	CD Warehouse	Jumbo Video	Music-Go-Round	TFM	TFM/Top Forty			
Startup Cost	120K-150K	125K-300K	193K-242K	125K-200K	125K-200K			
Franchise Fee	15K	25K-50K	20K	15K	15K			
Royalty	5%	5%	3%	5%	5%			
Advertising Fee	2.25%	3%	$500/YR		1%			
Financing Provided	Y	Y	Y	N	Y			
Experience Required	N	N	N					
Passive Ownership	D	N	N		A			
In Business Since	1992	1987	1986	1976	1974			
Franchised Since	1992	1989	1994	1980	1985			
Franchised Units 1996				13				
1997	96	63	34	17	17			
1998	288	65	58					
Company Owned 1996				20				
1997	34	0	4	2	2			
1998	33	2	7					
Number of Units U.S.	313	0	65		0			
Canada	8	67	0		19			
Foreign	8	0	0		0			
Projected New U.S.			35					
Canada		15						
Foreign								
Corporate Employees	40	21	200		9			
Contract Length	10/10	10/10	10/10		5/5			
Expand in Territory	Y	Y	N		Y			
Full-Time Employees	1-2	6	2		2			
Part-Time Employees	3	17	3		4			
Conversions	Y	Y	Y		Y			
Site Selection Assist.	Y	Y	Y		Y			
Lease Negotiation Assist.	Y	Y	Y		Y			
Site Space Required	1500-2000	1200-4000	2500		1400			
Development Agreement	Y	N	Y		N			
Develop. Agree. Term			3					
Sub-franchising	N	Y	N		N			

Retail Industry   Music, Video

CD Warehouse

1204 Sovereign Row
Oklahoma City, OK 73108
Buy/sell/trade pre-owned CD's, top 100 CD's, DVD, games & music
Phone: 405-949-2422   Accepts collect calls? N
Toll Free: 800-641-9394   FAX: 405-949-2566
Internet: cdwarehouse.com
Suitable Sites: AC, FB, SC
Concentration: 55 in TX, 29 in FL, 17 in OH
Expansion: All United States, Canada, Foreign
Registered: CA,FL,IL,IN,MD,MI,MN,NY,OR,RI,VA,WA,WI,DC
Field Support: CP, EO, ST, SO, IC, FC, H, N
Training: 1 week Oklahoma City, OK

Jumbo Video

5360 S Service Rd #201
Burlington, ON L7L-5L1 CANADA
Video, dvd & games sale & rental, movie reltd merchandise, candy
Phone: 905-634-4244   Accepts collect calls?
Toll Free: FAX: 905-632-2964
Internet: www.jumbovideo.com
Suitable Sites: SC
Concentration: 52 in ON, 5 in MB, 4 in BC
Expansion: Canada
Registered:
Field Support: EO, ST, SO, FC, N
Training: 4 days head office
2 weeks on-site

Music-Go-Round

4200 Dahlberg Dr
Minneapolis, MN 55422-4837
Music store buy/sell/trade/consign musical instruments & gear
Phone: 612-520-8419   Accepts collect calls? N
Toll Free: 800-645-7298   FAX: 612-520-8489
Internet: www.musicgoround.com
Suitable Sites: AC, FB, PC, SC, SF
Concentration: 11 in MN, 9 in IL, 4 in WI
Expansion: All United States, Canada
Registered: CA,FL,HI,IL,IN,MD,MI,MN,ND,NY,OR,RI,SD,VA,WA,WI,DC
Field Support: DP, EO, ST, SO, IC, $FC, H, N
Training: 12 days home office

TFM

10333 174th St
Edmonton, AB T5S-1H1 CANADA
CD's cassettes videos
Phone: 403-489-2324   Accepts collect calls?
Toll Free: FAX:
Internet:
Suitable Sites:
Concentration:
Expansion: N, Canada
Registered:
Field Support:
Training:

TFM/Top Forty

10333- 174 St
Edmonton, AB T5S-1H1 CANADA

Phone: 403-483-3217   Accepts collect calls?
Toll Free: 800-661-9931   FAX: 403-486-7528
Internet:
Suitable Sites: RM
Concentration: 7 in AB, 5 in SK, 3 in BC
Expansion: N, Canada
Registered: AB
Field Support: EO, ST, SO, IC, FC, N
Training: 1 week HQ
1 week in store
2 days refresher on-site

Retail Industry

Nature, Ecology

	EcoSmarte Planet Friendly	The Great Wilderness Company, Inc.	The Nature of Things Store	Nature's 10				
Startup Cost	100K-245K	275K	168K-288K	48K-760K				
Franchise Fee	15K-30K	30K	25K	27K				
Royalty	0%	5%	5%	5%				
Advertising Fee	0%	1%	1%	0.5%				
Financing Provided	Y	Y	Y	N				
Experience Required		N						
Passive Ownership	D	N	D	A				
In Business Since	1994	1989	1989	1993				
Franchised Since	1996	1994	1991	1995				
Franchised Units 1996								
1997	4	18	11	2				
1998		12	12					
Company Owned 1996								
1997	2	1	5	1				
1998		1	5					
Number of Units U.S.	6	0	17	3				
Canada	0	13	0	0				
Foreign	0	0	0	0				
Projected New U.S.			3					
Canada		2						
Foreign								
Corporate Employees	10	7	4	3				
Contract Length	5/5	5/5	10/10	5/5/5				
Expand in Territory	Y	Y	Y	N				
Full-Time Employees	2	3	1	5				
Part-Time Employees	4	2	4	2				
Conversions	N			Y				
Site Selection Assist.	Y	Y	Y	Y				
Lease Negotiation Assist.	Y	Y	Y	Y				
Site Space Required	1500	2000	1500-1800	1500				
Development Agreement	Y	N	N	N				
Develop. Agree. Term	5							
Sub-franchising	N	Y	N	N				

Retail Industry

Nature, Ecology

EcoSmarte Planet Friendly
730 West 78th St
Richfield, MN 55423

Phone: 612-866-1200 — Accepts collect calls?
Toll Free: 800-466-7946 — FAX: 612-866-0152
Internet: www.ecosmarte.com
Suitable Sites: HO, SC, SF
Concentration: 1 in AZ, 1 in MN, 1 in CA
Expansion: SE, Canada, Foreign
Registered:
Field Support: CP, EO, ST, $SO, $FC, H
Training: 10 days phoenix, AZ
7 days Minneapolis, MN

The Great Wilderness Company, Inc.
3365 Harvester Rd
Burlington, ON L7N-3N2 CANADA

Phone: 905-631-5300 — Accepts collect calls? N
Toll Free: — FAX: 905-631-6303
Internet:
Suitable Sites: RM
Concentration: 9 in ON, 3 in BC, 3 in PQ
Expansion: Canada
Registered: AB
Field Support: EO, $ST, SO, IC, N
Training: 4 weeks Ontario, Canada

The Nature of Things Store
10700 W Venture Dr
Franklin, WI 53132
Science & nature products, educational books & games, gifts
Phone: 414-529-2192 — Accepts collect calls?
Toll Free: 800-283-2921 — FAX: 414-529-2253
Internet: mmradaj@execpc.com
Suitable Sites: RM
Concentration: 7 in WI, 5 in MO, 1 in CO
Expansion: All United States
Registered: FL,IL,IN,MI,MN,NY,SD,WI
Field Support: DP, EO, ST, SO, FC, H, N
Training: 1 week corporate office/stores

Nature's 10
Box 890
North Sioux City, SD 57105

Phone: 712-546-6123 — Accepts collect calls?
Toll Free: 800-610-8610 — FAX: 712-546-7699
Internet:
Suitable Sites: FB, RM, SC
Concentration: 3 in SD
Expansion: All United States
Registered:
Field Support: EO, ST, $SO, H, N
Training: 10 days Sioux City, IA
3 days Bismarck, ND

Retail Industry

Party Supplies

	Paper Warehouse Franchising Inc	Party City Corp	Party Land Inc					
Startup Cost	146K-375K	275K	275K					
Franchise Fee	19K-25K	35K	35K					
Royalty	4%	4%	5%					
Advertising Fee	0							
Financing Provided	N	N	Y					
Experience Required	N		N					
Passive Ownership	A		A					
In Business Since	1983	1986	1986					
Franchised Since	1987	1990	1988					
Franchised Units 1996	55	148	72					
1997	50	152	83					
1998	49							
Company Owned 1996	60	19	15					
1997	64	77	7					
1998	88							
Number of Units U.S.	25		63					
Canada	0		4					
Foreign	0		20					
Projected New U.S.	11		75					
Canada	2		6					
Foreign	2		35					
Corporate Employees	5		25					
Contract Length	10		10					
Expand in Territory	Y		Y					
Full-Time Employees	3-4							
Part-Time Employees	3-4							
Conversions	Y		Y					
Site Selection Assist.	Y		Y					
Lease Negotiation Assist.	Y		Y					
Site Space Required	4000-9000		6000					
Development Agreement	Y		Y					
Develop. Agree. Term	10		10					
Sub-franchising	N		Y					

Retail Industry

Party Supplies

Paper Warehouse Franchising Inc

7630 Excelsior Blvd
Saint Louis Park, MN 55426-4504
Discount party supplies & greeting cards
    Phone: 612-936-1000   Accepts collect calls? N
Toll Free: 800-229-1792   FAX: 612-936-9800
    Internet: www.paperwarehouse.com
Suitable Sites: AC, FB, PC, SC, SF
Concentration: 5 in CO, 5 in AZ, 5 in SD
    Expansion: All United States, Canada, Foreign
    Registered: CA,FL,IL,IN,MD,MI,MN,ND,NY,OR,RI,SD,VA,WA,WI
Field Support: CP, EO, ST, SO, FC, H, N
    Training: 5 days classroom & in-store Minneapolis HQ

Party City Corp

400 Commons Wy #C
Rockaway, NJ 07866
Discount party supplies
    Phone: Accepts collect calls?
Toll Free: 800-883-2100   FAX:
    Internet:
Suitable Sites:
Concentration:
    Expansion: CA,HI,IL,IN,MI,NY, Foreign
    Registered:
Field Support:
    Training:

Party Land Inc

5215 Militia Hill Rd
Plymouth Meeting, PA 19462
Party supplies & balloons
    Phone: 610-941-6200   Accepts collect calls?
Toll Free: 800-778-9563   FAX: 610-941-6301
    Internet: www.partyland.com
Suitable Sites: AC, FB, M, PC, SC, SF
Concentration: 14 in PA, 6 in TX, 5 in NJ
    Expansion: All United States, Canada, Foreign
    Registered: CA,FL,HI,IL,IN,MD,MI,MN,ND,NY,OR,RI,SD,VA,WA,WI,DC
Field Support: EO, ST, SO, FC, H, N
    Training: 7 days at corporate HQ
        21 days at franchise location

Retail Industry

Water

	Culligan Water Conditioning	Pure Water Ultima	Purified Water To Go					
Startup Cost	103K-220K	ON-GOING	65K-85K					
Franchise Fee	5K	0	19.5K					
Royalty	0.5-5%	0	4-6%					
Advertising Fee		0	$150-200/MO					
Financing Provided	N	N	Y					
Experience Required								
Passive Ownership		N	D					
In Business Since	1936	1968	1992					
Franchised Since	1938	1995	1995					
Franchised Units 1996	795							
1997	793	8	28					
1998								
Company Owned 1996	23							
1997	26	0	1					
1998								
Number of Units U.S.		0	29					
Canada		0	0					
Foreign		8	0					
Projected New U.S.								
Canada								
Foreign								
Corporate Employees		2	9					
Contract Length		5/5	10/10					
Expand in Territory		Y	Y					
Full-Time Employees		7	1					
Part-Time Employees			2					
Conversions								
Site Selection Assist.		N	Y					
Lease Negotiation Assist.		N	Y					
Site Space Required		4500	1000					
Development Agreement		N	Y					
Develop. Agree. Term			10					
Sub-franchising		Y	N					

Retail Industry   Water

Culligan Water Conditioning
1 Culligan Pkwy
Northbrook, IL 60062-6209
Water-related products & services
    Phone: 847-205-5823   Accepts collect calls?
    Toll Free: FAX:
    Internet:
Suitable Sites:
Concentration:
    Expansion: All United States, Canada
    Registered:
Field Support:
    Training:

Pure Water Ultima
PO Box 83226
Lincoln, NE 68501

    Phone: 402-467-9300   Accepts collect calls?
    Toll Free: 800-875-5915   FAX: 402-467-9393
    Internet: www.purewaterinc.com
Suitable Sites:
Concentration:
    Expansion: N, Foreign
    Registered: N
Field Support: EO, ST, FC, N
    Training: 3 days Norway
           3 days Japan
           4 days Guam

Purified Water To Go
5160 S Valley View Blvd #112
Las Vegas, NV 89118

    Phone: 702-895-9350   Accepts collect calls?
    Toll Free: 800-976-9283   FAX: 702-895-9306
    Internet: www.watertogo.com
Suitable Sites: SC, SF
Concentration: 4 in NV, 4 in WA, 4 in CA
    Expansion: All United States, Canada, Foreign
    Registered: CA, WA, WI
Field Support: CP, EO, ST, SO, IC, FC, H, N
    Training: 5 days corp office Las Vegas, NV

Retail Industry   Other Retail (Spread 1 of 2)

	Butterfields, Etc.	Candleman Corporation	The Connoisseur	Consumer Casket USA	Crown Trophy	The Flag Shop	Gateway Newstands	John Simmons
Startup Cost	150K-225K	150K-350K	125K-150K	75K-85K	70K-85K	70K-90K	50K-200K	110K-185K
Franchise Fee	20K	25K	29.5K	25K	20K	25K	VAR.	15K
Royalty	4-5%	6%	6%	5%	5%	4%	3%	4.50%
Advertising Fee		0%	3%	1%	$100/MO.	2%	0%	0%
Financing Provided	Y	Y	N	Y	N	N	Y	N
Experience Required				N		N		
Passive Ownership	N	N	D	N	N	A	N	D
In Business Since	1979	1991	1975	95	1978	1974	1983	1985
Franchised Since	1986	1992	1989	96	1987	1988	1983	1985
Franchised Units 1996								
1997	26	76	6		44	6	285	1
1998								
Company Owned 1996								
1997	0	11	1		1	1	0	1
1998								
Number of Units U.S.	26	85	7	4	45	0	66	3
Canada	0	2	0		0	7	222	0
Foreign	0	0	0		0	0	1	0
Projected New U.S.				7				
Canada								
Foreign								
Corporate Employees		24	4		10	27	11	4
Contract Length	10	10/10	10/10	5	10/10	10/10	5-10/5	5/1
Expand in Territory		N	Y	Y	Y	Y	Y	Y
Full-Time Employees		1	1	2	1	3	1	2
Part-Time Employees		4-5	2	1	3	1	2	1-3
Conversions	Y	N	N	Y	N	Y	N	N
Site Selection Assist.	Y	Y	Y	Y	Y	Y	Y	Y
Lease Negotiation Assist.	Y	Y	Y	N	Y	Y	Y	Y
Site Space Required		800-1200	1500	2000	1250	1200	100-1000	2000
Development Agreement		N	Y	N	N	N	N	N
Develop. Agree. Term			10/10					
Sub-franchising		N	Y	N	N	Y	Y	Y

Retail Industry   **Other Retail (Spread 1 of 2)**

Butterfields, Etc.
1040 Wm Hilton Pkwy Circle Bldg
Hilton Head Island, SC 29928

Phone: 803-842-6000	Accepts collect calls?
Toll Free:	FAX: 803-842-6999
Internet:	

Suitable Sites:
Concentration:
    Expansion:
    Registered:
Field Support:
    Training: 2 weeks

Candleman Corporation
1021 Industrial Park Rd PO Box 731
Brainerd, MN 56401

Phone: 218-829-0592	Accepts collect calls?
Toll Free: 800-328-3453	FAX: 218-825-2449
Internet: www.candleman.com	

Suitable Sites: RM
Concentration: 6 in FL, 5 in WA, 5 in MN
    Expansion: All United States, Canada, Foreign
    Registered: CA,FL,HI,IL,IN,MD,MI,MN,ND,NY,OR,RI,SD,VA,WA,WI,DC
Field Support: DP, CP, EO, ST, SO, IC, FC, H, N
    Training: 1 week training center
            3-4 days on-site
            on-going as needed

The Connoisseur
201 Torrance Blvd
Redondo Beach, CA 90277

Phone: 310-374-9768	Accepts collect calls?
Toll Free:	FAX: 310-372-9097
Internet:	

Suitable Sites: FB, RM, SC
Concentration: 2 in CO, 2 in CA, 1 in IL
    Expansion: All United States
    Registered: CA,FL,HI,IL,IN,MD,MI,MN,ND,NY,OR,RI,SD,VA,WA,WI,DC
Field Support: DP, CP, EO, ST, SO, IC, FC
    Training: 1 week HQ

Consumer Casket USA
5044 Peach St.
Erie, PA 16509
Funeral and memorial merchandise

Phone: 814-866-7777	Accepts collect calls? N
Toll Free: 800-611-8778	FAX: 814-864-7732
Internet: www.ccusa.com	

Suitable Sites: M, RM, SC
Concentration:
    Expansion: All United States, Canada, Foreign
    Registered: CA,FL,MI,NY,DC
Field Support:
    Training:

Crown Trophy
1 Odell Plaza
Yonkers, NY 10701

Phone: 914-964-8366	Accepts collect calls?
Toll Free: 800-583-8228	FAX: 914-963-4841
Internet:	

Suitable Sites: SF
Concentration: 14 in NY, 5 in NJ, 3 in PA
    Expansion: All United States
    Registered: CA,FL,IL,MD,MN,MI,NY,OR,SD,WI
Field Support: EO, ST, SO, FC, H, N
    Training: 1 week corporate office
            1 week on-site

The Flag Shop
1755 West 4th Ave
Vancouver, BC V6J-1M2   CANADA

Phone: 604-736-8161	Accepts collect calls?
Toll Free: 800-663-8681	FAX: 604-736-6439
Internet: www.flagshop.com	

Suitable Sites: FB, SC, SF
Concentration: 2 in BC, 2 in AB, 1 in NS
    Expansion: N, Canada
    Registered: AB
Field Support: DP, CP, EO, ST, $SO, IC, $FC, H, N
    Training: 3 weeks Vancouver, BC
            1 week franchise location

Gateway Newstands
30 E Beaver Creek Rd #206
Richmond Hill, ON L4B-1J2   CANADA

Phone: 905-886-8900	Accepts collect calls?
Toll Free: 800-942-5351	FAX: 905-886-8904
Internet:	

Suitable Sites: RM, SF, OTHER
Concentration: 193 in ON, 19 in IL, 16 in NY
    Expansion: All United States, Canada, Foreign
    Registered:
Field Support: CP, EO, ST, SO, IC, H
    Training: 2 weeks in store

John Simmons
36 W Calhoun Ave
Memphis, TN 38103

Phone: 901-526-5567	Accepts collect calls?
Toll Free: 800-737-5567	FAX: 901-526-5605
Internet:	

Suitable Sites: SC
Concentration: 1 in TN, 1 in VA
    Expansion: SE, SE, Midwest
    Registered: IN,VA
Field Support: EO, ST, SO, FC, N
    Training: 1-3 days HQ
            4-7 days on-site
            5-7 days market

Retail Industry   Other Retail (Spread 2 of 2)

	Papyrus	Shefield & Sons	Successories	Wicks 'N' Sticks	Yard Cards			
Startup Cost	205K-417K	69K-130K	144K-238K	153.6K-249.3K	5K-15K			
Franchise Fee	29.5K	10K	35K	25K	1K+			
Royalty	6%	2%	2%	6%	5%			
Advertising Fee	1%	2%	1%	1%	0%			
Financing Provided	Y	N	N	Y	N			
Experience Required		N						
Passive Ownership	D	D	D		D			
In Business Since	1973	1976	1985	1968	1983			
Franchised Since	1988	1976	1992	1968	1986			
Franchised Units 1996								
1997	90	63	47	218	7			
1998		61						
Company Owned 1996								
1997	40	2	52	4	1			
1998		1						
Number of Units U.S.	130	0	96	222	8			
Canada	0	65	3	0	0			
Foreign	0	0	0	0	0			
Projected New U.S.								
Canada		2						
Foreign								
Corporate Employees	30	9	150	37	2			
Contract Length	10/5/5	5/5	5/5	10/5/5/5	20/5/5			
Expand in Territory	Y	Y	Y	Y	Y			
Full-Time Employees	1-2	1	2	1-2				
Part-Time Employees	4	1	2	2	1-2			
Conversions	Y	Y						
Site Selection Assist.	Y	Y	Y	Y	N			
Lease Negotiation Assist.	Y	Y	Y	Y				
Site Space Required	1000	350-500	800-1200	1000-2000				
Development Agreement	Y	N	N	N	N			
Develop. Agree. Term								
Sub-franchising	N	N	Y	Y	N			

Retail Industry

Papyrus
954 60th St
Oakland, CA 94608

Phone: 510-428-0166   Accepts collect calls?
Toll Free: 888-922-9555   FAX: 510-428-0615
Internet:
Suitable Sites: RM, SF
Concentration:
    Expansion: All United States, Canada
    Registered: CA,FL,HI,IL,IN,MD,MI,MN,NY,OR,RI,VA,WA,WI,DC,AB
Field Support: DP, CP, EO, ST, SO, IC, FC, H, N
    Training: 9 days corporate HQ

Shefield & Sons
2265 W Railway St Box 490
Abbotsford, BC V2S-5Z5   CANADA
Traditional "smoke shop", extensive selection of tobacco product
Phone: 604-859-1014   Accepts collect calls? N
Toll Free: FAX: 604-859-1711
    Internet: www.shefieldgourmet.com
Suitable Sites: K, M, OC, RM, SC
Concentration: 27 in BC, 17 in ON, 13 in AB
    Expansion: N
    Registered: AB
Field Support: EO, ST, SO, H, N
    Training: 1 week on-site

Successories
2520 Diehl Rd
Aurora, IL 60504

Phone: 630-820-7000   Accepts collect calls?
Toll Free: 800-621-1423   FAX: 630-820-3856
Internet:
Suitable Sites: RM, SC
Concentration: 11 in IL, 8 in CA, 6 in FL
    Expansion: Various Markets, Canada
    Registered: CA,FL,HI,IL,IN,MD,MI,MN,ND,NY,OR,RI,SD,VA,WA,WI,DC
Field Support: CP, EO, ST, SO, $IC, $FC, H
    Training: 5 days Lombard, IL

Wicks 'N' Sticks
PO Box 4586
Houston, TX 77210-4586

Phone: 281-874-3642   Accepts collect calls?
Toll Free: 888-559-4257   FAX: 281-874-3678
Internet:
Suitable Sites: RM
Concentration: 26 in TX, 15 in NY, 15 in FL
    Expansion: All United States
    Registered: CA,IL,IN,MD,MI,MN,NY,ND,OR,RI,SD,VA,WA,WI
Field Support: DP, EO, ST, SO, IC, FC, H, N
    Training: 2 weeks Houston, TX

Yard Cards
PO Box 618
Teays, WV 25569

Phone: 304-757-6944   Accepts collect calls?
Toll Free: 800-655-6944   FAX: 304-757-6944
Internet: www.members.aol/yardcards
Suitable Sites: HO
Concentration: 3 in IL, 2 in MO, 1 in WV
    Expansion: All United States
    Registered: IL,MD
Field Support: $FC, N
    Training: as needed

Security Systems Industry

	AirSoPure	Custom Homewatch International	Dynamark Security Centers	Fire Defense Centers	Paystation	ProShred Security	Roll-A-Way	Safe Not Sorry
Startup Cost	19.2K-21.4K	4K-10K	42K-46K	42.5K	7.5K	218K	25K-45K	11K-39K
Franchise Fee	15K	3K-7K	15K	19.5K	10K	35K	6.6K-18.5K	10K
Royalty	0%	3%	100/MO	10%	0%	8%	0%	8%
Advertising Fee	2%	2%	1%	2%	0%	0%	0%	2%
Financing Provided	N	N	Y	Y	N	Y	N	N
Experience Required						N		N
Passive Ownership	D	A	D	A	N	N	D	N
In Business Since	1995	1988	1975	1973	1955	1985	1955	1997
Franchised Since	1997	1989	1984	1986	1995	1990	1994	1997
Franchised Units 1996								0
1997	7	45	130	17	10	22	25	9
1998								18
Company Owned 1996								0
1997	1	0	4	44	4	1	4	0
1998								0
Number of Units U.S.	4	0	133	61	0	7	29	18
Canada	1	45	0	0	14	15	0	0
Foreign	3	0	1	0	0	1	0	0
Projected New U.S.								50
Canada								10
Foreign								5
Corporate Employees	20	2	97	12	40	15	30	5
Contract Length	5/5	5/5	10/10	10/10	5/5	5/5/5/5	10/5/5	5
Expand in Territory	Y	Y	Y	Y	Y	Y	Y	Y
Full-Time Employees	1		1	2		5	2	1-3
Part-Time Employees			1		1	2	2	1-3
Conversions			Y	N		Y		Y
Site Selection Assist.	N	N	Y	Y	N	N	N	N
Lease Negotiation Assist.			N	Y		N	N	N
Site Space Required			600	1500				
Development Agreement	N	N	N	N	N	N	N	N
Develop. Agree. Term								
Sub-franchising	Y	N	N	N	N	N	N	N

Security Systems Industry

AirSoPure

15400 Knoll Trail #106
Dallas, TX 75248

Phone: 972-960-9400	Accepts collect calls?
Toll Free: 800-752-3322	FAX: 972-960-9395

Internet:
Suitable Sites: HO
Concentration: 1 in NV, 1 in OK, 1 in TX
Expansion: All United States, Canada, Foreign
Registered: 0
Field Support: CP, EO, ST, $FC, H, N
Training: 1 week Dallas, TX

Custom Homewatch International

2094 Tomat Ave
Kelowna, BC V1Z-3C5 CANADA

Phone: 250-769-4329	Accepts collect calls?
Toll Free: 800-713-2888	FAX: 250-769-4329

Internet:
Suitable Sites:
Concentration: 14 in ON, 14 in BC, 10 in AB
Expansion: All United States, Canada
Registered: WA,AB
Field Support:
Training: 1 day Kelowna, BC

Dynamark Security Centers

19833 Leitersburg Pike PO Box 2068
Hagerstown, MD 21742

Phone: 301-797-2124	Accepts collect calls?
Toll Free: 800-342-4243	FAX: 301-797-2189

Internet:
Suitable Sites:
Concentration: 13 in PA, 10 in VA, 8 in MD
Expansion: All United States, Canada, Foreign
Registered: IL,IN,MD,MI,NY,RI,VA,WI
Field Support: EO, ST, SO, IC, FC, H, N
Training: 2 days HQ

Fire Defense Centers

3919 Morton St
Jacksonville, FL 32217

Phone: 904-731-0244	Accepts collect calls?
Toll Free: 800-554-3028	FAX:

Internet:
Suitable Sites: WR
Concentration: 20 in FL
Expansion: All United States
Registered: CA,FL,HI,IL,IN,MD,MI,MN,ND,NY,OR,RI,SD,VA,WA,WI,DC
Field Support: DP, CP, EO, ST, SO, IC, FC, H, N
Training: 2 weeks HQ

Paystation

5155 Spectrum Way Unit 17
Mississauga, ON L4W-5A1 CANADA

Phone: 905-625-8500	Accepts collect calls?
Toll Free: 800-268-1440	FAX: 905-625-6254

Internet: www.paymaster.ca
Suitable Sites: HO
Concentration: ON, AB
Expansion: All United States, Canada, Foreign
Registered:
Field Support: FC, H
Training: 5 days Toronto, ON

ProShred Security

2200 Lakeshore Blvd W #102
Toronto, ON M8V-1E4 CANADA
Mobile shredding service, business to business

Phone: 416-251-4272	Accepts collect calls? N
Toll Free: 800-461-9760	FAX: 416-251-7121

Internet: proshred@proshred.com
Suitable Sites:
Concentration: 8 in ON, 3 in CA, 2 in FL
Expansion: All United States, Canada, Foreign
Registered: CA,FL,MD,MI,OR,DC
Field Support: DP, EO, ST, FC, H, N
Training: 9 days Toronto, ON
2 days local

Roll-A-Way

10601 Oak St N E
Saint Petersburg, FL 33716
Rolling security & storm shutters

Phone: 813-576-6044	Accepts collect calls?
Toll Free: 800-683-9505	FAX: 813-579-9410

Internet:
Suitable Sites:
Concentration: 2 in NY, 2 in CA, 2 in FL
Expansion: All United States, Canada, Foreign
Registered: CA,FL,MD,NY,RI,VA,WA,WI
Field Support: CP, EO, ST, IC, $FC
Training: 2 weeks St Petersburg, FL

Safe Not Sorry

421 W Union Ave
Bound Brook, NJ 08805
Home safety incl consult & install focus on child-proofing

Phone: 888-469-2900	Accepts collect calls? N
Toll Free: 888-469-3900	FAX: 908-469-7405

Internet: www.safenotsorry.com
Suitable Sites: HO, K
Concentration: 11 in NJ, 3 in PA, 2 in CT
Expansion: All United States, Canada, Foreign
Registered: CA,FL,HI,IL,IN,MD,MI,MN,ND,NY,OR,RI,SD,VA,WA,WI,DC
Field Support: IC, FC, H, N
Training: marketing
operations
product installation

Security Systems Industry

	Shred-It	Sonitrol	V.I.D.E.O. Security Process (VSP)				
Startup Cost	350K-450K	250K-600K	6K				
Franchise Fee	55K	20K-50K	29.9K				
Royalty	5%	2.50%	7%				
Advertising Fee	1.5%	N/A	0%				
Financing Provided	Y	N	N				
Experience Required			N				
Passive Ownership	N	N	D				
In Business Since	1988	1964	1989				
Franchised Since	1992	1965	1995				
Franchised Units 1996							
1997	38	155	1				
1998							
Company Owned 1996							
1997	15	25	1				
1998							
Number of Units U.S.	39	177	0				
Canada	10	1	2				
Foreign	4	2	0				
Projected New U.S.							
Canada			2				
Foreign							
Corporate Employees	40	11	2				
Contract Length	10/10/10	10/10	5/5				
Expand in Territory	Y	N	Y				
Full-Time Employees	6	VAR	2-3				
Part-Time Employees							
Conversions							
Site Selection Assist.	Y	N	Y				
Lease Negotiation Assist.	Y	N					
Site Space Required	1500		250				
Development Agreement	Y	N	N				
Develop. Agree. Term	10/10						
Sub-franchising	N	N	N				

Security Systems Industry

Security Systems (Spread 2 of 2)

Shred-It

2359 Royal Windsor Dr, Unit 15
Mississauga, ON L5J-1K5 CANADA

Phone: 905-855-2856
Accepts collect calls?
Toll Free:
FAX: 905-855-0466
Internet:
Suitable Sites: LI, OTHER
Concentration: 6 in CA, 4 in FL, 2 in OH
Expansion: All United States, Canada, Foreign
Registered: CA, FL, IL, IN, MD, MI, NY, WA, WI, DC, AB
Field Support: CP, EO, ST, SO, FC, H, N
Training: 2 weeks Mississauga, ON

Sonitrol

211 North Union #350
Alexandria, VA 22314

Phone: 703-684-6606
Accepts collect calls?
Toll Free: 800-326-7475
FAX: 703-684-6612
Internet: www.sonitrol.com
Suitable Sites:
Concentration: 24 in CA, 14 in FL, 11 in NY
Expansion: All United States
Registered: FL,IL,VA
Field Support: EO, $ST, SO, $FC, H, N
Training: 1 week business training on-site
1 week technical training

V.I.D.E.O. Security Process (VSP)

1800 The Collegeway
Mississauga, ON L5L-5S4 CANADA

Phone: 905-608-8655
Accepts collect calls? N
Toll Free:
FAX: 905-608-8654
Internet:
Suitable Sites: HO
Concentration: 2 in ON
Expansion: Canada
Registered: AB
Field Support: ST, N
Training: 1 week Toronto on
1 week franchisee's location
continual research & supp

Sports and Recreation Industry   **Apparel, Equipment**

	A. J. Barnes Bicycle Emporium	The Athlete's Foot	Bike Line	Play It Again Sports	Soccer Post Intl Franchise Corp	The Sport Shoe	Sports Traders	
Startup Cost	100K-115K	175K-350K	130K-176K	170K-205K	91.5K-132K	300K+	150K	
Franchise Fee	25K	25K	24.5K	25K	19.5K	25K	25K	
Royalty	6%	5%	4%	5%	4%	4%	$500/MO	
Advertising Fee	0%	1%	3%	5%		4%	0	
Financing Provided	Y	Y	Y	Y	N	N	Y	
Experience Required							N	
Passive Ownership	A	D	D	D		D	D	
In Business Since	1989	1971	1983	1983	1978	1974	1983	
Franchised Since	1992	1972	1991	1988	1991	1989	1987	
Franchised Units 1996					14		33	
1997	34	361	55	689	22	5	33	
1998							33	
Company Owned 1996					3		1	
1997	0	271	17	4	3	18	1	
1998							1	
Number of Units U.S.	14	359	72	623		23	3	
Canada	0	2	0	69		0	30	
Foreign	20	271	0	1		0		
Projected New U.S.							0	
Canada							6	
Foreign							0	
Corporate Employees	5	180	12	283		20	40	
Contract Length	10/10	10/5	10/10	10/10		10/5/5	10	
Expand in Territory	Y	Y	Y	Y		Y		
Full-Time Employees	2	2	1	3		2-4		
Part-Time Employees	1	6	2	2		6-8		
Conversions	N	Y	Y	Y		Y	Y	
Site Selection Assist.	Y	Y	Y	Y		Y		
Lease Negotiation Assist.	Y	Y	Y	Y		Y		
Site Space Required	2000	1200	3000	2500-3000		4000	2500	
Development Agreement	Y	Y	N	N		Y	N	
Develop. Agree. Term	10	10						
Sub-franchising	N	N	N	N		N	Y	

Sports and Recreation Industry   ## Apparel, Equipment

A. J. Barnes Bicycle Emporium
14230 Stirrup Ln
West Palm Beach, FL 33414

Phone: 901-368-1144   Accepts collect calls?
Toll Free: 888-252-2453   FAX: 888-252-2454
Internet: www.ajbarnes.com
Suitable Sites: SC
Concentration: 11 in FL, 2 in GA, 1 in TN
Expansion: All United States, Foreign
Registered: FL
Field Support: DP, EO, ST, SO, IC, FC, H, N
Training: 14 days west palm beach, FL
3 days on location

The Athlete's Foot
1950 Vaughn Rd
Kennesaw, GA 30144

Phone: 770-514-4718   Accepts collect calls?
Toll Free: 800-524-6444   FAX: 770-514-4903
Internet: www.theathletesfoot.com
Suitable Sites: FB, RM, SC, SF
Concentration:
Expansion: All United States, Canada, Foreign
Registered: CA,FL,HI,IL,IN,MD,MI,MN,ND,NY,OR,RI,SD,VA,WA,WI,DC
Field Support: CP, EO, ST, SO, $IC, FC, H, N
Training: 1 week HQ in Atlanta
1 week opening on location

Bike Line
1035 Andrew Dr
West Chester, PA 19380

Phone: 610-429-4370   Accepts collect calls?
Toll Free: 800-537-2654   FAX: 610-429-4295
Internet: www.bikeline.com
Suitable Sites: SC, SF
Concentration: 23 in PA, 6 in NJ, 3 in MD
Expansion: All United States
Registered: FL,IL,MD,MI,MN,VA
Field Support: CP, EO, ST, SO, IC, FC, H, N
Training: 2 weeks Westchester, PA

Play It Again Sports
4200 Dahlberg Dr
Minneapolis, MN 55422

Phone: 612-520-8500   Accepts collect calls?
Toll Free: 800-842-4370   FAX: 612-520-8501
Internet: www.playitagainsports.com
Suitable Sites: FB, SC
Concentration: 67 in CA, 38 in ON, 34 in MI
Expansion: All United States, Canada
Registered: CA,FL,HI,IL,IN,MD,MI,MN,ND,NY,OR,RI,SD,VA,WA,WI,DC
Field Support: CP, EO, ST, SO, IC, FC, H, N
Training: 2.5 days Minneapolis, MN
2.5 days Minneapolis, m
5 days Minneapolis, MN

Soccer Post Intl Franchise Corp
111 Melrose Dr
New Rochelle, NY 10804
Soccer retail store
Phone: 914-235-9161   Accepts collect calls?
Toll Free: FAX:
Internet:
Suitable Sites:
Concentration:
Expansion: CA,IL,MI,NY, Canada
Registered:
Field Support:
Training:

The Sport Shoe
1770 Corporate Dr #500
Norcross, GA 30093

Phone: 770-279-7494   Accepts collect calls?
Toll Free: 800-944-7463   FAX: 770-279-7180
Internet:
Suitable Sites: FB, SC
Concentration: 2 in GA, 1 in TN, 1 in NC
Expansion: SE, SE
Registered: FL
Field Support: EO, $ST, SO, $IC, $FC
Training: 6-8 weeks corp office

Sports Traders
508 Discovery St
St Victoria, BC V8T-1G8   CANADA
Quality sports name brands at affordable prices, new & used
Phone: 250-383-6443   Accepts collect calls? N
Toll Free: 800-792-3111   FAX: 250-383-8481
Internet: traders@islandnet.com
Suitable Sites: AC, DA, FB, M, PC, RM, SC, SF
Concentration: 12 in BC, 7 in OT, 3 in AB
Expansion: All United States, Canada
Registered:
Field Support: EO, ST, SO, IC, FC, H, N
Training: 7 days Victoria head office
7 days on-site

Sports and Recreation Industry

Golf Specialty (Spread 1 of 2)

	Dynamic Golf Centres	Empowered Womens Golf Shops	Golf Augusta Pro Shops	Golf USA	International Golf	Las Vegas Golf & Tennis	MacBirdie Golf Gifts	Professional Golf Shops	Nevada Bob's
Startup Cost	300K-525K	280K	350K-700K	140K-330K	250K-300K	530K-750K	62K-122K	275K-295K
Franchise Fee	25K	25K	40K	30K-40K	42K	40K	12.5K	37.5K-57.5K
Royalty	3%	3%	5%	2%	2%	3%	5%	2%
Advertising Fee	2%		1%	1%	0%	2%	1-3%	N/A
Financing Provided	N	Y	N	N	Y	Y	Y	N
Experience Required	N		N	N		N		
Passive Ownership	A		D	D	D	D	A	N
In Business Since	1985	1993	1994	1986	1976	1974	1989	1974
Franchised Since	1987	1996	1995	1989	1981	1984	1994	1978
Franchised Units 1996		0						
1997	11	0	11	129	54	41	10	257
1998	14	4		126		40		
Company Owned 1996		1						
1997	1	1	1	2	6	7	1	55
1998	1			7		9		
Number of Units U.S.	0		12	115	60	41	11	205
Canada	15		0	5	0	0	0	45
Foreign	0		0	6	0	2	0	62
Projected New U.S.		6	6	12		10		
Canada	5			1		4		
Foreign				2				
Corporate Employees	4		10	18	15	38	6	72
Contract Length	5/5	10	10/10	20/20	15/15	15/15	5/5	10/10
Expand in Territory	Y	Y	Y	Y	Y	Y	Y	Y
Full-Time Employees	3		3	2	2-3	4	1	3
Part-Time Employees	3		4	1	2-3	3	5	2
Conversions	Y	Y	Y	Y	Y	Y	N	
Site Selection Assist.	Y	Y	Y	Y	Y	Y	Y	Y
Lease Negotiation Assist.	Y	Y	Y	Y	Y	Y	Y	N
Site Space Required	4000		4000	2500-4500	3500	6000-1000	800-1400	4000
Development Agreement	Y	N	N	Y	N	N	Y	N
Develop. Agree. Term	5			4			5	
Sub-franchising	N		N	N	N	N	N	N

Sports and Recreation Industry   **Golf Specialty (Spread 1 of 2)**

Dynamic Golf Centres
2025 Sheppard Ave E #2109
Toronto, ON M2J-1V7 CANADA
Retail golf equipment, related accessories & svcs, club repair
    Phone: 416-490-9855   Accepts collect calls? N
    Toll Free: FAX: 416-490-9792
    Internet: www.dynamicgolf.com
Suitable Sites: LI, RM, SC, SF
Concentration: 13 in ON, 1 in BC, 1 in QUE
    Expansion: Canada
    Registered: AB
Field Support: CP, EO, ST, SO, IC, FC, N
    Training: 1 week corporate office
        1 week closet centres
        1 week new centre

Empowered Womens Golf Shops
5344 Beltline Rd
Dallas, TX 75240
Women's golf clothes clubs & clinics
    Phone: 972-233-8807   Accepts collect calls? N
    Toll Free: 800-533-7309   FAX: 972-233-9079
    Internet: empoweredgolf.com
Suitable Sites: AC, SC
Concentration:
    Expansion: CA, Canada, Foreign
    Registered: CA, IL, MI, VA
Field Support:
    Training:

Golf Augusta Pro Shops
217 Bobby Jones Expwy
Augusta, GA 30907

    Phone: 706-863-9905   Accepts collect calls? N
    Toll Free: 800-465-3051   FAX: 706-863-9909
    Internet: www.golfaugustaproshops.com
Suitable Sites: AC, FB, PC, SC, SF
Concentration: 3 in NC, 2 in PA
    Expansion: All United States, Canada
    Registered: FL, IN, MI, MN, NY, VA, WI
Field Support: CP, ST, SO, IC, H, N
    Training: 2 weeks Augusta, GA

Golf USA
3705 W Memorial Rd #801
Oklahoma City, OK 73134
Discount golf retail stores, complete w/ pro-line equip, apparel
    Phone: 405-751-0015   Accepts collect calls? N
    Toll Free: 800-488-1107   FAX: 405-755-0065
    Internet: www.golfusainc.com
Suitable Sites: FB, SC, SF
Concentration: 6 in TX, 5 in FL, 6 in NE
    Expansion: All United States, Canada, Foreign
    Registered: CA, FL, HI, IL, IN, MD, MI, MN, NY, OR, RI, SD, VA, WA, WI, AB
Field Support: DP, CP, EO, ST, SO, IC, FC, H, N
    Training: 1 week Oklahoma City, OK
        4 days locally

International Golf
9101 N Thornydale Rd
Tucson, AZ 85742

    Phone: 520-744-1840   Accepts collect calls?
    Toll Free: 800-204-2600   FAX: 520-744-2076
    Internet:
Suitable Sites: FB, SC, SF
Concentration: 12 in MI, 6 in OK, 6 in CA
    Expansion: All United States, Canada, Foreign
    Registered: CA, FL, HI, IL, IN, MD, MI, MN, ND, NY, OR, RI, SD, VA, WA, WI, DC
Field Support: DP, CP, EO, ST, SO, IC, $FC, H, N
    Training: 10-14 days Oklahoma City, OK
        7 days on-site

Las Vegas Golf & Tennis
5325 S Valley View Blvd #10
Las Vegas, NV 89118
Off course retail pro-shop specialize in golf & tennis equipment
    Phone: 702-798-5500x218   Accepts collect calls? N
    Toll Free: 800-873-5110x218   FAX: 702-798-6847
    Internet: www.lvgolf.com
Suitable Sites: FB, SC, SF
Concentration: 12 in CA, 5 in MI, 3 in TX
    Expansion: All United States, Canada, Foreign
    Registered: CA, FL, HI, NY, OR, WA, WI, DC, IL, IN, MD, MI, MN, VA
Field Support: CP, EO, ST, SO, IC, FC, H, N
    Training: 2 weeks Las Vegas corp office

MacBirdie Golf Gifts
5250 W 73rd St #I
Minneapolis, MN 55439

    Phone: 612-830-1033   Accepts collect calls?
    Toll Free: 800-343-1033   FAX: 612-830-1055
    Internet: www.macbirdie.com
Suitable Sites: RM
Concentration: 2 in MN, 2 in TX
    Expansion: All United States, Canada
    Registered: CA, FL, HI, IL, IN, MD, MI, MN, ND, NY, OR, RI, SD, VA, WA, WI, DC
Field Support: $DP, CP, EO, ST, SO, $IC, $FC, H, N
    Training: 1 week corporate office
        3-5 days in-store

Nevada Bob's Professional Golf Shops
4043 S Eastern Ave
Las Vegas, NV 89119

    Phone: 702-451-3333   Accepts collect calls?
    Toll Free: 800-348-2627   FAX: 702-451-9378
    Internet: www.nevadabob.com
Suitable Sites: FB, SC
Concentration: 50 in CA, 20 in ON, 23 in UK
    Expansion: Midwest, SE, NE, Canada, Foreign
    Registered: CA, FL, HI, IL, IN, MD, MI, MN, ND, NY, OR, RI, VA, WA, WI, DC
Field Support: EO, ST, SO, FC, H, N
    Training: 1 week Las Vegas, NV

Sports and Recreation Industry

Golf Specialty (Spread 2 of 2)

	Pro Golf Discount	Strokes	Team Golf Corp	Woody's Wood Shops				
Startup Cost	300K-700K	60K-80K	15K-35K	85K-185K				
Franchise Fee	24.5K-49.5K	25K	15K	22K				
Royalty	2.5-3%	1-0%	VAR.	6%				
Advertising Fee	0%	1-0%		2%				
Financing Provided	N	Y	N	Y				
Experience Required	N							
Passive Ownership	D	A		D				
In Business Since	1961	1994	1993	1978				
Franchised Since	1974	1996	1994	1980				
Franchised Units 1996			3					
1997	166	22	4	26				
1998								
Company Owned 1996			1					
1997	0	1	1	13				
1998	1							
Number of Units U.S.	144	23		33				
Canada	20	0		6				
Foreign	5	0		0				
Projected New U.S.	24							
Canada	10							
Foreign	10							
Corporate Employees	25	8		21				
Contract Length	30/20	20/20		15/15				
Expand in Territory	Y	Y		N				
Full-Time Employees	2-3	1		1				
Part-Time Employees	2-3	1		4				
Conversions	Y	Y		Y				
Site Selection Assist.	Y	Y		Y				
Lease Negotiation Assist.	Y	Y		Y				
Site Space Required	5000-7000	1000-2000		2800-3400				
Development Agreement	Y	Y		Y				
Develop. Agree. Term	NEG.			15				
Sub-franchising	N	N		Y				

Sports and Recreation Industry

Pro Golf Discount
32751 Middlebelt Rd
Farmington Hills, MI 48334-1726

Phone: 248-737-0553   Accepts collect calls?
Toll Free: 800-776-4653   FAX: 248-737-9077
Internet:
Suitable Sites: FB, SC
Concentration: 15 in MI, 14 in CA, 9 in FL
    Expansion: All United States, Canada, Foreign
    Registered: CA,FL,HI,IL,IN,MD,MI,MN,ND,NY,OR,RI,SD,VA,WA,WI,DC,AB
Field Support: CP, EO, ST, SO, IC, FC, H, N
    Training: 2 weeks corp office in MI

Strokes
3012 Spring St
Redwood City, CA 94063
Custom golf clubs & related products
    Phone: 650-369-4100   Accepts collect calls?
Toll Free: 800-973-1111   FAX: 650-368-9316
    Internet:
Suitable Sites: SC, SF
Concentration: 21 in CA, 1 in WA, 1 in TX
    Expansion: West Coast, Sun Belt, Canada, Foreign
    Registered: CA
Field Support: DP, CP, EO, ST, SO, IC, FC, H, N
    Training: 5 days San Francisco/bay area, CA
        5 days redondo beach, CA

Team Golf Corp
1776 Woodstead Ct #213
The Woodlands, TX 77380
Golf event planning/admin/travel services
    Phone: 281-362-7777   Accepts collect calls?
Toll Free: 800-282-8326   FAX:
    Internet:
Suitable Sites:
Concentration:
    Expansion: MI,NY
    Registered:
Field Support:
    Training:

Woody's Wood Shops
20 Queensberry St #12a
Boston, MA 02215

    Phone: 617-839-5471   Accepts collect calls?
Toll Free: FAX: 617-547-3245
    Internet:
Suitable Sites: FB, WR
Concentration: 16 in CA, 8 in OR, 3 in WA
    Expansion: All United States, Canada
    Registered:
Field Support: DP, EO, ST, FC, $H, $N
    Training: 3 weeks HQ
        2 weeks on-site
        on-going

Sports and Recreation Industry   Memorabilia, Collectibles

	Fan-A-Mania	Field of Dreams	Pro Image	Sports Fantastic			
Startup Cost	80K-150K	145K-269K	130.5K-214.5K	25K-72K			
Franchise Fee	7.5K-19.5K	32.5K	19.5K	20K			
Royalty	3.5%	6%	4%	5%			
Advertising Fee		3%		1%			
Financing Provided	Y	N	Y	Y			
Experience Required	N	N		N			
Passive Ownership	D	D		D			
In Business Since	1993	1990	1985	1992			
Franchised Since	1996	1991	1985	1996			
Franchised Units 1996	4		169	1			
1997	11	25	91	1			
1998	15	32		1			
Company Owned 1996	4		60	2			
1997	4	0	0	2			
1998	6	0		2			
Number of Units U.S.	17	23		3			
Canada	2						
Foreign	2	1					
Projected New U.S.	15			6			
Canada	4						
Foreign	4						
Corporate Employees	7	9		6			
Contract Length	10/10/10	7		10/5/5			
Expand in Territory	Y	Y		Y			
Full-Time Employees	2	1		2			
Part-Time Employees	2+	2		2			
Conversions	Y			Y			
Site Selection Assist.	Y	Y		Y			
Lease Negotiation Assist.	Y	Y		Y			
Site Space Required	1500-2500	900-1400		1000			
Development Agreement	Y	Y		N			
Develop. Agree. Term	10/10/10	7					
Sub-franchising	Y	Y		N			

Sports and Recreation Industry

Memorabilia, Collectibles

Fan-A-Mania
3855 S, 500 West #R
Salt Lake City, UT 84115
Entertainment & sports stores
Phone: 801-288-9120   Accepts collect calls? Y
Toll Free: 800-770-9120   FAX: 801-288-9210
Internet:
Suitable Sites: K, M
Concentration: 3 in PA, 2 in TX
Expansion: All United States, Canada, Foreign
Registered: NY,VA,AB
Field Support: EO, ST, SO, FC, H, N
Training: 4 days corp HQ
7 days on-site
periodic in field

Field of Dreams
42620 Caroline Ct
Palm Desert, CA 92211
Retail stores selling sports personality & celebrity gifts
Phone: 760-776-1010   Accepts collect calls? Y
Toll Free: 800-589-6648   FAX: 760-779-0217
Internet: dreamsmail@aol.com
Suitable Sites: RM
Concentration: 3 in GA, 4 in CA, 3 in FL
Expansion: All United States, Canada, Foreign
Registered: CA,FL,MI,OR,IL,IN,DC
Field Support: EO, ST, SO, $FC, H
Training: 10 days Orlando, FL

Pro Image
563 W 500 South #330
Bountiful, UT 84010
Sports apparel store
Phone: 801-296-9999   Accepts collect calls?
Toll Free: FAX:
Internet:
Suitable Sites:
Concentration:
Expansion: Canada, Foreign
Registered:
Field Support:
Training:

Sports Fantastic
1919 South 40th St Ste 202
Lincoln, NE 68506
Sports memorabilia, cards and collectibles
Phone: 402-434-5620   Accepts collect calls? N
Toll Free: 800-865-2378   FAX: 402-434-5624
Internet: www.franchisedevelopers.com
Suitable Sites: RM, SC, SF
Concentration: 3 in NE
Expansion: All United States
Registered: MD,VA
Field Support: $CP, EO, ST, SO, H, N
Training: 1 week NE
1 week on-site

Sports and Recreation Industry   Tanning

	Everlasting Tan Club	Fabutan Sun Tan Studios	Sunbanque Island Tanning	Tan World	Tropi-Tan, Inc.			
Startup Cost	150K-230K	35K-50K	30K-40K	55K-85K	75K-250K			
Franchise Fee	10K	15K	5K	20K	12K			
Royalty	$900/MO.	6%	3%	6%	4.50%			
Advertising Fee		1%	5%	2%	3.5%			
Financing Provided	Y	N	Y	Y	Y			
Experience Required		N		N	N			
Passive Ownership		A	D	D	A			
In Business Since	1992	1979	1983	1995	1980			
Franchised Since	1996	1985	1984	1996	1986			
Franchised Units 1996	0	40		3				
1997	0	48	11	3	4			
1998		64		3				
Company Owned 1996	1	12		2				
1997	1	11	4	2	6			
1998		13		2				
Number of Units U.S.		0	7	5	10			
Canada		77	8		0			
Foreign		0	0		0			
Projected New U.S.		2		4				
Canada		20						
Foreign		0						
Corporate Employees		52	7	6	20			
Contract Length		10	5/5	10/10	10/5			
Expand in Territory		Y	Y	Y	N			
Full-Time Employees		1-2	2	2	2			
Part-Time Employees		2-3	1	6	2			
Conversions		N	Y	Y	Y			
Site Selection Assist.		Y	Y	Y	Y			
Lease Negotiation Assist.		Y	Y	Y	Y			
Site Space Required		800-1200	1000	2500	2500			
Development Agreement		N	Y	N	Y			
Develop. Agree. Term			5		5			
Sub-franchising		Y	Y	N	N			

Sports and Recreation Industry   Tanning

Everlasting Tan Club
709 Johnnie Dodds Blvd
Mount Pleasant, SC 29464
Tanning salons & products
    Phone: Accepts collect calls?
    Toll Free: 888-826-2582   FAX:
    Internet:
Suitable Sites:
Concentration:
    Expansion: IN,MI, Canada
    Registered:
Field Support:
    Training:

Fabutan Sun Tan Studios
Unit 101, 208 - 57th Ave SW
Calgary, AB T2H-2K8 CANADA
Indoor tanning salon
    Phone: 403-640-2100   Accepts collect calls? N
    Toll Free: 800-565-3658   FAX: 403-640-2116
    Internet: www.fabutan.com
Suitable Sites: AC, DA, FB, M, OC, RM, SC, SF, WF
Concentration: 37 in AB, 16 in BC, 12 in ONT
    Expansion: Canada
    Registered:
Field Support:
    Training:

Sunbanque Island Tanning
2533a Yonge St
Toronto, ON M4P-2H9 CANADA

    Phone: 416-488-5838   Accepts collect calls? N
    Toll Free: FAX: 416-488-3712
    Internet: sunbanque@bigfoot.com
Suitable Sites: AC, FB, SF
Concentration: 8 in ON, 7 in MA
    Expansion: All United States, Canada, Foreign
    Registered:
Field Support: DP, CP, EO, ST, SO, IC, FC, N
    Training: 2 weeks HQ

Tan World
1919 South 40th St Ste 202
Lincoln, NE 68506
Full service tanning salon
    Phone: 402-434-5620   Accepts collect calls? N
    Toll Free: 800-865-2378   FAX: 402-434-5624
    Internet: www.tanworld.com
Suitable Sites: SC
Concentration: 4 in IA, 1 in NE
    Expansion: All United States
    Registered:
Field Support: $CP, EO, ST, SO, H, N
    Training: 1 week IA
                1 week on-site

Tropi-Tan, Inc.
5152 Commerce Dr
Flint, MI 48507
Indoor tanning salon, full-line tanning lotions, clothing, etc
    Phone: 810-230-6789   Accepts collect calls? N
    Toll Free: 800-642-4826   FAX: 810-230-1115
    Internet:
Suitable Sites: FB, SC
Concentration: 10 in MI
    Expansion: All United States
    Registered: MI
Field Support: $DP, $CP, $EO, $ST, SO, IC, $FC, H
    Training: 1 week corporate office
                1 week on-site

Sports and Recreation Industry   Other Sports and Recreation (Spread 1 of 2)

	American Darters Association	American Poolplayers Association	Cinema Grill	Hauntrepreneurs, Ltd.	Hoop Mountain	Martial Arts America	Outdoor Connection	Hockey Training Centers	PuckMasters
Startup Cost	1.5K-2.8K	4.3K-6.2K	400K	30K-98K	30K	52.5K-66.5K	6.7K-10.2K	75K-115K
Franchise Fee		VAR	20K	15K	20K	20K	5.8K	20K
Royalty	20%	20%	3%	10%	5%	6%	1-4%	6%
Advertising Fee	N/A	N/A	0%	$1000			1%	
Financing Provided	N	Y	Y	Y	Y	N	Y	Y
Experience Required								
Passive Ownership	N	N	D	A	D		N	
In Business Since	1990	1980	1995	1985	1985	1994	1988	1993
Franchised Since	1991	1982	1995	1987	1995	1997	1989	1996
Franchised Units 1996								2
1997	75	222	29	17	6	0	93	6
1998							98	
Company Owned 1996						0		0
1997	0	2	1	0	1	1	3	1
1998							3	
Number of Units U.S.	75	212	20	21	5		101	
Canada	0	12	0	0	2		0	
Foreign	0	0	0	0	0		0	
Projected New U.S.							12	
Canada								
Foreign								
Corporate Employees	10	40+	7	5	1		5	
Contract Length	1.5/5	2/5	10/10	5/5	10/10		5/5	
Expand in Territory	Y		Y	Y	N		N	
Full-Time Employees	VAR	VAR	40					
Part-Time Employees				70			1-2	
Conversions			N		N			
Site Selection Assist.	N	Y	Y	Y	Y		N	
Lease Negotiation Assist.			Y		Y			
Site Space Required			10000	30 acres				
Development Agreement	N	N	Y	Y	N		N	
Develop. Agree. Term			10	5				
Sub-franchising	N	N	N	Y	N		N	

Sports and Recreation Industry

Other Sports and Recreation (Spread 1 of 2)

American Darters Association
1000 Lake Saint Louis Blvd #310
Lake Saint Louis, MO 63367

    Phone: 314-625-8621   Accepts collect calls?
Toll Free: FAX: 314-625-2975
    Internet: www.adadarters.com
Suitable Sites: HO
Concentration: TX, RI, MO
    Expansion: All United States
    Registered: CA,FL,HI,IL,IN,MD,MI,MN,ND,NY,RI,SD,VA,WA,WI
Field Support: $CP, EO, ST, FC, H, N
    Training: 3 days Lake Saint Louis MO

American Poolplayers Association
1000 Lake St Louis Blvd #325
Lake Saint Louis, MO 63367

    Phone: 314-625-8611   Accepts collect calls?
Toll Free: 800-372-2536   FAX: 314-625-2975
    Internet: www.budweiser.com.rules.html
Suitable Sites: HO
Concentration: 19 in IL, 14 in FL, 13 in CA
    Expansion: All United States, Canada
    Registered: CA,FL,HI,IL,IN,MD,MI,MN,NY,ND,RI,SD,VA,WA,WI
Field Support: DP, ST, FC, N
    Training: 6 days apa home office

Cinema Grill
PO Box 28467
Atlanta, GA 30358

    Phone: 404-250-9536   Accepts collect calls? N
Toll Free: FAX: 404-845-0718
    Internet: www.cinemagrill.com
Suitable Sites: FB, RM, SC
Concentration: 3 in VA, 3 in MD, 2 in NC
    Expansion: All United States
    Registered: CA,FL,IL,IN,MD,MN,NY,ND,VA,WI,DC
Field Support: EO, ST, IC, $FC, $H, N
    Training: 2 weeks site

Hauntrepreneurs, Ltd.
16 Orangewood Dr
Liverpool, NY 13090

    Phone: 315-652-8295   Accepts collect calls?
Toll Free: 800-344-2868   FAX: 315-652-8298
    Internet:
Suitable Sites:
Concentration: 8 in NY, 2 in PA, 1 in MA
    Expansion: All United States, Canada, Foreign
    Registered: CA,FL,HI,IL,IN,MD,MI,MN,ND,NY,OR,RI,SD,VA,WA,WI,DC
Field Support: EO, ST, SO, FC, H, N
    Training: 4 days Syracuse NY

Hoop Mountain
PO Box 242
Hathorne, MA 01937

    Phone: 508-774-7730   Accepts collect calls?
Toll Free: 800-519-8445   FAX:
    Internet:
Suitable Sites:
Concentration: 2 in MA, 2 in NC, 1 in FL
    Expansion: All United States, Foreign
    Registered: FL
Field Support: EO, ST
    Training: 4 days Boston MA

Martial Arts America
29911 Aventura #E
Rancho Santa Margarita, CA 92688
Family martial arts centers
      Phone: Accepts collect calls?
Toll Free: 800-596-5900   FAX:
    Internet:
Suitable Sites:
Concentration:
    Expansion: CA,MD
    Registered:
Field Support:
    Training:

Outdoor Connection
1001 E Cliff Rd
Burnsville, MN 55337
Fishing & hunting travel service
      Phone: 316-488-3166   Accepts collect calls? N
Toll Free: FAX: 316-488-2619
    Internet: www.outdoor-connection.com
Suitable Sites: HO
Concentration: 13 in MN, 9 in IL, 7 in IA
    Expansion: All United States, Canada, Foreign
    Registered: IL,IN,MI,MN,SD,WA,WI,CA,FL,OR,VA
Field Support: $FC, N
    Training: 1.5 days corporate office in KS

PuckMasters Hockey Training Centers
1655 Broadway St #102
Port Coquitlam, BC V3C-2M7 CANADA
Hockey training centers
      Phone: Accepts collect calls?
Toll Free: 800-663-2331   FAX:
    Internet:
Suitable Sites:
Concentration:
    Expansion: All United States, Canada, Foreign
    Registered:
Field Support:
    Training:

Sports and Recreation Industry   Other Sports and Recreation (Spread 2 of 2)

	Golf Courses Of America	Themed Miniature Golf Courses Putt-Putt	United Studios of Self-Defense Inc					
Startup Cost	100K-5M	250K-400K	83K					
Franchise Fee	5K-30K	N/A	27K					
Royalty	3%	N/A	5%					
Advertising Fee	2%	N/A						
Financing Provided	Y	N	N					
Experience Required		N						
Passive Ownership	A	A						
In Business Since	1954	1977	1968					
Franchised Since	1955	1985	1988					
Franchised Units 1996			131					
1997	255	12	121					
1998	179							
Company Owned 1996			0					
1997	8	4	0					
1998	7							
Number of Units U.S.	186	16						
Canada	1	0						
Foreign	21	0						
Projected New U.S.	12							
Canada								
Foreign	2							
Corporate Employees	34	5						
Contract Length	40	UNLIMITED						
Expand in Territory	N	Y						
Full-Time Employees		2						
Part-Time Employees		2						
Conversions								
Site Selection Assist.	Y	Y						
Lease Negotiation Assist.	Y	Y						
Site Space Required	2-10 a cres	30000						
Development Agreement	N	N						
Develop. Agree. Term								
Sub-franchising	N	N						

Sports and Recreation Industry

Other Sports and Recreation (Spread 2 of 2)

Putt-Putt Golf Courses Of America
PO Box 35237 3007 Ft Bragg Rd
Fayetteville, NC 28303-0237

Phone: 910-485-7131   Accepts collect calls?
Toll Free: FAX: 910-485-1122
Internet: www.putt-putt.com
Suitable Sites: AC, ES
Concentration: 25 in NC, 28 in TX, 21 in OH
Expansion: All United States, Canada, Foreign
Registered: CA,FL,HI,IL,IN,MD,MI,MN,ND,NY,OR,RI,SD,VA,WA,WI,DC
Field Support: EO, ST, $FC, H, N
Training: 1 week Fayetteville NC
     3-7 days franchisee's location

Themed Miniature Golf Courses
PO Box 2435
Myrtle Beach, SC 29578-2435
Elaborate & beautiful miniature golf courses/family entertain.
Phone: 843-236-4733   Accepts collect calls?
Toll Free: FAX: 843-249-2118
Internet:
Suitable Sites: FB, RM, SF, WF
Concentration: SC, FL, TX
Expansion: All United States, Canada
Registered:
Field Support: CP, EO, ST
Training:

United Studios of Self-Defense Inc
26826 Vista Terrace Bldg 18
El Toro, CA 92630
Martial arts studio
Phone: 714-588-7925   Accepts collect calls?
Toll Free: FAX:
Internet:
Suitable Sites:
Concentration:
Expansion: CA
Registered:
Field Support:
Training:

Travel Industry

	Admiral of The Fleet Cruise Centers	Algonquin Travel	Carlson Wagonlit Travel	Condotels	Cruise Holidays International	Cruise Lines Reservation Center	Cruise Vacations	CruiseOne / The Travel Company
Startup Cost	100K-150K	150K	6.6K-156.2K	20.42K-117.5K	100K-150K	2K-3K	100K	14K-26K
Franchise Fee	25K	35K	$INCLUDED	5K	29.5K	.5K-1K	39.9K	9.8K
Royalty	0.50%	6-10%	VAR	3%	1%	1%	1%	4%
Advertising Fee	1%	1.5-6%	VAR		$275/MO	0%	$200/MO	0%
Financing Provided	N	Y	N	Y	N	Y	Y	Y
Experience Required		N			N	N		N
Passive Ownership	N	N	D		D	A	D	N
In Business Since	1994	1964	1900	1982	1984	1989	1991	1992
Franchised Since	1994	1978	1984	1989	1984	1990	1991	1993
Franchised Units 1996		95		4				
1997	2	97	1388	4	200	24	4	323
1998		100			210			403
Company Owned 1996		0		0	0			
1997	3	0	416	0	0	1	1	0
1998		1			0			
Number of Units U.S.	5		1404		165	25	0	403
Canada	0	100	0		55	0	5	0
Foreign	0		400		0	0	0	0
Projected New U.S.					20			200
Canada					5			
Foreign					0			
Corporate Employees	1	15	80		41	10	15	35
Contract Length	15/10	10	3-10/3-10		7/7	10/10	10/10	1/1
Expand in Territory	Y	Y	Y		Y	Y	Y	N
Full-Time Employees	3	3	VAR		2	1	2	1
Part-Time Employees	3	2			1		1	
Conversions	Y	Y	Y		Y	Y	N	Y
Site Selection Assist.	Y	Y	Y		Y	N	Y	N
Lease Negotiation Assist.	Y	Y	Y		Y	N	Y	N
Site Space Required	1500	700			600-900	100	750	
Development Agreement	N	Y	N		N	Y	N	N
Develop. Agree. Term		10				20		
Sub-franchising	N	N	N		N	Y	Y	N

Travel Industry   Travel (Spread 1 of 2)

Admiral of The Fleet Cruise Centers
3202 Meander Ln #A
Olympia, WA 98502

    Phone: 360-438-1191   Accepts collect calls?
Toll Free: 800-877-7447   FAX: 360-438-2618
    Internet:
Suitable Sites: SC
Concentration: 4 in WA, 1 in TX
    Expansion: NW
    Registered:
Field Support: CP, EO, ST, SO, IC, H, N
    Training: 2 weeks Olympia WA

Algonquin Travel
657 Bronson Ave
Ottawa, ON K1S-4E7 CANADA
Full-service travel agencies
    Phone: 613-233-7713   Accepts collect calls? N
Toll Free: 800-668-1743   FAX: 613-233-7805
    Internet: franchise@algtravel.com
Suitable Sites:
Concentration:
    Expansion:
    Registered: AB
Field Support: DP, EO, ST, SO, FC, H, N
    Training: 3 weeks Ottawa

Carlson Wagonlit Travel
PO Box 59159
Minneapolis, MN 55459-8207

    Phone: 800-337-2537   Accepts collect calls?
Toll Free: 800-678-8241   FAX: 813-579-0529
    Internet: www.travel.carlson.com
Suitable Sites: FB, RM, SC, SF, OTHER
Concentration: 160 in CA, 80 in MN, 55 in TX
    Expansion: All United States
    Registered: MN,NY,DC
Field Support: $ST, SO, $FC, $H, $N
    Training: 2 weeks Minneapolis
        on-site for start-ups
        2 days Minneapolis for conversio

Condotels
2703 Hwy 17 S
Myrtle Beach, SC 29582
Condo lodging/management services
    Phone: Accepts collect calls?
Toll Free: 800-852-6636   FAX:
    Internet:
Suitable Sites:
Concentration:
    Expansion: SE,S,SE,W
    Registered:
Field Support:
    Training:

Cruise Holidays International
9665 Chesapeake Dr #401
San Diego, CA 92123
Cruise specialty agencies
    Phone: 619-279-4780   Accepts collect calls? N
Toll Free: 800-866-7245   FAX: 619-279-4788
    Internet: www.cruiseholidays.com
Suitable Sites: DA, FB, M, OC, RM, SC, SF
Concentration: 32 in CA, 17 in BC, 17 in ON
    Expansion: All United States, Canada
    Registered: CA,FL,HI,IL,IN,MD,MI,MN,ND,NY,OR,RI,SD,VA,WA,WI,DC
Field Support: DP, CP, EO, $ST, SO, $FC, H, N
    Training: 8-10 days Miami
        2 weeks San Diego

Cruise Lines Reservation Center
9229 Kaufman Place
Brooklyn, NY 11236
Cruise & vacation travel agency, tour packages, hotels, rentals
    Phone: 718-763-4259   Accepts collect calls? N
Toll Free: FAX: 718-444-3332
    Internet:
Suitable Sites: ES, FB, HO, IP, M, OC, RM, SF, WF, OTHER
Concentration: 25 in NY
    Expansion: All United States, Canada, Foreign
    Registered: NY
Field Support: $DP, CP, EO, ST, $SO, IC, FC, H, N
    Training: 1 day HQ

Cruise Vacations
2025 W Broadway
Vancouver, BC V6J-1Z6 CANADA

    Phone: 604-731-5546   Accepts collect calls?
Toll Free: 800-555-7447   FAX: 604-736-6513
    Internet:
Suitable Sites: HO, RM
Concentration: 5 in BC
    Expansion: All United States, Canada
    Registered:
Field Support: $CP, EO, ST, SO, $FC, H, N
    Training: 2 weeks head office
        1 week on a cruise

CruiseOne / The Travel Company
10 Fairway Dr #200
Deerfield Beach, FL 33441-1802

    Phone: 954-480-9265   Accepts collect calls? N
Toll Free: 800-892-3928   FAX: 954-428-6588
    Internet: www.cruiseone.com
Suitable Sites: HO
Concentration: 40 in CA, 40 in FL, 33 in TX
    Expansion: All United States
    Registered: CA,FL,HI,IL,IN,MD,MI,MN,ND,NY,OR,RI,SD,VA,WA,WI,DC
Field Support: DP, CP, EO, ST, IC, $FC, H, $N
    Training: 6 days Ft Lauderdale FL

Travel Industry   Travel (Spread 2 of 2)

	Empress Travel	GalaxSea Cruises & Tours	InHouse Travel Group LLC	Kirby Tours	TPI Travel Services	Travel Network	Travel Professionals International	Uniglobe Travel
Startup Cost		61.9K-92.5K	800-3.6K	25K-100K	5K	10K-100K	120K-168K	90K-150K
Franchise Fee		5K-25K	2.45K-5.95K	15K	1.5K	5K-30K	27.5K	25K-45K
Royalty		$2-750MO	1-4%	5%	$75	$350-750/MO	5%	.2-1%
Advertising Fee				5%	0%	$200/MO	1%	$407-814/MO
Financing Provided	N	N	Y	Y	Y	Y	N	N
Experience Required	Y					N		
Passive Ownership	A			D	D	D	D	D
In Business Since	1973	1988	1995	1919	1987	1982	1982	1979
Franchised Since		1989	1996	1995	1988	1983	1983	1980
Franchised Units 1996	63	67	25			365		
1997	75	72	111	0	650	507	71	1056
1998	83					569		
Company Owned 1996	0	0	1			1		
1997		0	1	5	1	1	1	0
1998						1		
Number of Units U.S.	160			3	559	505	72	700
Canada	0			1	40	3	0	226
Foreign	0			2	52	51	0	130
Projected New U.S.						50		
Canada						8		
Foreign						25		
Corporate Employees	11			10	15	25	15	85
Contract Length	10-20			5/5	3/3	15/15	10/10	10/5
Expand in Territory	Y			Y	Y	Y	Y	Y
Full-Time Employees				2		2	4	4
Part-Time Employees				2	1	1		1
Conversions	Y			Y	Y	Y	Y	Y
Site Selection Assist.	Y			Y	N	Y	Y	Y
Lease Negotiation Assist.				Y		Y	Y	Y
Site Space Required				500		400-1000	1000	1200
Development Agreement	N			N	Y	Y	Y	Y
Develop. Agree. Term					10	20	15	25
Sub-franchising	N			N	N	Y	N	Y

Travel Industry

Travel (Spread 2 of 2)

Empress Travel
465 Smith St
Farmingdale, NY 11735
Business development, supplier overrides air/tour/car
Phone: 516-420-9200   Accepts collect calls? N
Toll Free: 800-282-8440   FAX: 516-420-0511
Internet: empresstrvl.com
Suitable Sites: ES, FB, M, OC, SC, SF
Concentration: 40 in NY, 43 in NJ
Expansion: All United States
Registered: MD NY VA DC
Field Support: DP, CP, EO, ST, SO, IC, FC, H, N
Training: seminar/academy's
in-office training

GalaxSea Cruises & Tours
13150 Coit Rd #125
Dallas, TX 75240
Cruise & vacation travel store
Phone: 972-671-1040   Accepts collect calls?
Toll Free: FAX:
Internet:
Suitable Sites:
Concentration:
Expansion: All United States
Registered:
Field Support:
Training:

InHouse Travel Group LLC
190 E Westminster Ave
Lake Forest, IL 60045
Homebased travel agency
Phone: 847-234-8750   Accepts collect calls?
Toll Free: FAX:
Internet:
Suitable Sites:
Concentration:
Expansion: All United States, Canada, Foreign
Registered:
Field Support:
Training:

Kirby Tours
2451 S Telegraph Rd
Dearborn, MI 48124

Phone: 313-278-2224   Accepts collect calls?
Toll Free: 800-521-0711   FAX: 313-278-9569
Internet: www.kirbytours.com
Suitable Sites:
Concentration: 1 in MI, 1 in MD, 1 in NY
Expansion: All United States, Canada, Foreign
Registered: CA,FL,HI,IL,IN,MD,MI,MN,ND,NY,OR,RI,SD,VA,WA,WI,DC
Field Support: $EO, ST, SO, $IC, $FC, H, $N
Training: 1 week Dearborn MI

TPI Travel Services
3030 Rocky Point #100
Tampa, FL 33607

Phone: 813-281-5671   Accepts collect calls?
Toll Free: 800-393-7767   FAX: 813-281-2304
Internet: www.tpitravel.com
Suitable Sites: HO
Concentration: 120 in CA, 45 in FL, 30 in IL
Expansion: All United States, Canada, Foreign
Registered: CA,FL,IL
Field Support: DP, CP, $EO, $ST, IC, $FC, N
Training: 3 days Tampa FL
5 days Atlanta GA

Travel Network
560 Sylvan Ave
Englewood Cliffs, NJ 07632
Full-service travel agency w/ locations in strip center/Wal-Mart
Phone: 201-567-8500   Accepts collect calls? Y
Toll Free: 800-669-9000   FAX: 201-567-4405
Internet: www.travelnetwork.com
Suitable Sites: AC, FB, HO, K, M, OC, PC, RM, SC, SF, WF
Concentration: 65 in NY, 32 in NJ, 26 in CA
Expansion: All United States, Canada, Foreign
Registered: CA,FL,IL,IN,MD,MI,MN,NY,OR,RI,VA,WA,WI,DC AB
Field Support: DP, CP, EO, ST, SO, IC, FC, H, N
Training: 1 week Calif.
1 week Orlando FL
1 week on site

Travel Professionals International
312 Whittington Pkwy #203
Louisville, KY 40223

Phone: 502-423-9966   Accepts collect calls?
Toll Free: 800-626-2469   FAX: 502-327-9024
Internet: www.travelprof.com
Suitable Sites: SF
Concentration: 16 in FL, 13 in KY, 6 in MS
Expansion: All United States, Canada
Registered: CA,FL,IN,MI,OR,VA,WA
Field Support: $DP, CP, EO, ST, SO, $FC, H, N
Training: 5 days regional office
10 days on-site

Uniglobe Travel
1199 W Pender St #900
Vancouver, BC V6E-2R1 CANADA

Phone: 604-718-2600   Accepts collect calls?
Toll Free: 800-590-4111   FAX: 604-718-2678
Internet: www.uniglobe.com
Suitable Sites: FB, RM, SC, SF
Concentration: 134 in CA, 63 in OH, 57 in TX
Expansion: All United States, Canada, Foreign
Registered: CA,FL,HI,IL,IN,MD,MI,MN,ND,NY,OR,RI,SD,VA,WA,WI,DC
Field Support: $CP, EO, ST, $FC, $H, $N
Training: 1 week Vancouver BC Canada
1 week local regional office
1 week franchisee's office/store

Part III

Alphabetical Tables Listing Franchises by Category

Franchises by Start-up Costs

The beginning is the most important part of the work.
— PLATO

Appendix A is sorted by the average start-up cost. Franchises with no entry are listed first. Key: K = thousands, M = millions.

Start-up Costs	Franchise Name	Page	Start-up Costs	Franchise Name	Page
	American Lenders Service Co.	114		Liqui-Green Lawn & Tree Care	162
	Apartment Selector	386		McDonald's Restaurants of Canada Limited	334
	Better Homes Realty	386		Meineke Discount Mufflers	76
	Biologix	150		Monsieur Muffler	76
	Bullets Corporation of America, Inc.	332		Mr. Rooter Corp.	178
	Dairy Queen	316		Open Pantry Food Marts	230
	Dec-K-ing	188		Option Care	238
	Empress Travel	472		Sbarro, The Italian Eatery	338
	Era Franchise Systems	388		Talent Tree Staffing Services	250
	H & R Block	200		Travelcenters of America, Inc.	96
	Holiday Hospitality	270		VR Business Brokers	112
	Hospitality International	270		White Hen Pantry	232
	Houlihan's Restaurant Group	416	N/A	Cash Converters USA	192
	Lindy – Gertie's	378	N/A	Elmer's Pancake & Steak House	412

Start-up Costs	Franchise Name	Page	Start-up Costs	Franchise Name	Page
N/A	Leadership Management, Inc.	116	5K	TPI Travel Services	472
On-going	Pure Water Ultima	446	4.3–6.2K	American Poolplayers Association	466
Var.	Affordable Car Rental	66	5.3K	Novus Windshield Repair	86
Var.	Arrow Prescription Center	236	1–10K	Custom Auto Restoration Systems	70
Var	Better Homes & Gardens Real Estate Service	386	5.5K	Hayes Handpiece Franchises Inc	236
Var.	Budget Car & Truck Rental	66	1.5–10K	Infinity Video Productions Inc	280
Var.	Certicare	84	6K	V.I.D.E.O. Security Process (VSP)	454
Var.	Choice Hotels Intl	268	6K	Valet Express	198
Var.	Conroys 1-800-Flowers	432	3.6–8.7K	Resort Maps Franchise Inc	110
Var.	Denny's Inc	400	4.9–7.7K	Window & Wall Creations	262
Var.	Fosters Freeze, Incorporated	316	5–8K	Triple Check Income Tax Service	200
Var.	Holiday Inn Worldwide	270	4.35–8.9K	Decorating Den Painting & Home Imp	188
Var.	International Mergers & Acquisitions	112	6.8K	Diamond Seal Inc	190
Var.	Jay Roberts & Associates	128	4–10K	Custom Homewatch International	452
Var.	Payless Car Rental System	66	6–8K	Glass Magnum	176
Var.	Radisson Hotels Worldwide	272	5–9.5K	Gymn' Around Kids	138
Var.	Val-Pak Direct Marketing	110	5K CDN– 10K CDN	Model Managers Int'l	116
0.45K	KCS Applications	170	7.5K	CPR+	236
to 0.5K	Jan-Pro Franchising Int'l Inc	154	7.5K	Paystation	452
1K	Full Circle Image	424	5.1–10K	Calculated Couples	194
1.3–1.8K	Benihana of Tokyo	408	2.93–12.9K	America's Choice Int'l Inc.	386
0.78–2.5K	ProForce USA	158	~8K	21st Century Auto Alliance	96
1.5–2.8K	American Darters Association	466	8.2K	Diversified Dental Services	236
2–2.3K	Pee Wee Workout	138	6.7–10.2K	Outdoor Connection	466
0.8–3.6K	InHouse Travel Group LLC	472	8–10K	Patty-Cakes International, Inc.	144
1.5–3K	Hawkeye's Home Sitters	274	1.36– 16.85K	Jazzercise Inc	234
2.5K+	Wedding Gown Specialists/Restoration	198	4–15K	Decorating Den Interiors	262
2–3K	Cruise Lines Reservation Center	470	7–12K	Aqua Bio Technologies	150
3K	Our Weigh	242	7–12K	Stork News of America	144
2.5–4.5K	Pre-Fit	140	9.5K	Laser Chem "White Glove" Commercial Cleaning	154
3.95K	CarpetMate	146	6.3–13K	Elephant House Inc	436
4K	Airbag Options	88	6.75– 12.85K	Special Delivery Photos Inc	280
1–7.5K	Hollywood Weight Loss Centre	242	9.9K+	The Sports Section	282
4.62K	Kumon Math & Reading Center	216	10K	AccounTax Services	106
5K	Bingo Bugle Newspaper	290	10K	American Institute of Small Business	214
5K	Bright Beginnings	108	10K	InnSuites Hotels	270
5K	Cleaning Consultant Services	152	10K	The Sleeping Giant Within Inc.	216
5K	Decor-At-Your-Door International	258	10K	Turbo Management Systems Ltd.	118
5K	Empire Business Brokers	112	10K	Universal Business Consultants	130
5K	Nationwide Floor & Window Coverings	256			
5K	Points for Profits	110			
5K	Profit-On-Hold	110			

Start-up Costs	Franchise Name	Page
5–15K	Window Gang	160
5–15K	Yard Cards	450
6.5–13.5K	Serv U-1st	158
6.5–13.6K	United Capital Mortgage Assistance	192
7.8–12.5K	Gymsters, Inc.	138
4.6–16K	Heaven's Best	146
10.8K	Kitchen Solvers	182
8.3–13.3K	Stretch-N-Grow of America	140
2–20K	SaniBrite	158
5.1–17.1K	Elliott & Company Appraisers	388
7.6–15.7K	Home Helpers	206
11.7K	Kwik Dry International	154
10–14K	Tenniskids	140
12K	Classy Maids USA	166
2–22K	National Maintenance Contractors	156
10–15K	Furniture Medic	176
12.5K+	7-Eleven Convenience Stores	224
5–20K	Miracle Method	182
3.31–22K	The Homesteader	290
6.1–19.3K	Service One	158
25–50K	Showhomes of America	390
10–16.5K	Ambic Building Inspection Consult	382
11.5–15K	Accounting Business Systems	106
6–20.6K	Kinderdance International	138
9–18K	Oil Butler International	60
7.5–20K	Building Services of America	150
14K	Mini Maid Service Systems Of Canada	168
14.5K	Electronic Tax Filers	200
10–20K	Almost Heaven, Ltd.	438
12–18K	MaidPro	166
15K	Brite Site	150
15K+	PersoNet–The Personnel Network	254
5–25K	Critter Control	382
12–20K	I.B. Nuts & Fruit Too	228
6.25–25.75K	Critter Control Inc	210
9–23K	Hour Hands	166
9.2–23K	Property Damage Appraisers	178
13–20K	BMR Bath Master Reglazing Ltd.	170
9.8–23.4K	Building Systems Analysis Inc.	382
8.5K-25K	Maintain Cleaning Systems	156
6.9–27.6K	Chem-Dry Carpet/Drapery/Upholstery	146

Start-up Costs	Franchise Name	Page
7.5–27K	Window Butler	168
10–25K	Kitchen Tune-Up	182
10–25K	Room-Mate Referral Service Centers	390
15–20K	Canine Counselors	274
15–20K	Computer U Learning Centers	212
15–20K	Lifestyle Mobile Carpet Showroom	256
15–20K	Lindelle Studios	280
15–20K	Pressed 4 Time	198
5–30K	ApparelMaster USA	196
16–20K	Homeowners Concept	390
18K+	The Book Rack	422
7–29K	Candy Bouquet International	218
6.7–29.9K	Metropolitan Institute of Health Careers	116
11.45–25.4K	A Wonderful Wedding	210
12–25K	Guardsman WoodPro	184
18.5K	JDI Cleaning Systems	154
3.4–34K	Tower Cleaning Systems	160
12.4–25.4K	LedgerPlus	106
9.5K-28.5K	Superglass Windshield Repair	86
15–24K	Dent Zone	70
19.5K+	Perma Glaze	170
19.7K+	Professional Carpet Systems	148
7.7–31.9K	Dealer Specialties Int'l Inc	96
15.95–23.95K	Tee Signs Plus	110
14–26K	CruiseOne/The Travel Company	470
15–25K	EconoTax	200
15–25K	Manufacturing Management Associates	128
1–39K	Odyssey Art Centers	136
20K+	IC Solutions Inc	124
20K	Jantize America	154
20K	Old Fashioned Egg Cream Co Inc	378
20K	Professional House Doctors, Inc.	384
19.2–21.4K	AirSoPure	452
11–30K	DuraClean International	152
16–25K	Baby's Away	132
6–35K	BladeRunner Mobile Sharpening	176
7–34K	Budget Blinds	262
2.9–40K	Jani-King International	154
20–23K	Video Data Services	428
3–40K	AeroWest & WestAir Sanitation Services	150

Start-up Costs	Franchise Name	Page
17.8–25.8K	National Property Inspections, Inc.	384
15–30K	Castles Unlimited	388
15–30K	Fabri-Zone Cleaning Systems	146
15–30K	Greetings	108
15–30K	Homewatch Caregivers	206
15–30K	Safe-T-Child	144
20–25K	Pets Are Inn	276
20–25.7K	Home Instead Senior Care	248
17–29K	Merchant Advertising Systems	108
23.5K	Cartex Limited	88
9.25–38K	Home Guide Magazine	290
4.4–43.1K	RACS International	158
16–32K	Chem-Dry Carpet/Upholstery (Canada)	146
24K	Wee Watch Private Home Day Care	132
15.9–32.7K	Pillar To Post	384
22–27K	Proforma	286
24.5K	Perma Ceram Enterprises	182
10–40K	Citizens Against Crime	214
11–39K	Safe Not Sorry	452
15–35K	Team Golf Corp	460
20–30K	Enviro Masters Lawn Care	162
20–30K	Head Over Heels	138
25K	Criterium Engineers	382
25K	Franklin Traffic Service	126
25K	London Cleaners	198
25K	Performance Marketing Concepts Inc	110
25K	TRC Staffing Services	252
15.2–34.9K	Altracolor Systems	88
15.5–35K	Complete Music	208
1–50K	Service Center	130
16.4–34.9K	Diet Center Worldwide	242
26K	Carpet Network	256
18.5–35K	Floor Coverings International	256
18.5–35K	Permacrete Systems	190
27K	Yellow Jacket Direct Mail Advertising	110
15–40K	Color-Glo International	170
15–40K	HouseMaster, The Home Inspection Professionals	384
25–30K	Connect.Ad	108
25–30K	Diet Light Weight Loss System	242
5–50K	Look No-Fault Auto Insurance Agencies	128
5–50K	Sunbelt Business Brokers	112

Start-up Costs	Franchise Name	Page
13.9–42K	Surface Specialists Systems	172
21–35K	Certa Propainters Ltd	188
28K+	Yogi Bear Jellystone Park Camp-Resorts	266
18.5–38.5K	House Doctors Handyman Service	176
28.5K	Magis Fund Raising Specialists	128
18–40K	Happy & Healthy Products	320
19.4–39.9K	BrickKicker	382
29.9K	Appletree Art Publishers	420
10–50K	Group Trans-Action Brokerage Services	388
10–50K	Perfumes Etc.	100
10–50K	Worldwide Information Services	424
15–45K	Help-U-Sell	388
20–40K	Jet-Black Sealcoating & Repair	178
20–40K	Lady of America	234
25–35K	Bevinco	126
30K	Boston Bartenders School Associates	116
30K	Fast-Fix Jewelry Repairs	56
30K	Hoop Mountain	466
30K	Langenwalter Carpet Dyeing	146
20.95–39.2K	Last Flight Out	436
26.9–34K	Bathcrest	170
30.5K	Chip King	86
17.5–44.6K	Hometeam Inspection Service	382
11.7–50.5K	Bone Appetit Bakery	276
18–44.5K	I N V U Portraits	280
25.3–37.6K	Creative Colors Int'l Inc	174
26–37K	World Inspection Network	384
28–35K	Fudge Co.	218
12.7–50.6K	Castart	188
22.7–42.1K	ComputerTots/Computer Explorers	134
15.5–49.5K	Assist-2-Sell	386
25–40K	Critter Care of America	274
25–40K	EnviroFree Inspections	382
11–55K	Steam Brothers Professional Cleaning & Restoration	148
24.9–41.4K	Merry Maids	168
6.5–60K	E.P.I.C. Systems, Inc.	152
25–42K	Maid To Perfection	166
30.8–36.3K	Soft Touch Interiors	258
23.5–44.3K	Energy Wise	152
20–49K	ServiceMaster Residential/Commercial (Canada)	168

Start-up Costs	Franchise Name	Page
17.1–52.9K	Rich's Chimney Fix-It	184
20–50K	Fortune Practice Management	126
20–50K	Window Perfect	262
25–45K	Roll-A-Way	452
28–42K	High Touch–High Tech	142
30–40K	Sunbanque Island Tanning	464
35K	Ceiling Doctor	176
35K	Quik Internet	124
35K	The Visual Image	282
15.1–56.8K	Coldwell Banker Residential Affiliates	388
19–55K	Rental Guide	290
28–46K	Rent 'N Drive	68
27.5–47K	Trimark	110
15–60K	Acctcorp	106
25–50K	The Buyer's Agent	386
25–50K	Buyer's Resource	386
25–50K	Checkmate	250
25–50K	Little Scientists	136
25–50K	Terminix Termite & Pest Control	384
25–50K	Worldwide Refinishing Systems, Inc.	182
35–40K	Dr. Vinyl & Assoc.	174
35–40K	Grower Direct Fresh Cut Flowers	432
35–40K	Maid Brigade Services	166
37.7K	Successful Introduction	194
37.75K	Borvin Beverage	230
38.5K	Roto-Static International	148
25–53K	Drapery Works Systems	262
30–48K	Jackson Hewitt Tax Service	200
28.6–50.8K	Fortune Personnel Consultants	244
20–60K	DuctBusters/Buster Enterprises Inc	176
30–50K	Bath Fitter	182
30–50K	Home Cleaning Centers	166
35–45K	Adventures In Advertising	108
35–45K	Capital Carpet Cleaning	146
40K	Impressions On Hold International	108
40K	Nutrite	164
5–75K	Pack Mart	202
27.8–52.6K	The Cleaning Authority	166
31.5–49.5K	Professional Dynametric Programs/PDP	116
36–45K	Sears Driver Training	216
41K	Lawn Doctor	162

Start-up Costs	Franchise Name	Page
15.25–67.6K	Mister Mobile On-Site Oil Changes	60
7.8–76.8K	Coverall Cleaning Concepts	152
20–65K	Signs First	120
25–60K	Sale By Owner Systems	390
35–50K	By Owner Reality Network	386
35–50K	Fabutan Sun Tan Studios	464
35–50K	L A Weight Loss Centers Inc	242
35–50K	Nitro-Green Professional Lawn & Tree Care	162
35–50K	Proventure Business Group, Inc.	112
42.5K	Fire Defense Centers	452
41–45K	E.K. Williams & Co.	106
41–45K	General Business Services	126
7–80.5K	O.P.E.N. Cleaning Systems	156
42–46K	Dynamark Security Centers	452
40–49K	Dent Doctor	70
26.65–63K	Fast Bucks Development LLC	192
25–65K	Amerispec Home Inspection Service	382
30–60K	Tri-Color Carpet Dyeing And Cleaning	148
40–50K	Terra Systems	164
45K	Deckare Services	176
31.3–59.9K	ServPro	160
35.9–57.4K	Comprehensive Business Services	126
47K	The Office Alternative	128
32.5–62.5K	New York Burrito-Gourmet Wraps	340
26–69.5K	La Smoothie Franchises Inc	324
13.3–82.5K	Four Seasons Sunrooms	190
10–87K	American Mobile Sound	208
25–72K	Sports Fantastic	462
32–65K	Saf-T Auto Centers	80
48.5–51K	Handle With Care Packaging Store	202
25–75K	Aire-Master of America	150
25–75K	Steamatic	148
30–70K	Schumacher Garage Door Franchise	186
35–65K	FutureKids Inc	134
35–65K	Insulated Dry Roof Systems	190
40–60K	Padgett Business Services	106
40–60K	Screen Printing USA	286
50K	Boz Hot Dogs	336
50K	Mom's Bake At Home Pizza	374
50K	The Peanut Club	144
50K	Professional Polish	158

Start-up Costs	Franchise Name	Page
50K	Sparkle Wash	160
50K	Tradebank International	130
50K	Value Line Maintenance Systems	160
to 50K	Workenders	168
50K+Credi	Naturalawn of America	162
33.6–67.1K	ServiceMaster Residential/Commercial	168
44–60K	Oh Mighty Ices Franchise Corp	320
50–55K	Beverly Hills Weight Loss & Wellness	242
45–63K	RadioShack	428
37.5–70.6K	Lemon Tree, A Unisex Haircutting Est.	104
15.9–92.3K	National Hygiene/Lien	156
21.2–88K	Joy Carpet Dry Cleaning	146
10–100K	Travel Network	472
10–100K	Unishippers Association	204
35–75K	Atwork Personnel Services	246
40–70K	U.S. Lawns	164
45–65K	Fox's Pizza Den	364
45–65K	Gwynne Learning Academy	214
50–60K	The Maids	168
50–60K	Molly Maid	168
50–60K	Radio Shack International	428
55K	Aero-Colours	88
55K	The Mad Science Group	144
55K	One Hour Motophoto & Portrait Studio	280
55K	Rynker Ribbon Xchange Inc.	128
47.6–63.7K	The Screen Machine	178
22.5–89.2K	MaxCare Professional Cleaning Systems	156
25–87K	Slats Blind Cleaning	178
9.3–103K	Her Real Estate	390
41.9–70.7K	Around Your Neck	52
56.3K	The Screenmobile	184
44.8–68.2K	Haynes Pet Centre Franchising Inc	274
40–74K	B-Dry System	188
57K	Auto Purchase Consulting	90
47–67.5K	Barbizon Schools of Modeling	116
28.9–86K	Rainbow International Carpet Care & Restoration Specialist	148
34–81K	Malibu Gallery	420
40–75K	Southern Maid Donuts	302
40–75K	Yipes Stripes	98
55–60K	CottageCare	166
51–65K	DentPro	70

Start-up Costs	Franchise Name	Page
44.4–72K	Crestcom International, Ltd.	214
38.4–78.6K	Re-Bath	172
48–70K	Four Star Pizza	364
39–79.5K	Game Force Franchising	434
52.5–66.5K	Martial Arts America	466
16.4–102.8K	The Car Phone Store	428
to 120K	Minuteman Press International	286
40–80K	The Different Twist Pretzel Co.	306
45–75K	Gent's Formal Wear	54
50–70K	Academy for Mathematics & Science	214
50–70K	Genius Kid Academy	134
50–70K	Moe's Italian Sandwiches	348
60K	Boomerang GameWare	434
60K	Potts Doggie Shop	336
60K	Super Lawns	164
52–70K	Auto One Glass & Accessories	58
58–65K	Spring Crest Drapery Centers	262
25–99K	Roto-Rooter	178
25–100K	Kirby Tours	472
25–100K	Practical Rent A Car	66
39–86K	The Brake Shop	74
50–75K	American Concrete Raising	188
50–75K	Marble Renewal	170
30–98K	Hauntrepreneurs, Ltd.	466
46–82K	Chowderhead's Seafood Restaurants	352
30–100K	Coit Services	152
30–100K	L. A. Smoothie Healthmart & Cafe	226
50–80K	The Fourth R	142
50–80K	Scoopers Ice Cream	314
50–80K	Speedy Transmission Centers	82
54–76K	Craters & Freighters	202
55–75K	American Sign Shops	120
65K	The Pet Pantry International	276
65K	X-Bankers Check Cashing	192
49.5–81K	Cookies In Bloom	298
39.5–93.3K	Archadeck	188
33.5–100K	Slimmer Image Weight Loss Clinics	242
51–83K	Sanford Rose Associates	244
67K	U-Wash Doggie	274
49.6–84.8K	Emerald Green Lawn Care	162
49.8–85K	Balloons & Bears	436

Start-up Costs	Franchise Name	Page
19.5–116.5K	Business Information Int'l Inc	108
62.4–75K	The Car Wash Guys/Gals	94
20.42–117.5K	Condotels	470
38–100K	Wheelchair Getaways	68
40–100K	Colors On Parade	94
50–90K	Brake Centers of America	74
55–85K	Tan World	464
60–80K	Emack & Bolio's Ice Cream & Yogurt	312
60–80K	Pretzels Plus	306
60–80K	Snip N' Clip Haircut Shops	104
60–80K	Strokes	460
65–75K	Pony Mailbox & Business Centers	204
56–85K	Packaging And Shipping Specialist	202
55–86.3K	Aloette Cosmetics	100
22–120K	Paceco Financial Services	114
56.8–85.5K	The Soda Fountain	396
45–99K	Signs & More In 24	120
6–138.5K	Heel Quik	52
45–100K	Handyman Connection	190
50–95K	Chili Chompers	230
60–85K	Planet Earth Recycling	96
65–80K	Hydro Physics Pipe Inspection	154
49–97K	United States Seamless, Inc.	186
59–89K	Service-Tech Corporation	160
50–100K	Interface Financial Group	114
50–100K	Nutri-Lawn, Ecology-Friendly Lawn Care	164
50–100K	PuroFirst International	158
50–100K	Renaissance Executive Forums	118
50–100K	Seniors for Seniors/Seniors for Business	254
50–100K	Sterling Optical	240
50–100K	Swisher Hygiene	160
50–100K	Total Medical Compliance	238
65–85K	Little King	378
65–85K	Purified Water To Go	446
65–85K	Ruffin's Pet Centres	276
70–80K	First Choice Haircutters (U.S.) Inc.	102
75K	AJ Texas Hots	336
75K	Kids Team	142
75K	Weed Man	164
52–100K	Confidential Business Connection	112

Start-up Costs	Franchise Name	Page
3–150K	Peyron Tax Service	200
54.6–99K	The Medicine Shoppe	238
108.25–153.8K	The More Space Place	264
65–89K	Amigo Mobility Center	236
61.9–92.5K	GalaxSea Cruises & Tours	472
25–130K	Shoe Stop	52
35–120K	Profusion Systems	170
42.5–112.5K	Cost Cutters Family Hair Care	102
5–150K	A Quicki Services	206
70–85K	Crown Trophy	448
75–80K	United Energy Partners	190
62–97K	Carpet Master	256
60–100K	Mr. Jim's Pizza	366
60–100K	Thundercloud Subs	360
65–95K	Apple Auto Glass	86
70–90K	Aim Mail Centers	202
70–90K	Auto-Lab Diagnostic & Tune-Up Centers	84
70–90K	The Flag Shop	448
70–90K	Parcel Plus	204
75–85K	Consumer Casket USA	448
75–85K	TechnoKids	136
80K	Money Concepts (Canada)	114
80K	Pizza Man, He Delivers	368
80K	Victory Lane Quick Oil Change	62
58–103K	Pak Mail Centers of America	204
6.6–156.2K	Carlson Wagonlit Travel	470
28–135K	Stuckey's Express	228
65–100K	Mobil Ambition USA LC	108
75–90K	Mister Transmission	82
83K	United Studios of Self-Defense Inc	468
47.8–120.8K	Naut-A-Care Marine Services, Inc.	96
55.6–114.3K	Children's Orchard	142
20–150K	Re/Max International	390
44–126K	Sobik's Subs	358
75–95K	Buck's Pizza Franchising, Inc.	362
75–95K	Lentz USA Service Centers	76
80–90K	Sign-A-Rama	120
85K	Edelweiss Deli Express/Sub Express	348
85K	National Tenant Network	390

Start-up Costs	Franchise Name	Page
85K	Steaks To Go	354
60.8–109.8K	PestMaster Services	384
53–118K	H R C Int'l Inc	102
56.2–115.1K	Signs Now	120
75–100K	AccuStaff Inc	250
75–100K	Airbag Service	88
75–100K	American Leak Detection	176
75–100K	Ca$h Plus	192
75–100K	Family Pizza	364
50–127K	Matco Tools	64
54.8–122.7K	Brown Baggers	348
60–120K	United Consumers Club	210
70–110K	Good For You! Fruit & Yogurt Ltd.	318
90K	EndRust Auto Appearance Centers	70
90K	Vinylgraphics Custom Sign Centres	122
62–122K	MacBirdie Golf Gifts	458
35–150K	Foliage Design Systems	432
60–125K	Fantastic Sams	102
75–110K	ATS Personnel	246
81–106K	LawCorps Legal Staffing Services	250
64.4–123.9K	Power Smoothie	322
40–150K	International News	290
60–130K	Picture Hits	280
70–120K	Auto Accent Centers	58
75–115K	PuckMasters Hockey Training Centers	466
95K	Kennedy Transmission	82
47–146K	Rennsport	96
55–138K	Bahama Buck's Original Shaved Ice Co.	320
60.7–132.3K	We Care Hair	104
80–115K	Ronzio Pizza	370
85–110K	J.W. Tumbles, A Children's Gym	138
48.3–148.5K	Commission Express	126
61–135.86K	Econo Lube N' Tune	84
65–132K	The Honors Learning Center	216
82–116K	FastFrame U S A	420
99/Kit	Elegance Jewelry	56
69–130K	Shefield & Sons	450

Start-up Costs	Franchise Name	Page
100K	Admiral Subs	356
100K	Arodal	150
100K	Beneficial Health & Beauty	100
100K	Cruise Vacations	470
100K	IMBC	124
100K+	Kernels	228
100K	Kiddie Kobbler	142
100K	Laund-Ur-Mutt	274
100K	Tempaco	438
50–150K	National Homecraft	156
50–150K	Sandwich Tree Restaurants	350
75–125K	Biozhem Skin Care Centers	100
75–125K	Sport Clips	104
80–120K	American Transmissions	82
88–116K	Kid To Kid	142
35–170K	Merle Norman Cosmetics	100
5–200K	Master Care	156
80–125K	Panda Shoes	52
85–120K	Postnet Postal & Business Centers	204
90–115K	Pak Mail Centers (Canada)	204
95–110K	Just Legs	52
81–124.5K	Faro's Franchise Systems	364
75–131K	Wild Bird Centers of America, Inc.	278
10–200K	Coldwell Banker Affiliates (Canada)	388
60–150K	Dunhill Staffing Systems, Inc.	246
75–135K	Great Earth Vitamins	226
85–125K	Hungry Howie's Pizza & Subs	366
95–115K	Cottman Transmission	82
89–122K	Management Recruiters	244
79–134K	Morrone's Italian Ices	314
89–125K	Postal Annex+	204
86.6–127.6K	Great Clips	102
100–115K	A. J. Barnes Bicycle Emporium	456
75–140K	Cookie Bouquet/Cookies By Design	298
75–140K	Reface It Kitchen Systems	182
90–125K	MarbleLife	170
95–120K	Sangsters Health Centres	226
85–132K	Pasta To Go	378
100–120K	Health Force	248
110K	Larry's Giant Subs	356
85–135K	Wild Birds Unlimited	278

Start-up Costs	Franchise Name	Page
90–130K	Envirobate	152
95–125K	Cafe La France	416
33.75–188.5K	Bunnies Fresh Juice & Smoothie Bar	324
86.5–135.8K	PrideStaff	250
82.7–140.2K	The Pretzel Twister	306
91.5–132K	Soccer Post Intl Franchise Corp	456
99.5–125K	Estrella Insurance	126
100–125K	Cafe By George/Cookies By George	298
100–125K	Custom Cuts	102
100–125K	TechStaff	250
50–175K	Lord's & Lady's Hair Salons	104
75–150K	Sub Station Ii	358
75–150K	Yogen Fruz Worldwide	318
90–135K	Made In Japan, Teriyaki Experience	346
95–130K	Z Land, Inc.	124
98–127K	Lee Myles Transmissions	82
72–154.4K	Mighty Distribution System of America Inc	64
75.5–152.5K	City Looks Salons Int'l	102
89–139K	Cyber Exchange Software And Computers	424
96–132K	The T O L Franchise Group	100
110–119K	American Brake Service	74
80–149K	ElDorado Stone	190
100–130K	Pro-Cuts	104
60–170K	The Griddle Family Restaurants	400
80–150K	Fan-A-Mania	462
80–150K	Gymboree	138
80–150K	Medichair	238
80–150K	Pizza Pizza Limited	368
80–150K	Saint Cinnamon Bake Shoppe	296
85–145K	Once Upon A Child	144
62.8–168.6K	Two Men And A Truck	210
116.8K	Wetzel's Pretzels	306
73.8–160K	Mr. GoodCents Subs & Pasta	358
100–134K	EB's Express	338
81–153K	All American Frozen Yogurt/Ice Cream	318
83–151K	Signs By Tomorrow	120
75–160K	Kilwin's Chocolates Franchise	218
75–160K	Nach-O Fast	340

Start-up Costs	Franchise Name	Page
85–150K	2001 Flavors Plus Potatoes	312
85–150K	Snappy Tomato Pizza	370
90–145K	Today's Temporary	252
118K	Yesterday's Furniture & Country Store	260
100–137K	Taco Hut America Inc	406
70–167K	Terri's Consign & Design Furnishings	258
104.3–133K	McCoy's Cake & Pie Shop	310
111–127K	Labor Force	246
97–142K	Snelling Personnel Services	246
120K	Environmental Biotech	154
120K	Pizza Nova	368
120K	United Printing Unlimited	288
70–170K	Millicare Environmental Services	156
90–150K	Street Corner News	290
90–150K	Uniglobe Travel	472
90–150K	Wild Bird Marketplace	278
66.2–175K	Subway	360
32.8–209K	Rent-A-Wreck of America	68
100–142.9K	FutureKids (Canada)	134
110–135K	Mail Boxes Etc. (Canada)	202
110–135K	United Check Cashing	192
95–150K	Link Staffing Services	246
95–150K	Magic Wok	346
95–150K	Remedy Intelligent Staffing	250
45–202K	Pizzas By Marchelloni	370
44–204K	The Coffee Beanery	220
83.5–165.3K	Juice Connection	324
100–150K	Admiral of The Fleet Cruise Centers	470
100–150K	Cruise Holidays International	470
100–150K	Express Personnel Services	246
100–150K	Hairlines	102
100–150K	Its About Games	434
100–150K	Johnny's New York Style Pizza	366
100–150K	Rita's Italian Ice	322
100–150K	Treats	310
100–150K	We Care Home Health Services	248
100–150K	Zero's Subs	360
120–130K	ATL International	96
125K	FastSigns	120

Start-up Costs	Franchise Name	Page	Start-up Costs	Franchise Name	Page
125K	Milex Tune-Ups And Brakes	84	81–193K	Valvoline Instant Oil Change	62
125K	Shine Factory	94	100–175K	Moxie Java	222
125K	Transmission USA	82	125–150K	The Connoisseur	448
50–200K	Century 21 Real Estate	388	95–180K	Shefield Gourmet	222
50–200K	Gateway Newstands	448	106.3–169.5K	Tony Maroni's Famous Gourmet Pizza	370
75–175K	Candy Express	218	72.5–203.5K	U-Save Auto Rental of America Inc	68
90–160K	PretzelMaker	306	118.7–157.4K	Lube Depot	60
89–162K	Sylvan Learning Centers	216	94.6–183.8K	Erbert & Gerbert's Subs & Clubs	356
126K	The Great Frame Up	420	110–169K	Checkcare Systems	192
75.7–176.4K	Norrell Services	254	115–165K	Papa Murphy's	374
105.5–147K	A Shade Better	264	140K	Bagelz – The Bagel Bakery	292
110–145K	NurseFinders	248	140K	Verlo Mattress Factory Stores	260
80–175K	Cap'n Taco	340	30–250K	Tom's Foods	228
85–170K	Pet Valu	276	99.5–185K	The Closet Factory	180
86–171K	Tropik Sun Fruit & Nut	228	73.8–212K	ABC Seamless	186
110–150K	Donut Delite Cafe	300	120–168K	Travel Professionals International	472
110–150K	The Little Gym International, Inc.	138	117.9–170.7K	Computer Doctor	424
110–150K	Marco's Pizza	366	90.5–198.5K	Smoothie King	322
110–150K	Staff Builders Home Health Care	248	126.5–163.1K	Tunex International, Inc.	84
130K	Cindy's Cinnamon Rolls	296	100–190K	P.J.'S Coffee & Tea	222
100–161K	Ziebart Tidycar	94	140–150K	Speedy Printing Centers	288
69–192K	Boardwalk Fries	336	140–150K	Taco Villa	342
99–163.5K	Dollar Discount Stores	426	80–210K	Arthur Treacher's Fish & Chips	352
76.5–187K	Domino's Pizza Inc	362	121–172K	Cold Stone Creamery	312
64–200K	Mister Money – USA	128	118.5–175.6K	Huntington Learning Center	216
105–160K	Color Me Mine	420	110–185K	John Simmons	448
105–160K	Top Value Muffler & Brake Shops	78	139–159K	Jiffy Lube International Inc	60
120–145K	La Pizza Loca	366	100–200K	Baldinos Giant Jersey Subs	356
133K	Glamour Shots	280	100–200K	Blimpie Subs And Salads	356
110–160K	Framing & Art Centres	420	100–200K	Croissant + Plus	308
120–150K	CD Warehouse	440	100–200K	John Casablancas Modeling/Career Center	116
135K	World Trade Network	130	100–200K	Miracle-Ear	238
20–250K	Express One	202	100–200K	SlumberLand International	258
85–185K	Woody's Wood Shops	460	120–180K	MicroPlay Video Games	434
90–180K	1 Potato 2	376	125–175K	Kitchen Wizards	182
90–180K	The Gourmet Cup	220	125–175K	The Master Mechanic	80
95–175K	My Friend's Place	378			
94.8–176K	Petrucci's Ice Cream Co.	314			
110–161K	Re Tool	438			
108.6–163.7K	Mail Boxes Etc.	202			

Start-up Costs	Franchise Name	Page
125–175K	New York Fries	378
125–175K	The Sandwich Board	348
150K	Algonquin Travel	470
150K	East of Chicago Pizza Company	364
150K+	FCI Franchising Inc	64
150K	Jersey Mike's Franchise Systems, Inc.	348
150K	Mr. Front-End	76
150K	Sports Traders	456
150K	Subs Plus	360
150K+	Thrifty Rent-A-Car	68
150K+	Tippy's Taco House	342
50–250K	Dairy Belle Freeze	320
75–225K	California Closet Company	180
138–164K	Merlin's Muffler & Brake	76
131–171.5K	Tilden for Brakes Car Care Centers	74
122.5–181.4K	AWC Commercial Window Coverings	262
102–204K	Wing Machine	330
130–176K	Bike Line	456
91–216K	Heavenly Ham	230
22.5–285K	Medicap Pharmacy	236
98–210K	Sox Appeal	52
135–175K	Monsieur Felix & Mr. Norton Cookies	298
150–160K	Brown's Chicken & Pasta	328
112.4–197.9K	General Nutrition Centers	226
110–203K	I Can't Believe It's Yogurt	318
115–200K	Active Green + Ross Tire & Automotive Centre	92
65–250K	Captain Tony's Pizza & Pasta Emporium	362
88–227K	Eagle Cleaners	196
90–225K	Gelato Amare	314
129.6–187.3K	Ace America's Cash Express	192
117–200K	Blue Chip Cookies	298
135–185K	McBeans	222
160K	A Buck Or Two Stores	426
160K	The Goddard Schools	134
160K	Madame Et Monsieur	234
121.7–200.6K	Snap-On Tools	438
103–220K	Culligan Water Conditioning	446

Start-up Costs	Franchise Name	Page
76.4–246.8K	Hogi Yogi Sandwiches & Frozen Yogurt	348
142–182K	Submarina	358
125–200K+	Nu-Look 1-Hr. Cleaners	198
125–200K	TFM	440
125–200K	TFM/Top Forty	440
130–195K	Roli Boli	380
135–190K	Blenz Coffee	220
150–175K	AAMCO Transmissions	82
150–175K	Baskin-Robbins Canada	312
150–175K	For Olde Times Sake	436
150–175K	Ho-Lee-Chow	346
75–250K	Jackpot Convenience Stores	224
75–250K	Tropi-Tan, Inc.	464
113–213K	Rocky Mountain Chocolate Factory	218
129–199K	Quizno's Classic Subs	358
130–199K	Renzios	380
100–230K	Pizza Pit	368
140–190K	Elephant Walk Gift Galleries	436
140–190K	True Friends	278
145–185K	Lox of Bagels	294
150–180K	Greco Pizza Donair	364
165K	Great Steak & Potato Company	326
158–174K	Marble Slab Creamery	314
139–194K	Wallpapers To Go	264
145–188K	Between Rounds Bagel Deli & Bakery	292
134–200K	Port of Subs	358
126–209K	Antonello's	338
154.5–181.5K	Figaro's Italian Kitchen	338
110–227.7K	KitchenPro	262
136.7–202K	CompuTemp Inc	250
120–220K	KwiK-Kopy Printing (Canada)	284
75–265K	Great Outdoor Sub Shops	356
90–250K	CTI Computer Training Institutes	212
100–245K	EcoSmarte Planet Friendly	442
130.5–214.5K	Pro Image	462
142–203K	Precision Tune Auto Care	84
150–199K	Philly Connection	326

Start-up Costs	Franchise Name	Page
100–250K	Le Peep	418
100–250K	Tire Warehouse Central	92
125–225K	ClucK-U Chicken	328
125–225K	Grandma Lee's Bakery Cafe	308
125–225K	Men's Hair Now	104
150–200K	Clintar Groundskeeping Services	162
150–200K	Interim Healthcare	248
175K	PC Professor	212
149–202.5K	Joey's Only Seafood Restaurant	418
126.8–225K	Totally Wireless	428
139.5–213.5K	The Better Back Store	236
3.5–350K	CleanNet USA	152
147–207K	ASI Sign Systems Inc	120
130–226K	Pizza Factory Inc.	368
178.4K	Jimmy John's Gourmet Sandwich Shops	348
125–232K	Candy HQ/Sweets From Heaven	218
170–190K	Le Print Express	286
180K	Pro-Tect	384
119.7–242.7K	Gingiss Formalwear	54
130–235K	Relax The Back Franchising Co	238
165–200K	P.A.M.'S Coffee & Tea Co.	222
128–240K	Closettec	180
120–250K	Hobbytown USA	434
135–235K	Ameci Pizza & Pasta	362
150–220K	Sir Speedy (Canada)	286
170–200K	LubePros International, Inc.	60
70–300K	Lisa's Tea Treasures	220
161–213K	Tuffy Auto Service Centers	88
100–275K	Bassett's Original Turkey	328
150–225K	Butterfields, Etc.	448
150–225K	Jerry's Subs & Pizza	356
150–225K	Talking Book World	422
170–205K	Play It Again Sports	456
175–200K	Tutor Time Child Care Learning Center	132
75–300K	Pepe's Mexican Restaurant	406
176–199.95K	Nacho Nana's Worldwide Inc	340
111.1–265K	Mr. Hero	358

Start-up Costs	Franchise Name	Page
189.9K	Maaco Auto Painting & Bodyworks	70
150–230K	Everlasting Tan Club	464
170–210K	Bourbon Street Candy Company	218
180–200K	Mmmarvellous Mmmuffins	304
190K	Nancy's Pizzeria	366
144–238K	Successories	450
169–214K	Everything Yogurt & Salad Cafe	318
90–295K	Juice World	230
143–245K	Naked Furniture	258
120–270K	Berlitz Franchising Corp.	214
180–210K	Flamers Charbroiled Hamburgers & Chicken	332
195K	Maaco Auto Painting & Bodyworks (Canada)	70
134–257K	Just-A-Buck	426
146–245K	Mrs. Fields Cookies	298
151.2–240K	Auntie Anne's Hand-Rolled Soft Pretzels	306
159.9–233.9K	Copy Copy	284
170–225K	Video Impact	430
145.1–250K	EDO Japan	408
129–267K	Zuzu Mexican Food	406
117.5–280.5K	Charley's Steakery	412
47.3–351.7K	Baskin-Robbins USA Co	312
100–300K	Chef's Fried Chicken	328
100–300K	Chicago's Pizza	362
100–300K	ELS Language Centers	214
150–250K	Baby News Childrens Stores	142
150–250K	Ben & Jerry's	312
150–250K	Diamond Dave's Taco Company	340
150–250K	Discount Car & Truck Rentals	66
150–250K	First Optometry Eye Care Centers	240
150–250K	King Bear Auto Service Centers	80
150–250K	Minute Muffler And Brake	76
150–250K	Mountain Mike's Pizza	366
150–250K	Nutter's Bulk And Natural Foods	226
175–225K	Goldberg's New York Bagels	292
200K	Donut Inn	300
200K	Firstat Nursing Services	248
153.6–249.3K	Wicks 'N' Sticks	450

Start-up Costs	Franchise Name	Page
191.4–470.2K	Taco Bell Corp	342
175–500K	Tinder Box International	436
225–450K	Champion Auto Stores	64
250–425K	Harvey Washbangers	196
161.2–522.5K	IncrediPet	276
249–435K	New Horizons Computer Learning Center	212
340–352K	American Wholesale Thermographers	284
160–535.5K	Taco John's Int'l Inc	342
200–500K	ExecuTrain Corp.	212
200–500K	The Pizza Ranch	368
200–500K	Rodan Jewellers/Simply Charming	56
200–500K	Thrifty Car Rental (Canada)	68
250–450K	Buscemi's International	376
250–450K	Indy Lube	60
256.4–447.9K	Alphagraphics Printshops of the Future	284
175–550K	Interstate Dairy Queen	316
264–475K	Colortyme	428
273–467K	Team Tires Plus Ltd	92
296–449K	Expressions In Fabrics	258
150–600K	Jenny Craig Weight Loss Centres	242
250–500K	Barnie's Coffee & Tea Company	220
350–400K	Banners Restaurants	398
292–460K	One Stop Undercar	78
51–712K	Huddle House	396
320–450K	Hubb's Pub	416
130–650K	Oil Can Henry's International	62
260–522K	GCO Carpet Outlet	256
354–441K	BCT	284
41.5–758.3K	Sandler Sales Institute	118
150–650K	Stuft Pizza & Brewing	370
300–500K	Smitty's	402
350–450K	Humpty's Family Restaurant	400
350–450K	Shred-It	454
400K	Cinema Grill	466
48–760K	Nature's 10	442
275–550K	Mikes Restaurants	400
300–525K	Dynamic Golf Centres	458
208–619K	World Gym	234

Start-up Costs	Franchise Name	Page
317–522K	Famous Sam's Inc	410
250–600K	Sonitrol	454
350–500K	Easyriders	90
361–495K	Copy Club	284
216–644.5K	Farmer Boys Hamburgers	332
400–471.3K	Round Table Franchise Corp	370
330–565K	East Shore Athletic Club	234
395–500K	Jungle Jim's Restaurants	400
150–750K	Manchu Wok (U.S.)	346
300–600K	Baker Street Artisan Breads & Cafe	308
300–600K	FatBurger	332
400–500K	Chesapeake Bagel Bakery	292
382.1–522.7K	Checkers Drive-In Restaurants	376
150–761K	Bruster's Old-Fashioned Ice Cream & Yogurt	312
315.5–630.5K	El Pollo Loco	340
350–600K	Arthur Rutenberg Homes	188
425–525K	Imagine That Discovery Museums	134
186–765.5K	Speedee Oil Change & Tune-Up	62
423.5–568.5K	Hard Times Cafe	378
250–750K	Superior Walls of America	190
300–700K	Pro Golf Discount	460
500K	Chemstation International	150
7.5–1M	Truly Nolen	178
350–700K	Golf Augusta Pro Shops	458
50–1M	Joe Loue Tout Rent All	66
407.6–646.4K	McDonald's	334
100–1M	Hudson's Grill of America	416
350–750K	Q Lube	62
450–650K	Bobby Rubino's Place for Ribs	392
510–600K	Harvey's Restaurants	400
466–679K	Del Taco	340
150–1.0M	Sunshine Cafe	418
400–750K	Golden Chick	330
339–832K	Back Yard Burgers	332
512.8–659.7K	Longbranch Steakhouse & Saloon Inc	412
425–750K	BW-3 Franchise Systems Inc	228

Start-up Costs	Franchise Name	Page	Start-up Costs	Franchise Name	Page
450–750K	Bw-3 Buffalo Wild Wings	328	475–1.8M	Golds Gym	234
347.7–868K	Red Hot & Blue	418	784.58–1.5M	Culver Franchising System Inc	320
350–900K	Donatos Pizza	362	300–2M	Little Professor Book Centers	422
500–750K	Grease Monkey International	60	700–1.6M	Fuddruckers	416
500–750K	–Bob's Steakhouses	412	800–1.5M	Culvers Franchising System	376
530–750K	Las Vegas Golf & Tennis	458	800–1.5M	The Krystal Company	334
309–976K	Mazzio's Pizza	366	711–1.6M	Ponderosa Steakhouse	412
300–1M	Buddy's Bar-B-Q	354	875–1.5M	Friendly's Ice Cream Corporation	400
300–1M	Hartz Chicken	330	600–1.8M	Big Boy Restaurant & Bakery	398
500–800K	Long John Silver's	352	218–2.2M	Super 8 Motels Inc	272
550–750K	Arctic Circle	320	839–1.6M	Tumbleweed LLC	414
550–800K	Express Oil Change	60	1.19–1.25M	Hardee's Food Systems	332
550–800K	Saint Louis Bread Company, Inc.	310	880–1.6M	The Ground Round	394
600–750K	Kelsey's Restaurants	400	500–2M	Home & Garden Showplace	162
175–1.2M	Bojangles' Restaurants Inc	328	500–2M	Hq Business Centers	126
425.2–962.5K	Bennett's Bar-B-Que Inc	392	1.3M	Krispy Kreme Doughnuts	300
300–1.1M	Burger King (Canada)	332	135–2.5M	Pearle Vision Center	240
400–1M	Dog N' Suds Drive-In Restaurants	416	1.0–1.8M	Pizzeria Uno Chicago Bar & Grill	370
500–900K	Sonic Drive-In	334	70–2.75M	Star Mart	230
700K	Chelsea Street Pub & Grill	394	902.9–1.95M	Arby's	354
450–1M	Wienerschnitzel	336	514–2.4M	Village Inn Restaurants	402
50–1.5M	Happy Joe's Pizza & Ice Cream Parlor	364	1.3–1.7M	Kids R Kids Quality Learning Centers	136
100–1.5M	UncleSam's Convenient Store	224	1.3–1.7M	Western Steer Family Steakhouse/WSMP	414
400–1.2M	Dairy Queen Canada Inc.	316	1.53–1.56M	Shooters International Inc	418
450–1.2M	Buffalo's Cafe	398	1.3–1.8M	Primrose Schools	136
450–1.3M	Dickey's Barbecue Pit Restaurants	392	811–2.3M	Western Sizzlin'	414
800–950K	Boston Pizza	362	1.1–2.1M	Bennigan's	398
730–1.03M	Colter's Bar-B-Q	392	337.2–2.9M	Ramada Franchise Systems Inc	272
300–1.5M	J. D. Byrider Systems	90	350–3M	Dunkin' Donuts	300
833.5–1M	Captain D's Seafood	352	1.1–2.4M	Steak 'N Shake	354
300–1.6M	Schlotzsky's Deli	350	1.2–2.3M	Sirloin Stockade Family Steakhouse	412
700–1.2M	KFC	330	1.5–2.5M	AmericInn International	268
1M+	Damon's International	398	1–3M	Motel 6	270
500–1.5M	High Wheeler Ice Cream Parlour/Rest.	314	1.6–2.5M	Perkins Family Restaurants	402
700–1.3M	St. Hubert Bar-B-Q	392	1.5–2.67M	Copeland's of New Orleans	410
915–1.1M	East Side Mario's	404	1.2–3.3M	Golden Corral Family Steakhouse	412
635–1.4M	Bonanza	398	1.2–3.3M	Golden Corral Franchising Systems Inc	412
100–2M	Dollar Rent A Car	66	1.5–3M	Ashbury Suites & Inns	268
815–1.3M	The Ground Round Restaurant	394			
1–1.2M	Swiss Chalet/Swiss Chalet Plus Restaurants	410			

Franchises by Franchise Fee

Man is not the sum of what he has but the totality of what he does not yet have, of what he might have.

— JEAN PAUL SARTRE

Appendix B is sorted by the average franchise fee. Franchises with no entry are listed first. Key: K = thousands, M = millions.

Franchise Fee	Franchise Name	Page	Franchise Fee	Franchise Name	Page
	American Darters Association	466		Travelcenters of America, Inc.	96
	American Lenders Service Co.	114		Worldwide Information Services	424
	Boz Hot Dogs	336	0	Almost Heaven, Ltd.	438
	Bullets Corporation of America, Inc.	332	0	Champion Auto Stores	64
	Coffee Time Donuts	300	0	Domino's Pizza Inc	362
	Dec-K-ing	188	0	Elegance Jewelry	56
	Empress Travel	472	0	Emack & Bolio's Ice Cream & Yogurt	312
	H & R Block	200	0	FCI Franchising Inc	64
	Leadership Management, Inc.	116	0	Home & Garden Showplace	162
	Liqui-Green Lawn & Tree Care	162	0	Lawn Doctor	162
	Madame Et Monsieur	234	0	Le Peep	418
	Petro Stopping Centers	96	0	Le Print Express	286
	Pizza Nova	368	0	Lisa's Tea Treasures	220
	Tom's Foods	228	0	Matco Tools	64

Franchise Fee	Franchise Name	Page	Franchise Fee	Franchise Name	Page
0	Merle Norman Cosmetics	100	2K	Jay Roberts & Associates	128
0	Norrell Services	254	2K	Look No-Fault Auto Insurance Agencies	128
0	Our Weigh	242	2.3K	Serv U-1st	158
0	Perma Ceram Enterprises	182	2.5K	AccounTax Services	106
0	PrideStaff	250	2.5K	Cleaning Consultant Services	152
0	Property Damage Appraisers	178	2.5K	Cluck-U Chicken	328
0	Pure Water Ultima	446	2.5K	Dealer Specialties Int'l Inc	96
0	Tire Warehouse Central	92	2.5K	Stuckey's Express	228
0	TRC Staffing Services	252	2.9K	Heaven's Best	146
0	Triple Check Income Tax Service	200	3K	Peyron Tax Service	200
Included	Baker's Dozen Donuts	300	3K	Pony Mailbox & Business Centers	204
Included	Carlson Wagonlit Travel	470	3.5K+	Affordable Car Rental	66
Included	Ho-Lee-Chow	346	3.5K	Bathcrest	170
N/A	Cash Converters USA	192	3.9K	Better Homes & Gardens Real Estate Service	386
N/A	Custom Auto Restoration Systems	70	3.9K	BMR Bath Master Reglazing Ltd.	170
N/A	Themed Miniature Golf Courses	468	4K	Decor-At-Your-Door International	258
N/A	Wedding Gown Specialists/Restoration	198	2.45–5.95K	InHouse Travel Group LLC	472
Var.	7-Eleven Convenience Stores	224	1.5–7.5K	Hollywood Weight Loss Centre	242
Var.	American Poolplayers Association	466	4.5K	21st Century Auto Alliance	96
Var.	Certicare	84	4.5K	Help-U-Sell	388
Var.	Days Inns of America Inc	268	4.5K	Homeowners Concept	390
Var.	Discount Car & Truck Rentals	66	4.9K	Diet Center Worldwide	242
Var.	EndRust Auto Appearance Centers	70	3–7K	Custom Homewatch International	452
Var.	Gateway Newslands	448	3–7K	Oil Butler International	60
Var.	Holiday Inn Worldwide	270	5K	American Institute of Small Business	214
Var.	Howard Johnson Intl Inc	270	5K	Apple Auto Glass	86
Var.	Ramada Franchise Systems Inc	272	5K	Bingo Bugle Newspaper	290
Var.	Thrifty Rent-A-Car	68	5K	Brite Site	150
1	Atwork Personnel Services	246	5K	Calculated Couples	194
325–650	Jazzercise Inc	234	5K	Color-Glo International	170
500	Health Mart	236	5K	Condotels	470
500	Kumon Math & Reading Center	216	5K	Culligan Water Conditioning	446
.5–1K	Cruise Lines Reservation Center	470	5K	Diet Light Weight Loss System	242
1K	BladeRunner Mobile Sharpening	176	5K	The Different Twist Pretzel Co.	306
1K	Val-Pak Direct Marketing	110	5K	Fabri-Zone Cleaning Systems	146
1K+	Yard Cards	450	5K	Glass Magnum	176
1.35K	Aqua Bio Technologies	150	5K	The Homesteader	290
1.5K	Grand Rental Station/Taylor Rental	428	5K	I.B. Nuts & Fruit Too	228
1.5K	Pee Wee Workout	138	5K	Profit-On-Hold	110
1.5K	TPI Travel Services	472	5K+	Rent-A-Wreck of America	68
2K	AeroWest & WestAir Sanitation Services	150	5K	Roto-Rooter	178
2K	Four Star Pizza	364	5K	Slimmer Image Weight Loss Clinics	242

Franchise Fee	Franchise Name	Page	Franchise Fee	Franchise Name	Page
5K	Snap-On Tools	438	8.5K	Gymn' Around Kids	138
5K	Southern Maid Donuts	302	8.5K	Resort Maps Franchise Inc	110
5K	Sunbanque Island Tanning	464	8.5K	United States Seamless, Inc.	186
3.5–7K	Hawkeye's Home Sitters	274	8.55K	CarpetMate	146
5.4K	Superglass Windshield Repair	86	2.5–15K	2001 Flavors Plus Potatoes	312
1–10K	Capital Carpet Cleaning	146	8.9K	Empire Business Brokers	112
1–10K	Perfumes Etc.	100	9K	Maid To Perfection	166
5.8K	Outdoor Connection	466	9K	Snelling Personnel Services	246
3.9–7.9K	Decorating Den Painting & Home Imp	188	6–12.5K	Kitchen Tune-Up	182
6K	The Book Rack	422	5–14K	Buyer's Resource	386
6K	Kwik Dry International	154	9.5K	Accounting Business Systems	106
6K	Points for Profits	110	9.5K	Canine Counselors	274
2.5–10K	Apartment Selector	386	9.5K	Connect.Ad	108
6.4K	DuraClean International	152	9.5K	Econo Lube N' Tune	84
6.5K	E.P.I.C. Systems, Inc.	152	9.5K	Erbert & Gerbert's Subs & Clubs	356
6.9K	Boston Bartenders School Associates	116	9.5K	Hungry Howie's Pizza & Subs	366
6.99K	United Capital Mortgage Assistance	192	9.5K	KCS Applications	170
6–8K	Manufacturing Management Associates	128	9.5K	Lindy – Gertie's	378
7K	Assist-2-Sell	386	3.5–16K	Jantize America	154
7K	Maintain Cleaning Systems	156	9.8K	CruiseOne/The Travel Company	470
7K	Patty-Cakes International, Inc.	144	6.9–12.9K	The BrickKicker	382
5–10K	Jackpot Convenience Stores	224	9.9K	Altracolor Systems	88
5–10K	Sunbelt Business Brokers	112	9.9K	Better Homes Realty	386
7.5K	CPR+	236	9.9K	Classy Maids USA	166
7.5K+	Diamond Seal Inc	190	9.9K	Elliott & Company Appraisers	388
7.5K	Electronic Tax Filers	200	9.9K	Lindelle Studios	280
7.5K	IC Solutions Inc	124	9.9K	Metropolitan Institute of Health Careers	116
7.5K	Indy Lube	60	9.9K+	The Sports Section	282
7.5K	Jet-Black Sealcoating & Repair	178	10K	Admiral Subs	356
7.5K	Magis Fund Raising Specialists	128	10K	Airbag Options	88
7.5K	Radio Shack International	428	10K	Bagelz – The Bagel Bakery	292
7.9K	MaidPro	166	10K	Baldinos Giant Jersey Subs	356
7.9K	Window & Wall Creations	262	10K	Buck's Pizza Franchising, Inc.	362
.95–15K	SaniBrite	158	10K	Carvel Ice Cream Bakery	312
8K	Baby's Away	132	10K	Chicago's Pizza	362
8K	Fox's Pizza Den	364	10K	EconoTax	200
8K	Home Guide Magazine	290	10K	Everlasting Tan Club	464
1.5–15K	Building Services of America	150	10K	Faro's Franchise Systems	364
1.5–15K	Pack Mart	202	10K	First Optometry Eye Care Centers	240
8.3K	Laser Chem "White Glove" Commercial Cleaning	154	10K	Hospitality International	270
			10K	InnSuites Hotels	270
7–10K	Stork News of America	144	10K	Interim Healthcare	248

Franchise Fee	Franchise Name	Page	Franchise Fee	Franchise Name	Page
10K	International Mergers & Acquisitions	112	11.5K	Chowderhead's Seafood Restaurants	352
10K	Kids Team	142	3–20K	Quikava – Coffees By Chock Full O' Nuts	222
10K	La Pizza Loca	366	5–18K	Steamatic	148
10K	Lemon Tree – A Unisex Haircutting Est.	104	6–17K	Group Trans-Action Brokerage Services	388
10K	Mini Maid Service Systems Of Canada	168	7–16K	America's Choice Int'l Inc.	386
10K	Monsieur Muffler	76	3.5–20K	Pizza Inn Inc	368
10K	Moxie Java	222	8.5–15K	Medicap Pharmacy	236
10K	Mr. Front-End	76	11.9K+	Nationwide Floor & Window Coverings	256
10K	Mr. Jim's Pizza	366	11.9K	Tee Signs Plus	110
10K	Nutrite	164	12K	ABC Seamless	186
10K	Open Pantry Food Marts	230	12K+	Aire-Master of America	150
10K	Paystation	452	12K	Brake Centers of America	74
10K+	Pet Habitat	276	12K	Golds Gym	234
10K	The Pizza Ranch	368	12K	Gymsters, Inc.	138
10K	Planet Earth Recycling	96	12K	I N V U Portraits	280
10K	Proventure Business Group, Inc.	112	12K	LedgerPlus	106
10K	RadioShack	428	12K	Lifestyle Mobile Carpet Showroom	256
10K	Ronzio Pizza	370	12K	Marco's Pizza	366
10K	Safe Not Sorry	452	12K	Pretzels Plus	306
10K	Shefield & Sons	450	12K	Subs Plus	360
10K	SlumberLand International	258	12K	Tropi-Tan, Inc.	464
10K	Snip N' Clip Haircut Shops	104	12K	World Trade Network	130
10K	Sobik's Subs	358	3.5–20.5K	Candy Bouquet International	218
10K	Special Delivery Photos Inc	280	7.5–16.5K	USA Baby	144
10K	Straw Hat Pizza	370	9–15K	L. A. Smoothie Healthmart & Cafe	226
10K	Subway	360	9–15K	La Smoothie Franchises Inc	324
10K+	Tenniskids	140	6–18.3K	Service One	158
10K	Thundercloud Subs	360	0–25K	Minute Muffler And Brake	76
10K	Wing Machine	330	10–15K	Gent's Formal Wear	54
2.5–17.5K	Heel Quik	52	10–15K	Mobil Ambition USA LC	108
7.6–12.6K	Stretch-N-Grow of America	140	10–15K	Old Fashioned Egg Cream Co Inc	378
10.5K	Coit Services	152	10–15K	Signs First	120
10.5K	JDI Cleaning Systems	154	10–15K	Top Value Muffler & Brake Shops	78
10.5K	Sub Station Ii	358	12.5K	AccuStaff Inc	250
1–20K	National Maintenance Contractors	156	12.5K	ATS Personnel	246
6–15K	American Mobile Sound	208	12.5K	Bath Fitter	182
6.5–15K	Kinderdance International	138	12.5K	Biologix	150
11K	Castles Unlimited	388	12.5K+	Business Information Int'l Inc	108
8–14K	Kitchen Solvers	182	12.5K	Ceiling Doctor	176
2.5–20K	TCBY Treats	318	12.5K	Comprehensive Business Services	126
7.5–15K	Four Seasons Sunrooms	190	12.5K	Cookies In Bloom	298
7.5–15K	Room-Mate Referral Service Centers	390	12.5K	Cousins Subs	356

Franchise Fee	Franchise Name	Page
12.5K	Critter Care of America	274
12.5K	Dairy Belle Freeze	320
12.5K+	Dollar Rent A Car	66
12.5K	Donut Inn	300
12.5K	Energy Wise	152
12.5K	Head Over Heels	138
12.5K	Kitchen Wizards	182
12.5K	Lady of America	234
12.5K	Last Flight Out	436
12.5K	Little King	378
12.5K	Lube Depot	60
12.5K	MacBirdie Golf Gifts	458
12.5K	Magic Wok	346
12.5K+	MaxCare Professional Cleaning Systems	156
12.5K	Moe's Italian Sandwiches	348
12.5K	Mr. GoodCents Subs & Pasta	358
12.5K	New York Burrito-Gourmet Wraps	340
12.5K	Pressed 4 Time	198
12.5K	The Resume Hut	254
12.5K	Safe-T-Child	144
12.5K	U-Wash Doggie	274
12.5K	Valet Express	198
12.5K	Wee Watch Private Home Day Care	132
12.5K	Worldwide Refinishing Systems, Inc.	182
12.5K	Zero's Subs	360
5–20K	Window Gang	160
7.5–17.5K	A Quicki Services	206
6.6–18.5K	Roll-A-Way	452
12.75K	World Gym	234
7.5–18K	Coldwell Banker Affiliates (Canada)	388
9–16.8K	The Cleaning Authority	166
13K	Signs & More In 24	120
10–16.5K	Ambic Building Inspection Consult	382
7–19.8K	VR Business Brokers	112
9.9–16.9K	Window Butler	168
7.5–19.5K	Fan-A-Mania	462
9–18K	Cyber Exchange Software And Computers	424
12.5–15K	Fudge Co.	218
7.5–20K	All American Frozen Yogurt/Ice Cream	318
7.5–20K	Coldwell Banker Residential Affiliates	388
10–18K	The Medicine Shoppe	238
14K	Floor Coverings International	256

Franchise Fee	Franchise Name	Page
14.5K	Deckare Services	176
14.5K	Drapery Works Systems	262
14.5K	Home Instead Senior Care	248
14.5K	Roto-Static International	148
14.5K	Speedy Transmission Centers	82
14.5K	X-Bankers Check Cashing	192
7–22K	The Fourth R	142
14.7K	Professional Carpet Systems	148
14.9K	Auto Accent Centers	58
14.9K	Budget Blinds	262
14.9K	The Buyer's Agent	386
10–20K	Acctcorp	106
10–20K	Captain Tony's Pizza & Pasta Emporium	362
10–20K	Commission Express	126
10–20K	Talent Tree Staffing Services	250
12.5–17.5K	Building Systems Analysis Inc.	382
12–18K	Critter Control Inc	210
12–18K	Guardsman WoodPro	184
15K	AirSoPure	452
15K	American Concrete Raising	188
15K	American Sign Shops	120
15K	ApparelMaster USA	196
15K	Arrow Prescription Center	236
15K	Auto Purchase Consulting	90
15K	Baby News Childrens Stores	142
15K	Bahama Buck's Original Shaved Ice Co.	320
15K	Beneficial Health & Beauty	100
15K	Beverly Hills Weight Loss & Wellness	242
15K	Biozhem Skin Care Centers	100
15K	Buscemi's International	376
15K	Cafe La France	416
15K	Cap'n Taco	340
15K	CD Warehouse	440
15K	Certa Propainters Ltd	188
15K	Churchs Chicken	328
15K	Diamond Dave's Taco Company	340
15K	Dynamark Security Centers	452
15K	Enviro Masters Lawn Care	162
15K	EnviroFree Inspections	382
15K	Express Mart Convenient Store	224
15K	Fabutan Sun Tan Studios	464
15K	Family Pizza	364

Franchise Fee	Franchise Name	Page
15K	Fast Eddie's	376
15K	Gingiss Formalwear	54
15K	Glamour Shots	280
15K	Golden Chick	330
15K	Greco Pizza Donair	364
15K	Greetings	108
15K	Hauntrepreneurs, Ltd.	466
15K	Haynes Pet Centre Franchising Inc	274
15K	Hogi Yogi Sandwiches & Frozen Yogurt	348
15K	The Honors Learning Center	216
15K	Huddle House	396
15K	I Can't Believe It's Yogurt	318
15K	John Simmons	448
15K	Just Legs	52
15K	Kirby Tours	472
15K	Knights Franchise Systems Inc	270
15K	Larry's Giant Subs	356
15K	Link Staffing Services	246
15K	McCoy's Cake & Pie Shop	310
15K	Mom's Bake At Home Pizza	374
15K	Nach-O Fast	340
15K	Novus Windshield Repair	86
15K	Oh Mighty Ices Franchise Corp	320
15K	Pepe's Mexican Restaurant	406
15K	PersoNet – The Personnel Network	254
15K	Pets Are Inn	276
15K	Popeyes Chicken & Biscuits	330
15K	Potts Doggie Shop	336
15K	Professional House Doctors, Inc.	384
15K	Rainbow International Carpet Care & Restoration Specialist	148
15K	Renzios	380
15K	Saf-T Auto Centers	80
15K	Sale By Owner Systems	390
15K	Schumacher Garage Door Franchise	186
15K	Scoopers Ice Cream	314
15K	Shoe Stop	52
15K	Sirloin Stockade Family Steakhouse	412
15K	Snappy Tomato Pizza	370
15K	The Soda Fountain	396
15K	Sparkle Wash	160
15K	Sport Clips	104

Franchise Fee	Franchise Name	Page
15K	Spring Crest Drapery Centers	262
15K	Star Mart	230
15K	Taco Hut America Inc	406
15K	Taco Mayo	342
15K	Team Golf Corp	460
15K	TFM	440
15K	TFM/Top Forty	440
15K+	Thrifty Car Rental (Canada)	68
15K	Truly Nolen	178
15K	Tubby's Submarines	360
15K	U-Save Auto Rental of America Inc	68
15K	Wallpapers To Go	264
15K	Wild Bird Marketplace	278
15K	Window Perfect	262
15K	Yaya's Flame Broiled Chicken	330
15K+CDN	Model Managers Int'l	116
5–25K	The Coffee Beanery	220
5–25K	GalaxSea Cruises & Tours	472
5–25K	Marble Renewal	170
to 15K	Baskin-Robbins USA Co	312
12.8–17.8K	Happy & Healthy Products	320
7.8–22.8K	Dent Doctor	70
15.5K	Carpet Network	256
15.5K	Complete Music	208
7.5–24K	DuctBusters/Buster Enterprises Inc	176
10.9–20.9K	Pillar To Post	384
15.9K	Decorating Den Interiors	262
12.5–19.5K	City Looks Salons Int'l	102
12.5–19.5K	Cost Cutters Family Hair Care	102
12.5–19.5K	We Care Hair	104
14.5–17.5K	Express Personnel Services	246
16K	Chem-Dry Carpet/Upholstery (Canada)	146
16K	East of Chicago Pizza Company	364
16K	Millicare Environmental Services	156
16K	Port of Subs	358
2.7–29.5K	ProForce USA	158
12.5–20K	Era Franchise Systems	388
15–17.5K	Rich's Chimney Fix-It	184
7.5–25K	The Car Phone Store	428
7.5–25K	Re/Max International	390
8.5–24K	HouseMaster, The Home Inspection Professionals	384

Franchise Fee	Franchise Name	Page
16.4K	Furniture Medic	176
16.5K	By Owner Reality Network	386
16.5K	Home Cleaning Centers	166
16.5K	Miracle Method	182
16.5K	Mr. Hero	358
8.5–24.5K	Pre-Fit	140
16–17.5K	Pizza Pit	368
10.9–22.9K	House Doctors Handyman Service	176
16.9K	Maid Brigade Services	166
16.9K	Molly Maid	168
17K	Hayes Handpiece Franchises Inc	236
17K	Remedy Intelligent Staffing	250
3–31.5K	RACS International	158
10–25K	H R C Int'l Inc	102
10–25K	Jerry's Subs & Pizza	356
13.5–21.5K	Merry Maids	168
15.5–19.5K	Children's Orchard	142
15–20K	Bojangles' Restaurants Inc	328
17.5K	The Bone Appetit Bakery	276
17.5K	Ca$h Plus	192
17.5K	Cheeburger Cheeburger	332
17.5K	Express Oil Change	60
17.5K	Great Clips	102
17.5K	The Griddle Family Restaurants	400
17.5K	Kennedy Transmission	82
17.5K	The Maids	168
17.5K	Mickey Finn's Sports Cafe	418
17.5K	Mr. Rooter Corp.	178
17.5K	My Friend's Place	378
17.5K	Petro's Chili & Chips	380
17.5K	The Pretzel Twister	306
17.5K	Pro-Tect	384
17.5K	Rider's Hobby Shops	434
17.5K	Sandwich Tree Restaurants	350
17.5K	Slats Blind Cleaning	178
17.5K	Street Corner News	290
17.5K	Super Lawns	164
17.5K	Tri-Color Carpet Dyeing And Cleaning	148
17.5K	Wheelchair Getaways	68
5–30K	Putt-Putt Golf Courses Of America	468
5–30K	The Taco Maker	342
5–30K	Travel Network	472

Franchise Fee	Franchise Name	Page
16.5–19.5K	CottageCare	166
18K	Between Rounds Bagel Deli & Bakery	292
18K	Blimpie Subs And Salads	356
18K	Cold Stone Creamery	312
18K	Convenient Food Mart	224
18K	Dollar Discount Stores	426
18K	Ecomat	196
18K	Emerald Green Lawn Care	162
18K	Langenwalter Carpet Dyeing	146
18K	Signal Graphics Printing	286
18K	Soft Touch Interiors	258
18K	Tacotime	342
18K	United Printing Unlimited	288
18K	Wild Birds Unlimited	278
1–35K	Service Center	130
18.5K	Diversified Dental Services	236
18.5K	Figaro's Italian Kitchen	338
18.5K	Infinity Video Productions Inc	280
18.5K	Jersey Mike's Franchise Systems, Inc.	348
18.5K	Permacrete Systems	190
18.5K	Pizzas By Marchelloni	370
12.5–25K	Around Your Neck	52
12.5–25K	Century 21 Real Estate	388
12.5–25K	Citizens Against Crime	214
12.5–25K	Jimmy John's Gourmet Sandwich Shops	348
4–33.6K	Tower Cleaning Systems	160
13.9–23.9K	Amerispec Home Inspection Service	382
13.9–23.9K	Home Helpers	206
18.9K	Chem-Dry Carpet/Drapery/Upholstery	146
18.9K	Gelato Amare	314
19K	Caterina's	376
19K	Service-Tech Corporation	160
19K	Tunex International, Inc.	84
13.5–25.5K	Merchant Advertising Systems	108
15–24K	Critter Control	382
19.5K	American Brake Service	74
19.5K	American Speedy Printing Centers	284
19.5K	Arthur Treacher's Fish & Chips	352
19.5K	Charley's Steakery	412
19.5K	Dr. Vinyl & Assoc.	174
19.5K	FastFrame U S A	420
19.5K	Fire Defense Centers	452

Franchise Fee	Franchise Name	Page	Franchise Fee	Franchise Name	Page
19.5K	Game Force Franchising	434	20K	Arctic Circle	320
19.5K	Health Force	248	20K	Auto-Lab Diagnostic & Tune-Up Centers	84
19.5K	Hobbytown USA	434	20K	Boomerang GameWare	434
19.5K	Hour Hands	166	20K	Bourbon Street Candy Company	218
19.5K	Hydro Physics Pipe Inspection	154	20K	The Brake Shop	74
19.5K	Mister Mobile On-Site Oil Changes	60	20K	Brown Baggers	348
19.5K	Naked Furniture	258	20K	Budget Car & Truck Rental	66
19.5K	Nitro-Green Professional Lawn & Tree Care	162	20K	Butterfields, Etc.	448
19.5K+	Perma Glaze	170	20K	Captain D's Seafood	352
19.5K	Pro Image	462	20K	The Car Wash Guys/Gals	94
19.5K	Proforma	286	20K	Car-X Muffler & Brake	76
19.5K	Purified Water To Go	446	20K	Certigard/Petro-Canada	88
19.5K	Rocky Mountain Chocolate Factory	218	20K	Chicken Delight	328
19.5K	Signs By Tomorrow	120	20K	Chip King	86
19.5K	Soccer Post Intl Franchise Corp	456	20K	Cinema Grill	466
19.5K	Speedy Printing Centers	288	20K	Color Me Mine	420
19.5K	Steaks To Go	354	20K	Comet One-Hour Cleaners	196
19.5K	Successful Introduction	194	20K	Computer Doctor	424
19.5K	Taco John's Int'l Inc	342	20K	Computer U Learning Centers	212
19.5K	Trimark	110	20K	Cookie Bouquet/Cookies By Design	298
19.5K	United Check Cashing	192	20K	Crown Trophy	448
19.5K	Wild Bird Centers of America, Inc.	278	20K	Dent Zone	70
19.6K	NurseFinders	248	20K	Donut Delite Cafe	300
9.5–30K	Surface Specialists Systems	172	20K	Edelweiss Deli Express/Sub Express	348
19.8K	Signs Now	120	20K	EDO Japan	408
10.9–28.9K	The Hometeam Inspection Service	382	20K	Fast Bucks Development LLC	192
19.9K	World Inspection Network	384	20K	FastSigns	120
19.95K	Eagle Cleaners	196	20K	Framing & Art Centres	420
10–30K	Croissant + Plus	308	20K	Frozen Fusion Fruit Smoothies	320
10–30K	Pizza Delight	368	20K	Frullati Cafe	348
10–30K	Team Tires Plus Ltd	92	20K	Full Circle Image	424
11.5–28.5K	ServiceMaster Residential/Commercial (Canada)	168	20K	Godfather's Pizza	364
			20K	The Great American Bagel	292
15–25K	Dog N' Suds Drive-In Restaurants	416	20K	Great Steak & Potato Company	326
15–25K	Gloria Jean's Gourmet Coffees	220	20K	Happy Joe's Pizza & Ice Cream Parlor	364
15–25K	Labor Force	246	20K	Hartz Chicken	330
15–25K	Panchero's Mexican Grill	342	20K	Harvey Washbangers	196
15–25K	Showhomes of America	390	20K+	Hilton Inns	268
20K	1 Potato 2	376	20K	Hoop Mountain	466
20K	A Wonderful Wedding	210	20K	Its About Games	434
20K	Aloette Cosmetics	100	20K	Jacadi	52
20K	Antonello's	338	20K	Joe Loue Tout Rent All	66

Franchise Fee	Franchise Name	Page
20K	Joy Carpet Dry Cleaning	146
20K	Juice Connection	324
20K	Juice World	230
20K	Kid To Kid	142
20K	Kiddie Kobbler	142
20K	Kilwin's Chocolates Franchise	218
20K	Kwik-Kopy Printing (Canada)	284
20K	Lentz USA Service Centers	76
20K	Long John Silver's	352
20K	Malibu Gallery	420
20K	Manchu Wok (U.S.)	346
20K	Martial Arts America	466
20K	Morrone's Italian Ices	314
20K	Mountain Mike's Pizza	366
20K	Music-Go-Round	440
20K	Nancy's Pizzeria	366
20K	Nu-Look 1-Hr. Cleaners	198
20K	Once Upon A Child	144
20K	Orange Julius Canada Inc.	322
20K	P.J.'S Coffee & Tea	222
20K	The Pet Pantry International	276
20K	Pet Valu	276
20K	Petrucci's Ice Cream Co.	314
20K	Philly Connection	326
20K	Picture Hits	280
20K	Pizza Factory Inc.	368
20K	The Potato Sack	230
20K	Power Smoothie	322
20K	PuckMasters Hockey Training Centers	466
20K	Quizno's Classic Subs	358
20K	Re Tool	438
20K	Rent 'N Drive	68
20K	Roli Boli	380
20K	Ruffin's Pet Centres	276
20K	Schlotzsky's Deli	350
20K	Sears Driver Training	216
20K	The Second Cup	222
20K	Sir Speedy	286
20K	Sir Speedy (Canada)	286
20K	Smoothie King	322
20K	Sox Appeal	52
20K	Sports Fantastic	462
20K	The Steak Escape	354
20K	Sterling Optical	240
20K	Submarina	358
20K+	Super 8 Motels Inc	272
20K	The T O L Franchise Group	100
20K	Taco Villa	342
20K	Tan World	464
20K	TechnoKids	136
20K	Tippy's Taco House	342
20K	Tire Time Rentals	92
20K	Today's Temporary	252
20K	Tony Maroni's Famous Gourmet Pizza	370
20K	Tropik Sun Fruit & Nut	228
20K	Tuffy Auto Service Centers	88
20K	Two Men And A Truck	210
20K	Victory Lane Quick Oil Change	62
20K	Video Data Services	428
20K	Ward's Restaurants	418
20K	Western Sizzlin'	414
20K	Wetzel's Pretzels	306
20K	Wienerschnitzel	336
20K	Zuka Juice	324
20K avg	Amigo Mobility Center	236
20K(CAN)	Dufferin Game Room Store	434
5–35K	Colors On Parade	94
19–22K	Terra Systems	164
8–33K	Jani-King International	154
14.7–26.5K	ServiceMaster Residential/Commercial	168
20.8K	Women's Health Boutique	238
21K	Big O Tires	92
9–33K	Steam Brothers Professional Cleaning & Restoration	148
15–27.5K	Reface It Kitchen Systems	182
21.5K	Aim Mail Centers	202
21.5K	Criterium Engineers	382
21.5K	Handle With Care Packaging Store	202
21.5K	Homewatch Caregivers	206
21.5K	Parcel Plus	204
17.8–25.8K	National Property Inspections, Inc.	384
19–25K	Marble Slab Creamery	314
19–25K	Paper Warehouse Franchising Inc	444
22K	The Better Back Store	236

Franchise Fee	Franchise Name	Page	Franchise Fee	Franchise Name	Page
22K	Johnny's New York Style Pizza	366	24.5K	Lamar's Donuts	300
22K	Woody's Wood Shops	460	24.5K	Lox of Bagels	294
15–29.9K	ComputerTots/Computer Explorers	134	24.5K	Packaging And Shipping Specialist	202
15–30K	Ace America's Cash Express	192	24.5K	Steak-Out	232
15–30K	Dairy Queen	316	24.5K	Totally Kool	52
15–30K	EcoSmarte Planet Friendly	442	9.5–40K	Clean 'N' Press America	196
15–30K	Re-Bath	172	24.8K	Craters & Freighters	202
15–30K	Seniors for Seniors/Seniors for Business	254	24.9K	Postnet Postal & Business Centers	204
1–44K	Jan-Pro Franchising Int'l Inc	154	10–40K	Dunkin' Donuts	300
22.5K	Abra Auto Body & Glass	70	15–35K	John Casablancas Modeling/Career Center	116
22.5K	Bevinco	126	15–35K	Option Care	238
22.5K	Creative Cakery	308	20–30K	Fantastic Sams	102
22.5K	Doubledave's Pizzaworks Restaurant	404	25K	A. J. Barnes Bicycle Emporium	456
22.5K	Dry Cleaning Station	196	25K	Active Green + Ross Tire & Automotive Centre	92
22.5K	Le Croissant Shop	310	25K	Admiral of The Fleet Cruise Centers	470
22.5K	The More Space Place	264	25K	Aero-Colours	88
22.5K	PestMaster Services	384	25K	AJ Texas Hots	336
22.5K	PretzelMaker	306	25K	Ameci Pizza & Pasta	362
22.5K	Rita's Italian Ice	322	25K	American Transmissions	82
22.5K	Workenders	168	25K	AmericInn International	268
22.75K	The Office Alternative	128	25K	Ashbury Suites & Inns	268
18–28K	Yogi Bear Jellystone Park Camp-Resorts	266	25K	The Athlete's Foot	456
21.5–24.5K	Mister Money – USA	128	25K	ATL International	96
15.5–31K	Confidential Business Connection	112	25K	AWC Commercial Window Coverings	262
16.5–30K	Archadeck	188	25K	Back Yard Burgers	332
23.5K	Cartex Limited	88	25K	Bagelsmith Restaurants & Food Stores	292
23.5K	Checkmate	250	25K	Balloons & Bears	436
23.5K	The Mad Science Group	144	25K	Barnie's Coffee & Tea Company	220
12.9–34.8K	Mighty Distribution System of America Inc	64	25K	Baskin-Robbins Canada	312
23.9K	Postal Annex+	204	25K	Bassett's Original Turkey	328
24K	Auto One Glass & Accessories	58	25K	Batteries Plus	64
24K	Elephant House Inc	436	25K	Blenz Coffee	220
24K	Great Harvest Bread Co.	308	25K	Boardwalk Fries	336
24K	Odyssey Art Centers	136	25K	Borvin Beverage	230
24K	Pak Mail Centers of America	204	25K	Breadsmith	308
24K	Terri's Consign & Design Furnishings	258	25K	Brown's Chicken & Pasta	328
24K	Turbo Management Systems Ltd.	118	25K	Buffalo Wings & Rings	398
24K	Ziebart Tidycar	94	25K	Building Blocks Franchise Corp	142
9–39.5K	California Closet Company	180	25K	Buns Master Bakery Systems	308
24.5K	Air Brook Limousine	210	25K	BW-3 Buffalo Wild Wings	328
24.5K	Bike Line	456	25K	BW-3 Franchise Systems Inc	228
24.5K	Bunnies Fresh Juice & Smoothie Bar	324	25K	Cafe By George/Cookies By George	298

Franchise Fee	Franchise Name	Page	Franchise Fee	Franchise Name	Page
25K	Caffe Appassionato	220	25K	Grandma Lee's Bakery Cafe	308
25K	Candleman Corporation	448	25K	Great American Cookie Company, Inc.	298
25K	Carpet Master	256	25K	The Great Frame Up	420
25K	Champion Cleaners Franchise Inc.	196	25K	Great Outdoor Sub Shops	356
25K	Chef's Fried Chicken	328	25K	Great Wraps	378
25K	Chemstation International	150	25K	Grower Direct Fresh Cut Flowers	432
25K	Chesapeake Bagel Bakery	292	25K	Gwynne Learning Academy	214
25K	Chili Chompers	230	25K	Hammett's Learning World	214
25K	Cici's Pizza	362	25K	High Wheeler Ice Cream Parlour/Rest.	314
25K	Cindy's Cinnamon Rolls	296	25K	Hudson's Grill of America	416
25K	Colortyme	428	25K	Humpty's Family Restaurant	400
25K	Computer Renaissance	424	25K	Imagine That Discovery Museums	134
25K	Consumer Casket USA	448	25K	IncrediPet	276
25K	Copy Copy	284	25K	Interface Financial Group	114
25K	Cottman Transmission	82	25K	Interstate Dairy Queen	316
25K	Country Clutter	436	25K	J.W. Tumbles, A Children's Gym	138
25K	Custom Cuts	102	25K	Jackson Hewitt Tax Service	200
25K	Del Taco	340	25K	Joey's Only Seafood Restaurant	418
25K+	DentPro	70	25K	Jungle Jim's Restaurants	400
25K	Dickey's Barbecue Pit Restaurants	392	25K	Just-A-Buck	426
25K	Dynamic Golf Centres	458	25K	K-Bob's Steakhouses	412
25K	East Shore Athletic Club	234	25K	Kampgrounds of America/KOA	266
25K	Easyriders	90	25K	Kernels	228
25K	EB's Express	338	25K	KFC	330
25K	Elephant Walk Gift Galleries	436	25K	King Bear Auto Service Centers	80
25K	Empowered Womens Golf Shops	458	25K	KitchenPro	262
25K	English Butler Canada	206	25K	Krispy Kreme Doughnuts	300
25K	Envirobate	152	25K	Kwik Kopy Printing	284
25K	Everything Yogurt & Salad Cafe	318	25K	Laund-Ur-Mutt	274
25K	Fast-Fix Jewelry Repairs	56	25K	LawCorps Legal Staffing Services	250
25K	First Choice Haircutters (U.S.) Inc.	102	25K	LazerQuick	286
25K	Firstat Nursing Services	248	25K	Lee Myles Transmissions	82
25K	The Flag Shop	448	25K	Little Scientists	136
25K	Flamers Charbroiled Hamburgers & Chicken	332	25K	London Cleaners	198
25K	For Olde Times Sake	436	25K	Lord's & Lady's Hair Salons	104
25K	Fosters Freeze, Incorporated	316	25K	LubePros International, Inc.	60
25K	Franklin Traffic Service	126	25K	Maaco Auto Painting & Bodyworks (Canada)	70
25K	GCO Carpet Outlet	256	25K	Made In Japan, Teriyaki Experience	346
25K	Gigglebees	416	25K	Mamma Ilardo's	338
25K	Goldberg's New York Bagels	292	25K	The Master Mechanic	80
25K	Good For You! Fruit & Yogurt Ltd.	318	25K	Mazzio's Pizza	366
25K	The Gourmet Cup	220	25K	McBeans	222

Franchise Fee	Franchise Name	Page	Franchise Fee	Franchise Name	Page
25K	Medichair	238	25K	The Sandwich Board	348
25K	Meineke Discount Mufflers	76	25K	Sangsters Health Centres	226
25K	Midas (Canada)	76	25K	The Screen Machine	178
25K	Milex Tune-Ups And Brakes	84	25K	Screen Printing USA	286
25K	Mister Transmission	82	25K	The Screenmobile	184
25K	Mmmarvellous Mmmuffins	304	25K	ServPro	160
25K	Monsieur Felix & Mr. Norton Cookies	298	25K	Shefield Gourmet	222
25K	Motel 6	270	25K	The Sleeping Giant Within Inc.	216
25K	Mrs. Fields Cookies	298	25K	The Sport Shoe	456
25K	My Favorite Muffin	304	25K	Sports Traders	456
25K	Nacho Nana's Worldwide Inc	340	25K	Spot-Not Car Washes	94
25K	The Nature of Things Store	442	25K	Strokes	460
25K	New York Fries	378	25K	Stuft Pizza & Brewing	370
25K	Nutri-Lawn, Ecology-Friendly Lawn Care	164	25K	Sunshine Cafe	418
25K	Oil Can Henry's International	62	25K	Talking Book World	422
25K	One Hour Martinizing	198	25K	TechStaff	250
25K	P.A.M.'S Coffee & Tea Co.	222	25K	Tilden for Brakes Car Care Centers	74
25K	Paceco Financial Services	114	25K	Transmission USA	82
25K	Pak Mail Centers (Canada)	204	25K	Treats	310
25K	Panda Shoes	52	25K	Truck Options	58
25K	Papa Murphy's	374	25K	True Friends	278
25K	Pasta To Go	378	25K	UncleSam's Convenient Store	224
25K	Pastel's Cafe	380	25K	Valvoline Instant Oil Change	62
25K	The Peanut Club	144	25K	Video Impact	430
25K	Penn Stations East Coast Subs	358	25K	Vinylgraphics Custom Sign Centres	122
25K	Performance Marketing Concepts Inc	110	25K	We Care Home Health Services	248
25K	Petland	276	25K	Western Steer Family Steakhouse/WSMP	414
25K	Pizza Man – He Delivers	368	25K	White Hen Pantry	232
25K	Play It Again Sports	456	25K	Wicks 'N' Sticks	450
25K	Precision Tune Auto Care	84	25K	Yellow Jacket Direct Mail Advertising	110
25K	Pretzel Time	306	25K	Yogen Fruz Worldwide	318
25K	Pro-Cuts	104	25K	Z-Teca	344
25K	Professional Polish	158	25K	Zuzu Mexican Food	406
25K	Profusion Systems	170	25K avg	MarbleLife	170
25K	Q Lube	62	25.9K	Alphagraphics Printshops Of The Future	284
25K	Quik Internet	124	15–38K	Dunhill Staffing Systems, Inc.	246
25K	Relax The Back Franchising Co	238	27K	Nature's 10	442
25K	Rennsport	96	27K	United Studios of Self-Defense Inc	468
25K	Robin's Donuts	300	19.5–35K	Barbizon Schools of Modeling	116
25K	Round Table Franchise Corp	370	20–35K	High Touch-High Tech	142
25K	Rynker Ribbon Xchange Inc.	128	25–30K	Naut-A-Care Marine Services, Inc.	96
25K	Saint Cinnamon Bake Shoppe	296	27.5K	Adventures In Advertising	108

Franchise Fee	Franchise Name	Page	Franchise Fee	Franchise Name	Page
27.5K	Creative Colors Int'l Inc	174	30K	Ben & Jerry's	312
27.5K	General Nutrition Centers	226	30K+	Berlitz Franchising Corp.	214
27.5K	Kohr Bros. Frozen Custard	320	30K	Big City Bagels Inc	292
27.5K	Travel Professionals International	472	30K	Bonanza	398
27.5K	Yesterday's Furniture & Country Store	260	30K	Bruster's Old-Fashioned Ice Cream & Yogurt	312
35–20K	L A Weight Loss Centers Inc	242	30K	Buddy's Bar-B-Q	354
5–50K	Pinch-A-Penny	426	30K	Candy HQ/Sweets From Heaven	218
26–30K	Merlin's Muffler & Brake	76	30K	Checkers Drive-In Restaurants	376
28K	Grease Monkey International	60	30K	Chelsea Street Pub & Grill	394
12.5–45K	Checkcare Systems	192	30K	Clintar Groundskeeping Services	162
29K	Environmental Biotech	154	30K	Closettec	180
29K	St. Jerome Restaurant	402	30K	Colter's Bar-B-Q	392
29K	U.S. Lawns	164	30K	CompuTemp Inc	250
29K	Villa Pizza	372	30K	Conroys 1-800-Flowers	432
25–34K	Weed Man	164	30K	Copy Club	284
29.5K	Academy for Mathematics & Science	214	30K	Country Inns & Suites by Carlson	268
29.5K	Blue Chip Cookies	298	30K	CTI Computer Training Institutes	212
29.5K	The Connoisseur	448	30K+	ELS Language Centers	214
29.5K	Cruise Holidays International	470	30K	ExecuTrain	116
29.5K	La Salsa Fresh Mexican Grill	340	30K	Expressions In Fabrics	258
29.5K	MicroPlay Video Games	434	30K	Famous Sam's Inc	410
29.5K	Naturalawn of America	162	30K	Farmer Boys Hamburgers	332
29.5K	Papyrus	450	30K	FatBurger	332
29.5K	Professional Dynametric Programs/PDP	116	30K	Friendly's Ice Cream Corporation	400
29.5K	Staff Builders Home Health Care	248	30K	The Goddard Schools	134
9.5–50K	National Hygiene/Lien	156	30K	The Great Canadian Bagel	292
29.9K	Appletree Art Publishers	420	30K	Great Earth Vitamins	226
29.9K	Mail Boxes Etc.	202	30K	The Great Wilderness Company, Inc.	442
29.9K	Mail Boxes Etc. (Canada)	202	30K	Hard Times Cafe	378
29.9K	V.I.D.E.O. Security Process (VSP)	454	30K	Heavenly Ham	230
10–50K	Dollar Rent A Car (Canada)	66	30K	International News	290
10–50K	Shine Factory	94	30K	Learning Express	136
10–50K	Unishippers Association	204	30K	Lemstone Books	422
25–35K	Airbag Service	88	30K	Living Lighting	258
25–35K	Candy Express	218	30K	M & M Meat Shops	230
30K	AAMCO Transmissions	82	30K	Maaco Auto Painting & Bodyworks	70
30K	Academy of Learning	134	30K	Manhattan Bagel Co Inc	294
30K	American Wholesale Thermographers	284	30K	Manhattan Bagel Company	294
30K	Ashley Avery's Collectables	436	30K	National Tenant Network	390
30K	Auntie Anne's Hand-Rolled Soft Pretzels	306	30K	Nutter's Bulk And Natural Foods	226
30K	Baker Street Artisan Breads & Cafe	308	30K	Pearle Vision Center	240
30K	Banners Restaurants	398	30K	Pizza Pizza Limited	368

Franchise Fee	Franchise Name	Page
30K	Ponderosa Steakhouse	412
30K	PuroFirst International	158
30K	Radisson Hotels Worldwide	272
30K	Red Hot & Blue	418
30K	Select Sandwich	350
30K	Sonic Drive-In	334
30K	Speedee Oil Change & Tune-Up	62
30K	Steak 'N Shake	354
30K	Superior Walls of America	190
30K	Tinder Box International	436
30K	Tradebank International	130
30K+	Universal Business Consultants	130
30K	Value Line Maintenance Systems	160
30K	Verlo Mattress Factory Stores	260
30K	Z Land, Inc.	124
12.8–48K	Castart	188
32K	Yipes Stripes	98
32.5K	Field of Dreams	462
32.5K	The Krystal Company	334
33K	Huntington Learning Center	216
28.5–39.5K	The Closet Factory	180
34.5K	Padgett Business Services	106
20–50K	Sonitrol	454
25–45K	Uniglobe Travel	472
30–40K	Golf USA	458
30–40K	Western Medical Services	248
35K	A Shade Better	264
35K	Aaron's Rental Purchase	428
35K	Algonquin Travel	470
35K	BCT	284
35K	Bennett's Bar-B-Que Inc	392
35K	Buffalo's Cafe	398
35K	Cultures Restaurants	376
35K	Culver Franchising System Inc	320
35K	Culvers Franchising System	376
35K	Dairy Queen Canada Inc.	316
35K	Deck The Walls	420
35K	Denny's Inc	400
35K	Donatos Pizza	362
35K	E.K. Williams & Co.	106
35K	El Pollo Loco	340
35K	Elmer's Pancake & Steak House	412

Franchise Fee	Franchise Name	Page
35K	FutureKids Inc	134
35K	General Business Services	126
35K	Gymboree	138
35K	Hairlines	102
35K	Hardee's Food Systems	332
35K	Jiffy Lube International Inc	60
35K	Knowledge Development Centers Inc	128
35K	Miracle Auto Painting & Body Repair	72
35K	Norwalk – The Furniture Idea	258
35K	One Hour Motophoto & Portrait Studio	280
35K	One Hour Motophoto & Portrait Studio (Canada)	280
35K	Paradise Bakery & Cafe	310
35K	Party City Corp	444
35K	Party Land Inc	444
35K	Pizzeria Uno Chicago Bar & Grill	370
35K	ProShred Security	452
35K	Radisson Hotels International	270
35K+	Ramada Franchise Canada, Inc.	272
35K	Rental Guide	290
35K	Saint Louis Bread Company, Inc.	310
35K	Sandler Sales Institute	118
35K	SealMaster	158
35K	Smitty's	402
35K	Successories	450
35K	Tumbleweed LLC	414
35K	Village Inn Restaurants	402
35K/unit	Applebee's International	416
36K	United Energy Partners	190
6–67.5K	O.P.E.N. Cleaning Systems	156
24.5–49.5K	Pro Golf Discount	460
37K	Impressions On Hold International	108
15–60K	B-Dry System	188
25–50K	Choice Hotels Intl	268
25–50K	Doubletree Hotel Systems	268
25–50K	Insulated Dry Roof Systems	190
25–50K	Jumbo Video	440
25–50K	Terminix Termite & Pest Control	384
35–40K	U.S. Franchise Systems	272
37.5K	Arby's	354
37.5K	Kids R Kids Quality Learning Centers	136
37.5K	The Little Gym International, Inc.	138

Franchise Fee	Franchise Name	Page
37.5K	Sign-A-Rama	120
37.5K	Strings Italian Cafe	404
34–42K	Sylvan Learning Centers	216
38K	Your Office USA	130
39K	J. D. Byrider Systems	90
39.5K	Estrella Insurance	126
7.5–71.9K	Coverall Cleaning Concepts	152
39.9K	Cruise Vacations	470
30–50K	ExecuTrain Corp.	212
40K	A. L. Van Houtte	376
40K	Atlanta Bread Co	308
40K	Big Boy Restaurant & Bakery	398
40K	Burger King (Canada)	332
40K	C. B. S. Interactive Multimedia	212
40K	East Side Mario's	404
40K	Fortune Personnel Consultants	244
40K	Golden Corral Family Steakhouse	412
40K	Golden Corral Franchising Systems Inc	412
40K	Golf Augusta Pro Shops	458
40K	The Ground Round	394
40K	The Ground Round Restaurant	394
40K	Hawthorn Suites/Hawthorn Suites Ltd	268
40K	Houlihan's Restaurant Group	416
40K	Kelsey's Restaurants	400
40K	Kiddie Academy International	134
40K	Las Vegas Golf & Tennis	458
40K	PC Professor	212
40K	Perkins Family Restaurants	402
40K	Sanford Rose Associates	244
40K	Wendy's Restaurants of Canada Inc.	334
2.5–80K	Her Real Estate	390
42K	Fortune Practice Management	126
42K	International Golf	458
42K	Tutor Time Child Care Learning Center	132
35–50K	Tim Hortons	310
35–52.5K	Crestcom International, Ltd.	214
28–60K	Miracle-Ear	238
29–60K	New Horizons Computer Learning Center	212
44.5K	Minuteman Press International	286
45K	McDonald's	334
45K	McDonald's Restaurants of Canada Limited	334
45K	Mikes Restaurants	400

Franchise Fee	Franchise Name	Page
45K	Sbarro, The Italian Eatery	338
45K	Taco Bell Corp	342
37.5–57.5K	Nevada Bob's Professional Golf Shops	458
48.5K	Primrose Schools	136
49.5K	American Leak Detection	176
49.5K	Money Concepts (Canada)	114
49.5K	Renaissance Executive Forums	118
33.3–66.6K	Sutton Homes Franchising Corp	238
15–85K	Swisher Hygiene	160
25–75K	Handyman Connection	190
25–75K	National Homecraft	156
25–75K	Palace Entertainment & Bullwinkles Restaurant	402
25–75K	Totally Wireless	428
50K	A Buck Or Two Stores	426
50K	Arodal	150
50K	Benihana of Tokyo	408
50K	Bennigan's	398
50K	Bobby Rubino's Place for Ribs	392
50K	Bright Beginnings	108
50K	Damon's International	398
50K	ElDorado Stone	190
50K	Fuddruckers	416
50K	FutureKids (Canada)	134
50K	Genius Kid Academy	134
50K+	Holiday Hospitality	270
50K	Hubb's Pub	416
50K	Jenny Craig Weight Loss Centres	242
50K	Longbranch Steakhouse & Saloon Inc	412
50K	Tempaco	438
2.5–100K	Practical Rent A Car	66
55K	Shred-It	454
55K	United Consumers Club	210
37–75K	Little Professor Book Centers	422
35–80K	Color Your World	438
35–80K	Total Medical Compliance	238
20–100K	Foliage Design Systems	432
40–80K	One Stop Undercar	78
60K	Arthur Rutenberg Homes	188
60K	St. Hubert Bar-B-Q	392
62K	IMBC	124
50–75K	Harvey's Restaurants	400

Table C

Franchises by Industry/Business Specialty

A man to carry on a successful business must have imagination. He must see things as in a vision, a dream of the whole thing.
— CHARLES M. SCHWAB

Appendix C is sorted by industry and business specialty.

Industry	Business Specialty	Franchise Name	Page
Apparel	Formalwear	McMaid Inc.	57
Apparel Industry	Clothing	Around Your Neck	52
Apparel Industry	Clothing	Heel Quik	52
Apparel Industry	Clothing	Jacadi	52
Apparel Industry	Clothing	Just Legs	52
Apparel Industry	Clothing	Panda Shoes	52
Apparel Industry	Clothing	Shoe Stop	52
Apparel Industry	Clothing	Sox Appeal	52
Apparel Industry	Clothing	Totally Kool	52
Apparel Industry	Formal Wear	Gent's Formal Wear	54
Apparel Industry	Formal Wear	Gingiss Formalwear	54
Apparel Industry	Jewelry	Elegance Jewelry	56
Apparel Industry	Jewelry	Fast-Fix Jewelry Repairs	56
Apparel Industry	Jewelry	Rodan Jewellers/Simply Charming	56
Automotive Industry	Auto Accessories	Auto Accent Centers	58

Industry	Business Specialty	Franchise Name	Page
Automotive Industry	Auto Accessories	Auto One Glass & Accessories	58
Automotive Industry	Auto Accessories	Truck Options	58
Automotive Industry	Oil Change, Lube	Express Oil Change	60
Automotive Industry	Oil Change, Lube	Grease Monkey International	60
Automotive Industry	Oil Change, Lube	Indy Lube	60
Automotive Industry	Oil Change, Lube	Jiffy Lube International Inc	60
Automotive Industry	Oil Change, Lube	Lube Depot	60
Automotive Industry	Oil Change, Lube	LubePros International, Inc.	60
Automotive Industry	Oil Change, Lube	Mister Mobile On-Site Oil Changes	60
Automotive Industry	Oil Change, Lube	Oil Butler International	60
Automotive Industry	Oil Change, Lube	Oil Can Henry's International	62
Automotive Industry	Oil Change, Lube	Q Lube	62
Automotive Industry	Oil Change, Lube	Speedee Oil Change & Tune-Up	62
Automotive Industry	Oil Change, Lube	Valvoline Instant Oil Change	62
Automotive Industry	Oil Change, Lube	Victory Lane Quick Oil Change	62
Automotive Industry	Parts, Tools	Batteries Plus	64
Automotive Industry	Parts, Tools	Champion Auto Stores	64
Automotive Industry	Parts, Tools	FCI Franchising Inc	64
Automotive Industry	Parts, Tools	Matco Tools	64
Automotive Industry	Parts, Tools	Mighty Distribution System of America Inc	64
Automotive Industry	Rentals	Affordable Car Rental	66
Automotive Industry	Rentals	Budget Car & Truck Rental	66
Automotive Industry	Rentals	Discount Car & Truck Rentals	66
Automotive Industry	Rentals	Dollar Rent A Car	66
Automotive Industry	Rentals	Dollar Rent A Car (Canada)	66
Automotive Industry	Rentals	Joe Loue Tout Rent All	66
Automotive Industry	Rentals	Payless Car Rental System	66
Automotive Industry	Rentals	Practical Rent A Car	66
Automotive Industry	Rentals	Rent 'N Drive	68
Automotive Industry	Rentals	Rent-A-Wreck of America	68
Automotive Industry	Rentals	Thrifty Car Rental (Canada)	68
Automotive Industry	Rentals	Thrifty Rent-A-Car	68
Automotive Industry	Rentals	U-Save Auto Rental of America Inc	68
Automotive Industry	Rentals	Wheelchair Getaways	68
Automotive Industry	Repair: Body	Abra Auto Body & Glass	70
Automotive Industry	Repair: Body	Custom Auto Restoration Systems	70
Automotive Industry	Repair: Body	Dent Doctor	70
Automotive Industry	Repair: Body	Dent Zone	70
Automotive Industry	Repair: Body	DentPro	70
Automotive Industry	Repair: Body	EndRust Auto Appearance Centers	70
Automotive Industry	Repair: Body	Maaco Auto Painting & Bodyworks	70
Automotive Industry	Repair: Body	Maaco Auto Painting & Bodyworks (Canada)	70
Automotive Industry	Repair: Body	Miracle Auto Painting & Body Repair	72

Table C – Franchises by Industry/Business Specialty   513

Industry	Business Specialty	Franchise Name	Page
Automotive Industry	Repair: Brakes	American Brake Service	74
Automotive Industry	Repair: Brakes	Brake Centers of America	74
Automotive Industry	Repair: Brakes	The Brake Shop	74
Automotive Industry	Repair: Brakes	Tilden for Brakes Car Care Centers	74
Automotive Industry	Repair: Exhaust, Brakes, Suspension	Car-X Muffler & Brake	76
Automotive Industry	Repair: Exhaust, Brakes, Suspension	Lentz USA Service Centers	76
Automotive Industry	Repair: Exhaust, Brakes, Suspension	Meineke Discount Mufflers	76
Automotive Industry	Repair: Exhaust, Brakes, Suspension	Merlin's Muffler & Brake	76
Automotive Industry	Repair: Exhaust, Brakes, Suspension	Midas (Canada)	76
Automotive Industry	Repair: Exhaust, Brakes, Suspension	Minute Muffler And Brake	76
Automotive Industry	Repair: Exhaust, Brakes, Suspension	Monsieur Muffler	76
Automotive Industry	Repair: Exhaust, Brakes, Suspension	Mr. Front-End	76
Automotive Industry	Repair: Exhaust, Brakes, Suspension	One Stop Undercar	78
Automotive Industry	Repair: Exhaust, Brakes, Suspension	Top Value Muffler & Brake Shops	78
Automotive Industry	Repair: General	King Bear Auto Service Centers	80
Automotive Industry	Repair: General	The Master Mechanic	80
Automotive Industry	Repair: General	Saf-T Auto Centers	80
Automotive Industry	Repair: Transmission	AAMCO Transmissions	82
Automotive Industry	Repair: Transmission	American Transmissions	82
Automotive Industry	Repair: Transmission	Cottman Transmission	82
Automotive Industry	Repair: Transmission	Kennedy Transmission	82
Automotive Industry	Repair: Transmission	Lee Myles Transmissions	82
Automotive Industry	Repair: Transmission	Mister Transmission	82
Automotive Industry	Repair: Transmission	Speedy Transmission Centers	82
Automotive Industry	Repair: Transmission	Transmission USA	82
Automotive Industry	Repair: Tune-ups	Auto-Lab Diagnostic & Tune-Up Centers	84
Automotive Industry	Repair: Tune-ups	Certicare	84
Automotive Industry	Repair: Tune-ups	Econo Lube N' Tune	84
Automotive Industry	Repair: Tune-ups	Milex Tune-Ups And Brakes	84
Automotive Industry	Repair: Tune-ups	Precision Tune Auto Care	84
Automotive Industry	Repair: Tune-ups	Tunex International, Inc.	84
Automotive Industry	Repair: Windshield, Glass	Apple Auto Glass	86
Automotive Industry	Repair: Windshield, Glass	Chip King	86
Automotive Industry	Repair: Windshield, Glass	Novus Windshield Repair	86
Automotive Industry	Repair: Windshield, Glass	Superglass Windshield Repair	86

Industry	Business Specialty	Franchise Name	Page
Automotive Industry	Repair: Other	Aero-Colours	88
Automotive Industry	Repair: Other	Airbag Options	88
Automotive Industry	Repair: Other	Airbag Service	88
Automotive Industry	Repair: Other	Altracolor Systems	88
Automotive Industry	Repair: Other	Cartex Limited	88
Automotive Industry	Repair: Other	Certigard/Petro-Canada	88
Automotive Industry	Repair: Other	Tuffy Auto Service Centers	88
Automotive Industry	Sales, Brokerage	Auto Purchase Consulting	90
Automotive Industry	Sales, Brokerage	Easyriders	90
Automotive Industry	Sales, Brokerage	J. D. Byrider Systems	90
Automotive Industry	Tires	Active Green + Ross Tire & Automotive Centre	92
Automotive Industry	Tires	Big O Tires	92
Automotive Industry	Tires	Team Tires Plus Ltd	92
Automotive Industry	Tires	Tire Time Rentals	92
Automotive Industry	Tires	Tire Warehouse Central	92
Automotive Industry	Wash, Detail, Protect	The Car Wash Guys/Gals	94
Automotive Industry	Wash, Detail, Protect	Colors On Parade	94
Automotive Industry	Wash, Detail, Protect	Shine Factory	94
Automotive Industry	Wash, Detail, Protect	Spot-Not Car Washes	94
Automotive Industry	Wash, Detail, Protect	Ziebart Tidycar	94
Automotive Industry	Other Automotive	21st Century Auto Alliance	96
Automotive Industry	Other Automotive	ATL International	96
Automotive Industry	Other Automotive	Dealer Specialties Int'l Inc	96
Automotive Industry	Other Automotive	Naut-A-Care Marine Services, Inc.	96
Automotive Industry	Other Automotive	Petro Stopping Centers	96
Automotive Industry	Other Automotive	Planet Earth Recycling	96
Automotive Industry	Other Automotive	Rennsport	96
Automotive Industry	Other Automotive	Travelcenters of America, Inc.	96
Automotive Industry	Other Automotive	Yipes Stripes	98
Beauty Industry	Cosmetics	Aloette Cosmetics	100
Beauty Industry	Cosmetics	Beneficial Health & Beauty	100
Beauty Industry	Cosmetics	Biozhem Skin Care Centers	100
Beauty Industry	Cosmetics	Merle Norman Cosmetics	100
Beauty Industry	Cosmetics	Perfumes Etc.	100
Beauty Industry	Cosmetics	The T O L Franchise Group	100
Beauty Industry	Hair Care	City Looks Salons Int'l	102
Beauty Industry	Hair Care	Cost Cutters Family Hair Care	102
Beauty Industry	Hair Care	Custom Cuts	102
Beauty Industry	Hair Care	Fantastic Sams	102
Beauty Industry	Hair Care	First Choice Haircutters (U.S.) Inc.	102
Beauty Industry	Hair Care	Great Clips	102
Beauty Industry	Hair Care	H R C Int'l Inc	102
Beauty Industry	Hair Care	Hairlines	102

Table C – Franchises by Industry/Business Specialty   515

Industry	Business Specialty	Franchise Name	Page
Beauty Industry	Hair Care	Lemon Tree – A Unisex Haircutting Est.	104
Beauty Industry	Hair Care	Lord's & Lady's Hair Salons	104
Beauty Industry	Hair Care	Men's Hair Now	104
Beauty Industry	Hair Care	Pro-Cuts	104
Beauty Industry	Hair Care	Snip N' Clip Haircut Shops	104
Beauty Industry	Hair Care	Sport Clips	104
Beauty Industry	Hair Care	We Care Hair	104
Business Service Industry	Accounting, Collections	AccounTax Services	106
Business Service Industry	Accounting, Collections	Accounting Business Systems	106
Business Service Industry	Accounting, Collections	Acctcorp	106
Business Service Industry	Accounting, Collections	E.K. Williams & Co.	106
Business Service Industry	Accounting, Collections	LedgerPlus	106
Business Service Industry	Accounting, Collections	Padgett Business Services	106
Business Service Industry	Advertising, Promotion	Adventures In Advertising	108
Business Service Industry	Advertising, Promotion	Bright Beginnings	108
Business Service Industry	Advertising, Promotion	Business Information Int'l Inc	108
Business Service Industry	Advertising, Promotion	Connect.Ad	108
Business Service Industry	Advertising, Promotion	Greetings	108
Business Service Industry	Advertising, Promotion	Impressions On Hold International	108
Business Service Industry	Advertising, Promotion	Merchant Advertising Systems	108
Business Service Industry	Advertising, Promotion	Mobil Ambition USA LC	108
Business Service Industry	Advertising, Promotion	Performance Marketing Concepts Inc	110
Business Service Industry	Advertising, Promotion	Points for Profits	110
Business Service Industry	Advertising, Promotion	Profit-On-Hold	110
Business Service Industry	Advertising, Promotion	Resort Maps Franchise Inc	110
Business Service Industry	Advertising, Promotion	Tee Signs Plus	110
Business Service Industry	Advertising, Promotion	Trimark	110
Business Service Industry	Advertising, Promotion	Val-Pak Direct Marketing	110
Business Service Industry	Advertising, Promotion	Yellow Jacket Direct Mail Advertising	110
Business Service Industry	Brokerage, Sales	Confidential Business Connection	112
Business Service Industry	Brokerage, Sales	Empire Business Brokers	112
Business Service Industry	Brokerage, Sales	International Mergers & Acquisitions	112
Business Service Industry	Brokerage, Sales	Proventure Business Group, Inc.	112
Business Service Industry	Brokerage, Sales	Sunbelt Business Brokers	112
Business Service Industry	Brokerage, Sales	VR Business Brokers	112
Business Service Industry	Finance	American Lenders Service Co.	114
Business Service Industry	Finance	Interface Financial Group	114
Business Service Industry	Finance	Money Concepts (Canada)	114
Business Service Industry	Finance	Paceco Financial Services	114
Business Service Industry	Job Training	Barbizon Schools of Modeling	116
Business Service Industry	Job Training	Boston Bartenders School Associates	116
Business Service Industry	Job Training	ExecuTrain	116

Industry	Business Specialty	Franchise Name	Page
Business Service Industry	Job Training	John Casablancas Modeling/Career Center	116
Business Service Industry	Job Training	Leadership Management, Inc.	116
Business Service Industry	Job Training	Metropolitan Institute of Health Careers	116
Business Service Industry	Job Training	Model Managers Int'l	116
Business Service Industry	Job Training	Professional Dynametric Programs/PDP	116
Business Service Industry	Job Training	Renaissance Executive Forums	118
Business Service Industry	Job Training	Sandler Sales Institute	118
Business Service Industry	Job Training	Turbo Management Systems Ltd.	118
Business Service Industry	Signs	American Sign Shops	120
Business Service Industry	Signs	ASI Sign Systems Inc	120
Business Service Industry	Signs	FastSigns	120
Business Service Industry	Signs	Sign-A-Rama	120
Business Service Industry	Signs	Signs By Tomorrow	120
Business Service Industry	Signs	Signs First	120
Business Service Industry	Signs	Signs & More In 24	120
Business Service Industry	Signs	Signs Now	120
Business Service Industry	Signs	Vinylgraphics Custom Sign Centres	122
Business Service Industry	Telecom, Internet	IC Solutions Inc	124
Business Service Industry	Telecom, Internet	IMBC	124
Business Service Industry	Telecom, Internet	Quik Internet	124
Business Service Industry	Telecom, Internet	Z Land, Inc.	124
Business Service Industry	Other Business Service	Bevinco	126
Business Service Industry	Other Business Service	Commission Express	126
Business Service Industry	Other Business Service	Comprehensive Business Services	126
Business Service Industry	Other Business Service	Estrella Insurance	126
Business Service Industry	Other Business Service	Fortune Practice Management	126
Business Service Industry	Other Business Service	Franklin Traffic Service	126
Business Service Industry	Other Business Service	General Business Services	126
Business Service Industry	Other Business Service	Hq Business Centers	126
Business Service Industry	Other Business Service	Jay Roberts & Associates	128
Business Service Industry	Other Business Service	Knowledge Development Centers Inc	128
Business Service Industry	Other Business Service	Look No-Fault Auto Insurance Agencies	128
Business Service Industry	Other Business Service	Magis Fund Raising Specialists	128
Business Service Industry	Other Business Service	Manufacturing Management Associates	128
Business Service Industry	Other Business Service	Mister Money – USA	128
Business Service Industry	Other Business Service	The Office Alternative	128
Business Service Industry	Other Business Service	Rynker Ribbon Xchange Inc.	128
Business Service Industry	Other Business Service	Service Center	130
Business Service Industry	Other Business Service	Tradebank International	130
Business Service Industry	Other Business Service	Universal Business Consultants	130
Business Service Industry	Other Business Service	World Trade Network	130
Business Service Industry	Other Business Service	Your Office USA	130

Table C – Franchises by Industry/Business Specialty   517

Industry	Business Specialty	Franchise Name	Page
Child Development Industry	Child Care	Baby's Away	132
Child Development Industry	Child Care	Tutor Time Child Care Learning Center	132
Child Development Industry	Child Care	Wee Watch Private Home Day Care	132
Child Development Industry	Child Education	Academy of Learning	134
Child Development Industry	Child Education	ComputerTots/Computer Explorers	134
Child Development Industry	Child Education	FutureKids (Canada)	134
Child Development Industry	Child Education	FutureKids Inc	134
Child Development Industry	Child Education	Genius Kid Academy	134
Child Development Industry	Child Education	The Goddard Schools	134
Child Development Industry	Child Education	Imagine That Discovery Museums	134
Child Development Industry	Child Education	Kiddie Academy International	134
Child Development Industry	Child Education	Kids R Kids Quality Learning Centers	136
Child Development Industry	Child Education	Learning Express	136
Child Development Industry	Child Education	Little Scientists	136
Child Development Industry	Child Education	Odyssey Art Centers	136
Child Development Industry	Child Education	Primrose Schools	136
Child Development Industry	Child Education	TechnoKids	136
Child Development Industry	Child Fitness	Gymboree	138
Child Development Industry	Child Fitness	Gymn' Around Kids	138
Child Development Industry	Child Fitness	Gymsters, Inc.	138
Child Development Industry	Child Fitness	Head Over Heels	138
Child Development Industry	Child Fitness	J.W. Tumbles, A Children's Gym	138
Child Development Industry	Child Fitness	Kinderdance International	138
Child Development Industry	Child Fitness	The Little Gym International, Inc.	138
Child Development Industry	Child Fitness	Pee Wee Workout	138
Child Development Industry	Child Fitness	Pre-Fit	140
Child Development Industry	Child Fitness	Stretch-N-Grow of America	140
Child Development Industry	Child Fitness	Tenniskids	140
Child Development Industry	Other Child Development	Baby News Childrens Stores	142
Child Development Industry	Other Child Development	Building Blocks Franchise Corp	142
Child Development Industry	Other Child Development	Children's Orchard	142
Child Development Industry	Other Child Development	The Fourth R	142
Child Development Industry	Other Child Development	High Touch-High Tech	142
Child Development Industry	Other Child Development	Kid To Kid	142
Child Development Industry	Other Child Development	Kiddie Kobbler	142
Child Development Industry	Other Child Development	Kids Team	142
Child Development Industry	Other Child Development	The Mad Science Group	144
Child Development Industry	Other Child Development	Once Upon A Child	144
Child Development Industry	Other Child Development	Patty-Cakes International, Inc.	144
Child Development Industry	Other Child Development	The Peanut Club	144
Child Development Industry	Other Child Development	Safe-T-Child	144
Child Development Industry	Other Child Development	Stork News of America	144

Table C – Franchises by Industry/Business Specialty 519

Industry	Business Specialty	Franchise Name	Page
Cleaning and Repair Industry	Commercial Cleaning	Millicare Environmental Services	156
Cleaning and Repair Industry	Commercial Cleaning	National Homecraft	156
Cleaning and Repair Industry	Commercial Cleaning	National Hygiene/Lien	156
Cleaning and Repair Industry	Commercial Cleaning	National Maintenance Contractors	156
Cleaning and Repair Industry	Commercial Cleaning	O.P.E.N. Cleaning Systems	156
Cleaning and Repair Industry	Commercial Cleaning	Professional Polish	158
Cleaning and Repair Industry	Commercial Cleaning	ProForce USA	158
Cleaning and Repair Industry	Commercial Cleaning	PuroFirst International	158
Cleaning and Repair Industry	Commercial Cleaning	RACS International	158
Cleaning and Repair Industry	Commercial Cleaning	SaniBrite	158
Cleaning and Repair Industry	Commercial Cleaning	SealMaster	158
Cleaning and Repair Industry	Commercial Cleaning	Serv U-1st	158
Cleaning and Repair Industry	Commercial Cleaning	Service One	158
Cleaning and Repair Industry	Commercial Cleaning	Service-Tech Corporation	160
Cleaning and Repair Industry	Commercial Cleaning	ServPro	160
Cleaning and Repair Industry	Commercial Cleaning	Sparkle Wash	160
Cleaning and Repair Industry	Commercial Cleaning	Swisher Hygiene	160
Cleaning and Repair Industry	Commercial Cleaning	Tower Cleaning Systems	160
Cleaning and Repair Industry	Commercial Cleaning	Value Line Maintenance Systems	160
Cleaning and Repair Industry	Commercial Cleaning	Window Gang	160
Cleaning and Repair Industry	Lawn Care, Landscaping	Clintar Groundskeeping Services	162
Cleaning and Repair Industry	Lawn Care, Landscaping	Emerald Green Lawn Care	162
Cleaning and Repair Industry	Lawn Care, Landscaping	Enviro Masters Lawn Care	162
Cleaning and Repair Industry	Lawn Care, Landscaping	Home & Garden Showplace	162
Cleaning and Repair Industry	Lawn Care, Landscaping	Lawn Doctor	162
Cleaning and Repair Industry	Lawn Care, Landscaping	Liqui-Green Lawn & Tree Care	162
Cleaning and Repair Industry	Lawn Care, Landscaping	Naturalawn of America	162
Cleaning and Repair Industry	Lawn Care, Landscaping	Nitro-Green Professional Lawn & Tree Care	162
Cleaning and Repair Industry	Lawn Care, Landscaping	Nutri-Lawn, Ecology-Friendly Lawn Care	164
Cleaning and Repair Industry	Lawn Care, Landscaping	Nutrite	164
Cleaning and Repair Industry	Lawn Care, Landscaping	Super Lawns	164
Cleaning and Repair Industry	Lawn Care, Landscaping	Terra Systems	164
Cleaning and Repair Industry	Lawn Care, Landscaping	U.S. Lawns	164
Cleaning and Repair Industry	Lawn Care, Landscaping	Weed Man	164
Cleaning and Repair Industry	Residential Cleaning	Classy Maids USA	166
Cleaning and Repair Industry	Residential Cleaning	The Cleaning Authority	166
Cleaning and Repair Industry	Residential Cleaning	CottageCare	166
Cleaning and Repair Industry	Residential Cleaning	Home Cleaning Centers	166
Cleaning and Repair Industry	Residential Cleaning	Hour Hands	166
Cleaning and Repair Industry	Residential Cleaning	Maid Brigade Services	166
Cleaning and Repair Industry	Residential Cleaning	Maid To Perfection	166
Cleaning and Repair Industry	Residential Cleaning	MaidPro	166

Table C – Franchises by Industry/Business Specialty   521

Industry	Business Specialty	Franchise Name	Page
Construction Industry	Kitchens, Baths, Cabinets	Miracle Method	182
Construction Industry	Kitchens, Baths, Cabinets	Perma Ceram Enterprises	182
Construction Industry	Kitchens, Baths, Cabinets	Reface It Kitchen Systems	182
Construction Industry	Kitchens, Baths, Cabinets	Worldwide Refinishing Systems, Inc.	182
Construction Industry	Repair, Reconstruction	Guardsman WoodPro	184
Construction Industry	Repair, Reconstruction	Rich's Chimney Fix-It	184
Construction Industry	Repair, Reconstruction	The Screenmobile	184
Construction Industry	Windows, Doors, Siding	ABC Seamless	186
Construction Industry	Windows, Doors, Siding	Schumacher Garage Door Franchise	186
Construction Industry	Windows, Doors, Siding	United States Seamless, Inc.	186
Construction Industry	Other Construction	American Concrete Raising	188
Construction Industry	Other Construction	Archadeck	188
Construction Industry	Other Construction	Arthur Rutenberg Homes	188
Construction Industry	Other Construction	B-Dry System	188
Construction Industry	Other Construction	Castart	188
Construction Industry	Other Construction	Certa Propainters Ltd	188
Construction Industry	Other Construction	Dec-K-ing	188
Construction Industry	Other Construction	Decorating Den Painting & Home Imp	188
Construction Industry	Other Construction	Diamond Seal Inc	190
Construction Industry	Other Construction	ElDorado Stone	190
Construction Industry	Other Construction	Four Seasons Sunrooms	190
Construction Industry	Other Construction	Handyman Connection	190
Construction Industry	Other Construction	Insulated Dry Roof Systems	190
Construction Industry	Other Construction	Permacrete Systems	190
Construction Industry	Other Construction	Superior Walls of America	190
Construction Industry	Other Construction	United Energy Partners	190
Consumer Service Industry	Consumer Finance	Ace America's Cash Express	192
Consumer Service Industry	Consumer Finance	Ca$h Plus	192
Consumer Service Industry	Consumer Finance	Cash Converters USA	192
Consumer Service Industry	Consumer Finance	Checkcare Systems	192
Consumer Service Industry	Consumer Finance	Fast Bucks Development LLC	192
Consumer Service Industry	Consumer Finance	United Capital Mortgage Assistance	192
Consumer Service Industry	Consumer Finance	United Check Cashing	192
Consumer Service Industry	Consumer Finance	X-Bankers Check Cashing	192
Consumer Service Industry	Dating Services	Calculated Couples	194
Consumer Service Industry	Dating Services	Successful Introduction	194
Consumer Service Industry	Dry Cleaning, Laundry	ApparelMaster USA	196
Consumer Service Industry	Dry Cleaning, Laundry	Champion Cleaners Franchise Inc.	196
Consumer Service Industry	Dry Cleaning, Laundry	Clean 'N' Press America	196
Consumer Service Industry	Dry Cleaning, Laundry	Comet One-Hour Cleaners	196
Consumer Service Industry	Dry Cleaning, Laundry	Dry Cleaning Station	196
Consumer Service Industry	Dry Cleaning, Laundry	Eagle Cleaners	196

Industry	Business Specialty	Franchise Name	Page
Consumer Service Industry	Dry Cleaning, Laundry	Ecomat	196
Consumer Service Industry	Dry Cleaning, Laundry	Harvey Washbangers	196
Consumer Service Industry	Dry Cleaning, Laundry	London Cleaners	198
Consumer Service Industry	Dry Cleaning, Laundry	Nu-Look 1-Hr. Cleaners	198
Consumer Service Industry	Dry Cleaning, Laundry	One Hour Martinizing	198
Consumer Service Industry	Dry Cleaning, Laundry	Pressed 4 Time	198
Consumer Service Industry	Dry Cleaning, Laundry	Valet Express	198
Consumer Service Industry	Dry Cleaning, Laundry	Wedding Gown Specialists/Restoration	198
Consumer Service Industry	Income Tax	EconoTax	200
Consumer Service Industry	Income Tax	Electronic Tax Filers	200
Consumer Service Industry	Income Tax	H & R Block	200
Consumer Service Industry	Income Tax	Jackson Hewitt Tax Service	200
Consumer Service Industry	Income Tax	Peyron Tax Service	200
Consumer Service Industry	Income Tax	Triple Check Income Tax Service	200
Consumer Service Industry	Packaging, Mailing, Shipping	Aim Mail Centers	202
Consumer Service Industry	Packaging, Mailing, Shipping	Craters & Freighters	202
Consumer Service Industry	Packaging, Mailing, Shipping	Express One	202
Consumer Service Industry	Packaging, Mailing, Shipping	Handle With Care Packaging Store	202
Consumer Service Industry	Packaging, Mailing, Shipping	Mail Boxes Etc.	202
Consumer Service Industry	Packaging, Mailing, Shipping	Mail Boxes Etc. (Canada)	202
Consumer Service Industry	Packaging, Mailing, Shipping	Pack Mart	202
Consumer Service Industry	Packaging, Mailing, Shipping	Packaging And Shipping Specialist	202
Consumer Service Industry	Packaging, Mailing, Shipping	Pak Mail Centers (Canada)	204
Consumer Service Industry	Packaging, Mailing, Shipping	Pak Mail Centers of America	204
Consumer Service Industry	Packaging, Mailing, Shipping	Parcel Plus	204
Consumer Service Industry	Packaging, Mailing, Shipping	Pony Mailbox & Business Centers	204
Consumer Service Industry	Packaging, Mailing, Shipping	Postal Annex+	204
Consumer Service Industry	Packaging, Mailing, Shipping	Postnet Postal & Business Centers	204
Consumer Service Industry	Packaging, Mailing, Shipping	Unishippers Association	204
Consumer Service Industry	Personal Services	A Quicki Services	206
Consumer Service Industry	Personal Services	English Butler Canada	206
Consumer Service Industry	Personal Services	Home Helpers	206
Consumer Service Industry	Personal Services	Homewatch Caregivers	206
Consumer Service Industry	Special Event Services	American Mobile Sound	208
Consumer Service Industry	Special Event Services	Complete Music	208
Consumer Service Industry	Other Consumer Service	A Wonderful Wedding	210
Consumer Service Industry	Other Consumer Service	Air Brook Limousine	210
Consumer Service Industry	Other Consumer Service	Critter Control Inc	210
Consumer Service Industry	Other Consumer Service	Two Men And A Truck	210
Consumer Service Industry	Other Consumer Service	United Consumers Club	210
Education Industry	Computer Training	C. B. S. Interactive Multimedia	212
Education Industry	Computer Training	Computer U Learning Centers	212

Table C – Franchises by Industry/Business Specialty   523

Industry	Business Specialty	Franchise Name	Page
Education Industry	Computer Training	CTI Computer Training Institutes	212
Education Industry	Computer Training	ExecuTrain Corp.	212
Education Industry	Computer Training	New Horizons Computer Learning Center	212
Education Industry	Computer Training	PC Professor	212
Education Industry	Other Education	Academy for Mathematics & Science	214
Education Industry	Other Education	American Institute of Small Business	214
Education Industry	Other Education	Berlitz Franchising Corp.	214
Education Industry	Other Education	Citizens Against Crime	214
Education Industry	Other Education	Crestcom International, Ltd.	214
Education Industry	Other Education	ELS Language Centers	214
Education Industry	Other Education	Gwynne Learning Academy	214
Education Industry	Other Education	Hammett's Learning World	214
Education Industry	Other Education	The Honors Learning Center	216
Education Industry	Other Education	Huntington Learning Center	216
Education Industry	Other Education	Kumon Math & Reading Center	216
Education Industry	Other Education	Sears Driver Training	216
Education Industry	Other Education	The Sleeping Giant Within Inc.	216
Education Industry	Other Education	Sylvan Learning Centers	216
Food Industry	Candy	Bourbon Street Candy Company	218
Food Industry	Candy	Candy Bouquet International	218
Food Industry	Candy	Candy Express	218
Food Industry	Candy	Candy HQ/Sweets From Heaven	218
Food Industry	Candy	Fudge Co.	218
Food Industry	Candy	Kilwin's Chocolates Franchise	218
Food Industry	Candy	Rocky Mountain Chocolate Factory	218
Food Industry	Coffees, Teas	Barnie's Coffee & Tea Company	220
Food Industry	Coffees, Teas	Blenz Coffee	220
Food Industry	Coffees, Teas	Brew Thru	220
Food Industry	Coffees, Teas	Caffe Appassionato	220
Food Industry	Coffees, Teas	The Coffee Beanery	220
Food Industry	Coffees, Teas	Gloria Jean's Gourmet Coffees	220
Food Industry	Coffees, Teas	The Gourmet Cup	220
Food Industry	Coffees, Teas	Lisa's Tea Treasures	220
Food Industry	Coffees, Teas	McBeans	222
Food Industry	Coffees, Teas	Moxie Java	222
Food Industry	Coffees, Teas	P.A.M.'S Coffee & Tea Co.	222
Food Industry	Coffees, Teas	P.J.'S Coffee & Tea	222
Food Industry	Coffees, Teas	Quikava – Coffees By Chock Full O' Nuts	222
Food Industry	Coffees, Teas	The Second Cup	222
Food Industry	Coffees, Teas	Shefield Gourmet	222
Food Industry	Convenience Stores	7-Eleven Convenience Stores	224
Food Industry	Convenience Stores	Convenient Food Mart	224

Industry	Business Specialty	Franchise Name	Page
Food Industry	Convenience Stores	Express Mart Convenient Store	224
Food Industry	Convenience Stores	Jackpot Convenience Stores	224
Food Industry	Convenience Stores	UncleSam's Convenient Store	224
Food Industry	Health Food, Vitamins	General Nutrition Centers	226
Food Industry	Health Food, Vitamins	Great Earth Vitamins	226
Food Industry	Health Food, Vitamins	L. A. Smoothie Healthmart & Cafe	226
Food Industry	Health Food, Vitamins	Nutter's Bulk And Natural Foods	226
Food Industry	Health Food, Vitamins	Sangsters Health Centres	226
Food Industry	Snack Foods	Bw-3 Franchise Systems Inc	228
Food Industry	Snack Foods	I.B. Nuts & Fruit Too	228
Food Industry	Snack Foods	Kernels	228
Food Industry	Snack Foods	Stuckey's Express	228
Food Industry	Snack Foods	Tom's Foods	228
Food Industry	Snack Foods	Tropik Sun Fruit & Nut	228
Food Industry	Other Food	Borvin Beverage	230
Food Industry	Other Food	Chili Chompers	230
Food Industry	Other Food	Heavenly Ham	230
Food Industry	Other Food	Juice World	230
Food Industry	Other Food	M & M Meat Shops	230
Food Industry	Other Food	Open Pantry Food Marts	230
Food Industry	Other Food	The Potato Sack	230
Food Industry	Other Food	Star Mart	230
Food Industry	Other Food	Steak-Out	232
Food Industry	Other Food	White Hen Pantry	232
Health Industry	Adult Fitness	East Shore Athletic Club	234
Health Industry	Adult Fitness	Golds Gym	234
Health Industry	Adult Fitness	Jazzercise Inc	234
Health Industry	Adult Fitness	Lady of America	234
Health Industry	Adult Fitness	Madame Et Monsieur	234
Health Industry	Adult Fitness	World Gym	234
Health Industry	Medical Supplies	Amigo Mobility Center	236
Health Industry	Medical Supplies	Arrow Prescription Center	236
Health Industry	Medical Supplies	The Better Back Store	236
Health Industry	Medical Supplies	CPR+	236
Health Industry	Medical Supplies	Diversified Dental Services	236
Health Industry	Medical Supplies	Hayes Handpiece Franchises Inc	236
Health Industry	Medical Supplies	Health Mart	236
Health Industry	Medical Supplies	Medicap Pharmacy	236
Health Industry	Medical Supplies	Medichair	238
Health Industry	Medical Supplies	The Medicine Shoppe	238
Health Industry	Medical Supplies	Miracle-Ear	238
Health Industry	Medical Supplies	Option Care	238

Table C – Franchises by Industry/Business Specialty   525

Industry	Business Specialty	Franchise Name	Page
Health Industry	Medical Supplies	Relax The Back Franchising Co	238
Health Industry	Medical Supplies	Sutton Homes Franchising Corp	238
Health Industry	Medical Supplies	Total Medical Compliance	238
Health Industry	Medical Supplies	Women's Health Boutique	238
Health Industry	Optical Supplies	First Optometry Eye Care Centers	240
Health Industry	Optical Supplies	Pearle Vision Center	240
Health Industry	Optical Supplies	Sterling Optical	240
Health Industry	Weight Loss and Control	Beverly Hills Weight Loss & Wellness	242
Health Industry	Weight Loss and Control	Diet Center Worldwide	242
Health Industry	Weight Loss and Control	Diet Light Weight Loss System	242
Health Industry	Weight Loss and Control	Hollywood Weight Loss Centre	242
Health Industry	Weight Loss and Control	Jenny Craig Weight Loss Centres	242
Health Industry	Weight Loss and Control	L A Weight Loss Centers Inc	242
Health Industry	Weight Loss and Control	Our Weigh	242
Health Industry	Weight Loss and Control	Slimmer Image Weight Loss Clinics	242
Human Resources Industry	Executive-search Personnel	Fortune Personnel Consultants	244
Human Resources Industry	Executive-search Personnel	Management Recruiters	244
Human Resources Industry	Executive-search Personnel	Sanford Rose Associates	244
Human Resources Industry	General Personnel	ATS Personnel	246
Human Resources Industry	General Personnel	Atwork Personnel Services	246
Human Resources Industry	General Personnel	Dunhill Staffing Systems, Inc.	246
Human Resources Industry	General Personnel	Express Personnel Services	246
Human Resources Industry	General Personnel	Labor Force	246
Human Resources Industry	General Personnel	Link Staffing Services	246
Human Resources Industry	General Personnel	Snelling Personnel Services	246
Human Resources Industry	Medical Personnel	Firstat Nursing Services	248
Human Resources Industry	Medical Personnel	Health Force	248
Human Resources Industry	Medical Personnel	Home Instead Senior Care	248
Human Resources Industry	Medical Personnel	Interim Healthcare	248
Human Resources Industry	Medical Personnel	NurseFinders	248
Human Resources Industry	Medical Personnel	Staff Builders Home Health Care	248
Human Resources Industry	Medical Personnel	We Care Home Health Services	248
Human Resources Industry	Medical Personnel	Western Medical Services	248
Human Resources Industry	Temporary Personnel	AccuStaff Inc	250
Human Resources Industry	Temporary Personnel	Checkmate	250
Human Resources Industry	Temporary Personnel	CompuTemp Inc	250
Human Resources Industry	Temporary Personnel	LawCorps Legal Staffing Services	250
Human Resources Industry	Temporary Personnel	PrideStaff	250
Human Resources Industry	Temporary Personnel	Remedy Intelligent Staffing	250
Human Resources Industry	Temporary Personnel	Talent Tree Staffing Services	250
Human Resources Industry	Temporary Personnel	TechStaff	250
Human Resources Industry	Temporary Personnel	Today's Temporary	252

Industry	Business Specialty	Franchise Name	Page
Human Resources Industry	Temporary Personnel	TRC Staffing Services	252
Human Resources Industry	Other Human Resources	Norrell Services	254
Human Resources Industry	Other Human Resources	PersoNet-The Personnel Network	254
Human Resources Industry	Other Human Resources	The Resume Hut	254
Human Resources Industry	Other Human Resources	Seniors for Seniors/Seniors for Business	254
Interior Design Industry	Carpet	Carpet Master	256
Interior Design Industry	Carpet	Carpet Network	256
Interior Design Industry	Carpet	Floor Coverings International	256
Interior Design Industry	Carpet	GCO Carpet Outlet	256
Interior Design Industry	Carpet	Lifestyle Mobile Carpet Showroom	256
Interior Design Industry	Carpet	Nationwide Floor & Window Coverings	256
Interior Design Industry	Furnishings	Decor-At-Your-Door International	258
Interior Design Industry	Furnishings	Expressions In Fabrics	258
Interior Design Industry	Furnishings	Living Lighting	258
Interior Design Industry	Furnishings	Naked Furniture	258
Interior Design Industry	Furnishings	Norwalk – The Furniture Idea	258
Interior Design Industry	Furnishings	SlumberLand International	258
Interior Design Industry	Furnishings	Soft Touch Interiors	258
Interior Design Industry	Furnishings	Terri's Consign & Design Furnishings	258
Interior Design Industry	Furnishings	Verlo Mattress Factory Stores	260
Interior Design Industry	Furnishings	Yesterday's Furniture & Country Store	260
Interior Design Industry	Window Coverings	AWC Commercial Window Coverings	262
Interior Design Industry	Window Coverings	Budget Blinds	262
Interior Design Industry	Window Coverings	Decorating Den Interiors	262
Interior Design Industry	Window Coverings	Drapery Works Systems	262
Interior Design Industry	Window Coverings	KitchenPro	262
Interior Design Industry	Window Coverings	Spring Crest Drapery Centers	262
Interior Design Industry	Window Coverings	Window Perfect	262
Interior Design Industry	Window Coverings	Window & Wall Creations	262
Interior Design Industry	Other Interior Design	A Shade Better	264
Interior Design Industry	Other Interior Design	The More Space Place	264
Interior Design Industry	Other Interior Design	Wallpapers To Go	264
Lodging Industry	Campgrounds	Kampgrounds of America/KOA	266
Lodging Industry	Campgrounds	Yogi Bear Jellystone Park Camp-Resorts	266
Lodging Industry	Hotels, Motels	AmericInn International	268
Lodging Industry	Hotels, Motels	Ashbury Suites & Inns	268
Lodging Industry	Hotels, Motels	Choice Hotels Intl	268
Lodging Industry	Hotels, Motels	Country Inns & Suites by Carlson	268
Lodging Industry	Hotels, Motels	Days Inns of America Inc	268
Lodging Industry	Hotels, Motels	Doubletree Hotel Systems	268
Lodging Industry	Hotels, Motels	Hawthorn Suites/Hawthorn Suites Ltd	268
Lodging Industry	Hotels, Motels	Hilton Inns	268

Table C – Franchises by Industry/Business Specialty 527

Industry	Business Specialty	Franchise Name	Page
Lodging Industry	Hotels, Motels	Holiday Hospitality	270
Lodging Industry	Hotels, Motels	Holiday Inn Worldwide	270
Lodging Industry	Hotels, Motels	Hospitality International	270
Lodging Industry	Hotels, Motels	Howard Johnson Intl Inc	270
Lodging Industry	Hotels, Motels	InnSuites Hotels	270
Lodging Industry	Hotels, Motels	Knights Franchise Systems Inc	270
Lodging Industry	Hotels, Motels	Motel 6	270
Lodging Industry	Hotels, Motels	Radisson Hotels International	270
Lodging Industry	Hotels, Motels	Radisson Hotels Worldwide	272
Lodging Industry	Hotels, Motels	Ramada Franchise Canada, Inc.	272
Lodging Industry	Hotels, Motels	Ramada Franchise Systems Inc	272
Lodging Industry	Hotels, Motels	Super 8 Motels Inc	272
Lodging Industry	Hotels, Motels	U.S. Franchise Systems	272
Pets Industry	Pet Care	Canine Counselors	274
Pets Industry	Pet Care	Critter Care of America	274
Pets Industry	Pet Care	Hawkeye's Home Sitters	274
Pets Industry	Pet Care	Haynes Pet Centre Franchising Inc	274
Pets Industry	Pet Care	Laund-Ur-Mutt	274
Pets Industry	Pet Care	U-Wash Doggie	274
Pets Industry	Pet Supplies	The Bone Appetit Bakery	276
Pets Industry	Pet Supplies	IncrediPet	276
Pets Industry	Pet Supplies	Pet Habitat	276
Pets Industry	Pet Supplies	The Pet Pantry International	276
Pets Industry	Pet Supplies	Pet Valu	276
Pets Industry	Pet Supplies	Petland	276
Pets Industry	Pet Supplies	Pets Are Inn	276
Pets Industry	Pet Supplies	Ruffin's Pet Centres	276
Pets Industry	Pet Supplies	True Friends	278
Pets Industry	Pet Supplies	Wild Bird Centers of America, Inc.	278
Pets Industry	Pet Supplies	Wild Bird Marketplace	278
Pets Industry	Pet Supplies	Wild Birds Unlimited	278
Photography Industry	Photography	Glamour Shots	280
Photography Industry	Photography	I N V U Portraits	280
Photography Industry	Photography	Infinity Video Productions Inc	280
Photography Industry	Photography	Lindelle Studios	280
Photography Industry	Photography	One Hour Motophoto & Portrait Studio	280
Photography Industry	Photography	One Hour Motophoto & Portrait Studio (Canada)	280
Photography Industry	Photography	Picture Hits	280
Photography Industry	Photography	Special Delivery Photos Inc	280
Photography Industry	Photography	The Sports Section	282
Photography Industry	Photography	The Visual Image	282
Printing and Copying Industry	Printing and Copying	Alphagraphics Printshops Of The Future	284

Industry	Business Specialty	Franchise Name	Page
Printing and Copying Industry	Printing and Copying	American Speedy Printing Centers	284
Printing and Copying Industry	Printing and Copying	American Wholesale Thermographers	284
Printing and Copying Industry	Printing and Copying	BCT	284
Printing and Copying Industry	Printing and Copying	Copy Club	284
Printing and Copying Industry	Printing and Copying	Copy Copy	284
Printing and Copying Industry	Printing and Copying	Kwik Kopy Printing	284
Printing and Copying Industry	Printing and Copying	Kwik-Kopy Printing (Canada)	284
Printing and Copying Industry	Printing and Copying	LazerQuick	286
Printing and Copying Industry	Printing and Copying	Le Print Express	286
Printing and Copying Industry	Printing and Copying	Minuteman Press International	286
Printing and Copying Industry	Printing and Copying	Proforma	286
Printing and Copying Industry	Printing and Copying	Screen Printing USA	286
Printing and Copying Industry	Printing and Copying	Signal Graphics Printing	286
Printing and Copying Industry	Printing and Copying	Sir Speedy	286
Printing and Copying Industry	Printing and Copying	Sir Speedy (Canada)	286
Printing and Copying Industry	Printing and Copying	Speedy Printing Centers	288
Printing and Copying Industry	Printing and Copying	United Printing Unlimited	288
Publishing Industry	Publishing	Bingo Bugle Newspaper	290
Publishing Industry	Publishing	Home Guide Magazine	290
Publishing Industry	Publishing	The Homesteader	290
Publishing Industry	Publishing	International News	290
Publishing Industry	Publishing	Rental Guide	290
Publishing Industry	Publishing	Street Corner News	290
Quick-service Industry	Bakery: Bagels	Bagelsmith Restaurants & Food Stores	292
Quick-service Industry	Bakery: Bagels	Bagelz – The Bagel Bakery	292
Quick-service Industry	Bakery: Bagels	Between Rounds Bagel Deli & Bakery	292
Quick-service Industry	Bakery: Bagels	Big City Bagels Inc	292
Quick-service Industry	Bakery: Bagels	Chesapeake Bagel Bakery	292
Quick-service Industry	Bakery: Bagels	Goldberg's New York Bagels	292
Quick-service Industry	Bakery: Bagels	The Great American Bagel	292
Quick-service Industry	Bakery: Bagels	The Great Canadian Bagel	292
Quick-service Industry	Bakery: Bagels	Lox of Bagels	294
Quick-service Industry	Bakery: Bagels	Manhattan Bagel Co Inc	294
Quick-service Industry	Bakery: Bagels	Manhattan Bagel Company	294
Quick-service Industry	Bakery: Cinnamon Rolls	Cindy's Cinnamon Rolls	296
Quick-service Industry	Bakery: Cinnamon Rolls	Saint Cinnamon Bake Shoppe	296
Quick-service Industry	Bakery: Cookies	Blue Chip Cookies	298
Quick-service Industry	Bakery: Cookies	Cafe By George/Cookies By George	298
Quick-service Industry	Bakery: Cookies	Cookie Bouquet/Cookies By Design	298
Quick-service Industry	Bakery: Cookies	Cookies In Bloom	298
Quick-service Industry	Bakery: Cookies	Great American Cookie Company, Inc.	298
Quick-service Industry	Bakery: Cookies	Monsieur Felix & Mr. Norton Cookies	298

Table C – Franchises by Industry/Business Specialty   529

Industry	Business Specialty	Franchise Name	Page
Quick-service Industry	Bakery: Cookies	Mrs. Fields Cookies	298
Quick-service Industry	Bakery: Doughnuts	Baker's Dozen Donuts	300
Quick-service Industry	Bakery: Doughnuts	Coffee Time Donuts	300
Quick-service Industry	Bakery: Doughnuts	Donut Delite Cafe	300
Quick-service Industry	Bakery: Doughnuts	Donut Inn	300
Quick-service Industry	Bakery: Doughnuts	Dunkin' Donuts	300
Quick-service Industry	Bakery: Doughnuts	Krispy Kreme Doughnuts	300
Quick-service Industry	Bakery: Doughnuts	Lamar's Donuts	300
Quick-service Industry	Bakery: Doughnuts	Robin's Donuts	300
Quick-service Industry	Bakery: Doughnuts	Southern Maid Donuts	302
Quick-service Industry	Bakery: Muffins	Mmmarvellous Mmmuffins	304
Quick-service Industry	Bakery: Muffins	My Favorite Muffin	304
Quick-service Industry	Bakery: Pretzels	Auntie Anne's Hand-Rolled Soft Pretzels	306
Quick-service Industry	Bakery: Pretzels	The Different Twist Pretzel Co.	306
Quick-service Industry	Bakery: Pretzels	Pretzel Time	306
Quick-service Industry	Bakery: Pretzels	The Pretzel Twister	306
Quick-service Industry	Bakery: Pretzels	PretzelMaker	306
Quick-service Industry	Bakery: Pretzels	Pretzels Plus	306
Quick-service Industry	Bakery: Pretzels	Wetzel's Pretzels	306
Quick-service Industry	Bakery: Other	Atlanta Bread Co	308
Quick-service Industry	Bakery: Other	Baker Street Artisan Breads & Cafe	308
Quick-service Industry	Bakery: Other	Breadsmith	308
Quick-service Industry	Bakery: Other	Buns Master Bakery Systems	308
Quick-service Industry	Bakery: Other	Creative Cakery	308
Quick-service Industry	Bakery: Other	Croissant + Plus	308
Quick-service Industry	Bakery: Other	Grandma Lee's Bakery Cafe	308
Quick-service Industry	Bakery: Other	Great Harvest Bread Co.	308
Quick-service Industry	Bakery: Other	Le Croissant Shop	310
Quick-service Industry	Bakery: Other	McCoy's Cake & Pie Shop	310
Quick-service Industry	Bakery: Other	Paradise Bakery & Cafe	310
Quick-service Industry	Bakery: Other	Saint Louis Bread Company, Inc.	310
Quick-service Industry	Bakery: Other	Tim Hortons	310
Quick-service Industry	Bakery: Other	Treats	310
Quick-service Industry	Frozen: Ice Cream	2001 Flavors Plus Potatoes	312
Quick-service Industry	Frozen: Ice Cream	Baskin-Robbins Canada	312
Quick-service Industry	Frozen: Ice Cream	Baskin-Robbins USA Co	312
Quick-service Industry	Frozen: Ice Cream	Ben & Jerry's	312
Quick-service Industry	Frozen: Ice Cream	Bruster's Old-Fashioned Ice Cream & Yogurt	312
Quick-service Industry	Frozen: Ice Cream	Carvel Ice Cream Bakery	312
Quick-service Industry	Frozen: Ice Cream	Cold Stone Creamery	312
Quick-service Industry	Frozen: Ice Cream	Emack & Bolio's Ice Cream & Yogurt	312
Quick-service Industry	Frozen: Ice Cream	Gelato Amare	314

Industry	Business Specialty	Franchise Name	Page
Quick-service Industry	Frozen: Ice Cream	High Wheeler Ice Cream Parlour/Rest.	314
Quick-service Industry	Frozen: Ice Cream	Marble Slab Creamery	314
Quick-service Industry	Frozen: Ice Cream	Morrone's Italian Ices	314
Quick-service Industry	Frozen: Ice Cream	Petrucci's Ice Cream Co.	314
Quick-service Industry	Frozen: Ice Cream	Scoopers Ice Cream	314
Quick-service Industry	Frozen: Soft-serve	Dairy Queen	316
Quick-service Industry	Frozen: Soft-serve	Dairy Queen Canada Inc.	316
Quick-service Industry	Frozen: Soft-serve	Fosters Freeze, Incorporated	316
Quick-service Industry	Frozen: Soft-serve	Interstate Dairy Queen	316
Quick-service Industry	Frozen: Yogurt	All American Frozen Yogurt/Ice Cream	318
Quick-service Industry	Frozen: Yogurt	Everything Yogurt & Salad Cafe	318
Quick-service Industry	Frozen: Yogurt	Good For You! Fruit & Yogurt Ltd.	318
Quick-service Industry	Frozen: Yogurt	I Can't Believe It's Yogurt	318
Quick-service Industry	Frozen: Yogurt	TCBY Treats	318
Quick-service Industry	Frozen: Yogurt	Yogen Fruz Worldwide	318
Quick-service Industry	Frozen: Other	Arctic Circle	320
Quick-service Industry	Frozen: Other	Bahama Buck's Original Shaved Ice Co.	320
Quick-service Industry	Frozen: Other	Culver Franchising System Inc	320
Quick-service Industry	Frozen: Other	Dairy Belle Freeze	320
Quick-service Industry	Frozen: Other	Frozen Fusion Fruit Smoothies	320
Quick-service Industry	Frozen: Other	Happy & Healthy Products	320
Quick-service Industry	Frozen: Other	Kohr Bros. Frozen Custard	320
Quick-service Industry	Frozen: Other	Oh Mighty Ices Franchise Corp	320
Quick-service Industry	Frozen: Other	Orange Julius Canada Inc.	322
Quick-service Industry	Frozen: Other	Power Smoothie	322
Quick-service Industry	Frozen: Other	Rita's Italian Ice	322
Quick-service Industry	Frozen: Other	Smoothie King	322
Quick-service Industry	Juices & Smoothies	Bunnies Fresh Juice & Smoothie Bar	324
Quick-service Industry	Juices & Smoothies	Juice Connection	324
Quick-service Industry	Juices & Smoothies	La Smoothie Franchises Inc	324
Quick-service Industry	Juices & Smoothies	Zuka Juice	324
Quick-service Industry	Meals: Cheese-steak	Great Steak & Potato Company	326
Quick-service Industry	Meals: Cheese-steak	Philly Connection	326
Quick-service Industry	Meals: Chicken, Turkey	Bassett's Original Turkey	328
Quick-service Industry	Meals: Chicken, Turkey	Bojangles' Restaurants Inc	328
Quick-service Industry	Meals: Chicken, Turkey	Brown's Chicken & Pasta	328
Quick-service Industry	Meals: Chicken, Turkey	Bw-3 Buffalo Wild Wings	328
Quick-service Industry	Meals: Chicken, Turkey	Chef's Fried Chicken	328
Quick-service Industry	Meals: Chicken, Turkey	Chicken Delight	328
Quick-service Industry	Meals: Chicken, Turkey	Churchs Chicken	328
Quick-service Industry	Meals: Chicken, Turkey	Cluck-U Chicken	328
Quick-service Industry	Meals: Chicken, Turkey	Golden Chick	330

Table C – Franchises by Industry/Business Specialty   531

Industry	Business Specialty	Franchise Name	Page
Quick-service Industry	Meals: Chicken, Turkey	Hartz Chicken	330
Quick-service Industry	Meals: Chicken, Turkey	KFC	330
Quick-service Industry	Meals: Chicken, Turkey	Popeyes Chicken & Biscuits	330
Quick-service Industry	Meals: Chicken, Turkey	Wing Machine	330
Quick-service Industry	Meals: Chicken, Turkey	Yaya's Flame Broiled Chicken	330
Quick-service Industry	Meals: Hamburgers	Back Yard Burgers	332
Quick-service Industry	Meals: Hamburgers	Bullets Corporation of America, Inc.	332
Quick-service Industry	Meals: Hamburgers	Burger King (Canada)	332
Quick-service Industry	Meals: Hamburgers	Cheeburger Cheeburger	332
Quick-service Industry	Meals: Hamburgers	Farmer Boys Hamburgers	332
Quick-service Industry	Meals: Hamburgers	FatBurger	332
Quick-service Industry	Meals: Hamburgers	Flamers Charbroiled Hamburgers & Chicken	332
Quick-service Industry	Meals: Hamburgers	Hardee's Food Systems	332
Quick-service Industry	Meals: Hamburgers	The Krystal Company	334
Quick-service Industry	Meals: Hamburgers	McDonald's	334
Quick-service Industry	Meals: Hamburgers	McDonald's Restaurants of Canada Limited	334
Quick-service Industry	Meals: Hamburgers	Sonic Drive-In	334
Quick-service Industry	Meals: Hamburgers	Wendy's Restaurants of Canada Inc.	334
Quick-service Industry	Meals: Hot Dogs	AJ Texas Hots	336
Quick-service Industry	Meals: Hot Dogs	Boardwalk Fries	336
Quick-service Industry	Meals: Hot Dogs	Boz Hot Dogs	336
Quick-service Industry	Meals: Hot Dogs	Potts Doggie Shop	336
Quick-service Industry	Meals: Hot Dogs	Wienerschnitzel	336
Quick-service Industry	Meals: Italian	Antonello's	338
Quick-service Industry	Meals: Italian	EB's Express	338
Quick-service Industry	Meals: Italian	Figaro's Italian Kitchen	338
Quick-service Industry	Meals: Italian	Mamma Ilardo's	338
Quick-service Industry	Meals: Italian	Sbarro, The Italian Eatery	338
Quick-service Industry	Meals: Mexican	Cap'n Taco	340
Quick-service Industry	Meals: Mexican	Del Taco	340
Quick-service Industry	Meals: Mexican	Diamond Dave's Taco Company	340
Quick-service Industry	Meals: Mexican	El Pollo Loco	340
Quick-service Industry	Meals: Mexican	La Salsa Fresh Mexican Grill	340
Quick-service Industry	Meals: Mexican	Nach-O Fast	340
Quick-service Industry	Meals: Mexican	Nacho Nana's Worldwide Inc	340
Quick-service Industry	Meals: Mexican	New York Burrito-Gourmet Wraps	340
Quick-service Industry	Meals: Mexican	Panchero's Mexican Grill	342
Quick-service Industry	Meals: Mexican	Taco Bell Corp	342
Quick-service Industry	Meals: Mexican	Taco John's Int'l Inc	342
Quick-service Industry	Meals: Mexican	The Taco Maker	342
Quick-service Industry	Meals: Mexican	Taco Mayo	342
Quick-service Industry	Meals: Mexican	Taco Villa	342

Industry	Business Specialty	Franchise Name	Page
Quick-service Industry	Meals: Mexican	Tacotime	342
Quick-service Industry	Meals: Mexican	Tippy's Taco House	342
Quick-service Industry	Meals: Mexican	Z-Teca	344
Quick-service Industry	Meals: Oriental	Ho-Lee-Chow	346
Quick-service Industry	Meals: Oriental	Made In Japan, Teriyaki Experience	346
Quick-service Industry	Meals: Oriental	Magic Wok	346
Quick-service Industry	Meals: Oriental	Manchu Wok (U.S.)	346
Quick-service Industry	Meals: Sandwiches, Soups, Salad	Brown Baggers	348
Quick-service Industry	Meals: Sandwiches, Soups, Salad	Edelweiss Deli Express/Sub Express	348
Quick-service Industry	Meals: Sandwiches, Soups, Salad	Frullati Cafe	348
Quick-service Industry	Meals: Sandwiches, Soups, Salad	Hogi Yogi Sandwiches & Frozen Yogurt	348
Quick-service Industry	Meals: Sandwiches, Soups, Salad	Jersey Mike's Franchise Systems, Inc.	348
Quick-service Industry	Meals: Sandwiches, Soups, Salad	Jimmy John's Gourmet Sandwich Shops	348
Quick-service Industry	Meals: Sandwiches, Soups, Salad	Moe's Italian Sandwiches	348
Quick-service Industry	Meals: Sandwiches, Soups, Salad	The Sandwich Board	348
Quick-service Industry	Meals: Sandwiches, Soups, Salad	Sandwich Tree Restaurants	350
Quick-service Industry	Meals: Sandwiches, Soups, Salad	Schlotzsky's Deli	350
Quick-service Industry	Meals: Sandwiches, Soups, Salad	Select Sandwich	350
Quick-service Industry	Meals: Seafood	Arthur Treacher's Fish & Chips	352
Quick-service Industry	Meals: Seafood	Captain D's Seafood	352
Quick-service Industry	Meals: Seafood	Chowderhead's Seafood Restaurants	352
Quick-service Industry	Meals: Seafood	Long John Silver's	352
Quick-service Industry	Meals: Steak, BBQ	Arby's	354
Quick-service Industry	Meals: Steak, BBQ	Buddy's Bar-B-Q	354
Quick-service Industry	Meals: Steak, BBQ	The Steak Escape	354
Quick-service Industry	Meals: Steak, BBQ	Steak 'N Shake	354
Quick-service Industry	Meals: Steak, BBQ	Steaks To Go	354
Quick-service Industry	Meals: Submarine Sandwiches	Admiral Subs	356
Quick-service Industry	Meals: Submarine Sandwiches	Baldinos Giant Jersey Subs	356
Quick-service Industry	Meals: Submarine Sandwiches	Blimpie Subs And Salads	356
Quick-service Industry	Meals: Submarine Sandwiches	Cousins Subs	356
Quick-service Industry	Meals: Submarine Sandwiches	Erbert & Gerbert's Subs & Clubs	356
Quick-service Industry	Meals: Submarine Sandwiches	Great Outdoor Sub Shops	356
Quick-service Industry	Meals: Submarine Sandwiches	Jerry's Subs & Pizza	356
Quick-service Industry	Meals: Submarine Sandwiches	Larry's Giant Subs	356
Quick-service Industry	Meals: Submarine Sandwiches	Mr. GoodCents Subs & Pasta	358
Quick-service Industry	Meals: Submarine Sandwiches	Mr. Hero	358
Quick-service Industry	Meals: Submarine Sandwiches	Penn Stations East Coast Subs	358
Quick-service Industry	Meals: Submarine Sandwiches	Port of Subs	358
Quick-service Industry	Meals: Submarine Sandwiches	Quizno's Classic Subs	358
Quick-service Industry	Meals: Submarine Sandwiches	Sobik's Subs	358
Quick-service Industry	Meals: Submarine Sandwiches	Sub Station Ii	358

Table C – Franchises by Industry/Business Specialty 533

Industry	Business Specialty	Franchise Name	Page
Quick-service Industry	Meals: Submarine Sandwiches	Submarina	358
Quick-service Industry	Meals: Submarine Sandwiches	Subs Plus	360
Quick-service Industry	Meals: Submarine Sandwiches	Subway	360
Quick-service Industry	Meals: Submarine Sandwiches	Thundercloud Subs	360
Quick-service Industry	Meals: Submarine Sandwiches	Tubby's Submarines	360
Quick-service Industry	Meals: Submarine Sandwiches	Zero's Subs	360
Quick-service Industry	Pizza: Dine-in or Delivery	Ameci Pizza & Pasta	362
Quick-service Industry	Pizza: Dine-in or Delivery	Boston Pizza	362
Quick-service Industry	Pizza: Dine-in or Delivery	Buck's Pizza Franchising, Inc.	362
Quick-service Industry	Pizza: Dine-in or Delivery	Captain Tony's Pizza & Pasta Emporium	362
Quick-service Industry	Pizza: Dine-in or Delivery	Chicago's Pizza	362
Quick-service Industry	Pizza: Dine-in or Delivery	Cici's Pizza	362
Quick-service Industry	Pizza: Dine-in or Delivery	Domino's Pizza Inc	362
Quick-service Industry	Pizza: Dine-in or Delivery	Donatos Pizza	362
Quick-service Industry	Pizza: Dine-in or Delivery	East of Chicago Pizza Company	364
Quick-service Industry	Pizza: Dine-in or Delivery	Family Pizza	364
Quick-service Industry	Pizza: Dine-in or Delivery	Faro's Franchise Systems	364
Quick-service Industry	Pizza: Dine-in or Delivery	Four Star Pizza	364
Quick-service Industry	Pizza: Dine-in or Delivery	Fox's Pizza Den	364
Quick-service Industry	Pizza: Dine-in or Delivery	Godfather's Pizza	364
Quick-service Industry	Pizza: Dine-in or Delivery	Greco Pizza Donair	364
Quick-service Industry	Pizza: Dine-in or Delivery	Happy Joe's Pizza & Ice Cream Parlor	364
Quick-service Industry	Pizza: Dine-in or Delivery	Hungry Howie's Pizza & Subs	366
Quick-service Industry	Pizza: Dine-in or Delivery	Johnny's New York Style Pizza	366
Quick-service Industry	Pizza: Dine-in or Delivery	La Pizza Loca	366
Quick-service Industry	Pizza: Dine-in or Delivery	Marco's Pizza	366
Quick-service Industry	Pizza: Dine-in or Delivery	Mazzio's Pizza	366
Quick-service Industry	Pizza: Dine-in or Delivery	Mountain Mike's Pizza	366
Quick-service Industry	Pizza: Dine-in or Delivery	Mr. Jim's Pizza	366
Quick-service Industry	Pizza: Dine-in or Delivery	Nancy's Pizzeria	366
Quick-service Industry	Pizza: Dine-in or Delivery	Pizza Delight	368
Quick-service Industry	Pizza: Dine-in or Delivery	Pizza Factory Inc.	368
Quick-service Industry	Pizza: Dine-in or Delivery	Pizza Inn Inc	368
Quick-service Industry	Pizza: Dine-in or Delivery	Pizza Man – He Delivers	368
Quick-service Industry	Pizza: Dine-in or Delivery	Pizza Nova	368
Quick-service Industry	Pizza: Dine-in or Delivery	Pizza Pit	368
Quick-service Industry	Pizza: Dine-in or Delivery	Pizza Pizza Limited	368
Quick-service Industry	Pizza: Dine-in or Delivery	The Pizza Ranch	368
Quick-service Industry	Pizza: Dine-in or Delivery	Pizzas By Marchelloni	370
Quick-service Industry	Pizza: Dine-in or Delivery	Pizzeria Uno Chicago Bar & Grill	370
Quick-service Industry	Pizza: Dine-in or Delivery	Ronzio Pizza	370
Quick-service Industry	Pizza: Dine-in or Delivery	Round Table Franchise Corp	370

Industry	Business Specialty	Franchise Name	Page
Quick-service Industry	Pizza: Dine-in or Delivery	Snappy Tomato Pizza	370
Quick-service Industry	Pizza: Dine-in or Delivery	Straw Hat Pizza	370
Quick-service Industry	Pizza: Dine-in or Delivery	Stuft Pizza & Brewing	370
Quick-service Industry	Pizza: Dine-in or Delivery	Tony Maroni's Famous Gourmet Pizza	370
Quick-service Industry	Pizza: Dine-in or Delivery	Villa Pizza	372
Quick-service Industry	Pizza: Take and Bake	Mom's Bake At Home Pizza	374
Quick-service Industry	Pizza: Take and Bake	Papa Murphy's	374
Quick-service Industry	Other Quick-service	1 Potato 2	376
Quick-service Industry	Other Quick-service	A. L. Van Houtte	376
Quick-service Industry	Other Quick-service	Buscemi's International	376
Quick-service Industry	Other Quick-service	Caterina's	376
Quick-service Industry	Other Quick-service	Checkers Drive-In Restaurants	376
Quick-service Industry	Other Quick-service	Cultures Restaurants	376
Quick-service Industry	Other Quick-service	Culvers Franchising System	376
Quick-service Industry	Other Quick-service	Fast Eddie's	376
Quick-service Industry	Other Quick-service	Great Wraps	378
Quick-service Industry	Other Quick-service	Hard Times Cafe	378
Quick-service Industry	Other Quick-service	Lindy – Gertie's	378
Quick-service Industry	Other Quick-service	Little King	378
Quick-service Industry	Other Quick-service	My Friend's Place	378
Quick-service Industry	Other Quick-service	New York Fries	378
Quick-service Industry	Other Quick-service	Old Fashioned Egg Cream Co Inc	378
Quick-service Industry	Other Quick-service	Pasta To Go	378
Quick-service Industry	Other Quick-service	Pastel's Cafe	380
Quick-service Industry	Other Quick-service	Petro's Chili & Chips	380
Quick-service Industry	Other Quick-service	Renzios	380
Quick-service Industry	Other Quick-service	Roli Boli	380
Real Estate Industry	Property Inspection	Ambic Building Inspection Consult	382
Real Estate Industry	Property Inspection	Amerispec Home Inspection Service	382
Real Estate Industry	Property Inspection	The BrickKicker	382
Real Estate Industry	Property Inspection	Building Systems Analysis Inc.	382
Real Estate Industry	Property Inspection	Criterium Engineers	382
Real Estate Industry	Property Inspection	Critter Control	382
Real Estate Industry	Property Inspection	EnviroFree Inspections	382
Real Estate Industry	Property Inspection	The Hometeam Inspection Service	382
Real Estate Industry	Property Inspection	HouseMaster, The Home Inspection Professionals	384
Real Estate Industry	Property Inspection	National Property Inspections, Inc.	384
Real Estate Industry	Property Inspection	PestMaster Services	384
Real Estate Industry	Property Inspection	Pillar To Post	384
Real Estate Industry	Property Inspection	Pro-Tect	384
Real Estate Industry	Property Inspection	Professional House Doctors, Inc.	384
Real Estate Industry	Property Inspection	Terminix Termite & Pest Control	384

Table C – Franchises by Industry/Business Specialty   535

Industry	Business Specialty	Franchise Name	Page
Real Estate Industry	Property Inspection	World Inspection Network	384
Real Estate Industry	Other Real Estate	America's Choice Int'l Inc.	386
Real Estate Industry	Other Real Estate	Apartment Selector	386
Real Estate Industry	Other Real Estate	Assist-2-Sell	386
Real Estate Industry	Other Real Estate	Better Homes & Gardens Real Estate Service	386
Real Estate Industry	Other Real Estate	Better Homes Realty	386
Real Estate Industry	Other Real Estate	The Buyer's Agent	386
Real Estate Industry	Other Real Estate	Buyer's Resource	386
Real Estate Industry	Other Real Estate	By Owner Reality Network	386
Real Estate Industry	Other Real Estate	Castles Unlimited	388
Real Estate Industry	Other Real Estate	Century 21 Real Estate	388
Real Estate Industry	Other Real Estate	Coldwell Banker Affiliates (Canada)	388
Real Estate Industry	Other Real Estate	Coldwell Banker Residential Affiliates	388
Real Estate Industry	Other Real Estate	Elliott & Company Appraisers	388
Real Estate Industry	Other Real Estate	Era Franchise Systems	388
Real Estate Industry	Other Real Estate	Group Trans-Action Brokerage Services	388
Real Estate Industry	Other Real Estate	Help-U-Sell	388
Real Estate Industry	Other Real Estate	Her Real Estate	390
Real Estate Industry	Other Real Estate	Homcowners Concept	390
Real Estate Industry	Other Real Estate	National Tenant Network	390
Real Estate Industry	Other Real Estate	Re/Max International	390
Real Estate Industry	Other Real Estate	Room-Mate Referral Service Centers	390
Real Estate Industry	Other Real Estate	Sale By Owner Systems	390
Real Estate Industry	Other Real Estate	Showhomes of America	390
Restaurant Industry	Barbecue	Bennett's Bar-B-Que Inc	392
Restaurant Industry	Barbecue	Bobby Rubino's Place for Ribs	392
Restaurant Industry	Barbecue	Colter's Bar-B-Q	392
Restaurant Industry	Barbecue	Dickey's Barbecue Pit Restaurants	392
Restaurant Industry	Barbecue	St. Hubert Bar-B-Q	392
Restaurant Industry	Burgers	Chelsea Street Pub & Grill	394
Restaurant Industry	Burgers	The Ground Round	394
Restaurant Industry	Burgers	The Ground Round Restaurant	394
Restaurant Industry	Diner Style	Huddle House	396
Restaurant Industry	Diner Style	The Soda Fountain	396
Restaurant Industry	Family Style	Banners Restaurants	398
Restaurant Industry	Family Style	Bennigan's	398
Restaurant Industry	Family Style	Big Boy Restaurant & Bakery	398
Restaurant Industry	Family Style	Bonanza	398
Restaurant Industry	Family Style	Bridgeman's Restaurants Inc	398
Restaurant Industry	Family Style	Buffalo Wings & Rings	398
Restaurant Industry	Family Style	Buffalo's Cafe	398
Restaurant Industry	Family Style	Damon's International	398

Industry	Business Specialty	Franchise Name	Page
Restaurant Industry	Family Style	Denny's Inc	400
Restaurant Industry	Family Style	Friendly's Ice Cream Corporation	400
Restaurant Industry	Family Style	The Griddle Family Restaurants	400
Restaurant Industry	Family Style	Harvey's Restaurants	400
Restaurant Industry	Family Style	Humpty's Family Restaurant	400
Restaurant Industry	Family Style	Jungle Jim's Restaurants	400
Restaurant Industry	Family Style	Kelsey's Restaurants	400
Restaurant Industry	Family Style	Mikes Restaurants	400
Restaurant Industry	Family Style	Palace Entertainment & Bullwinkles Restaurant	402
Restaurant Industry	Family Style	Perkins Family Restaurants	402
Restaurant Industry	Family Style	Smitty's	402
Restaurant Industry	Family Style	St. Jerome Restaurant	402
Restaurant Industry	Family Style	Village Inn Restaurants	402
Restaurant Industry	Italian	Doubledave's Pizzaworks Restaurant	404
Restaurant Industry	Italian	East Side Mario's	404
Restaurant Industry	Italian	Strings Italian Cafe	404
Restaurant Industry	Mexican	Pepe's Mexican Restaurant	406
Restaurant Industry	Mexican	Taco Hut America Inc	406
Restaurant Industry	Mexican	Zuzu Mexican Food	406
Restaurant Industry	Oriental	Benihana of Tokyo	408
Restaurant Industry	Oriental	EDO Japan	408
Restaurant Industry	Specialty Style	Copeland's of New Orleans	410
Restaurant Industry	Specialty Style	Famous Sam's Inc	410
Restaurant Industry	Specialty Style	Swiss Chalet/Swiss Chalet Plus Restaurants	410
Restaurant Industry	Steak Houses	Charley's Steakery	412
Restaurant Industry	Steak Houses	Elmer's Pancake & Steak House	412
Restaurant Industry	Steak Houses	Golden Corral Family Steakhouse	412
Restaurant Industry	Steak Houses	Golden Corral Franchising Systems Inc	412
Restaurant Industry	Steak Houses	K-Bob's Steakhouses	412
Restaurant Industry	Steak Houses	Longbranch Steakhouse & Saloon Inc	412
Restaurant Industry	Steak Houses	Ponderosa Steakhouse	412
Restaurant Industry	Steak Houses	Sirloin Stockade Family Steakhouse	412
Restaurant Industry	Steak Houses	Tumbleweed LLC	414
Restaurant Industry	Steak Houses	Western Sizzlin'	414
Restaurant Industry	Steak Houses	Western Steer Family Steakhouse/WSMP	414
Restaurant Industry	Other Restaurant	Applebee's International	416
Restaurant Industry	Other Restaurant	Cafe La France	416
Restaurant Industry	Other Restaurant	Dog N' Suds Drive-In Restaurants	416
Restaurant Industry	Other Restaurant	Fuddruckers	416
Restaurant Industry	Other Restaurant	Gigglebees	416
Restaurant Industry	Other Restaurant	Houlihan's Restaurant Group	416
Restaurant Industry	Other Restaurant	Hubb's Pub	416

Table C – Franchises by Industry/Business Specialty   537

Industry	Business Specialty	Franchise Name	Page
Restaurant Industry	Other Restaurant	Hudson's Grill of America	416
Restaurant Industry	Other Restaurant	Joey's Only Seafood Restaurant	418
Restaurant Industry	Other Restaurant	Le Peep	418
Restaurant Industry	Other Restaurant	Mickey Finn's Sports Cafe	418
Restaurant Industry	Other Restaurant	Red Hot & Blue	418
Restaurant Industry	Other Restaurant	Shooters International Inc	418
Restaurant Industry	Other Restaurant	Sunshine Cafe	418
Restaurant Industry	Other Restaurant	TGI Friday's Hospitality Worldwide	418
Restaurant Industry	Other Restaurant	Ward's Restaurants	418
Retail Industry	Art, Prints, Framing	Appletree Art Publishers	420
Retail Industry	Art, Prints, Framing	Color Me Mine	420
Retail Industry	Art, Prints, Framing	Deck The Walls	420
Retail Industry	Art, Prints, Framing	FastFrame U S A	420
Retail Industry	Art, Prints, Framing	Framing & Art Centres	420
Retail Industry	Art, Prints, Framing	The Great Frame Up	420
Retail Industry	Art, Prints, Framing	Malibu Gallery	420
Retail Industry	Books, Audiobooks	The Book Rack	422
Retail Industry	Books, Audiobooks	Lemstone Books	422
Retail Industry	Books, Audiobooks	Little Professor Book Centers	422
Retail Industry	Books, Audiobooks	Talking Book World	422
Retail Industry	Computer Sales and Service	Computer Doctor	424
Retail Industry	Computer Sales and Service	Computer Renaissance	424
Retail Industry	Computer Sales and Service	Cyber Exchange Software And Computers	424
Retail Industry	Computer Sales and Service	Full Circle Image	424
Retail Industry	Computer Sales and Service	Worldwide Information Services	424
Retail Industry	Discount Stores	A Buck Or Two Stores	426
Retail Industry	Discount Stores	Dollar Discount Stores	426
Retail Industry	Discount Stores	Just-A-Buck	426
Retail Industry	Discount Stores	Pinch-A-Penny	426
Retail Industry	Electronics	Aaron's Rental Purchase	428
Retail Industry	Electronics	The Car Phone Store	428
Retail Industry	Electronics	Colortyme	428
Retail Industry	Electronics	Grand Rental Station/Taylor Rental	428
Retail Industry	Electronics	Radio Shack International	428
Retail Industry	Electronics	RadioShack	428
Retail Industry	Electronics	Totally Wireless	428
Retail Industry	Electronics	Video Data Services	428
Retail Industry	Electronics	Video Impact	430
Retail Industry	Flowers	Conroys 1-800-Flowers	432
Retail Industry	Flowers	Foliage Design Systems	432
Retail Industry	Flowers	Grower Direct Fresh Cut Flowers	432
Retail Industry	Games, Hobby	Boomerang GameWare	434

Table C – Franchises by Industry/Business Specialty   539

Industry	Business Specialty	Franchise Name	Page
Retail Industry	Other Retail	Papyrus	450
Retail Industry	Other Retail	Shefield & Sons	450
Retail Industry	Other Retail	Successories	450
Retail Industry	Other Retail	Wicks 'N' Sticks	450
Retail Industry	Other Retail	Yard Cards	450
Security Systems Industry	Security Systems	AirSoPure	452
Security Systems Industry	Security Systems	Custom Homewatch International	452
Security Systems Industry	Security Systems	Dynamark Security Centers	452
Security Systems Industry	Security Systems	Fire Defense Centers	452
Security Systems Industry	Security Systems	Paystation	452
Security Systems Industry	Security Systems	ProShred Security	452
Security Systems Industry	Security Systems	Roll-A-Way	452
Security Systems Industry	Security Systems	Safe Not Sorry	452
Security Systems Industry	Security Systems	Shred-It	454
Security Systems Industry	Security Systems	Sonitrol	454
Security Systems Industry	Security Systems	V.I.D.E.O. Security Process (VSP)	454
Sports and Recreation Industry	Apparel, Equipment	A. J. Barnes Bicycle Emporium	456
Sports and Recreation Industry	Apparel, Equipment	The Athlete's Foot	456
Sports and Recreation Industry	Apparel, Equipment	Bike Line	456
Sports and Recreation Industry	Apparel, Equipment	Play It Again Sports	456
Sports and Recreation Industry	Apparel, Equipment	Soccer Post Intl Franchise Corp	456
Sports and Recreation Industry	Apparel, Equipment	The Sport Shoe	456
Sports and Recreation Industry	Apparel, Equipment	Sports Traders	456
Sports and Recreation Industry	Golf Specialty	Dynamic Golf Centres	458
Sports and Recreation Industry	Golf Specialty	Empowered Womens Golf Shops	458
Sports and Recreation Industry	Golf Specialty	Golf Augusta Pro Shops	458
Sports and Recreation Industry	Golf Specialty	Golf USA	458
Sports and Recreation Industry	Golf Specialty	International Golf	458
Sports and Recreation Industry	Golf Specialty	Las Vegas Golf & Tennis	458
Sports and Recreation Industry	Golf Specialty	MacBirdie Golf Gifts	458
Sports and Recreation Industry	Golf Specialty	Nevada Bob's Professional Golf Shops	458
Sports and Recreation Industry	Golf Specialty	Pro Golf Discount	460
Sports and Recreation Industry	Golf Specialty	Strokes	460
Sports and Recreation Industry	Golf Specialty	Team Golf Corp	460
Sports and Recreation Industry	Golf Specialty	Woody's Wood Shops	460
Sports and Recreation Industry	Memorabilia, Collectibles	Fan-A-Mania	462
Sports and Recreation Industry	Memorabilia, Collectibles	Field of Dreams	462
Sports and Recreation Industry	Memorabilia, Collectibles	Pro Image	462
Sports and Recreation Industry	Memorabilia, Collectibles	Sports Fantastic	462
Sports and Recreation Industry	Tanning	Everlasting Tan Club	464
Sports and Recreation Industry	Tanning	Fabutan Sun Tan Studios	464
Sports and Recreation Industry	Tanning	Sunbanque Island Tanning	464

Franchises by Products and Services

If man has good corn, or wood, or boards, or pigs to sell, or can make better chairs or knives, crucibles, or church organs, than anybody else, you will find a broad, hard-beaten road to his house, tho' it be in the woods.

— RALPH WALDO EMERSON

Appendix D is sorted by the franchise's brief description of their products or services. Those listed first gave no description.

Franchise Name	Page	Franchise Name	Page
1 Potato 2	376	Admiral of The Fleet Cruise Centers	470
2001 Flavors Plus Potatoes	312	Admiral Subs	356
A Buck Or Two Stores	426	Adventures In Advertising	108
A. J. Barnes Bicycle Emporium	456	AeroWest & WestAir Sanitation Services	150
A. L. Van Houtte	376	Affordable Car Rental	66
A Shade Better	264	Air Brook Limousine	210
AAMCO Transmissions	82	AirSoPure	452
Aaron's Rental Purchase	428	All American Frozen Yogurt/Ice Cream	318
Abra Auto Body & Glass	70	Almost Heaven, Ltd.	438
Academy for Mathematics & Science	214	Aloette Cosmetics	100
Academy of Learning	134	Alphagraphics Printshops Of The Future	284
Accounting Business Systems	106	Ameci Pizza & Pasta	362
Ace America's Cash Express	192	American Brake Service	74
Active Green + Ross Tire & Automotive Centre	92	American Concrete Raising	188

Franchise Name	Page	Franchise Name	Page
Guardsman WoodPro	184	I Can't Believe It's Yogurt	318
Gwynne Learning Academy	214	Imagine That Discovery Museums	134
Gymn' Around Kids	138	InnSuites Hotels	270
Hairlines	102	Insulated Dry Roof Systems	190
Hammett's Learning World	214	Interface Financial Group	114
Handle With Care Packaging Store	202	Interim Healthcare	248
Handyman Connection	190	International Golf	458
Happy & Healthy Products	320	International Mergers & Acquisitions	112
Happy Joe's Pizza & Ice Cream Parlor	364	International News	290
Hard Times Cafe	378	Interstate Dairy Queen	316
Hartz Chicken	330	Jani-King International	154
Harvey Washbangers	196	Jantize America	154
Harvey's Restaurants	400	Jay Roberts & Associates	128
Hauntrepreneurs, Ltd.	466	JDI Cleaning Systems	154
Head Over Heels	138	Jenny Craig Weight Loss Centres	242
Health Mart	236	Jerry's Subs & Pizza	356
Heavenly Ham	230	Jet-Black Sealcoating & Repair	178
Help-U-Sell	388	Jimmy John's Gourmet Sandwich Shops	348
Her Real Estate	390	Joe Loue Tout Rent All	66
High Touch-High Tech	142	Joey's Only Seafood Restaurant	418
High Wheeler Ice Cream Parlour/Rest.	314	John Casablancas Modeling/Career Center	116
Hilton Inns	268	John Simmons	448
Ho-Lee-Chow	346	Johnny's New York Style Pizza	366
Hobbytown USA	434	Juice World	230
Holiday Hospitality	270	Just Legs	52
Hollywood Weight Loss Centre	242	Just-A-Buck	426
Home Cleaning Centers	166	K-Bob's Steakhouses	412
Home Instead Senior Care	248	Kampgrounds of America/KOA	266
Homeowners Concept	390	Kelsey's Restaurants	400
The Honors Learning Center	216	KFC	330
Hoop Mountain	466	Kiddie Kobbler	142
Houlihan's Restaurant Group	416	Kids Team	142
House Doctors Handyman Service	176	Kirby Tours	472
HouseMaster, The Home Inspection Professionals	384	Kitchen Wizards	182
Hq Business Centers	126	Krispy Kreme Doughnuts	300
Hubb's Pub	416	Kwik Dry International	154
Hudson's Grill of America	416	Kwik-Kopy Printing (Canada)	284
Humpty's Family Restaurant	400	L. A. Smoothie Healthmart & Cafe	226
Hungry Howie's Pizza & Subs	366	La Pizza Loca	366
Huntington Learning Center	216	La Salsa Fresh Mexican Grill	340
Hydro Physics Pipe Inspection	154	Labor Force	246
I.B. Nuts & Fruit Too	228	Langenwalter Carpet Dyeing	146

Franchise Name	Page	Franchise Name	Page
Nu-Look 1-Hr. Cleaners	198	Pizza Nova	368
NurseFinders	248	Pizza Pit	368
Nutrite	164	Pizzas By Marchelloni	370
Nutter's Bulk And Natural Foods	226	Planet Earth Recycling	96
O.P.E.N. Cleaning Systems	156	Play It Again Sports	456
Oil Butler International	60	Ponderosa Steakhouse	412
Once Upon A Child	144	Pony Mailbox & Business Centers	204
One Hour Martinizing	198	Popeyes Chicken & Biscuits	330
One Stop Undercar	78	Port of Subs	358
Open Pantry Food Marts	230	Postal Annex+	204
Option Care	238	Postnet Postal & Business Centers	204
Our Weigh	242	The Potato Sack	230
P.A.M.'S Coffee & Tea Co.	222	Potts Doggie Shop	336
P.J.'S Coffee & Tea	222	Practical Rent A Car	66
Paceco Financial Services	114	Precision Tune Auto Care	84
Pack Mart	202	Pressed 4 Time	198
Pak Mail Centers (Canada)	204	Pretzel Time	306
Panchero's Mexican Grill	342	PretzelMaker	306
Panda Shoes	52	Pro Golf Discount	460
Papa Murphy's	374	Pro-Tect	384
Papyrus	450	Professional Carpet Systems	148
Paradise Bakery & Cafe	310	Professional Polish	158
Parcel Plus	204	Profit-On-Hold	110
Pasta To Go	378	Proforma	286
Pastel's Cafe	380	Profusion Systems	170
Paystation	452	Property Damage Appraisers	178
Pearle Vision Center	240	Pure Water Ultima	446
Pee Wee Workout	138	Purified Water To Go	446
Pepe's Mexican Restaurant	406	PuroFirst International	158
Permacrete Systems	190	Putt-Putt Golf Courses Of America	468
PestMaster Services	384	Q Lube	62
Pet Habitat	276	Quizno's Classic Subs	358
The Pet Pantry International	276	RACS International	158
Pet Valu	276	Radio Shack International	428
Petland	276	Ramada Franchise Canada, Inc.	272
Pets Are Inn	276	Re-Bath	172
Peyron Tax Service	200	Re/Max International	390
Pillar To Post	384	Red Hot & Blue	418
Pinch-A-Penny	426	Reface It Kitchen Systems	182
Pizza Delight	368	Remedy Intelligent Staffing	250
Pizza Factory Inc.	368	Renaissance Executive Forums	118
Pizza Man – He Delivers	368	Rennsport	96

Franchise Name	Page	Franchise Name	Page
Talent Tree Staffing Services	250	USA Baby	144
TCBY Treats	318	V.I.D.E.O. Security Process (VSP)	454
TechnoKids	136	Val-Pak Direct Marketing	110
TechStaff	250	Value Line Maintenance Systems	160
Terminix Termite & Pest Control	384	Valvoline Instant Oil Change	62
Terra Systems	164	Victory Lane Quick Oil Change	62
Terri's Consign & Design Furnishings	258	Video Data Services	428
TFM/Top Forty	440	Video Impact	430
TGI Friday's Hospitality Worldwide	418	Vinylgraphics Custom Sign Centres	122
Thrifty Car Rental (Canada)	68	VR Business Brokers	112
Thundercloud Subs	360	Wallpapers To Go	264
Tilden for Brakes Car Care Centers	74	Ward's Restaurants	418
Tim Hortons	310	We Care Home Health Services	248
Tippy's Taco House	342	Wedding Gown Specialists/Restoration	198
Today's Temporary	252	Wee Watch Private Home Day Care	132
Tony Maroni's Famous Gourmet Pizza	370	Weed Man	164
Total Medical Compliance	238	Wendy's Restaurants of Canada Inc.	334
Totally Wireless	428	Western Medical Services	248
Tower Cleaning Systems	160	Western Sizzlin'	414
TPI Travel Services	472	Western Steer Family Steakhouse/WSMP	414
Tradebank International	130	White Hen Pantry	232
Transmission USA	82	Wicks 'N' Sticks	450
Travel Professionals International	472	Wienerschnitzel	336
TRC Staffing Services	252	Wild Bird Marketplace	278
Treats	310	Wild Birds Unlimited	278
Tri-Color Carpet Dyeing And Cleaning	148	Window Perfect	262
Triple Check Income Tax Service	200	Wing Machine	330
Tropik Sun Fruit & Nut	228	Woody's Wood Shops	460
Truck Options	58	World Inspection Network	384
Truly Nolen	178	World Trade Network	130
Tubby's Submarines	360	Worldwide Information Services	424
Tuffy Auto Service Centers	88	Yard Cards	450
Tutor Time Child Care Learning Center	132	Yaya's Flame Broiled Chicken	330
U.S. Franchise Systems	272	Yellow Jacket Direct Mail Advertising	110
UncleSam's Convenient Store	224	Yipes Stripes	98
Uniglobe Travel	472	Yogen Fruz Worldwide	318
Unishippers Association	204	Your Office USA	130
United Check Cashing	192	Ziebart Tidycar	94
United Energy Partners	190	Zuzu Mexican Food	406
United Printing Unlimited	288		

Brief Description	Franchise Name	Page
24 varieties of fresh baked bagels, 21 flavours of cream cheese	The Great Canadian Bagel	292
24hr diner-style restaurant- always open, always fresh	Huddle House	396
24hr retail digital imaging to high speed copying, fast paced	Copy Club	284
5–10 yr. old used car, sub-prime financing	J. D. Byrider Systems	90
7 days, 24 hrs coffee, donut, deli restaurant, pastries, soups	Robin's Donuts	300
Accounting, bookkeeping, taxation & financial planning	AccounTax Services	106
Acrylic asphalt sealing	KCS Applications	170
Adult fast food, hot subs, feature romanburger, Philly-steak etc	Mr. Hero	358
Advertising system	Mobil Ambition USA LC	108
Affordable prices and quality service for the whole family	Lemon Tree – A Unisex Haircutting Est.	104
Airbag deactivation services	Airbag Options	88
All types of computer generated signs, graphics & lettering	Signs By Tomorrow	120
Alzheimer/personal care homes	Sutton Homes Franchising Corp	238
America's #1 cigar-gift franchise	Tinder Box International	436
Art classes/fine art based upon art history	Odyssey Art Centers	136
Assist and act as counsel to non-profit organizations campaigns	Magis Fund Raising Specialists	128
Authentic east coast style subs incl Philly cheesesteak	Penn Stations East Coast Subs	358
Auto, furniture & marine repair & appearance conditioning	Dr. Vinyl & Assoc.	174
Auto lube & tune/brakes/other services	Econo Lube N' Tune	84
Auto painting & body work	Maaco Auto Painting & Bodyworks (Canada)	70
Auto parts	FCI Franchising Inc	64
Auto rentals/auto sales	Payless Car Rental System	66
Auto services center	Certicare	84
Auto/truck accessories,security,auto glass,detailing	Auto One Glass & Accessories	58
Automotive lubrication & filter maint.	Oil Can Henry's International	62
Automotive service – under car specialists	Meineke Discount Mufflers	76
Baby equipment & supplies rental for traveling/visiting parents	Baby's Away	132
Bagel bakery & deli	Manhattan Bagel Co Inc	294
Bagels, sandwiches, soups & salads	Bagelz-The Bagel Bakery	292
Bakery cafe specialize in gourmet cookies & specialty gifts	Cafe By George/Cookies By George	298
Bakery goods & light lunches	Baker's Dozen Donuts	300
Bakery/cafe	Atlanta Bread Co	308
Balloons bears flowers gift baskets cards	Balloons & Bears	436
Barbecue restaurant	Bennett's Bar-B-Que Inc	392
Bath & kitchen refinishing, bathtubs, tile, showers, countertops	Miracle Method	182
Bath & kitchen-remodeling options, refinish & recolor tub/wall	Worldwide Refinishing Systems, Inc.	182
Bathroom & kitchen reglazing	Perma Ceram Enterprises	182
Bathtub, sink, tile, cupboard & countertop resurfacing	BMR Bath Master Reglazing Ltd.	170
Batteries for all types of uses, retail & commercial	Batteries Plus	64
Better bread, better subs, provided by better people	Cousins Subs	356
Bingo & gambling news	Bingo Bugle Newspaper	290
Boat to boat oil changing, bilge steam cleaning & carpet clean	Naut-A-Care Marine Services, Inc.	96

Brief Description	Franchise Name	Page
Body & collision repairs, auto refinishing	Miracle Auto Painting & Body Repair	72
Books, video, software, seminars on how to set up & run business	American Institute of Small Business	214
Brakes, exhaust, ride control, steering systems, a/c, tires, oil	Car-X Muffler & Brake	76
Brakes/exhaust/suspension/oil & lube	Merlin's Muffler & Brake	76
Bridal guides & shows	A Wonderful Wedding	210
Budget price family haircut shops, open 7 days & nights, no appt	Snip N' Clip Haircut Shops	104
Buffalo wings	Bw-3 Franchise Systems Inc	228
Business brokerage	Sunbelt Business Brokers	112
Business brokers, intermediary, M & A for private companies	Proventure Business Group, Inc.	112
Business development, supplier overrides air/tour/car	Empress Travel	472
Business referral network	Universal Business Consultants	130
Business services	Aim Mail Centers	202
Business & tourist information maps	Resort Maps Franchise Inc	110
Butter burgers/frozen custard	Culver Franchising System Inc	320
Buy/sell/trade pre-owned CD's, top 100 CD's, DVD, games & music	CD Warehouse	440
Cabinet & nook restoration, new cabinet doors, custom cabinets	Kitchen Tune-Up	182
Cakes & pies	McCoy's Cake & Pie Shop	310
Car rental franchises	Rent-A-Wreck of America	68
Career consultancy providing resumes, career assessment, etc	The Resume Hut	254
Carpet cleaning service	CarpetMate	146
Carpet dry extraction cleaning, upholstery & drapery cleaning	Joy Carpet Dry Cleaning	146
Carpet, upholstery, ceiling, wall & hard floor cleaning	Roto-Static International	148
Carry out & delivery thin pizza, stuffed pizza, sandwich, salads	Nancy's Pizzeria	366
Casual dining restaurant specialize in chicken wings & curly fry	Buffalo Wings & Rings	398
Casual dining sports entertainment restaurant bbq ribs prime rib	Damon's International	398
Casual western family-style steakhouse	Longbranch Steakhouse & Saloon Inc	412
Catering to children's parties, children's indoor playground	The Peanut Club	144
CD's cassettes videos	TFM	440
Centers repair, rebuild & recondition auto & std transmissions	Speedy Transmission Centers	82
Check cashing and related services	X-Bankers Check Cashing	192
Check cashing services	Fast Bucks Development LLC	192
Cheesesteaks, grilled sandwiches, salads, frys	Great Steak & Potato Company	326
Chemical carpet & upholstery cleaning	Heaven's Best	146
Chicken & biscuits, wide variety of breakfast biscuits/side item	Bojangles' Restaurants Inc	328
Child care centers	Kids R Kids Quality Learning Centers	136
Child protection & security	Safe-T-Child	144
Children's/mom's retail clothing	Totally Kool	52
Chock full o' nuts (NYSE:CHF) drive-thru coffee cafe	Quikava – Coffees By Chock Full O' Nuts	222
Chocolate, fudge, ice cream	Kilwin's Chocolates Franchise	218
Christian book, gift & music stores	Lemstone Books	422
Classroom & private instruction of PC's for mature adults	Computer U Learning Centers	212
Clean-up & reconstruction after fire & flood, janitorial svcs	ServiceMaster Residential/Commercial (Canada)	168

Brief Description	Franchise Name	Page
Direct sales of mens clothing/image consulting	Around Your Neck	52
Direct-mail advertising in print on behalf of local business	Trimark	110
Discount golf retail stores, complete w/ pro-line equip, apparel	Golf USA	458
Discount party supplies	Party City Corp	444
Discount party supplies & greeting cards	Paper Warehouse Franchising Inc	444
Discount real estate company	Assist-2-Sell	386
Dollar store	Dollar Discount Stores	426
Donuts & baked goods	Lamar's Donuts	300
Donuts, pastries, croissants, muffins, bagels, catering	Donut Inn	300
Drive-in featuring hamburgers, Coneys, ice-cream & spec. drinks	Sonic Drive-In	334
Dry cleaning delivery service	Valet Express	198
Dry cleaning & laundry services	Champion Cleaners Franchise Inc.	196
Duct & hvac-system cleaning, indoor air quality testing	DuctBusters/Buster Enterprises Inc	176
Early child care learning centers w/ age appropriate curriculum	Kiddie Academy International	134
Economy motels	Super 8 Motels Inc	272
Educational toy store	Building Blocks Franchise Corp	142
Egg cream drinks & specialty confections	Old Fashioned Egg Cream Co Inc	378
Elaborate & beautiful miniature golf courses/family entertain.	Themed Miniature Golf Courses	468
Electronic filing to IRS/state & refund anticipation loans	Electronic Tax Filers	200
Employee leasing	Checkmate	250
Employment services	AccuStaff Inc	250
English language training courses for academic/professional dev.	ELS Language Centers	214
Entertainment & sports stores	Fan-A-Mania	462
Environmental & building science services	Professional House Doctors, Inc.	384
Environmental services to the food service & hospitality indust.	Biologix	150
Executive search services thru global network w/ specialists	Sanford Rose Associates	244
Existing business & franchise sales, financial brokering	Empire Business Brokers	112
Expert carpet care & restoration services, water/smoke/fire dam.	Rainbow International Carpet Care & Restoration Specialist	148
Extended-stay suite hotels	Hawthorn Suites/Hawthorn Suites Ltd	268
Family haircare centers providing quality haircuts, affordable $	Pro-Cuts	104
Family martial arts centers	Martial Arts America	466
Family steakhouse/buffet & bakery	Golden Corral Franchising Systems Inc	412
Family-style restaurant/soda fountain	Bridgeman's Restaurants Inc	398
Fast food takeout & delivery	Pizza Pizza Limited	368
Fast oil change	Jiffy Lube International Inc	60
Fine collectibles	Ashley Avery's Collectables	436
Finished architectural signs/planning svcs.	ASI Sign Systems Inc	120
Fishing & hunting travel service	Outdoor Connection	466
Flavored popcorn	Kernels	228
Flowers gifts & related products	Conroys 1-800-Flowers	432
Foreclosure prevention services	United Capital Mortgage Assistance	192
Formalwear specialist, rental & sales of men's & boys formalwear	Gingiss Formalwear	54

Brief Description	Franchise Name	Page
Gourmet coffee bar, specialty beverages, traditional smoke-shop	Shefield Gourmet	222
Gourmet sandwiches, subs, salads, soup, philly's, breakfast	Edelweiss Deli Express/Sub Express	348
Greeting card distribution	Elephant House Inc	436
Grounds care svc provider for fortune 500 industrial companies	Clintar Groundskeeping Services	162
Gym & fitness centers	Golds Gym	234
Gym/fitness center, sell memberships, clothing, accessories	World Gym	234
Gymnastics, sports, karate for children 4 mos to 12 yrs	The Little Gym International, Inc.	138
Hair care, beauty supplies & tanning	We Care Hair	104
Hair replacements	H R C Int'l Inc	102
Hamburger, Krystal chik, french fries, etc.	The Krystal Company	334
Hand crafted quality mattresses at a comfortable price	Verlo Mattress Factory Stores	260
Hand rolled soft pretzels & sandwiches on pretzel roll	Pretzels Plus	306
Hand-rolled pizza buffet & delivery	Doubledave's Pizzaworks Restaurant	404
Hand-rolled soft pretzels	Wetzel's Pretzels	306
Hand-twisted soft pretzels & fruit shakes	The Pretzel Twister	306
Hands-on after-school science learning ages 3–10	Little Scientists	136
Health beverages & products	Bunnies Fresh Juice & Smoothie Bar	324
Health services/weight loss counseling	L A Weight Loss Centers Inc	242
heating & cooling parts & supplies for industrial & commercial	Tempaco	438
High quality framing and art gallery	Malibu Gallery	420
Hockey training centers	PuckMasters Hockey Training Centers	466
Home health care & health staffing services	Health Force	248
Home improvement specializing in seamless steel siding	United States Seamless, Inc.	186
Home safety incl consult & install focus on child-proofing	Safe Not Sorry	452
Home/building inspections	Ambic Building Inspection Consult	382
Homebased travel agency	InHouse Travel Group LLC	472
Homemade ice cream, yogurt, sherbet, waffle cones, cakes	Bruster's Old-Fashioned Ice Cream & Yogurt	312
Homemade Italian ices, ice-cream, ice-cream cakes	Morrone's Italian Ices	314
Homemade super-premium ice cream, yogurt, smoothies, coffee, etc	Gelato Amare	314
Hot dogs & hamburgers	AJ Texas Hots	336
Hot & spicy foods, chili-themed clothing & gifts	Chili Chompers	230
Hot wings & southwestern food served in kick-back, old-west fun	Buffalo's Cafe	398
Hotels	Holiday Inn Worldwide	270
Hotels	Howard Johnson Intl Inc	270
Hotels	Knights Franchise Systems Inc	270
Hotels & inns	Days Inns of America Inc	268
Hotels inns suites & resorts	Choice Hotels Intl	268
Hotels/inns/resorts/cruise ships	Radisson Hotels Worldwide	272
Hotels/suites & inns	Ashbury Suites & Inns	268
Ice cream & frozen yogurt	Cold Stone Creamery	312
Ice cream, water ice, yogurt, cakes	Petrucci's Ice Cream Co.	314
Ice cream & yogurt	Baskin-Robbins USA Co	312

Brief Description	Franchise Name	Page
Mobile airbag system repair for the collision industry	Airbag Service	88
Mobile auto paint repair process serve dealership, fleet, indiv.	Aero-Colours	88
Mobile auto paint restoration system	Altracolor Systems	88
Mobile car wash turnkey franchise	The Car Wash Guys/Gals	94
Mobile disc jockey entertainment service	Complete Music	208
Mobile fitness program for children ages 2–12	Gymsters, Inc.	138
Mobile floor & window coverings. Carpet, vinyl, hardwood, etc	Nationwide Floor & Window Coverings	256
Mobile floor-covering and window treatment business	Carpet Network	256
Mobile on-site auto reconditioning svcs, paint/dent/interior rep	Colors On Parade	94
Mobile plastic/vinyl/leather/restor/rpr	Creative Colors Int'l Inc	174
Mobile preschool fitness program/health club for children	Pre-Fit	140
Mobile retail floor covering business, soft & hard flooring	Floor Coverings International	256
Mobile screening service. Window & door screens. New or re-screen	The Screen Machine	178
Mobile service business specialize in interior repair	Cartex Limited	88
Mobile sharpening system	BladeRunner Mobile Sharpening	176
Mobile shredding service, business to business	ProShred Security	452
Mobile windshield repair & replacement	Novus Windshield Repair	86
Modeling courses & related services	Model Managers Int'l	116
Monthly accounting & tax for small business	Padgett Business Services	106
More than 25 varieties of sourdough-based breads and bagels, etc	Saint Louis Bread Company, Inc.	310
Motivational/human development training	The Sleeping Giant Within Inc.	216
Motor vehicle lubrication services	Mister Mobile On-Site Oil Changes	60
Music store buy/sell/trade/consign musical instruments & gear	Music-Go-Round	440
National network reporting of tenant performance data, screening	National Tenant Network	390
Natural organic-based fertilization, weed/insect/disease control	Naturalawn of America	162
Neighborhood bakery specialize in whole-wheat breads	Great Harvest Bread Co.	308
New media, information technology & business computer training	C. B. S. Interactive Multimedia	212
New & used auto rentals	U-Save Auto Rental of America Inc	68
New & used video games	Game Force Franchising	434
New & used video games	Its About Games	434
Newspaper for new homeowners	The Homesteader	290
Non-medical in-home elder care	Home Helpers	206
Nonmedical personal care services to the elderly	Homewatch Caregivers	206
North american franchiser of family oriented campgrounds	Yogi Bear Jellystone Park Camp-Resorts	266
Nostalgic memorabilia	For Olde Times Sake	436
Off course retail pro-shop specialize in golf & tennis equipment	Las Vegas Golf & Tennis	458
Offers delicious fruit smoothies, fresh squeeze juices, sandwich	Power Smoothie	322
Offers full-line, full-service community oriented book stores	Little Professor Book Centers	422
Office space & support services	The Office Alternative	128
Oil change & lubrication services	Lube Depot	60
Old fashion car hop curb service drive-in restaurant	Dog N' Suds Drive-In Restaurants	416
"On hold" advertising service (on hold telephone messages)	Impressions On Hold International	108

Brief Description	Franchise Name	Page
One hour photo finishing & other related imaging services	One Hour Motophoto & Portrait Studio	280
One stop packaging, shipping & business support svcs, internet	Pak Mail Centers of America	204
One-stop printing & copying centers, computer svcs, offset print	LazerQuick	286
Organic & enviro considerate lawn care	Enviro Masters Lawn Care	162
Originator of 100% plus(r) commission program	Castles Unlimited	388
Over 100 breakfst/lunch/dinner items dine-in/take-out/drive-thru	Farmer Boys Hamburgers	332
Owner operated repair shop	Saf-T Auto Centers	80
Owner-assisted real estate marketing	America's Choice Int'l Inc.	386
Paint free dent repair of minor dents, door dings & hail damage	Dent Doctor	70
Painting & home-improvement services	Decorating Den Painting & Home Imp	188
Paintless dent repair service	Dent Zone	70
Paintless dent repair system of auto body repair	DentPro	70
Parent-child participation play program	Gymboree	138
Party supplies & balloons	Party Land Inc	444
Patented, hot carbonating carpet & upholstery cleaning	Chem-Dry Carpet/Drapery/Upholstery	146
Pet shop & grooming service	Haynes Pet Centre Franchising Inc	274
Pet supplies superstore	IncrediPet	276
Pharmacy franchise company	Medicap Pharmacy	236
Philly cheesesteaks, specialty sandwiches & premium ice cream	Philly Connection	326
Photo-finishing & digital imaging svcs, sell cameras, film, etc	One Hour Motophoto & Portrait Studio (Canada)	280
Pictorial community real estate adv magazine	Home Guide Magazine	290
Pictorial rental property magazine	Rental Guide	290
Pizza	Domino's Pizza Inc	362
Pizza	Round Table Franchise Corp	370
Pizza & chicken	The Pizza Ranch	368
Pizza, hoagies, stromboli & cheese stix	Buck's Pizza Franchising, Inc.	362
Pizza, hot subs, cheesebread & salad for carry-out & delivery	Marco's Pizza	366
Pizza, pasta & microbrewery	Stuft Pizza & Brewing	370
Pizza, pasta, salads	Pizza Inn Inc	368
Pizza, salad, dessert, pasta buffets + pizza take-out, family	Cici's Pizza	362
Pizza, salads & sandwiches	Straw Hat Pizza	370
Pizza & subs	Faro's Franchise Systems	364
Pizza, subs & pasta	East of Chicago Pizza Company	364
Pizza, subs & salad delivery	Mr. Jim's Pizza	366
Pizza, subs, salads thru delivery, dine-in, pickup window, cater	Donatos Pizza	362
Pizza/sandwiches/pasta/drinks	Chicago's Pizza	362
Portrait photography studio	Picture Hits	280
Precision mechanics hand tools, service equip & diagnostic comp.	Matco Tools	64
Preschool learning center	The Goddard Schools	134
Private buying service; our members purchase goods at wholesale	United Consumers Club	210
Products for back pain relief/prevention	Relax The Back Franchising Co	238
Products & services for post breast surgery, pre/post natal etc.	Women's Health Boutique	238

Brief Description	Franchise Name	Page
Professional cleaning services for commercial, offices, medical	E.P.I.C. Systems, Inc.	152
Professional dating service	Successful Introduction	194
Professional home inspection services incl pest, radon, septic, etc	The Hometeam Inspection Service	382
Professional janitorial services	Laser Chem "White Glove" Commercial Cleaning	154
Professional new car & truck buying, financing, leasing	Auto Purchase Consulting	90
Professional pharmacies specialize in prescription & health-care	The Medicine Shoppe	238
Professional residential & commercial cleaning & restoration	ServPro	160
Professional & temporary staffing, executive, technical	Dunhill Staffing Systems, Inc.	246
Proof-of-purchase ad plan for broadcast stations	Points for Profits	110
Property inspections	Building Systems Analysis Inc.	382
Provide commercial contract cleaning for buildings & offices	Master Care	156
Provide parents w/ unique, bronzed keepsake of child hand & foot	Patty-Cakes International, Inc.	144
Provides all forms of home medical equipment and supplies	Medichair	238
Provides busy homeowners w/ window cleaning & maintenance	Window Butler	168
Provides law firms and corp legal depts w/temp legal staff	LawCorps Legal Staffing Services	250
Providing highest levels of quality drycleaning & superior svc	Eagle Cleaners	196
QSR solution for G&C and other markets, flame broiled burger/BBQ	Bullets Corporation of America, Inc.	332
Quality educational child-care w/ emphasis on devel. Whole child	Primrose Schools	136
Quality sports name brands at affordable prices, new & used	Sports Traders	456
Quick, casual restaurant serving 1/3lb gourmet burgers & chicken	Back Yard Burgers	332
Quick lube services	Indy Lube	60
Quick serve eat in/take-out specialize in chowder & seafood	Chowderhead's Seafood Restaurants	352
Quick service hamburger restaurants	Hardee's Food Systems	332
Quick service restaurants, multiple concepts	Dairy Queen Canada Inc.	316
Quick service restaurants, multiple concepts	Orange Julius Canada Inc.	322
Quick-service gourmet wraps & fresh fruit smoothies, beer & wine	New York Burrito-Gourmet Wraps	340
Quick-service pizza & Italian restaurant	Villa Pizza	372
Real estate brokerage specialize exclusive buyer representation	The Buyer's Agent	386
Real estate commission factoring	Commission Express	126
Recycled office products – inkjet, laser toner cartridge, ribbon	Full Circle Image	424
Recycling print media cartridges: ribbons, inkjets, lasers	Rynker Ribbon Xchange Inc.	128
Rent audiobooks w/ no due dates & sell audiobooks at discount	Talking Book World	422
Rent-to-own tires & custom wheels	Tire Time Rentals	92
Rental or long-term leasing of wheelchair accessible vans	Wheelchair Getaways	68
Repair crystal, plate-glass, auto-glass	Glass Magnum	176
Repair of brake, steering & exhaust systems, oil changes & a/c	Lentz USA Service Centers	76
Repair, replace & service auto/manual transmissions & related	Lee Myles Transmissions	82
Repair & sales of residential garage door openers, door repair	Schumacher Garage Door Franchise	186
Res. Comm. & ind. Building inspection & engineering consulting	Criterium Engineers	382
Resale of overnight freight services (DHL) w/ other trans. Modes	Express One	202
Resid. Cleaning, yard work, chores, minor repairs	Hour Hands	166
Residential and small commercial inspection services	Amerispec Home Inspection Service	382

Brief Description	Franchise Name	Page
Sports-themed haircutters for men & boys	Sport Clips	104
Staffing services	PrideStaff	250
Staffing/human resource consulting/payroll svcs/employee leasing	PersoNet-The Personnel Network	254
Steak/chicken/sandwich delivery	Steaks To Go	354
Steaks chicken fish & salad bar/bakery	Sirloin Stockade Family Steakhouse	412
Stone chip repairs, windshield replace, insurance inspections	Chip King	86
Submarine sandwiches and salads	Subway	360
Submarine sandwiches, cakes & pastries baked on-site	Subs Plus	360
Subs & salads	Blimpie Subs And Salads	356
Sunrooms, solariums, conservatories and porch enclosures	Four Seasons Sunrooms	190
Super premium ice cream + yogurt	Emack & Bolio's Ice Cream & Yogurt	312
Supplemental education	Kumon Math & Reading Center	216
SW theme, specialize in chips, chili & delicious toppings	Petro's Chili & Chips	380
Tanning salons & products	Everlasting Tan Club	464
Tax preparation, electronic filing	H & R Block	200
Tax return preparation features custom software, electronic file	Jackson Hewitt Tax Service	200
Teaching tennis to children ages 2–10	Tenniskids	140
The original frozen custard since 1919 simple and unique concept	Kohr Bros. Frozen Custard	320
Tires & automotive services	Team Tires Plus Ltd	92
Top quality house cleaning on a scheduled or one-time basis	Merry Maids	168
Traditional printing, digital imaging, high speed color copying	Kwik Kopy Printing	284
Traditional "smoke shop," extensive selection of tobacco product	Shefield & Sons	450
Train to take photographs on-site for preschools & pet shops	The Visual Image	282
Training facility rentals	Knowledge Development Centers Inc	128
Transmission repair service	Mister Transmission	82
Travelcenters on major hwys serving pro truck driver & motorist	Travelcenters of America, Inc.	96
Tropical theme frozen dessert specialize gourmet shaved ice	Bahama Buck's Original Shaved Ice Co.	320
True brake specialty shop	Brake Centers of America	74
Unique hand-craft gift gallery	Elephant Walk Gift Galleries	436
Unique portraits in creative settings, sepia, B&W, hand colored	I N V U Portraits	280
Up-scale Italian restaurant featuring pizza, pasta, calzone, etc	Mazzio's Pizza	366
Upscale apparel, shoes, furniture, cosmetics for newborn – size 12	Jacadi	52
Upscale bagel bakery cafe & deli	Big City Bagels Inc	292
Upscale bagel deli bakery – catering svcs and delivery	Between Rounds Bagel Deli & Bakery	292
Upscale childrens' resale store, parents buy/sell kids used item	Kid To Kid	142
Upscale community advertising/neighbor welcoming service	Bright Beginnings	108
Upscale custom living room furniture retail storewide selection	Norwalk – The Furniture Idea	258
Upscale plaza hotels, suite hotels, hotels, resorts, cruise ship	Radisson Hotels International	270
Upscale residential maid service, window clean, carpet clean	Maid To Perfection	166
Urban/rural wildlife management	Critter Control Inc	210
Used car, truck and van rentals	Rent 'N Drive	68
Used-car window stickers	Dealer Specialties Int'l Inc	96

Franchises by Geographic Area

A place in the sun.
— BERNHARD VON BÜLOW

Appendix E is sorted by the U.S. state or Canadian province abbreviation.

State or Province	Franchise Name	Page	State or Province	Franchise Name	Page
AB	Certigard/Petro-Canada	88	AL	Express Oil Change	60
AB	EDO Japan	408	AL	GCO Carpet Outlet	256
AB	Fabutan Sun Tan Studios	464	AL	Head Over Heels	138
AB	Grower Direct Fresh Cut Flowers	432	AL	Patty-Cakes International, Inc.	144
AB	Hawkeye's Home Sitters	274	AR	Candy Bouquet International	218
AB	Humpty's Family Restaurant	400	AR	Dent Doctor	70
AB	Joey's Only Seafood Restaurant	418	AR	Marble Renewal	170
AB	Minute Muffler And Brake	76	AR	TCBY Treats	318
AB	Nutter's Bulk And Natural Foods	226	AZ	Alphagraphics Printshops Of The Future	284
AB	Pastel's Cafe	380	AZ	Bahama Buck's Original Shaved Ice Co.	320
AB	Shine Factory	94	AZ	Calculated Couples	194
AB	Smitty's	402	AZ	Castart	188
AB	TFM	440	AZ	Cold Stone Creamery	312
AB	TFM/Top Forty	440	AZ	Doubletree Hotel Systems	268

State or Province	Franchise Name	Page
AZ	Famous Sam's Inc	410
AZ	For Olde Times Sake	436
AZ	Frozen Fusion Fruit Smoothies	320
AZ	Gwynne Learning Academy	214
AZ	InnSuites Hotels	270
AZ	International Golf	458
AZ	International Mergers & Acquisitions	112
AZ	The Little Gym International, Inc.	138
AZ	Nacho Nana's Worldwide Inc	340
AZ	New York Burrito-Gourmet Wraps	340
AZ	O.P.E.N. Cleaning Systems	156
AZ	Perma Glaze	170
AZ	Re-Bath	172
AZ	Service Center	130
AZ	Terri's Consign & Design Furnishings	258
AZ	Truly Nolen	178
BC	Banners Restaurants	398
BC	Blenz Coffee	220
BC	BMR Bath Master Reglazing Ltd.	170
BC	Boston Pizza	362
BC	Chem-Dry Carpet/Upholstery (Canada)	146
BC	Cruise Vacations	470
BC	Custom Homewatch International	452
BC	Dec-K-ing	188
BC	Edelweiss Deli Express/Sub Express	348
BC	The Flag Shop	448
BC	Good For You! Fruit & Yogurt Ltd.	318
BC	The Gourmet Cup	220
BC	Jungle Jim's Restaurants	400
BC	Just Legs	52
BC	Master Care	156
BC	McBeans	222
BC	Pet Habitat	276
BC	PuckMasters Hockey Training Centers	466
BC	The Resume Hut	254
BC	Rodan Jewellers/Simply Charming	56
BC	Rynker Ribbon Xchange Inc.	128
BC	Sandwich Tree Restaurants	350
BC	Shefield Gourmet	222
BC	Shefield & Sons	450
BC	Speedy Printing Centers	288
BC	Sports Traders	456

State or Province	Franchise Name	Page
BC	Uniglobe Travel	472
CA	2001 Flavors Plus Potatoes	312
CA	AeroWest & WestAir Sanitation Services	150
CA	Aim Mail Centers	202
CA	Ameci Pizza & Pasta	362
CA	American Leak Detection	176
CA	American Mobile Sound	208
CA	Auto Purchase Consulting	90
CA	AWC Commercial Window Coverings	262
CA	Baby News Childrens Stores	142
CA	Better Homes Realty	386
CA	Big City Bagels Inc	292
CA	Biozhem Skin Care Centers	100
CA	Blue Chip Cookies	298
CA	Bright Beginnings	108
CA	Budget Blinds	262
CA	Ca$h Plus	192
CA	California Closet Company	180
CA	The Car Wash Guys/Gals	94
CA	Caterina's	376
CA	Cindy's Cinnamon Rolls	296
CA	Clean 'N' Press America	196
CA	The Closet Factory	180
CA	Coit Services	152
CA	Color Me Mine	420
CA	Comprehensive Business Services	126
CA	Computer U Learning Centers	212
CA	The Connoisseur	448
CA	Country Clutter	436
CA	Coverall Cleaning Concepts	152
CA	CPR+	236
CA	Creative Cakery	308
CA	Cruise Holidays International	470
CA	Dairy Belle Freeze	320
CA	Decor-At-Your-Door International	258
CA	Del Taco	340
CA	DentPro	70
CA	Donut Inn	300
CA	Easyriders	90
CA	Econo Lube N' Tune	84
CA	El Pollo Loco	340
CA	Energy Wise	152

State or Province	Franchise Name	Page	State or Province	Franchise Name	Page
CA	Expressions In Fabrics	258	CA	Papyrus	450
CA	Fantastic Sams	102	CA	Paradise Bakery & Cafe	310
CA	Farmer Boys Hamburgers	332	CA	PestMaster Services	384
CA	FastFrame U S A	420	CA	Pizza Factory Inc.	368
CA	FatBurger	332	CA	Pizza Man – He Delivers	368
CA	Field of Dreams	462	CA	Points for Profits	110
CA	Fortune Practice Management	126	CA	Postal Annex+	204
CA	Fosters Freeze, Incorporated	316	CA	PrideStaff	250
CA	FutureKids Inc	134	CA	Remedy Intelligent Staffing	250
CA	Gloria Jean's Gourmet Coffees	220	CA	Renaissance Executive Forums	118
CA	Golds Gym	234	CA	Round Table Franchise Corp	370
CA	Great Earth Vitamins	226	CA	Schumacher Garage Door Franchise	186
CA	Gymboree	138	CA	The Screen Machine	178
CA	Gymsters, Inc.	138	CA	The Screenmobile	184
CA	H R C Int'l Inc	102	CA	Sir Speedy	286
CA	Hayes Handpiece Franchises Inc	236	CA	Slats Blind Cleaning	178
CA	Help-U-Sell	388	CA	Soft Touch Interiors	258
CA	Hilton Inns	268	CA	Spring Crest Drapery Centers	262
CA	Home Cleaning Centers	166	CA	Star Mart	230
CA	Hq Business Centers	126	CA	Straw Hat Pizza	370
CA	Infinity Video Productions Inc	280	CA	Strings Italian Cafe	404
CA	J.W. Tumbles, A Children's Gym	138	CA	Strokes	460
CA	Jazzercise Inc	234	CA	Stuft Pizza & Brewing	370
CA	Jenny Craig Weight Loss Centres	242	CA	Submarina	358
CA	Juice Connection	324	CA	Taco Bell Corp	342
CA	Juice World	230	CA	Tenniskids	140
CA	La Pizza Loca	366	CA	Totally Wireless	428
CA	La Salsa Fresh Mexican Grill	340	CA	Triple Check Income Tax Service	200
CA	Langenwalter Carpet Dyeing	146	CA	U-Wash Doggie	274
CA	Lisa's Tea Treasures	220	CA	United Studios of Self-Defense Inc	468
CA	Lox of Bagels	294	CA	VR Business Brokers	112
CA	Madame Et Monsieur	234	CA	Western Medical Services	248
CA	Mail Boxes Etc.	202	CA	Wetzel's Pretzels	306
CA	Martial Arts America	466	CA	Wienerschnitzel	336
CA	Merle Norman Cosmetics	100	CA	World Gym	234
CA	Miracle Auto Painting & Body Repair	72	CA	Yellow Jacket Direct Mail Advertising	110
CA	Mountain Mike's Pizza	366	CA	Your Office USA	130
CA	Naut-A-Care Marine Services, Inc.	96	CA	Z Land, Inc.	124
CA	New Horizons Computer Learning Center	212	CO	Baby's Away	132
CA	One Stop Undercar	78	CO	Bennett's Bar-B-Que Inc	392
CA	Palace Entertainment & Bullwinkles Restaurant	402	CO	The Better Back Store	236
			CO	Big O Tires	92

State or Province	Franchise Name	Page	State or Province	Franchise Name	Page
CO	Confidential Business Connection	112	FL	A. J. Barnes Bicycle Emporium	456
CO	Copy Copy	284	FL	Accounting Business Systems	106
CO	Craters & Freighters	202	FL	Aqua Bio Technologies	150
CO	Crestcom International, Ltd.	214	FL	Arby's	354
CO	Game Force Franchising	434	FL	Arthur Rutenberg Homes	188
CO	Grease Monkey International	60	FL	Arthur Treacher's Fish & Chips	352
CO	Handle With Care Packaging Store	202	FL	Ashbury Suites & Inns	268
CO	Homewatch Caregivers	206	FL	ATS Personnel	246
CO	Hydro Physics Pipe Inspection	154	FL	Barbizon Schools of Modeling	116
CO	Laund-Ur-Mutt	274	FL	Barnie's Coffee & Tea Company	220
CO	Le Peep	418	FL	BCT	284
CO	Miracle Method	182	FL	Benihana of Tokyo	408
CO	Mister Money – USA	128	FL	Bobby Rubino's Place for Ribs	392
CO	Pak Mail Centers of America	204	FL	The Book Rack	422
CO	Performance Marketing Concepts Inc	110	FL	Canine Counselors	274
CO	PretzelMaker	306	FL	Capital Carpet Cleaning	146
CO	Professional Dynametric Programs/PDP	116	FL	Captain Tony's Pizza & Pasta Emporium	362
CO	Profusion Systems	170	FL	Checkers Drive-In Restaurants	376
CO	Quizno's Classic Subs	358	FL	Cheeburger Cheeburger	332
CO	Re/Max International	390	FL	Classy Maids USA	166
CO	Renzios	380	FL	CompuTemp Inc	250
CO	Rocky Mountain Chocolate Factory	218	FL	Connect.Ad	108
CO	Sale By Owner Systems	390	FL	CruiseOne/The Travel Company	470
CO	Signal Graphics Printing	286	FL	Custom Auto Restoration Systems	70
CO	Sutton Homes Franchising Corp	238	FL	Diversified Dental Services	236
CO	Village Inn Restaurants	402	FL	DuctBusters/Buster Enterprises Inc	176
CO	Window & Wall Creations	262	FL	Eagle Cleaners	196
CO	Z-Teca	344	FL	Environmental Biotech	154
CT	Arrow Prescription Center	236	FL	Estrella Insurance	126
CT	Bagelz – The Bagel Bakery	292	FL	Fast-Fix Jewelry Repairs	56
CT	Between Rounds Bagel Deli & Bakery	292	FL	Fire Defense Centers	452
CT	Brake Centers of America	74	FL	First Choice Haircutters (U.S.) Inc.	102
CT	The Car Phone Store	428	FL	Firstat Nursing Services	248
CT	Carvel Ice Cream Bakery	312	FL	Flamers Charbroiled Hamburgers & Chicken	332
CT	Little Scientists	136	FL	Foliage Design Systems	432
CT	Saf-T Auto Centers	80	FL	Gent's Formal Wear	54
CT	Subway	360	FL	Happy & Healthy Products	320
CT	Totally Kool	52	FL	High Touch-High Tech	142
CT	X-Bankers Check Cashing	192	FL	Home Guide Magazine	290
DC	LawCorps Legal Staffing Services	250	FL	Hour Hands	166
DE	Trimark	110	FL	Hubb's Pub	416
DE	Yipes Stripes	98	FL	Interface Financial Group	114

State or Province	Franchise Name	Page	State or Province	Franchise Name	Page
FL	Interim Healthcare	248	FL	Workenders	168
FL	Kinderdance International	138	FL	Worldwide Information Services	424
FL	Lady of America	234	GA	A Quicki Services	206
FL	Larry's Giant Subs	356	GA	Aaron's Rental Purchase	428
FL	Last Flight Out	436	GA	American Brake Service	74
FL	LedgerPlus	106	GA	The Athlete's Foot	456
FL	Longbranch Steakhouse & Saloon Inc	412	GA	Atlanta Bread Co	308
FL	Manchu Wok (U.S.)	346	GA	Baldinos Giant Jersey Subs	356
FL	Mister Mobile On-Site Oil Changes	60	GA	Blimpie Subs And Salads	356
FL	Mobil Ambition USA LC	108	GA	Buffalo's Cafe	398
FL	The More Space Place	264	GA	Building Systems Analysis Inc.	382
FL	National Homecraft	156	GA	Checkcare Systems	192
FL	Nu-Look 1-Hr. Cleaners	198	GA	Chesapeake Bagel Bakery	292
FL	Old Fashioned Egg Cream Co Inc	378	GA	Chili Chompers	230
FL	Pack Mart	202	GA	Churchs Chicken	328
FL	Payless Car Rental System	66	GA	Cinema Grill	466
FL	PC Professor	212	GA	Colors On Parade	94
FL	PersoNet-The Personnel Network	254	GA	ExecuTrain	116
FL	Pillar To Post	384	GA	ExecuTrain Corp.	212
FL	Pinch-A-Penny	426	GA	Floor Coverings International	256
FL	Potts Doggie Shop	336	GA	Golf Augusta Pro Shops	458
FL	Power Smoothie	322	GA	Great American Cookie Company, Inc.	298
FL	The Pretzel Twister	306	GA	Great Wraps	378
FL	ProForce USA	158	GA	Hawthorn Suites/Hawthorn Suites Ltd	268
FL	PuroFirst International	158	GA	Haynes Pet Centre Franchising Inc	274
FL	Rental Guide	290	GA	Heavenly Ham	230
FL	Roll-A-Way	452	GA	Heel Quik	52
FL	Service One	158	GA	Holiday Hospitality	270
FL	Shooters International Inc	418	GA	Holiday Inn Worldwide	270
FL	Sign-A-Rama	120	GA	Hospitality International	270
FL	Signs Now	120	GA	Huddle House	396
FL	Sobik's Subs	358	GA	Johnny's New York Style Pizza	366
FL	Speedy Transmission Centers	82	GA	Kids R Kids Quality Learning Centers	136
FL	Superglass Windshield Repair	86	GA	Lifestyle Mobile Carpet Showroom	256
FL	Tempaco	438	GA	Maid Brigade Services	166
FL	Total Medical Compliance	238	GA	MaxCare Professional Cleaning Systems	156
FL	TPI Travel Services	472	GA	Mighty Distribution System of America Inc	64
FL	Truck Options	58	GA	Millicare Environmental Services	156
FL	Tutor Time Child Care Learning Center	132	GA	My Friend's Place	378
FL	U.S. Lawns	164	GA	Nitro-Green Professional Lawn & Tree Care	162
FL	Val-Pak Direct Marketing	110	GA	Norrell Services	254
FL	Valet Express	198	GA	Padgett Business Services	106

State or Province	Franchise Name	Page	State or Province	Franchise Name	Page
GA	Philly Connection	326	IL	The Great American Bagel	292
GA	Popeyes Chicken & Biscuits	330	IL	The Great Frame Up	420
GA	Primrose Schools	136	IL	Hairlines	102
GA	Professional Carpet Systems	148	IL	Home & Garden Showplace	162
GA	Rennsport	96	IL	InHouse Travel Group LLC	472
GA	The Sport Shoe	456	IL	Jay Roberts & Associates	128
GA	The Sports Section	282	IL	Jimmy John's Gourmet Sandwich Shops	348
GA	Steak-Out	232	IL	Kwik Dry International	154
GA	Steaks To Go	354	IL	Lemstone Books	422
GA	Tom's Foods	228	IL	Lindy – Gertie's	378
GA	Tradebank International	130	IL	Liqui-Green Lawn & Tree Care	162
GA	TRC Staffing Services	252	IL	LubePros International, Inc.	60
GA	U.S. Franchise Systems	272	IL	Manufacturing Management Associates	128
GA	Video Impact	430	IL	McDonald's	334
GA	Wedding Gown Specialists/Restoration	198	IL	Merlin's Muffler & Brake	76
IA	Better Homes & Gardens Real Estate Service	386	IL	Milex Tune-Ups And Brakes	84
IA	Diamond Dave's Taco Company	340	IL	My Favorite Muffin	304
IA	Happy Joe's Pizza & Ice Cream Parlor	364	IL	Nancy's Pizzeria	366
IA	Medicap Pharmacy	236	IL	National Hygiene/Lien	156
IA	Panchero's Mexican Grill	342	IL	Option Care	238
IA	The Pizza Ranch	368	IL	Pepe's Mexican Restaurant	406
IA	Professional House Doctors, Inc.	384	IL	Pizzas By Marchelloni	370
IA	Roto-Rooter	178	IL	Pre-Fit	140
IA	United Printing Unlimited	288	IL	Successories	450
ID	By Owner Reality Network	386	IL	Transmission USA	82
ID	Heaven's Best	146	IL	Tropik Sun Fruit & Nut	228
ID	Moxie Java	222	IL	USA Baby	144
IL	American Concrete Raising	188	IL	White Hen Pantry	232
IL	Boz Hot Dogs	336	IN	Chicago's Pizza	362
IL	The BrickKicker	382	IN	Dog N' Suds Drive-In Restaurants	416
IL	Brite Site	150	IN	E.P.I.C. Systems, Inc.	152
IL	Brown's Chicken & Pasta	328	IN	Indy Lube	60
IL	Budget Car & Truck Rental	66	IN	J. D. Byrider Systems	90
IL	Car-X Muffler & Brake	76	IN	Kids Team	142
IL	Cash Converters USA	192	IN	RACS International	158
IL	Certicare	84	IN	Steak 'N Shake	354
IL	Creative Colors Int'l Inc	174	IN	Sunshine Cafe	418
IL	Culligan Water Conditioning	446	IN	United Consumers Club	210
IL	Cyber Exchange Software And Computers	424	IN	Wild Birds Unlimited	278
IL	Drapery Works Systems	262	KS	Applebee's International	416
IL	DuraClean International	152	KS	Building Services of America	150
IL	Gingiss Formalwear	54	KS	CottageCare	166

State or Province	Franchise Name	Page	State or Province	Franchise Name	Page
KS	Mr. GoodCents Subs & Pasta	358	MA	Learning Express	136
KS	Sirloin Stockade Family Steakhouse	412	MA	Lord's & Lady's Hair Salons	104
KS	Snip N' Clip Haircut Shops	104	MA	MaidPro	166
KY	Greetings	108	MA	Pizzeria Uno Chicago Bar & Grill	370
KY	IncrediPet	276	MA	Pressed 4 Time	198
KY	KFC	330	MA	Proventure Business Group, Inc.	112
KY	Long John Silver's	352	MA	Quikava – Coffees By Chock Full O' Nuts	222
KY	Peyron Tax Service	200	MA	Woody's Wood Shops	460
KY	Snappy Tomato Pizza	370	MB	Chicken Delight	328
KY	Travel Professionals International	472	MB	Medichair	238
KY	Tumbleweed LLC	414	MD	ATL International	96
KY	Valvoline Instant Oil Change	62	MD	Boardwalk Fries	336
KY	Wheelchair Getaways	68	MD	Candy Express	218
LA	Altracolor Systems	88	MD	Choice Hotels Intl	268
LA	Bunnies Fresh Juice & Smoothie Bar	324	MD	The Cleaning Authority	166
LA	Chef's Fried Chicken	328	MD	CleanNet USA	152
LA	Copeland's of New Orleans	410	MD	Decorating Den Interiors	262
LA	Critter Care of America	274	MD	Decorating Den Painting & Home Imp	188
LA	L. A. Smoothie Healthmart & Cafe	226	MD	Dynamark Security Centers	452
LA	La Smoothie Franchises Inc	324	MD	Interstate Dairy Queen	316
LA	Metropolitan Institute of Health Careers	116	MD	Jerry's Subs & Pizza	356
LA	P.J.'S Coffee & Tea	222	MD	Kiddie Academy International	134
LA	Profit-On-Hold	110	MD	KitchenPro	262
LA	Smoothie King	322	MD	Maid To Perfection	166
LA	Speedee Oil Change & Tune-Up	62	MD	Mamma Ilardo's	338
MA	Academy of Learning	134	MD	Merchant Advertising Systems	108
MA	Adventures In Advertising	108	MD	Naturalawn of America	162
MA	Baskin-Robbins USA Co	312	MD	Parcel Plus	204
MA	Boston Bartenders School Associates	116	MD	Rent-A-Wreck of America	68
MA	Castles Unlimited	388	MD	Sandler Sales Institute	118
MA	Closettec	180	MD	Signs By Tomorrow	120
MA	Dunkin' Donuts	300	MD	Stuckey's Express	228
MA	EB's Express	338	MD	Super Lawns	164
MA	Emack & Bolio's Ice Cream & Yogurt	312	MD	Sylvan Learning Centers	216
MA	Friendly's Ice Cream Corporation	400	MD	United Capital Mortgage Assistance	192
MA	Fuddruckers	416	MD	Wild Bird Centers of America, Inc.	278
MA	The Ground Round	394	ME	Chowderhead's Seafood Restaurants	352
MA	The Ground Round Restaurant	394	ME	Criterium Engineers	382
MA	Hammett's Learning World	214	ME	Successful Introduction	194
MA	The Homesteader	290	MI	American Speedy Printing Centers	284
MA	Hoop Mountain	466	MI	American Transmissions	82
MA	Jan-Pro Franchising Int'l Inc	154	MI	Amigo Mobility Center	236

State or Province	Franchise Name	Page	State or Province	Franchise Name	Page
MI	Antonello's	338	MN	Abra Auto Body & Glass	70
MI	Auto One Glass & Accessories	58	MN	Aero-Colours	88
MI	Auto-Lab Diagnostic & Tune-Up Centers	84	MN	American Institute of Small Business	214
MI	Big Boy Restaurant & Bakery	398	MN	AmericInn International	268
MI	The Brake Shop	74	MN	Bridgeman's Restaurants Inc	398
MI	Buscemi's International	376	MN	Bw-3 Buffalo Wild Wings	328
MI	Cartex Limited	88	MN	Candleman Corporation	448
MI	Children's Orchard	142	MN	Carlson Wagonlit Travel	470
MI	The Coffee Beanery	220	MN	Champion Auto Stores	64
MI	Critter Control	382	MN	City Looks Salons Int'l	102
MI	Critter Control Inc	210	MN	Color-Glo International	170
MI	CTI Computer Training Institutes	212	MN	Computer Renaissance	424
MI	Domino's Pizza Inc	362	MN	Cost Cutters Family Hair Care	102
MI	EnviroFree Inspections	382	MN	Country Inns & Suites by Carlson	268
MI	Faro's Franchise Systems	364	MN	Dairy Queen	316
MI	First Optometry Eye Care Centers	240	MN	Dry Cleaning Station	196
MI	Fudge Co.	218	MN	EcoSmarte Planet Friendly	442
MI	Guardsman WoodPro	184	MN	Envirobate	152
MI	High Wheeler Ice Cream Parlour/Rest.	314	MN	Full Circle Image	424
MI	Hungry Howie's Pizza & Subs	366	MN	Great Clips	102
MI	IMBC	124	MN	Its About Games	434
MI	Jantize America	154	MN	Jet-Black Sealcoating & Repair	178
MI	Kilwin's Chocolates Franchise	218	MN	Kennedy Transmission	82
MI	Kirby Tours	472	MN	MacBirdie Golf Gifts	458
MI	Lentz USA Service Centers	76	MN	Miracle-Ear	238
MI	Little Professor Book Centers	422	MN	Music-Go-Round	440
MI	Look No-Fault Auto Insurance Agencies	128	MN	Novus Windshield Repair	86
MI	Molly Maid	168	MN	Once Upon A Child	144
MI	Pasta To Go	378	MN	Outdoor Connection	466
MI	Pets Are Inn	276	MN	Paper Warehouse Franchising Inc	444
MI	Pro Golf Discount	460	MN	Play It Again Sports	456
MI	Rich's Chimney Fix-It	184	MN	Radisson Hotels International	270
MI	Rider's Hobby Shops	434	MN	Radisson Hotels Worldwide	272
MI	Talking Book World	422	MN	Re Tool	438
MI	Top Value Muffler & Brake Shops	78	MN	SlumberLand International	258
MI	Tropi-Tan, Inc.	464	MN	Sox Appeal	52
MI	Tubby's Submarines	360	MN	Team Tires Plus Ltd	92
MI	Two Men And A Truck	210	MN	We Care Hair	104
MI	Victory Lane Quick Oil Change	62	MO	21st Century Auto Alliance	96
MI	Yaya's Flame Broiled Chicken	330	MO	Aire-Master of America	150
MI	Ziebart Tidycar	94	MO	American Darters Association	466
MN	1 Potato 2	376	MO	American Poolplayers Association	466

State or Province	Franchise Name	Page	State or Province	Franchise Name	Page
MO	Balloons & Bears	436	NC	Window Gang	160
MO	Biologix	150	ND	ABC Seamless	186
MO	Custom Cuts	102	ND	Steam Brothers Professional Cleaning & Restoration	148
MO	Dr. Vinyl & Assoc.	174			
MO	FCI Franchising Inc	64	ND	United States Seamless, Inc.	186
MO	H & R Block	200	NE	The Bone Appetit Bakery	276
MO	Houlihan's Restaurant Group	416	NE	Brown Baggers	348
MO	I.B. Nuts & Fruit Too	228	NE	Complete Music	208
MO	The Medicine Shoppe	238	NE	Dent Zone	70
MO	Saint Louis Bread Company, Inc.	310	NE	Fast Bucks Development LLC	192
MO	The Sleeping Giant Within Inc.	216	NE	Godfather's Pizza	364
MO	Slimmer Image Weight Loss Clinics	242	NE	Hobbytown USA	434
MO	Spot-Not Car Washes	94	NE	Home Instead Senior Care	248
MO	Street Corner News	290	NE	Lamar's Donuts	300
MO	Surface Specialists Systems	172	NE	Little King	378
MO	Taco Hut America Inc	406	NE	The Maids	168
MO	United Energy Partners	190	NE	Malibu Gallery	420
MO	Yesterday's Furniture & Country Store	260	NE	Mickey Finn's Sports Cafe	418
MS	EconoTax	200	NE	National Property Inspections, Inc.	384
MS	U-Save Auto Rental of America Inc	68	NE	Pure Water Ultima	446
MS	Ward's Restaurants	418	NE	Rent 'N Drive	68
MT	Great Harvest Bread Co.	308	NE	Sports Fantastic	462
MT	Kampgrounds of America/KOA	266	NE	Tan World	464
MT	Value Line Maintenance Systems	160	NF	Elegance Jewelry	56
NB	English Butler Canada	206	NH	Buyer's Resource	386
NB	Pizza Delight	368	NH	Moe's Italian Sandwiches	348
NC	American Sign Shops	120	NH	Tire Warehouse Central	92
NC	BladeRunner Mobile Sharpening	176	NJ	Affordable Car Rental	66
NC	Bojangles' Restaurants Inc	328	NJ	Air Brook Limousine	210
NC	Electronic Tax Filers	200	NJ	Ambic Building Inspection Consult	382
NC	Elliott & Company Appraisers	388	NJ	Bagelsmith Restaurants & Food Stores	292
NC	Gelato Amare	314	NJ	Berlitz Franchising Corp.	214
NC	Golden Corral Family Steakhouse	412	NJ	Carpet Network	256
NC	Golden Corral Franchising Systems Inc	412	NJ	Century 21 Real Estate	388
NC	Hardee's Food Systems	332	NJ	Cluck-U Chicken	328
NC	Krispy Kreme Doughnuts	300	NJ	Coldwell Banker Residential Affiliates	388
NC	Meineke Discount Mufflers	76	NJ	Days Inns of America Inc	268
NC	Putt-Putt Golf Courses Of America	468	NJ	ELS Language Centers	214
NC	Stork News of America	144	NJ	Era Franchise Systems	388
NC	Swisher Hygiene	160	NJ	Goldberg's New York Bagels	292
NC	Terra Systems	164	NJ	HouseMaster, The Home Inspection Professionals	384
NC	Western Steer Family Steakhouse/WSMP	414			

State or Province	Franchise Name	Page	State or Province	Franchise Name	Page
NJ	Howard Johnson Intl Inc	270	NY	Cruise Lines Reservation Center	470
NJ	Huntington Learning Center	216	NY	Dunhill Staffing Systems, Inc.	246
NJ	Imagine That Discovery Museums	134	NY	Ecomat	196
NJ	Jersey Mike's Franchise Systems, Inc.	348	NY	Empire Business Brokers	112
NJ	Knights Franchise Systems Inc	270	NY	Empress Travel	472
NJ	Kumon Math & Reading Center	216	NY	Everything Yogurt & Salad Cafe	318
NJ	Lawn Doctor	162	NY	Express Mart Convenient Store	224
NJ	Lee Myles Transmissions	82	NY	Fortune Personnel Consultants	244
NJ	Manhattan Bagel Co Inc	294	NY	Four Seasons Sunrooms	190
NJ	Manhattan Bagel Company	294	NY	Franklin Traffic Service	126
NJ	Oil Butler International	60	NY	Hauntrepreneurs, Ltd.	466
NJ	Party City Corp	444	NY	Health Force	248
NJ	Ramada Franchise Systems Inc	272	NY	Jacadi	52
NJ	Roli Boli	380	NY	John Casablancas Modeling/Career Center	116
NJ	Safe Not Sorry	452	NY	Just-A-Buck	426
NJ	Super 8 Motels Inc	272	NY	KCS Applications	170
NJ	The T O L Franchise Group	100	NY	King Bear Auto Service Centers	80
NJ	Travel Network	472	NY	Le Croissant Shop	310
NJ	Villa Pizza	372	NY	Lemon Tree – A Unisex Haircutting Est.	104
NM	K-Bob's Steakhouses	412	NY	Men's Hair Now	104
NS	Greco Pizza Donair	364	NY	Minuteman Press International	286
NS	Permacrete Systems	190	NY	Odyssey Art Centers	136
NS	St. Jerome Restaurant	402	NY	Perma Ceram Enterprises	182
NV	Assist-2-Sell	386	NY	Pro-Tect	384
NV	Elephant Walk Gift Galleries	436	NY	Sbarro, The Italian Eatery	338
NV	Las Vegas Golf & Tennis	458	NY	Soccer Post Intl Franchise Corp	456
NV	Nevada Bob's Professional Golf Shops	458	NY	Staff Builders Home Health Care	248
NV	The Pet Pantry International	276	NY	Sterling Optical	240
NV	Port of Subs	358	NY	Tilden for Brakes Car Care Centers	74
NV	Postnet Postal & Business Centers	204	NY	Video Data Services	428
NV	Practical Rent A Car	66	OH	A Shade Better	264
NV	Purified Water To Go	446	OH	ApparelMaster USA	196
NV	Quik Internet	124	OH	Auto Accent Centers	58
NV	True Friends	278	OH	B-Dry System	188
NY	AccuStaff Inc	250	OH	Buffalo Wings & Rings	398
NY	AJ Texas Hots	336	OH	Building Blocks Franchise Corp	142
NY	America's Choice Int'l Inc.	386	OH	Bw-3 Franchise Systems Inc	228
NY	Appletree Art Publishers	420	OH	Cap'n Taco	340
NY	Bourbon Street Candy Company	218	OH	Charley's Steakery	412
NY	Carpet Master	256	OH	Chemstation International	150
NY	Conroys 1-800-Flowers	432	OH	Convenient Food Mart	224
NY	Crown Trophy	448	OH	Damon's International	398

State or Province	Franchise Name	Page	State or Province	Franchise Name	Page
OH	Dealer Specialties Int'l Inc	96	OK	Express Personnel Services	246
OH	Deckare Services	176	OK	Glamour Shots	280
OH	Diet Center Worldwide	242	OK	Golf USA	458
OH	Donatos Pizza	362	OK	Impressions On Hold International	108
OH	East of Chicago Pizza Company	364	OK	Mazzio's Pizza	366
OH	Emerald Green Lawn Care	162	OK	Paceco Financial Services	114
OH	Great Steak & Potato Company	326	OK	Room-Mate Referral Service Centers	390
OH	Handyman Connection	190	OK	Sonic Drive-In	334
OH	Her Real Estate	390	OK	Taco Mayo	342
OH	Home Helpers	206	OK	Thrifty Rent-A-Car	68
OH	The Hometeam Inspection Service	382	ON	A Buck Or Two Stores	426
OH	House Doctors Handyman Service	176	ON	Academy for Mathematics & Science	214
OH	Knowledge Development Centers Inc	128	ON	AccounTax Services	106
OH	Lube Depot	60	ON	Active Green + Ross Tire & Automotive Centre	92
OH	Magic Wok	346	ON	Algonquin Travel	470
OH	Magis Fund Raising Specialists	128	ON	Apple Auto Glass	86
OH	Maintain Cleaning Systems	156	ON	Arodal	150
OH	Management Recruiters	244	ON	Baker's Dozen Donuts	300
OH	Marco's Pizza	366	ON	Baskin-Robbins Canada	312
OH	Matco Tools	64	ON	Bevinco	126
OH	Mr. Hero	358	ON	Buns Master Bakery Systems	308
OH	Norwalk – The Furniture Idea	258	ON	Burger King (Canada)	332
OH	The Office Alternative	128	ON	C. B. S. Interactive Multimedia	212
OH	One Hour Martinizing	198	ON	Cafe By George/Cookies By George	298
OH	One Hour Motophoto & Portrait Studio	280	ON	Chip King	86
OH	Pee Wee Workout	138	ON	Clintar Groundskeeping Services	162
OH	Penn Stations East Coast Subs	358	ON	Coffee Time Donuts	300
OH	Petland	276	ON	Coldwell Banker Affiliates (Canada)	388
OH	Proforma	286	ON	Color Your World	438
OH	Sanford Rose Associates	244	ON	Cultures Restaurants	376
OH	Scoopers Ice Cream	314	ON	Dairy Queen Canada Inc.	316
OH	SealMaster	158	ON	Discount Car & Truck Rentals	66
OH	Service-Tech Corporation	160	ON	Dollar Rent A Car (Canada)	66
OH	Sparkle Wash	160	ON	Donut Delite Cafe	300
OH	The Steak Escape	354	ON	Dufferin Game Room Store	434
OH	Travelcenters of America, Inc.	96	ON	Dynamic Golf Centres	458
OH	Tuffy Auto Service Centers	88	ON	East Side Mario's	404
OH	Window Butler	168	ON	Enviro Masters Lawn Care	162
OH	World Trade Network	130	ON	Fabri-Zone Cleaning Systems	146
OH	Yogi Bear Jellystone Park Camp-Resorts	266	ON	Fast Eddie's	376
OK	CD Warehouse	440	ON	Framing & Art Centres	420
OK	Dollar Rent A Car	66	ON	FutureKids (Canada)	134

State or Province	Franchise Name	Page
ON	Gateway Newstands	448
ON	Genius Kid Academy	134
ON	Grandma Lee's Bakery Cafe	308
ON	The Great Canadian Bagel	292
ON	The Great Wilderness Company, Inc.	442
ON	The Griddle Family Restaurants	400
ON	Harvey's Restaurants	400
ON	Ho-Lee-Chow	346
ON	International News	290
ON	JDI Cleaning Systems	154
ON	Jumbo Video	440
ON	Kelsey's Restaurants	400
ON	Kernels	228
ON	Kiddie Kobbler	142
ON	Kwik-Kopy Printing (Canada)	284
ON	Le Print Express	286
ON	Living Lighting	258
ON	London Cleaners	198
ON	M & M Meat Shops	230
ON	Maaco Auto Painting & Bodyworks (Canada)	70
ON	Made In Japan, Teriyaki Experience	346
ON	Mail Boxes Etc. (Canada)	202
ON	The Master Mechanic	80
ON	McDonald's Restaurants of Canada Limited	334
ON	MicroPlay Video Games	434
ON	Midas (Canada)	76
ON	Mini Maid Service Systems Of Canada	168
ON	Mister Transmission	82
ON	Mmmarvellous Mmmuffins	304
ON	Model Managers Int'l	116
ON	Money Concepts (Canada)	114
ON	Mr. Front-End	76
ON	New York Fries	378
ON	Nutri-Lawn, Ecology-Friendly Lawn Care	164
ON	One Hour Motophoto & Portrait Studio (Canada)	280
ON	Orange Julius Canada Inc.	322
ON	P.A.M.'S Coffee & Tea Co.	222
ON	Pak Mail Centers (Canada)	204
ON	Paystation	452
ON	The Peanut Club	144
ON	Pizza Nova	368

State or Province	Franchise Name	Page
ON	Pizza Pizza Limited	368
ON	ProShred Security	452
ON	Ramada Franchise Canada, Inc.	272
ON	Robin's Donuts	300
ON	Roto-Static International	148
ON	Ruffin's Pet Centres	276
ON	Saint Cinnamon Bake Shoppe	296
ON	The Sandwich Board	348
ON	SaniBrite	158
ON	Sears Driver Training	216
ON	The Second Cup	222
ON	Select Sandwich	350
ON	Seniors for Seniors/Seniors for Business	254
ON	ServiceMaster Residential/Commercial (Canada)	168
ON	Shred-It	454
ON	Sir Speedy (Canada)	286
ON	Subs Plus	360
ON	Sunbanque Island Tanning	464
ON	Swiss Chalet/Swiss Chalet Plus Restaurants	410
ON	Taco Villa	342
ON	TechnoKids	136
ON	Thrifty Car Rental (Canada)	68
ON	Tim Hortons	310
ON	Treats	310
ON	V.I.D.E.O. Security Process (VSP)	454
ON	Vinylgraphics Custom Sign Centres	122
ON	We Care Home Health Services	248
ON	Wee Watch Private Home Day Care	132
ON	Weed Man	164
ON	Wendy's Restaurants of Canada Inc.	334
ON	Wing Machine	330
ON	Yogen Fruz Worldwide	318
ONT	Perfumes Etc.	100
OR	All American Frozen Yogurt/Ice Cream	318
OR	Diet Light Weight Loss System	242
OR	Elmer's Pancake & Steak House	412
OR	Figaro's Italian Kitchen	338
OR	Glass Magnum	176
OR	Insulated Dry Roof Systems	190
OR	LazerQuick	286
OR	National Tenant Network	390

State or Province	Franchise Name	Page	State or Province	Franchise Name	Page
OR	Oil Can Henry's International	62	PA	Tower Cleaning Systems	160
OR	Serv U-1st	158	PA	United Check Cashing	192
OR	Tacotime	342	PA	Wild Bird Marketplace	278
OR	Turbo Management Systems Ltd.	118	PQ	A. L. Van Houtte	376
PA	AAMCO Transmissions	82	PQ	Croissant + Plus	308
PA	Aloette Cosmetics	100	PQ	Monsieur Muffler	76
PA	Auntie Anne's Hand-Rolled Soft Pretzels	306	PQ	Nutrite	164
PA	Baker Street Artisan Breads & Cafe	308	PQ	Panda Shoes	52
PA	Bassett's Original Turkey	328	QC	Group Trans-Action Brokerage Services	388
PA	Bike Line	456	QC	Joe Loue Tout Rent All	66
PA	Bruster's Old-Fashioned Ice Cream & Yogurt	312	QC	The Mad Science Group	144
PA	Buck's Pizza Franchising, Inc.	362	QC	Mikes Restaurants	400
PA	Candy HQ/Sweets From Heaven	218	QC	Monsieur Felix & Mr. Norton Cookies	298
PA	CarpetMate	146	QC	St. Hubert Bar-B-Q	392
PA	Certa Propainters Ltd	188	RI	Beverly Hills Weight Loss & Wellness	242
PA	Consumer Casket USA	448	RI	Cafe La France	416
PA	Cottman Transmission	82	RI	Ronzio Pizza	370
PA	The Different Twist Pretzel Co.	306	SC	A Wonderful Wedding	210
PA	Dollar Discount Stores	426	SC	Butterfields, Etc.	448
PA	EndRust Auto Appearance Centers	70	SC	Checkmate	250
PA	Four Star Pizza	364	SC	Condotels	470
PA	Fox's Pizza Den	364	SC	Denny's Inc	400
PA	General Nutrition Centers	226	SC	East Shore Athletic Club	234
PA	The Goddard Schools	134	SC	Everlasting Tan Club	464
PA	Grand Rental Station/Taylor Rental	428	SC	Gymn' Around Kids	138
PA	L A Weight Loss Centers Inc	242	SC	Sub Station Ii	358
PA	Lindelle Studios	280	SC	Sunbelt Business Brokers	112
PA	Maaco Auto Painting & Bodyworks	70	SC	Themed Miniature Golf Courses	468
PA	Mom's Bake At Home Pizza	374	SD	Computer Doctor	424
PA	Morrone's Italian Ices	314	SD	Gigglebees	416
PA	Naked Furniture	258	SD	Kitchen Tune-Up	182
PA	Oh Mighty Ices Franchise Corp	320	SD	Nature's 10	442
PA	Party Land Inc	444	SK	Family Pizza	364
PA	Pet Valu	276	SK	Sangsters Health Centres	226
PA	Petrucci's Ice Cream Co.	314	TN	Amerispec Home Inspection Service	382
PA	Planet Earth Recycling	96	TN	Atwork Personnel Services	246
PA	The Potato Sack	230	TN	Back Yard Burgers	332
PA	Pretzels Plus	306	TN	Boomerang GameWare	434
PA	Rita's Italian Ice	322	TN	Buddy's Bar-B-Q	354
PA	Screen Printing USA	286	TN	Business Information Int'l Inc	108
PA	Superior Walls of America	190	TN	The Buyer's Agent	386
PA	Tinder Box International	436	TN	Captain D's Seafood	352

State or Province	Franchise Name	Page	State or Province	Franchise Name	Page
TN	Champion Cleaners Franchise Inc.	196	TX	Deck The Walls	420
TN	Furniture Medic	176	TX	Dickey's Barbecue Pit Restaurants	392
TN	Harvey Washbangers	196	TX	Doubledave's Pizzaworks Restaurant	404
TN	The Honors Learning Center	216	TX	E.K. Williams & Co.	106
TN	John Simmons	448	TX	Elephant House Inc	436
TN	The Krystal Company	334	TX	Empowered Womens Golf Shops	458
TN	Merry Maids	168	TX	FastSigns	120
TN	Our Weigh	242	TX	Frullati Cafe	348
TN	Perkins Family Restaurants	402	TX	GalaxSea Cruises & Tours	472
TN	Petro's Chili & Chips	380	TX	General Business Services	126
TN	Picture Hits	280	TX	Golden Chick	330
TN	ServiceMaster Residential/Commercial	168	TX	Great Outdoor Sub Shops	356
TN	ServPro	160	TX	Hartz Chicken	330
TN	Signs First	120	TX	Health Mart	236
TN	The Soda Fountain	396	TX	Hudson's Grill of America	416
TN	Special Delivery Photos Inc	280	TX	I Can't Believe It's Yogurt	318
TN	Terminix Termite & Pest Control	384	TX	IC Solutions Inc	124
TN	Tri-Color Carpet Dyeing And Cleaning	148	TX	Jani-King International	154
TN	The Visual Image	282	TX	Jiffy Lube International Inc	60
TN	Western Sizzlin'	414	TX	Joy Carpet Dry Cleaning	146
TX	7-Eleven Convenience Stores	224	TX	Kitchen Wizards	182
TX	Ace America's Cash Express	192	TX	Kwik Kopy Printing	284
TX	Airbag Options	88	TX	Labor Force	246
TX	AirSoPure	452	TX	Leadership Management, Inc.	116
TX	American Lenders Service Co.	114	TX	Link Staffing Services	246
TX	American Wholesale Thermographers	284	TX	Marble Slab Creamery	314
TX	Apartment Selector	386	TX	MarbleLife	170
TX	Around Your Neck	52	TX	Motel 6	270
TX	Ashley Avery's Collectables	436	TX	Mr. Jim's Pizza	366
TX	ASI Sign Systems Inc	120	TX	Mr. Rooter Corp.	178
TX	Bennigan's	398	TX	NurseFinders	248
TX	Bonanza	398	TX	Packaging And Shipping Specialist	202
TX	Ceiling Doctor	176	TX	Pearle Vision Center	240
TX	Chelsea Street Pub & Grill	394	TX	Petro Stopping Centers	96
TX	Cici's Pizza	362	TX	Pizza Inn Inc	368
TX	Citizens Against Crime	214	TX	Ponderosa Steakhouse	412
TX	Colortyme	428	TX	Pro-Cuts	104
TX	Colter's Bar-B-Q	392	TX	Professional Polish	158
TX	Comet One-Hour Cleaners	196	TX	Property Damage Appraisers	178
TX	Cookie Bouquet/Cookies By Design	298	TX	Radio Shack International	428
TX	Cookies In Bloom	298	TX	RadioShack	428
TX	Copy Club	284			

State or Province	Franchise Name	Page	State or Province	Franchise Name	Page
TX	Rainbow International Carpet Care & Restoration Specialist	148	UT	Q Lube	62
TX	Relax The Back Franchising Co	238	UT	The Taco Maker	342
TX	Safe-T-Child	144	UT	Tee Signs Plus	110
TX	Schlotzsky's Deli	350	UT	Tunex International, Inc.	84
TX	Showhomes of America	390	UT	Unishippers Association	204
TX	Snelling Personnel Services	246	UT	Zuka Juice	324
TX	Southern Maid Donuts	302	VA	Archadeck	188
TX	Sport Clips	104	VA	Borvin Beverage	230
TX	Steamatic	148	VA	Brew Thru	220
TX	Stretch-N-Grow of America	140	VA	Bullets Corporation of America, Inc.	332
TX	Talent Tree Staffing Services	250	VA	Commission Express	126
TX	Team Golf Corp	460	VA	ComputerTots/Computer Explorers	134
TX	TGI Friday's Hospitality Worldwide	418	VA	Hard Times Cafe	378
TX	Thundercloud Subs	360	VA	Hollywood Weight Loss Centre	242
TX	Tippy's Taco House	342	VA	Jackson Hewitt Tax Service	200
TX	Tire Time Rentals	92	VA	Kohr Bros. Frozen Custard	320
TX	Today's Temporary	252	VA	Precision Tune Auto Care	84
TX	UncleSam's Convenient Store	224	VA	Red Hot & Blue	418
TX	Universal Business Consultants	130	VA	Sonitrol	454
TX	Wallpapers To Go	264	VA	Zero's Subs	360
TX	Wicks 'N' Sticks	450	VT	Bath Fitter	182
TX	Window Perfect	262	VT	Ben & Jerry's	312
TX	Women's Health Boutique	238	VT	Resort Maps Franchise Inc	110
TX	Worldwide Refinishing Systems, Inc.	182	WA	Acctcorp	106
TX	Zuzu Mexican Food	406	WA	Admiral of The Fleet Cruise Centers	470
UT	Arctic Circle	320	WA	Admiral Subs	356
UT	Bathcrest	170	WA	Airbag Service	88
UT	Beneficial Health & Beauty	100	WA	Bingo Bugle Newspaper	290
UT	Chem-Dry Carpet/Drapery/Upholstery	146	WA	Caffe Appassionato	220
UT	Diamond Seal Inc	190	WA	Cleaning Consultant Services	152
UT	Express One	202	WA	ElDorado Stone	190
UT	Fan-A-Mania	462	WA	The Fourth R	142
UT	Hogi Yogi Sandwiches & Frozen Yogurt	348	WA	Jackpot Convenience Stores	224
UT	I N V U Portraits	280	WA	National Maintenance Contractors	156
UT	Kid To Kid	142	WA	Papa Murphy's	374
UT	Laser Chem "White Glove" Commercial Cleaning	154	WA	Pony Mailbox & Business Centers	204
UT	Mrs. Fields Cookies	298	WA	Reface It Kitchen Systems	182
UT	Nach-O Fast	340	WA	Shoe Stop	52
UT	Pretzel Time	306	WA	Tony Maroni's Famous Gourmet Pizza	370
UT	Pro Image	462	WA	World Inspection Network	384
			WI	Batteries Plus	64
			WI	Breadsmith	308

Franchises by Total Units

By a sample we may judge of the whole piece.
— MIGUEL DE CERVANTES

Appendix F is sorted by the total franchise units reported in 1998. Franchises with no entry are listed first, then from the fewest to the most.

Total Units	Franchise Name	Page	Total Units	Franchise Name	Page
	1 Potato 2	376		AccounTax Services	106
	2001 Flavors Plus Potatoes	312		Accounting Business Systems	106
	7-Eleven Convenience Stores	224		AccuStaff Inc	250
	A Buck Or Two Stores	426		Ace America's Cash Express	192
	A. J. Barnes Bicycle Emporium	456		Active Green + Ross Tire & Automotive Centre	92
	A. L. Van Houtte	376		Admiral of The Fleet Cruise Centers	470
	A Quicki Services	206		Admiral Subs	356
	A Shade Better	264		Adventures In Advertising	108
	A Wonderful Wedding	210		AeroWest & WestAir Sanitation Services	150
	AAMCO Transmissions	82		Affordable Car Rental	66
	Aaron's Rental Purchase	428		Air Brook Limousine	210
	ABC Seamless	186		Airbag Options	88
	Academy for Mathematics & Science	214		AirSoPure	452
	Academy of Learning	134		AJ Texas Hots	336

Total Units	Franchise Name	Page	Total Units	Franchise Name	Page
	The Book Rack	422		Carlson Wagonlit Travel	470
	Boomerang GameWare	434		Carpet Master	256
	Borvin Beverage	230		Carpet Network	256
	Boston Bartenders School Associates	116		CarpetMate	146
	Boston Pizza	362		Carvel Ice Cream Bakery	312
	The Brake Shop	74		Cash Converters USA	192
	Breadsmith	308		Castart	188
	Brew Thru	220		Castles Unlimited	388
	The BrickKicker	382		Caterina's	376
	Bridgeman's Restaurants Inc	398		Ceiling Doctor	176
	Brite Site	150		Century 21 Real Estate	388
	Brown's Chicken & Pasta	328		Certa Propainters Ltd	188
	Buddy's Bar-B-Q	354		Certicare	84
	Budget Car & Truck Rental	66		Certigard/Petro-Canada	88
	Building Blocks Franchise Corp	142		Champion Auto Stores	64
	Building Services of America	150		Champion Cleaners Franchise Inc.	196
	Building Systems Analysis Inc.	382		Charley's Steakery	412
	Bunnies Fresh Juice & Smoothie Bar	324		Checkcare Systems	192
	Buns Master Bakery Systems	308		Checkers Drive-In Restaurants	376
	Burger King (Canada)	332		Checkmate	250
	Buscemi's International	376		Chef's Fried Chicken	328
	Business Information Int'l Inc	108		Chelsea Street Pub & Grill	394
	Butterfields, Etc.	448		Chem-Dry Carpet/Upholstery (Canada)	146
	Buyer's Resource	386		Chemstation International	150
	Bw-3 Buffalo Wild Wings	328		Chesapeake Bagel Bakery	292
	Bw-3 Franchise Systems Inc	228		Chicago's Pizza	362
	By Owner Reality Network	386		Chicken Delight	328
	Cafe By George/Cookies By George	298		Children's Orchard	142
	Cafe La France	416		Chili Chompers	230
	Caffe Appassionato	220		Chip King	86
	Calculated Couples	194		Choice Hotels Intl	268
	California Closet Company	180		Churchs Chicken	328
	Candleman Corporation	448		Cindy's Cinnamon Rolls	296
	Candy Express	218		Cinema Grill	466
	Candy HQ/Sweets From Heaven	218		Classy Maids USA	166
	Canine Counselors	274		Clean 'N' Press America	196
	Cap'n Taco	340		The Cleaning Authority	166
	Capital Carpet Cleaning	146		Cleaning Consultant Services	152
	Captain D's Seafood	352		The Closet Factory	180
	Captain Tony's Pizza & Pasta Emporium	362		Closettec	180
	The Car Phone Store	428		Cluck-U Chicken	328
	The Car Wash Guys/Gals	94		The Coffee Beanery	220

Total Units	Franchise Name	Page
	EconoTax	200
	EcoSmarte Planet Friendly	442
	EDO Japan	408
	El Pollo Loco	340
	ElDorado Stone	190
	Elegance Jewelry	56
	Elephant House Inc	436
	Elmer's Pancake & Steak House	412
	Emack & Bolio's Ice Cream & Yogurt	312
	Emerald Green Lawn Care	162
	EndRust Auto Appearance Centers	70
	Energy Wise	152
	English Butler Canada	206
	Enviro Masters Lawn Care	162
	Envirobate	152
	EnviroFree Inspections	382
	Environmental Biotech	154
	Era Franchise Systems	388
	Erbert & Gerbert's Subs & Clubs	356
	Estrella Insurance	126
	Everlasting Tan Club	464
	ExecuTrain	116
	ExecuTrain Corp.	212
	Express Oil Change	60
	Express Personnel Services	246
	Expressions In Fabrics	258
	Fabri-Zone Cleaning Systems	146
	Family Pizza	364
	Famous Sam's Inc	410
	Faro's Franchise Systems	364
	Fast Bucks Development LLC	192
	Fast Eddie's	376
	FastFrame U S A	420
	FatBurger	332
	FCI Franchising Inc	64
	Figaro's Italian Kitchen	338
	Fire Defense Centers	452
	First Choice Haircutters (U.S.) Inc.	102
	First Optometry Eye Care Centers	240
	Firstat Nursing Services	248
	The Flag Shop	448
	Flamers Charbroiled Hamburgers & Chicken	332

Total Units	Franchise Name	Page
	Floor Coverings International	256
	For Olde Times Sake	436
	Fortune Personnel Consultants	244
	Four Seasons Sunrooms	190
	Four Star Pizza	364
	The Fourth R	142
	Fox's Pizza Den	364
	Franklin Traffic Service	126
	Friendly's Ice Cream Corporation	400
	Frozen Fusion Fruit Smoothies	320
	Fuddruckers	416
	Fudge Co.	218
	Furniture Medic	176
	FutureKids (Canada)	134
	FutureKids Inc	134
	GalaxSea Cruises & Tours	472
	Game Force Franchising	434
	Gateway Newstands	448
	GCO Carpet Outlet	256
	General Business Services	126
	General Nutrition Centers	226
	Genius Kid Academy	134
	Gent's Formal Wear	54
	Gigglebees	416
	Glamour Shots	280
	Glass Magnum	176
	The Goddard Schools	134
	Godfather's Pizza	364
	Goldberg's New York Bagels	292
	Golden Chick	330
	Golden Corral Family Steakhouse	412
	Golds Gym	234
	Golf Augusta Pro Shops	458
	Grand Rental Station/Taylor Rental	428
	Grandma Lee's Bakery Cafe	308
	Grease Monkey International	60
	The Great American Bagel	292
	Great American Cookie Company, Inc.	298
	Great Clips	102
	Great Earth Vitamins	226
	The Great Frame Up	420
	Great Outdoor Sub Shops	356

Total Units	Franchise Name	Page	Total Units	Franchise Name	Page
	Jimmy John's Gourmet Sandwich Shops	348		Le Print Express	286
	Joe Loue Tout Rent All	66		Leadership Management, Inc.	116
	Joey's Only Seafood Restaurant	418		Learning Express	136
	John Casablancas Modeling/Career Center	116		LedgerPlus	106
	John Simmons	448		Lifestyle Mobile Carpet Showroom	256
	Juice Connection	324		Lindelle Studios	280
	Juice World	230		Lindy – Gertie's	378
	Jungle Jim's Restaurants	400		Link Staffing Services	246
	Just Legs	52		Liqui-Green Lawn & Tree Care	162
	Just-A-Buck	426		Lisa's Tea Treasures	220
	K-Bob's Steakhouses	412		Little King	378
	KCS Applications	170		Little Scientists	136
	Kelsey's Restaurants	400		Living Lighting	258
	Kernels	228		Long John Silver's	352
	KFC	330		Longbranch Steakhouse & Saloon Inc	412
	Kiddie Academy International	134		Look No-Fault Auto Insurance Agencies	128
	Kiddie Kobbler	142		Lord's & Lady's Hair Salons	104
	Kids R Kids Quality Learning Centers	136		Lox of Bagels	294
	Kids Team	142		Lube Depot	60
	Kilwin's Chocolates Franchise	218		Maaco Auto Painting & Bodyworks	70
	Kinderdance International	138		Maaco Auto Painting & Bodyworks (Canada)	70
	King Bear Auto Service Centers	80		MacBirdie Golf Gifts	458
	Kirby Tours	472		The Mad Science Group	144
	Kitchen Tune-Up	182		Madame Et Monsieur	234
	Kitchen Wizards	182		Magic Wok	346
	KitchenPro	262		Magis Fund Raising Specialists	128
	Knights Franchise Systems Inc	270		Maid Brigade Services	166
	Knowledge Development Centers Inc	128		Mail Boxes Etc.	202
	Krispy Kreme Doughnuts	300		Mail Boxes Etc. (Canada)	202
	Kumon Math & Reading Center	216		Maintain Cleaning Systems	156
	Kwik Dry International	154		Mamma Ilardo's	338
	Kwik-Kopy Printing (Canada)	284		Management Recruiters	244
	L. A. Smoothie Healthmart & Cafe	226		Manchu Wok (U.S.)	346
	La Pizza Loca	366		Manhattan Bagel Co Inc	294
	La Salsa Fresh Mexican Grill	340		Manhattan Bagel Company	294
	La Smoothie Franchises Inc	324		Manufacturing Management Associates	128
	Labor Force	246		Marble Renewal	170
	Langenwalter Carpet Dyeing	146		Marble Slab Creamery	314
	Larry's Giant Subs	356		MarbleLife	170
	Last Flight Out	436		Marco's Pizza	366
	Le Croissant Shop	310		Martial Arts America	466
	Le Peep	418		Master Care	156

Total Units	Franchise Name	Page	Total Units	Franchise Name	Page
	Matco Tools	64		Naked Furniture	258
	MaxCare Professional Cleaning Systems	156		National Homecraft	156
	McBeans	222		National Hygiene/Lien	156
	McCoy's Cake & Pie Shop	310		National Maintenance Contractors	156
	McDonald's	334		National Property Inspections, Inc.	384
	Medicap Pharmacy	236		Nature's 10	442
	Men's Hair Now	104		Nevada Bob's Professional Golf Shops	458
	Merchant Advertising Systems	108		New Horizons Computer Learning Center	212
	Merlin's Muffler & Brake	76		New York Fries	378
	Metropolitan Institute of Health Careers	116		Nitro-Green Professional Lawn & Tree Care	162
	Mickey Finn's Sports Cafe	418		Norrell Services	254
	Mikes Restaurants	400		Norwalk – The Furniture Idea	258
	Milex Tune-Ups And Brakes	84		Nu-Look 1-Hr. Cleaners	198
	Mini Maid Service Systems Of Canada	168		Nutrite	164
	Minute Muffler And Brake	76		Nutter's Bulk And Natural Foods	226
	Minuteman Press International	286		O.P.E.N. Cleaning Systems	156
	Miracle Auto Painting & Body Repair	72		The Office Alternative	128
	Miracle Method	182		Oh Mighty Ices Franchise Corp	320
	Miracle-Ear	238		Oil Butler International	60
	Mister Mobile On-Site Oil Changes	60		Oil Can Henry's International	62
	Mister Money – USA	128		Old Fashioned Egg Cream Co Inc	378
	Mmmarvellous Mmmuffins	304		Once Upon A Child	144
	Mobil Ambition USA LC	108		One Hour Martinizing	198
	Model Managers Int'l	116		One Stop Undercar	78
	Moe's Italian Sandwiches	348		Open Pantry Food Marts	230
	Molly Maid	168		Option Care	238
	Mom's Bake At Home Pizza	374		Orange Julius Canada Inc.	322
	Money Concepts (Canada)	114		Our Weigh	242
	Monsieur Felix & Mr. Norton Cookies	298		P.J.'S Coffee & Tea	222
	The More Space Place	264		Paceco Financial Services	114
	Motel 6	270		Pack Mart	202
	Mountain Mike's Pizza	366		Padgett Business Services	106
	Moxie Java	222		Pak Mail Centers (Canada)	204
	Mr. Front-End	76		Panchero's Mexican Grill	342
	Mr. GoodCents Subs & Pasta	358		Panda Shoes	52
	Mr. Jim's Pizza	366		Papa Murphy's	374
	Mr. Rooter Corp.	178		Papyrus	450
	Mrs. Fields Cookies	298		Paradise Bakery & Cafe	310
	My Favorite Muffin	304		Parcel Plus	204
	My Friend's Place	378		Party City Corp	444
	Nach-O Fast	340		Party Land Inc	444
	Nacho Nana's Worldwide Inc	340		Pasta To Go	378

Total Units	Franchise Name	Page
	Pastel's Cafe	380
	Payless Car Rental System	66
	Paystation	452
	Pearle Vision Center	240
	Pee Wee Workout	138
	Penn Stations East Coast Subs	358
	Pepe's Mexican Restaurant	406
	Performance Marketing Concepts Inc	110
	Permacrete Systems	190
	PestMaster Services	384
	Pet Habitat	276
	The Pet Pantry International	276
	Pet Valu	276
	Petland	276
	Petro Stopping Centers	96
	Petro's Chili & Chips	380
	Pets Are Inn	276
	Peyron Tax Service	200
	Picture Hits	280
	Pillar To Post	384
	Pinch-A-Penny	426
	Pizza Delight	368
	Pizza Factory Inc.	368
	Pizza Inn Inc	368
	Pizza Man – He Delivers	368
	Pizza Nova	368
	Pizza Pizza Limited	368
	Pizzas By Marchelloni	370
	Planet Earth Recycling	96
	Play It Again Sports	456
	Points for Profits	110
	Ponderosa Steakhouse	412
	Pony Mailbox & Business Centers	204
	Popeyes Chicken & Biscuits	330
	Port of Subs	358
	Postal Annex+	204
	Postnet Postal & Business Centers	204
	The Potato Sack	230
	Potts Doggie Shop	336
	Practical Rent A Car	66
	Precision Tune Auto Care	84
	Pressed 4 Time	198

Total Units	Franchise Name	Page
	Pretzel Time	306
	The Pretzel Twister	306
	PretzelMaker	306
	Pro Image	462
	Pro-Cuts	104
	Pro-Tect	384
	Professional Carpet Systems	148
	Professional House Doctors, Inc.	384
	Professional Polish	158
	Profit-On-Hold	110
	ProForce USA	158
	Proforma	286
	Profusion Systems	170
	Property Damage Appraisers	178
	ProShred Security	452
	Proventure Business Group, Inc.	112
	PuckMasters Hockey Training Centers	466
	Pure Water Ultima	446
	Purified Water To Go	446
	PuroFirst International	158
	Q Lube	62
	Quizno's Classic Subs	358
	RACS International	158
	Radio Shack International	428
	RadioShack	428
	Radisson Hotels Worldwide	272
	Rainbow International Carpet Care & Restoration Specialist	148
	Ramada Franchise Canada, Inc.	272
	Ramada Franchise Systems Inc	272
	Re-Bath	172
	Re/Max International	390
	Red Hot & Blue	418
	Reface It Kitchen Systems	182
	Relax The Back Franchising Co	238
	Remedy Intelligent Staffing	250
	Renaissance Executive Forums	118
	Rennsport	96
	Rental Guide	290
	Renzios	380
	Rich's Chimney Fix-It	184
	Rider's Hobby Shops	434

Total Units	Franchise Name	Page	Total Units	Franchise Name	Page
	Rita's Italian Ice	322		Signal Graphics Printing	286
	Rocky Mountain Chocolate Factory	218		Signs & More In 24	120
	Rodan Jewellers/Simply Charming	56		Signs Now	120
	Roli Boli	380		Sir Speedy	286
	Roll-A-Way	452		Sir Speedy (Canada)	286
	Ronzio Pizza	370		Sirloin Stockade Family Steakhouse	412
	Room-Mate Referral Service Centers	390		Slats Blind Cleaning	178
	Roto-Rooter	178		Slimmer Image Weight Loss Clinics	242
	Roto-Static International	148		SlumberLand International	258
	Round Table Franchise Corp	370		Smitty's	402
	Ruffin's Pet Centres	276		Smoothie King	322
	Rynker Ribbon Xchange Inc.	128		Snap-On Tools	438
	Safe-T-Child	144		Snappy Tomato Pizza	370
	Saint Cinnamon Bake Shoppe	296		Snelling Personnel Services	246
	Sale By Owner Systems	390		Sobik's Subs	358
	Sandler Sales Institute	118		Soccer Post Intl Franchise Corp	456
	The Sandwich Board	348		The Soda Fountain	396
	Sandwich Tree Restaurants	350		Soft Touch Interiors	258
	Sanford Rose Associates	244		Sonitrol	454
	SaniBrite	158		Southern Maid Donuts	302
	Schlotzsky's Deli	350		Special Delivery Photos Inc	280
	Scoopers Ice Cream	314		Speedee Oil Change & Tune-Up	62
	Screen Printing USA	286		Speedy Printing Centers	288
	The Screenmobile	184		Speedy Transmission Centers	82
	SealMaster	158		The Sport Shoe	456
	Sears Driver Training	216		The Sports Section	282
	The Second Cup	222		Spot-Not Car Washes	94
	Select Sandwich	350		Spring Crest Drapery Centers	262
	Seniors for Seniors/Seniors for Business	254		St. Jerome Restaurant	402
	Serv U-1st	158		Staff Builders Home Health Care	248
	Service Center	130		Star Mart	230
	Service One	158		The Steak Escape	354
	Service-Tech Corporation	160		Steak 'N Shake	354
	ServiceMaster Residential/Commercial (Canada)	168		Steak-Out	232
	ServiceMaster Residential/Commercial	168		Steaks To Go	354
	ServPro	160		Steam Brothers Professional Cleaning & Restoration	148
	Shine Factory	94		Steamatic	148
	Shoe Stop	52		Sterling Optical	240
	Shooters International Inc	418		Stork News of America	144
	Showhomes of America	390		Street Corner News	290
	Shred-It	454		Stretch-N-Grow of America	140

Total Units	Franchise Name	Page	Total Units	Franchise Name	Page
	Strings Italian Cafe	404		Thundercloud Subs	360
	Strokes	460		Tilden for Brakes Car Care Centers	74
	Stuckey's Express	228		Tim Hortons	310
	Sub Station Ii	358		Tippy's Taco House	342
	Submarina	358		Tire Time Rentals	92
	Subs Plus	360		Today's Temporary	252
	Successful Introduction	194		Tony Maroni's Famous Gourmet Pizza	370
	Successories	450		Total Medical Compliance	238
	Sunbanque Island Tanning	464		Totally Wireless	428
	Sunbelt Business Brokers	112		Tower Cleaning Systems	160
	Sunshine Cafe	418		TPI Travel Services	472
	Super 8 Motels Inc	272		Tradebank International	130
	Super Lawns	164		Transmission USA	82
	Superglass Windshield Repair	86		Travel Professionals International	472
	Superior Walls of America	190		TRC Staffing Services	252
	Surface Specialists Systems	172		Treats	310
	Sutton Homes Franchising Corp	238		Tri-Color Carpet Dyeing And Cleaning	148
	Swisher Hygiene	160		Trimark	110
	Swiss Chalet/Swiss Chalet Plus Restaurants	410		Triple Check Income Tax Service	200
	Sylvan Learning Centers	216		Tropi-Tan, Inc.	464
	Taco Bell Corp	342		Tropik Sun Fruit & Nut	228
	Taco Hut America Inc	406		Truck Options	58
	Taco John's Int'l Inc	342		Truly Nolen	178
	Taco Villa	342		Tubby's Submarines	360
	Tacotime	342		Tuffy Auto Service Centers	88
	Talent Tree Staffing Services	250		Tumbleweed LLC	414
	TCBY Treats	318		Tutor Time Child Care Learning Center	132
	Team Golf Corp	460		Two Men And A Truck	210
	Team Tires Plus Ltd	92		U.S. Franchise Systems	272
	TechStaff	250		UncleSam's Convenient Store	224
	Tee Signs Plus	110		Uniglobe Travel	472
	Tempaco	438		Unishippers Association	204
	Tenniskids	140		United Capital Mortgage Assistance	192
	Terminix Termite & Pest Control	384		United Check Cashing	192
	Terra Systems	164		United Energy Partners	190
	Terri's Consign & Design Furnishings	258		United Printing Unlimited	288
	TFM	440		United Studios of Self-Defense Inc	468
	TFM/Top Forty	440		Universal Business Consultants	130
	TGI Friday's Hospitality Worldwide	418		USA Baby	144
	Themed Miniature Golf Courses	468		V.I.D.E.O. Security Process (VSP)	454
	Thrifty Car Rental (Canada)	68		Val-Pak Direct Marketing	110
	Thrifty Rent-A-Car	68		Valet Express	198

Total Units	Franchise Name	Page	Total Units	Franchise Name	Page
	Valvoline Instant Oil Change	62		Zuzu Mexican Food	406
	Victory Lane Quick Oil Change	62	0	Copy Club	284
	Video Data Services	428	0	The Resume Hut	254
	Video Impact	430	1	Confidential Business Connection	112
	Villa Pizza	372	1	Creative Cakery	308
	Vinylgraphics Custom Sign Centres	122	1	Pro Golf Discount	460
	VR Business Brokers	112	1	Schumacher Garage Door Franchise	186
	Wallpapers To Go	264	2	American Institute of Small Business	214
	Ward's Restaurants	418	2	Dec-K-ing	188
	We Care Hair	104	2	Dent Zone	70
	We Care Home Health Services	248	2	Joy Carpet Dry Cleaning	146
	Wedding Gown Specialists/Restoration	198	2	PC Professor	212
	Wee Watch Private Home Day Care	132	2	Pre-Fit	140
	Weed Man	164	2	Rent 'N Drive	68
	Wendy's Restaurants of Canada Inc.	334	2	Totally Kool	52
	Western Medical Services	248	3	Brown Baggers	348
	Western Sizzlin'	414	3	Hydro Physics Pipe Inspection	154
	Western Steer Family Steakhouse/WSMP	414	3	Laund-Ur-Mutt	274
	Wetzel's Pretzels	306	3	Odyssey Art Centers	136
	Wheelchair Getaways	68	3	The Peanut Club	144
	White Hen Pantry	232	3	Sports Fantastic	462
	Wicks 'N' Sticks	450	3	Turbo Management Systems Ltd.	118
	Wienerschnitzel	336	4	Bourbon Street Candy Company	218
	Wild Bird Centers of America, Inc.	278	4	C. B. S. Interactive Multimedia	212
	Wild Bird Marketplace	278	4	Chowderhead's Seafood Restaurants	352
	Wild Birds Unlimited	278	4	Empowered Womens Golf Shops	458
	Window Perfect	262	4	Gelato Amare	314
	Window & Wall Creations	262	4	Naut-A-Care Marine Services, Inc.	96
	Wing Machine	330	4	The Sleeping Giant Within Inc.	216
	Woody's Wood Shops	460	4	True Friends	278
	World Inspection Network	384	5	Arodal	150
	World Trade Network	130	5	PersoNet-The Personnel Network	254
	Worldwide Information Services	424	5	Re Tool	438
	Yard Cards	450	5	The T O L Franchise Group	100
	Yaya's Flame Broiled Chicken	330	5	Tan World	464
	Yellow Jacket Direct Mail Advertising	110	5	U-Wash Doggie	274
	Yesterday's Furniture & Country Store	260	6	LawCorps Legal Staffing Services	250
	Yipes Stripes	98	6	Merle Norman Cosmetics	100
	Your Office USA	130	6	Sox Appeal	52
	Z-Teca	344	7	Between Rounds Bagel Deli & Bakery	292
	Zero's Subs	360	7	Ecomat	196
	Ziebart Tidycar	94	7	Gymsters, Inc.	138

Total Units	Franchise Name	Page	Total Units	Franchise Name	Page
7	Homewatch Caregivers	206	21	P.A.M.'S Coffee & Tea Co.	222
7	Malibu Gallery	420	21	Professional Dynametric Programs/PDP	116
7	Perfumes Etc.	100	21	The Screen Machine	178
8	Brake Centers of America	74	21	Sport Clips	104
8	X-Bankers Check Cashing	192	21	The Visual Image	282
9	Cartex Limited	88	21	Workenders	168
10	Bahama Buck's Original Shaved Ice Co.	320	22	Diamond Seal Inc	190
10	Clintar Groundskeeping Services	162	22	PrideStaff	250
10	Farmer Boys Hamburgers	332	23	Acctcorp	106
10	InnSuites Hotels	270	23	Lamar's Donuts	300
10	Saf-T Auto Centers	80	23	National Tenant Network	390
11	BMR Bath Master Reglazing Ltd.	170	23	Pretzels Plus	306
12	MaidPro	166	24	DuctBusters/Buster Enterprises Inc	176
12	Shefield Gourmet	222	25	Biologix	150
13	Elliott & Company Appraisers	388	25	Buffalo Wings & Rings	398
13	The Great Wilderness Company, Inc.	442	25	Tunex International, Inc.	84
13	Power Smoothie	322	25	Value Line Maintenance Systems	160
13	Z Land, Inc.	124	26	Baby's Away	132
14	Computer U Learning Centers	212	26	International News	290
14	Elephant Walk Gift Galleries	436	26	London Cleaners	198
15	Donut Inn	300	27	ELS Language Centers	214
15	Dynamic Golf Centres	458	28	Boz Hot Dogs	336
15	Full Circle Image	424	28	Bruster's Old-Fashioned Ice Cream & Yogurt	312
15	Morrone's Italian Ices	314	28	Kid To Kid	142
16	Good For You! Fruit & Yogurt Ltd.	318	28	Stuft Pizza & Brewing	370
16	Window Butler	168	28	Talking Book World	422
16	Women's Health Boutique	238	29	Bright Beginnings	108
17	21st Century Auto Alliance	96	29	The Master Mechanic	80
17	Nationwide Floor & Window Coverings	256	30	Citizens Against Crime	214
17	The Nature of Things Store	442	31	Airbag Service	88
17	TechnoKids	136	32	Easyriders	90
18	Cheeburger Cheeburger	332	32	Field of Dreams	462
18	Safe Not Sorry	452	33	Deckare Services	176
19	The Bone Appetit Bakery	276	33	Dent Doctor	70
19	Jacadi	52	33	Fortune Practice Management	126
19	Palace Entertainment & Bullwinkles Restaurant	402	34	Ashley Avery's Collectables	436
20	American Wholesale Thermographers	284	34	Ca$h Plus	192
20	Edelweiss Deli Express/Sub Express	348	34	Sports Traders	456
20	Johnny's New York Style Pizza	366	34	Window Gang	160
20	Kennedy Transmission	82	35	Her Real Estate	390
21	Fan-A-Mania	462	35	I N V U Portraits	280
			35	Kohr Bros. Frozen Custard	320

Total Units	Franchise Name	Page	Total Units	Franchise Name	Page
35	Petrucci's Ice Cream Co.	314	60	Aero-Colours	88
36	Express One	202	60	Straw Hat Pizza	370
36	LubePros International, Inc.	60	62	Bath Fitter	182
38	Bullets Corporation of America, Inc.	332	62	Shefield & Sons	450
38	Nutri-Lawn, Ecology-Friendly Lawn Care	164	63	Abra Auto Body & Glass	70
39	City Looks Salons Int'l	102	63	Its About Games	434
39	Lentz USA Service Centers	76	65	The Buyer's Agent	386
40	Country Clutter	436	65	Music-Go-Round	440
40	Electronic Tax Filers	200	66	Criterium Engineers	382
40	U.S. Lawns	164	67	Computer Doctor	424
41	Buffalo's Cafe	398	67	Jumbo Video	440
41	The Gourmet Cup	220	69	Lemon Tree – A Unisex Haircutting Est.	104
41	Laser Chem "White Glove" Commercial Cleaning	154	69	Verlo Mattress Factory Stores	260
41	Medichair	238	70	Millicare Environmental Services	156
41	Top Value Muffler & Brake Shops	78	71	Bingo Bugle Newspaper	290
42	Signs First	120	72	Express Mart Convenient Store	224
43	Made In Japan, Teriyaki Experience	346	72	Yogi Bear Jellystone Park Camp-Resorts	266
43	New York Burrito-Gourmet Wraps	340	73	Health Force	248
43	Pizza Pit	368	74	Lemstone Books	422
44	Creative Colors Int'l Inc	174	77	Fabutan Sun Tan Studios	464
45	Aire-Master of America	150	79	Little Professor Book Centers	422
46	Home Helpers	206	80	Signs By Tomorrow	120
47	Foliage Design Systems	432	81	Philly Connection	326
47	Quikava – Coffees By Chock Full O' Nuts	222	82	Back Yard Burgers	332
47	Resort Maps Franchise Inc	110	83	Empress Travel	472
47	Sangsters Health Centres	226	83	Monsieur Muffler	76
47	Tire Warehouse Central	92	86	Lee Myles Transmissions	82
49	Las Vegas Golf & Tennis	458	87	Mister Transmission	82
51	CottageCare	166	88	Fast-Fix Jewelry Repairs	56
51	DentPro	70	89	The Pizza Ranch	368
51	Naturalawn of America	162	90	United Consumers Club	210
52	Aim Mail Centers	202	90	Zuka Juice	324
52	Buck's Pizza Franchising, Inc.	362	91	St. Hubert Bar-B-Q	392
52	Framing & Art Centres	420	93	Everything Yogurt & Salad Cafe	318
52	LazerQuick	286	94	Frullati Cafe	348
52	One Hour Motophoto & Portrait Studio (Canada)	280	94	Primrose Schools	136
55	Craters & Freighters	202	95	Kitchen Solvers	182
55	Empire Business Brokers	112	97	Eagle Cleaners	196
56	Nancy's Pizzeria	366	97	Snip N' Clip Haircut Shops	104
57	Group Trans-Action Brokerage Services	388	100	Quik Internet	124
58	Patty-Cakes International, Inc.	144	101	Algonquin Travel	470
			101	Outdoor Connection	466

Total Units	Franchise Name	Page	Total Units	Franchise Name	Page
102	Jackpot Convenience Stores	224	233	Gingiss Formalwear	54
103	United States Seamless, Inc.	186	239	Great Steak & Potato Company	326
110	American Lenders Service Co.	114	239	Robin's Donuts	300
111	East of Chicago Pizza Company	364	247	Midas (Canada)	76
112	NurseFinders	248	251	Mazzio's Pizza	366
113	Barnie's Coffee & Tea Company	220	258	M & M Meat Shops	230
113	Saint Louis Bread Company, Inc.	310	259	Bojangles' Restaurants Inc	328
115	The Little Gym International, Inc.	138	265	World Gym	234
120	Taco Mayo	342	266	Hospitality International	270
127	Conroys 1-800-Flowers	432	280	Gloria Jean's Gourmet Coffees	220
127	Dr. Vinyl & Assoc.	174	281	Cici's Pizza	362
129	Damon's International	398	282	Colors On Parade	94
130	Fosters Freeze, Incorporated	316	282	Heaven's Best	146
130	Tinder Box International	436	296	Amerispec Home Inspection Service	382
131	Great Harvest Bread Co.	308	300	Home & Garden Showplace	162
132	Mr. Hero	358	320	Candy Bouquet International	218
133	Golf USA	458	321	CD Warehouse	440
135	Donatos Pizza	362	350	Pak Mail Centers of America	204
136	L A Weight Loss Centers Inc	242	354	The Krystal Company	334
137	Paper Warehouse Franchising Inc	444	360	Lawn Doctor	162
139	MicroPlay Video Games	434	364	The Maids	168
146	Maid To Perfection	166	380	One Hour Motophoto & Portrait Studio	280
146	The Taco Maker	342	380	Radisson Hotels International	270
146	Travelcenters of America, Inc.	96	390	Hungry Howie's Pizza & Subs	366
149	Mighty Distribution System of America Inc	64	403	CruiseOne/The Travel Company	470
153	Interstate Dairy Queen	316	406	Gymboree	138
156	Budget Blinds	262	408	Worldwide Refinishing Systems, Inc.	182
161	The Great Canadian Bagel	292	424	FastSigns	120
164	Pizzeria Uno Chicago Bar & Grill	370	425	Sign-A-Rama	120
172	Sparkle Wash	160	449	Golden Corral Franchising Systems Inc	412
175	Lady of America	234	450	Rent-A-Wreck of America	68
178	Perma Glaze	170	450	U-Save Auto Rental of America Inc	68
181	Cookie Bouquet/Cookies By Design	298	454	Packaging And Shipping Specialist	202
182	Car-X Muffler & Brake	76	486	Novus Windshield Repair	86
183	House Doctors Handyman Service	176	497	Perkins Family Restaurants	402
186	Putt-Putt Golf Courses Of America	468	520	Kampgrounds of America/KOA	266
187	Perma Ceram Enterprises	182	570	Travel Network	472
192	Deck The Walls	420	783	Kwik Kopy Printing	284
194	Batteries Plus	64	836	Tom's Foods	228
197	Dunhill Staffing Systems, Inc.	246	889	Sbarro, The Italian Eatery	338
210	Cruise Holidays International	470	891	Cost Cutters Family Hair Care	102
211	Village Inn Restaurants	402	893	Meineke Discount Mufflers	76

Total Units	Franchise Name	Page	Total Units	Franchise Name	Page
1079	McDonald's Restaurants of Canada Limited	334	2862	Jackson Hewitt Tax Service	200
1222	Merry Maids	168	3912	Chem-Dry Carpet/Drapery/Upholstery	146
1248	The Medicine Shoppe	238	4920	Yogen Fruz Worldwide	318
1306	Fantastic Sams	102	5080	Jazzercise Inc	234
1901	Sonic Drive-In	334	7035	Jani-King International	154
2025	Blimpie Subs And Salads	356	8800	H & R Block	200
2042	CleanNet USA	152	13539	Subway	360
2686	Hardee's Food Systems	332			

Franchises by Royalty Percentages

I have known no man of genius who had not to pay ... for what the gods had given him.
— Sir Max Beerbohm

Appendix G is sorted by the average royalty. Franchises with no entry are listed first. Key: /wk = per week; /mo = per month; /qtr = per quarter; /yr = per year; /unit = per unit.

Royalty	Franchise Name	Page	Royalty	Franchise Name	Page
	21st Century Auto Alliance	96	0	Almost Heaven, Ltd.	438
	American Lenders Service Co.	114	0	American Institute of Small Business	214
	Bullets Corporation of America, Inc.	332	0	Appletree Art Publishers	420
	Empress Travel	472	0	Aqua Bio Technologies	150
	Glamour Shots	280	0	Bath Fitter	182
	H & R Block	200	0	Ben & Jerry's	312
	Liqui-Green Lawn & Tree Care	162	0	Biozhem Skin Care Centers	100
	Open Pantry Food Marts	230	0	BladeRunner Mobile Sharpening	176
	Petro Stopping Centers	96	0	Brew Thru	220
	Travelcenters of America, Inc.	96	0	Business Information Int'l Inc	108
	United States Seamless, Inc.	186	0	Calculated Couples	194
0	Academy of Learning	134	0	Candy Bouquet International	218
0	Affordable Car Rental	66	0	Capital Carpet Cleaning	146
0	AirSoPure	452	0	Champion Auto Stores	64

Royalty	Franchise Name	Page	Royalty	Franchise Name	Page
0	Citizens Against Crime	214	0	Worldwide Information Services	424
0	Cleaning Consultant Services	152	0	Z Land, Inc.	124
0	Custom Auto Restoration Systems	70	$0.5–1K	Stork News of America	144
0	Dec-K-ing	188	$0.50/ad	Trimark	110
0	Diet Light Weight Loss System	242	$1.55/gal.	Carvel Ice Cream Bakery	312
0	EcoSmarte Planet Friendly	442	10	Quik Internet	124
0	Elegance Jewelry	56	10% + $360	FutureKids (Canada)	134
0	Elephant House Inc	436	$100/mo	Bathcrest	170
0	Emack & Bolio's Ice Cream & Yogurt	312	$100/mo	Dynamark Security Centers	452
0	EndRust Auto Appearance Centers	70	$100/mo.	Stretch-N-Grow of America	140
0	FCI Franchising Inc	64	$100/wk	EnviroFree Inspections	382
0	Four Seasons Sunrooms	190	$105/mo	CarpetMate	146
0	Happy & Healthy Products	320	$110/mo	Langenwalter Carpet Dyeing	146
0	Health Mart	236	$12/audit	Bevinco	126
0	Home & Garden Showplace	162	$120/mo+5%	The Fourth R	142
0	I.B. Nuts & Fruit Too	228	$140/wk	Haynes Pet Centre Franchising Inc	274
0	I Can't Believe It's Yogurt	318	$15/coupon	Yellow Jacket Direct Mail Advertising	110
0	Leadership Management, Inc.	116	$150/mo	Accounting Business Systems	106
0	Lisa's Tea Treasures	220	$150/mo	Empire Business Brokers	112
0	Lox of Bagels	294	$175/mo	Kwik Dry International	154
0	Matco Tools	64	$175/mo	Service One	158
0	Merchant Advertising Systems	108	$191/wk	Fantastic Sams	102
0	Merle Norman Cosmetics	100	$192/mo	Chem-Dry Carpet/Drapery/Upholstery	146
0	Minute Muffler And Brake	76	$1K/mo	Le Print Express	286
0	Mom's Bake At Home Pizza	374	$1K/mo	Rich's Chimney Fix-It	184
0	Moxie Java	222	$2–750/mo	GalaxSea Cruises & Tours	472
0	Norwalk – The Furniture Idea	258	$200–400/wk	Captain Tony's Pizza & Pasta Emporium	362
0	Oh Mighty Ices Franchise Corp	320	$200/mo	Fox's Pizza Den	364
0	Our Weigh	242	$240/wk	Grower Direct Fresh Cut Flowers	432
0	Packaging And Shipping Specialist	202	$2400/yr	J.W. Tumbles, A Children's Gym	138
0	Paystation	452	$25/liner	Re-Bath	172
0	Perma Ceram Enterprises	182	$250/mo	Stuckey's Express	228
0	The Pet Pantry International	276	$29/student	Kumon Math & Reading Center	216
0	Pet Valu	276	$290/mo	Chem-Dry Carpet/Upholstery (Canada)	146
0	Points for Profits	110	3%/$300	Insulated Dry Roof Systems	190
0	Pure Water Ultima	446	3–5K	Hungry Howie's Pizza & Subs	366
0	Radio Shack International	428	3–6K/yr	Sunbelt Business Brokers	112
0	RadioShack	428	3.5%/$300/mo	Pressed 4 Time	198
0	Roll-A-Way	452	$3.5K/yr	Nutrite	164
0	Southern Maid Donuts	302	$300	Cartex Limited	88
0	The Sports Section	282	$300/mo	Madame Et Monsieur	234
0	Val-Pak Direct Marketing	110	$350–750/mo		
0	The Visual Image	282		Travel Network	472

Royalty	Franchise Name	Page	Royalty	Franchise Name	Page
$350/mo	Tri-Color Carpet Dyeing And Cleaning	148	7%/$300/mo	World Inspection Network	384
$350/yr	KCS Applications	170	7%/$350	Little Scientists	136
$375/qtr	International Mergers & Acquisitions	112	$700/mo	The Car Wash Guys/Gals	94
$3K/yr	Pony Mailbox & Business Centers	204	$75	TPI Travel Services	472
4%/$100/wk	Hollywood Weight Loss Centre	242	$75/mo	The Book Rack	422
4%/$1,333/mo	Truck Options	58	750/yr	Video Data Services	428
4%/$15/wk	Comprehensive Business Services	126	8%/$200 min	Elliott & Company Appraisers	388
4%/$200	ApparelMaster USA	196	8%/$75/wk	Diet Center Worldwide	242
4%/$8K min	Wild Birds Unlimited	278	$80/mo	Heaven's Best	146
4.5%/$250/W	The More Space Place	264	$800/vehcl	Weed Man	164
4.5K	Street Corner News	290	$900/mo	Everlasting Tan Club	464
40/Sign/yr	Tee Signs Plus	110	$908	Sandler Sales Institute	118
$400–1K/mo	Decorating Den Painting & Home Imp	188	$95/wk	Altracolor Systems	88
$46.50/unit	Miracle-Ear	238	Fixed	The Resume Hut	254
5%/$200/mo	BMR Bath Master Reglazing Ltd.	170	Flat	Group Trans-Action Brokerage Services	388
5%/$45/wk	Floor Coverings International	256	Flat	My Friend's Place	378
5%/$500	LazerQuick	286	Flat/Car	Practical Rent A Car	66
5%/$500	Yipes Stripes	98	N/A	Cash Converters USA	192
5%/$750 min	Ace America's Cash Express	192	N/A	Comet One-Hour Cleaners	196
5%/$9K/yr	The Better Back Store	236	N/A	Perma Glaze	170
5% or $175/wk			N/A	Themed Miniature Golf Courses	468
	Eagle Cleaners	196	N/A	Tradebank International	130
$50/mo	Snap-On Tools	438	to 1K/mo	Certa Propainters Ltd	188
$500/mo	AJ Texas Hots	336	Var.	7-Eleven Convenience Stores	224
$500/mo	Game Force Franchising	434	Var.	The Car Phone Store	428
$500/mo	Naut-A-Care Marine Services, Inc.	96	Var.	Carlson Wagonlit Travel	470
$500/mo	Saf-T Auto Centers	80	Var.	Castart	188
$500/mo	Sports Traders	456	Var.	Certicare	84
$550/van/yr	Wheelchair Getaways	68	Var.	Commission Express	126
$5K/mo	IMBC	124	Var.	East Shore Athletic Club	234
6%/$250 min	ComputerTots/Computer Explorers	134	Var.	FutureKids Inc	134
6%/$30/Car	Rent-A-Wreck of America	68	Var.	Golds Gym	234
6%/$350/wk	Tilden for Brakes Car Care Centers	74	Var.	Health Force	248
$6.5K/yr	World Gym	234	Var.	Home Guide Magazine	290
$.6/unit	Dealer Specialties Int'l Inc	96	Var.	Jay Roberts & Associates	128
$600–1K	Mobil Ambition USA LC	108	Var.	Link Staffing Services	246
$600/mo	Rynker Ribbon Xchange Inc.	128	Var.	Money Concepts (Canada)	114
7%	Arodal	150	Var.	National Hygiene/Lien	156
7%/$150	American Mobile Sound	208	Var.	Norrell Services	254
7%/$150/wk	Paceco Financial Services	114	Var.	Option Care	238
7%/$200	Pillar To Post	384	Var.	PersoNet – The Personnel Network	254
7%/$200 min	Furniture Medic	176	Var.	PrideStaff	250
7%/$250	Amerispec Home Inspection Service	382	Var.	Re/Max International	390

Royalty	Franchise Name	Page	Royalty	Franchise Name	Page
Var.	Remedy Intelligent Staffing	250	2–3% gross	Western Sizzlin'	414
Var.	Rental Guide	290	2.5%	Tom's Foods	228
Var.	Roto-Rooter	178	2.5%/.5%	J. D. Byrider Systems	90
Var.	Staff Builders Home Health Care	248	2.5%	Hobbytown USA	434
Var.	Team Golf Corp	460	2.5%	Le Peep	418
Var.	Today's Temporary	252	2.5%	Sonitrol	454
Var.	Triple Check Income Tax Service	200	2.5%	Terri's Consign & Design Furnishings	258
Var.	U-Save Auto Rental of America Inc	68	0.5–5%	Culligan Water Conditioning	446
Var.	Franklin Traffic Service	126	2.5–3%	Pro Golf Discount	460
0.2% volumn	United Check Cashing	192	0–6%	Pro-Cuts	104
0.3–0.5%	Firstat Nursing Services	248	1–5%	Aim Mail Centers	202
0.50%	Admiral of The Fleet Cruise Centers	470	1–5%	Better Homes & Gardens Real Estate Service	386
0.50%	Jackpot Convenience Stores	224	1–5%	Sonic Drive-In	334
1–0%	Strokes	460	2–4%	Doubletree Hotel Systems	268
0.2–1%	Uniglobe Travel	472	2–4%	Hubb's Pub	416
0.5–1%	Baskin-Robbins USA Co	312	2–4%	Medicap Pharmacy	236
1%	Baby News Childrens Stores	142	3%	Arctic Circle	320
1%	Baskin-Robbins Canada	312	3%	Beneficial Health & Beauty	100
1%	Cruise Holidays International	470	3%	Boomerang GameWare	434
1%	Cruise Lines Reservation Center	470	3%	Buck's Pizza Franchising, Inc.	362
1%	Cruise Vacations	470	3%	Captain D's Seafood	352
1%	Decor-At-Your-Door International	258	3%	Cinema Grill	466
1.3%	Grand Rental Station/Taylor Rental	428	3%	CleanNet USA	152
1.5%	Crestcom International, Ltd.	214	3%	Computer Doctor	424
2%	Big O Tires	92	3%	Computer Renaissance	424
2%	Bridgeman's Restaurants Inc	398	3%	Condotels	470
2%	Buscemi's International	376	3%	Connect.Ad	108
2%	Golf USA	458	3%	Custom Homewatch International	452
2%	Infinity Video Productions Inc	280	3%	Dollar Discount Stores	426
2%	International Golf	458	3%	Dynamic Golf Centres	458
2%	Nevada Bob's Professional Golf Shops	458	3%	Easyriders	90
2%	Nu-Look 1-Hr. Cleaners	198	3%	Empowered Womens Golf Shops	458
2%	Perfumes Etc.	100	3%	Environmental Biotech	154
2%	Shefield & Sons	450	3%	Fudge Co.	218
2%	Straw Hat Pizza	370	3%	Gateway Newstands	448
2%	Successories	450	3%	Homeowners Concept	390
2%	Total Medical Compliance	238	3%	IncrediPet	276
2–2.4%	Hq Business Centers	126	3%	InnSuites Hotels	270
0–5%	Humpty's Family Restaurant	400	3%	International News	290
0–5%	Signal Graphics Printing	286	3%	K-Bob's Steakhouses	412
1–4%	Bagelsmith Restaurants & Food Stores	292	3%	Las Vegas Golf & Tennis	458
1–4%	InHouse Travel Group LLC	472	3%	Little Professor Book Centers	422
1–4%	Outdoor Connection	466	3%	M & M Meat Shops	230

Royalty	Franchise Name	Page	Royalty	Franchise Name	Page
3%	Mazzio's Pizza	366	3.5%	Expressions In Fabrics	258
3%	Music-Go-Round	440	3.5%	The Ground Round Restaurant	394
3%	Planet Earth Recycling	96	3.5%	Rider's Hobby Shops	434
3%	Postnet Postal & Business Centers	204	2.5–5%	Signs By Tomorrow	120
3%	Profit-On-Hold	110	3–4.5%	Tim Hortons	310
3%	ProForce USA	158	3–4.5%	Wild Bird Centers of America, Inc.	278
3%	Putt-Putt Golf Courses Of America	468	2–6%	Coit Services	152
3%	Sirloin Stockade Family Steakhouse	412	3–5%	Express Oil Change	60
3%	SlumberLand International	258	3–5%	GCO Carpet Outlet	256
3%	Steaks To Go	354	3–5%	Marco's Pizza	366
3%	Stuft Pizza & Brewing	370	3–5%	Mister Money – USA	128
3%	Sunbanque Island Tanning	464	3–5%	Payless Car Rental System	66
3%	Superglass Windshield Repair	86	3–5%	Sparkle Wash	160
3%	Taco Hut America Inc	406	3–5%	Spring Crest Drapery Centers	262
3%	Team Tires Plus Ltd	92	4%	A Quicki Services	206
3%	Tippy's Taco House	342	4%	Adventures In Advertising	108
3%	Tire Warehouse Central	92	4%	Ameci Pizza & Pasta	362
3%	Tower Cleaning Systems	160	4%	Applebee's International	416
3%	Tumbleweed LLC	414	4%	Arby's	354
3%	USA Baby	144	4%	Ashbury Suites & Inns	268
3%	Western Steer Family Steakhouse/WSMP	414	4%	Back Yard Burgers	332
3%	Window Perfect	262	4%	Baker Street Artisan Breads & Cafe	308
3%	X-Bankers Check Cashing	192	4%	Banners Restaurants	398
1.5–5%	Cyber Exchange Software And Computers	424	4%	Bennigan's	398
0–7%	Lentz USA Service Centers	76	4%	Between Rounds Bagel Deli & Bakery	292
2–5%	ABC Seamless	186	4%	Big Boy Restaurant & Bakery	398
2–5%	Amigo Mobility Center	236	4%	Big City Bagels Inc	292
2–5%	Bright Beginnings	108	4%	Bike Line	456
2–5%	Dog N' Suds Drive-In Restaurants	416	4%	Biologix	150
2–5%	Dry Cleaning Station	196	4%	Blue Chip Cookies	298
2–5%	Top Value Muffler & Brake Shops	78	4%	Bobby Rubino's Place for Ribs	392
2.5–4.5%	Q Lube	62	4%	Bojangles' Restaurants Inc	328
3–4%	Batteries Plus	64	4%	Bonanza	398
3–4%	Country Inns & Suites by Carlson	268	4%	Buddy's Bar-B-Q	354
3–4%	Estrella Insurance	126	4%	Buffalo Wings & Rings	398
3–4%	Signs & More In 24	120	4%	Burger King (Canada)	332
3.5%	Bennett's Bar-B-Que Inc	392	4%	Champion Cleaners Franchise Inc.	196
3.5%	Copeland's of New Orleans	410	4%	Checkers Drive-In Restaurants	376
3.5%	Fan-A-Mania	462	4%	Chemstation International	150
3.5%	The Ground Round	394	4%	Chicago's Pizza	362
3.5%	Subs Plus	360	4%	Cici's Pizza	362
3.5%	Valet Express	198	4%	City Looks Salons Int'l	102
3.5%	Arthur Rutenberg Homes	188	4%	Color-Glo International	170

Royalty	Franchise Name	Page	Royalty	Franchise Name	Page
4%	Colortyme	428	4%	Just-A-Buck	426
4%	Colter's Bar-B-Q	392	4%	KFC	330
4%	CruiseOne/The Travel Company	470	4%	Kiddie Kobbler	142
4%	Culver Franchising System Inc	320	4%	Kids Team	142
4%	Culvers Franchising System	376	4%	Lemstone Books	422
4%	Dairy Queen Canada Inc.	316	4%	Living Lighting	258
4%	Damon's International	398	4%	Long John Silver's	352
4%	Denny's Inc	400	4%	Longbranch Steakhouse & Saloon Inc	412
4%	Diamond Dave's Taco Company	340	4%	Mister Mobile On-Site Oil Changes	60
4%	Dickey's Barbecue Pit Restaurants	392	4%	Motel 6	270
4%	Donatos Pizza	362	4%	Mr. Front-End	76
4%	Doubledave's Pizzaworks Restaurant	404	4%	Naked Furniture	258
4%	El Pollo Loco	340	4%	Nutter's Bulk And Natural Foods	226
4%	Elmer's Pancake & Steak House	412	4%	One Hour Martinizing	198
4%	Express Mart Convenient Store	224	4%	Palace Entertainment & Bullwinkles Restaurant	402
4%	Family Pizza	364	4%	Panda Shoes	52
4%	Faro's Franchise Systems	364	4%	Paper Warehouse Franchising Inc	444
4%	The Flag Shop	448	4%	Parcel Plus	204
4%	Fosters Freeze, Incorporated	316	4%	Party City Corp	444
4%	Friendly's Ice Cream Corporation	400	4%	Pepe's Mexican Restaurant	406
4%	Golden Chick	330	4%	Perkins Family Restaurants	402
4%	Golden Corral Family Steakhouse	412	4%	Pizza Factory Inc.	368
4%	Golden Corral Franchising Systems Inc	412	4%	Pizza Man – He Delivers	368
4%	The Great American Bagel	292	4%	The Pizza Ranch	368
4%	Great Outdoor Sub Shops	356	4%	Ponderosa Steakhouse	412
4%	Hard Times Cafe	378	4%	Potts Doggie Shop	336
4%	Hardee's Food Systems	332	4%	Pretzels Plus	306
4%	Hartz Chicken	330	4%	Pro Image	462
4%	Hawkeye's Home Sitters	274	4%	Radisson Hotels International	270
4%	Heel Quik	52	4%	Radisson Hotels Worldwide	272
4%	High Wheeler Ice Cream Parlour/Rest.	314	4%	Ramada Franchise Canada, Inc.	272
4%	Hospitality International	270	4%	Ramada Franchise Systems Inc	272
4%	Houlihan's Restaurant Group	416	4%	Re Tool	438
4%	Howard Johnson Intl Inc	270	4%	Reface It Kitchen Systems	182
4%	Huddle House	396	4%	Relax The Back Franchising Co	238
4%	Hudson's Grill of America	416	4%	Robin's Donuts	300
4%	Impressions On Hold International	108	4%	Ronzio Pizza	370
4%	Its About Games	434	4%	Round Table Franchise Corp	370
4%	Jacadi	52	4%	Ruffin's Pet Centres	276
4%	Joe Loue Tout Rent All	66	4%	Shooters International Inc	418
4%	Johnny's New York Style Pizza	366	4%	Slimmer Image Weight Loss Clinics	242
4%	Juice World	230	4%	Soccer Post Intl Franchise Corp	456
4%	Jungle Jim's Restaurants	400	4%	The Sport Shoe	456

Royalty	Franchise Name	Page	Royalty	Franchise Name	Page
4%	St. Hubert Bar-B-Q	392	4.5%	Gigglebees	416
4%	Steak 'N Shake	354	4.5%	Happy Joe's Pizza & Ice Cream Parlor	364
4%	Sub Station Ii	358	4.5%	John Simmons	448
4%	Sunshine Cafe	418	4.5%	Petland	276
4%	Superior Walls of America	190	4.5%	Tropi-Tan, Inc.	464
4%	Taco John's Int'l Inc	342	4.5%	Villa Pizza	372
4%	Taco Mayo	342	4.5%	Zuzu Mexican Food	406
4%	TCBY Treats	318	5.5–3.5%	Just Legs	52
4%	Tempaco	438	6–3%	Mr. Rooter Corp.	178
4%	TGI Friday's Hospitality Worldwide	418	4.5–5%	Home Cleaning Centers	166
4%	Thundercloud Subs	360	4.75%	Kid To Kid	142
4%	U.S. Lawns	164	3.6–6%	American Speedy Printing Centers	284
4%	Village Inn Restaurants	402	4.9%	Merlin's Muffler & Brake	76
4%	Wendy's Restaurants of Canada Inc.	334	4.9%	Dunkin' Donuts	300
4%	Wild Bird Marketplace	278	2–8%	DuraClean International	152
4%	Yaya's Flame Broiled Chicken	330	2–8%	General Business Services	126
3–5.25%	Choice Hotels Intl	268	3–7%	Maid To Perfection	166
3.5–5%	Hayes Handpiece Franchises Inc	236	3–7%	Sanford Rose Associates	244
5.5–3%	Help-U-Sell	388	4–6%	Cousins Subs	356
2–7%	PuroFirst International	158	4–6%	Fast Eddie's	376
3–6%	MaidPro	166	4–6%	Purified Water To Go	446
3–6%	Molly Maid	168	4–6%	Service-Tech Corporation	160
3–6%	Workenders	168	4–6%	Sir Speedy	286
3–6%	Worldwide Refinishing Systems, Inc.	182	4–6%	Valvoline Instant Oil Change	62
4–5%	Budget Blinds	262	5%	2001 Flavors Plus Potatoes	312
4–5%	Butterfields, Etc.	448	5%	A. L. Van Houtte	376
4–5%	Dairy Queen	316	5%	Aaron's Rental Purchase	428
4–5%	Handyman Connection	190	5%	Abra Auto Body & Glass	70
4–5%	Mamma Ilardo's	338	5%	AccounTax Services	106
4–5%	Pizza Inn Inc	368	5%	Active Green + Ross Tire & Automotive Centre	92
4–5%	Ward's Restaurants	418	5%	Admiral Subs	356
4.5%	Cheeburger Cheeburger	332	5%	Air Brook Limousine	210
4.5%	Coffee Time Donuts	300	5%	Aire-Master of America	150
4.5%	Joey's Only Seafood Restaurant	418	5%	All American Frozen Yogurt/Ice Cream	318
4.5%	Knights Franchise Systems Inc	270	5%	Aloette Cosmetics	100
4.5%	Krispy Kreme Doughnuts	300	5%	American Wholesale Thermographers	284
4.5%	The Krystal Company	334	5%	AmericInn International	268
4.5%	1 Potato 2	376	5%	Antonello's	338
4.5%	Baldinos Giant Jersey Subs	356	5%	Apartment Selector	386
4.5%	Caffe Appassionato	220	5%	Apple Auto Glass	86
4.5%	Castles Unlimited	388	5%	ASI Sign Systems Inc	120
4.5%	Closettec	180	5%	Assist-2-Sell	386
4.5%	Dairy Belle Freeze	320	5%	The Athlete's Foot	456

Royalty	Franchise Name	Page	Royalty	Franchise Name	Page
5%	Atlanta Bread Co	308	5%	Copy Copy	284
5%	Auto Accent Centers	58	5%	CPR+	236
5%	Auto One Glass & Accessories	58	5%	Craters & Freighters	202
5%	Bahama Buck's Original Shaved Ice Co.	320	5%	Creative Cakery	308
5%	Baker's Dozen Donuts	300	5%	Critter Care of America	274
5%	Bassett's Original Turkey	328	5%	Croissant + Plus	308
5%	Borvin Beverage	230	5%	Crown Trophy	448
5%	Bourbon Street Candy Company	218	5%	Cultures Restaurants	376
5%	Boz Hot Dogs	336	5%	Deckare Services	176
5%	Brown's Chicken & Pasta	328	5%	Del Taco	340
5%	Bruster's Old-Fashioned Ice Cream & Yogurt	312	5%	The Different Twist Pretzel Co.	306
5%	Budget Car & Truck Rental	66	5%	Diversified Dental Services	236
5%	Buffalo's Cafe	398	5%	Dufferin Game Room Store	434
5%	Building Blocks Franchise Corp	142	5%	East of Chicago Pizza Company	364
5%	Bunnies Fresh Juice & Smoothie Bar	324	5%	East Side Mario's	404
5%	Buns Master Bakery Systems	308	5%	EB's Express	338
5%	The Buyer's Agent	386	5%	ELS Language Centers	214
5%	Buyer's Resource	386	5%	Energy Wise	152
5%	Bw-3 Buffalo Wild Wings	328	5%	Enviro Masters Lawn Care	162
5%	Bw-3 Franchise Systems Inc	228	5%	Everything Yogurt & Salad Cafe	318
5%	Cafe La France	416	5%	Famous Sam's Inc	410
5%	Cap'n Taco	340	5%	Farmer Boys Hamburgers	332
5%	Car-X Muffler & Brake	76	5%	Fast Bucks Development LLC	192
5%	Carpet Master	256	5%	Fast-Fix Jewelry Repairs	56
5%	Carpet Network	256	5%	FatBurger	332
5%	Caterina's	376	5%	Figaro's Italian Kitchen	338
5%	CD Warehouse	440	5%	Flamers Charbroiled Hamburgers & Chicken	332
5%	Certigard/Petro-Canada	88	5%	Four Star Pizza	364
5%	Charley's Steakery	412	5%	Frozen Fusion Fruit Smoothies	320
5%	Checkcare Systems	192	5%	Fuddruckers	416
5%	Chelsea Street Pub & Grill	394	5%	Full Circle Image	424
5%	Chesapeake Bagel Bakery	292	5%	Gelato Amare	314
5%	Chicken Delight	328	5%	Glass Magnum	176
5%	Chili Chompers	230	5%	Godfather's Pizza	364
5%	Chip King	86	5%	Goldberg's New York Bagels	292
5%	Churchs Chicken	328	5%	Golf Augusta Pro Shops	458
5%	Cindy's Cinnamon Rolls	296	5%	Grease Monkey International	60
5%	Clean 'N' Press America	196	5%	Great Steak & Potato Company	326
5%	Cluck-U Chicken	328	5%	The Great Wilderness Company, Inc.	442
5%	Color Me Mine	420	5%	Greco Pizza Donair	364
5%	Consumer Casket USA	448	5%	Greetings	108
5%	Convenient Food Mart	224	5%	The Griddle Family Restaurants	400
5%	Cookies In Bloom	298	5%	Handle With Care Packaging Store	202

Royalty	Franchise Name	Page	Royalty	Franchise Name	Page
5%	Harvey Washbangers	196	5%	Manufacturing Management Associates	128
5%	Harvey's Restaurants	400	5%	McCoy's Cake & Pie Shop	310
5%	Hawthorn Suites/Hawthorn Suites Ltd	268	5%	Medichair	238
5%	Heavenly Ham	230	5%	Metropolitan Institute of Health Careers	116
5%	Her Real Estate	390	5%	Mickey Finn's Sports Cafe	418
5%	Hilton Inns	268	5%	Midas (Canada)	76
5%	Holiday Hospitality	270	5%	Mighty Distribution System of America Inc	64
5%	Holiday Inn Worldwide	270	5%	Miracle Auto Painting & Body Repair	72
5%	Home Instead Senior Care	248	5%	Moe's Italian Sandwiches	348
5%	Homewatch Caregivers	206	5%	Monsieur Felix & Mr. Norton Cookies	298
5%	Hoop Mountain	466	5%	Monsieur Muffler	76
5%	Indy Lube	60	5%	Morrone's Italian Ices	314
5%	Jerry's Subs & Pizza	356	5%	Mr. GoodCents Subs & Pasta	358
5%	Joy Carpet Dry Cleaning	146	5%	Mr. Jim's Pizza	366
5%	Juice Connection	324	5%	My Favorite Muffin	304
5%	Jumbo Video	440	5%	Nach-O Fast	340
5%	Kelsey's Restaurants	400	5%	Nancy's Pizzeria	366
5%	Kids R Kids Quality Learning Centers	136	5%	National Homecraft	156
5%	Kilwin's Chocolates Franchise	218	5%	Nationwide Floor & Window Coverings	256
5%	King Bear Auto Service Centers	80	5%	The Nature of Things Store	442
5%	Kirby Tours	472	5%	Nature's 10	442
5%	KitchenPro	262	5%	Old Fashioned Egg Cream Co Inc	378
5%	Knowledge Development Centers Inc	128	5%	Once Upon A Child	144
5%	Kohr Bros. Frozen Custard	320	5%	One Stop Undercar	78
5%	L. A. Smoothie Healthmart & Cafe	226	5%	P.J.'S Coffee & Tea	222
5%	La Pizza Loca	366	5%	Pack Mart	202
5%	La Salsa Fresh Mexican Grill	340	5%	Pak Mail Centers of America	204
5%	Lamar's Donuts	300	5%	Panchero's Mexican Grill	342
5%	Larry's Giant Subs	356	5%	Papa Murphy's	374
5%	Last Flight Out	436	5%	Party Land Inc	444
5%	Laund-Ur-Mutt	274	5%	Pasta To Go	378
5%	Le Croissant Shop	310	5%	Pastel's Cafe	380
5%	Learning Express	136	5%	Patty-Cakes International, Inc.	144
5%	Lifestyle Mobile Carpet Showroom	256	5%	The Peanut Club	144
5%	London Cleaners	198	5%	Permacrete Systems	190
5%	Lube Depot	60	5%	Pet Habitat	276
5%	LubePros International, Inc.	60	5%	Petro's Chili & Chips	380
5%	MacBirdie Golf Gifts	458	5%	Petrucci's Ice Cream Co.	314
5%	Magic Wok	346	5%	Peyron Tax Service	200
5%	Mail Boxes Etc.	202	5%	Philly Connection	326
5%	Maintain Cleaning Systems	156	5%	Pizzas By Marchelloni	370
5%	Manhattan Bagel Co Inc	294	5%	Pizzeria Uno Chicago Bar & Grill	370
5%	Manhattan Bagel Company	294	5%	Play It Again Sports	456

Royalty	Franchise Name	Page	Royalty	Franchise Name	Page
5%	Popeyes Chicken & Biscuits	330	5%	Super 8 Motels Inc	272
5%	Postal Annex+	204	5%	Surface Specialists Systems	172
5%	The Potato Sack	230	5%	Swiss Chalet/Swiss Chalet Plus Restaurants	410
5%	Power Smoothie	322	5%	The T O L Franchise Group	100
5%	The Pretzel Twister	306	5%	Tacotime	342
5%	PretzelMaker	306	5%	Talking Book World	422
5%	Pro-Tect	384	5%	Terra Systems	164
5%	Professional Polish	158	5%	TFM	440
5%	Quikava – Coffees By Chock Full O' Nuts	222	5%	TFM/Top Forty	440
5%	RACS International	158	5%	Thrifty Car Rental (Canada)	68
5%	Red Hot & Blue	418	5%	Thrifty Rent-A-Car	68
5%	Renzios	380	5%	Tony Maroni's Famous Gourmet Pizza	370
5%	Rocky Mountain Chocolate Factory	218	5%	Totally Kool	52
5%	Rodan Jewellers/Simply Charming	56	5%	Travel Professionals International	472
5%	Roli Boli	380	5%	Tuffy Auto Service Centers	88
5%	Room-Mate Referral Service Centers	390	5%	Tunex International, Inc.	84
5%	Roto-Static International	148	5%	UncleSam's Convenient Store	224
5%	Saint Louis Bread Company, Inc.	310	5%	United Capital Mortgage Assistance	192
5%	The Sandwich Board	348	5%	United Studios of Self-Defense Inc	468
5%	Sandwich Tree Restaurants	350	5%	Verlo Mattress Factory Stores	260
5%	Sangsters Health Centres	226	5%	We Care Home Health Services	248
5%	Schumacher Garage Door Franchise	186	5%	Wienerschnitzel	336
5%	Scoopers Ice Cream	314	5%	Yard Cards	450
5%	The Screen Machine	178	5%	Yesterday's Furniture & Country Store	260
5%	The Screenmobile	184	5%	Z-Teca	344
5%	SealMaster	158	5%	Zuka Juice	324
5%	Seniors for Seniors/Seniors for Business	254	5%/10C/SF	ElDorado Stone	190
5%	Shoe Stop	52	5%/1K	Mountain Mike's Pizza	366
5%	Shred-It	454	5%/4%	Tinder Box International	436
5%	Signs Now	120	5% gross	United Printing Unlimited	288
5%	Slats Blind Cleaning	178	5%/mo	Hour Hands	166
5%	Smitty's	402	5% w/cap	Auto-Lab Diagnostic & Tune-Up Centers	84
5%	Smoothie King	322	6-4%	Pizza Delight	368
5%	Snappy Tomato Pizza	370	7-3%	Kitchen Wizards	182
5%	Snip N' Clip Haircut Shops	104	7-3%	Maid Brigade Services	166
5%	Sobik's Subs	358	8-2%	E.K. Williams & Co.	106
5%	The Soda Fountain	396	to 5%	Jiffy Lube International Inc	60
5%	Sox Appeal	52	to 5%	La Smoothie Franchises Inc	324
5%	Sports Fantastic	462	3.3–7%	The Maids	168
5%	Spot-Not Car Washes	94	2–8.5%	United Energy Partners	190
5%	St. Jerome Restaurant	402	4.5–6%	Children's Orchard	142
5%	Steak-Out	232	5.3%	Service Center	130
5%	Strings Italian Cafe	404	6.9–3.9%	TechStaff	250

Royalty	Franchise Name	Page	Royalty	Franchise Name	Page
4–7%	Aero-Colours	88	6%	American Sign Shops	120
4–7%	Archadeck	188	6%	Arrow Prescription Center	236
4–7%	Dr. Vinyl & Assoc.	174	6%	Arthur Treacher's Fish & Chips	352
4–7%	Home Helpers	206	6%	Ashley Avery's Collectables	436
4–7%	Interstate Dairy Queen	316	6%	Auntie Anne's Hand-Rolled Soft Pretzels	306
4–7%	Women's Health Boutique	238	6%	B-Dry System	188
5–6%	Building Systems Analysis Inc.	382	6%	Balloons & Bears	436
5–6%	U.S. Franchise Systems	272	6%	Barnie's Coffee & Tea Company	220
5.5%	Domino's Pizza Inc	362	6%	BCT	284
5.5%	Jersey Mike's Franchise Systems, Inc.	348	6%	Benihana of Tokyo	408
5.5%	Mr. Hero	358	6%	Beverly Hills Weight Loss & Wellness	242
5.5%	Taco Bell Corp	342	6%	Blimpie Subs And Salads	356
5.5%	Zero's Subs	360	6%	The Bone Appetit Bakery	276
5.5%	CottageCare	166	6%	Brake Centers of America	74
5.5%	Country Clutter	436	6%	The BrickKicker	382
5.5%	The Medicine Shoppe	238	6%	Brown Baggers	348
5.5%	Oil Can Henry's International	62	6%	Ca$h Plus	192
5.5%	Pizza Pit	368	6%	Cafe By George/Cookies By George	298
5.5%	Port of Subs	358	6%	California Closet Company	180
4.5–7%	Gingiss Formalwear	54	6%	Candleman Corporation	448
4.5–7%	Kitchen Tune-Up	182	6%	Candy Express	218
4.5–7%	Snelling Personnel Services	246	6%	Candy HQ/Sweets From Heaven	218
5–6.5%	Steam Brothers Professional Cleaning & Restoration	148	6%	Century 21 Real Estate	388
5.8%	The Closet Factory	180	6%	Chef's Fried Chicken	328
4.3–7.5%	Penn Stations East Coast Subs	358	6%	Chowderhead's Seafood Restaurants	352
5.95%	Donut Inn	300	6%	Classy Maids USA	166
4–8%	Kwik Kopy Printing	284	6%	The Coffee Beanery	220
4–8%	Sutton Homes Franchising Corp	238	6%	Cold Stone Creamery	312
4.5–7.5%	VR Business Brokers	112	6%	Coldwell Banker Affiliates (Canada)	388
5–7%	Boardwalk Fries	336	6%	Coldwell Banker Residential Affiliates	388
5–7%	The Cleaning Authority	166	6%	Computer U Learning Centers	212
5–7%	Great Harvest Bread Co.	308	6%	Confidential Business Connection	112
5–7%	Meineke Discount Mufflers	76	6%	The Connoisseur	448
5–7%	Merry Maids	168	6%	Conroys 1-800-Flowers	432
5–7%	The Taco Maker	342	6%	Cookie Bouquet/Cookies By Design	298
6%	A Buck Or Two Stores	426	6%	Cost Cutters Family Hair Care	102
6%	A. J. Barnes Bicycle Emporium	456	6%	Creative Colors Int'l Inc	174
6%	A Shade Better	264	6%	Criterium Engineers	382
6%	Alphagraphics Printshops Of The Future	284	6%+	Critter Control	382
6%	Ambic Building Inspection Consult	382	6%	CTI Computer Training Institutes	212
6%	American Brake Service	74	6%	Deck The Walls	420
6%	American Concrete Raising	188	6%	Dent Doctor	70
			6%	Diamond Seal Inc	190

Royalty	Franchise Name	Page	Royalty	Franchise Name	Page
6%	Donut Delite Cafe	300	6%	Lindy – Gertie's	378
6%	Drapery Works Systems	262	6%	Little King	378
6%	Ecomat	196	6%	Lord's & Lady's Hair Salons	104
6%	Edelweiss Deli Express/Sub Express	348	6%	Made In Japan, Teriyaki Experience	346
6%	EDO Japan	408	6%	Mail Boxes Etc. (Canada)	202
6%	Elephant Walk Gift Galleries	436	6%	Malibu Gallery	420
6%	English Butler Canada	206	6%	Marble Slab Creamery	314
6%	Envirobate	152	6%	MarbleLife	170
6%	Era Franchise Systems	388	6%	Martial Arts America	466
6%	Express One	202	6%	The Master Mechanic	80
6%	Fabri-Zone Cleaning Systems	146	6%	MaxCare Professional Cleaning Systems	156
6%	Fabutan Sun Tan Studios	464	6%	Men's Hair Now	104
6%	FastSigns	120	6%	Millicare Environmental Services	156
6%	Field of Dreams	462	6%	Mini Maid Service Systems Of Canada	168
6%	Foliage Design Systems	432	6%	Minuteman Press International	286
6%	For Olde Times Sake	436	6%	Mrs. Fields Cookies	298
6%	Framing & Art Centres	420	6%	Nacho Nana's Worldwide Inc	340
6%	Frullati Cafe	348	6%	National Maintenance Contractors	156
6%	General Nutrition Centers	226	6%	New Horizons Computer Learning Center	212
6%	Gloria Jean's Gourmet Coffees	220	6%	New York Fries	378
6%	Good For You! Fruit & Yogurt Ltd.	318	6%	Novus Windshield Repair	86
6%	The Great Canadian Bagel	292	6%	Nutri-Lawn, Ecology-Friendly Lawn Care	164
6%	Great Clips	102	6%	Odyssey Art Centers	136
6%	Great Earth Vitamins	226	6%	The Office Alternative	128
6%	The Great Frame Up	420	6%	One Hour Motophoto & Portrait Studio	280
6%	Great Wraps	378	6%	One Hour Motophoto & Portrait Studio (Canada)	280
6%	Gymboree	138			
6%	H R C Int'l Inc	102	6%	Orange Julius Canada Inc.	322
6%	Hammett's Learning World	214	6%	Pak Mail Centers (Canada)	204
6%	Ho-Lee-Chow	346	6%	Papyrus	450
6%	Hogi Yogi Sandwiches & Frozen Yogurt	348	6%	Paradise Bakery & Cafe	310
6%	The Hometeam Inspection Service	382	6%	Picture Hits	280
6%	House Doctors Handyman Service	176	6%	Pinch-A-Penny	426
6%	I N V U Portraits	280	6%	Pizza Nova	368
6%	IC Solutions Inc	124	6%	Pizza Pizza Limited	368
6%	Imagine That Discovery Museums	134	6%	Professional Carpet Systems	148
6%	Jimmy John's Gourmet Sandwich Shops	348	6%	Professional House Doctors, Inc.	384
6%	Kennedy Transmission	82	6%	Profusion Systems	170
6%	Kitchen Solvers	182	6%	Proventure Business Group, Inc.	112
6%	Kwik-Kopy Printing (Canada)	284	6%	PuckMasters Hockey Training Centers	466
6%	Labor Force	246	6%	Quizno's Classic Subs	358
6%	LedgerPlus	106	6%	Rennsport	96
6%	Lemon Tree – A Unisex Haircutting Est.	104	6%	Rent 'N Drive	68

Royalty	Franchise Name	Page	Royalty	Franchise Name	Page
6%	Safe-T-Child	144	to 6%	MicroPlay Video Games	434
6%	Saint Cinnamon Bake Shoppe	296	5–7.5%	Miracle Method	182
6%	Sale By Owner Systems	390	5.5–7%	DuctBusters/Buster Enterprises Inc	176
6%	Schlotzsky's Deli	350	3–10%	ServPro	160
6%	Screen Printing USA	286	4–9%	ServiceMaster Residential/ Commercial (Canada)	168
6%	Sears Driver Training	216			
6%	Select Sandwich	350	5–8%	Academy for Mathematics & Science	214
6%	Sign-A-Rama	120	5–8%	Marble Renewal	170
6%	Signs First	120	5–8%	Steamatic	148
6%	Sir Speedy (Canada)	286	5–8%	Ziebart Tidycar	94
6%	Soft Touch Interiors	258	6.5%	Days Inns of America Inc	268
6%	Special Delivery Photos Inc	280	6.5%	Econo Lube N' Tune	84
6%	Speedee Oil Change & Tune-Up	62	6.5%	Grandma Lee's Bakery Cafe	308
6%	Speedy Printing Centers	288	6.5%	Erbert & Gerbert's Subs & Clubs	356
6%	Sport Clips	104	6.5%	Rita's Italian Ice	322
6%	The Steak Escape	354	9-4.5%	Padgett Business Services	106
6%	Submarina	358	6.9%	ATS Personnel	246
6%	Successful Introduction	194	4–10%	E.P.I.C. Systems, Inc.	152
6%	Swisher Hygiene	160	4–10%	ServiceMaster Residential/Commercial	168
6%	Taco Villa	342	6–8%	Discount Car & Truck Rentals	66
6%	Tan World	464	6–8%	Guardsman WoodPro	184
6%	TechnoKids	136	6–8%	Wee Watch Private Home Day Care	132
6%	Tenniskids	140	7%	AAMCO Transmissions	82
6%	Tire Time Rentals	92	7%	Airbag Options	88
6%	Tropik Sun Fruit & Nut	228	7%	American Transmissions	82
6%	True Friends	278	7%	Around Your Neck	52
6%	Tubby's Submarines	360	7%	ATL International	96
6%	Tutor Time Child Care Learning Center	132	7%	Baby's Away	132
6%	Two Men And A Truck	210	7%	Boston Pizza	362
6%	U-Wash Doggie	274	7%	Breadsmith	308
6%	Victory Lane Quick Oil Change	62	7%	Canine Counselors	274
6%	Video Impact	430	7%	Color Your World	438
6%	Wallpapers To Go	264	7%	CompuTemp Inc	250
6%	We Care Hair	104	7%	Copy Club	284
6%	Wetzel's Pretzels	306	7%	DentPro	70
6%	Wicks 'N' Sticks	450	7%	Dollar Rent A Car	66
6%	Window Gang	160	7%	Dollar Rent A Car (Canada)	66
6%	Wing Machine	330	7%	Dunhill Staffing Systems, Inc.	246
6%	Woody's Wood Shops	460	7%	First Choice Haircutters (U.S.) Inc.	102
6%	Yogen Fruz Worldwide	318	7%	Fortune Personnel Consultants	244
6%	Yogi Bear Jellystone Park Camp-Resorts	266	7%	The Goddard Schools	134
6%/5K	Better Homes Realty	386	7%	Great American Cookie Company, Inc.	298
6% min.	Your Office USA	130	7%	Gwynne Learning Academy	214

Royalty	Franchise Name	Page	Royalty	Franchise Name	Page
7%	Gymsters, Inc.	138	7.5%	By Owner Reality Network	386
7%	High Touch-High Tech	142	7.5%	Checkmate	250
7%	Interim Healthcare	248	7.5%	Cottman Transmission	82
7%	Jenny Craig Weight Loss Centres	242	7.5%	FastFrame U S A	420
7%	John Casablancas Modeling/Career Center	116	7.5%	HouseMaster, The Home Inspection Professionals	384
7%	Kiddie Academy International	134			
7%	L A Weight Loss Centers Inc	242	7.5%	Precision Tune Auto Care	84
7%	Laser Chem "White Glove" Commercial Cleaning	154	7–8.5%	Nitro-Green Professional Lawn & Tree Care	162
			6–10%	Algonquin Travel	470
7%	Lee Myles Transmissions	82	7–9%	Naturalawn of America	162
7%	Management Recruiters	244	8%	Acctcorp	106
7%	Manchu Wok (U.S.)	346	8%	Atwork Personnel Services	246
7%	McBeans	222	8%	Auto Purchase Consulting	90
7%	Milex Tune-Ups and Brakes	84	8%	Bagelz-The Bagel Bakery	292
7%	Mister Transmission	82	8%	Blenz Coffee	220
7%	Mmmarvellous Mmmuffins	304	8%	The Brake Shop	74
7%	New York Burrito-Gourmet Wraps	340	8%	Building Services of America	150
7%	NurseFinders	248	8%	Ceiling Doctor	176
7%	Oil Butler International	60	8%	Clintar Groundskeeping Services	162
7%	Pearle Vision Center	240	8%	Complete Music	208
7%	Primrose Schools	136	8%	Dent Zone	70
7%	Rainbow International Carpet Care & Restoration Specialist	148	8%	Electronic Tax Filers	200
			8%	First Optometry Eye Care Centers	240
7%	Sbarro, The Italian Eatery	338	8%	Gent's Formal Wear	54
7%	Speedy Transmission Centers	82	8%	The Gourmet Cup	220
7%	Terminix Termite & Pest Control	384	8%	Gymn' Around Kids	138
7%	Totally Wireless	428	8%	Hairlines	102
7%	Transmission USA	82	8%	Head Over Heels	138
7%	Treats	310	8%	The Honors Learning Center	216
7%	Truly Nolen	178	8%	Huntington Learning Center	216
7%	V.I.D.E.O. Security Process (VSP)	454	8%	Interface Financial Group	114
7%+	White Hen Pantry	232	8%	Jan-Pro Franchising Int'l Inc	154
7%	Window Butler	168	8%	Jet-Black Sealcoating & Repair	178
7%	World Trade Network	130	8%	Kampgrounds of America/KOA	266
7%+23%	Colors On Parade	94	8%	Kernels	228
5–10%	Pets Are Inn	276	8%	LawCorps Legal Staffing Services	250
6–9%	ExecuTrain	116	8%	The Little Gym International, Inc.	138
6–9%	ExecuTrain Corp.	212	8%	Maaco Auto Painting & Bodyworks	70
6–9%	Express Personnel Services	246	8%	Maaco Auto Painting & Bodyworks (Canada)	70
6–9%	Window & Wall Creations	262	8%	The Mad Science Group	144
6.5–8.5%	Emerald Green Lawn Care	162	8%	Magis Fund Raising Specialists	128
7.5%	Hydro Physics Pipe Inspection	154	8%	Mikes Restaurants	400
7.5%	Barbizon Schools of Modeling	116	8%	National Property Inspections, Inc.	384

Royalty	Franchise Name	Page	Royalty	Franchise Name	Page
8%	P.A.M.'S Coffee & Tea Co.	222	10%	Lawn Doctor	162
8%	PC Professor	212	10%	Lindelle Studios	280
8%	ProShred Security	452	10%	Model Managers Int'l	116
8%	Safe Not Sorry	452	10%	National Tenant Network	390
8%	Shefield Gourmet	222	10%	Pee Wee Workout	138
8%	Shine Factory	94	10%	Performance Marketing Concepts Inc	110
8%	The Sleeping Giant Within Inc.	216	10%	Resort Maps Franchise Inc	110
8%	Sterling Optical	240	10%	Showhomes of America	390
8%	Subway	360	10%	Turbo Management Systems Ltd.	118
8%	Vinylgraphics Custom Sign Centres	122	10%	Universal Business Consultants	130
8%	Western Medical Services	248	10%	Value Line Maintenance Systems	160
7–10%	America's Choice Int'l Inc.	386	10% max	Super Lawns	164
8–9%	Sylvan Learning Centers	216	5–15%	Master Care	156
8.5%	Airbag Service	88	6–15%	Kinderdance International	138
5–12.5%	AWC Commercial Window Coverings	262	6–15%	Serv U-1st	158
7–11%	Decorating Den Interiors	262	12%	Genius Kid Academy	134
8–10%	American Leak Detection	176	12%	Jackson Hewitt Tax Service	200
8–10%	Pre-Fit	140	6–18%	Critter Control Inc	210
9%	Jantize America	154	12.5%	McDonald's	334
9%	PestMaster Services	384	13%	JDI Cleaning Systems	154
9%	Pretzel Time	306	14%	EconoTax	200
9%	Proforma	286	0–30%	Professional Dynametric Programs/PDP	116
9%	The Second Cup	222	15%	Coverall Cleaning Concepts	152
9.5%	SaniBrite	158	15%	Look No-Fault Auto Insurance Agencies	128
9.5%	TRC Staffing Services	252	15%	O.P.E.N. Cleaning Systems	156
10%	A Wonderful Wedding	210	15%	Property Damage Appraisers	178
10%	Berlitz Franchising Corp.	214	16.5%	Unishippers Association	204
10%	Bingo Bugle Newspaper	290	17%	McDonald's Restaurants of Canada Limited	334
10%	Boston Bartenders School Associates	116	20%	American Darters Association	466
10%	Brite Site	150	20%	American Poolplayers Association	466
10%	C. B. S. Interactive Multimedia	212	20%	Renaissance Executive Forums	118
10%	Custom Cuts	102	20% Fee	Wedding Gown Specialists/Restoration	198
10%	Fire Defense Centers	452	to 20%	Jazzercise Inc	234
10%	Fortune Practice Management	126	22%	United Consumers Club	210
10%	Hauntrepreneurs, Ltd.	466	30%	AccuStaff Inc	250
10%	The Homesteader	290	35%	AeroWest & WestAir Sanitation Services	150
10%	Jani-King International	154	40%	Star Mart	230
10%	Lady of America	234	40% to $2M	Talent Tree Staffing Services	250

Part IV

Appendices

State Regulatory Agencies

California

Franchise Division

Department of Corporations

1115 11th Street

Sacramento, CA 95814

(916) 445-7205

Hawaii

Franchise and Securities Division

State Department of Commerce

P.O. Box 40

Honolulu, HI 96813

(808) 586-2722

Illinois

Franchise Division

Office of Attorney General

500 South Second Street

Springfield, IL 62706

(217) 782-4465

Indiana

Franchise Division

Office of Secretary of State

One North Capitol Street, Suite 560

Indianapolis, IN 46204

(317) 232-6576

Maryland

Franchise Office

Division of Securities

200 St.Paul Place, 20th Floor

Baltimore, MD 21202

(410) 576-6360

Michigan

Antitrust and Franchise Unit

Office of Attorney General

670 Law Building

Lansing, MI 48913

(517) 373-7117

Minnesota

Franchise Division
Department of Commerce
133 East Seventh Street
St. Paul, MN 55101
(612) 296-6328

New York

Franchise and Securities Division
State Department of Law
120 Broadway, 23rd Floor
New York, NY 10271
(212) 416-8211

North Dakota

Franchise Division
Office of Securities Commission
600 East Boulevard, 5th Floor
Bismarck, ND 58505
(701) 328-2910

Oregon

Corporate Securities Section
Department of Insurance and Finance
Labor and Industries Building
Salem, OR 97310
(503) 378-4387

Rhode Island

Franchise Office
Division of Securities
233 Richmond Street, Suite 232
Providence, RI 02903
(401) 277-3048

South Dakota

Franchise Office
Division of Securities
910 East Sioux Avenue
Pierre, SD 57501
(605) 773-4013

Virginia

Franchise Office
State Corporation Commission
1300 East Main Street
Richmond, VA 23219
(804) 371-9276

Washington

The Department of Financial Institutions
Securities Division
P.O. Box 9033
Olympia, WA 98507-9033
(360) 902-8760
FAX: (360) 586-5068

Wisconsin

Franchise Office
Wisconsin Securities Commission
P.O. Box 1768
Madison, WI 53701
(608) 266-3364

International Franchise Associations

International Franchise Associations

Associacao Portuguesa Da Franchise

Rua Castilho, 14,

1250 Lisbon, Portugal

Tel. 351-1-315 18 45

FAX: 351-1-315 18 45

Asociacion Argentina De Franchising

Sante Fe 995, Piso 4

Buenos Aires 1059, Argentina

Tel. 54 1 3935263

FAX: 54 1 3939260

Asociacion de Franchising de Chile

Director of International Affairs

Hernando de Aguirre 162, of. 904

Providencia, Santiago, Chile

Tel. 562 234 4189

FAX: 562 334 5719

email: 70501.2671@compuserve.com

Brazil Franchise Association

Av. Prof. Ascendino Reis

1548 CEP: 04027-000 – Sao Paulo – SP, Brazil

Tel. 55 11 573 9496

FAX: 55 11 575 5590

British Franchise Association

Thames View, Newtown Road,

 Henley on Thames

Oxfordshire, RG9 1HG

United Kingdom

Tel. 01491-578050   or   01491-578049

FAX: 01491-573517

Bulgarian Franchise Association

25 A Ochrid Street

BG-9000 Varna Bulgaria

Tel. 359 52 235 424

FAX: 59 52 600 724

email: 0644@main.infotel.bg

Colombian Franchise Association

A.A. 25200

Cali, Colombia, South America

Tel. 572 331 1086

FAX: 572 331 7138

Czech Franchise Association

Board of Directors

Rytirska 18, P.O. Box 706

CZ – 110 00 Praha 1

Tel. 0042 2 24215099

Danish Franchisors' Association

Amaliegade 37

DK-1256, Copenhagen K, Denmark

Tel. 45 33 15 60 11

FAX: 45 33 91 03 46

Ecuadorian Franchise Association

9 de Octubrey, Los Rios,

Edificio Finansur, Piso 16

Guayquil-Ecuador

Tel. (5934) 450097

FAX: (5934) 450150

email: Leonidas@Samerica.com

European Franchise Association

60, rue la Boetie

75008, Paris, France

Tel. 53.75.22.24

FAX: 53.75.22.20

Anas Group Inc.

62 Abassia St.

Cairo, Egypt

Tel. 20-2-484-3420

FAX: 20-2-295-5456

email: oanas@access.com.eg

Federation Belge de la Franchise

Bd. de L'Humanite 116/2

1070 Brussels

Tel. 0032 2 523 97 07

FAX: 0032 2 523 35 10

Federation of French Franchisese

60, rue La Boetie

75008 Paris, France

Tel. (33) 1 53 75 22 25

FAX: (33) 1 53 75 22 20

**Federation of Norwegian
Commercial and Service Enterprises**

P.O. Box 2483 Solli

0202 Oslo, Norway

Tel. 47 22 55 82 20

FAX: 47 22 55 82 25

Franchise Association of Austrailia & New Zealand

Suite 9, 6 Hunter Street

Parramatta, Sydney 2150 Australia

Tel. 61 2 8914933

FAX: 61 2 8914474

Franchise Association of Southern Africa

P.O. Box 31708

2117 Braamfontein, Republic of South Africa

Tel. 27 11 403-3468

FAX: 27 11 403-1279

Internet: http://www.infodoor.co.za/fasa/

email: fasa@infobahn.co.za

Hong Kong Franchise Association

22/F United Centre

95 Queensway, Hong Kong

Tel. 852 2823 1295

FAX: 852 2527 9843

Internet: http://www.franchise.org.hk

email: hkfa@franchise.org.hk

Hungarian Franchise Association

Margit krt. 15-17

Budapest H-1024 Hungary

Tel. 361 212 4124

FAX: 361 212 5712

email: 100324.454@compuserve.com

International Franchise Association

1350 New York Avenue NW, Suite 900

Washington, D.C. 20005-4709

Tel. (202) 628-8000

FAX: (202) 628-0812

Israel Franchise & Distribution Association

P.O. Box 3093 Herzeliya

Israel 46590

Tel. 972 9 576631

FAX: 972 9 576631

email: emmers@netvision.net.il

Israeli Franchise Association

44 Reines Street

Tel-Aviv, 64587

Tel. 972 3 5273111

FAX: 972 3 5245673

email: exhibiti@inter.net.il

Mexican Franchise Association

Insurgentes Sur 1783, #303

Colonia Guadalupe Inn

Mexico City C.P 01020, Mexico

Tel. (525) 524-8043

FAX: (525) 524-8043

National Franchise Association of Turkey – UFRAD

Selime Hatun Cami Sk 13/4

80040 Findikli – Istanbul, Turkey

Tel. 0212-252 55 61

FAX: 0212-252 55 61

Turkish Franchising Association

Selime Hatun Camii Sok

Ozlen Apt. No. 13/4

Gumussuyu – Istanbul, Turkey

Tel. 291 55 61

FAX: 291 55 61

Netherlands Franchise Association

Boomberglaan 12

NL-1217 RR Hilversum, The Netherlands

Tel. (31) 35 624 34 44

FAX: (31) 35 624 91 94

Polish Franchise Association

ul. Szpitalna 1 lok. 5

00-020 Warsaw, Poland

Tel. 48 22 680 30-39 ext. 120,123

FAX: 48 22 625 6956

Singapore International Franchise Association

71 Sophia Road

Singapore

Tel. 65 334-8200

FAX: 65 334-8211

email: frantech@pacific.net.sg

Swedish Franchise Association

Box 5512

S 114 85 Stockholm, Sweden

Tel. 46 86 608610

FAX: 46 86 627457

Swiss Franchise Association

Lowenstrasse 11, Postfach

CH – 8039 Zurich, Switzerland

Tel. 01 225 47 57

FAX: 01 225 47 77

Romanian Franchise Association

86, Bd. Aviatorilor, Bucharest 1, Romania

Tel. 401 210-4881

FAX: 401 210-4832

email: mbas@bah.logicnet.ro

The 1998 Franchise Redbook Questionnaire • Page 1 of 2

Thank you for taking the time to complete this form. Print any changes or additions in the white boxes. Return both pages in the provided reply envelope, or FAX them to (530)677-3391.

Franchise Name

Other names that are used by similar franchises under your organization †

Address

City | **State or Province**

Postal Code | **Country** | **Internet Address**

Phone | Toll Free | Alternate | Fax | **Will you accept collect calls? (Y/N)**

Please give a brief description of the products and services offered by your franchise(s).

FORM NO.

In Business Since

Franchising Since

Total Number of Corporate Employees

Number of	1996	1997	1998
Company Owned Units			
Number of Franchised Units			

	U.S.	Canada	Foreign
Number of Units 1998			
Projected NEW Units in 1999			

Please list the three states or provinces in which you have the greatest number of franchises, and the number of franchises in each area. →

State / Province			
Number of units			

Planned U.S. Expansion (List states or 'ALL')

Plan Canada Expansion? (Y/N)

Plan Foreign Expansion? (Y/N)

	CA	FL	HI	IL	IN	MD	MI	MN	ND	NY	OR	RI	SD	VA	WA	WI	DC	Alberta
Franchise Registered In																		

† Feel free to copy this form for additional franchises under your organization that are not adequately described with a single questionnaire.

The 1998 Franchise Redbook Questionnaire • Page 2 of 2

Do you provide **Financial Assistance?** (Y/N) ☐

Franchise Contract Length (years) 1ST/2ND/3RD ☐

Startup Costs· ☐

Royalty ☐

Do you allow **Sub-Franchising?** (Y/N) ☐

Passive Ownership? (allowed, discouraged OR not allowed) ☐

Franchise Fee ☐

Advertising Fee ☐

Does Franchise require **Previous Experience?** (Y/N) ☐

Site Space Required (sq.ft.) ☐

·Startup Costs are the total expenses required to get the franchise up and running but should **not** include the Franchise Fee.

Do you provide **Site Selection Assistance?** (Y/N) ☐

What types of sites are suitable for locating your franchise?

Anchored Center ☐   **Auto Mall** ☐   **Executive Suite** ☐   **Free Standing Building** ☐   **Food Court** ☐

Do you provide **Lease Negotiation Assistance?** (Y/N) ☐

Home Office ☐   **Industrial Park** ☐   **Kiosk** ☐   **Light Industrial** ☐   **Mall** ☐

Will you allow franchise to expand within its territory? (Y/N) ☐

Office Complex ☐   **Office+ Storage** ☐   **Power Center** ☐   **Regional Mall** ☐   **Strip Center** ☐

Store front ☐   **Water Front Area** ☐   **Ware-house** ☐   **Depends On Area** ☐   **Other** ☐

Do you offer an **Area Development Agreement?** (Y/N) ☐   → If you do, what is the term? ☐   Do you encourage existing **Independent Businesses** to convert into your **Franchise?** (Y/N) ☐   FORM NO.

Full Time Employees Required ☐

Training Provided (3 lines) ☐

Part Time Employees Required ☐

Field Support Provided (YES=service provided, FEE=at additional cost)

Central Data Processing ☐   **Central Purchasing** ☐   **Field Operations Evaluation** ☐

Field Training ☐   **Franchisor Conference** ☐   **Hotline** ☐

Initial Store Opening ☐   **Inventory Control** ☐   **Newsletter** ☐

Thank you for helping us provide accurate information The information below will only be used if we need to contact you regarding this questionnaire.

Name: _____

Position: _____

Phone: _____

Comments: _____

_____

_____

Bibliography

Bard, Ray and Henderson, Sheila. *Own Your Own Franchise: Everything You Need to Know about the Best Franchise Opportunities in America.* Reading, MA: Addison-Wesley, 1987.

Bond, Robert E. *Bond's Franchise Guide*, 12th Edition. Oakland, CA: Source Book Publications, 1999.

"Entrepreneur 20th Annual Franchise 500." *Entrepreneur* (January, 1999).

Foster, Dennis L. *The Rating Guide to Franchise.* New York, NY: Facts On File Publications, 1988.

Foster, Dennis L. *Franchising for Free.* New York, NY: John Wiley & Sons, Inc., 1988.

Franchise Opportunities, 23nd Edition. New York, NY: Sterling Publishing Co., Inc., 1995.

Franchise Opportunities Guide. Washington, DC: International Franchise Association, Fall/Winter, 1998–1999.

Franchising in the Economy, 1988–1990. New York: International Franchise Association Education Foundation, Inc. and Horwath International, International Franchise Association, 1990.

Jones, Constance. *220 Best Franchises to Buy.* New York, NY: The Philip Lief Group, 1987.

Keup, Edwin J. *Franchise Bible.* Grants Pass, OR: The Oasis Press, 1995.

Kostecka, Andrew, *Franchise Opportunities Handbook.* U.S. Department of Commerce: U.S. Government Printing Office, 22nd Annual Edition, 1991.

Ludden, LaVerne. *Franchise Opportunities Handbook.* Indianapolis, IN: JIST Works, Inc., 1999.

Rule, Roger C. *No Money Down Financing for Franchising.* Grants Pass, OR: The Oasis Press, 1999.

Sherman, Andrew J. *Franchising and Licensing: Two Ways to Build Your Business.* New York, NY: AMACON, 1991.

Index of Franchises

C

H

I

J

K

T

Please answer these questions to let us know how our products are working for you, and what we can do to serve you better. See other side for where to send this form.

The Franchise Redbook

1. The overall quality of information is: ☐ Excellent ☐ Good ☐ Fair ☐ Poor

2. This book is: ☐ Easy to use ☐ Helpful ☐ Too complicated ☐ Too elementary

3. The format is: ☐ Excellent ☐ Good ☐ Fair ☐ Poor

4. Did this book provide what you needed? ☐ Yes ☐ No

5. If not, what could be added? _____

6. What about the price? ☐ Lower than expected ☐ Fair ☐ Too expensive

7. From what perspective are you interested in this book? ☐ Prospective franchisee
   ☐ Existing franchisee ☐ Prospective franchisor ☐ Existing franchisor ☐ Franchise attorney
   ☐ Franchise consultant ☐ Franchise supplier ☐ Franchise advertising

8. How did you learn about this book? ☐ Referred by a friend ☐ Saw in a bookstore ☐ Saw in a library
   ☐ Used in a seminar ☐ Saw/heard review in: newspaper ___, magazine ___, radio/TV ___

9. Where did you buy this book? ☐ Bookstore ☐ Discount Store ☐ Catalog ☐ Office Supply
   ☐ Internet ☐ Consultant ☐ Association ☐ Publisher

10. Would you recommend this product to an associate? ☐ Yes ☐ No

11. Did you find an error in the information in this book? ☐ Yes ☐ No

11a. If yes, please note the page number and identify the error.

_____ _____
_____ _____
_____ _____
_____ _____

11b. If you would like to be contacted about the error you discovered, please provide your contact information
     and the best hours to call.

   Name: _____ Daytime phone number: _____

   e-mail address: _____ Best time to call: _____

12. What would you like to see included in this book in future editions?

_____
_____
_____

13. May we add your name to our mailing list?

   Name: _____ Title: _____

   Company: _____ Phone: _____

   Address: _____ City/State/Zip: _____

   e-mail (home): _____ e-mail (business): _____

After you complete this form:
you can FAX it to: Rcrwin70@aol.com

or

you can fold, seal, and stamp this form, and mail it to the address below.

fold

- -

Name: _____

Address: _____

City/State/Zip: _____

Place
Stamp
Here

Roger Rule

77-6461 Kilohama Street

Kailua-Kona, HI 96740

- -

fold

Tools that seamlessly integrate your business planning needs into Microsoft® Office

Now you can use Winning Business Plans in Color to create an effective business plan that gets results. This CD-ROM is available for any computer with Microsoft Windows 95/98 and Microsoft Office. Templates, financial worksheets, and other time-saving helpers accelerate your business planning and activities. The Winning Business Plans in Color CD-ROM includes:

- **Excel templates** that will compute Profit and Loss, Cash Flow, Market and Sales Forecasting, Break-Even Analysis, Income Statements, Balance Sheets, and Financial Ratios. Spreadsheet cells are linked and formulated so that when you input a change to your financials, all of your plan statistics and charts reflect the adjustments — automatically and without hassle.

- **Word business templates** that contain a complete business plan outline with a table of contents and five example business plans. Information from the Excel templates is instantly linked to the Word templates. Color charts and tables are automatically positioned in the document and are ready for professional output on your inkjet printer or service bureau.

- **The PowerPoint presentation** example provides you with a persuasive presentation tool and ideas. A complete help system is also provided.

- **Supplemental files** can also make your business life easier, like a non-disclosure agreement, an Average Selling Price and a Sales Seasonality Analysis.

Demo CD Available

If you're not sure if this is the right tool for your needs, simply ask for a demo CD-ROM showcasing this software (and others) from The Oasis Press®. And if you decide that you want the software, simply call for the unlockable key, which will make the software fully-functionable.

Order Today! 1-800-228-2275

Your special introductory price is only $59.95

Winning Business Plans in Color

New software from The Oasis Press®

From The Leading Publisher of Small Business Information
Books that save you time and money.

This all-in-one, easy-to-understand guide will get you started on the right foot. Packed with valuable information, *SmartStart Your (State) Business* will prepare you to deal with the federal, state, and local regulations imposed on small businesses. This concise, friendly, and up-to-the-minute source book details each critical step of starting your own business — from choosing a business structure to writing a top-notch business plan and the latest financing options available in your state.

SmartStart Your (State) Business   **Pages: varies**
Paperback: $19.95 (be sure to specify which state you prefer)

Explores every source of financing available for franchising, including many ways that require no money down. Reviews the preliminaries of financing, rating your credit, developing financial statements and understanding the necessary investment requirements.

No Money Down Financing for Franchising   **Pages: 240**
Paperback: $19.95   ISBN: 1-55571-462-5

This complete and practical guide includes sample documents and explains what the franchise system is and the precise benefits it offers. The Franchise Bible tells you what to expect from a franchise agreement and helps you avoid costly misunderstandings.

Franchise Bible   **Pages: 274**
Paperback: $24.95   ISBN: 1-55571-367-X

From The Leading Publisher of Small Business Information
Books that save you time and money.

Understand the economics of your business. Business Owner's Guide to Accounting & Bookkeeping explains the basic accounting principles that relate to any business, with step-by-step instructions for generating and interpreting accounting statements, spotting errors, and recognizing warning signs. It also covers how creditors view your financial statements.

**Business Owner's Guide to Accounting & Bookkeeping Pages: 184
Paperback: $19.95   ISBN: 1-55571-163-4**

This book will show you how to push the doors open, how the banking industry operates, and how to speak their language. It tells you how and why you should take a leading role in developing and nurturing a lasting partnership with your bank.

**The Small Business Insider's Guide to Bankers   Pages: 163
Paperback: $18.95   ISBN: 1-55571-400-5**

"...a handy reference source, not only when thinking about buying or selling a business, but during the process and long after the transaction is complete. All in all, The Secrets to Buying and Selling a Business is a winner."

— Alan Woods, Attorney
Woods, Kinney & Breithaupt, P.C.

**Secrets to Buying and Selling a Business   Pages: 300
Paperback: $24.95   ISBN: 1-55571-489-7**

ORDER DIRECT FROM THE PUBLISHER

The Oasis Press®

The Leading Publisher of Small Business Information

— 1-800-228-2275 —

[U.S. AND CANADA ONLY]

HOW TO ORDER

Mail: Send this completed order form and a check, money order or credit card information to:
PSI Research/The Oasis Press®, P.O. Box 3727, Central Point, Oregon 97502-0032

Fax: Available 24 hours a day, 7 days a week at 1-541-476-1479

Email: info@psi-research.com (Please include a phone number, should we need to contact you.)

Web: Purchase any of our products online at our Website at http://www.psi-research.com/oasis.htm

Inquiries and International Orders: Please call 1-541-479-9464

Indicate the quantity and price of the titles you would like:

5/99

TITLE	ISBN	BINDER	PAPERBACK	QTY.	TOTAL
Advertising Without An Agency	1-55571-429-3		☐ 19.95		
Before You Go Into Business Read This	1-55571-481-1		☐ 17.95		
Bottom Line Basics	1-55571-329-7 (B) ■ 1-55571-330-0 (P)	☐ 39.95	☐ 19.95		
BusinessBasics	1-55571-430-7		☐ 16.95		
The Business Environmental Handbook	1-55571-304-1 (B) ■ 1-55571-163-4 (P)	☐ 39.95	☐ 19.95		
Business Owner's Guide to Accounting and Bookkeeping	1-55571-381-5		☐ 19.95		
businessplan.com	1-55571-455-2		☐ 19.95		
Buyer's Guide to Business Insurance	1-55571-310-6 (B) ■ 1-55571-162-6 (P)	☐ 39.95	☐ 19.95		
California Corporation Formation Package	1-55571-368-8 (B) ■ 1-55571-464-1 (P)	☐ 39.95	☐ 29.95		
Collection Techniques for a Small Business	1-55571-312-2 (B) ■ 1-55571-171-5 (P)	☐ 39.95	☐ 19.95		
College Entrepreneur Handbook	1-55571-503-6		☐ 16.95		
A Company Policy & Personnel Workbook	1-55571-364-5 (B) ■ 1-55571-486-2 (P)	☐ 49.95	☐ 29.95		
Company Relocation Handbook	1-55571-091-3 (B) ■ 1-55571-092-1 (P)	☐ 39.95	☐ 19.95		
CompControl	1-55571-356-4 (B) ■ 1-55571-355-6 (P)	☐ 39.95	☐ 19.95		
Complete Book of Business Forms	1-55571-107-3		☐ 19.95		
Connecting Online	1-55571-403-X		☐ 21.95		
Customer Engineering	1-55571-360-2 (B) ■ 1-55571-359-9 (P)	☐ 39.95	☐ 19.95		
Develop and Market Your Creative Ideas	1-55571-383-1		☐ 15.95		
Developing International Markets	1-55571-433-1		☐ 19.95		
Doing Business in Russia	1-55571-375-0		☐ 19.95		
Draw the Line	1-55571-370-X		☐ 17.95		
The Essential Corporation Handbook	1-55571-342-4		☐ 21.95		
Essential Limited Liability Company Handbook	1-55571-362-9 (B) ■ 1-55571-361-0 (P)	☐ 39.95	☐ 21.95		
Export Now	1-55571-192-8 (B) ■ 1-55571-167-7 (P)	☐ 39.95	☐ 24.95		
Financial Decisionmaking	1-55571-435-8		☐ 19.95		
Financial Management Techniques	1-55571-116-2 (B) ■ 1-55571-124-3 (P)	☐ 39.95	☐ 19.95		
Financing Your Small Business	1-55571-160-X		☐ 19.95		
Franchise Bible	1-55571-366-1 (B) ■ 1-55571-367-X (P)	☐ 39.95	☐ 24.95		
The Franchise Redbook	1-55571-484-6		☐ 34.95		
Friendship Marketing	1-55571-399-8		☐ 18.95		
Funding High-Tech Ventures	1-55571-405-6		☐ 21.95		
Home Business Made Easy	1-55571-428-5		☐ 19.95		
Improving Staff Productivity	1-55571-456-0		☐ 16.95		
Information Breakthrough	1-55571-413-7		☐ 22.95		
Insider's Guide to Small Business Loans	1-55571-488-9		☐ 19.95		
InstaCorp™ Book & Software	1-55571-382-3		☐ 29.95		
Joysticks, Blinking Lights, and Thrills	1-55571-401-3		☐ 18.95		
Keeping Score: An Inside Look at Sports Marketing	1-55571-377-7		☐ 18.95		
Know Your Market	1-55571-341-6 (B) ■ 1-55571-333-5 (P)	☐ 39.95	☐ 19.95		
Leader's Guide: 15 Essential Skills	1-55571-434-X		☐ 19.95		
Legal Expense Defense	1-55571-349-1 (B) ■ 1-55571-348-3 (P)	☐ 39.95	☐ 19.95		
Legal Road Map for Consultants	1-55571-460-9		☐ 18.95		
Location, Location, Location	1-55571-376-9		☐ 19.95		
Mail Order Legal Guide	1-55571-193-6 (B) ■ 1-55571-190-1 (P)	☐ 45.00	☐ 29.95		
Managing People: A Practical Guide	1-55571-380-7		☐ 21.95		
Marketing for the New Millennium	1-55571-432-3		☐ 19.95		
Marketing Mastery	1-55571-358-0 (B) ■ 1-55571-357-2 (P)	☐ 39.95	☐ 19.95		
Money Connection	1-55571-352-1 (B) ■ 1-55571-351-3 (P)	☐ 39.95	☐ 24.95		
Moonlighting: Earning a Second Income at Home	1-55571-406-4		☐ 15.95		
Navigating the Marketplace: Growth Strategies for Small Business	1-55571-458-7		☐ 21.95		
No Money Down Financing for Franchising	1-55571-462-5		☐ 19.95		
Not Another Meeting!	1-55571-480-3		☐ 17.95		
People-Centered Profit Strategies	1-55571-517-6		☐ 18.95		

Sub-total for this side:

TITLE	ISBN	BINDER	PAPERBACK	QTY.	TOTAL
People Investment	1-55571-187-1 (B) ■ 1-55571-161-8 (P)	☐ 39.95	☐ 19.95		
Power Marketing for Small Business	1-55571-303-3 (B) ■ 1-55571-166-9 (P)	☐ 39.95	☐ 19.95		
Proposal Development	1-55571-067-0 (B) ■ 1-55571-431-5 (P)	☐ 39.95	☐ 21.95		
Prospecting for Gold	1-55571-483-8		☐ 14.95		
Public Relations Marketing	1-55571-459-5		☐ 19.95		
Raising Capital	1-55571-306-8 (B) ■ 1-55571-305-X (P)	☐ 39.95	☐ 19.95		
Renaissance 2000	1-55571-412-9		☐ 22.95		
Retail in Detail	1-55571-371-8		☐ 15.95		
The Rule Book of Business Plans for Startups	1-55571-519-2		☐ 18.95		
Secrets of High Ticket Selling	1-55571-436-6		☐ 19.95		
Secrets to Buying and Selling a Business	1-55571-489-7		☐ 24.95		
Secure Your Future	1-55571-335-1		☐ 19.95		
Selling Services	1-55571-461-7		☐ 18.95		
SmartStart Your (State) Business	varies per state		☐ 19.95		
Indicate which state you prefer:					
Small Business Insider's Guide to Bankers	1-55571-400-5		☐ 18.95		
Smile Training Isn't Enough	1-55571-422-6		☐ 19.95		
Start Your Business	1-55571-485-4		☐ 10.95		
Strategic Management for Small and Growing Firms	1-55571-465-X		☐ 24.95		
Successful Network Marketing	1-55571-350-5		☐ 15.95		
Surviving Success	1-55571-446-3		☐ 19.95		
TargetSmart!	1-55571-384-X		☐ 19.95		
Top Tax Saving Ideas for Today's Small Business	1-55571-463-3		☐ 16.95		
Truth About Teams	1-55571-482-X		☐ 18.95		
Twenty-One Sales in a Sale	1-55571-448-X		☐ 19.95		
WebWise	1-55571-501-X (B) ■ 1-55571-479-X (P)	☐ 29.95	☐ 19.95		
What's It Worth?	1-55571-504-4		☐ 22.95		
Which Business?	1-55571-390-4		☐ 18.95		
Write Your Own Business Contracts	1-55571-196-0 (B) ■ 1-55571-170-7 (P)	☐ 39.95	☐ 24.95		

Success Series

	ISBN		PAPERBACK	QTY.	TOTAL
50 Ways to Get Promoted	1-55571-506-0		☐ 10.95		
You Can't Go Wrong By Doing It Right	1-55571-490-0		☐ 14.95		

Oasis Software

	FORMAT	BINDER		QTY.	TOTAL
Company Policy Text Files	CD-ROM ☐		☐ 49.95		
Company Policy Text Files Book & Disk Package	CD-ROM ☐	☐ 89.95 (B)	☐ 69.95 (P)		
Financial Management Techniques Standalone	Floppy Disks ☐		☐ 99.95		
Financial Management Techniques Book & Disk Package	Floppy Disks ☐	☐ 129.95(B)	☐ 119.95 (P)		
Insurance Assistant	Floppy Disks ☐		☐ 29.95		
Insurance Assistant & Buyer's Guide to Business Insurance	Floppy Disks ☐	☐ 59.95 (B)	☐ 39.95 (P)		
Winning Business Plans in Color CD-ROM	CD-ROM ☐		☐ 59.95		

Ordered by: *Please give street address*

NAME _____ TITLE _____

COMPANY _____

STREET ADDRESS _____

CITY _____ STATE _____ ZIP _____

DAYTIME PHONE _____ EMAIL _____

Ship to: *If different than above*

NAME _____ TITLE _____

COMPANY _____

STREET ADDRESS _____

CITY _____ STATE _____ ZIP _____

DAYTIME PHONE _____

Shipping:

YOUR ORDER IS:	ADD:
0-25	5.00
25.01-50	6.00
50.01-100	7.00
100.01-175	9.00
175.01-250	13.00
250.01-500	18.00
500.01+	4% of total

Subtotal from other side	
Subtotal from this side	
Shipping	
TOTAL	

PLEASE CALL FOR RUSH SERVICE OPTIONS.
INTERNATIONAL ORDERS, PLEASE CALL FOR A QUOTE ON CURRENT SHIPPING RATES.

Payment Method:

☐ CHECK   ☐ MONEY ORDER
☐ AMERICAN EXPRESS   ☐ DISCOVER
☐ MASTERCARD   ☐ VISA

CREDIT CARD NUMBER

EXPIRATION (MM/YY)   NAME ON CARD (PLEASE PRINT)

SIGNATURE OF CARDHOLDER (REQUIRED)

OASIS PRESS
BOOKS & SOFTWARE

Fax this order form to: (541) 476-1479 or mail it to: P.O. Box 3727, Central Point, Oregon 97502
For more information about our products or to order online, visit http://www.psi-research.com